Kawasaki ZX600 & 636 (ZX-6R)

Service and Repair Manual

by Matthew Coombs and Phil Mather

UK and Europe models covered

(3541-272-7AC2)

ZX600F. 599 cc. 1995 to 1997
ZX600G. 599 cc. 1998 to 1999
ZX600H. 599 cc. 1998 (except UK)
ZX600J. 599 cc. 2000 to 2001
ZX636A. 636 cc. 2002

US models covered

ZX600F. 599 cc. 1995 to 1997
ZX600G. 599 cc. 1998 to 1999
ZX600H. 599 cc. 1998
ZX600J. 599 cc. 2000 to 2002

ABCDE
FGHIJ
KLM

A book in the **Haynes Service and Repair Manual Series**

ISBN **1 84425 065 2**

British Library Cataloguing in Publication Data
A catalogue record for this book is available from the British Library.

Library of Congress Catalog Card Number 2003108846

Printed in the USA

Haynes Publishing
Sparkford, Yeovil, Somerset, BA22 7JJ, England

Haynes North America, Inc
861 Lawrence Drive, Newbury Park, California 91320, USA

Editions Haynes S.A.
4, Rue de l'Abreuvoir, 92415 COURBEVOIE CEDEX, France

Haynes Publishing Nordiska AB
Box 1504, 751 45 UPPSALA, Sweden

Contents

LIVING WITH YOUR KAWASAKI ZX-6R

Introduction

Daily (pre-ride) checks

MAINTENANCE

Routine maintenance and servicing

Contents

Kawasaki The Green Meanies

by Julian Ryder

Kawasaki Heavy Industries

Kawasaki is a company of contradictions. It is the smallest of the big four Japanese manufacturers but the biggest company, it was the last of the four to make and market motorcycles yet it owns the oldest name in the Japanese industry, and it was the first to set up a factory in the USA. Kawasaki Heavy Industries, of which the motorcycle operation is but a small component, is a massive company with its heritage firmly in the old heavy industries like shipbuilding and railways; nowadays it is as much involved in aerospace as in motorcycles.

In fact it may be because of this that Kawasaki's motorcycles have always been quirky, you get the impression that they are designed by a small group of enthusiasts who are given an admirably free hand. More realistically, it may be that Kawasaki's designers have experience with techniques and materials from other engineering disciplines. Either way, Kawasaki have managed to be the factory who surprise us more than the rest. Quite often, they do this by totally ignoring a market segment the others are scrabbling over, but more often they hit us with pure, undiluted performance.

The origins of the company, and its name, go back to 1878 when Shozo Kawasaki set up a dockyard in Tokyo. By the late 1930s, the company was making its own steel in massive steelworks and manufacturing railway locos and rolling stock. In the run up to war, the Kawasaki Aircraft Company was set up in 1937 and it was this arm of the now giant operation that would look to motorcycle engine manufacture in post-war Japan.

They bought their high-technology experience to bear first on engines which were sold on to a number of manufacturers as original equipment. Both two- and four-stroke units were made, a 58 cc and 148 cc OHC unit. One of the customer companies was Meihatsu Heavy Industries, another company within the Kawasaki group, which in 1961 was shaken up and renamed Kawasaki Auto Sales. At the same time, the Akashi factory which was to be Kawasaki's main production facility until the Kobe earthquake of 1995, was opened. Shortly afterwards, Kawasaki took over the ailing Meguro company, Japan's oldest motorcycle maker, thus instantly obtaining a range of bigger bikes which were marketed as Kawasaki-Meguros. The following year, the first bike to be made and sold as a Kawasaki was produced, a 125 cc single called the B8 and in 1963 a motocross version, the B8M appeared.

The three cylinder two-stroke 750

Model development

Kawasaki's first appearance on a road-race circuit came in 1965 with a batch of disc-valve 125 twins. They were no match for the opposition from Japan in the shape of Suzuki and Yamaha or for the fading force of the factory MZs from East Germany. Only after the other Japanese factories had pulled out of the class did Kawasaki win, with British rider Dave Simmonds becoming World 125 GP Champion in 1969 on a bike that looked astonishingly similar to the original racer. That same year Kawasaki reorganised once again, this time merging three companies to form Kawasaki Heavy Industries. One of the new organisation's objectives was to take motorcycle production forward and exploit markets outside Japan.

KHI achieved that target immediately and set out their stall for the future with the astonishing and frightening H1. This three-cylinder air-cooled 500 cc two-stroke was arguably the first modern pure performance bike to hit the market. It hypnotised a whole generation of motorcyclists who'd never before encountered such a ferocious, wheelie inducing power band or such shattering straight-line speed allied to questionable handling. And as for the 750 cc version ...

The triples perfectly suited the late '60s, fitting in well with the student demonstrations of 1968 and the anti-establishment ethos of the Summer of Love. Unfortunately, the oil crisis would put an end to the thirsty strokers but Kawasaki had another high-performance ace up their corporate sleeve. Or rather they thought they did.

The 1968 Tokyo Show saw probably the single most significant new motorcycle ever made unveiled: the Honda CB750. At Kawasaki it caused a major shock, for they also had a 750 cc four, code-named New York Steak, almost ready to roll and it was a double, rather than single, overhead cam motor. Bravely, they took the decision to go ahead - but with the motor taken out to 900 cc. The result was the Z1, unveiled at the 1972 Cologne Show. It was a bike straight out of the same mould as the H1, scare stories spread about unmanageable power, dubious straight-line stability and frightening handling, none of which stopped the sales graph rocketing upwards and led to the coining of the term 'superbike'. While rising fuel prices cut short development of the big two-strokes, the Z1 went on to found a dynasty, indeed its genes can still be detected in Kawasaki's latest products like the ZZ-R1100 (Ninja ZX-11).

This is another characteristic of the way Kawasaki operates. Models quite often have very long lives, or gradually evolve. There is no major difference between that first Z1 and the air-cooled GPz range. Add water-cooling and you have the GPZ900, which in turn metamorphosed into the GPZ1000RX and then the ZX-10 and the ZZ-R1100. Indeed, the

The first Superbike, Kawasaki's 900 cc Z1

One of the two-stroke engined KH and KE range - the KE100B

The GT750 - a favourite hack for despatch riders

last three models share the same 58 mm stroke. The bikes are obviously very different but it's difficult to put your finger on exactly why.

Other models have remained effectively untouched for over a decade: the KH and KE single-cylinder air-cooled two-stroke learner bikes, the GT550 and 750 shaft-drive hacks favoured by big city despatch riders and the GPz305 being prime examples. It's only when they step outside the performance field that Kawasakis seems less sure. Their first factory customs were dire, you simply got the impression that the team that designed them didn't have their heart in the job. Only when the Classic range appeared in 1995 did they get it right.

The high-performance ZXR750

Racing success

Kawasaki also have a more focused approach to racing than the other factories. The policy has always been to race the road bikes and with just a couple of exceptions that's what they've done. Even Simmonds' championship winner bore a strong resemblance to the twins they were selling in the late '60s and racing versions of the 500 and 750 cc triples were also sold as over-the-counter racers, the H1R and H2R. The 500 was in the forefront of the two-stroke assault on MV Agusta but wasn't a Grand Prix winner. It was the 750 that made the impact and carried the factory's image in F750 racing against the Suzuki triples and Yamaha fours.

The factory's decision to use green, usually regarded as an unlucky colour in sport, meant its bikes and personnel stood out and the phrase 'Green Meanies' fitted them perfectly. The Z1 motor soon became a full 1000 cc and powered Kawasaki's assault in F1 racing, notably in endurance which Kawasaki saw as being most closely related to its road bikes.

That didn't stop them dominating 250 and 350 cc GPs with a tandem twin two-stroke in the late '70s and early '80s, but their path-breaking monocoque 500 while a race winner never won a world title. When Superbike arrived, Kawasaki's road 750s weren't as track-friendly as the opposition's out-and-out race replicas. This makes Scott Russell's World title on the ZXR750 in 1993 even more praiseworthy, for the homologation bike, the ZXR750RR, was much heavier and much more of a road bike than the Italian and Japanese competition.

The company's Supersport 600 contenders have similarly been more sports-tourers than race-replicas, yet they too have been competitive on the track. Indeed, the flagship bike, the ZZ-R1100, is most definitely a sports tourer capable of carrying two people and their luggage at high speed in comfort all day and then doing it again the next day. Try that on one of the race replicas and you'll be in need of a course of treatment from a chiropractor.

Through doing it their way Kawasaki developed a brand loyalty for their performance bikes that kept the Z1's derivatives in production until the mid-'80s and turned the bike into a classic in its model life. You could even argue that the Z1 lives on in the shape of the 1100 Zephyr's GPz1100-derived motor. And that's another Kawasaki invention, the retro bike. But when you look at what many commentators refer to as the retro boom, especially in Japan, you find that it is no such thing. It is the Zephyr boom. Just another example of Japan's most surprising motorcycle manufacturer getting it right again.

First Among Equals

The ZX-6R is Kawasaki's fourth-generation Supersport 600, and by far the sportiest. It isn't closely related to the third-generation 600, the sports-tourer ZZ-R600 (known as the Ninja ZX-6 in the US), it's really a scaled-down version of the ZX-9R, an out-and-out sportster, and shares much of the bigger bike's design architecture. Compared to the ZZ-R's 64 x 46.6 mm motor, the ZX-6R uses a short-stroke 66 x 43.8 mm bore and stroke with the chain drive to the camshafts at the right-hand end of the cylinder block, not in the centre.

The motor is smaller in all directions than its predecessor's and delivers a fraction under 100 real horsepower at the back wheel. But it's the way it does it that is really impressive. Not only does it have the strong top-end you'd expect, it has plenty of mid-range driveability too. The relocation of the camchain drive allowed Kawasaki to lose one crankshaft main bearing which allowed the crankcases to be narrowed while the valve angle was reduced substantially from 30 to 25 degrees, and the cylinder block was canted forward by 13 degrees more than the ZZ-R for a total lean of 28 degrees to reduce the overall height of the powerplant and give the carbs more downdraft effect. The chassis also follows the same basic layout as the 900; it's big slabby chassis is all aluminium, frame, sub-frame, swinging arm, the lot.

Any 600 cc four-cylinder bike will inevitably be compared to the Honda CBR600 that has dominated the class for so long, and the ZX-6R manages a very clever trick. It is nearly as civilised as the Honda (the main difference is that you can actually carry a pillion in comfort on the Honda) and just that little bit sportier while not being as difficult to live with as Suzuki's single-mindedly sporty GSX-R600. And in the class where things change year by year, the ZX-6R stayed unchanged save for graphics for the first three years of its life (the ZX600F models) without losing any of its edge. It sold nearly as well as the Honda and the road testers loved it too, especially that typically Kawasaki edge, a hint of the unruliness that made the company's name with its two-stroke triples and the mighty Z1.

The ZX600F (ZX-6R)

There were a few modifications when the ZX600G model arrived in 1998. The sub-frame now bolted to the main frame and the whole thing had a slightly reduced wheelbase. Stopping was also improved with six-piston front brake calipers replacing the original four-piston Tokicos. Cooling was also uprated by using the motor's coolant to cool the oil cooler fitted on the oil filter mount. There are more detail differences, and of course the change in wheelbase means the bodywork is all different, but the overall package has changed very little indeed overall. Riders in certain markets can also buy the ZX600H model which is fitted with a catalytic converter.

The ZX600G and H models were superseded by the ZX600J in 2000 with a host of engine and chassis improvements to ensure that the ZX-6R remained competative in the 600cc class. The modifed engine featured an all-aluminium linerless cylinder block, and was 4 kg lighter than the previous model's engine due to the fitting of lighter crankshaft and clutch assemblies, and magnesium castings for the valve cover, sump and clutch cover. Stick type ignition coils and a throttle position sensor were fitted and revised bodywork followed the lines of the ZX-9R.

The ZX600J continued in the US until the end of 2002 when it was discontinued. European markets got the ZX636A for 2002 which had a 2 mm increase in bore diameter to raise its capacity by 37 cc. All carburettor-engined ZX-6R models were discontinued for 2003 in favour of the fuel injected ZX636B and ZX600K models. The 599cc engine size has been retained to conform to the regulations for the World Supersport race series.

Acknowledgements

Our thanks are due to Paul Branson Motorcycles of Yeovil and Taylors Motorcycles of Crewkerne who supplied the machines featured in the illustrations throughout this manual. Thanks are also due to Kawasaki Motors (UK) Ltd for the supply of technical information and permission to use some of the line drawings featured. We would also like to thank NGK Spark Plugs (UK) Ltd for supplying the colour spark plug condition photos, the Avon Rubber Company for supplying information on tyre fitting and Draper Tools Ltd for some of the workshop tools shown.

Thanks are also due to Kawasaki Motors (UK) Ltd for supplying model photographs. The introduction 'Kawasaki – The Green Meanies' was written by Julian Ryder.

About this Manual

The aim of this manual is to help you get the best value from your motorcycle. It can do so in several ways. It can help you decide what work must be done, even if you choose to have it done by a dealer; it provides information and procedures for routine maintenance and servicing; and it offers diagnostic and repair procedures to follow when trouble occurs.

We hope you use the manual to tackle the work yourself. For many simpler jobs, doing it yourself may be quicker than arranging an appointment to get the motorcycle into a dealer and making the trips to leave it and pick it up. More importantly, a lot of money can be saved by avoiding the expense the shop must pass on to you to cover its labour and overhead costs. An added benefit is the sense of satisfaction and accomplishment that you feel after doing the job yourself.

References to the left or right side of the motorcycle assume you are sitting on the seat, facing forward.

We take great pride in the accuracy of information given in this manual, but motorcycle manufacturers make alterations and design changes during the production run of a particular motorcycle of which they do not inform us. No liability can be accepted by the authors or publishers for loss, damage or injury caused by any errors in, or omissions from, the information given.

Professional mechanics are trained in safe working procedures. However enthusiastic you may be about getting on with the job at hand, take the time to ensure that your safety is not put at risk. A moment's lack of attention can result in an accident, as can failure to observe simple precautions.

There will always be new ways of having accidents, and the following is not a comprehensive list of all dangers; it is intended rather to make you aware of the risks and to encourage a safe approach to all work you carry out on your bike.

Asbestos

● Certain friction, insulating, sealing and other products - such as brake pads, clutch linings, gaskets, etc. - contain asbestos. Extreme care must be taken to avoid inhalation of dust from such products since it is hazardous to health. If in doubt, assume that they do contain asbestos.

Fire

● Remember at all times that petrol is highly flammable. Never smoke or have any kind of naked flame around, when working on the vehicle. But the risk does not end there - a spark caused by an electrical short-circuit, by two metal surfaces contacting each other, by careless use of tools, or even by static electricity built up in your body under certain conditions, can ignite petrol vapour, which in a confined space is highly explosive. Never use petrol as a cleaning solvent. Use an approved safety solvent.

● Always disconnect the battery earth terminal before working on any part of the fuel or electrical system, and never risk spilling fuel on to a hot engine or exhaust.

● It is recommended that a fire extinguisher of a type suitable for fuel and electrical fires is kept handy in the garage or workplace at all times. Never try to extinguish a fuel or electrical fire with water.

Fumes

● Certain fumes are highly toxic and can quickly cause unconsciousness and even death if inhaled to any extent. Petrol vapour comes into this category, as do the vapours from certain solvents such as trichloro-ethylene. Any draining or pouring of such volatile fluids should be done in a well ventilated area.

● When using cleaning fluids and solvents, read the instructions carefully. Never use materials from unmarked containers - they may give off poisonous vapours.

● Never run the engine of a motor vehicle in an enclosed space such as a garage. Exhaust fumes contain carbon monoxide which is extremely poisonous; if you need to run the engine, always do so in the open air or at least have the rear of the vehicle outside the workplace.

The battery

● Never cause a spark, or allow a naked light near the vehicle's battery. It will normally be giving off a certain amount of hydrogen gas, which is highly explosive.

● Always disconnect the battery ground (earth) terminal before working on the fuel or electrical systems (except where noted).

● If possible, loosen the filler plugs or cover when charging the battery from an external source. Do not charge at an excessive rate or the battery may burst.

● Take care when topping up, cleaning or carrying the battery. The acid electrolyte, evenwhen diluted, is very corrosive and should not be allowed to contact the eyes or skin. Always wear rubber gloves and goggles or a face shield. If you ever need to prepare electrolyte yourself, always add the acid slowly to the water; never add the water to the acid.

Electricity

● When using an electric power tool, inspection light etc., always ensure that the appliance is correctly connected to its plug and that, where necessary, it is properly grounded (earthed). Do not use such appliances in damp conditions and, again, beware of creating a spark or applying excessive heat in the vicinity of fuel or fuel vapour. Also ensure that the appliances meet national safety standards.

● A severe electric shock can result from touching certain parts of the electrical system, such as the spark plug wires (HT leads), when the engine is running or being cranked, particularly if components are damp or the insulation is defective. Where an electronic ignition system is used, the secondary (HT) voltage is much higher and could prove fatal.

Remember...

✗ **Don't** start the engine without first ascertaining that the transmission is in neutral.

✗ **Don't** suddenly remove the pressure cap from a hot cooling system - cover it with a cloth and release the pressure gradually first, or you may get scalded by escaping coolant.

✗ **Don't** attempt to drain oil until you are sure it has cooled sufficiently to avoid scalding you.

✗ **Don't** grasp any part of the engine or exhaust system without first ascertaining that it is cool enough not to burn you.

✗ **Don't** allow brake fluid or antifreeze to contact the machine's paintwork or plastic components.

✗ **Don't** siphon toxic liquids such as fuel, hydraulic fluid or antifreeze by mouth, or allow them to remain on your skin.

✗ **Don't** inhale dust - it may be injurious to health (see Asbestos heading).

✗ **Don't** allow any spilled oil or grease to remain on the floor - wipe it up right away, before someone slips on it.

✗ **Don't** use ill-fitting spanners or other tools which may slip and cause injury.

✗ **Don't** lift a heavy component which may be beyond your capability - get assistance.

✗ **Don't** rush to finish a job or take unverified short cuts.

✗ **Don't** allow children or animals in or around an unattended vehicle.

✗ **Don't** inflate a tyre above the recommended pressure. Apart from overstressing the carcass, in extreme cases the tyre may blow off forcibly.

✓ **Do** ensure that the machine is supported securely at all times. This is especially important when the machine is blocked up to aid wheel or fork removal.

✓ **Do** take care when attempting to loosen a stubborn nut or bolt. It is generally better to pull on a spanner, rather than push, so that if you slip, you fall away from the machine rather than onto it.

✓ **Do** wear eye protection when using power tools such as drill, sander, bench grinder etc.

✓ **Do** use a barrier cream on your hands prior to undertaking dirty jobs - it will protect your skin from infection as well as making the dirt easier to remove afterwards; but make sure your hands aren't left slippery. Note that long-term contact with used engine oil can be a health hazard.

✓ **Do** keep loose clothing (cuffs, ties etc. and long hair) well out of the way of moving mechanical parts.

✓ **Do** remove rings, wristwatch etc., before working on the vehicle - especially the electrical system.

✓ **Do** keep your work area tidy - it is only too easy to fall over articles left lying around.

✓ **Do** exercise caution when compressing springs for removal or installation. Ensure that the tension is applied and released in a controlled manner, using suitable tools which preclude the possibility of the spring escaping violently.

✓ **Do** ensure that any lifting tackle used has a safe working load rating adequate for the job.

✓ **Do** get someone to check periodically that all is well, when working alone on the vehicle.

✓ **Do** carry out work in a logical sequence and check that everything is correctly assembled and tightened afterwards.

✓ **Do** remember that your vehicle's safety affects that of yourself and others. If in doubt on any point, get professional advice.

● If in spite of following these precautions, you are unfortunate enough to injure yourself, seek medical attention as soon as possible.

Frame and engine numbers

The frame serial number is stamped into the right side of the steering head. The engine number is stamped into the top of the crankcase on the right-hand side of the engine. Both of these numbers should be recorded and kept in a safe place so they can be furnished to law enforcement officials in the event of a theft. There is also a carburettor identification number on the intake side of each carburettor body, and a colour code label on the top of the rear mudguard under the passenger seat.

The frame serial number, engine serial number, carburettor identification number and colour code should also be kept in a handy place (such as with your driving licence) so they are always available when purchasing or ordering parts for your machine.

The procedures in this manual identify the bikes by model code. The model code or production year is printed on the colour code label, which is located on the top of the rear fender under the passenger seat.

Buying spare parts

Once you have found all the identification numbers, record them for reference when buying parts. Since the manufacturers change specifications, parts and vendors (companies that manufacture various components on the machine), providing the ID numbers is the only way to be reasonably sure that you are buying the correct parts.

Whenever possible, take the worn part to the dealer so direct comparison with the new component can be made. Along the trail from the manufacturer to the parts shelf, there are numerous places that the part can end up with the wrong number or be listed incorrectly.

The two places to purchase new parts for your motorcycle – the accessory store and the franchised dealer – differ in the type of parts they carry. While dealers can obtain virtually every part for your motorcycle, the accessory dealer is usually limited to normal high wear items such as shock absorbers, tune-up parts, various engine gaskets, cables, chains, brake parts, etc. Rarely will an accessory outlet have major suspension components, cylinders, transmission gears, or cases.

Used parts can be obtained for roughly half the price of new ones, but you can't always be sure of what you're getting. Once again, take your worn part to the wrecking yard (breaker) for direct comparison.

Whether buying new, used or rebuilt parts, the best course is to deal directly with someone who specialises in parts for your particular make.

Model	Country	Year	Code	Frame Nos.
ZX-6R	UK	1995	ZX600F1	ZX600F-000001 to 017000
ZX-6R	UK	1996	ZX600F2	ZX600F-017001 to 030000
ZX-6R	UK	1997	ZX600F3	ZX600F-030001 on
ZX-6R	UK	1998	ZX600G1	JKAZX600G-GA000001 on
ZX-6R	-	1998	ZX600H1	JKAZX600GHA000001 on
ZX-6R	UK	1999	ZX600G2	JKAZX600G-GA024001 on
ZX-6R	UK	2000	ZX600J1	JKAZX600J-JA000001 on
ZX-6R	UK	2001	ZX600J2	JKAZX600J-JA030001 on
ZX-6R	UK	2002	ZX636A1	JKBZX636A-AA000001 on
ZX-6R	US	1995	ZX600F1	JKAZX4F1-SA000001 to 017000
ZX-6R	US	1996	ZX600F2	JKAZX4F1-TA017001 to 030000
ZX-6R	US	1997	ZX600F3	JKAZX4F1-VA030001 on
ZX-6R	US	1998	ZX600G1	JKAZX4G1-WA000001 on
ZX-6R	US	1999	ZX600G2	not available
ZX-6R	US	2000	ZX600J1	JKAZX4J1-YA000001 on
ZX-6R	US	2001	ZX600J2	JKAZX4J1-1A030001 on
ZX-6R	US	2002	ZX600J3	JKAZX4J1-2A048001 on

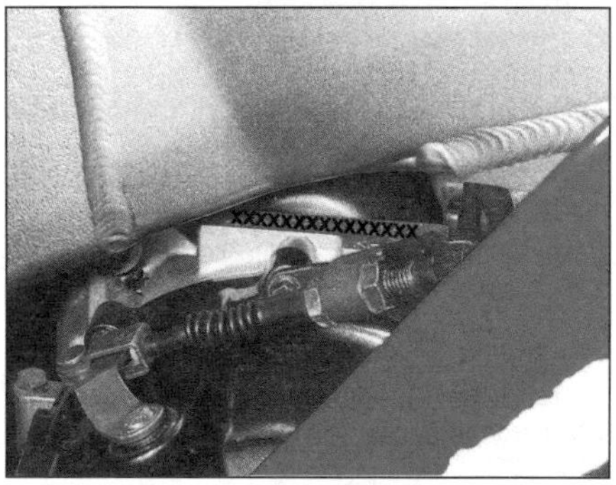

The engine number is stamped into the top of the crankcase on the right-hand side of the engine

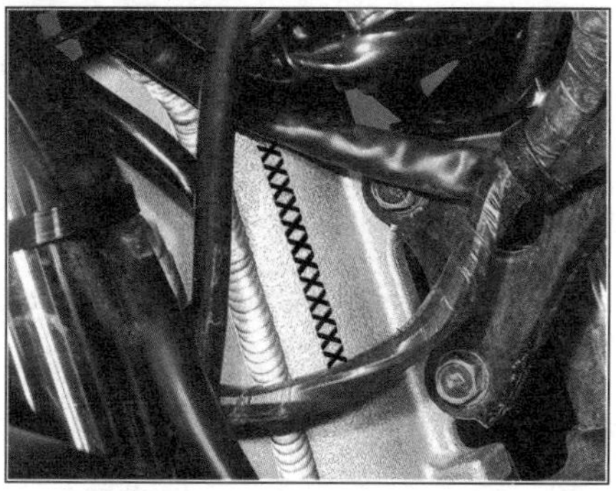

The frame number is stamped in the right-hand side of the steering head

Model development

ZX600F

The ZX-6R Ninja was first introduced in January 1995 as the model ZX600F1.

The engine was a light-weight, liquid cooled four-cylinder with double overhead camshafts driven by chain from the right-hand end of the crankshaft. The separate cylinder block was fitted with replaceable liners and the crankcases were split horizontally. The alternator and pick-up coil cover were made of magnesium.

A matrix-type oil cooler was mounted below the radiator and air was fed from the front, underside of the fairing to the air filter housing via Kawasaki's Twin Ram Air system.

Drive was transmitted to the six-speed gearbox via a multi-plate, four-spring clutch, and to the rear wheel by chain and sprockets.

The chassis comprised a twin-spar aluminium alloy frame with welded-on subframe and box-section, aluminium swingarm. Front suspension was by conventional, three-way adjustable telescopic forks and rear suspension was by a rising rate, three-way adjustable monoshock with remotely mounted gas reservoir.

Braking was by twin, semi-floating discs with four piston calipers at the front and a single disc with single piston caliper at the rear. Span adjusters were fitted to the clutch and front brake levers.

The ZX600F1 was available in Lime green and Pearl alpine white, Luminous rose opera and Pearl alpine white, Metallic eventide and Firecracker red.

The ZX600F2 was introduced in January 1996. Minor detail changes included an increase in the thickness of the front fork tube walls. The ZX600F2 was available in Candy persimmon red and Metallic violet royal, Lime green and Pearl alpine white, Firecracker red.

The ZX600F3 was introduced in October 1996. The bike was available in Candy persimmon red, Galaxy silver, Lime green.

ZX600G (and H)

The ZX600G1 was introduced in March 1998. The bike featured a larger air intake and stainless steel exhaust system. An open-loop catalytic converter was fitted in the exhaust system of California ZX600G models, and German and Swiss ZX600H models. A heat-exchanger type oil cooler was incorporated in the engine-cooling system.

The rear sub-frame was now bolted-on instead of welded. New, six piston calipers were fitted to the front brakes and the thickness of the front discs was increased.

The ZX600G1 was available in Ebony and Firecracker red, Ebony and Pearl chateau grey, Lime green and Metallic violet royal, Sunbeam red.

The ZX600G2 was introduced in October 1998. It was available in Firecracker red, Lime green, Pearl gentry grey.

ZX600J

The ZX600J1 was introduced in January 2000.

A number of revisions were aimed at reducing weight and increasing power. A new, linerless, plated cylinder block and hemi-squish cylinder head were fitted together with a new crankshaft, connecting rods and pistons. The ignition system was uprated with 'stick' spark plug cap ignition coils. The valve cover, oil sump, clutch cover and oil pump cover were made from magnesium. A catalytic converter was incorporated in the exhaust system of all models except those for the Australian market.

A new design of internally braced, extruded aluminium swingarm was introduced. The front brake calipers were modified with differential bore pistons and the diameter of the rear disc was reduced.

A new instrument cluster with LCD displays and LED warning lights was fitted. The new fairing with twin headlights was inspired by the ZX-9R.

The ZX600J1 was available in Ebony and lime green, Firecracker red, Galaxy silver and Black pearl, Sunbeam red and Ebony.

The ZX600J2 was introduced in January 2001. It was available in Candy lightning blue, Candy lightning blue and Metallic nocturne blue, Lime green and Pearl purplish black mica, Pearl chrome yellow and Pearl purplish black mica.

The ZX600J3 was introduced in 2003 for the US market only. It was available in Galaxy silver and Black pearl, Lime green and Black pearl, Passion red and Black pearl, Pearl chrome yellow.

ZX636A1

The ZX636A1 was introduced in February 2002 for the European market only. The increase in engine capacity was achieved by an increase in the cylinder bore diameter. It was available in Galaxy silver and Black pearl, Lime green and black pearl, Passion red and black pearl.

Performance data

Maximum power

ZX600F model ....98 bhp (73 kW) @ 12,600 rpm
ZX600G model ....100 bhp (74.5 kW) @ 12,500 rpm
ZX600J model ....109.5 bhp (81.6 kW) @ 12,500 rpm
ZX636A model ....111 bhp (82.7 kW) @ 12,500 rpm

Maximum torque

ZX600F model ....46.3 lbf ft (62.7 Nm) @ 9,500 rpm
ZX600G model ....45.6 lbf ft (61.8 Nm) @ 9,500 rpm
ZX600J model ....48 lbf ft (65 Nm) @ 10,000 rpm
ZX636A model ....52.4 lbf ft (71 Nm) @ 9,800 rpm

Top speed

ZX600F model ....161 mph (259 km/h)
ZX600G models ....166 mph (267 km/h)
ZX600J and ZX636A models ....168 mph (279 km/h)

Average fuel consumption

Miles per Imp gal, miles per litre, litres per 100 km
ZX600F model ....42 mpg, 9.2 mpl, 6.7 l/100 km
ZX600G, J and ZX636A models ...37.5 mpg, 8.2 mpl, 7.5 l/100 km

Fuel tank capacity

All models ....18 litres (3.96 Imp gal, 4.7 US gal)

Fuel tank range

ZX600F model ....165 miles (265 km)
ZX600G, J and ZX636A models ....148 miles (238 km)

Weights and dimensions

ZX600F models

Wheelbase	1415 mm
Overall length	2030 mm
Overall width	690 mm
Overall height	1130 mm
Ground clearance	120 mm
Seat height	810 mm
Weight (dry)	
California models	182.5 kg
All other models	182 kg

ZX600G and H models

Wheelbase	1400 mm
Overall length	
G models	2025 mm
H models	2055 mm
Overall width	715 mm
Overall height	1160 mm
Ground clearance	140 mm
Seat height	815 mm
Weight (dry)	
G models	
California models	178 kg
All other models	176 kg
H models	177 kg

ZX600J and ZX636A models

Wheelbase	1400 mm
Overall length	2030 mm
Overall width	730 mm
Overall height	1175 mm
Ground clearance	145 mm
Seat height	820 mm
Weight (dry)	
J model	
California models	173 kg
All other models	171 kg
A model	
California models	175 kg
All other models	174 kg

Engine

Type	Liquid cooled, in-line 4-cylinder
Capacity	
ZX600F,G, H and J models	599 cc
ZX636A models	636 cc
Bore	
ZX600F, G, H and J models	66 mm
ZX636A models	68 mm
Stroke	43.8 mm
Compression ratio	
ZX600F, G and H models	11.8:1
ZX600J and ZX636A models	12.8:1
Camshafts	DOHC, chain driven
Valves	4 valves per cylinder
Fuel system	
ZX600F models	4 x Keihin CVKD 36 carburettors
ZX600G and H models	4 x Mikuni BDSR 36R carburettors
ZX600J models	4 x Mikuni BDSR-36 carburettors
ZX636A models	4 x Mikuni BDSR-37 carburettors
Clutch	Wet multi-plate, cable operated
Transmission	6 speed constant mesh
Final drive	
Chain	EK 525MVXL (108 links)
Sprockets	15 tooth front/40 tooth rear

Chassis

Type	Twin spar, aluminium alloy
Rake	
ZX600F models	24.0°
All other models	23.5°
Trail	
ZX600F models	87 mm
ZX600G and H models	91 mm
ZX600J and ZX636A models	95 mm
Front suspension	
ZX600F models	41 mm diameter telescopic forks
All other models	46 mm diameter telescopic forks
Travel	120 mm
Adjustments	Spring pre-load, compression and rebound damping
Rear suspension	
Type	Rising rate with monoshock
Wheel travel	
ZX600F models	137 mm
All other models	135 mm
Adjustments	Spring pre-load, compression and rebound damping
Tyre sizes	
Front	
ZX600F models	120/60 ZR 17
ZX600G and H models	120/60 ZR 17 55W
ZX600J and ZX636A models	120/65 ZR 17 56W
Rear	
ZX600F models	160/60 ZR 17
ZX600G and H models	170/60 ZR 17 72W
ZX600J and ZX636A models	180/55 ZR 17 73W
Brakes	
Front	
ZX600F models	2 x discs with four-piston calipers
ZX600G and H models	2 x discs with six-piston calipers
ZX600J and ZX636A models	2 x discs with six-piston, differential bore calipers
Rear	disc with single-piston caliper

1 Engine/ transmission oil level check

Before you start:

✔ Support the motorcycle in an upright position, using an auxiliary stand if required. Make sure the motorcycle is on level ground.

✔ The oil level is viewed through the window in the clutch cover on the right-hand side of the engine. Wipe the glass clean before inspection to make the check easier.

Bike care:

● If you have to add oil frequently, you should check whether you have any oil leaks. If there is no sign of oil leakage from the joints and gaskets the engine could be burning oil (see *Fault Finding* in the Reference section).

The correct oil

● Modern, high-revving engines place great demands on their oil. It is very important that the correct oil for your bike is used.

● Always top up with a good quality oil of the specified type and viscosity and do not overfill the engine.

Oil type	API grade SE, SF or SG
Oil viscosity	SAE 10W40, 10W50, 20W40 or 20W50

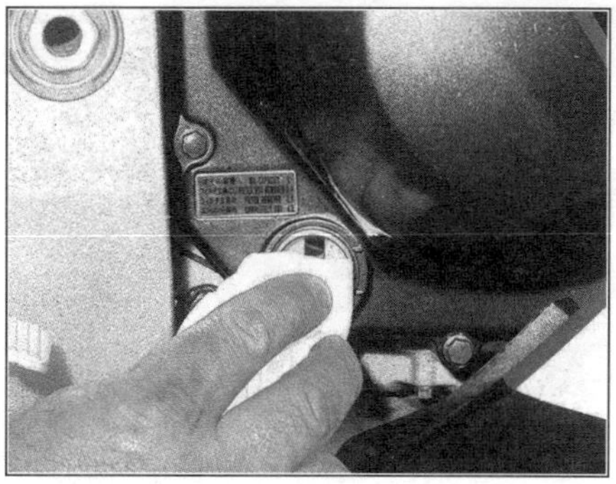

1 Wipe the oil level window in the clutch cover so that it is clean.

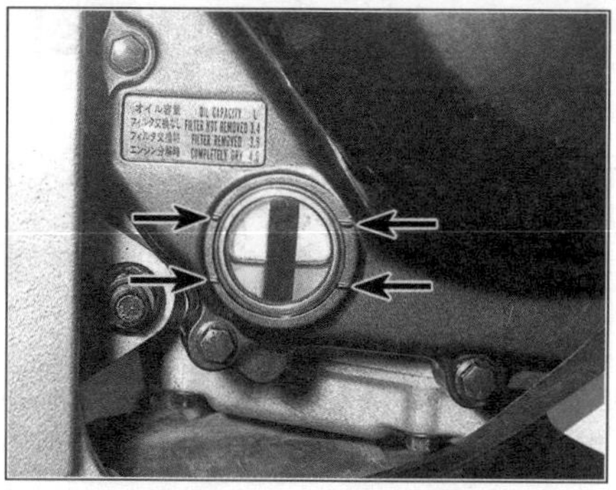

2 With the motorcycle held vertical, the oil level should lie between the upper and lower level lines marked on the clutch cover (arrowed).

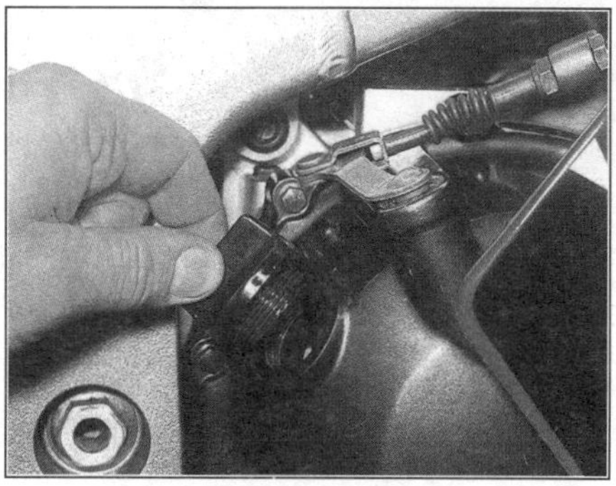

3 If the level is below the lower line, remove the filler cap from the top of the clutch cover.

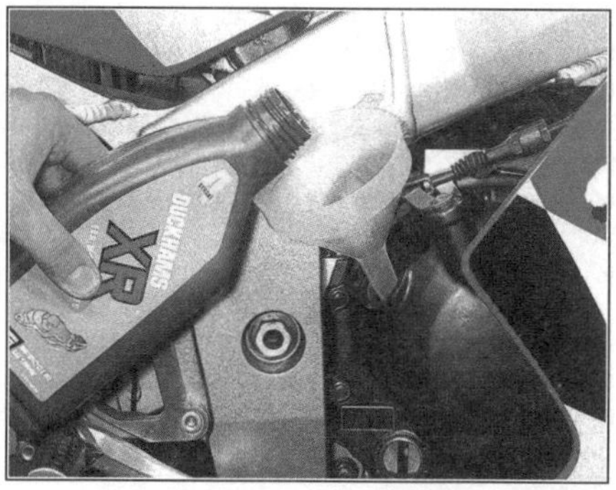

4 Top the engine up with the recommended grade and type of oil, to bring the level up to the upper line on the window.

2 Coolant level check

Before you start:

✔ Make sure you have a supply of coolant available (a mixture of 50% distilled water and 50% corrosion inhibited ethylene glycol anti-freeze is needed).

✔ Always check the coolant level when the engine is cold.

✔ Support the motorcycle in an upright position, using an auxiliary stand if required, whilst checking the level. Make sure the motorcycle is on level ground.

Bike care:

● Use only the specified coolant mixture. It is important that anti-freeze is used in the system all year round, and not just in the winter. Do not top the system up using only water, as the system will become too diluted.

● Do not overfill the reservoir tank. If the coolant is significantly above the F (full) level line at any time, the surplus should be siphoned or drained off to prevent the possibility of it being expelled out of the overflow hose.

● If the coolant level falls steadily, check the system for leaks (see Chapter 1). If no leaks are found and the level continues to fall, it is recommended that the machine is taken to a Kawasaki dealer for a pressure test.

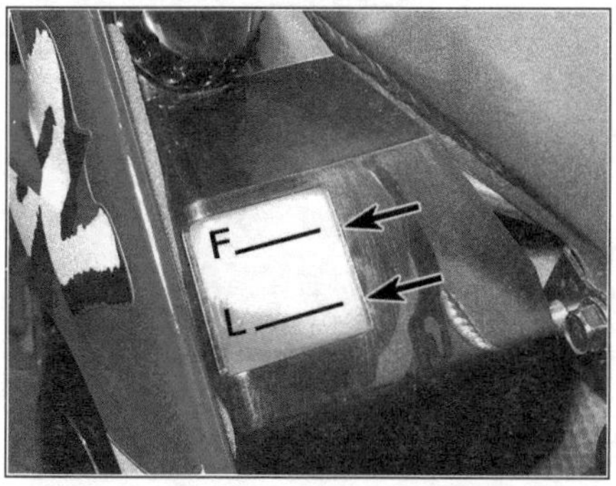

1 The coolant reservoir is located on the left-hand side of the engine. The coolant F and L (full and low) level lines (arrowed) are visible on the back of the reservoir.

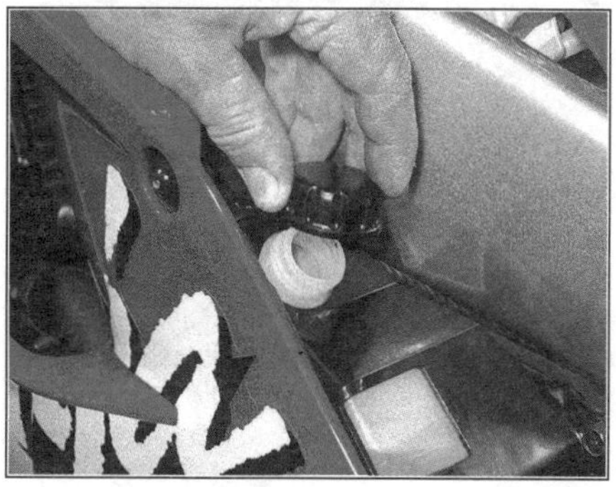

2 If the coolant level is not in between the F and L markings, remove the reservoir filler cap.

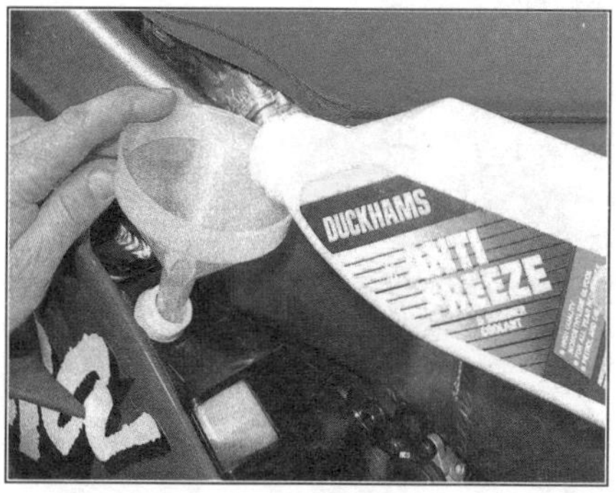

3 Top the coolant level up with the recommended coolant mixture. Fit the cap securely.

3 Brake fluid level checks

> ⚠ ***Warning: Brake hydraulic fluid can harm your eyes and damage painted surfaces, so use extreme caution when handling and pouring it and cover surrounding surfaces with rag. Do not use fluid that has been standing open for some time, as it absorbs moisture from the air which can cause a dangerous loss of braking effectiveness***

Before you start:

✔ Support the motorcycle in an upright position, using an auxiliary stand if required, and turn the handlebars until the top of the front master cylinder is as level as possible. The rear master cylinder reservoir is located below the seat on the right-hand side of the machine.

✔ Make sure you have the correct hydraulic fluid. DOT 4 is recommended.

✔ Wrap a rag around the reservoir being worked on to ensure that any spillage does not come into contact with painted surfaces.

✔ Access to the front reservoir cap screws is restricted by the windshield. Use a short or angled screwdriver to access the screws.

Bike care:

● The fluid in the front and rear brake master cylinder reservoirs will drop slightly as the brake pads wear down.

● If any fluid reservoir requires repeated topping-up this is an indication of an hydraulic leak somewhere in the system, which should be investigated immediately.

● Check for signs of fluid leakage from the hydraulic hoses and components – if found, rectify immediately.

● Check the operation of both brakes before taking the machine on the road; if there is evidence of air in the system (spongy feel to lever or pedal), it must be bled as described in Chapter 7.

1 On ZX600F models, the front brake fluid level is checked via the sightglass in the reservoir – it must be above the low level mark (arrowed).

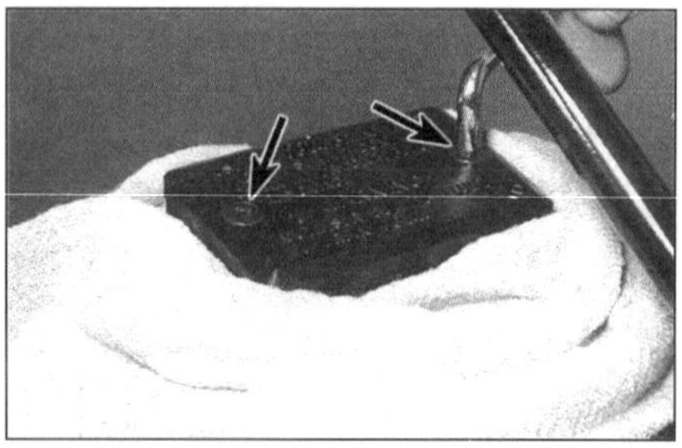

2 If the level is below the mark, remove the two screws (arrowed) to free the front brake fluid reservoir cover, and remove the cover, the diaphragm plate and the diaphragm.

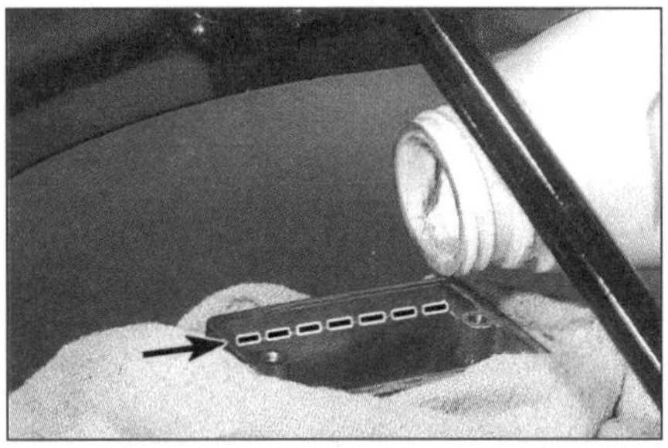

3 Top up with new clean DOT 4 hydraulic fluid until the level is up to the high level mark on the inside of the reservoir (arrowed). Do not overfill.

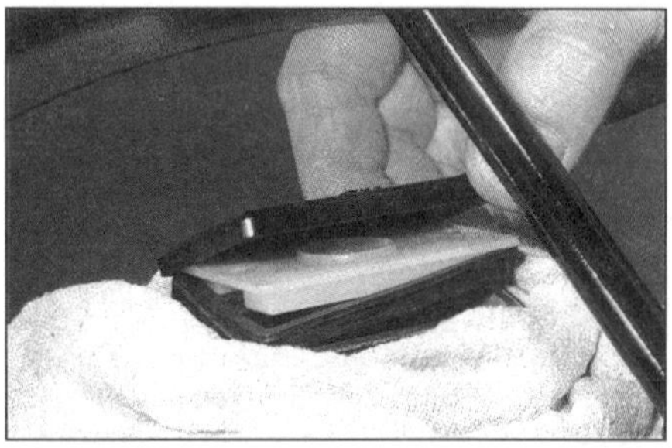

4 Ensure that the diaphragm is correctly seated before installing the plate and cover.

5 On ZX600G, H, J and ZX636A models, the front brake fluid level is visible through the reservoir body – it must be between the UPPER and LOWER level lines (arrowed).

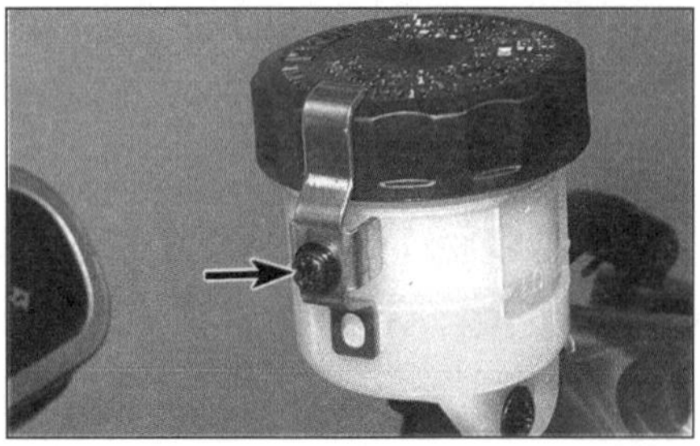

6 If the level is below the LOWER level line, remove the screw securing the cap clamp (arrowed) and remove the cap, the diaphragm plate and the diaphragm. Top up as described for the ZX600F model reservoir.

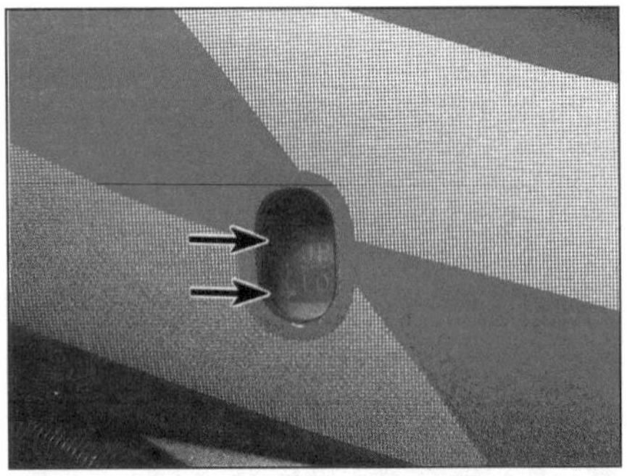

7 On ZX600F models, the rear brake fluid level is visible through the reservoir body via the aperture in the right-hand side panel – it must be between the UPPER and LOWER level lines (arrowed). If the level is below the LOWER level line, remove the seat (see Chapter 8).

8 On ZX600G, H, J and ZX636A models, the rear brake fluid level can be seen through the translucent body of the reservoir which is located under the seat on the right-hand side. The fluid must lie between the UPPER and LOWER level marks (arrowed).

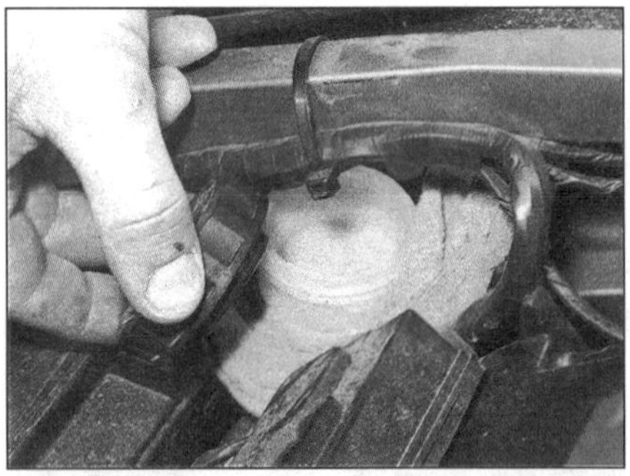

9 If the level is below the LOWER level line, on ZX600G, H, J and ZX636A models remove the cap clamp, then on all models unscrew the reservoir cap and remove the diaphragm plate and diaphragm. Top up with new clean hydraulic fluid of the recommended type, until the level is above the lower mark.

4 Tyre checks

Tyre care:

● Check the tyres carefully for cuts, tears, cracks, bulges, embedded nails or other sharp objects and excessive wear. Operation of the motorcycle with excessively worn tyres is extremely hazardous, as traction and handling are directly affected.

● Check the condition of the tyre valve and ensure the dust cap is in place.

● Pick out any stones or nails which may have become embedded in the tyre tread. If left, they will eventually penetrate through the casing and cause a puncture.

● If tyre damage is apparent, or unexplained loss of pressure is experienced, seek the advice of a tyre fitting specialist without delay.

The correct pressures:

● The tyres must be checked when **cold**, not immediately after riding. Note that low tyre pressures may cause the tyre to slip on the rim or come off. High tyre pressures will cause abnormal tread wear and unsafe handling.

● Use an accurate pressure gauge.

● Proper air pressure will increase tyre life and provide maximum stability and ride comfort.

Tyre pressures

Front (all models)	36 psi (2.5 bars)
Rear (ZX600F, G, H and J models)	41 psi (2.8 bars)
Rear (ZX636A model)	42 psi (2.9 bars)

Tyre tread depth:

● At the time of writing UK law requires that tread depth must be at least 1 mm over 3/4 of the tread breadth all the way around the tyre, with no bald patches. Many riders, however, consider 2 mm tread depth minimum to be a safer limit. Kawasaki recommend a minimum of 1 mm on the front, and 2 mm on the rear for normal speed riding or 3 mm for high speed riding.

● Many tyres now incorporate wear indicators in the tread. Identify the triangular pointer on the tyre sidewall to locate the indicator bar and replace the tyre if the tread has worn down to the bar.

1 Check the tyre pressures when the tyres are **cold** and keep them properly inflated.

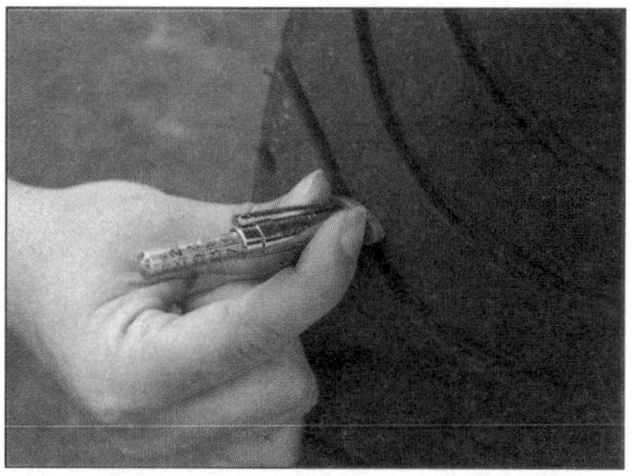

2 Measure tread depth at the centre of the tyre using a tread depth gauge.

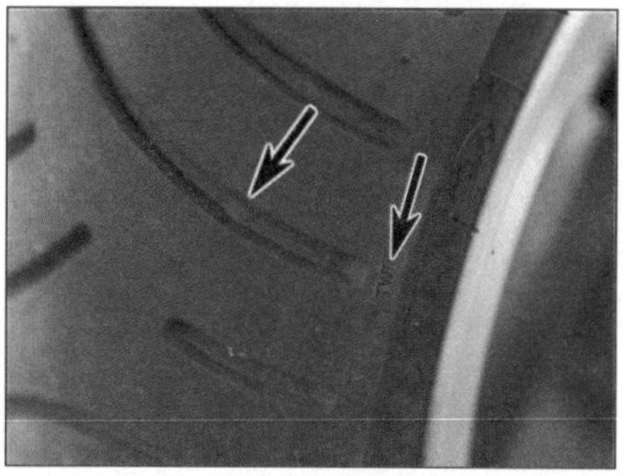

3 Tyre tread wear indicator bar and its location marking (usually either an arrow, a triangle or the letters TWI) on the sidewall (arrowed).

5 Suspension, steering and drive chain checks

Suspension and Steering:

- Check that the front and rear suspension operates smoothly without binding.
- Check that the suspension is adjusted as required (see Chapter 6).
- Check that the steering moves smoothly from lock-to-lock.
- Check the tightness of all nuts and bolts.

Final drive:

- Check that the drive chain slack isn't excessive, and adjust if necessary (see Chapter 1).
- If the chain looks dry, lubricate it (see Chapter 1).

6 Legal and safety checks

Lighting and signalling:

- Take a minute to check that the headlight, taillight, brake light, instrument lights and turn signals all work correctly.
- Check that the horn sounds when the switch is operated.
- A working speedometer graduated in mph is a statutory requirement in the UK.

Safety:

- Check that the throttle grip rotates smoothly and snaps shut when released, in all steering positions. Also check for the correct amount of the throttle and clutch cables (see Chapter 1).
- Check that the engine shuts off when the kill switch is operated.
- Check that sidestand return spring holds the stand securely up when retracted.

Fuel:

- This may seem obvious, but check that you have enough fuel to complete your journey. If you notice signs of fuel leakage – rectify the cause immediately.
- Ensure you use the correct grade unleaded fuel – see Chapter 4 Specifications.

Chapter 1
Routine maintenance and Servicing

Contents

Degrees of difficulty

Easy, suitable for novice with little experience	**Fairly easy,** suitable for beginner with some experience	**Fairly difficult,** suitable for competent DIY mechanic	**Difficult,** suitable for experienced DIY mechanic	**Very difficult,** suitable for expert DIY or professional

Engine

Spark plugs	
Type	NGK CR9E or ND U27ESR-N
Electrode gap	0.7 to 0.8 mm
Engine idle speed	
F models	1100 ± 50 rpm
All other models	1300 ± 50 rpm
Carburettor synchronisation – max. difference between carburettors	2 cm Hg (2.7 kPa)
Cylinder identification	from left to right, numbered 1, 2, 3 and 4
Valve clearances (COLD engine)	
F models	
Inlet valves	0.15 to 0.24 mm
Exhaust valves	0.22 to 0.31 mm
All other models	
Inlet valves	0.11 to 0.19 mm
Exhaust valves	0.22 to 0.31 mm
Cylinder compression	138 to 210 psi (9.7 to 14.8 Bar)
Oil pressure (with engine warm)	17 to 26 psi (1.2 to 1.8 Bar) @ 4000 rpm, oil @ 90°C

Cycle parts

Drive chain	
Freeplay	
F, G, H and J models	35 to 40 mm
A models	30 to 35 mm
Stretch limit (21 pin length – see text)	323 mm
Brake pad friction material minimum thickness	1 mm
Freeplay adjustments	
Clutch lever	2.0 to 3.0 mm
Throttle twistgrip	2.0 to 3.0 mm (see text)
Choke lever	2.0 to 3.0 mm
Brake pedal – distance below top of footrest	
F models	43 mm
All other models	57 mm
Tyre pressures and tread depth	see *Daily (pre-ride) checks*
Tyre sizes	see Chapter 7

Recommended lubricants and fluids

Drive chain lubricant	heavy motor oil (SAE 90) or aerosol lubricant suitable for O-ring chains
Engine/transmission oil type	API grade SE, SF or SG motor oil
Engine/transmission oil viscosity	SAE 10W40, 10W50, 20W40 or 20W50
Engine/transmission oil capacity	
Oil change	3.4 litres
Oil and filter change	3.6 litres
Following engine overhaul – dry engine, new filter	4.0 litres
Brake fluid	DOT 4
Wheel bearings	multi-purpose grease
Swingarm bearings	multi-purpose grease
Steering head bearings	multi-purpose grease
Inner cables	cable lubricant
Cable ends	multi-purpose grease
Lever and stand pivot points	motor oil
Throttle grip	multi-purpose grease or dry film lubricant

Torque settings

Air suction valve cover bolts	13 Nm
Coolant drain plug	
F models	12 Nm
G and H models	10 Nm
J and A models	9.8 Nm
Engine oil drain plug	20 Nm
Fork clamp bolts (bottom yoke)	20 Nm
Oil filter	
F, G and H models	10 Nm
J and A models	27 Nm
Oil gallery plug	15 Nm
Pick-up cover bolts	12 Nm
Rear axle nut	
F, G and H models	110 Nm
J models	125 Nm
A models	127 Nm
Spark plugs	13 Nm
Steering stem nut	49 Nm

Component locations on the right-hand side – F models

1. *Rear brake fluid reservoir*
2. *Battery*
3. *Clutch cable lower adjuster*
4. *Front brake fluid reservoir*
5. *Radiator pressure cap*
6. *Timing rotor cover*
7. *Engine idle speed adjuster*
8. *Engine oil level window*
9. *Engine oil filler cap*
10. *Rear brake light switch*
11. *Rear brake pedal height adjuster*

Component locations on the right-hand side – G, H, J and A models

1. *Battery*
2. *Rear brake fluid reservoir*
3. *Clutch cable lower adjuster*
4. *Front brake fluid reservoir*
5. *Radiator pressure cap*
6. *Timing rotor cover*
7. *Engine oil level window*
8. *Engine oil filler cap*
9. *Rear brake light switch*
10. *Rear brake pedal height adjuster*

Component locations on the left-hand side – F models

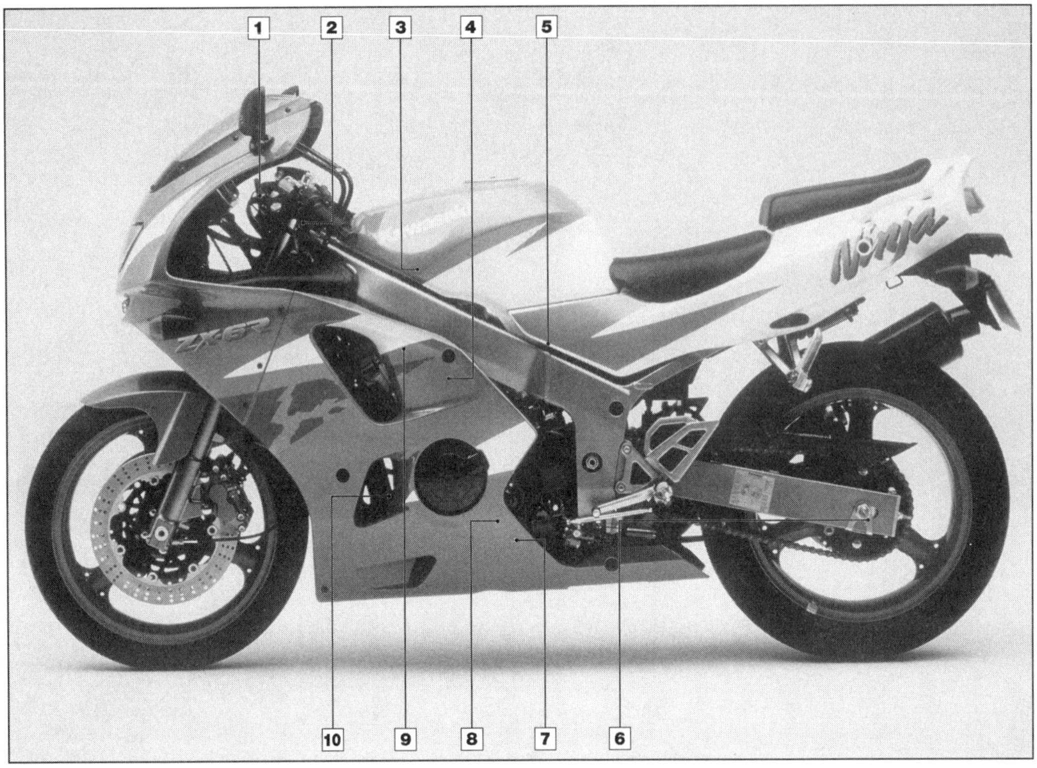

1. *Clutch cable upper adjuster*
2. *Steering head bearings*
3. *Air filter*
4. *Coolant reservoir*
5. *Fuel (in-line) filter*
6. *Drive chain adjuster*
7. *Engine oil drain plug*
8. *Coolant drain bolt*
9. *Air suction valves, spark plugs and valves*
10. *Engine oil filter*

Component locations on the left-hand side – G, H, J and A models

1. *Clutch cable upper adjuster*
2. *Steering head bearings*
3. *Air filter*
4. *Coolant reservoir*
5. *Engine idle speed adjuster*
6. *Fuel (in-line) filter*
7. *Drive chain adjuster*
8. *Engine oil drain plug*
9. *Coolant drain bolt*
10. *Air suction valves, spark plugs and valves*
11. *Engine oil filter*

Note: *The daily (pre-ride) checks at the beginning of the manual cover those items which should be inspected on a daily basis. Always perform the pre-ride inspection at every maintenance interval (in addition to the procedures listed). The intervals listed below are the intervals recommended by the manufacturer for the models covered in this manual. If in doubt, check with a Kawasaki dealer.*

Daily (pre-ride)

See *'Daily (pre-ride) checks'* at the beginning of this manual.

After the initial 500 miles (800 km)

Note: *This check is usually performed by a Kawasaki dealer after the first 500 miles (800 km) from new. Thereafter, maintenance is carried out according to the following intervals of the schedule.*

Every 200 miles (300 km)

Carry out all the items under the Daily (pre-ride) checks, plus the following

- ☐ Clean and lubricate the drive chain (Section 1).

Every 500 miles (800 km)

Carry out all the items under the Daily (pre-ride) checks, plus the following

- ☐ Check and adjust drive chain freeplay (Section 2).

Every 3000 miles (5000 km)

Carry out all the items under the Daily (pre-ride) checks and the 200 mile (300 km) and 500 mile (800 km) check, plus the following

- ☐ Clean and check the spark plugs (Section 3).
- ☐ Check the air suction valve (US models only) (Section 4).
- ☐ Check the evaporative emission control (EVAP) system (California models only) (Section 5).
- ☐ Change the engine oil (Section 6).
- ☐ Check the operation of the clutch (Section 7).
- ☐ Check for drive chain wear and stretch and sprocket wear (Section 8).
- ☐ Check the brake pads for wear (Section 9).
- ☐ Check the operation of the brakes, and for fluid leakage (Section 10).
- ☐ Check the steering head bearing freeplay (Section 11).
- ☐ Check the wheel and tyre condition, and the tyre tread depth (Section 12).
- ☐ Check and adjust the engine idle speed (Section 13).
- ☐ Check carburettor synchronisation (Section 14).
- ☐ Check and lubricate the stands, lever pivots and cables (Section 15).

Every 6000 miles (10,000 km) or twelve months

Carry out all the items under the 3000 mile (5000 km) check, plus the following:

- ☐ Check the valve clearances (Section 16).
- ☐ Clean the air filter element (Section 17).
- ☐ Check throttle/choke cable operation and freeplay (Section 18).
- ☐ Change the engine oil and renew the oil filter (Section 19).
- ☐ Check the cooling system (Section 20).
- ☐ Check the fuel hoses and system components (Section 21).
- ☐ Check the front and rear suspension (Section 22).
- ☐ Re-grease the swingarm and suspension linkage bearings (Section 23).
- ☐ Check the tightness of all nuts and bolts (Section 24).

Every 12,000 miles (20,000 km) or two years

Carry out all the items under the 6000 mile (10,000 km) check, plus the following:

- ☐ Change the brake fluid (Section 25).
- ☐ Re-grease the steering head bearings (Section 26).

Every 18,000 miles (30,000 km) or two years

Carry out all the items under the 6000 mile (10,000 km) check, plus the following:

- ☐ Change the front fork oil (Section 27).
- ☐ Change the coolant (Section 28).

Every two years

- ☐ Renew the brake master cylinder and caliper seals (Section 29).

Every four years

- ☐ Renew the brake hoses (Section 30).
- ☐ Renew the fuel hoses (Section 31).

Non-scheduled maintenance

- ☐ Check the battery (Section 32).
- ☐ Check the headlight aim (Section 33).
- ☐ Check the wheel bearings (Section 34).
- ☐ Check the cylinder compression (Section 35).
- ☐ Check the engine oil pressure (Section 36).

Note: *The daily (pre-ride) checks at the beginning of the manual cover those items which should be inspected on a daily basis. Always perform the pre-ride inspection at every maintenance interval (in addition to the procedures listed). The intervals listed below are the intervals recommended by the manufacturer for the models covered in this manual. If in doubt, check with a Kawasaki dealer.*

Daily (pre-ride)

See *'Daily (pre-ride) checks'* at the beginning of this manual.

After the initial 600 miles (1000 km)

Note: *This check is usually performed by a Kawasaki dealer after the first 600 miles (1000 km) from new. Thereafter, maintenance is carried out according to the following intervals of the schedule.*

Every 400 miles (600 km)

Carry out all the items under the Daily (pre-ride) checks, plus the following

- ☐ Clean and lubricate the drive chain (Section 1).

Every 600 miles (1000 km)

Carry out all the items under the Daily (pre-ride) checks, plus the following

- ☐ Check and adjust drive chain freeplay (Section 2).

Every 4000 miles (6000 km) or six months

Carry out all the items under the Daily (pre-ride) checks and the 400 mile (600 km) and 600 mile (1000 km) check, plus the following

- ☐ Clean and check the spark plugs (Section 3).
- ☐ Check the air suction valve (US models only) (Section 4).
- ☐ Check the evaporative emission control (EVAP) system (California models only) (Section 5).
- ☐ Change the engine oil (Section 6).
- ☐ Check the operation of the clutch (Section 7).
- ☐ Check for drive chain wear and stretch and sprocket wear (Section 8).
- ☐ Check the brake pads for wear (Section 9).
- ☐ Check the operation of the brakes, and for fluid leakage (Section 10).
- ☐ Check the steering head bearing freeplay (Section 11).
- ☐ Check the wheel and tyre condition, and the tyre tread depth (Section 12).
- ☐ Check and adjust the engine idle speed (Section 13).

Every 8000 miles (12,000 km) or twelve months

Carry out all the items under the 4000 mile (6000 km) check, plus the following:

- ☐ Check carburettor synchronisation (Section 14).
- ☐ Check and lubricate the stands, lever pivots and cables (Section 15).
- ☐ Check the valve clearances (Section 16).
- ☐ Clean the air filter element (Section 17).
- ☐ Check throttle/choke cable operation and freeplay (Section 18).
- ☐ Change the engine oil and renew the oil filter (Section 19).
- ☐ Check the cooling system (Section 20).
- ☐ Check the fuel hoses and system components (Section 21).
- ☐ Check the front and rear suspension (Section 22).
- ☐ Re-grease the swingarm and suspension linkage bearings (Section 23).
- ☐ Check the tightness of all nuts and bolts (Section 24).

Every 16,000 miles (24,000 km) or two years

Carry out all the items under the 8000 mile (12,000 km) check, plus the following:

- ☐ Change the brake fluid (Section 25).
- ☐ Re-grease the steering head bearings (Section 26).
- ☐ Change the front fork oil (Section 27).
- ☐ Change the coolant (Section 28).

Every four years

- ☐ Renew the brake master cylinder and caliper seals (Section 29).
- ☐ Renew the brake hoses (Section 30).
- ☐ Renew the fuel hoses (Section 31).

Non-scheduled maintenance

- ☐ Check the battery (Section 32).
- ☐ Check the headlight aim (Section 33).
- ☐ Check the wheel bearings (Section 34).
- ☐ Check the cylinder compression (Section 35).
- ☐ Check the engine oil pressure (Section 36).

Note: *The daily (pre-ride) checks at the beginning of the manual cover those items which should be inspected on a daily basis. Always perform the pre-ride inspection at every maintenance interval (in addition to the procedures listed). The intervals listed below are the intervals recommended by the manufacturer for the models covered in this manual. If in doubt, check with a Kawasaki dealer.*

Daily (pre-ride)

See *'Daily (pre-ride) checks'* at the beginning of this manual.

After the initial 600 miles (1000 km)

Note: *This check is usually performed by a Kawasaki dealer after the first 600 miles (1000 km) from new. Thereafter, maintenance is carried out according to the following intervals of the schedule.*

Every 400 miles (600 km)

Carry out all the items under the Daily (pre-ride) checks, plus the following

☐ Clean and lubricate the drive chain (Section 1).

Every 600 miles (1000 km)

Carry out all the items under the Daily (pre-ride) checks, plus the following

☐ Check and adjust drive chain freeplay (Section 2).

Every 4000 miles (6000 km) or six months

Carry out all the items under the Daily (pre-ride) checks and the 400 mile (600 km) and 600 mile (1000 km) check, plus the following

☐ Clean and check the spark plugs (Section 3).
☐ Check the air suction valve (US models only) (Section 4).
☐ Check the evaporative emission control (EVAP) system (California models only) (Section 5).
☐ Check the fuel hoses and system components – J and A models (Section 21).
☐ Change the engine oil (Section 6).
☐ Check the operation of the clutch (Section 7).
☐ Check for drive chain wear and stretch and sprocket wear (Section 8).
☐ Check the brake pads for wear (Section 9).
☐ Check the operation of the brakes, and for fluid leakage (Section 10).
☐ Check the steering head bearing freeplay (Section 11).
☐ Check the wheel and tyre condition, and the tyre tread depth (Section 12).

Every 8000 miles (12,000 km) or twelve months

Carry out all the items under the 4000 mile (6000 km) check, plus the following:

☐ Check and adjust the engine idle speed (Section 13).
☐ Check carburettor synchronisation (Section 14).
☐ Check and lubricate the stands, lever pivots and cables (Section 15).
☐ Check the valve clearances (Section 16).
☐ Clean the air filter element (Section 17).
☐ Check throttle/choke cable operation and freeplay (Section 18).
☐ Change the engine oil and renew the oil filter (Section 19).
☐ Check the cooling system (Section 20).
☐ Check the fuel hoses and system components – G and H models (Section 21).
☐ Check the front and rear suspension (Section 22).
☐ Re-grease the swingarm and suspension linkage bearings (Section 23).
☐ Check the tightness of all nuts and bolts (Section 24).

Every 16,000 miles (24,000 km) or two years

Carry out all the items under the 8000 mile (12,000 km) check, plus the following:

☐ Change the brake fluid (Section 25).
☐ Re-grease the steering head bearings (Section 26).
☐ Change the front fork oil (Section 27).
☐ Change the coolant (Section 28).

Every four years

☐ Renew the brake master cylinder and caliper seals (Section 29).
☐ Renew the brake hoses (Section 30).
☐ Renew the fuel hoses (Section 31).

Non-scheduled maintenance

☐ Check the battery (Section 32).
☐ Check the headlight aim (Section 33).
☐ Check the wheel bearings (Section 34).
☐ Check the cylinder compression (Section 35).
☐ Check the engine oil pressure (Section 36).

1 This Chapter is designed to help the home mechanic maintain his/her motorcycle for safety, economy, long life and peak performance.

2 Deciding where to start or plug into the routine maintenance schedule depends on several factors. If the warranty period on your motorcycle has just expired, and if it has been maintained according to the warranty standards, you may want to pick up routine maintenance as it coincides with the next mileage or calendar interval. If you have owned the machine for some time but have never performed any maintenance on it, then you may want to start at the nearest interval and include some additional procedures to ensure that nothing important is overlooked. If you have just had a major engine overhaul, then you may want to start the maintenance routine from the beginning. If you have a used machine and have no knowledge of its history or maintenance record, you may desire to combine all the checks into one large service initially and then settle into the maintenance schedule prescribed.

3 Before beginning any maintenance or repair, the machine should be cleaned thoroughly, especially around the oil filter, spark plugs, valve cover, side panels, carburettors, etc. Cleaning will help ensure that dirt does not contaminate the engine and will allow you to detect wear and damage that could otherwise easily go unnoticed.

4 Certain maintenance information is sometimes printed on decals attached to the motorcycle. If the information on the decals differs from that included here, use the information on the decal.

Maintenance procedures

1 Drive chain – cleaning and lubrication

Interval:
F1 model – every 200 miles (300 km)
All other models – every 400 miles (600 km)

1 Support the machine on an auxiliary stand so that the rear wheel is off the ground. Rotate the rear wheel whilst cleaning and lubricating the chain to access all the links.

2 Wash the chain in paraffin (kerosene), then wipe it off and allow it to dry, using compressed air if available. If the chain is excessively dirty it should be removed from the machine and allowed to soak in the paraffin (see Chapter 6).

Caution: Don't use petrol, solvent or other cleaning fluids which might damage the internal sealing properties of the chain. Don't use high-pressure water. The entire process shouldn't take longer than ten minutes – if it does, the O-rings in the chain rollers could be damaged.

3 The best time to lubricate the chain is after the motorcycle has been ridden, as when the chain is warm the lubricant penetrates the joints between the side plates better than when cold.

4 Apply the specified lubricant (see Specifications at the beginning of the Chapter) to the area where the side plates overlap – not to the middle of the rollers, covering the inside edge as well as the outside **(see illustration)**. After applying the lubricant, let it soak in for a few minutes before wiping off any excess.

> **HAYNES HiNT** ***Apply lubricant to the top of the lower chain run – centrifugal force will work it into the chain when the bike is moving.***

2 Drive chain – freeplay check and adjustment

Interval:
F1 model – every 500 miles (800 km)
All other models – every 600 miles (1000 km)

Check

1 A neglected drive chain won't last long and can quickly damage the sprockets. Routine chain adjustment will ensure maximum chain and sprocket life.

2 To check the chain, shift the transmission into neutral and make sure the ignition switch is OFF. Rotate the rear wheel until the chain is positioned with the tightest point at the centre of its bottom run, then place the machine on its sidestand. Make sure that the adjuster position marker is in the same position on each side relative to the notches in the swingarm **(see illustrations 2.6c and d)**.

3 Measure the amount of freeplay on the chain's bottom run, at a point midway between the two sprockets, then compare your measurement to the value listed in this Chapter's Specifications **(see illustration)**. Since the chain will rarely wear evenly, rotate the rear wheel so that another section of chain can be checked; do this several times to check the entire length of chain. In some cases where lubrication has been neglected, corrosion and galling may cause the links to bind and kink, which effectively shortens the chain's length. If the chain is tight between the sprockets, rusty or kinked, or if any of the pins are loose or the rollers damaged, it's time to fit a new one. If you find a tight area, mark it with felt pen or paint, and repeat the measurement after the bike has been ridden. If the chain's still tight in the same area, it may be damaged or worn. Because a tight or kinked chain can damage the transmission output shaft bearing, it's a good idea to renew it.

Adjustment

4 Rotate the rear wheel until the chain is positioned with the tightest point at the centre of its bottom run, then place the machine on its sidestand.

5 Remove the split pin from the rear axle nut, then slacken the nut **(see illustration)**.

1.4 Apply the oil to the top of the lower run where the sideplates overlap

2.3 Push up on the chain and measure the slack

2.5 Remove the split pin (arrowed) and slacken the axle nut – F models shown

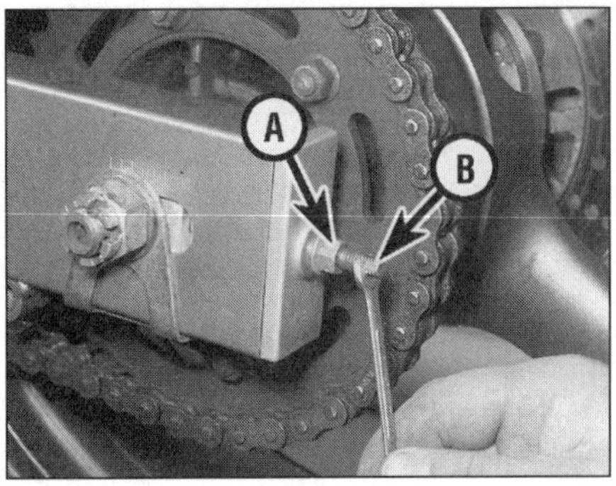

2.6a Adjuster locknut (A) and adjuster (B) – F models

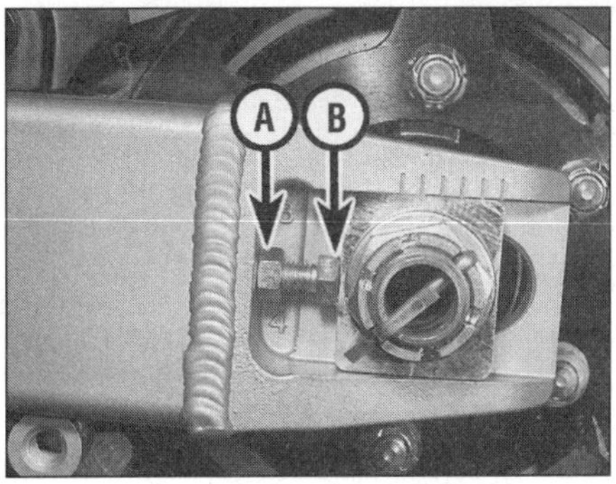

2.6b Adjuster locknut (A) and adjuster (B) – G, H, J and A models

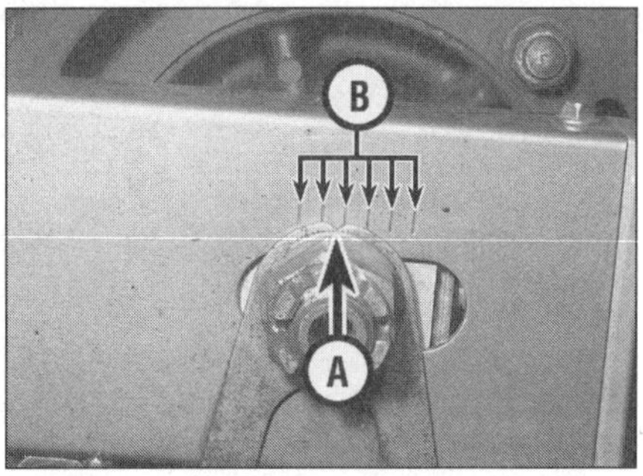

2.6c Align the cutout in the marker (A) with the same notch (B) on each side of the swingarm – F models

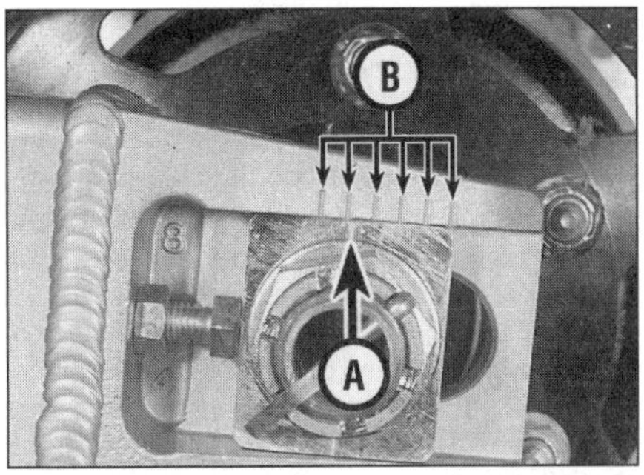

2.6d Align the cutout in the marker (A) with the same notch (B) on each side of the swingarm – G, H, J and A models

2.8a Tighten the axle nut to the specified torque . . .

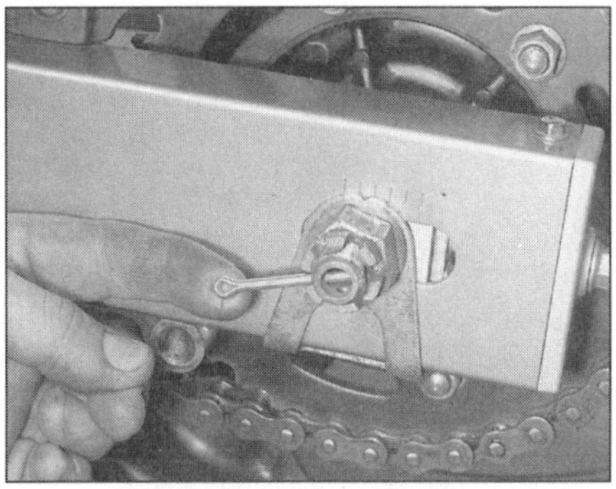
2.8b . . . then secure it using a new split pin

6 Slacken the adjuster locknut on each side of the swingarm, then turn the adjusters evenly until the amount of freeplay specified at the beginning of the Chapter is obtained at the centre of the bottom run of the chain **(see illustrations)**. On G, H, J and A models, if the chain was too tight and the adjusters have been turned in to create slack, push the rear wheel forward to ensure all the created slack is been taken up. Following chain adjustment, check that the cut-out on the top of each adjuster position marker is in the same position in relation to the marks on the swingarm **(see illustrations)**. It is important that both markers align with the same notch; if not, the rear wheel will be out of alignment with the front.

7 If there is a discrepancy in the positions of the markers, reset one of the adjusters so that its position is exactly the same as the other. Check the chain freeplay as described above and readjust if necessary.

8 Tighten the axle nut to the torque setting specified at the beginning of the Chapter, then tighten the adjuster locknuts securely **(see illustration)**. Fit a new split pin onto the axle nut **(see illustration)**.

3 Spark plugs – gap check and adjustment

Interval:

F1 model – every 3000 miles (5000 km)

All other models – every 4000 miles (6000 km)

1 Make sure your spark plug socket is the correct size before attempting to remove the plugs – a suitable one is supplied in the motorcycle's tool kit which is stored under the seat.

2 Remove the air filter housing (see Chapter 4).

3 Clean the area around the plug caps to prevent any dirt falling into the spark plug channels. If required, move aside or detach the vacuum valve components to improve access. **Note:** *On J and A models, the plug caps are integral with the ignition coils. To avoid damaging the wiring, always disconnect the connectors before removing the coil/caps **(see illustrations)**. Do not attempt to lever the coil/caps off the plugs or pull them off with pliers. Do not drop the coil/caps.*

4 Check that the cylinder location is marked on each plug lead, then pull the plug cap off each plug **(see illustration)**. Using either the

1

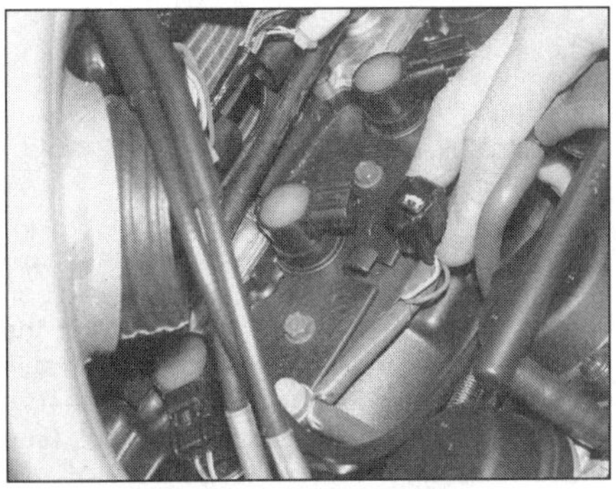
3.3a On J and A models, disconnect the coil/cap wiring connectors . . .

3.3b . . . then pull the coil/caps off the spark plugs

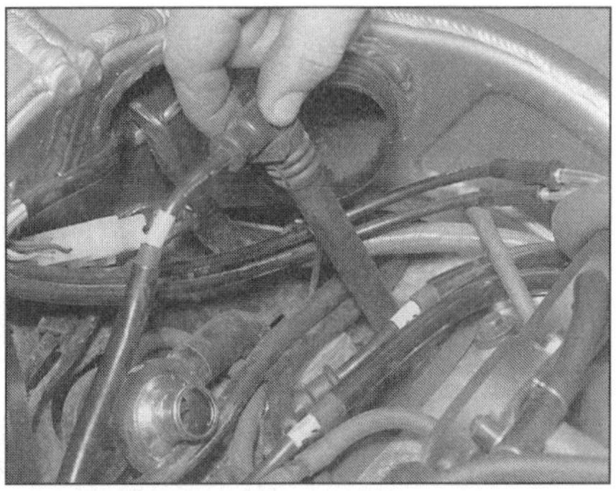
3.4a Remove the spark plug cap . . .

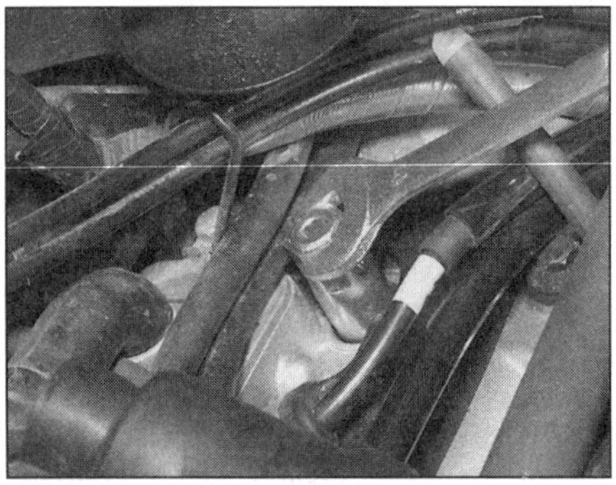

3.4b . . . then unscrew the spark plug

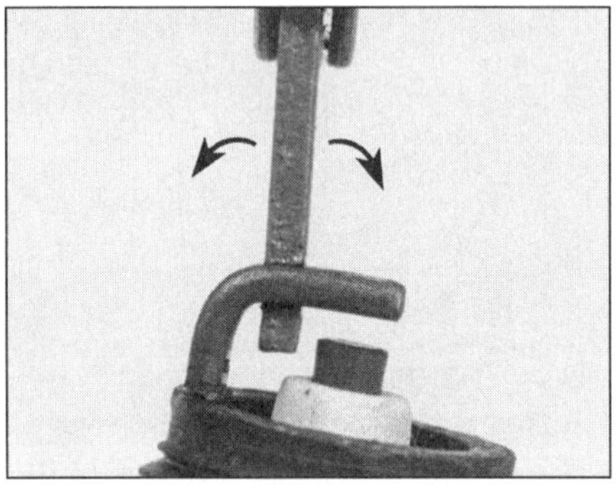

3.8c Adjust the electrode gap by bending the side electrode only

plug removing tool supplied in the bike's toolkit or a socket type wrench, unscrew the plugs from the cylinder head **(see illustration)**. Lay each plug out in relation to its cylinder; if either plug shows up a problem it will then be easy to identify the troublesome cylinder.

5 Inspect the electrodes for wear. Both the centre and side electrodes should have square edges and the side electrode should be of uniform thickness. Look for excessive deposits and evidence of a cracked or chipped insulator around the centre electrode. Compare your spark plugs to the colour spark plug reading chart at the end of this manual. Check the threads, the washer and the

4.1a Lift the vacuum valve switch bracket (arrowed) off the vacuum valve hoses . . .

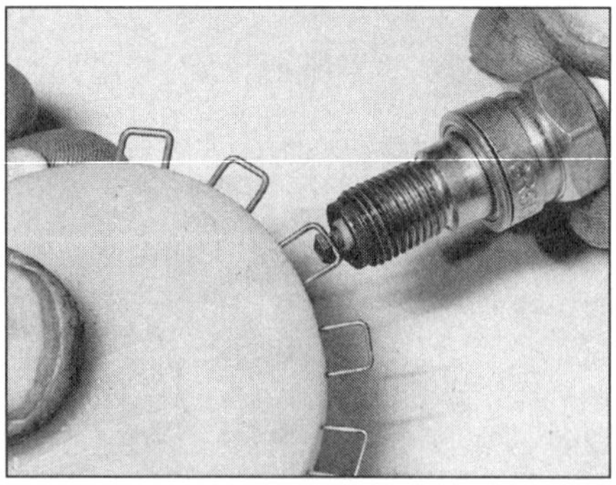

3.8a Using a wire type gauge to measure the spark plug electrode gap

3.9 Thread the plug in as far as possible turning the tool by hand

ceramic insulator body for cracks and other damage.

6 If the electrodes are not excessively worn, and if the deposits can be easily removed with a wire brush, the plugs can be re-gapped and re-used (if no cracks or chips are visible in the insulator). If in doubt concerning the condition of the plugs, fit new ones, as the expense is minimal.

7 Cleaning spark plugs by sandblasting is permitted, provided you clean the plugs with a high flash-point solvent afterwards.

8 Before installing the plugs, make sure they are the correct type and heat range and check the gap between the electrodes (they are not pre-set on new plugs). For best results, use a

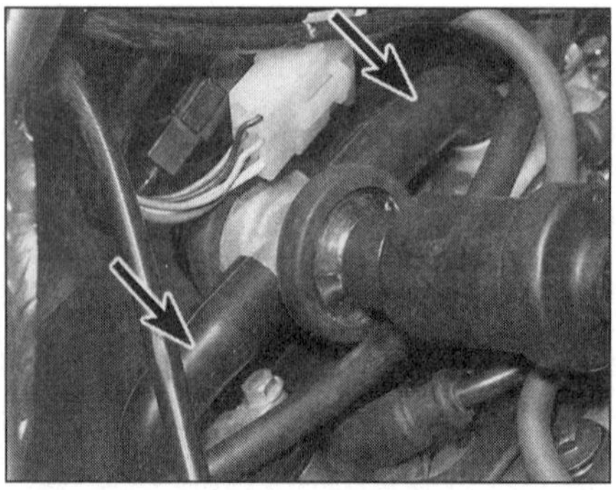

4.1b . . . then detach the hoses (arrowed) from the suction valve covers

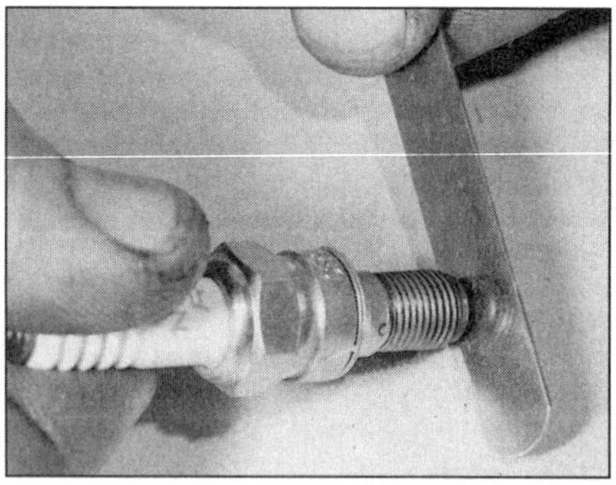

3.8b Using a feeler gauge to measure the spark plug electrode gap

wire-type gauge rather than a flat (feeler) gauge to check the gap **(see illustrations)**. Compare the gap to that specified and adjust as necessary. If the gap must be adjusted, bend the side electrode only and be very careful not to chip or crack the insulator nose **(see illustration)**. Make sure the washer is in place before installing each plug.

9 Since the cylinder head is made of aluminium, which is soft and easily damaged, thread the plugs into the heads by hand **(see illustration)**. Once the plugs are finger-tight, the job can be finished with the tool supplied or a socket. Tighten the spark plugs to the specified torque setting or according to the manufacturer's instructions on the packet – do not over-tighten them.

HAYNES HiNT

Stripped plug threads in the cylinder head can be repaired with a thread insert – see 'Tools and workshop tips' in the Reference section.

10 Reconnect the spark plug caps, making sure they are securely connected to the correct cylinder. On J and A models, reconnect the coil/cap wiring connectors.

11 Install the air filter housing (see Chapter 4).

4 Air suction valves – check

Interval:

F1 model – every 3000 miles (5000 km)

All other models – every 4000 miles (6000 km)

1 Remove the air filter housing (see Chapter 4). Lift the vacuum valve switch bracket off the vacuum valve hoses, then detach the vacuum valve hoses from the suction valve covers and displace the assembly, noting how it fits and where the hoses connect **(see illustrations)**.

2 Unscrew the bolts securing each suction valve cover to the valve cover, then lift the

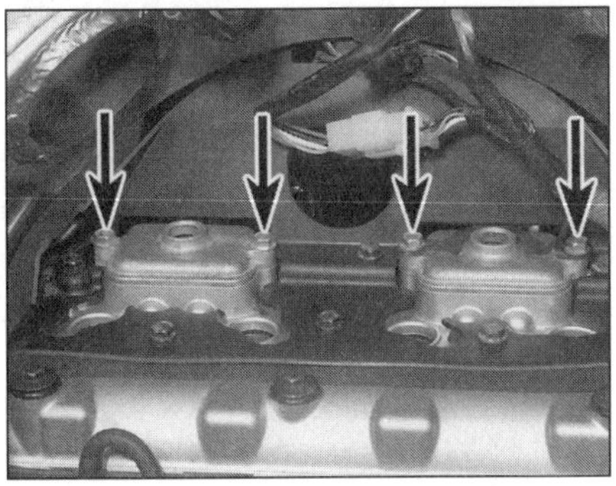

4.2 Suction valve cover bolts (arrowed)

covers off and remove the reed valve assemblies, noting which way up and round they fit **(see illustration)**.

3 Check the reeds for cracks, warpage and any other damage or deterioration **(see illustration)**. Also check the contact areas between the reeds and the reed holders, and the holders themselves, for any signs of damage or deterioration. Any carbon deposits or other foreign particles can be cleaned off using a high flash-point solvent. Renew the reed valve assemblies if there is any doubt about their condition. Also check the condition of the upper and lower gaskets and renew them if necessary.

4 Install the valve assemblies with their gaskets, making sure the wider section of the reed and the projection on the upper gasket face the rear, then install the covers and tighten the bolts to the torque setting specified at the beginning of the Chapter. On J and A models, apply a suitable non-permanent thread locking compound to the bolts before reassembly.

5 Install the vacuum valve and its switch, making sure the hoses are correctly and securely connected **(see illustrations 4.1b and a)**.

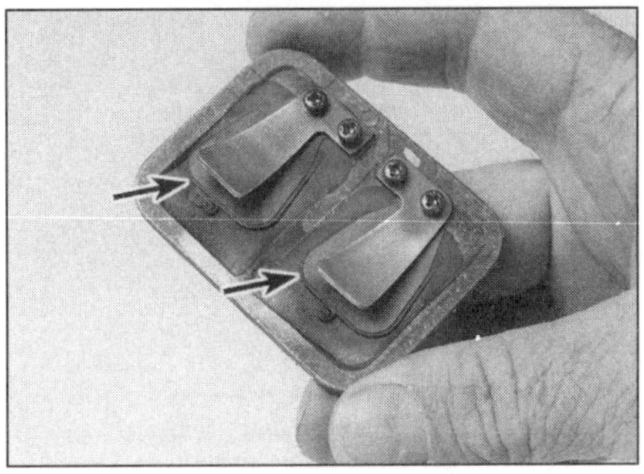

4.3 Check the reeds (arrowed) and their contact areas on the air suction valve for damage and wear as described

5 Evaporative emission control (EVAP) system - check (California models only)

Interval:
F1 model - every 3000 miles (5000 km)
All other models - every 4000 miles (6000 km)

1 Visually inspect all the EVAP system hoses for kinks and splits and any other damage or deterioration. Make sure that the hoses are securely connected with a clamp on each end. Renew any hoses that are damaged or deteriorated. Refer to Chapter 4 for further information and diagrams of the EVAP system and to the hose routing label on the bike.

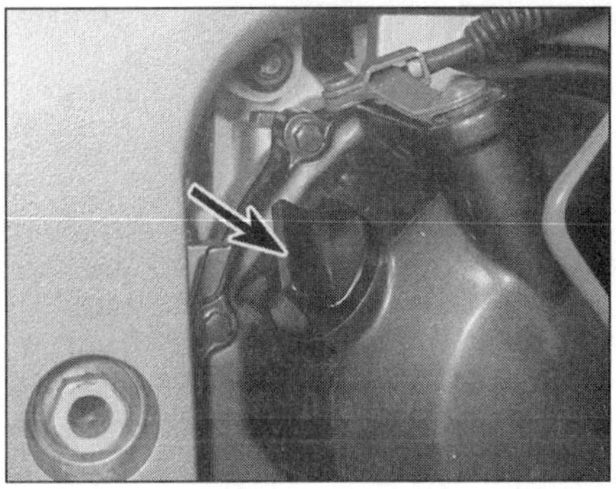

6.3 Unscrew the oil filler cap (arrowed) . . .

6 Engine - oil change

Interval:
F1 model - every 3000 miles (5000 km)
All other models - every 4000 miles (6000 km)

Warning: Be careful when draining the oil, as the exhaust pipes, the engine, and the oil itself can cause severe burns.

1 Regular oil changes are the single most important maintenance procedure you can perform on a motorcycle. The oil not only lubricates the internal parts of the engine, transmission and clutch, but it also acts as a coolant, a cleaner, a sealant, and a protectant. Because of these demands, the oil takes a terrific amount of abuse and should be changed often with new oil of the recommended grade and type. Saving a little money on the difference in cost between a good oil and a cheap oil won't pay off if the engine is damaged. The oil filter should be changed with every second oil change.

2 Before changing the oil, warm up the engine so the oil will drain easily.

3 Support the motorcycle upright using an auxiliary stand, and position a clean drain tray below the engine. Unscrew the oil filler cap on the clutch cover to vent the crankcase and to act as a reminder that there is no oil in the engine **(see illustration)**.

4 Next, unscrew the oil drain plug from the bottom of the engine and allow the oil to flow into the drain tray **(see illustrations)**. Check the condition of the drain plug sealing washer. If it is damaged or deformed discard it and use a new one.

5 When the oil has completely drained, fit the sealing washer over the drain plug, using a new one if necessary, then fit the plug to the sump and tighten it to the torque setting specified at the beginning of the Chapter **(see illustrations)**.

6.4a . . . and the oil drain plug (arrowed) . . .

6.4b . . . and allow the oil to completely drain

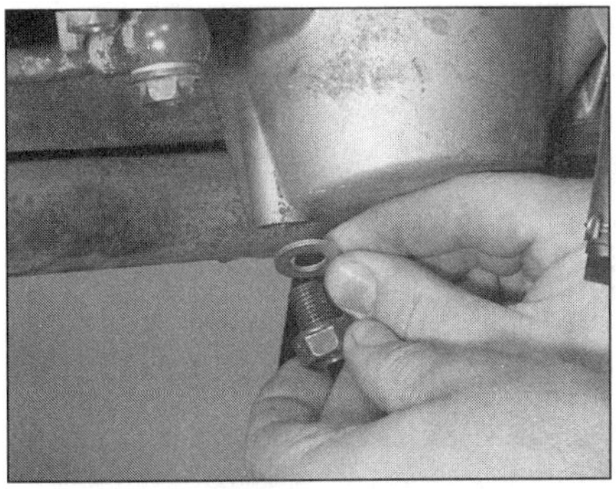

6.5a Do not forget the sealing washer and use a new one if necessary

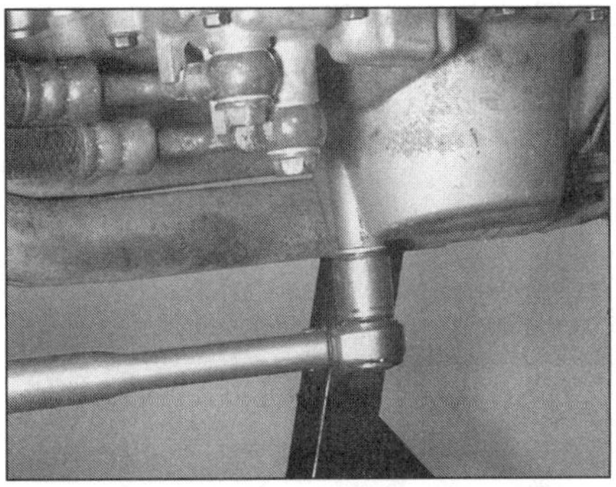

6.5b Tighten the drain plug to the specified torque setting

Avoid overtightening, as damage to the sump will result.

6 Refill the crankcase to the proper level using the recommended type and amount of oil (see *Specifications*). With the motorcycle held vertical, the oil level should lie between the upper and lower level lines on the inspection window in the clutch cover (see *Daily (pre-ride) checks*). Install the filler cap. Start the engine and let it run for two or three minutes (make sure that the oil pressure light extinguishes after a few seconds). Shut it off, wait a few minutes, then check the oil level. If necessary, add more oil to bring the level up to the high level line on the inspection window. Check around the drain plug for leaks.

> HAYNES HiNT *Saving a little money on the difference between good and cheap oils won't pay off if the engine is damaged as a result.*

7 The old oil drained from the engine cannot be re-used and should be disposed of properly. Check with your local refuse disposal company, disposal facility or environmental agency to see whether they will accept the used oil for recycling. Don't pour used oil into drains or onto the ground.

> HAYNES HiNT *Check the old oil carefully – if it is very metallic coloured, then the engine is experiencing wear from break-in (new engine) or from insufficient lubrication. If there are flakes or chips of metal in the oil, then something is drastically wrong internally and the engine will have to be disassembled for inspection and repair. If there are pieces of fibre-like material in the oil, the clutch is experiencing excessive wear and should be checked.*

7 Clutch – check

Interval:
F1 model – every 3000 miles (5000 km)
All other models – every 4000 miles (6000 km)

1 Periodic adjustment of the clutch cable is necessary to compensate for wear in the clutch plates and stretch of the cable. Check that the amount of freeplay at the clutch lever is within the specifications listed at the beginning of the Chapter **(see illustration)**. If adjustment is required, it can be made at either the lever end of the cable or at the clutch end.

2 To adjust the freeplay at the lever on F, G and H models, first loosen the adjuster locking ring, then on all models turn the adjuster in or out until the required amount of freeplay is obtained **(see illustrations)**. To increase freeplay, turn the adjuster clockwise. To reduce freeplay, turn the adjuster anti-clockwise. After adjustment on F, G and H models, tighten the locking ring securely against the lever bracket.

3 If all the adjustment has been taken up at the lever, first reset the adjuster at the lever end of the cable. On F, G and H models there should be 5 to 6 mm of thread visible between the adjuster head and the locking ring. On J and A models, there should be 5 to 6 mm of thread visible between the adjuster head and the bracket.

4 Pull back the rubber boot on the adjuster at the clutch end of the cable and fully slacken the locknuts, then pull the outer cable so that it is tight **(see illustration)**. Retighten the locknuts against the bracket and refit the rubber boot. Now set the correct amount of freeplay using the adjuster at the clutch end of the cable as described in Step 2. Subsequent adjustments can be made using the lever adjuster only, until again all the adjustment has been taken up. If all the adjustment on both adjusters has been taken up, fit a new cable (see Chapter 2).

5 Push the release lever on the clutch cover forward until it stops. At this point the angle between the release lever and the cable should be approximately 60°. If not, and the cable freeplay is set correctly, the clutch should be inspected for wear (see Chapter 2).

6 On F, G and H models, the clutch lever has a span adjuster which alters the distance of the lever from the handlebar **(see illustration)**.

7.1 Measure the amount of freeplay between the clutch lever and bracket as shown

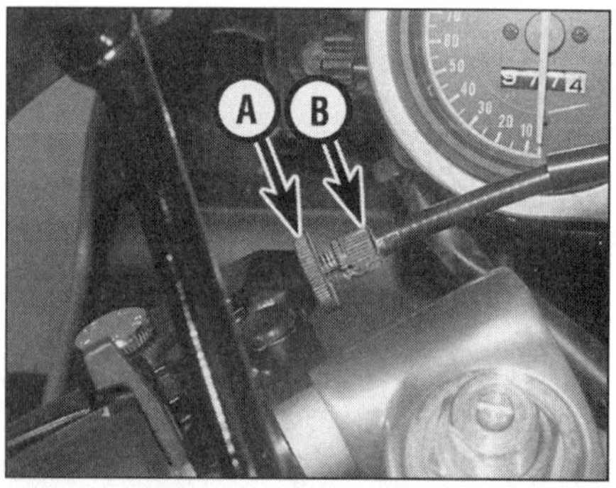

7.2a Loosen the lockring (A) and turn the adjuster (B) as required – F, G and H models

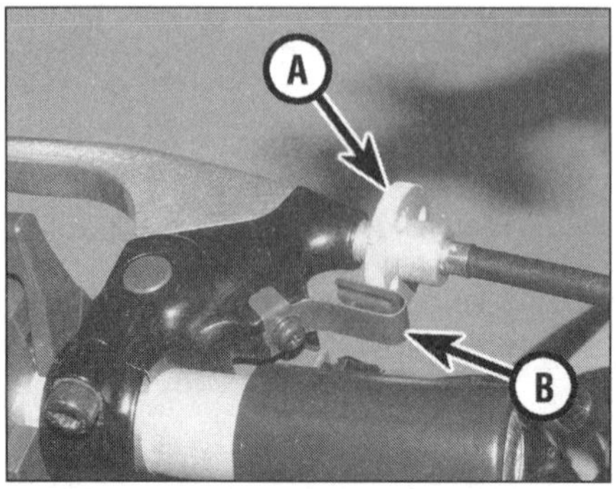

7.2b Adjuster (A) is secured by spring clip (B) – J and A models

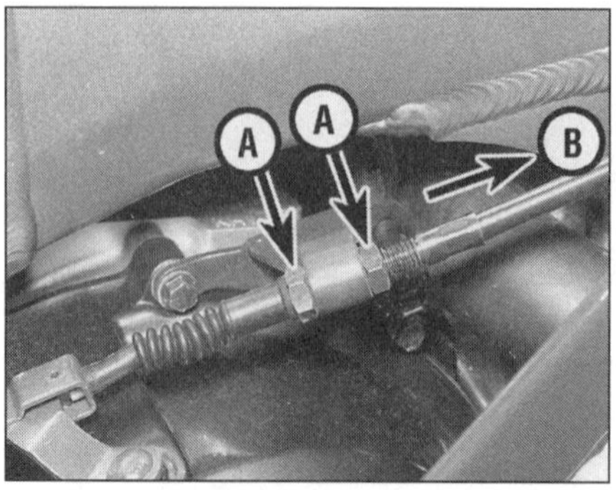

7.4 Slacken the locknuts (A) and pull the cable in the direction shown (B)

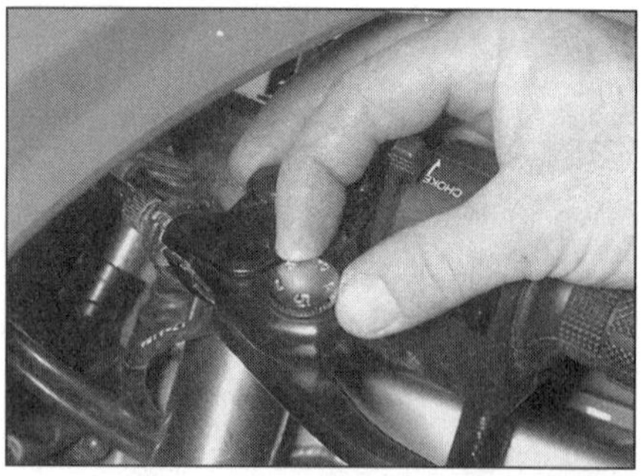

7.6 Pull the lever away from the handlebar and adjust the dial as required – F, G and H models

8.2a The chainguard is secured by two screws (arrowed)

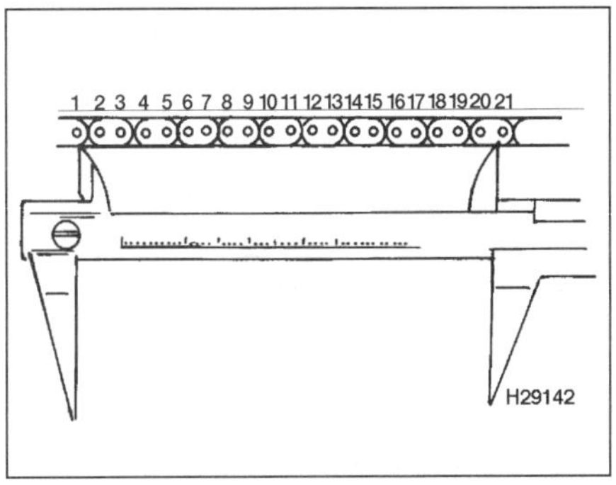

8.2b Measure the distance between 21 pins as shown to determine chain stretch

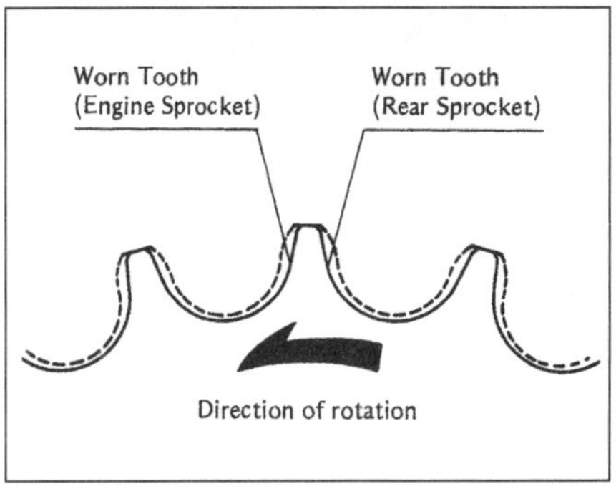

8.3 Check the teeth on both sprockets to determine whether they are excessively worn

Pull the lever away from the handlebar and turn the adjuster dial until the setting which best suits the rider is obtained. There are five positions. Align the number for the setting required with the triangular mark on the lever bracket.

8 Drive chain and sprockets – wear and stretch check

Interval:
F1 model – every 3000 miles (5000 km)
All other models – every 4000 miles (6000 km)

1 Check the entire length of the chain for damaged rollers, cracked sideplates, loose links and pins, and fit a new chain if damage is found. If the chain has reached the end of its adjustment, it must be renewed.

2 The amount of chain stretch can be measured and compared to the stretch limit specified at the beginning of the Chapter. Remove the screws securing the chainguard to the swingarm and remove the guard, noting how it fits **(see illustration)**. Hang a 10 kg (22 lb) weight from the bottom run of the chain. Measure along the top run the length of 21 pins (from the centre of the 1st pin to the centre of the 21st pin) and compare the result with the service limit specified at the beginning of the Chapter **(see illustration)**. Rotate the rear wheel so that several sections of the chain are measured. If any of the measurements exceeds the service limit the chain must be renewed (see Chapter 6). **Note:** *It is good practice to renew the chain and sprockets as a set.*

3 Remove the engine sprocket cover (see Chapter 6). Check the teeth on the engine sprocket and the rear wheel sprocket for wear **(see illustration)**.

4 Inspect the drive chain slider on the swingarm for excessive wear and renew it if necessary (see Chapter 6).

9 Brake pads – wear check

Interval:
F1 model – every 3000 miles (5000 km)
All other models – every 4000 miles (6000 km)

1 Each brake pad has wear indicator steps, lines, cutouts or grooves that can be viewed without removing the pads from the caliper **(see illustrations)**. If the pads are worn to or beyond the wear limit, they must be renewed. If the pads are dirty or if you are in doubt as to the amount of friction material remaining, remove them for inspection (see Chapter 7) and measure the thickness of the friction material. If the thickness of the material remaining is 1 mm or less, fit new pads. **Note:** *Some after-market pads may use different indicators to those on the original equipment as shown.*

2 Refer to Chapter 7 for details of pad renewal.

10 Brake system – check

Interval:
F1 model – every 3000 miles (5000 km)
All other models – every 4000 miles (6000 km)

1 A routine general check of the brake system will ensure that any problems are discovered and remedied before the rider's safety is jeopardised.

2 Check the brake lever and pedal for loose connections, improper or rough action, excessive play, bends, and other damage. Replace any damaged parts with new ones (see Chapter 7).

3 Make sure all brake fasteners are tight. Check the brake pads for wear (see Section 9) and make sure the fluid level in the reservoirs is correct (see *Daily (pre-ride) checks*). Look for leaks at the hose connections and check for cracks in the hoses **(see illustration)**. If the lever or pedal is spongy, bleed the brakes (see Chapter 7).

4 Make sure the brake light operates when the front brake lever is depressed. The front brake light switch is not adjustable. If it fails to operate properly, check it (see Chapter 9).

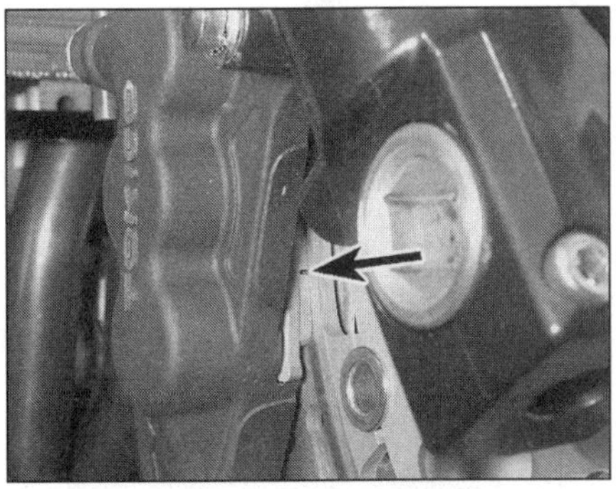

9.1a Front brake pad wear indicator groove (arrowed)

9.1b Rear brake pad wear indicator cutouts (arrowed)

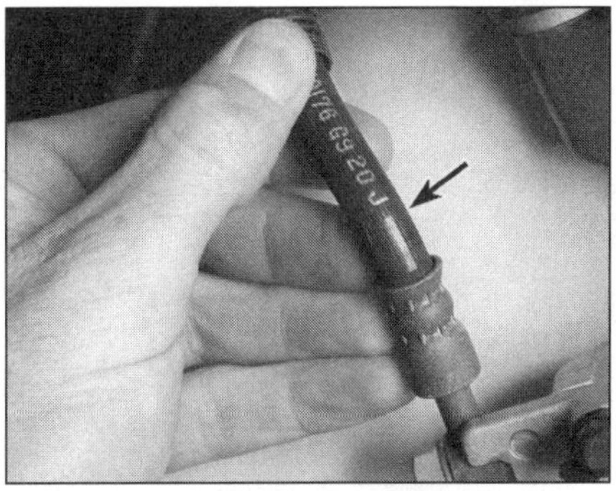

10.3 Flex the brake hoses and check for cracks, bulges and leaking fluid

10.5 Hold the switch and turn the adjusting nut as required

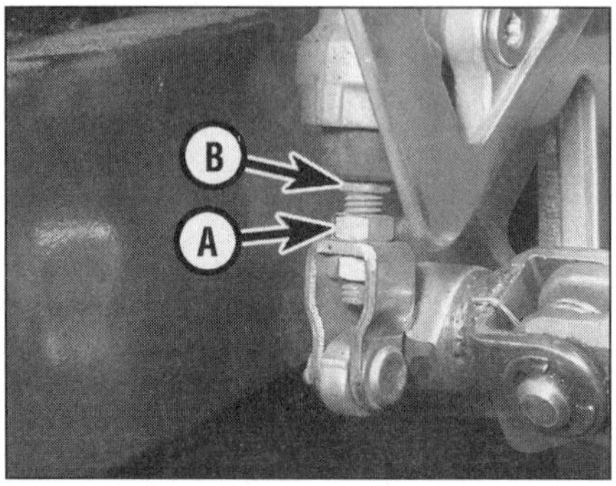

10.6b Slacken the locknut (A) and turn the pushrod using the hex (B)

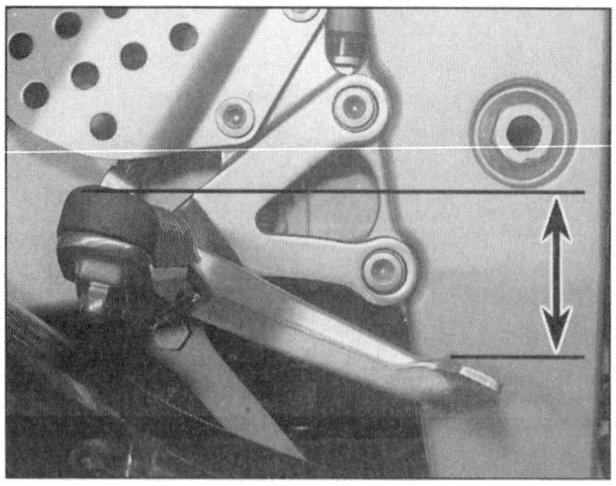

10.6a Measure the distance between the pedal tip and the top of the footrest as shown

10.7 Pull the lever away from the handlebar and adjust the dial as required

5 Make sure the brake light is activated after about 10 mm of brake pedal travel or just before the rear brake takes effect. If adjustment is necessary, hold the switch and turn the adjusting nut on the switch body until the brake light is activated when required **(see illustration)**. If the switch doesn't operate the brake lights, check it (see Chapter 9).

6 Check the position of the brake pedal. Kawasaki recommend that the distance from the pedal tip to the top of the rider's footrest should be as specified at the beginning of the Chapter **(see illustration)**. If the pedal height is incorrect, or if the rider's preference is different, slacken the clevis locknut on the master cylinder pushrod, then turn the pushrod using a spanner on the hex at the top of the rod until the pedal is at the correct or desired height **(see illustration)**. If access to the pushrod is too restricted, remove the footrest bracket mounting bolts, then draw the bracket away from the frame, taking care not to twist or strain the brake hoses. On completion tighten the locknut securely. Adjust the rear brake light switch after adjusting the pedal height (see Step 5).

7 The front brake lever has a span adjuster which alters the distance of the lever from the handlebar **(see illustration)**. Pull the lever away from the handlebar and turn the adjuster dial until the setting which best suits the rider is obtained. There are four positions on F models and five on all other models. Align the number for the setting required with the triangular mark on the lever bracket.

11 Steering head bearings – freeplay check and adjustment

Interval:
F1 model – every 3000 miles (5000 km)
All other models – every 4000 miles (6000 km)

1 The steering head bearings can become dented, rough or loose during normal use of the machine. In extreme cases, worn or loose steering head bearings can cause steering wobble – a condition that is potentially dangerous.

Check

2 Place the motorcycle on an auxiliary stand. Raise the front wheel off the ground either by having an assistant push down on the rear, or by removing the lower fairing panels (see Chapter 8) and placing a support under the engine.

3 Point the front wheel straight-ahead and slowly move the handlebars from side-to-side. Any dents or roughness in the bearing races will be felt and the bars will not move smoothly and freely. With the wheel pointing straight-ahead, tap the end of each bar in turn. The handlebars should travel to the full-lock position under the force of gravity alone. If not, and it is not due to interference from wiring or cables, the bearings are over-tight.

4 Next, grasp the fork sliders and try to move them forward and backward **(see illustration)**. Any looseness in the steering head bearings will be felt as front-to-rear movement of the forks. If play is felt in the bearings, adjust the steering head as follows.

> **HAYNES HiNT** ***Freeplay in the fork due to worn fork bushes can be misinterpreted for steering head bearing play – do not confuse the two.***

Adjustment

5 Remove the upper fairing (see Chapter 8) and the air filter housing (see Chapter 4). Slacken the steering stem nut, then slacken the fork clamp bolts in the bottom yoke **(see illustrations)**.

11.4 Checking for play in the steering head bearings

11.5a Slacken the steering stem nut (arrowed) . . .

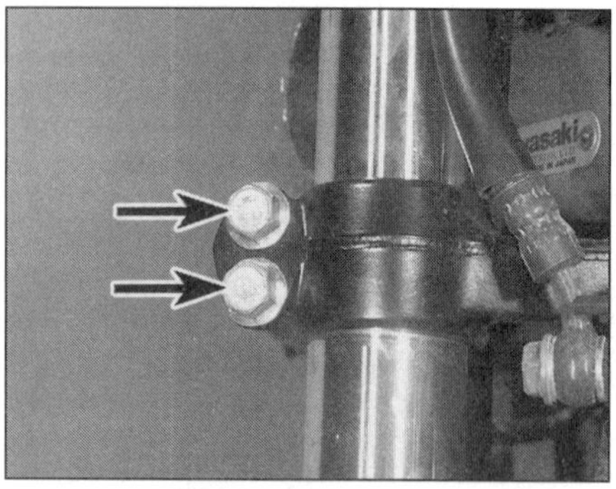

11.5b . . . and the bottom yoke clamp bolts (arrowed) for each fork

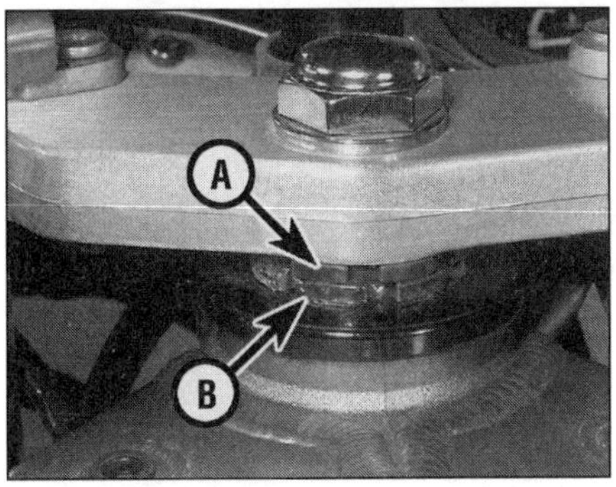

11.6 Adjuster ring locknut (A) and adjuster ring (B)

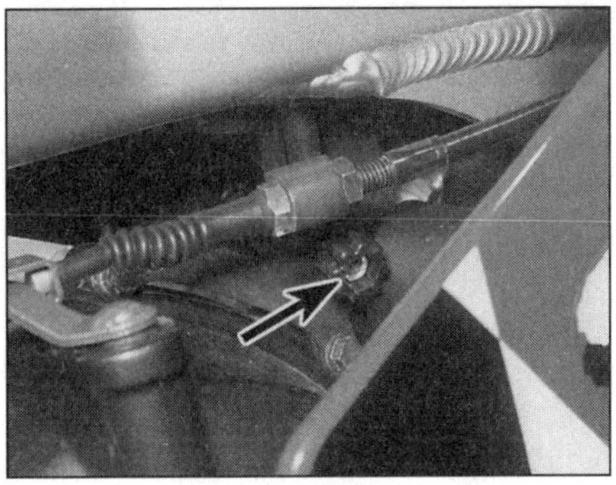
13.3a Idle speed adjuster (arrowed) – F models

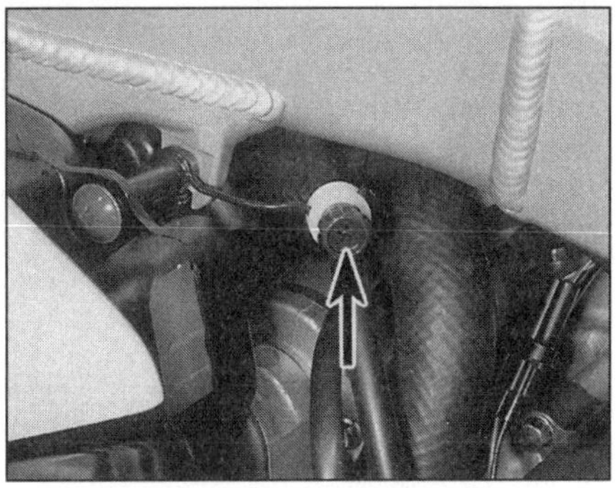
13.3b Idle speed adjuster (arrowed) – G, H, J and A models

6 Using a suitable C-spanner or drift located in one of the notches in the adjuster ring locknut, slacken the locknut **(see illustration)**. Now initially slacken the adjuster ring, then tighten or slacken it a little bit at a time as required until all freeplay in the bearings is removed, yet the steering is able to move freely from side to side. Do not turn the adjuster ring more than 1/8 turn at a time. The object is to set the adjuster ring so that the bearings are under a very light loading, just enough to remove any freeplay. Tighten the locknut lightly against the adjuster ring and check the bearings again.

Caution: Take great care not to apply excessive pressure because this will cause premature failure of the bearings.

7 If the bearings cannot be set up properly, or if there is any binding, roughness or notchiness, they will have to be removed for inspection or renewal (see Chapter 6).

8 With the bearings correctly adjusted, tighten the steering stem nut and the fork clamp bolts to the torque settings specified at the beginning of the Chapter.

9 Re-check the bearing adjustment as described above and re-adjust if necessary.

10 Install the air filter housing (see Chapter 4) and the upper fairing (see Chapter 8).

12 Wheels and tyres – check

Interval:
F1 model – every 3000 miles (5000 km)
All other models – every 4000 miles (6000 km)

Wheels

1 The cast wheels used on all models are virtually maintenance free, but they should be kept clean and checked periodically for cracks and other damage. Also check the wheel runout and alignment (see Chapter 7). Never attempt to repair damaged cast wheels; they must be replaced with new ones. Check the valve rubber for signs of damage or deterioration and have it renewed if necessary. Also, make sure the valve stem cap is in place and tight.

Tyres

2 Check the tyre condition and tread depth thoroughly – see *Daily (pre-ride) checks*.

13 Engine – idle speed check and adjustment

Interval:
F1 model – every 3000 miles (5000 km)
F2 and F3 models – every 4000 miles (6000 km)
G, H, J and A models – every 8000 miles (12,000 km)

1 The idle speed should be checked and adjusted before and after the carburettors are synchronised (balanced) and when it is obviously too high or too low. Before adjusting the idle speed, make sure the valve clearances and spark plug gaps are correct. Also, turn the handlebars back-and-forth and see if the idle speed changes as this is done. If it does, the throttle cable may not be adjusted correctly, or may be worn out. This is a dangerous condition that can cause loss of control of the bike. Be sure to correct this problem before proceeding.

2 The engine should be at normal operating temperature, which is usually reached after 10 to 15 minutes of stop and go riding. Support the motorcycle upright on an auxiliary stand, and make sure the transmission is in neutral.

3 With the engine idling in neutral, adjust the idle speed by turning the adjusting screw in or out until the idle speed listed in this Chapter's Specifications is obtained. The idle speed adjusting screw is located by the clutch cover on the right-hand side of the engine on F models, and by the coolant reservoir on the left-hand side of the engine on all other models **(see illustrations)**.

4 Snap the throttle open and shut a few times, then recheck the idle speed. If necessary, repeat the adjustment procedure.

5 If a smooth, steady idle can't be achieved, the fuel/air mixture may be incorrect (see Chapter 4) or the carburettors may need synchronising (see Section 14). Also check the air suction valves (see Section 4).

14 Carburettors – synchronisation

Interval:
F1 model – every 3000 miles (5000 km)
All other models – every 8000 miles (12,000 km)

Warning: Petrol (gasoline) is extremely flammable, so take extra precautions when you work on any part of the fuel system. Don't smoke or allow open flames or bare light bulbs near the work area, and don't work in a garage where a natural gas-type appliance is present. If you spill any fuel on your skin, rinse it off immediately with soap and water. When you perform any kind of work on the fuel system, wear safety glasses and have a fire extinguisher suitable for a Class B type fire (flammable liquids) on hand.

Warning: Take great care not to burn your hand on the hot engine unit when accessing the gauge take-off points on the intake manifolds. Do not allow exhaust gases to build up in the work area; either perform the check outside or use an exhaust gas extraction system.

1 Carburettor synchronisation is simply the process of adjusting the carburettors so they pass the same amount of fuel/air mixture to each cylinder. This is done by measuring the vacuum produced in each cylinder. Carburettors that are out of synchronisation will result in decreased fuel mileage, increased engine temperature, less than ideal throttle response and higher vibration levels. Before synchronising the carburettors, make sure the valve clearances are properly set.

2 To properly synchronise the carburettors, you will need a set of four vacuum gauges or calibrated tubes (manometer) to indicate engine vacuum. **Note:** *Because of the nature of the synchronisation procedure and the need for special instruments, most owners leave the task to a Kawasaki dealer.*

3 Start the engine and let it run until it reaches normal operating temperature, then shut it off.

4 On F, G and H models displace the

14.4 Intake manifold take-off stubs (arrowed) – F, G and H models

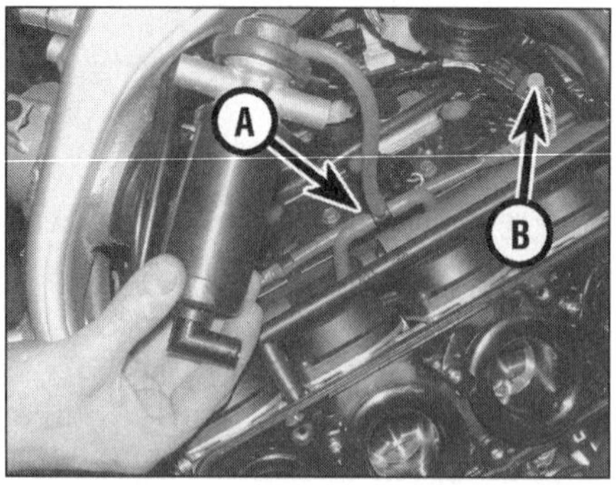

14.5 Vacuum hose T-piece (A) and blanking plug (B) – J and A models

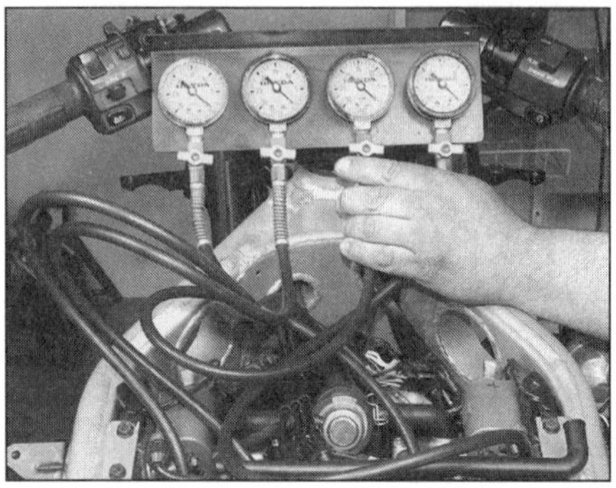

14.6 Carburettor vacuum gauge set-up

14.11 Carburettor synchronisation screws (arrowed)

carburettors from the intake manifolds to access the vacuum take-off stubs (see Chapter 4). There is no need to disconnect the throttle or choke cables. Remove the blanking caps or hoses from the take-off stubs, noting which hoses fit where **(see illustration)**.

5 On J and A models, remove the air filter housing to access the vacuum take-off hoses (see Chapter 4). Disconnect the hoses from the No. 2 and No. 3 manifolds at the T-piece and remove the blanking plugs from the No. 1 and No. 4 hoses **(see illustration)**.

6 Connect the gauge hoses to the take-off stubs or to the vacuum hoses with adapters **(see illustration)**. Make sure there are no air leaks as false readings will result.

7 On F, G and H models, fit the carburettors back into the manifolds and tighten the clamps. On all models, install the air filter housing (see Chapter 4).

8 Arrange a temporary fuel supply, either by using a small temporary tank or by using an extra long fuel hose to the now remote fuel tank.

9 Start the engine and let it idle. If the gauges are fitted with damping adjustment, set this so that the needle flutter is just eliminated but so that they can still respond to small changes in pressure.

10 The vacuum readings for all of the cylinders should be the same. If the vacuum readings vary, proceed as follows.

11 The carburettors are adjusted by turning the synchronising screws situated in-between each carburettor, in the throttle linkage **(see illustration)**. **Note:** *Do not press down on the screws whilst adjusting them, otherwise a false reading will be obtained.* First synchronise the outer left carburettor (No. 1) to the inner left carburettor (No. 2) using the left-hand synchronising screw until the readings are the same. Then synchronise the outer right carburettor (No. 4) to the inner right carburettor (No. 3) using the right-hand synchronising screw. Finally synchronise the left-hand carburettors (Nos. 1 and 2) to the right-hand carburettors (Nos. 3 and 4) using the centre synchronising screw. When all the carburettors are synchronised, open and close the throttle quickly to settle the linkage, and recheck the gauge readings, readjusting if necessary.

12 When the adjustment is complete, recheck the vacuum readings, then adjust the idle speed (see Section 13) until the idle speed listed in this Chapter's Specifications is obtained.

13 Detach the temporary fuel supply, then remove the air filter housing. On F, G and H models, displace the carburettors (see Chapter 4). Remove the gauge hoses, then install the vacuum hoses and/or blanking caps onto the carburettor take-off stubs.

14 On F, G and H models, install the carburettors. On all models, install the air filter housing and fuel tank (see Chapter 4).

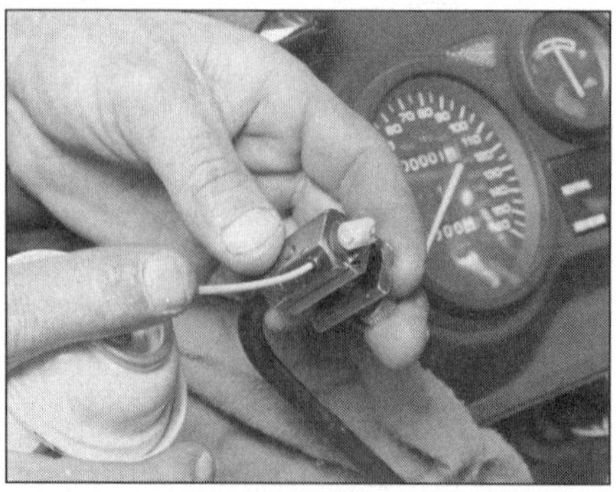

15.3a Lubricating a cable with a pressure lubricator. Make sure the tool seals around the inner cable

15 Sidestand, lever pivots and cables – lubrication

Interval:
F1 model – every 3000 miles (5000 km)
All other models – every 8000 miles (12,000 km)

1 Since the controls, cables and various other components of a motorcycle are exposed to the elements, they should be lubricated periodically to ensure safe and trouble-free operation.

2 The footrests, clutch and brake levers, brake pedal, gearchange lever linkage and sidestand pivot should be lubricated frequently. In order for the lubricant to be applied where it will do the most good, the component should be disassembled. However, if chain and cable lubricant is being used, it can be applied to the pivot joint gaps and will usually work its way into the areas where friction occurs. If motor oil or light grease is being used, apply it sparingly as it may attract dirt (which could cause the controls to bind or wear at an accelerated rate). **Note:** *One of the best lubricants for the control lever pivots is a dry-film lubricant (available from many sources by different names).*

3 To lubricate the cables, disconnect the relevant cable at its upper end, then lubricate the cable with a pressure adapter, or if one is not available, using the set-up shown **(see illustrations)**. See Chapter 4 for the choke

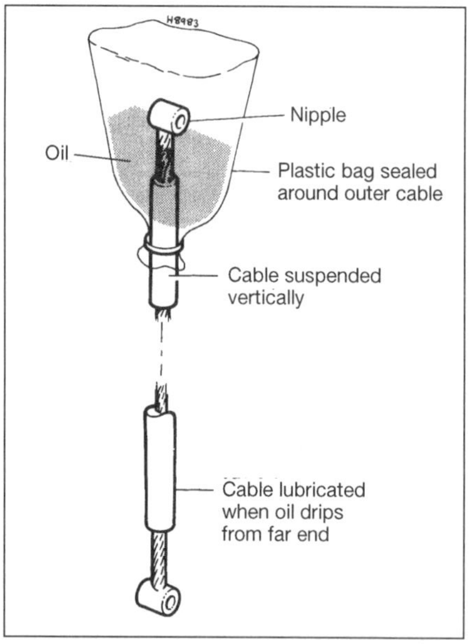

15.3b Lubricating a cable with a makeshift funnel and motor oil

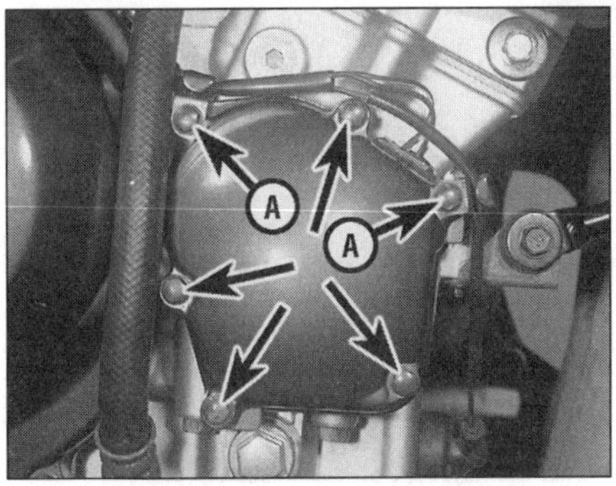

16.4a The pick-up coil cover is secured by six bolts (arrowed) – note the wiring clamps (A)

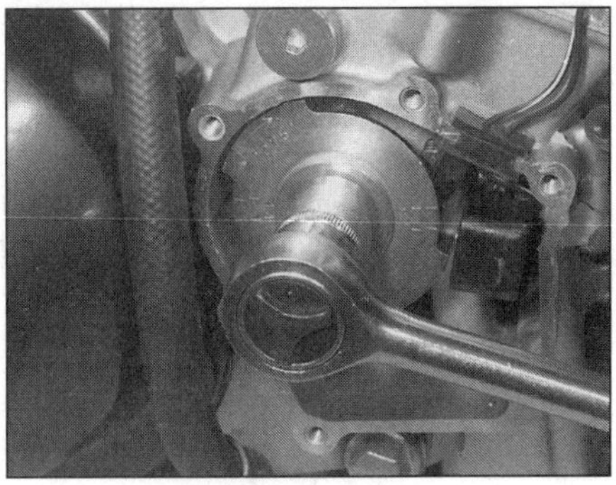

16.4b Turn the engine using a socket on the rotor hex . . .

16.5a . . . until the T 1.4 mark aligns with the crankcase rear mating surfaces (arrowed)

and throttle cable removal procedures, and Chapter 2 for the clutch cable.

4 On F models, the speedometer cable should be removed (see Chapter 9), the inner cable withdrawn from the outer cable and lubricated with motor oil or cable lubricant. Do not lubricate the upper few inches of the cable as the lubricant may travel up into the instrument head.

16 Valve clearances – check and adjustment

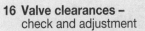

Interval:

F1 model – every 6000 miles (10,000 km)
All other models – every 8000 miles (12,000 km)

1 The engine must be completely cool for this maintenance procedure, so let the machine sit overnight before beginning. Remove the lower fairing panels (See Chapter 8). On F models, unscrew the radiator mounting bolts and displace the radiator for access (see Chapter 3) – there is no need to drain the system or disconnect the hoses.

2 Remove the valve cover (see Chapter 2). Unscrew the spark plugs to allow the engine to be turned over easier (see Section 3).

3 Make a chart or sketch of all four valve positions so that a note of each clearance can be made against the relevant valve.

4 Unscrew the bolts securing the pick-up coil cover to the right-hand side crankcase cover, noting the positions of the wiring clamps **(see illustration)**. The engine can be rotated using a 17 mm socket on the timing rotor hex (F models) or timing rotor bolt, turning it in a clockwise direction only **(see illustration)**. ***Caution: On F models, DO NOT use the timing rotor Allen bolt to turn the crankshaft – it may snap or strip out. Also be sure to turn the engine in its normal direction of rotation.***

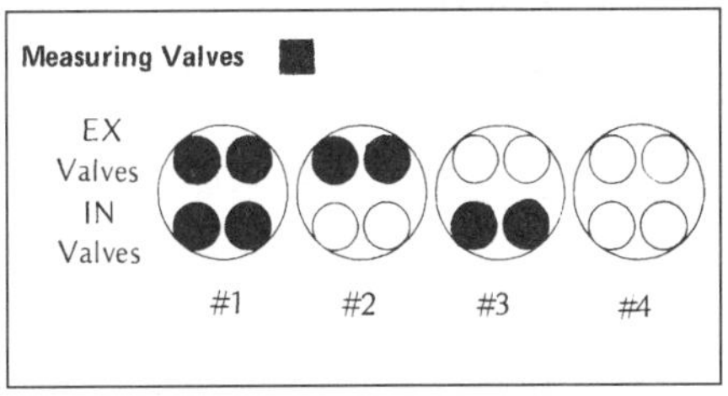

16.6 With no. 1 cylinder at TDC on the compression stroke, the shaded valves can be checked

5 Rotate the engine until the T 1.4 mark on the rotor aligns with the rear mating surfaces of the crankcase halves **(see illustration)**. At this point either No. 1 cylinder or No. 4 cylinder will be at top dead centre (TDC) on the compression stroke. Check the position of the cam lobes on No. 1 cylinder. If they are facing away from each other and are not depressing the valves, No. 1 cylinder is at TDC on the compression stroke **(see illustration)**. If the cam lobes on No. 1 cylinder are facing each other and are depressing the valves, the lobes on No. 4 cylinder will be facing away from each other and No. 4 is at TDC on the compression stroke.

6 With No. 1 cylinder at TDC on the compression stroke, the following valves can be checked **(see illustration)**:

a) No. 1, inlet and exhaust
b) No. 2, exhaust
c) No. 3, inlet

7 With No. 4 cylinder at TDC on the compression stroke, the following valves can be checked **(see illustration)**:

a) No. 2, inlet
b) No. 3, exhaust
c) No. 4, inlet and exhaust

8 Insert a feeler gauge of the same thickness as the correct valve clearance (see Specifications) between the cam base and follower of each valve and check that it is a firm sliding fit – you should feel a slight drag when the you pull the gauge out **(see illustration and 16.5b)**. If not, use the feeler gauges to obtain the exact clearance. Record the measured clearance on the chart.

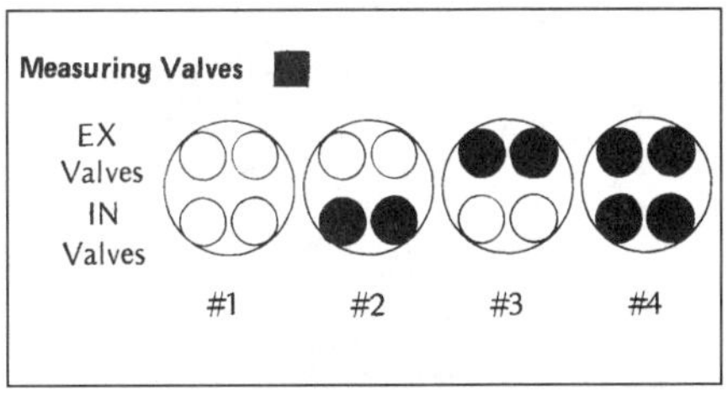

16.7 With no. 4 cylinder at TDC on the compression stroke, the shaded valves can be checked

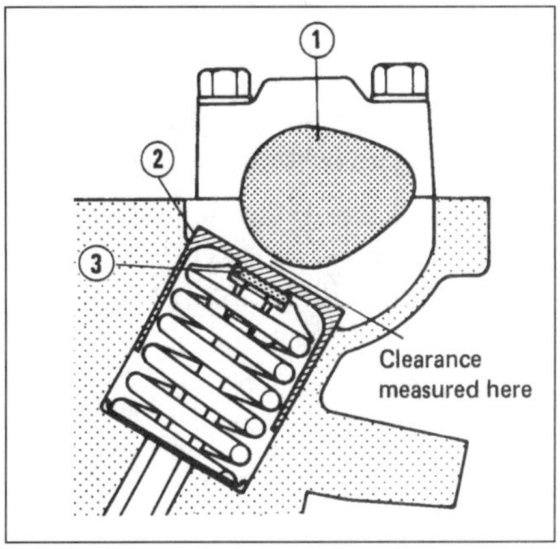

16.5b Note the position of the cam lobes – with the cylinder at TDC on the compression stroke they should not be depressing the valves and should be facing away from each other

1 Cam lobe 2 Follower 3 Shim

9 When one set of valve clearances have been checked, rotate the engine through 360° and measure the clearance of the remaining valves using the method described in Step 8.

10 When all clearances have been measured and charted, identify whether the clearance

16.8 Insert the feeler gauge between the cam base and the follower

16.12a Lift the follower out of its bore . . .

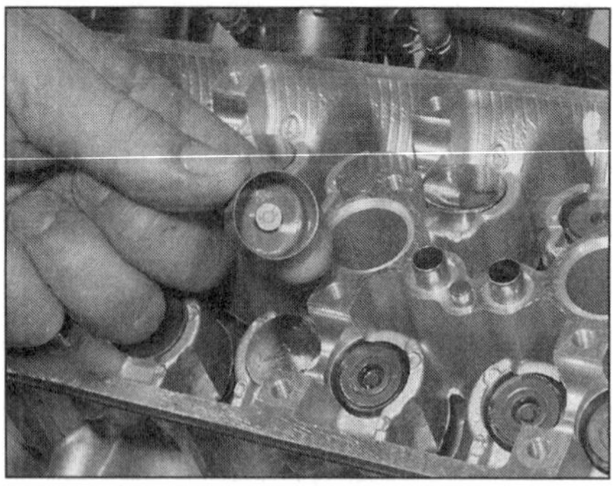

16.12b . . . and retrieve the shim either from inside the follower . . .

16.12c . . . or from the top of the valve

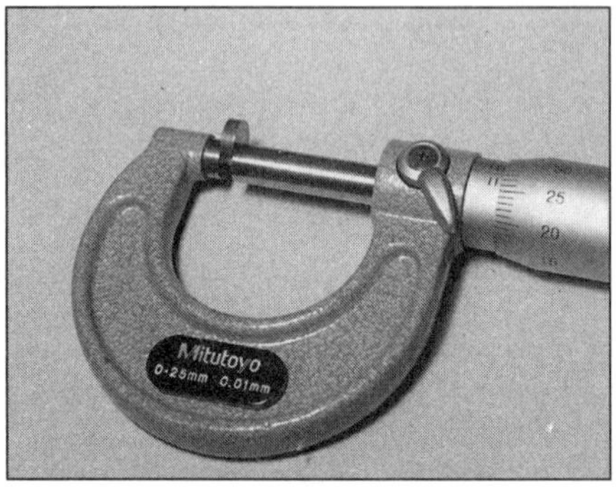

16.13 Measure the shim using a micrometer

on any valve falls outside that specified. If it does, the shim between the follower and the valve must be replaced with one of a thickness which will restore the correct clearance.

11 Shim replacement requires removal of the camshafts (see Chapter 2). There is no need to remove both camshafts if shims from only one side of the engine need replacing.

12 With the camshaft removed, remove the cam follower of the valve in question, then either retrieve the shim from the inside of the follower or pick it out of the top of the valve using a small screwdriver and a pair of pliers **(see illustrations)**.

13 A size mark should be stamped on the face of the shim – refer to the shim selection charts for reference. If the mark is not visible the shim thickness will have to be measured. It is recommended that the shim is measured anyway to check that it has not worn **(see illustration)**. Shims are available in 0.05 mm increments from 2.50 mm to 3.50 mm.

14 Using the appropriate shim selection chart, find where the measured valve clearance and existing shim thickness values intersect and read off the shim size required **(see illustrations)**. Obtain the replacement shim, then lubricate it with molybdenum disulphide grease or engine oil and fit it into its recess in the top of the valve **(see illustration)**.

15 Lubricate the follower with molybdenum

	PRESENT SHIM																				
PART No. (92180 -)	1014	1016	1018	1020	1022	1024	1026	1028	1030	1032	1034	1036	1038	1040	1042	1044	1046	1048	1050	1052	1054
MARK	50	55	60	65	70	75	80	85	90	95	00	05	10	15	20	25	30	35	40	45	50
THICKNESS (mm)	2.50	2.55	2.60	2.65	2.70	2.75	2.80	2.85	2.90	2.95	3.00	3.05	3.10	3.15	3.20	3.25	3.30	3.35	3.40	3.45	3.50
VALVE CLEARANCE MEASUREMENT																					
0.00 ~ 0.04				2.50	2.55	2.60	2.65	2.70	2.75	2.80	2.85	2.90	2.95	3.00	3.05	3.10	3.15	3.20	3.25	3.30	3.35
0.05 ~ 0.09			2.50	2.55	2.60	2.65	2.70	2.75	2.80	2.85	2.90	2.95	3:00	3.05	3.10	3.15	3.20	3.25	3.30	3.35	3.40
0.10 ~ 0.14		2.50	2.55	2.60	2.65	2.70	2.75	2.80	2.85	2.90	2.95	3.00	3.05	3.10	3.15	3.20	3.25	3.30	3.35	3.40	3.45
0.15 ~ 0.24	SPECIFIED CLEARANCE/NO CHANGE REQUIRED																				
0.25 ~ 0.29	2.55	2.60	2.65	2.70	2.75	2.80	2.85	2.90	2.95	3.00	3.05	3.10	3.15	3.20	3.25	3.30	3.35	3.40	3.45	3.50	
0.30 ~ 0.34	2.60	2.65	2.70	2.75	2.80	2.85	2.90	2.95	3.00	3.05	3.10	3.15	3.20	3.25	3.30	3.35	3.40	3.45	3.50		
0.35 ~ 0.39	2.65	2.70	2.75	2.80	2.85	2.90	2.95	3.00	3.05	3.10	3.15	3.20	3.25	3.30	3.35	3.40	3.45	3.50			
0.40 ~ 0.44	2.70	2.75	2.80	2.85	2.90	2.95	3.00	3.05	3.10	3.15	3.20	3.25	3.30	3.35	3.40	3.45	3.50				
0.45 ~ 0.49	2.75	2.80	2.85	2.90	2.95	3.00	3.05	3.10	3.15	3.20	3.25	3.30	3.35	3.40	3.45	3.50					
0.50 ~ 0.54	2.80	2.85	2.90	2.95	3.00	3.05	3.10	3.15	3.20	3.25	3.30	3.35	3.40	3.45	3.50						
0.55 ~ 0.59	2.85	2.90	2.95	3.00	3.05	3.10	3.15	3.20	3.25	3.30	3.35	3.40	3.45	3.50							
0.60 ~ 0.64	2.90	2.95	3.00	3.05	3.10	3.15	3.20	3.25	3.30	3.35	3.40	3.45	3.50								
0.65 ~ 0.69	2.95	3.00	3.05	3.10	3.15	3.20	3.25	3.30	3.35	3.40	3.45	3.50									
0.70 ~ 0.74	3.00	3.05	3.10	3.15	3.20	3.25	3.30	3.35	3.40	3.45	3.50										
0.75 ~ 0.79	3.05	3.10	3.15	3.20	3.25	3.30	3.35	3.40	3.45	3.50											
0.80 ~ 0.84	3.10	3.15	3.20	3.25	3.30	3.35	3.40	3.45	3.50												
0.85 ~ 0.89	3.15	3.20	3.25	3.30	3.35	3.40	3.45	3.50													
0.90 ~ 0.94	3.20	3.25	3.30	3.35	3.40	3.45	3.50														
0.95 ~ 0.99	3.25	3.30	3.35	3.40	3.45	3.50															
1.00 ~ 1.04	3.30	3.35	3.40	3.45	3.50																
1.05 ~ 1.09	3.35	3.40	3.45	3.50																	
1.10 ~ 1.14	3.40	3.45	3.50																		
1.15 ~ 1.19	3.45	3.50																			
1.20 ~ 1.24	3.50																				

16.14a Shim selection chart – inlet valve (F models)

	PRESENT SHIM																				
PART No. (92180 -)	1014	1016	1018	1020	1022	1024	1026	1028	1030	1032	1034	1036	1038	1040	1042	1044	1046	1048	1050	1052	1054
MARK	50	55	60	65	70	75	80	85	90	95	00	05	10	15	20	25	30	35	40	45	50
THICKNESS (mm)	2.50	2.55	2.60	2.65	2.70	2.75	2.80	2.85	2.90	2.95	3.00	3.05	3.10	3.15	3.20	3.25	3.30	3.35	3.40	3.45	3.50
VALVE CLEARANCE MEASUREMENT																					
0.00 ~ 0.02						2.50	2.55	2.60	2.65	2.70	2.75	2.80	2.85	2.90	2.95	3.00	3.05	3.10	3.15	3.20	3.25
0.03 ~ 0.06					2.50	2.55	2.60	2.65	2.70	2.75	2.80	2.85	2.90	2.95	3.00	3.05	3.10	3.15	3.20	3.25	3.30
0.07 ~ 0.11				2.50	2.55	2.60	2.65	2.70	2.75	2.80	2.85	2.90	2.95	3.00	3.05	3.10	3.15	3.20	3.25	3.30	3.35
0.12 ~ 0.16			2.50	2.55	2.60	2.65	2.70	2.75	2.80	2.85	2.90	2.95	3.00	3.05	3.10	3.15	3.20	3.25	3.30	3.35	3.40
0.17 ~ 0.21		2.50	2.55	2.60	2.65	2.70	2.75	2.80	2.85	2.90	2.95	3.00	3.05	3.10	3.15	3.20	3.25	3.30	3.35	3.40	3.45
0.22 ~ 0.31	SPECIFIED CLEARANCE/NO CHANGE REQUIRED																				
0.32 ~ 0.36	2.55	2.60	2.65	2.70	2.75	2.80	2.85	2.90	2.95	3.00	3.05	3.10	3.15	3.20	3.25	3.30	3.35	3.40	3.45	3.50	
0.37 ~ 0.41	2.60	2.65	2.70	2.75	2.80	2.85	2.90	2.95	3.00	3.05	3.10	3.15	3.20	3.25	3.30	3.35	3.40	3.45	3.50		
0.42 ~ 0.46	2.65	2.70	2.75	2.80	2.85	2.90	2.95	3.00	3.05	3.10	3.15	3.20	3.25	3.30	3.35	3.40	3.45	3.50			
0.47 ~ 0.51	2.70	2.75	2.80	2.85	2.90	2.95	3.00	3.05	3.10	3.15	3.20	3.25	3.30	3.35	3.40	3.45	3.50				
0.52 ~ 0.56	2.75	2.80	2.85	2.90	2.95	3.00	3.05	3.10	3.15	3.20	3.25	3.30	3.35	3.40	3.45	3.50					
0.57 ~ 0.61	2.80	2.85	2.90	2.95	3.00	3.05	3.10	3.15	3.20	3.25	3.30	3.35	3.40	3.45	3.50						
0.62 ~ 0.66	2.85	2.90	2.95	3.00	3.05	3.10	3.15	3.20	3.25	3.30	3.35	3.40	3.45	3.50							
0.67 ~ 0.71	2.90	2.95	3.00	3.05	3.10	3.15	3.20	3.25	3.30	3.35	3.40	3.45	3.50								
0.72 ~ 0.76	2.95	3.00	3.05	3.10	3.15	3.20	3.25	3.30	3.35	3.40	3.45	3.50									
0.77 ~ 0.81	3.00	3.05	3.10	3.15	3.20	3.25	3.30	3.35	3.40	3.45	3.50										
0.82 ~ 0.86	3.05	3.10	3.15	3.20	3.25	3.30	3.35	3.40	3.45	3.50											
0.87 ~ 0.91	3.10	3.15	3.20	3.25	3.30	3.35	3.40	3.45	3.50												
0.92 ~ 0.96	3.15	3.20	3.25	3.30	3.35	3.40	3.45	3.50													
0.97 ~ 1.01	3.20	3.25	3.30	3.35	3.40	3.45	3.50														
1.02 ~ 1.06	3.25	3.30	3.35	3.40	3.45	3.50															
1.07 ~ 1.11	3.30	3.35	3.40	3.45	3.50																
1.12 ~ 1.16	3.35	3.40	3.45	3.50																	
1.17 ~ 1.21	3.40	3.45	3.50																		
1.22 ~ 1.26	3.45	3.50																			
1.27 ~ 1.31	3.50																				

16.14b Shim selection chart – exhaust valve (F models)

	PRESENT SHIM																				
PART No. (92180 -)	1014	1016	1018	1020	1022	1024	1026	1028	1030	1032	1034	1036	1038	1040	1042	1044	1046	1048	1050	1052	1054
MARK	50	55	60	65	70	75	80	85	90	95	00	05	10	15	20	25	30	35	40	45	50
THICKNESS (mm)	2.50	2.55	2.60	2.65	2.70	2.75	2.80	2.85	2.90	2.95	3.00	3.05	3.10	3.15	3.20	3.25	3.30	3.35	3.40	3.45	3.50
VALVE CLEARANCE MEASUREMENT																					
0.00 ~ 0.05			2.50	2.55	2.60	2.65	2.70	2.75	2.80	2.85	2.90	2.95	3.00	3.05	3.10	3.15	3.20	3.25	3.30	3.35	3.40
0.06 ~ 0.10		2.50	2.55	2.60	2.65	2.70	2.75	2.80	2.85	2.90	2.95	3.00	3.05	3.10	3.15	3.20	3.25	3.30	3.35	3.40	3.45
0.11 ~ 0.19	SPECIFIED CLEARANCE/NO CHANGE REQUIRED																				
0.20 ~ 0.24	2.55	2.60	2.65	2.70	2.75	2.80	2.85	2.90	2.95	3.00	3.05	3.10	3.15	3.20	3.25	3.30	3.35	3.40	3.45	3.50	
0.25 ~ 0.29	2.60	2.65	2.70	2.75	2.80	2.85	2.90	2.95	3.00	3.05	3.10	3.15	3.20	3.25	3.30	3.35	3.40	3.45	3.50		
0.30 ~ 0.34	2.65	2.70	2.75	2.80	2.85	2.90	2.95	3.00	3.05	3.10	3.15	3.20	3.25	3.30	3.35	3.40	3.45	3.50			
0.35 ~ 0.39	2.70	2.75	2.80	2.85	2.90	2.95	3.00	3.05	3.10	3.15	3.20	3.25	3.30	3.35	3.40	3.45	3.50				
0.40 ~ 0.44	2.75	2.80	2.85	2.90	2.95	3.00	3.05	3.10	3.15	3.20	3.25	3.30	3.35	3.40	3.45	3.50					
0.45 ~ 0.49	2.80	2.85	2.90	2.95	3.00	3.05	3.10	3.15	3.20	3.25	3.30	3.35	3.40	3.45	3.50						
0.50 ~ 0.54	2.85	2.90	2.95	3.00	3.05	3.10	3.15	3.20	3.25	3.30	3.35	3.40	3.45	3.50							
0.55 ~ 0.59	2.90	2.95	3.00	3.05	3.10	3.15	3.20	3.25	3.30	3.35	3.40	3.45	3.50								
0.60 ~ 0.64	2.95	3.00	3.05	3.10	3.15	3.20	3.25	3.30	3.35	3.40	3.45	3.50									
0.65 ~ 0.69	3.00	3.05	3.10	3.15	3.20	3.25	3.30	3.35	3.40	3.45	3.50										
0.70 ~ 0.74	3.05	3.10	3.15	3.20	3.25	3.30	3.35	3.40	3.45	3.50											
0.75 ~ 0.79	3.10	3.15	3.20	3.25	3.30	3.35	3.40	3.45	3.50												
0.80 ~ 0.84	3.15	3.20	3.25	3.30	3.35	3.40	3.45	3.50													
0.85 ~ 0.89	3.20	3.25	3.30	3.35	3.40	3.45	3.50														
0.90 ~ 0.94	3.25	3.30	3.35	3.40	3.45	3.50															
0.95 ~ 0.99	3.30	3.35	3.40	3.45	3.50																
1.00 ~ 1.04	3.35	3.40	3.45	3.50																	
1.05 ~ 1.09	3.40	3.45	3.50																		
1.10 ~ 1.14	3.45	3.50																			
1.15 ~ 1.19	3.50																				

16.14c Shim selection chart – inlet valve (G, H, J and A models)

	PRESENT SHIM																				
PART No. (92180 -)	1014	1016	1018	1020	1022	1024	1026	1028	1030	1032	1034	1036	1038	1040	1042	1044	1046	1048	1050	1052	1054
MARK	50	55	60	65	70	75	80	85	90	95	00	05	10	15	20	25	30	35	40	45	50
THICKNESS (mm)	2.50	2.55	2.60	2.65	2.70	2.75	2.80	2.85	2.90	2.95	3.00	3.05	3.10	3.15	3.20	3.25	3.30	3.35	3.40	3.45	3.50
VALVE CLEARANCE MEASUREMENT																					
0.00 ~ 0.02						2.50	2.55	2.60	2.65	2.70	2.75	2.80	2.85	2.90	2.95	3.00	3.05	3.10	3.15	3.20	3.25
0.03 ~ 0.06					2.50	2.55	2.60	2.65	2.70	2.75	2.80	2.85	2.90	2.95	3.00	3.05	3.10	3.15	3.20	3.25	3.30
0.07 ~ 0.11				2.50	2.55	2.60	2.65	2.70	2.75	2.80	2.85	2.90	2.95	3.00	3.05	3.10	3.15	3.20	3.25	3.30	3.35
0.12 ~ 0.16			2.50	2.55	2.60	2.65	2.70	2.75	2.80	2.85	2.90	2.95	3.00	3.05	3.10	3.15	3.20	3.25	3.30	3.35	3.40
0.17 ~ 0.21		2.50	2.55	2.60	2.65	2.70	2.75	2.80	2.85	2.90	2.95	3.00	3.05	3.10	3.15	3.20	3.25	3.30	3.35	3.40	3.45
0.22 ~ 0.31	SPECIFIED CLEARANCE/NO CHANGE REQUIRED																				
0.32 ~ 0.36	2.55	2.60	2.65	2.70	2.75	2.80	2.85	2.90	2.95	3.00	3.05	3.10	3.15	3.20	3.25	3.30	3.35	3.40	3.45	3.50	
0.37 ~ 0.41	2.60	2.65	2.70	2.75	2.80	2.85	2.90	2.95	3.00	3.05	3.10	3.15	3.20	3.25	3.30	3.35	3.40	3.45	3.50		
0.42 ~ 0.46	2.65	2.70	2.75	2.80	2.85	2.90	2.95	3.00	3.05	3.10	3.15	3.20	3.25	3.30	3.35	3.40	3.45	3.50			
0.47 ~ 0.51	2.70	2.75	2.80	2.85	2.90	2.95	3.00	3.05	3.10	3.15	3.20	3.25	3.30	3.35	3.40	3.45	3.50				
0.52 ~ 0.56	2.75	2.80	2.85	2.90	2.95	3.00	3.05	3.10	3.15	3.20	3.25	3.30	3.35	3.40	3.45	3.50					
0.57 ~ 0.61	2.80	2.85	2.90	2.95	3.00	3.05	3.10	3.15	3.20	3.25	3.30	3.35	3.40	3.45	3.50						
0.62 ~ 0.66	2.85	2.90	2.95	3.00	3.05	3.10	3.15	3.20	3.25	3.30	3.35	3.40	3.45	3.50							
0.67 ~ 0.71	2.90	2.95	3.00	3.05	3.10	3.15	3.20	3.25	3.30	3.35	3.40	3.45	3.50								
0.72 ~ 0.76	2.95	3.00	3.05	3.10	3.15	3.20	3.25	3.30	3.35	3.40	3.45	3.50									
0.77 ~ 0.81	3.00	3.05	3.10	3.15	3.20	3.25	3.30	3.35	3.40	3.45	3.50										
0.82 ~ 0.86	3.05	3.10	3.15	3.20	3.25	3.30	3.35	3.40	3.45	3.50											
0.87 ~ 0.91	3.10	3.15	3.20	3.25	3.30	3.35	3.40	3.45	3.50												
0.92 ~ 0.96	3.15	3.20	3.25	3.30	3.35	3.40	3.45	3.50													
0.97 ~ 1.01	3.20	3.25	3.30	3.35	3.40	3.45	3.50														
1.02 ~ 1.06	3.25	3.30	3.35	3.40	3.45	3.50															
1.07 ~ 1.11	3.30	3.35	3.40	3.45	3.50																
1.12 ~ 1.16	3.35	3.40	3.45	3.50																	
1.17 ~ 1.21	3.40	3.45	3.50																		
1.22 ~ 1.26	3.45	3.50																			
1.27 ~ 1.31	3.50																				

16.14d Shim selection chart – exhaust valve (G, H, J and A models)

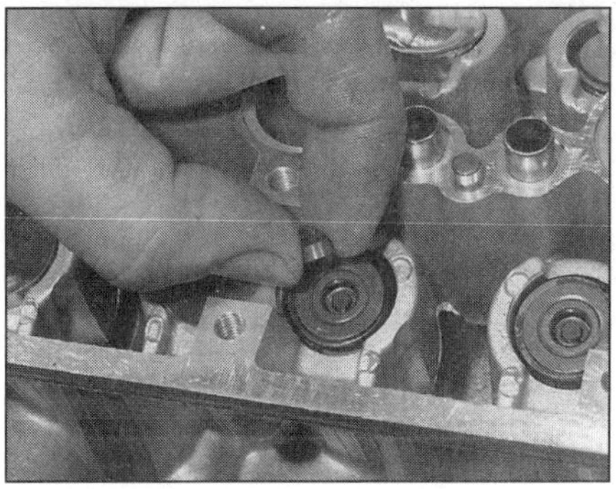

16.14e Fit the shim into the recess in the top of the valve . . .

disulphide grease or engine oil and install it onto the valve **(see illustration)**. Repeat the process for any other valves until the clearances are correct, then install the camshafts (see Chapter 2).

16 Rotate the crankshaft several turns to seat the new shim, then check the clearances again.

17 Install all disturbed components in a reverse of the removal sequence. Apply a smear of sealant to the crankcase joints on the mating surface with the pick-up coil cover and to the rubber wiring grommet **(see illustration)**. Apply a suitable non-permanent thread locking compound to the top middle cover bolt. Install the pick-up coil cover using a new gasket and tighten its bolts to the specified torque setting, not forgetting to secure the wiring clamps with the top front and rear cover bolts **(see illustration and 16.4a)**.

17 Air filter – cleaning

Interval:

F1 model – every 6000 miles (10,000 km)
All other models – every 8000 miles (12,000 km)

1 Remove the fuel tank (see Chapter 4). Detach the crankcase breather hose and, on F

16.15 . . . then install the follower

16.17a Apply the sealant as described . . .

16.17b . . . then fit a new gasket

models, the vacuum valve hose, from the air filter cover **(see illustration)**.

2 Unscrew the bolts securing the air filter cover to the filter housing **(see illustration)**. Remove the cover and withdraw the filter element from the housing **(see illustrations)**.

3 Soak the element in a high flash-point solvent until it is clean, then if compressed air is available, use it to dry the element, directing the air from the inside out **(see illustration)**. Otherwise dry it by shaking it or leaving it in the open air for a while.

4 Check the element and its cage for signs of damage. If the element is torn or cannot be cleaned, fit a new one. On F1 models, the filter should be renewed after every five cleanings (30,000 miles (50,000 km)).

5 Soak a clean lint-free rag in motor oil, then smear the rag over the upper (grey) side of the filter element. Install the filter by reversing the removal procedure, making sure the grey side is facing up.

Caution: If the machine is continually ridden in dusty conditions, the filter should be cleaned more frequently.

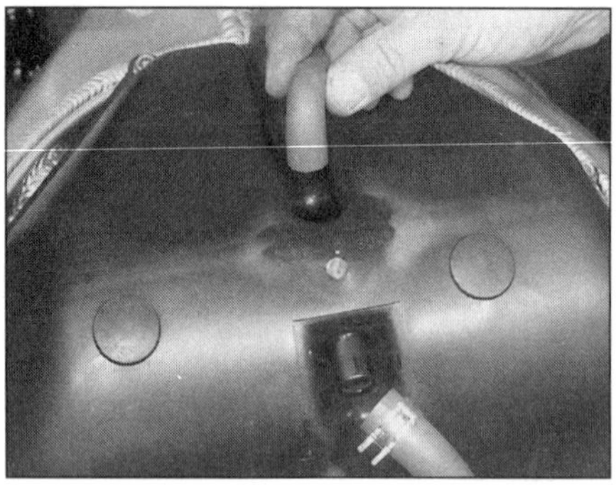

17.1 Detach the breather hose and the vacuum valve hose (where fitted) from their unions

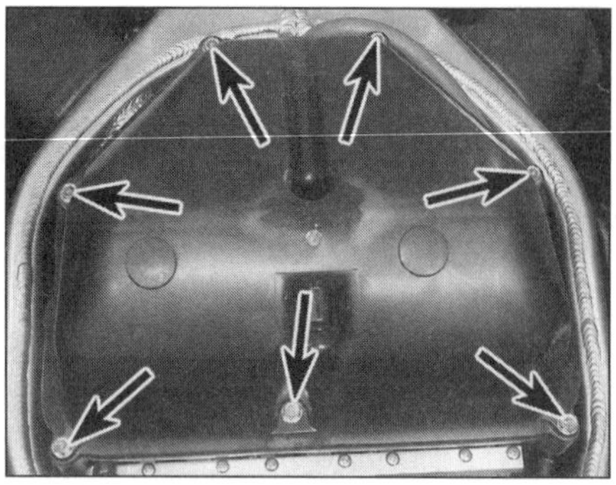

17.2a Unscrew the bolts (arrowed) and remove the cover . . .

17.2b . . . and the filter element

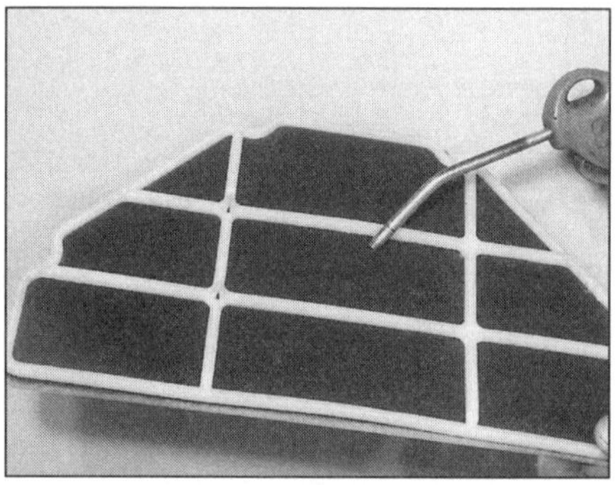

17.3 Direct the air from the inside (grey side) of the element

18 Throttle and choke cables – check and freeplay adjustment

Interval:
F1 model – every 6000 miles (10,000 km)
All other models – every 8000 miles (12,000 km)

Throttle cable

1 Make sure the throttle grip rotates easily from fully closed to fully open with the front wheel turned at various angles. The grip should return automatically from fully open to fully closed when released.

2 If the throttle sticks, this is probably due to a cable fault. Remove the cables (see Chapter 4) and lubricate them (see Section 15). Install the cables, making sure they are correctly routed. If this fails to improve the operation of the throttle, the cables must be renewed. Note that in very rare cases the fault could lie in the carburettors rather than the cables, necessitating the removal of the carburettors and inspection of the throttle linkage (see Chapter 4).

3 With the throttle operating smoothly, check for a small amount of freeplay in the twistgrip and compare the amount to that listed in this Chapter's Specifications **(see illustration)**. If it's incorrect, adjust the cables to correct it.

F models

4 Freeplay adjustments can be made at the handlebar end of the cables. Loosen the lockring on the accelerator cable where it leaves the handlebar **(see illustration)**. Turn the adjuster until the specified amount of freeplay is obtained (see this Chapter's Specifications), then retighten the lockring.

5 If the cables can't be adjusted within specifications, screw the adjuster all the way in, then set the adjusters at the carburettor end of the cable using the same procedure **(see illustration)**. Remove the air filter housing for access to the adjusters (see Chapter 4). If the cables still can't be adjusted within specifications, use the adjuster at the handlebar end again. Otherwise, fit new cables (see Chapter 4).

G, H, J and A models

6 Freeplay adjustments can be made at the handlebar end of the cables. Loosen the

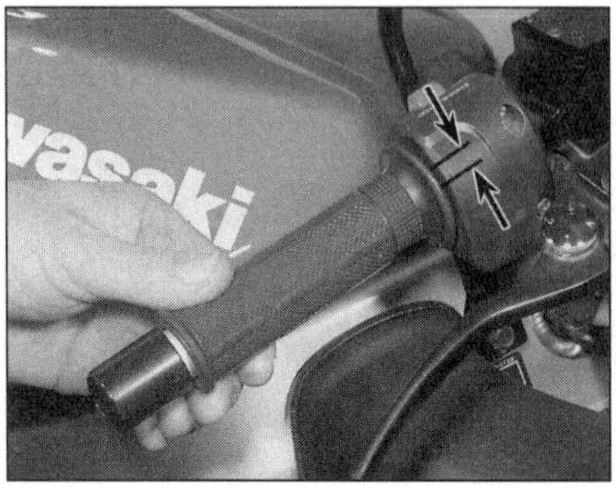

18.3 Check the amount of freeplay in the twistgrip

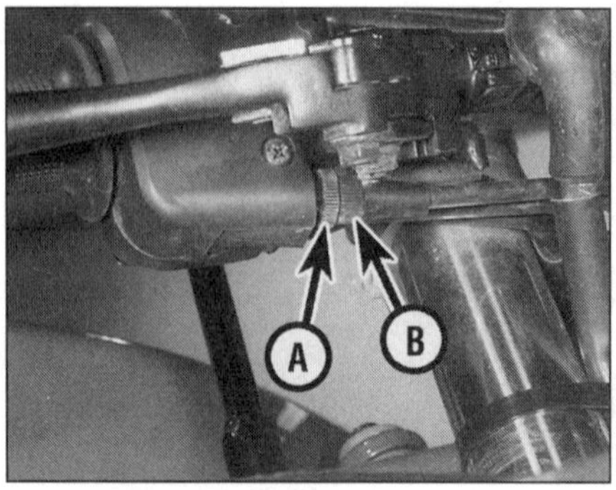

18.4 Loosen the lockring (A) and turn the adjuster (B) as required

18.5 Throttle cable adjusters (arrowed) – carburettor end

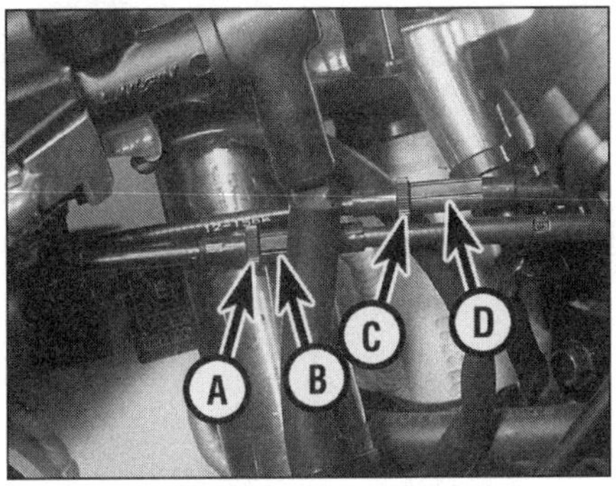

18.6 Lockring (A), adjuster (B) – accelerator cable. Lockring (C), adjuster (D) – decelerator cable

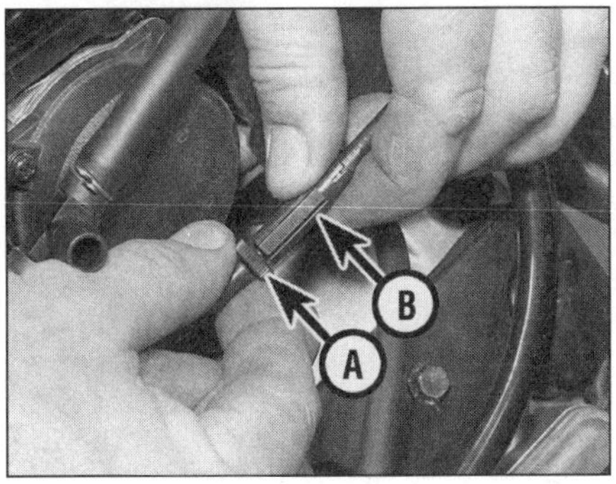

18.11a Choke cable adjuster (F models) – lockring (A), adjuster (B)

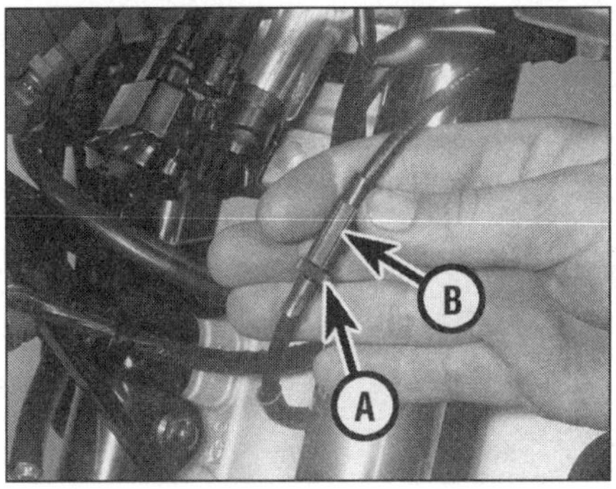

18.11b Choke cable adjuster (G, H, J and A models) – lockring (A), adjuster (B)

lockrings on both cables **(see illustration)**. Turn the adjusters fully in to provide maximum freeplay in both cables. Now turn the decelerator cable adjuster out until there is no freeplay in the throttle when it is in the closed position, then tighten the lockring. Now turn the accelerator cable adjuster until the specified amount of freeplay is obtained (see this Chapter's Specifications), then tighten the lockring.

7 If the cables can't be adjusted within specifications, fit new ones (see Chapter 4).

Warning: Turn the handlebars all the way through their travel with the engine idling. Idle speed should not change. If it does, the cable may be routed incorrectly. Correct this condition before riding the bike.

8 Check again that the throttle twistgrip operates smoothly and snaps shut quickly when released.

Choke cable

9 If the choke does not operate smoothly this is probably due to a cable fault. Remove the cable (see Chapter 4) and lubricate it (see Section 15). Install the cable, routing it so it takes the smoothest route possible.

10 Check for a small amount of freeplay (see Specifications) in the cable before the plungers in the carburettors move.

11 On F models, freeplay adjustments are made at the adjuster at the carburettor end of the cable **(see illustration)**. Remove the air filter housing for access to the adjuster (see Chapter 4). On all other models the adjuster is at the handlebar end of the cable **(see illustration)**. Loosen the lockring and turn the adjuster until the specified amount of freeplay is obtained (see Specifications), then retighten the lockring. If this fails to improve the operation of the choke, the cable must be renewed. Note that in very rare cases the fault could lie in the carburettors rather than the cable, necessitating the removal of the carburettors and inspection of the choke valves (see Chapter 4).

19 Engine – oil and oil filter change

Interval:

F1 model – every 6000 miles (10,000 km)
All other models – every 8000 miles (12,000 km)

Warning: Be careful when draining the oil, as the exhaust pipes, the engine, and the oil itself can cause severe burns.

1 Regular oil and filter changes are the single most important maintenance procedure you can perform on a motorcycle. The oil not only lubricates the internal parts of the engine, transmission and clutch, but it also acts as a coolant, a cleaner, a sealant, and a protectant. Because of these demands, the oil takes a terrific amount of abuse and should be changed often with new oil of the recommended grade and type. Saving a little money on the difference in cost between a good oil and a cheap oil won't pay off if the engine is damaged. The oil filter should be changed with every second oil change.

2 Before changing the oil, warm up the engine so the oil will drain easily. Remove the left-hand lower fairing panel (see Chapter 8).

3 Support the motorcycle upright using an auxiliary stand, and position a clean drain tray below the engine. Unscrew the oil filler cap on the clutch cover to vent the crankcase and to act as a reminder that there is no oil in the engine **(see illustration 6.3)**.

4 Next, unscrew the oil drain plug from the bottom of the engine and allow the oil to flow into the drain tray **(see illustrations 6.4a and b)**. Check the condition of the drain plug sealing washer. If it is damaged or deformed discard it and use a new one.

5 When the oil has completely drained, fit the sealing washer over the drain plug, then fit the plug to the sump and tighten it to the torque setting specified at the beginning of the Chapter **(see illustrations 6.5a and b)**. Avoid overtightening, as damage to the sump will result.

6 Now place the drain tray below the oil filter. Unscrew the filter using an oil filter wrench or strap and tip any residual oil into the drain tray **(see illustration)**.

7 Smear clean engine oil onto the rubber seal on the new filter, then screw it onto the engine **(see illustrations)**. Tighten the filter to the specified torque setting using a filter wrench.

19.6 Use an appropriate filter removing tool to unscrew the filter

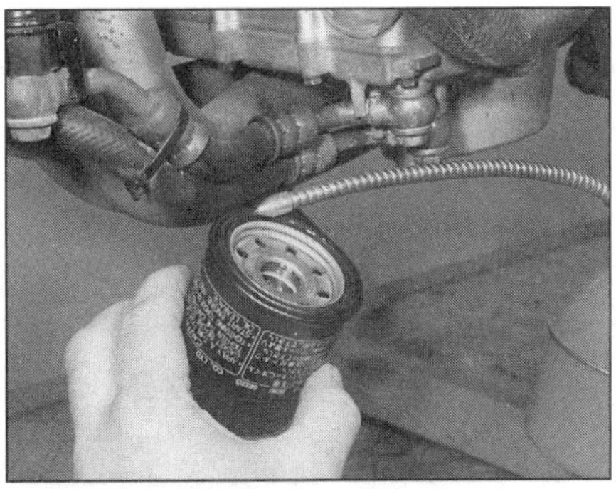

19.7a Smear oil onto the sealing ring . . .

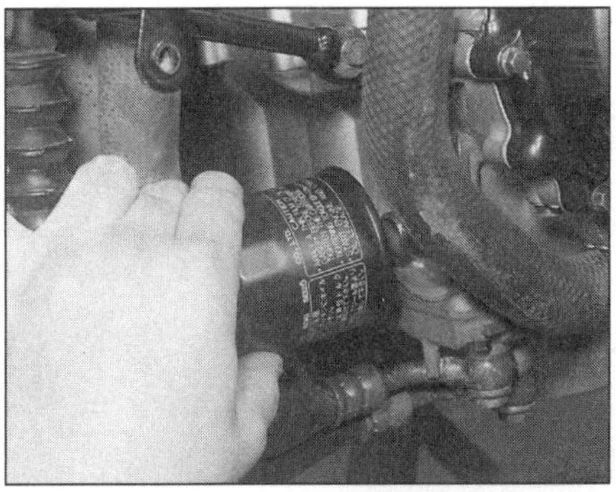

19.7b . . . then install the filter . . .

19.7c ... and tighten it as described

On F, G and H models, if a filter wrench is not available, tighten the filter by hand, about 3/4 of a turn after the rubber seal contacts the engine. On J and A models, the filter must be tightened to the specified torque setting **(see illustration)**.

8 Refill the crankcase to the proper level using the recommended type and amount of oil (see *Specifications* at the beginning of the Chapter). With the motorcycle held vertical, the oil level should lie between the upper and lower level lines on the inspection window in the clutch cover (see *Daily (pre-ride) checks*). Install the filler cap. Start the engine and let it run for two or three minutes (make sure that the oil pressure light extinguishes after a few seconds). Shut it off, wait a few minutes, then check the oil level. If necessary, add more oil to bring the level up to the high level line on the inspection window. Check around the drain plug and the oil filter for leaks.

> **HAYNES HiNT** *Saving a little money on the difference between good and cheap oils won't pay off if the engine is damaged as a result.*

9 The old oil drained from the engine cannot be re-used and should be disposed of properly. Check with your local refuse disposal company, disposal facility or environmental agency to see whether they will accept the used oil for recycling. Don't pour used oil into drains or onto the ground.

> **HAYNES HiNT** *Check the old oil carefully – if it is very metallic coloured, then the engine is experiencing wear from break-in (new engine) or from insufficient lubrication. If there are flakes or chips of metal in the oil, then something is drastically wrong internally and the engine will have to be disassembled for inspection and repair. If there are pieces of fibre-like material in the oil, the clutch is experiencing excessive wear and should be checked.*

20 Cooling system – check

Interval:

F1 model – every 6000 miles (10,000 km)
All other models – every 8000 miles (12,000 km)

Warning: ***The engine must be cool before beginning this procedure.***

1 Check the coolant level (see *Daily (pre-ride) checks*).

2 Remove the lower fairing panels and, on F, G and H models, the right-hand trim panel in the upper fairing (see Chapter 8). The entire cooling system should be checked for evidence of leakage. Examine each rubber coolant hose along its entire length. Look for cracks, abrasions and other damage. Squeeze each hose at various points. They should feel firm, yet pliable, and return to their original shape when released. If they are dried out or hard, fit new ones.

3 Check for evidence of leaks at each cooling system joint. Tighten the hose clips carefully to prevent future leaks.

4 Check the radiator for leaks and other damage. Leaks in the radiator leave tell-tale scale deposits or coolant stains on the outside of the core below the leak. If leaks are noted, remove the radiator (see Chapter 3) and have it repaired at a radiator shop or replace it with a new one.

Caution: Do not use a liquid leak stopping compound to try to repair leaks.

5 Check the radiator fins for mud, dirt and insects, which may impede the flow of air through the radiator. If the fins are dirty, remove the radiator (see Chapter 3) and clean it using water or low pressure compressed air directed through the fins from the back. If the fins are bent or distorted, straighten them carefully with a screwdriver. If the air flow is restricted by bent or damaged fins over more than 30% of the radiator's surface area, renew the radiator.

6 Remove the pressure cap from the radiator filler neck by turning it anti-clockwise until it reaches a stop **(see illustration)**. If you hear a hissing sound (indicating there is still pressure in the system), wait until it stops. Now press down on the cap and continue turning the cap until it can be removed. Check the condition of the coolant in the system. If it is rust-coloured or if accumulations of scale are visible, drain, flush and refill the system with new coolant (See Section 28). Check the cap seal for cracks and other damage. If in doubt about the pressure cap's condition, have it tested by a Kawasaki dealer or replace it with a new one. Install the cap by turning it clockwise until it reaches the first stop then push down on the cap and continue turning until it can turn further.

7 Check the antifreeze content of the coolant with an antifreeze hydrometer. Sometimes coolant looks like it's in good condition, but might be too weak to offer adequate protection. If the hydrometer indicates a weak mixture, drain, flush and refill the system (see Section 28).

8 Start the engine and let it reach normal operating temperature, then check for leaks again. As the coolant temperature increases, the fan should come on automatically and the temperature should begin to drop. If it does not, refer to Chapter 3 and check the fan and fan circuit carefully.

9 If the coolant level is consistently low, and no evidence of leaks can be found, have the entire system pressure checked by a Kawasaki dealer.

10 Check the drainage hole on the underside of the water pump cover **(see illustration)**.

20.6 Radiator pressure cap (arrowed)

20.10 Check the drainage hole (arrowed) for evidence of leakage

20.11 Detach the heater filter from the coolant hoses

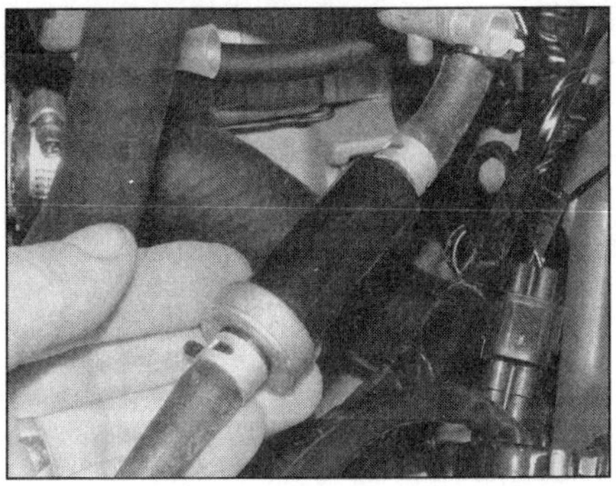

20.13 Location of the carburettor heater valve

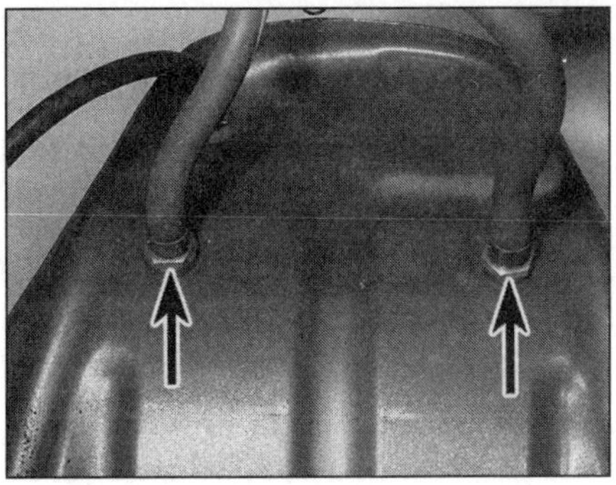

21.5 Fuel tank filters (arrowed) - F models

21.7 In-line fuel filter location (arrowed)

Leakage from this hole indicates failure of the pump's mechanical seal – refer to Chapter 3.

11 On models with a carburettor heater system, remove the fuel tank (see Chapter 4) and partially drain the cooling system (see Section 28 of this Chapter). Release the clips securing the coolant hoses to the carburettor heater filter on the left-hand side of the cylinder head and detach the filter **(see illustration)**.

12 Withdraw the filter gauze from the filter body and clean off any sediment with a soft brush or compressed air. Inspect the filter gauze for damage and fit a new one if necessary. Install the gauze in the filter body, then reconnect the coolant hoses and secure them with the clips.

13 Release the clips securing the coolant hoses to the heater valve at the rear of the cylinder head on the right-hand side **(see illustration)**. The valve should be open at room temperature; check by blowing through it. If the valve is closed, fit a new one. Reconnect the coolant hoses and secure them with the clips.

14 Top-up the coolant system (see *Daily (pre-ride) checks*).

21 Fuel system - check

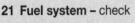

Interval:

F1 model - every 6000 miles (10,000 km)
F2, F3, G and H models - every 8000 miles (12,000 km)
J and A models - every 4000 miles (6000 km)

Warning: Petrol (gasoline) is extremely flammable, so take extra precautions when you work on any part of the fuel system. Don't smoke or allow open flames or bare light bulbs near the work area, and don't work in a garage where a natural gas-type appliance is present. If you spill any fuel on your skin, rinse it off immediately with soap and water. When you perform any kind of work on the fuel system, wear safety glasses and have a fire extinguisher suitable for a Class B type fire (flammable liquids) on hand.

Check

1 Remove the fuel tank (see Chapter 4) and check the tank, the fuel tap, and the fuel hose(s) for signs of leakage, damage or deterioration. Renew any hoses which are cracked or deteriorated.

2 On F models, if the fuel hose union to tank joint is leaking, unscrew the filter and fit a new O-ring (see Step 4). On G, H , J and A models, if the tap to tank joint is leaking, tighten the fixing screws. If leakage persists, remove the tap and fit a new O-ring (see Chapter 4).

3 If the fuel tap body is leaking, remove the tap and tighten the assembly screws (see Chapter 4). If leakage persists undo the screws and disassemble the tap, noting how the components fit. Inspect all components for wear or damage. New gaskets and O-rings are available, otherwise a new tap must be fitted.

4 If the carburettor gaskets are leaking, the carburettors should be disassembled and rebuilt using new gaskets and seals (see Chapter 4).

Filter cleaning/renewal

5 On F models, there are two filters mounted in the fuel tank which may become clogged and should be removed and cleaned periodically. In order to clean the filters, the fuel tank must be removed and drained (see Chapter 4). Detach the fuel hoses, noting which fits where, and unscrew the filters from the base of the tank **(see illustration)**. Clean them thoroughly; if they are severely blocked or torn, replace them with new ones. Install the filters, using new O-rings if the old ones are in any way damaged or deteriorated, and attach the fuel hoses. The ON hose is marked yellow and attaches to the taller filter. The RES hose is marked white and attaches to the shorter filter. Make sure the hoses are secured by their clamps .

6 On all other models, the fuel tank filter is integral with the fuel tap. Remove the fuel tank and the fuel tap (see Chapter 4). Clean the gauze filters to remove all traces of dirt and fuel sediment. Check the gauze for holes. If any are found, a new tap body will have to be fitted. Check the condition of the O-ring and gasket and renew them if they are damaged or deteriorated.

7 On all models there is also an in-line fuel filter fitted in the fuel pipe from the tap to the fuel pump **(see illustration)**. Remove the fuel tank (see Chapter 4). Lift the filter off its lug and slip the rubber boot back. Check the condition of the filter – if it is clean, undamaged and free of residue it can be used. Otherwise a new one should be fitted. Have a rag handy to soak up any residual fuel and disconnect the pipes from the filter. Slip the filter out of its boot and install the new filter so that its arrow points in the direction of fuel flow (i.e. towards the pump). Secure the pipes to the filter with the retaining clips. Install the fuel tank (see Chapter 4), turn the tap ON and check that there are no fuel leaks.

22 Suspension - check

Interval:

F1 model - every 6000 miles (10,000 km)
All other models - every 8000 miles (12,000 km)

1 The suspension components must be maintained in top operating condition to ensure rider safety. Loose, worn or damaged suspension parts which will seriously affect the motorcycle's stability and control.

Front suspension

2 While standing alongside the motorcycle, apply the front brake and push down on the handlebars to compress the forks several times. See if they move up-and-down smoothly without binding. If binding is felt, the forks should be disassembled and inspected (see Chapter 6).

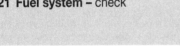

3 Inspect the area above the dust seal for signs of oil leaks, then carefully lever off the dust seal using a flat-bladed screwdriver and inspect the area around the fork seal **(see**

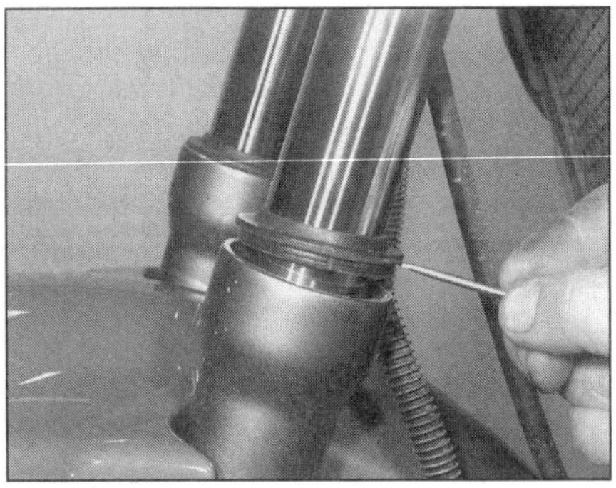

22.3 Checking for leakage of the fork seals

22.8a Checking for play in the swingarm bearings

22.8b Checking for play in the suspension and linkage

illustration). If leakage is evident, the seals must be renewed (see Chapter 6).

4 Check the tightness of all suspension nuts and bolts to be sure none have worked loose. Refer to the torque settings specified at the beginning of Chapter 6.

5 The forks are adjustable for spring pre-load, rebound damping and compression damping and it is essential that both fork kegs are adjusted equally (see Chapter 6).

Rear suspension

6 Inspect the rear shock for fluid leaks and tightness of its mountings. If leakage is found, fit a new shock (see Chapter 6).

7 With the aid of an assistant to support the bike, compress the rear suspension several times. It should move up and down freely without binding. If any binding is felt, the worn or faulty component must be identified and renewed. The problem could be caused by the shock absorber, the suspension linkage components or the swingarm components.

8 Support the motorcycle using an auxiliary stand so that the rear wheel is off the ground. Grab the swingarm and rock it from side to side – there should be no discernible movement at the rear **(see illustration)**. If there's a little movement or a slight clicking can be heard, inspect the tightness of all the rear suspension mounting bolts and nuts, referring to the torque settings specified at the beginning of Chapter 6, and re-check for movement. Next, grasp the top of the rear wheel and pull it upwards – there should be no discernible freeplay before the shock absorber begins to compress **(see illustration)**. Any freeplay felt in either check indicates worn bearings in the swingarm, or worn shock absorber or suspension linkage mountings. The worn components must be renewed (see Chapter 6).

9 To make an accurate assessment of the swingarm bearings, remove the rear wheel (see Chapter 7) and the shock absorber (see Chapter 6). Grasp the rear of the swingarm with one hand and place your other hand at the junction of the swingarm and the frame. Try to move the rear of the swingarm from side-to-side. Any wear (play) in the bearings should be felt as movement between the swingarm and the frame at the front. If there is any play the swingarm will be felt to move forward and backward at the front (not from side-to-side). Next, move the swingarm up and down through its full travel. It should move freely, without any binding or rough spots. If any play in the swingarm is noted or if the swingarm does not move freely, remove the swingarm and inspect the bearings (see Chapter 6).

23 Swingarm and suspension linkage bearings – lubrication

Interval:
F1 model – every 6000 miles (10,000 km)
All other models – every 8000 miles (12,000 km)

1 Over a period of time the grease will harden or work out from behind the seals.

2 On F, G and H models the swingarm is not equipped with grease nipples. Remove the swingarm and suspension linkage as described in Chapter 6 to grease the bearings.

3 On J and A models, two grease nipples are fitted in the swingarm and three in the suspension linkage arm. Clean any road dirt off the nipples before applying the grease gun. Support the bike with the weight off the rear suspension, then pump general purpose grease into each bearing until new grease emerges from behind the seal at each end of the component **(see illustration)**. Wipe off any surplus grease.

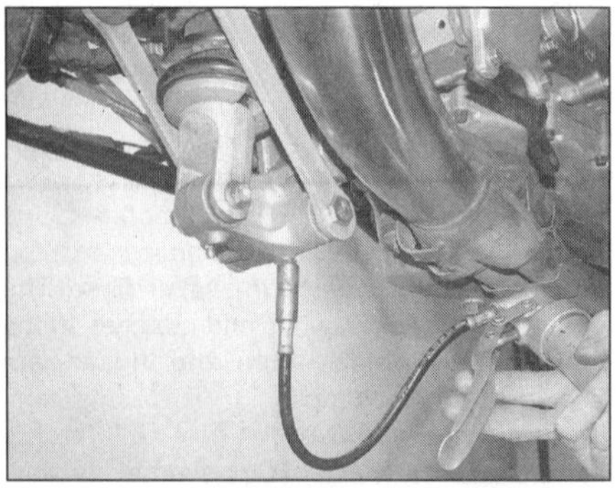

23.3 Greasing the suspension linkage bearings – J and A models

24 Nuts and bolts – tightness check

Interval:
F1 model – every 6000 miles (10,000 km)
All other models – every 8000 miles (12,000 km)

1 Since vibration of the machine tends to loosen fasteners, all nuts, bolts, screws, etc. should be periodically checked for proper tightness.

2 Pay particular attention to the following:
Spark plugs
Engine oil drain plug
Gearchange lever bolt
Footrest and stand bolts
Engine mounting bolts
Shock absorber mounting bolts
Handlebar bolts
Front axle and axle clamp bolts
Front fork clamp bolts (top and bottom yoke)
Rear axle nut
Swingarm pivot nut
Brake caliper mounting bolts
Brake hose banjo bolts and caliper bleed valves
Brake disc bolts and rear sprocket nuts
Exhaust system bolts/nuts

3 If a torque wrench is available, use it along with the torque specifications at the beginning of this, or the appropriate, Chapter.

25 Brake fluid – change

Interval:
F1 model – every 12,000 miles (20,000 km)
All other models – every 16,000 miles (24,000 km)

1 The brake fluid should be changed at the prescribed interval or whenever a master cylinder or caliper overhaul is carried out. Follow the procedure described in the brake bleeding section in Chapter 7. Ensure that all the old fluid is pumped from the hydraulic system and that the level in the fluid reservoir is checked and the brakes tested before riding the motorcycle.

> **HAYNES HiNT** *Old brake fluid is invariably much darker in colour than new fluid, making it easy to see when all old fluid has been expelled from the system.*

26 Steering head bearings - lubrication

Interval:
F1 model –
every 12,000 miles (20,000 km)
All other models –
every 16,000 miles (24,000 km)

1 Disassemble the steering head to re-grease the bearings. Refer to Chapter 6 for details.

27 Front forks - oil change

Interval:
F1 model –
every 18,000 miles (30,000 km)
All other models –
every 16,000 miles (24,000 km)

1 Fork oil degrades over a period of time and loses its damping qualities. Refer to Chapter 6 for front fork removal, oil draining and refilling, following the relevant steps. The forks do not need to be completely disassembled.

28 Cooling system - draining, flushing and refilling

Interval:
F1 model –
every 18,000 miles (30,000 km)
All other models –
every 16,000 miles (24,000 km)

Warning: Allow the engine to cool completely before performing this maintenance operation. Also, don't allow antifreeze to come into contact with your skin or the painted surfaces of the motorcycle. Rinse off spills immediately with plenty of water. Antifreeze is highly toxic if ingested. Never leave antifreeze lying around in an open container or in puddles on the floor; children and pets are attracted by its sweet smell and may drink it. Check with local authorities (councils) about disposing of antifreeze. Many communities have collection centres which will see that antifreeze is disposed of safely. Antifreeze is also combustible, so don't store it near open flames.

Draining

1 Remove the lower fairing panels and, on F, G and H models, the right-hand trim panel in the upper fairing (see Chapter 8). Remove the pressure cap by turning it anti-clockwise until it reaches a stop **(see illustration 20.6)**. If you hear a hissing sound, indicating there is still pressure in the system, wait until it stops. Now press down on the cap and continue turning until it can be removed.

2 Position a suitable container beneath the water pump. Remove the coolant drain plug and its sealing washer and allow the coolant to completely drain from the system **(see illustration)**. Retain the old sealing washer for use during flushing.

3 Remove the coolant reservoir cap. Place a suitable container underneath the reservoir, then release the clamp securing the radiator overflow hose to the base of the reservoir. Detach the hose and allow the coolant to drain into the container **(see illustration)**. Rinse the inside of the reservoir with clean water and reconnect the overflow hose.

Flushing

4 Flush the system with clean tap water by inserting a garden hose in the radiator filler neck. Allow the water to run through the system until it is clear. If there is a lot of rust in the water, remove the radiator and have it cleaned professionally (see Chapter 3).

5 Ensure the drain hole is clear, then install the drain plug using the old sealing washer.

6 Fill the cooling system with clean water mixed with a flushing compound. Make sure the flushing compound is compatible with aluminium components, and follow the manufacturer's instructions carefully.

7 Start the engine and allow it to reach normal operating temperature. Let it run for about ten minutes.

8 Stop the engine. Let it cool for a while, then cover the pressure cap with a heavy rag and turn it anti-clockwise to the first stop, releasing any pressure that may be present in the system. Once the hissing stops, push down on the cap and remove it completely.

9 Drain the system once again.

10 Fill the system with clean water and repeat the procedure in Steps 7 to 9.

Refilling

11 Fit a new sealing washer to the drain plug and tighten it to the torque setting specified at the beginning of the Chapter.

12 Fill the system with the proper coolant mixture (see this Chapter's Specifications) **(see illustration)**. **Note:** *Pour the coolant in slowly to minimise the amount of air entering the system.*

13 When the system is full (all the way up to the top of the radiator filler neck), install the pressure cap. Also top up the coolant reservoir to the UPPER level mark (see *Daily (pre-ride) checks*). Fit the reservoir cap.

14 Start the engine and allow it to idle for 2 to 3 minutes. Flick the throttle twistgrip part open 3 or 4 times, so that the engine speed rises to approximately 4000 – 5000 rpm, then stop the engine. Any air trapped in the system should have bled back to the radiator filler neck.

15 Let the engine cool then remove the pressure cap as described in Step 8. Check that the coolant level is still up to the radiator filler neck. If it's low, add the specified mixture until it reaches the top of the filler neck. Refit the cap.

16 Check the coolant level in the reservoir and top up if necessary.

17 Check the system for leaks.

18 Do not dispose of the old coolant by pouring it down the drain. Instead pour it into a heavy plastic container, cap it tightly and

28.2 Unscrew the drain plug and allow the coolant to drain

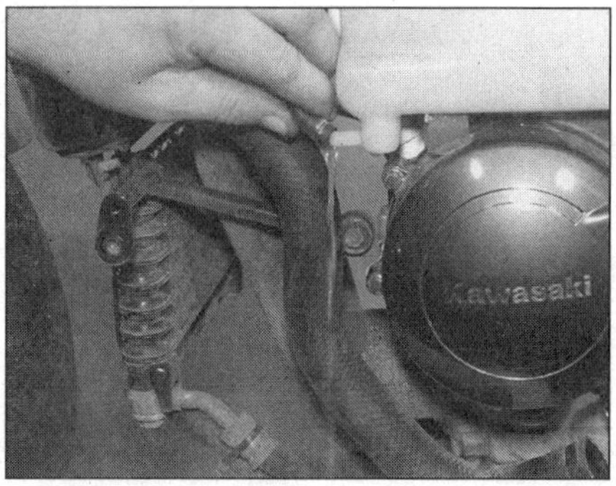

28.3 Also drain the coolant reservoir

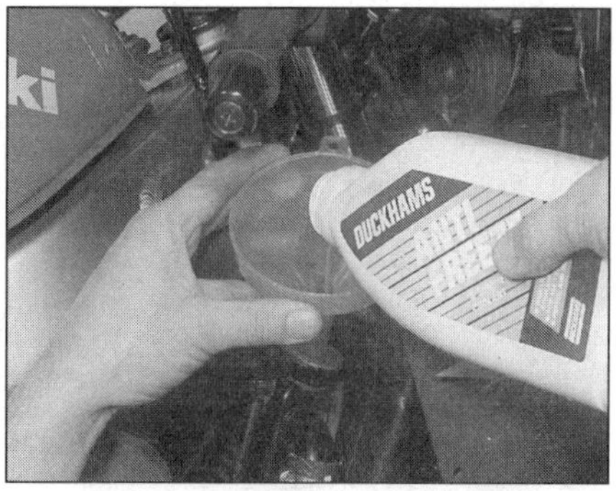

28.12 Filling the cooling system

take it into an authorised disposal site or service station – see **Warning** at the beginning of this Section.

29 Brake caliper and master cylinder – seal renewal

Interval:
F1 model – every two years
All other models – every four years

1 Refer to Chapter 7 and dismantle the components to fit new seals.

30 Brake hose – renewal

Interval:
All models – every four years

1 The hoses should be renewed regardless of their condition.

2 Refer to Chapter 7 and disconnect the brake hoses from the master cylinders and calipers. Always fit new banjo union sealing washers.

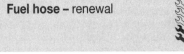

31 Fuel hose – renewal

Interval:
All models – every four years

Warning: Petrol (gasoline) is extremely flammable, so take extra precautions when you work on any part of the fuel system. Don't smoke or allow open flames or bare light bulbs near the work area, and don't work in a garage where a natural gas-type appliance is present. If you spill any fuel on your skin, rinse it off immediately with soap and water. When you perform any kind of work on the fuel system, wear safety glasses and have a fire extinguisher suitable for a Class B type fire (flammable liquids) on hand.

1 The hoses should be renewed regardless of their condition.

2 Remove the fuel tank (see Chapter 4). Disconnect the fuel hoses from the fuel tank and/or tap, the fuel pump and the carburettors, noting the routing of each hose and where it connects (see Chapter 4). It is advisable to make a sketch of the various hoses before removing them to ensure they are correctly installed.

3 Secure each new hose to its unions using new clamps. Run the engine and check that there are no leaks before taking the machine out on the road.

Non-scheduled maintenance

32 Battery – check

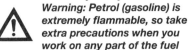

1 All models covered in this manual are fitted with a sealed battery, and therefore require no maintenance. **Note:** *Do not attempt to remove the battery caps to check the electrolyte level or battery specific gravity. Removal will damage the caps, resulting in electrolyte leakage and battery damage.* All that should be done is to periodically check that its terminals are clean and tight and that the casing is not damaged or leaking. See Chapter 9 for further details.

2 If the machine is not in regular use, disconnect the battery and give it a refresher charge every month to six weeks, as described in Chapter 9.

33 Headlight aim – check and adjustment

Note: *An improperly adjusted headlight may cause problems for oncoming traffic or provide poor, unsafe illumination of the road ahead. Before adjusting the headlight aim, be sure to consult with local traffic laws and regulations. Machines in use in the UK should refer to MOT Test Checks in the Reference section.*

1 The headlight beam can adjusted both horizontally and vertically. Before making any adjustment, check that the tyre pressures are correct and the suspension is adjusted as required. Make any adjustments to the headlight aim with the machine on level ground, with the fuel tank half full and with an assistant sitting on the seat. If the bike is usually ridden with a passenger on the back, have a second assistant to do this.

2 On F, G and H models, horizontal adjustment is made by turning the adjuster screw with a Phillips screwdriver. On F models, the adjuster is on the left-hand side of the headlight casing; on G and H models, it is on the right-hand side **(see illustrations)**.

3 On F, G and H models, vertical adjustment is made by turning the adjuster knob with your fingers. On F models, the horizontal adjuster is on the right-hand side of the headlight casing; on G and H models, it is on the left-hand side **(see illustrations 33.2a and 2b)**.

4 On J and A models both the headlights can be adjusted individually. Vertical adjustment is

33.2a Horizontal adjuster (A), vertical adjuster (B) – F models

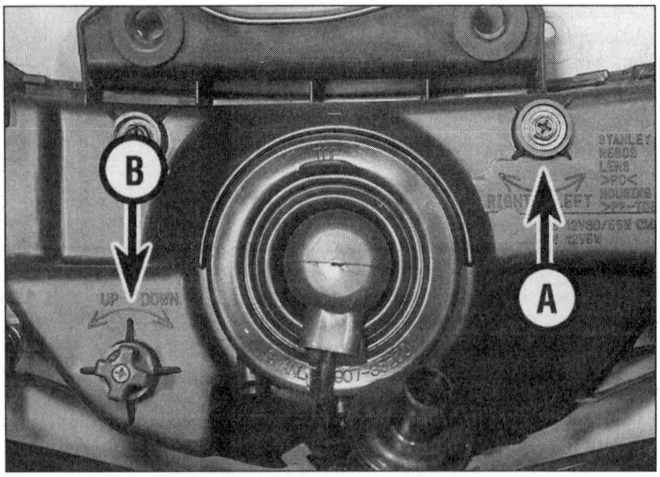

33.2b Horizontal adjuster (A), vertical adjuster (B) – G and H models

33.4 Vertical adjuster (A), horizontal adjuster (B) – J and A models

36.3 Remove the plug (arrowed) and connect the gauge adapter in its place

made by turning the upper adjuster, horizontal adjustment is made by turning the lower adjuster **(see illustration)**.

34 Wheel bearings – check

1 Support the motorcycle upright using an auxiliary stand. Check for any play in the bearings by pushing and pulling the wheel against the hub. Also rotate the wheel and check that it rotates smoothly. If any play is detectable in the hub, or if the wheel does not rotate smoothly (and this is not due to brake or transmission drag), the wheel must be removed and the bearings inspected for wear or damage (see Chapter 7).

35 Engine – cylinder compression check

1 Among other things, poor engine performance may be caused by leaking valves, incorrect valve clearances, a leaking head gasket, or worn pistons, rings and/or cylinder walls. A cylinder compression check will help pinpoint these conditions and can also indicate the presence of excessive carbon deposits in the cylinder heads.

2 The only tools required are a compression gauge and a spark plug wrench. A compression gauge with a threaded end for the spark plug hole is preferable to the type which requires hand pressure to maintain a tight seal. Depending on the outcome of the initial test, a squirt-type oil can may also be needed.

3 Make sure the valve clearances are correctly set (see Section 16) and that the cylinder head bolts are tightened to the correct torque setting (see Chapter 2).

4 Refer to *Fault Finding Equipment* in the Reference section for details of the compression test. Compression specifications are given at the beginning of this Chapter.

36 Engine – oil pressure check

1 To check the oil pressure, a suitable gauge and adapter piece (which screws into the crankcase) will be needed. Kawasaki provide a kit (part nos. 57001-164 and 57001-1278) for this purpose.

2 Warm the engine up to normal operating temperature then stop it. Remove the fairing right-hand lower panel for access to the take-off point (see Chapter 8).

3 Unscrew the oil gallery plug below the pick-up coil cover and swiftly screw the adapter into the crankcase threads **(see illustration)**. Connect the gauge to the adapter.

4 Start the engine and increase the engine speed to 4000 rpm whilst watching the gauge reading. The oil pressure should be similar to that given in the Specifications at the start of this Chapter.

5 If the pressure is significantly lower than the standard, either the pressure regulator is stuck open, the oil pump is faulty, the oil strainer or filter is blocked, or there is other engine damage. Begin diagnosis by checking the oil filter, strainer and regulator, then the oil pump (see Chapter 2). If those items check out okay, chances are the bearing oil clearances are excessive and the engine needs to be overhauled.

6 If the pressure is too high, either an oil passage is clogged, the regulator is stuck closed or the wrong grade of oil is being used.

7 Stop the engine and unscrew the gauge and adapter from the crankcase.

8 Check the condition of the oil gallery plug O-ring and fit a new one if necessary. Apply a suitable silicone sealant to the threads of the plug, then install the plug and tighten it to the torque setting specified at the beginning of the Chapter. Check the oil level (see *Daily (pre-ride) checks*). Refit the fairing lower panel.

Notes

Chapter 2
Engine, clutch and transmission

Contents

Degrees of difficulty

Easy, suitable for novice with little experience	**Fairly easy,** suitable for beginner with some experience	**Fairly difficult,** suitable for competent DIY mechanic	**Difficult,** suitable for experienced DIY mechanic	**Very difficult,** suitable for expert DIY or professional

Specifications

General

Bore	
F, G, H and J models	66.0 mm
A models	68.0 mm
Stroke	43.8 mm
Displacement	599 cc
Compression ratio	
F, G and H models	11.8 : 1
J and A models	12.8 : 1
Cylinder numbering	1-2-3-4 (from left to right)
Firing order	1-2-4-3

Camshafts

	Standard	Minimum
Lobe height (F models)		
Inlet	35.143 to 35.257 mm	35.04 mm
Exhaust	34.394 to 34.406 mm	34.29 mm
Lobe height (G, H, J and A models)		
Inlet	35.146 to 35.254 mm	35.04 mm
Exhaust	34.345 to 34.453 mm	34.24 mm
Bearing oil clearance	0.038 to 0.081 mm	0.17 mm
Journal diameter	23.940 to 23.962 mm	23.91 mm
Bearing journal inside diameter	24.000 to 24.021 mm	24.08 mm
Camshaft runout	0.02 mm or less	0.1 mm
Cam chain 20-link length	127.0 to 127.36 mm	128.9 mm

Cylinder head

Cylinder head warpage limit	0.05 mm

Valves and valve springs

Valve clearances	see Chapter 1
Valve stem runout	
Standard	0.01 mm or less
Maximum	0.05 mm
Valve stem diameter	
Inlet valve	
Standard	3.975 to 3.990 mm
Minimum	3.960 mm
Exhaust valve	
Standard	3.955 to 3.970 mm
Minimum	3.940 mm
Valve guide inside diameter (inlet and exhaust)	
Standard	4.000 to 4.012 mm
Maximum	4.08 mm
Valve stem-to-guide clearance (by direct measurement)	
Inlet valve	
Standard	0.010 to 0.037 mm
Maximum	0.12 mm
Exhaust valve	
Standard	0.030 to 0.057 mm
Maximum	0.14 mm
Valve stem-to-guide clearance (by wobble method – see text)	
Inlet valve	
Standard	0.03 to 0.12 mm
Maximum	0.29 mm
Exhaust valve	
Standard	0.10 to 0.18 mm
Maximum	0.35 mm
Valve seat width (inlet and exhaust)	0.5 to 1.0 mm
Valve spring free length	
Inlet	
Inner spring	
Standard	44.1 mm
Maximum	42.6 mm
Outer spring	
Standard	48.2 mm
Maximum	46.6 mm
Exhaust	
F1 models	
Standard	49.5 mm
Maximum	48.1 mm
F2 and F3 models	
Standard	49.03 mm
Maximum	47.7 mm
G, H, J and A models	
Standard	49.0 mm
Maximum	47.6 mm

Cylinder block

Bore diameter	
F, G and H models	
Standard	66.000 to 66.012 mm
Maximum	66.10 mm
J models	
Standard	65.960 to 65.972 mm
Maximum	66.06 mm
A models	
Standard	68.000 to 68.012 mm
Maximum	68.10 mm

Pistons

Piston diameter	
F models	
Standard	65.940 to 65.960 mm
Minimum	65.79 mm
G and H models	
Cylinders 1 and 2	
Standard	65.930 to 65.950 mm
Minimum	65.78 mm
Cylinders 3 and 4	
Standard	65.910 to 65.920 mm
Minimum	65.76 mm
J models	
Standard	65.935 to 65.950 mm
Minimum	65.78 mm
A models	
Standard	67.975 to 67.990 mm
Minimum	67.83 mm
Piston-to-cylinder clearance	
F models	0.040 to 0.072 mm
G and H models	
Cylinders 1 and 2	0.050 to 0.082 mm
Cylinders 3 and 4	0.080 to 0.102 mm
J and A models	0.010 to 0.037 mm
Piston ring-to-groove clearance	
Top ring	
Standard	0.05 to 0.09 mm
Maximum	0.19 mm
Second ring	
Standard	0.03 to 0.07 mm
Maximum	0.17 mm
Piston ring groove width	
Top ring	
Standard	0.84 to 0.86 mm
Maximum	0.94 mm
Second ring	
Standard	0.82 to 0.84 mm
Maximum	0.92 mm
Piston ring thickness	
Top ring and second rings	
Standard	0.77 to 0.79 mm
Minimum	0.7 mm
Piston ring end gap	
Top ring	
Standard	0.15 to 0.30 mm
Maximum	0.6 mm
Second ring	
Standard	
G and H models	0.30 to 0.45 mm
F, J and A models	0.35 to 0.50 mm
Maximum	0.8 mm

Oil pump

Oil pressure (with engine warm)	17 to 26 psi (1.2 to 1.8 Bar) @ 4000 rpm, oil at 90°C

Crankshaft and bearings

Crankshaft endplay	
Standard	0.05 to 0.20 mm
Maximum	0.40 mm
Crankshaft runout	
Standard	0.02 mm or less
Maximum	0.05 mm
Main bearing oil clearance	
F, G, H and J models	
Standard	0.014 to 0.038 mm
Maximum	0.070 mm
A models	
Standard	0.024 to 0.059 mm
Maximum	0.090 mm
Crankcase main bearing bore diameter	
'O' mark on crankcase	33.000 to 33.008 mm
No mark on crankcase	33.009 to 33.016 mm
Main bearing journal diameter	
No mark on crank web	29.984 to 29.994 mm
'1' mark on crank web	29.995 to 30.000 mm

Connecting rods and bearings

Connecting rod big-end side clearance	
Standard	0.13 mm to 0.33 mm
Maximum	0.50 mm
Connecting rod bearing oil clearance	
F, G, H and J models	
Standard	0.031 to 0.059 mm
Maximum	0.10 mm
A models	
Standard	0.035 to 0.064 mm
Maximum	0.10 mm
Connecting rod big-end inside diameter	
No mark on side of rod	33.000 to 33.008 mm
'O' mark on side of rod	33.009 to 33.016 mm
Connecting rod journal (crankpin) diameter	
No mark on crank web	29.984 to 29.994 mm
'O' mark on crank web	29.995 to 30.000 mm

Clutch

Spring free length			
Standard	82.1 mm		
Minimum	78.0 mm		
Friction and plain plate warpage			
Standard	0.2 mm or less		
Maximum	0.3 mm		
Friction plate thickness (all models)			
Standard	2.72 to 2.88 mm		
Maximum	2.2 mm		
Plain plate thickness	**Thin**	**Standard**	**Thick**
F, G and H models	2.0 mm	2.3 mm	2.6 mm
J and A models	1.4 mm	1.6 mm	2.0 mm
Clutch plate pack width			
F, G and H models	43.3 to 43.9 mm		
J and A models	37.7 to 38.3 mm		

Transmission

Gear ratios (no. of teeth)	
Primary reduction	2.022 to 1 (89/44T)
1st gear	2.923 to 1 (38/13T)
2nd gear	2.062 to 1 (33/16T)
3rd gear	1.631 to 1 (31/19T)
4th gear	1.380 to 1 (29/21T)
5th gear	1.217 to 1 (28/23T)
6th gear	1.083 to 1 (26/24T)
Final reduction	2.666 to 1 (40/15T)

Selector drum and forks

Selector fork end thickness	
Standard	5.9 to 6.0 mm
Minimum	5.8 mm
Selector fork groove width in pinions	
Standard	6.05 to 6.15 mm
Maximum	6.25 mm
Selector fork guide pin diameter	
Standard	5.9 to 6.0 mm
Minimum	5.8 mm
Selector drum groove width	
Standard	6.05 to 6.20 mm
Maximum	6.3 mm

Torque specifications

Engine mountings

Collar clamp bolts (F, G and H models)	23 Nm
Mounting adjuster locknuts (J and A models)	49 Nm
Mounting bolt nuts	44 Nm
Mounting bracket bolts	
F, G and H models	23 Nm
J and A models	25 Nm

Engine bottom end

Connecting rod cap nuts	
F, G and H models	
Old rods, new bolts and nuts	24 Nm + 120° (see text)
New rods, new bolts and nuts, supplied individually	24 Nm + 120° (see text)
New rods, new bolts and nuts, supplied as an assembly	22 Nm + 120° (see text)
J models	15 Nm + 160° (see text)
A models	15 Nm
Crankcase bolts	
F models	
Lower crankcase 8 mm bolts	31 Nm
Lower crankcase 6 mm bolts	12 Nm
Upper crankcase 7 mm bolts	20 Nm
Upper crankcase 6 mm bolts	12 Nm
G, H, J and A models	
Lower crankcase 8 mm bolts	
G and H models	31 Nm
J and A models	30 Nm
Lower crankcase 6 mm bolts (external)	18 Nm
Lower crankcase 6 mm bolts (within crankcase)	12 Nm
Upper crankcase 7 mm bolts	20 Nm
Upper crankcase 6 mm bolts	12 Nm
Crankcase breather plate bolts	
F, G and H models	10 Nm
J and A models	9.8 Nm
Gearchange shaft centralising spring locating pin	
F, G and H models	29 Nm
J and A models	28 Nm
Oil pipe holder bolts	
F models	12 Nm
G, H, J and A models	13 Nm
Selector drum stopper arm bolt	
F models	10 Nm
G, H, J and A models	13 Nm
Selector drum stopper plate bolt	12 Nm
Selector drum/fork shaft retainer plate bolt	
F models	12 Nm
G, H, J and A models	13 Nm
Selector drum/fork shaft retainer plate screw	
F models	12 Nm
G, H, J and A models	5.4 Nm
Starter clutch bolts	
F models	33 Nm
G, H, J and A models	34 Nm

Torque specifications (continued)

Engine top end

Baffle plate bolts	
F models	12 Nm
G, H, J and A models	5.9 Nm
Cam chain rear guide pivot bolt	25 Nm
Cam chain tensioner cap bolt (G and H models)	5.4 Nm
Cam chain tensioner mounting bolts	
F models	12 Nm
G, H, J and A models	11 Nm
Camshaft holder bolts	12 Nm
Cylinder head bolts	
10 mm bolts	
Initial setting	20 Nm
Final setting	49 Nm
6 mm bolt	12 Nm
Engine side cover bolts	12 Nm
Oil hose banjo bolt	25 Nm
Valve cover bolts	9.8 Nm

Clutch

Clutch cover bolts	12 Nm
Clutch cover noise damper bolts	5.9 Nm
Clutch hub nut	
F, G and H models	130 Nm
J and A models	135 Nm
Clutch spring bolts	8.8 Nm

Engine lubrication system

External oil line banjo bolts	25 Nm
Oil pressure relief valve	15 Nm
Oil pressure switch	15 Nm
Oil pump driven gear bolt (F models)	12 Nm
Oil sump bolts	
F, G and H models	12 Nm
J and A models	11 Nm
Water pump impeller bolt	9.8 Nm

1 General information

The engine/transmission unit is of the water-cooled, in-line, four-cylinder design, installed transversely across the frame. The sixteen valves are operated by double overhead camshafts which are chain driven off the crankshaft. The engine/transmission assembly is constructed from aluminium alloy. The crankcase is divided horizontally.

The crankcase incorporates a wet sump, pressure-fed lubrication system which uses a gear-driven, dual-rotor oil pump, an oil filter and by-pass valve assembly, a relief valve and an oil pressure switch.

Power from the crankshaft is routed to the transmission via the clutch, which is of the wet, multi-plate type and is gear-driven off the crankshaft. The transmission is a six-speed, constant-mesh unit.

2 Operations possible with the engine in the frame

The components and assemblies listed below can be removed without having to remove the engine from the frame. If, however, a number of areas require attention at the same time, removal of the engine is recommended.

Gear selector mechanism external components
Water pump
Starter motor
Alternator and starter clutch
Clutch assembly
Oil sump, oil pump and relief valve
Valve cover, camshafts, followers and shims
Cam chain tensioner
Cylinder head (F, G, H and J models)
Cylinder block and pistons (F models only)
*Selector drum and forks (see **Note** at the beginning of Section 30)*

3 Operations requiring engine removal

It is necessary to remove the engine/transmission assembly from the frame to remove the cylinder head on A models and the cylinder block and pistons on G, H, J and A models.

On all models the engine/transmission assembly must be removed from the frame and the crankcase halves separated to remove the following components:

Crankshaft, connecting rods and bearings
Transmission shafts
Cam chain

4 Major engine repair – general note

1 It is not always easy to determine when or if an engine should be completely overhauled, as a number of factors must be considered.

2 High mileage is not necessarily an indication that an overhaul is needed, while low mileage, on the other hand, does not preclude the need for an overhaul. Frequency of servicing is probably the single most important consideration. An engine that has regular and frequent oil and filter changes, as well as other required maintenance, will most likely give many miles of reliable service. Conversely, a neglected engine, or one which has not been broken in properly, may require an overhaul very early in its life.

3 Exhaust smoke and excessive oil consumption are both indications that piston rings and/or valve guides are in need of attention. Make sure oil leaks are not responsible before deciding that the rings and guides are bad. Refer to Chapter 1 and perform a cylinder compression check to determine for certain the nature and extent of the work required.

4 Low oil pressure is usually an indicator of excessive crankshaft bearing wear or a worn out oil pump. To check the oil pressure, refer to Chapter 1. If the oil pressure is lower than specified, inspect the oil passages for clogging, and inspect the oil pump, oil pressure relief valves and the crankshaft bearing inserts for excessive wear.

5 If the engine is making obvious knocking or rumbling noises, the connecting rod and/or main bearings are probably at fault.

6 Loss of power, rough running, excessive valve train noise and high fuel consumption rates may also point to the need for an overhaul, especially if they are all present at the same time. If a complete tune-up does not remedy the situation, major mechanical work is the only solution.

7 An engine overhaul generally involves restoring the internal parts to the specifications of a new engine. The piston rings, main and connecting rod bearings are usually renewed during a major overhaul. The valve seats are re-ground and, if necessary, re-cut by a specialist engineer, since they are usually in less than perfect condition at this point. The end result should be a like-new engine that will give as many trouble free miles as the original.

8 Before beginning the engine overhaul, read through all of the related procedures to familiarise yourself with the scope and requirements of the job. Overhauling an engine is not all that difficult, but it is time consuming. Plan on the motorcycle being tied up for a minimum of two weeks. Check on the availability of parts and make sure that any necessary special tools, equipment and supplies are obtained in advance.

9 Most work can be done with typical workshop hand tools, although a number of precision measuring tools are required for inspecting parts to determine if they must be renewed. Often a dealer service department or motorcycle repair shop will handle the inspection of parts and offer advice concerning reconditioning and renewal.

HAYNES HiNT ***As a general rule, time is the primary cost of an overhaul so it doesn't pay to install worn or substandard parts.***

10 As a final note, to ensure maximum life and minimum trouble from a rebuilt engine, everything must be assembled with care in a spotlessly clean environment.

5 Engine – removal and installation

Warning: Engine removal and installation should be done with the aid of at least one assistant – and preferably two – to avoid back injuries, or injuries that could occur if the engine is dropped. An hydraulic or mechanical floor jack should be used to support and lower the engine if possible. Always make sure the motorcycle is properly supported and secure.

Removal

1 Support the bike securely in an upright position using an auxiliary stand. Work can be made easier by raising the machine to a suitable working height on an hydraulic ramp or a suitable platform. Make sure the motorcycle is secure and will not topple over (see *Tools and Workshop Tips* in the Reference section). Apply the front brake and secure the lever in that position using a cable tie.

2 If the engine is dirty, particularly around its mountings, wash it thoroughly before starting any major dismantling work. This will make work much easier and rule out the possibility of caked on lumps of dirt falling into some vital component.

3 Remove the seats, the side panels and the lower fairing panels (see Chapter 8). Though not strictly necessary, it is also advisable to remove the upper fairing to improve access and clearance and to prevent the possibility of damaging it (see Chapter 8).

4 Remove the fuel tank and the air filter housing (see Chapter 4).

5 On F, G and H models, lift the vacuum valve switch bracket off the vacuum valve hoses, then detach the vacuum valve switch hose from the carburettors and remove the switch, noting how it fits and where the hoses connect **(see illustration)**. Also detach the vacuum valve hoses from the suction valve covers and the carburettors and remove the valve, noting how it fits and where the hoses connect. On J and A models, detach the vacuum valve hoses from the suction valve covers, then detach the valve switch hose from the carburettors and lift off the valve assembly **(see illustration)**.

6 Drain the coolant and the engine oil (see Chapter 1).

7 On F models, remove the ignition coils (see Chapter 5). On G and H models, check that the cylinder location is marked on each plug lead, then pull the spark plug cap off each spark plug. On J and A models, check that the cylinder location is marked on each ignition coil/cap wiring connector, then disconnect the connectors and carefully remove the coil/caps. **Note:** *Do not attempt to lever the coil/caps off the plugs or pull them off with pliers. Do not drop the coil/caps.* Temporarily undo the right-hand suction valve cover bolt and detach the earth (ground) wire from the coil/cap wiring loom **(see illustration)**. Release the loom from the clips along the back edge of the valve cover baffle plate and secure it clear of the engine.

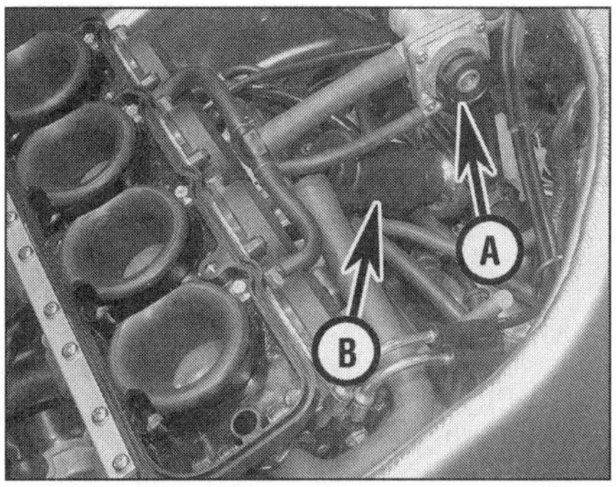

5.5a Remove the vacuum valve switch (A) and the vacuum valve (B), noting where their hoses connect – F, G and H models

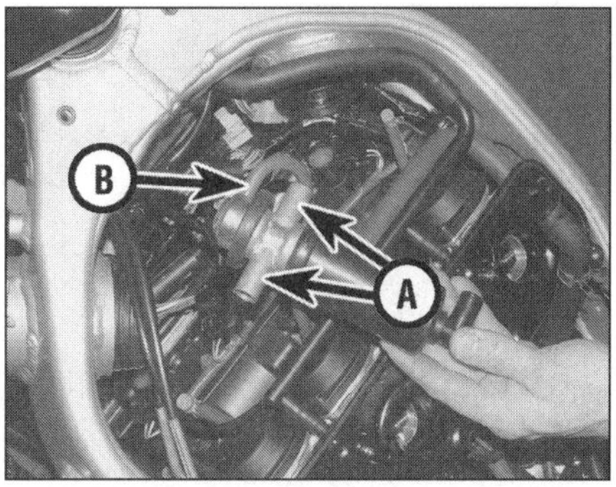

5.5b Detach the hoses from the suction valves (A) and the carburettors (B) – J and A models

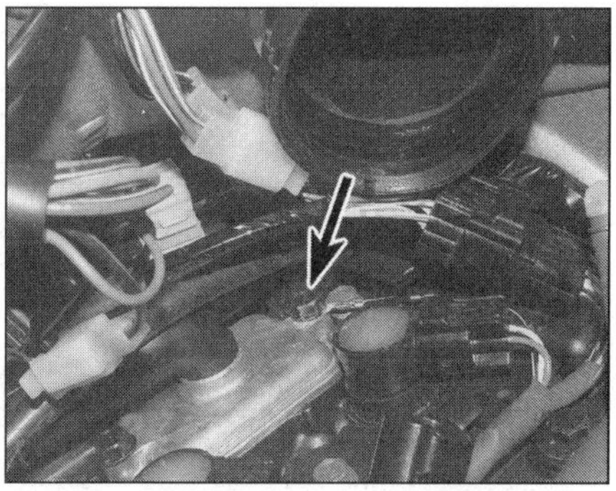

5.7 Detach the earth (ground) wire (arrowed) from the suction valve cover

5.10 Unscrew the bolts (arrowed) and remove the baffle plate and insulating pad

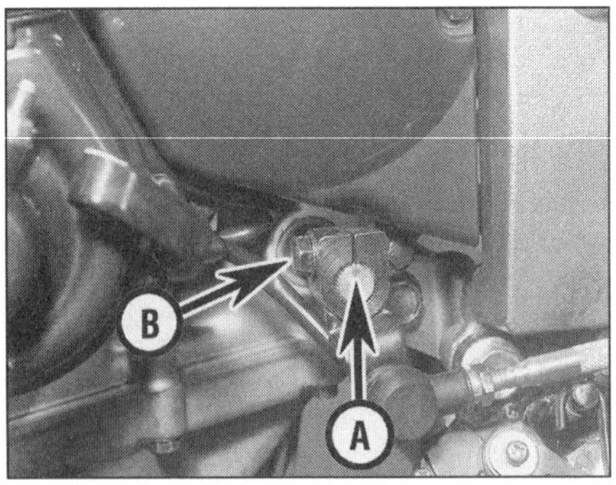

5.13 Make an alignment mark as shown (A), then unscrew the bolt (B) and slide the arm off the shaft

8 Remove the carburettors (see Chapter 4) and plug the inlet openings with rags.

9 Remove the radiator and coolant reservoir, and on F models, remove the oil cooler (see Chapter 3).

10 Unscrew the bolts securing the baffle plate to the valve cover and remove the plate and its insulating pad, noting how they fit **(see illustration)**.

11 Remove the exhaust system (see Chapter 4).

12 Disconnect the lower end of the clutch cable from the release lever and bracket (see Section 19).

13 Make an alignment mark between the gearchange linkage arm and the shaft so that they can be correctly aligned on installation (a small dot of paint on the shaft aligned with the split in the arm is best). Unscrew the linkage arm pinch bolt and slide the arm off the shaft **(see illustration)**.

14 Remove the engine sprocket cover, then remove the sprocket nut and detach the sprocket and chain from the engine (see Chapter 6). On G and H models, position the speed sensor clear so that it does not impede engine removal.

15 Disconnect the alternator wiring connector **(see illustration)**. Disconnect the neutral switch and sidestand switch wiring connectors, then disconnect the combined pick-up coil/oil pressure switch/coolant temperature sensor wiring connector **(see illustrations)**. **Note:** *On J and A models, the pick-up coil, coolant temperature sensor, oil pressure switch, neutral switch and sidestand switch are all routed through the same connector.* Release the wiring from any clips or ties, noting its routing, and coil it on top of the crankcase so that it does not impede engine removal.

16 Pull back the rubber cover on the starter motor terminal, then unscrew the nut or bolt and disconnect the lead **(see illustration)**.

17 Remove the bolt securing the battery earth (ground) cable to the engine case **(see illustration)**.

18 Position a jack under the engine with a block of wood between the jack head and sump. Make sure the jack is centrally positioned so the engine will not topple in any direction when the last mounting bolt is removed. Take the weight of the engine on the jack, but make sure the weight of the motorcycle itself is not supported as this will place strain on the engine bolts and make then difficult to remove.

19 On F, G and H models, slacken the clamp bolts which secure the engine mounting collars. On F models, the collars are on the upper and lower rear mounting

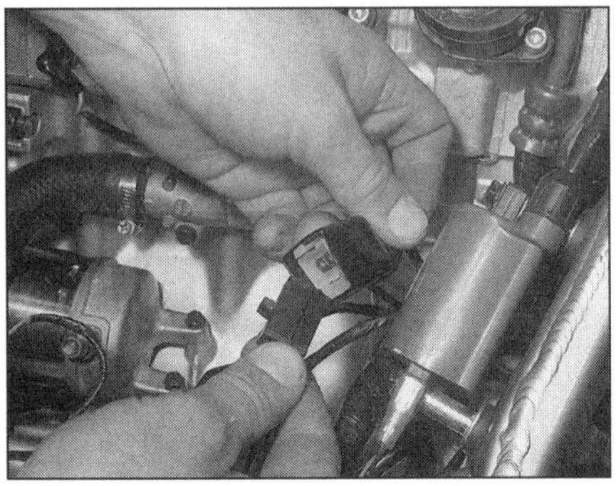

5.15a Disconnect the alternator wiring connector

5.15b Disconnect the neutral switch wiring connector . . .

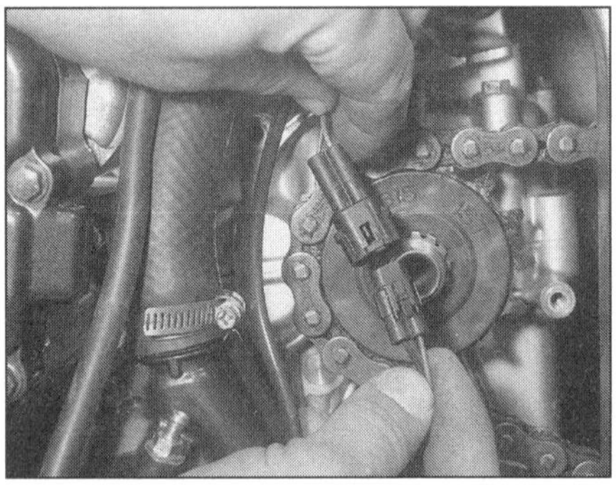

5.15c . . . the sidestand switch wiring connector . . .

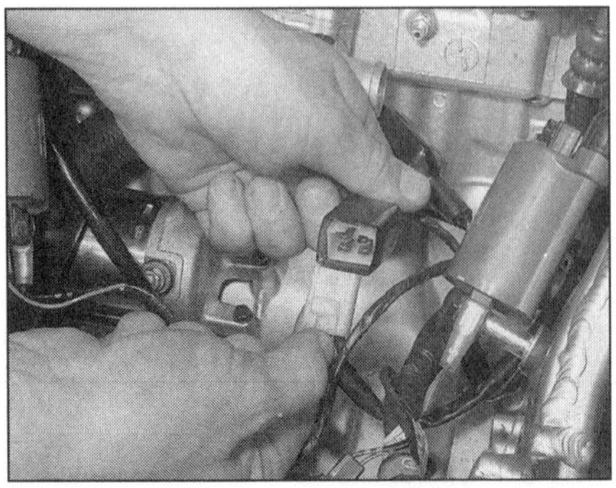

5.15d . . . and the pick-up coil/oil pressure switch/coolant temperature sensor wiring connector – F, G and H models

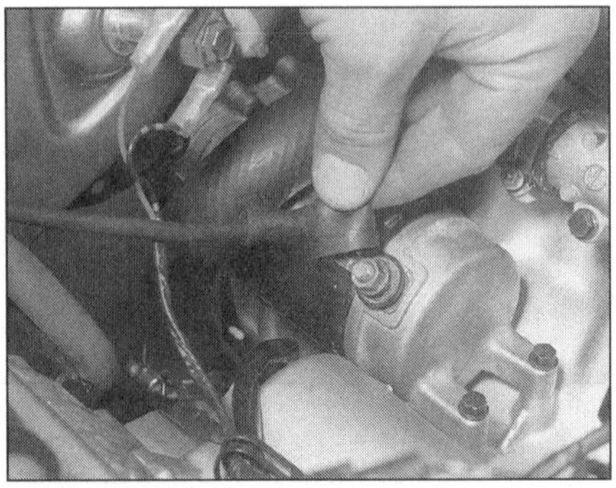

5.16 Pull back the terminal cover and detach the starter lead

5.17 Unscrew the bolt (arrowed) securing the earth lead

5.19a Upper rear mounting bolt collar clamp bolt (arrowed) – F models

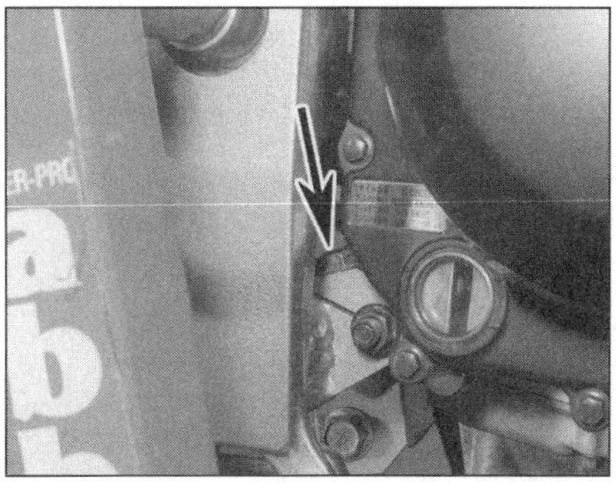

5.19b Lower rear mounting bolt collar clamp bolt (arrowed) – F, G and H models

5.19c Right-hand front mounting bolt collar clamp bolt (arrowed) – G and H models

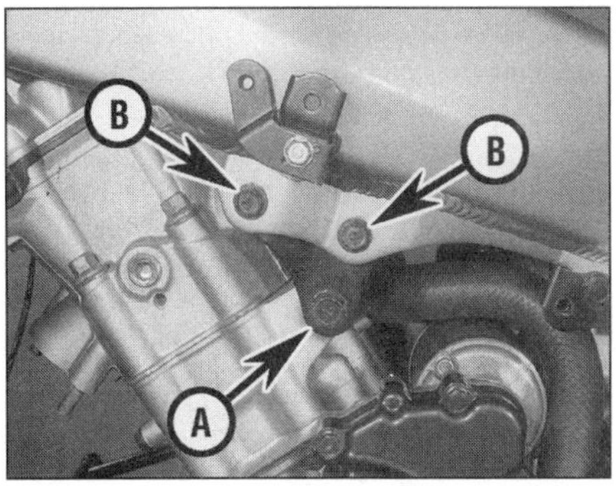

5.20a Left-hand front mounting bolt (A) and bracket bolts (B) – F models

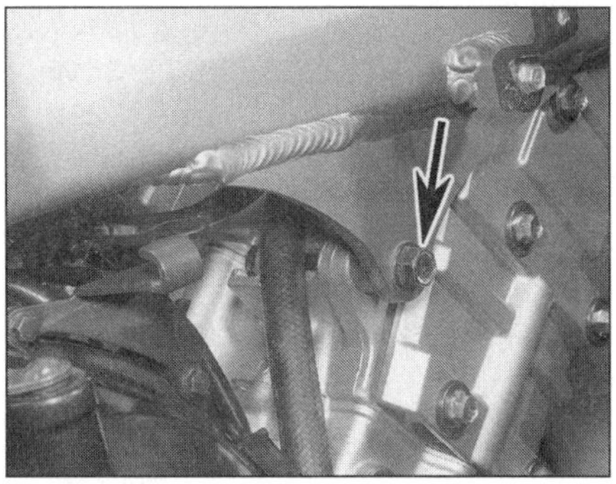

5.20b Right-hand front mounting bolt (arrowed)

5.20c Rear mounting bolts (arrowed)

TOOL TiP

For the locknut, a peg spanner can be made by cutting an old 19 mm socket as shown – measure the width and depth of the slots in the locknut to determine the size of the castellations on the socket. It is important to use a tool to which a torque wrench can be applied on installation.

bolts **(see illustrations)**. On G and H models, the collars are on the lower rear and right-hand front mounting bolts **(see illustration)**.

20 Again make sure the engine is properly supported on the jack, and have an assistant support it as well. Remove the engine mounting nuts and bolts **(see illustrations)**. On F models, remove the bolts securing the engine bracket for the left-hand front mounting bolt and remove the bracket **(see illustration)**. On G, H, J and A models, note the spacer fitted on the upper rear mounting bolt on the left-hand side **(see illustration)**. On J and A models, using either the Kawasaki service tool (pt. no. 57001-1450) or a suitable peg spanner (see ***Tool Tip***), slacken the locknuts on the engine mounting adjusters on the right-hand side of the frame **(see**

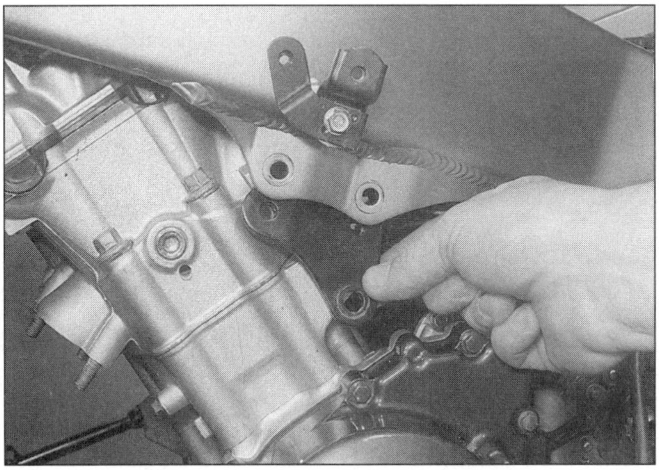

5.20d On F models, remove the bracket

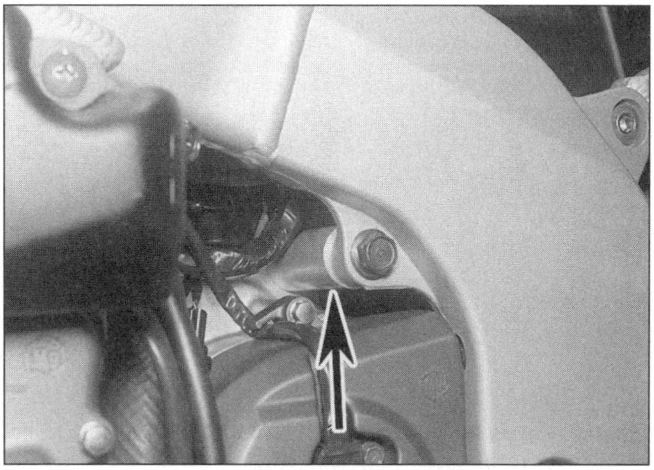

5.20e On G, H, J and A models, note the spacer (arrowed)

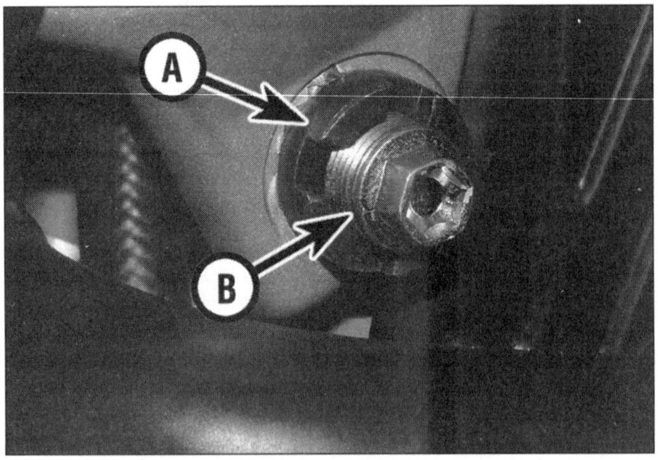

5.20f On J and A models, slacken the locknuts (A) and adjusters (B) on the right-hand upper front . . .

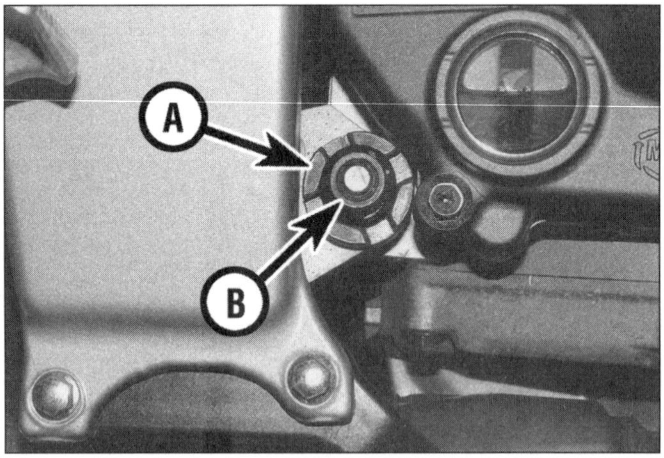

5.20g . . . and lower rear engine mountings

illustrations). Now slacken the adjusters so that there is clearance between them and the engine unit.

21 Slowly and carefully lower the engine unit and manoeuvre it out of the side of the frame, making sure the drive chain does not hook up on the transmission output shaft.

22 With the aid of an assistant lift the engine unit off the jack and position it carefully onto the work surface. On F, G and H models, if required, remove the engine mounting collars from the frame, noting how they fit.

Installation

23 On G, H, J and A models, before positioning the engine, loosen the bolts securing the engine mounting bracket to the inside of the right-hand side of the frame **(see illustration)**. On F, G and H models, ensure the engine mounting collars are installed in the clamps in the frame, but do not yet tighten the clamp bolts **(see illustration)**. On J and A models, ensure the mounting adjusters are screwed fully into the frame.

24 With the aid of an assistant place the engine unit on top of the jack and block of wood and carefully raise the engine unit into the frame. Position the drive chain over the transmission output shaft as you manoeuvre the engine, just before it is finally in position.

25 On F models, install the engine mounting bracket for the left-hand front mounting bolt and tighten its bolts to the torque setting specified at the beginning of the Chapter **(see illustrations 5.20d and a)**.

26 Once the engine is in position, install the mounting bolts and tighten them finger-tight. Make sure the captive nuts for the front mounting bolts are located in their cutouts **(see illustration)**. On G, H, J and A models, do not forget the spacer between the frame and the left-hand side of the engine on the upper rear mounting bolt **(see illustration 5.20e)**.

27 On F, G and H models, tighten the rear mounting bolt nuts (while counter-holding the bolts) and the front mounting bolts to the specified torque setting **(see illustrations 5.20c, b and a)**. Now tighten the collar clamp bolts, and on G and H models the mounting bracket bolts, to the specified torque **(see illustrations 5.19a, b and c, and 5.23a)**.

28 On J and A models, turn the lower mounting adjuster until there is no clearance between the adjuster and the engine unit, then tighten the bolts on the bracket on the inside of the right-hand side of the frame. Tighten the rear mounting bolt nuts (while counter-holding the bolts) and the front left-hand mounting bolt to the specified torque setting. Using the same tool as on removal, tighten the locknut on the lower engine mounting adjuster to the specified torque setting. Temporarily remove the upper right-hand mounting bolt, then turn the upper mounting adjuster until there is no clearance between the adjuster and the engine unit. Install the bolt and tighten it to the specified torque, then tighten the adjuster locknut.

29 The remainder of installation is essentially the reverse of removal, noting the following:

- Tighten the baffle plate bolts to the specified torque.
- Use new gaskets at all exhaust pipe connections.
- Align the punch marks on the gearchange lever linkage arm and shaft when installing the arm onto the shaft, and tighten the pinch bolt securely **(see illustration 5.13)**.
- Make sure all wires, cables and hoses are correctly routed and connected, and secured by any clips or ties.
- Refill the engine with oil and coolant (see Chapter 1).
- Adjust the throttle and clutch cable freeplay and idle speed (see Chapter 1).
- Adjust the drive chain (see Chapter 1).
- Start the engine and check for any oil or coolant leaks before installing the fairing panels.

5.23a On G, H, J and A models, slacken the mounting bracket bolts (arrowed)

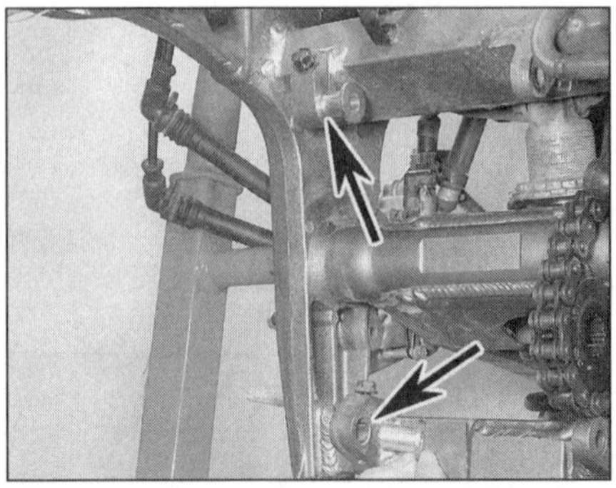

5.23b Fit the collars into their correct locations (arrowed) – F models shown

5.26 Make sure the front mounting bolt nuts are located in their cutouts (arrowed)

6 Engine disassembly and reassembly – general information

Disassembly

1 Before disassembling the engine, the external surfaces of the unit should be thoroughly cleaned and degreased. This will prevent contamination of the engine internals, and will also make working a lot easier and cleaner. A high flash-point solvent, such as paraffin (kerosene) can be used, or better still, a proprietary engine degreaser such as Gunk. Use old paintbrushes and toothbrushes to work the solvent into the various recesses of the engine casings. Take care to exclude solvent or water from the electrical components and inlet and exhaust ports.

Warning: The use of petrol (gasoline) as a cleaning agent should be avoided because of the risk of fire.

2 When clean and dry, arrange the unit on the workbench, leaving suitable clear area for working. Gather a selection of small containers and plastic bags so that parts can be grouped together in an easily identifiable manner. Some paper and a pen should be on hand so that notes can be made and labels attached where necessary. A supply of clean rag is also required.

3 Before commencing work, read through the appropriate section so that some idea of the necessary procedure can be gained. When removing components it should be noted that great force is seldom required, unless specified. In many cases, a component's reluctance to be removed is indicative of an incorrect approach or removal method – if in any doubt, re-check with the text.

4 An engine support stand made from short lengths of 2 x 4 inch wood bolted together into a rectangle will help support the engine **(see illustration)**. The perimeter of the mount should be just big enough to accommodate the sump within it so that the engine rests on its crankcase.

5 When disassembling the engine, keep 'mated' parts together (including gears, cylinders, pistons, connecting rods, valves, etc. that have been in contact with each other during engine operation). These 'mated' parts must be reused or renewed as an assembly.

6 A complete engine/transmission disassembly should be done in the following general order with reference to the appropriate Sections.

Remove the cylinder head
Remove the cylinder block
Remove the pistons
Remove the oil sump
Remove the clutch
Remove the gearchange mechanism external components
Remove the alternator rotor/starter clutch (see Chapter 9)
Separate the crankcase halves

6.4 An engine support made from pieces of 2 x 4 inch wood

Remove the crankshaft and connecting rods
Remove the transmission shafts/gears
Remove the selector drum and forks

Reassembly

7 Reassembly is accomplished by reversing the general disassembly sequence.

7 Valve cover – removal and installation

Note: *The valve cover can be removed with the engine in the frame. If the engine has been removed, ignore the steps which don't apply.*

Removal

1 Remove the lower fairing panels (see Chapter 8).

2 Remove the carburettors (see Chapter 4).

3 On G and H models, remove the radiator (see Chapter 3).

4 Detach the vacuum valve switch and valve from the vacuum hoses from the carburettors and suction valve covers and remove the valve assembly, noting how it fits and where the hoses connect **(see illustrations 5.5a and b)**.

5 On F, G and H models, check that the cylinder location is marked on each plug lead, then pull the spark plug cap off each spark plug. On J and A models, check that the cylinder location is marked on each ignition coil/cap wiring connector, then disconnect the connectors and carefully remove the coil/caps. **Note:** *Do not attempt to lever the coil/caps off the plugs or pull them off with pliers. Do not drop the coil/caps*

6 Unscrew the bolts securing the baffle plate to the valve cover and remove the plate and its insulating pad, noting how they fit **(see illustration 5.10)**.

7 Unscrew the bolts securing the cover to the right-hand side of the engine and remove the cover and rubber insulator **(see illustration)**.

8 Remove the valve cover bolts and lift the cover off the cylinder head **(see illustration)**. If it is stuck, do not try to lever it off with a screwdriver. Tap it gently around the sides with a rubber hammer or block of wood to dislodge it. Note the position of the dowels and remove them for safekeeping if they are loose.

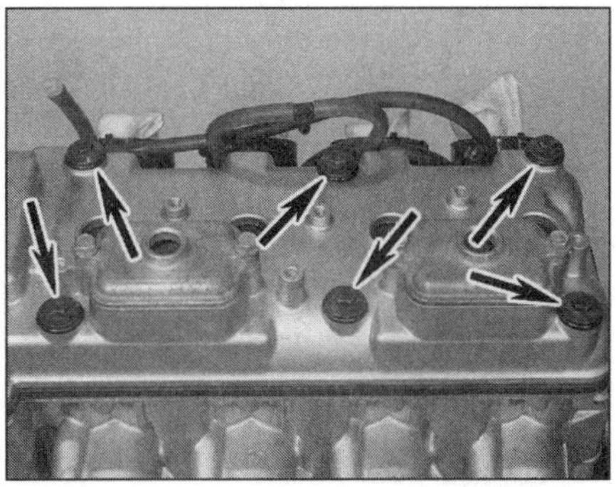

7.8 The valve cover is secured by six bolts (arrowed)

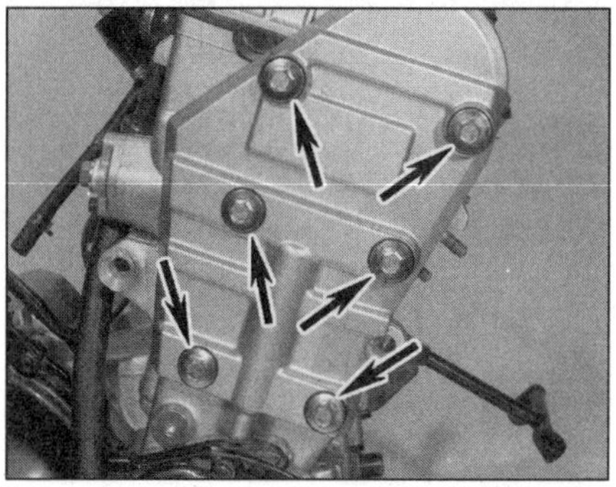

7.7 The side cover is secured by six bolts (arrowed)

Installation

9 Peel the gasket from the valve cover. If it is damaged or shows signs of general deterioration, renew it. Check that the spark plug hole gaskets and the dowels are properly positioned on the camshaft holder. Renew any of the gaskets if they are damaged or have deteriorated.

10 Clean the mating surfaces of the cylinder head and the valve cover with a suitable solvent. Apply a thin film of silicone sealant to the half-circle cutouts on each side of the head **(see illustration)**.

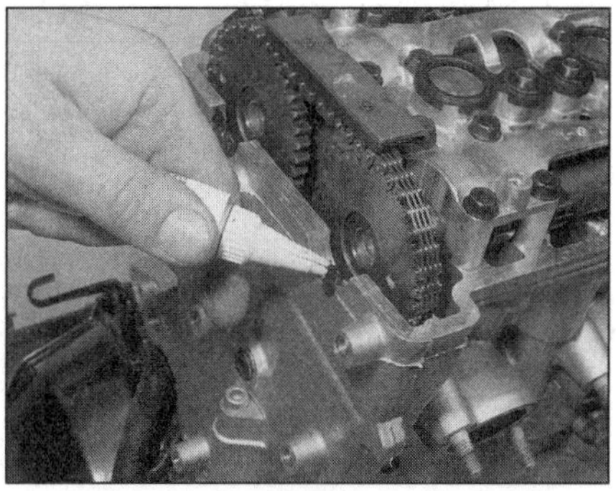

7.10 Apply a silicone sealant to the cutouts . . .

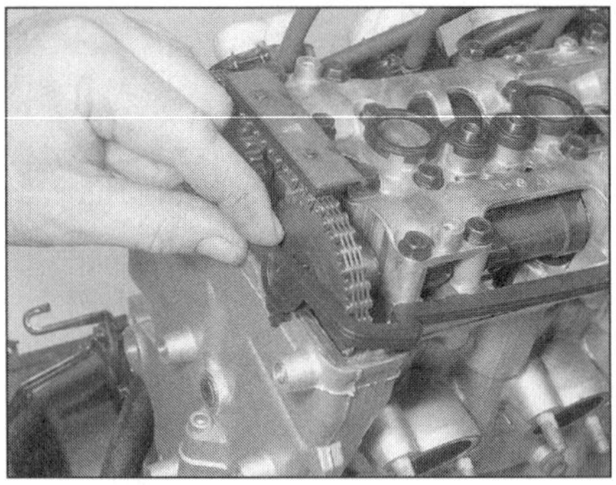

7.11a ... then fit the gasket ...

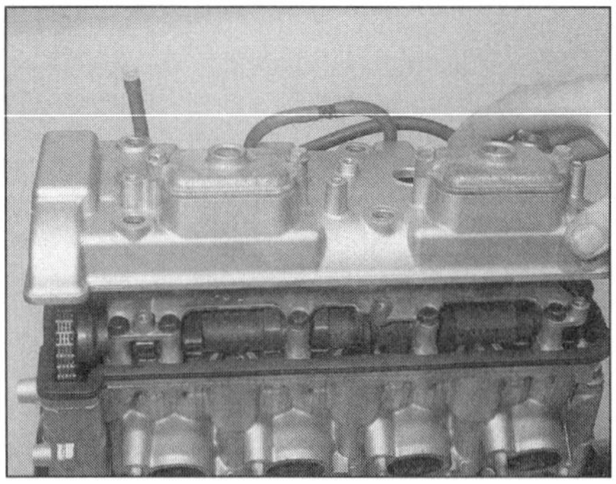

7.11b ... and the valve cover

7.13a Locate the rubber insulator ...

7.13b ... then fit the cover and tighten the bolts

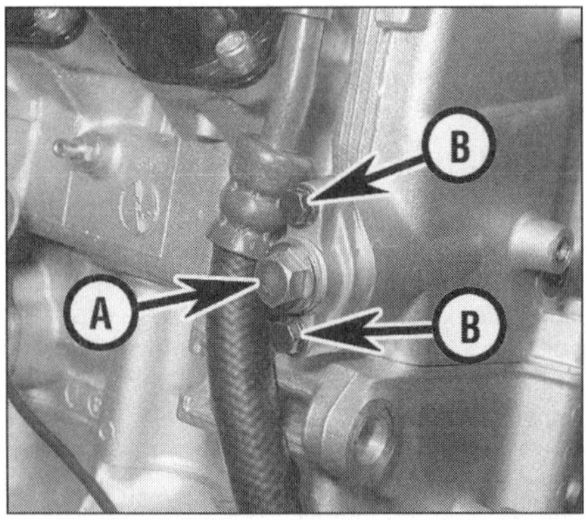

8.3 Tensioner cap bolt (A) and mounting bolts (B)

11 Fit the gasket onto the cover **(see illustration)**. Position the cover on the cylinder head, making sure the gasket doesn't slip out of place **(see illustration)**.

12 Check the seals on the valve cover bolts and fit new ones if they are damaged or have deteriorated. Fit the seals metal side uppermost. Install the bolts, tightening them evenly to the torque listed in this Chapter's Specifications.

13 Check the seals on the side cover bolts; if they're cracked or worn, renew them. Locate the rubber insulator on the side of the engine, then fit the cover and tighten the bolts to the specified torque **(see illustrations)**.

14 The remainder of installation is the reverse of removal. Tighten the baffle plate bolts to the specified torque.

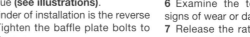

8 Cam chain tensioner – removal and installation

Note: *This procedure can be performed with the engine in the frame.*

F models

Caution: Once you start to remove the tensioner bolts, you must remove the tensioner all the way and reset it before tightening the bolts. The tensioner extends itself and locks in place, so if you loosen the bolts partway and then retighten them, the tensioner or cam chain will be damaged.

Removal

1 Remove the carburettors (see Chapter 4).

2 Remove the ignition coil for cylinders 2 and 3 (see Chapter 5).

3 Unscrew the tensioner spring cap bolt and withdraw the spring from the tensioner body **(see illustration)**.

4 Unscrew the two tensioner mounting bolts and withdraw the tensioner from the back of the cylinder block **(see illustration 8.3)**.

5 Discard the tensioner body O-ring as a new one must be used.

Inspection

6 Examine the tensioner components for signs of wear or damage.

7 Release the ratchet mechanism from the tensioner plunger and check that the plunger moves freely in and out of the tensioner body **(see illustration 8.9)**.

8 If the tensioner or any of its components are worn or damaged, or if the plunger is seized in the body, the tensioner must be renewed. Individual components are not available.

Installation

9 Release the ratchet mechanism and press the tensioner plunger all the way into the tensioner body **(see illustration)**.

10 Fit a new O-ring onto the tensioner body, then install the tensioner in the engine, making sure the plate on the end of the plunger faces up **(see illustrations)**. Apply a suitable non-permanent thread locking compound to the

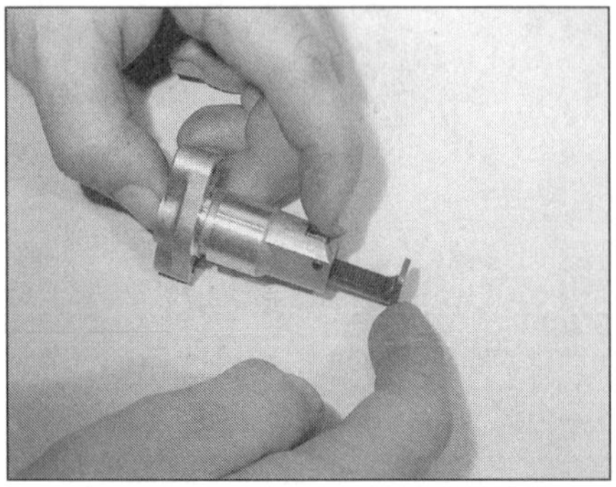

8.9 Release the ratchet and push the plunger into the body

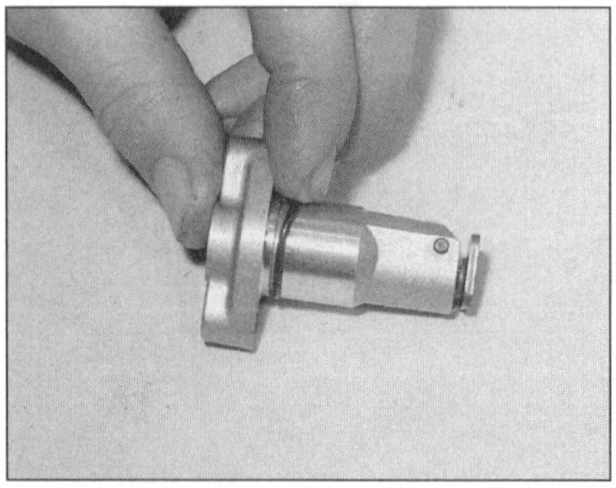

8.10a Fit a new O-ring ...

8.10b ... then install the tensioner ...

mounting bolts and tighten them to the torque setting specified at the beginning of the Chapter.

11 Check the condition of the sealing washer on the cap bolt and renew it if it is worn or damaged. Install the spring and cap bolt and tighten the bolt securely **(see illustration)**.

12 It is advisable to remove the valve cover (see Section 7) and check that the cam chain is tensioned and all the timing marks are in alignment (see Section 9). If the chain is slack, the tensioner plunger did not release when the spring and cap bolt were installed. Remove the tensioner and re-check it. Also remove the pick-up coil cover (see Section 9) and turn the crankshaft through two full turns using a socket or spanner on the timing rotor hex. This will allow the tensioner to set itself properly. Check the timing marks again (see Section 9), then install the covers (see Sections 7 and 9).

Caution: DO NOT use the timing rotor Allen bolt to turn the crankshaft – it may snap or strip out. Also be sure to turn the engine in its normal direction of rotation.

13 Install the remaining components in the reverse order of removal.

G and H models

Caution: Once you start to remove the tensioner bolts, you must remove the tensioner all the way and reset it before tightening the bolts. The tensioner extends itself and locks in place, so if you loosen the bolts partway and then retighten them, the tensioner or cam chain will be damaged. Do not rotate the crankshaft once the tensioner has been removed.

Removal

14 Remove the carburettors (see Chapter 4).

15 Remove the ignition coil for cylinders 1 and 4 (see Chapter 5).

16 Slacken the tensioner cap bolt, then unscrew the two tensioner mounting bolts and withdraw the tensioner from the back of the cylinder block **(see illustration 8.3)**.

17 Discard the tensioner body O-ring as a new one must be used.

Inspection

18 Examine the tensioner components for signs of wear or damage.

19 Remove the tensioner cap bolt. Discard the O-ring as a new one must be used. Using a flat-bladed screwdriver, turn the slotted end of the tensioner clockwise to release the tension and allow the plunger to retract into the tensioner body **(see illustration 8.22)**. Remove the screwdriver and check that the tensioner plunger springs back out of the tensioner body.

20 If the tensioner is worn or damaged, or if the plunger is seized in the body or the spring mechanism broken, the tensioner must be renewed. The internal components of the tensioner are not available individually.

Installation

21 Fit a new O-ring onto the tensioner body.

22 If not already done, remove the tensioner cap bolt. Discard the O-ring as a new one must be used. Using a flat-bladed screwdriver, turn the slotted end of the tensioner clockwise to release the tension and allow the plunger to be pushed fully into the tensioner body **(see illustration)**. Keep the screwdriver located in the slotted end of the tensioner to prevent the plunger springing back out. If a new tensioner is being fitted, it will come with a special key that is easier to use than a screwdriver, and it keeps itself in place rather than having to be held whilst installing the tensioner.

23 Keeping the screwdriver located, fit the tensioner into the cylinder block, making sure the arrow on the left-hand side of the tensioner points up. Install the tensioner mounting bolts and tighten them to the torque setting specified at the beginning of the Chapter.

Caution: Do not allow the screwdriver to turn the slotted end anti-clockwise when installing the tensioner as it will not set properly.

24 Remove the screwdriver or key from the end of the tensioner. As the slotted end turns itself back, the tensioner automatically sets itself to the correct tension against the cam chain. It is advisable to remove the valve cover (see Section 7) and check that the cam chain is tensioned and that the timing marks are all in alignment. If the chain is slack, the tensioner plunger did not release when the screwdriver was removed. Remove the tensioner and re-check it. Also remove the pick-up cover (see Section 9) and turn the crankshaft through two full turns using a socket or spanner on the timing rotor hex. This will allow the tensioner to set itself properly. Check the timing marks again (see Section 9), then install the covers (see Sections 7 and 9).

Caution: DO NOT use the timing rotor Allen bolt to turn the crankshaft – it may snap or strip out. Also be sure to turn the engine in its normal direction of rotation.

25 Fit a new O-ring onto the tensioner cap bolt and tighten it to the specified torque setting.

26 Install the remaining components in the reverse order of removal.

J and A models

Caution: Once you start to remove the tensioner bolts, you must remove the tensioner all the way and reset it before tightening the bolts. The tensioner extends itself and locks in place, so if you loosen the bolts partway and then retighten them, the tensioner or cam chain will be damaged. Do not rotate the crankshaft once the tensioner has been removed.

Removal

27 Remove the carburettors (see Chapter 4).

28 Unscrew the tensioner cap bolt and remove the bolt and washer. Withdraw the spring and rod from the tensioner body.

29 Unscrew the tensioner mounting bolts and withdraw the tensioner from the back of the cylinder block. Discard the tensioner body O-ring as a new one must be used on reassembly.

Inspection

30 Examine the tensioner components for signs of wear or damage.

31 Release the ratchet mechanism from the tensioner plunger and check that the plunger moves freely in and out of the tensioner body **(see illustration 8.9)**.

32 If the tensioner or any of its components are worn or damaged, or if the plunger is seized in the body, the tensioner must be renewed. Individual components are not available.

2

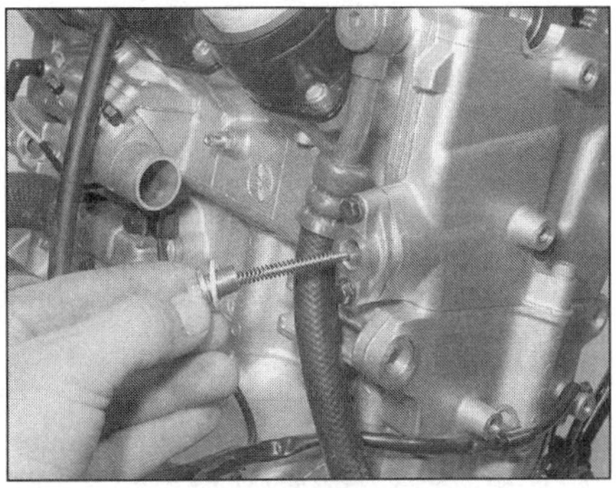

8.11 . . . followed by the spring and cap bolt assembly

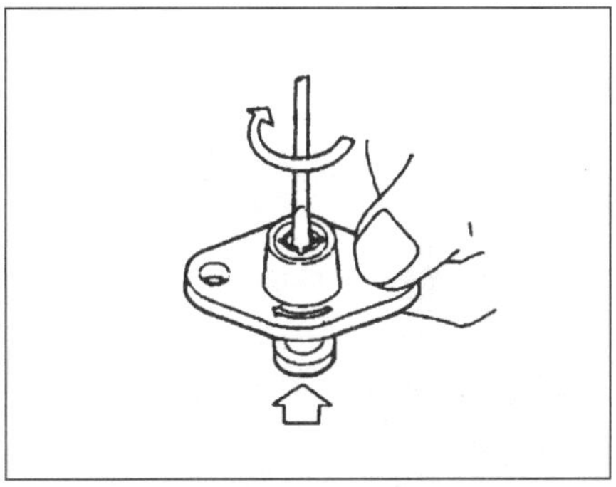

8.22 Turn the slotted end of the tensioner clockwise using a screwdriver as shown and push the plunger into the body

TOOL TIP

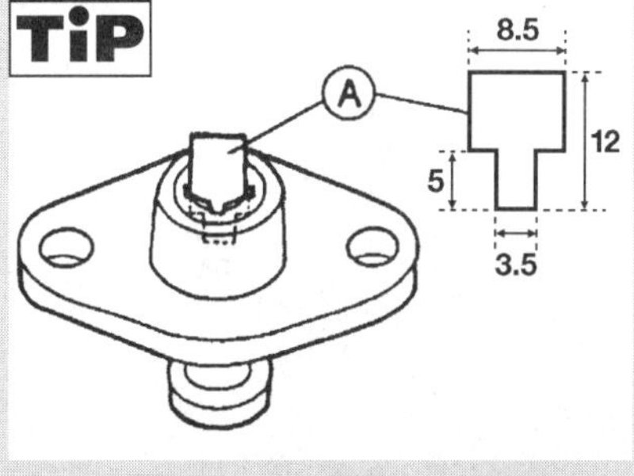

If required, a copy of the Kawasaki key (A) can be made to the dimensions shown using a 0.8 mm thick piece of mild sheet steel or aluminium.

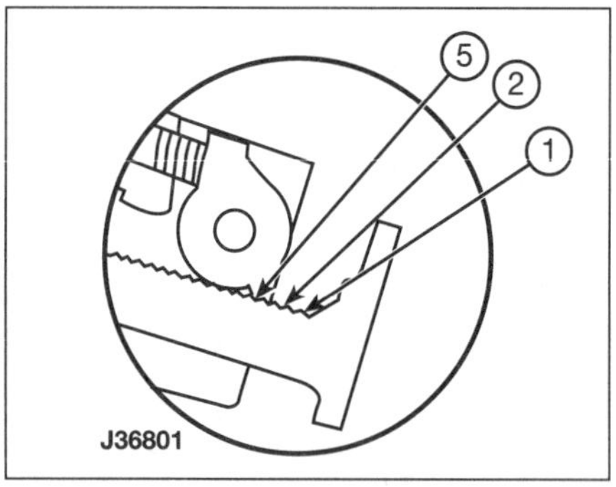

8.34 Set the position of the plunger so that its 5th notch aligns with the ratchet latch

9.1 Remove the spark plug hole rubbers and dowels

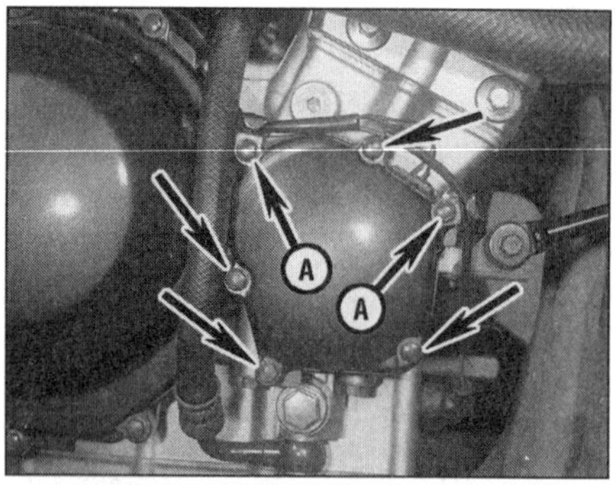

9.2 The pick-up coil cover is secured by six bolts – note the wiring clamps (A)

Installation

33 Fit a new O-ring onto the tensioner body.

34 Release the latch on the ratchet mechanism and press the tensioner plunger into the tensioner body until the ratchet engages with the fifth notch on the plunger **(see illustration)**.

35 Install the tensioner into the cylinder block with the ratchet facing up, then tighten the mounting bolts to the specified torque setting.

36 Check the condition of the sealing washer on the cap bolt and renew it if it is worn or damaged. Install the spring and cap bolt and tighten the bolt securely.

37 Remove the pick-up coil cover (see Section 9) and turn the crankshaft through two full turns using a socket or spanner on the timing rotor hex. This will allow the tensioner to set itself properly. Remove the valve cover (see Section 7) and check that the cam chain is tensioned and all the timing marks are in alignment (see Section 9). If the chain is slack, the tensioner plunger did not release when the spring and cap bolt were installed. Remove the tensioner again and re-check it. Check the timing marks again (see Section 9), then install the covers (see Sections 7 and 9).

Caution: DO NOT use the timing rotor Allen bolt to turn the crankshaft – it may snap or strip out. Also be sure to turn the engine in its normal direction of rotation.

38 Install the remaining components in the reverse order of removal.

9.3a Turn the engine using a socket on the rotor hex . . .

9.3b . . . until the T 1.4 mark aligns with the crankcase mating surfaces (arrowed) – F, G and H models . . .

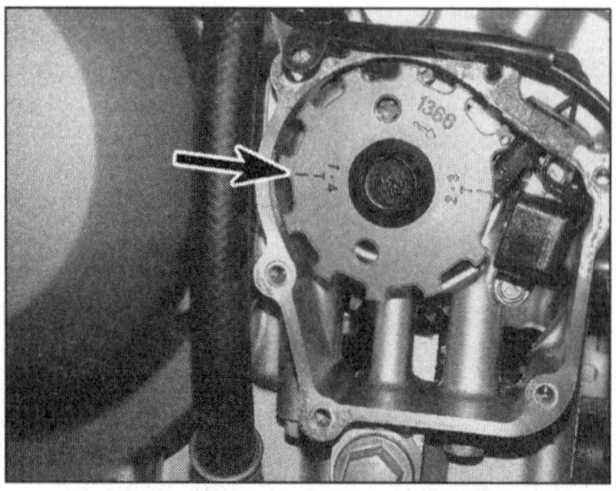

9.3c . . . and J and A models

9.5 Camshaft holder bolts (arrowed), cam chain top guide (A)

9 Camshafts and followers – removal, inspection and installation

Note: *This procedure can be performed with the engine in the frame.*

Removal

1 Remove the valve cover (see Section 7). Also remove the four spark plug hole gaskets and the dowels **(see illustration)**.

2 Unscrew the bolts securing the pick-up coil cover to the right-hand side crankcase, noting the positions of the wiring clamps **(see illustration)**.

3 The engine can be rotated using a 17 mm socket on the timing rotor hex (F models) or timing rotor bolt, turning it in a clockwise direction only **(see illustration)**. Rotate the engine until the T 1.4 mark on the timing rotor aligns with the rear mating surfaces of the crankcase halves **(see illustrations)**.

Caution: On F models, DO NOT use the timing rotor Allen bolt to turn the crankshaft – it may snap or strip out. Also be sure to turn the engine in its normal direction of rotation.

4 Remove the cam chain tensioner (see Section 8).

5 Unscrew the camshaft holder bolts evenly and a little at a time in a criss-cross pattern, until they are all loose, then lift off the cam chain top guide and the holder **(see illustration)**.

Caution: If the bearing cap bolts aren't loosened evenly, the camshaft may bind.

6 Look for marks on the camshafts. The inlet camshaft should have a 117 IN mark and the exhaust camshaft should have a 117 EX mark. If you can't find these marks, label the camshafts to ensure they are installed in their

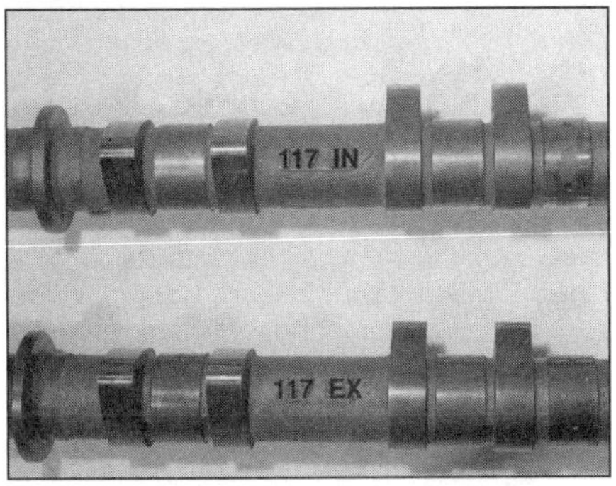

9.6a Identify the inlet and exhaust camshafts . . .

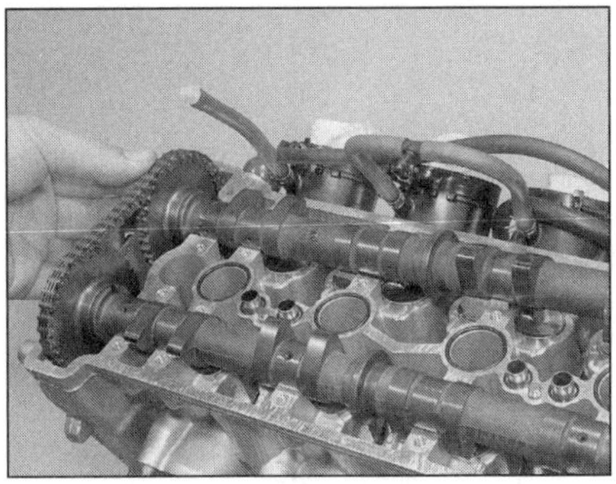
9.6b . . . then remove them from the head

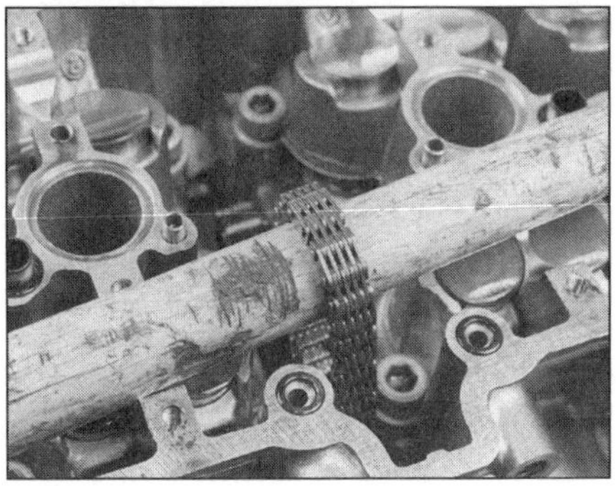
9.7 A length of broom handle makes a good hanger for the cam chain to prevent it dropping into the engine

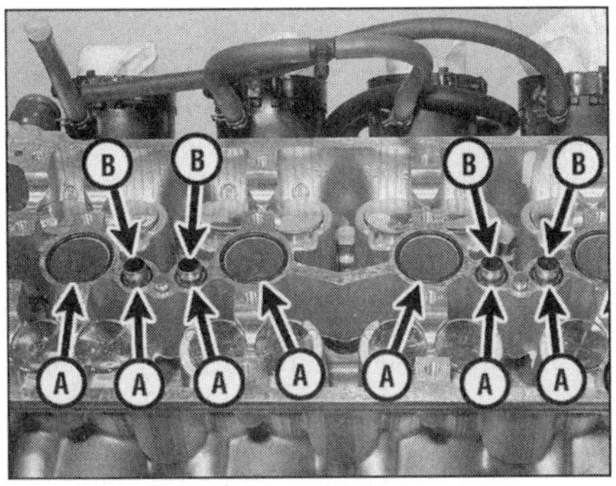

9.8a Remove the O-rings (A) and dowels (B)

9.8b Lift each follower out of its bore . . .

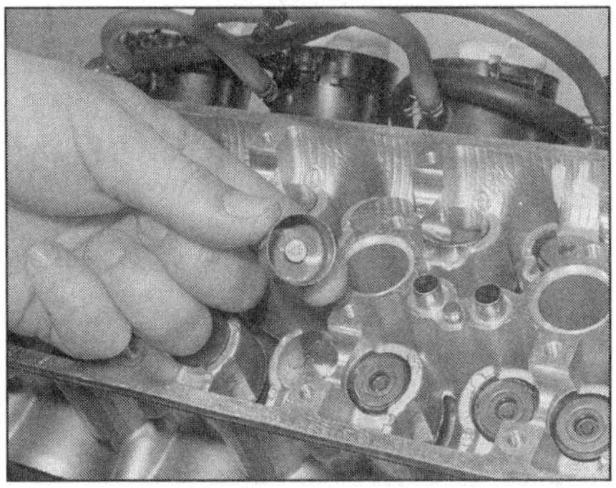
9.8c . . . and retrieve the shim either from inside the follower . . .

original locations **(see illustration)**. Pull up on the cam chain and carefully guide one camshaft out **(see illustration)**. With the chain still held taut, remove the other camshaft.

7 While the camshafts are out, don't allow the cam chain to go slack and do not rotate the crankshaft – the chain may drop down and bind between the crankshaft and case, which could damage these components. Wire the chain to another component or secure it using a rod of some sort to prevent it from dropping **(see illustration)**. Also, cover the top of the cylinder head with a rag to prevent foreign objects from falling into the engine.

8 Remove the O-rings from around the spark plug holes and remove the dowels if they are loose **(see illustration)**. Discard the O-rings as new ones must be used. Obtain a container which is divided into sixteen compartments, and label each compartment with the location of its corresponding valve in the cylinder head and whether it belongs with an inlet or an exhaust valve. If a container is not available, use labelled plastic bags. Using a magnet if necessary, lift each follower out of the cylinder head and store it in its corresponding compartment in the container **(see illustration)**. The shim is likely to stick to the inside of the follower so take great care not to lose it when removing the follower. Remove the shims from either the followers or from the recess in the top of the valves and store each one with its respective follower **(see illustrations)**.

Inspection

9 Inspect the bearing surfaces of the camshaft holder and the cylinder head and the corresponding journals on the camshaft. Look for score marks, deep scratches and evidence of spalling (a pitted appearance) **(see illustration)**.

10 Check the camshaft lobes for heat discoloration (blue appearance), score marks, chipped areas, flat spots and spalling **(see illustration)**. Measure the height of each lobe

9.8d . . . or from the top of the valve

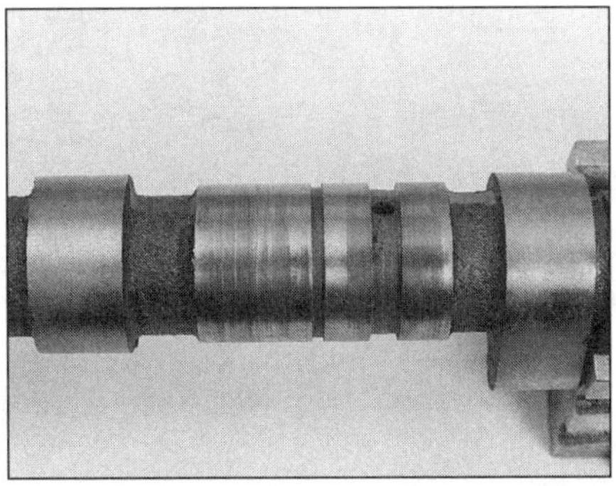
9.9 Check the journal surfaces of the camshaft for scratches or wear

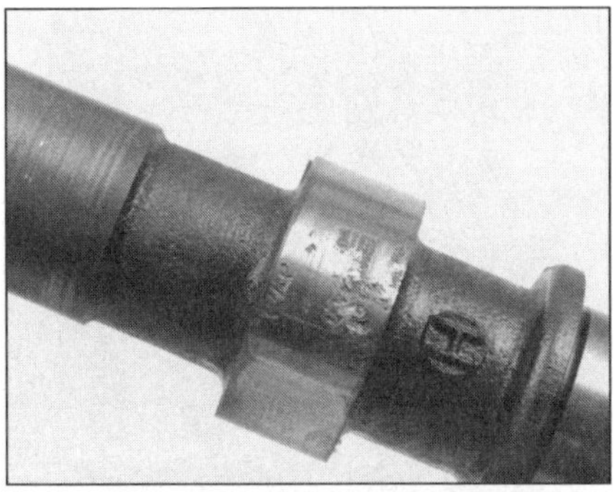
9.10a Check the lobes of the camshaft for wear – here's an example of damage requiring camshaft repair or renewal

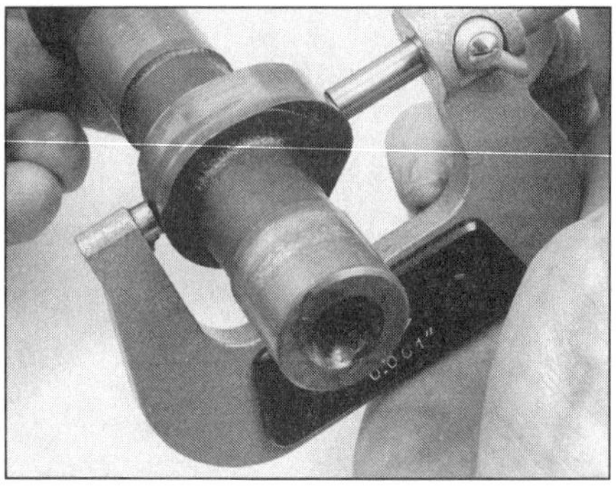

9.10b Measure the height of the camshaft lobes with a micrometer

with a micrometer **(see illustration)** and compare the results to the minimum lobe height listed in this Chapter's Specifications. If damage is noted or wear is excessive, the camshaft must be renewed.

11 Check the camshaft runout by supporting each end of the camshaft on V-blocks, and measuring any runout at the journals using a dial gauge. If the runout exceeds the specified limit the camshaft must be renewed.

> **HAYNES HiNT** *Refer to Tools and Workshop Tips in the Reference section for details of how to read a micrometer and dial gauge.*

12 Next, check the camshaft bearing oil clearances. Clean the camshaft journals, the bearing surfaces in the cylinder head and camshaft holder with a clean lint-free cloth, then lay the cams in place in the cylinder head. Engage the cam chain with the sprockets, so the camshafts don't turn as the camshaft holder bolts are tightened.

13 Cut eight strips of Plastigauge and lay one piece on each camshaft journal along the camshaft centreline **(see illustration)**. Install the camshaft holder and holder bolts. On F, G and H models, tighten the bolts evenly and a little at a time in a criss-cross pattern until the specified torque is reached. On J and A models, first tighten the bolts evenly to seat the camshafts, then tighten them to the specified torque in the specified sequence **(see illustration 9.23c)**. While doing this, don't let the camshafts rotate.

9.13 Lay a strip of Plastigauge on each bearing journal along the camshaft centreline

14 Now unscrew the bolts evenly and a little at a time in a criss-cross pattern, and carefully lift off the camshaft holder.

15 To determine the oil clearance, compare the crushed Plastigauge (at its widest point) on each journal to the scale printed on the Plastigauge container **(see illustration)**. Compare the results to this Chapter's Specifications. If the oil clearance is greater than specified, measure the diameter of the camshaft journals and the bearing inside diameters to determine which component is worn beyond its service limit. Measure the camshaft journals with a micrometer **(see illustration)**. To measure the bearing inside diameters, first install the camshaft holder without the camshafts and tighten the bolts to the specified torque as described in Step 13, then measure the diameters with a telescoping gauge and micrometer (see *Tools and Workshop Tips* in the Reference section).

> **HAYNES HiNT** *Before renewing camshafts or the cylinder head and bearing caps because of wear or damage, check with local machine shops specialising in motorcycle engine work. In the case of the camshafts, it may be possible for cam lobes to be welded, reground and hardened, at a cost far lower than that of a new camshaft. If the bearing surfaces in the cylinder head are damaged, it may be possible for them to be bored out to accept bearing inserts. Because of the high cost of a new cylinder head, we recommend that all options be explored before condemning it as trash!*

16 Except in cases of oil starvation, the cam chain wears very little. If the chain has stretched excessively, which makes it difficult to maintain proper tension, fit a new one. Refer to Section 28 for chain stretch measurement and renewal. Inspect the front (exhaust side) and rear (inlet side) cam chain guides. If they are damaged or excessively worn they should be renewed (see Section 28).

17 Check the camshaft sprockets for wear and other damage. If the sprockets are worn, it is likely the cam chain is also worn, and so is the sprocket on the crankshaft. If severe wear is apparent, the entire engine should be disassembled for inspection. If the sprockets are worn or damaged, the camshafts must be renewed as the sprockets are integral with them.

18 Inspect the outer surfaces of the cam followers for evidence of scoring or other damage. If a follower is in poor condition, it is probable that the bore in which it works is also damaged. Check for clearance between the followers and their bores. Whilst no specifications are given, if slack is excessive, fit new followers. If the bores are

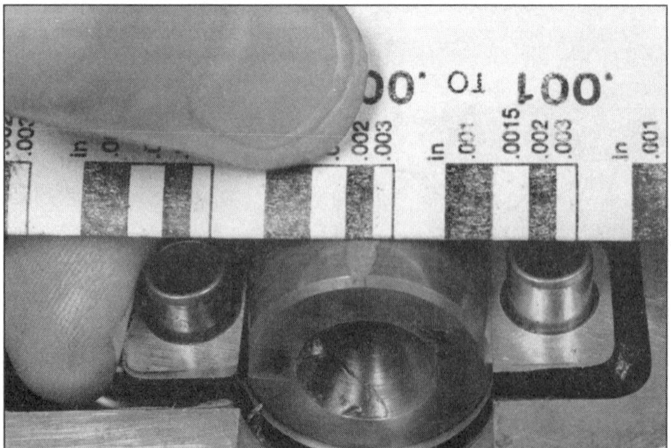

9.15a Compare the width of the crushed Plastigauge to the scale printed on the Plastigauge container

9.15b Measure the cam bearing journals with a micrometer

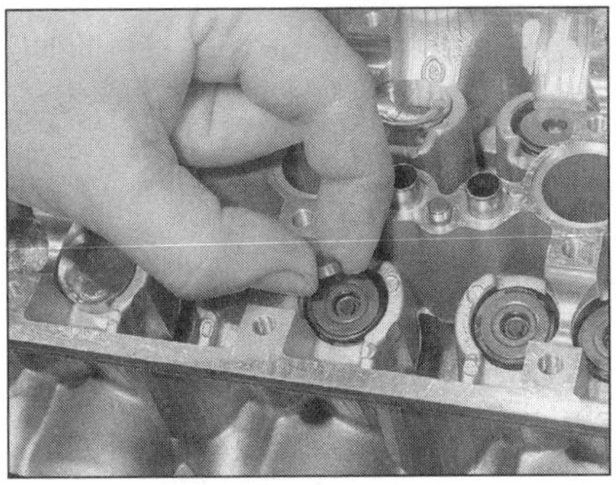

9.19a Fit the shim into the recess in the top of the valve . . .

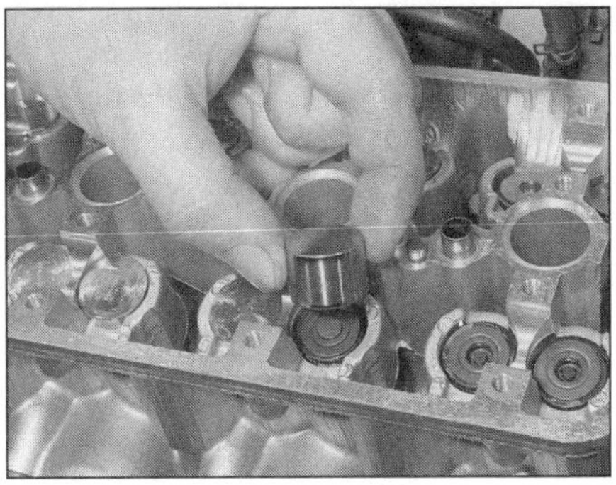

9.19b . . . then install the follower

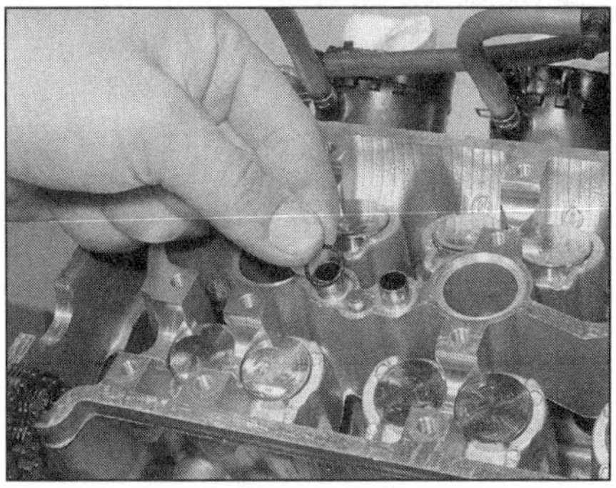

9.20a Fit a new O-ring around each dowel . . .

seriously out-of-round or tapered, the cylinder head and the followers must be renewed.

Installation

19 Lubricate each shim and its follower with molybdenum disulphide grease or engine oil and install them in the cylinder head **(see illustrations)**. Make sure each shim is correctly seated in the top of the valve assembly, and make sure each follower fits squarely in its bore. **Note:** *It is most important that the shims and followers are returned to their original valves otherwise the valve clearances will be inaccurate.*

20 Make sure the bearing surfaces in the cylinder head and the camshaft holder are clean, then apply engine oil to each of them. Fit the dowels if removed, then fit a new O-ring around each dowel adjacent to the spark plug holes, and around each spark plug hole **(see illustrations)**.

21 Verify that the T 1.4 mark on the timing rotor is still aligned (see Step 3) **(see illustration 9.3b or c)**. When installing the camshafts, align the marks on the camshaft sprockets exactly with the cylinder head surface **(see illustration)**. The EX mark on the sprocket must be facing forwards, towards the exhaust, and the IN mark must be facing backwards, towards the inlet side. Do not mix the camshafts up **(see illustration 9.6a)**. Apply engine oil (or a coat of engine assembly lube or molybdenum disulphide grease if new camshafts are being fitted) to the lobes. Make sure the camshaft bearing journals are clean, then lay the exhaust camshaft (marked 117 EX) onto the front of the head **(see illustration)**. Fit the cam chain around the sprocket. When fitting the chain, pull up on the front run to remove all slack from it. Now lay the inlet camshaft (marked 117 IN) onto the rear of the head and fit the cam chain around the sprocket, making sure there is no slack in the chain between the camshafts **(see illustration)**.

22 Count the number of chain link pins between the front EX mark and the rear IN mark **(see illustration)**. There should be 30 link pins and no slack in the chain between the two sprockets, or in the front run of the chain. Any slack in the chain must be in the rear run, so that it is taken up by the tensioner when it is installed.

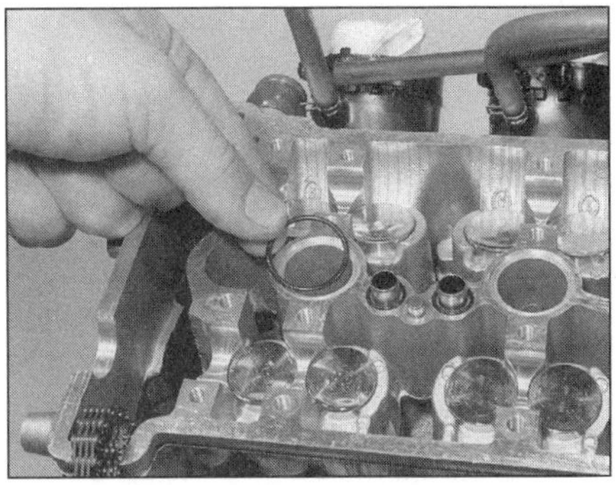

9.20b . . . and spark plug hole

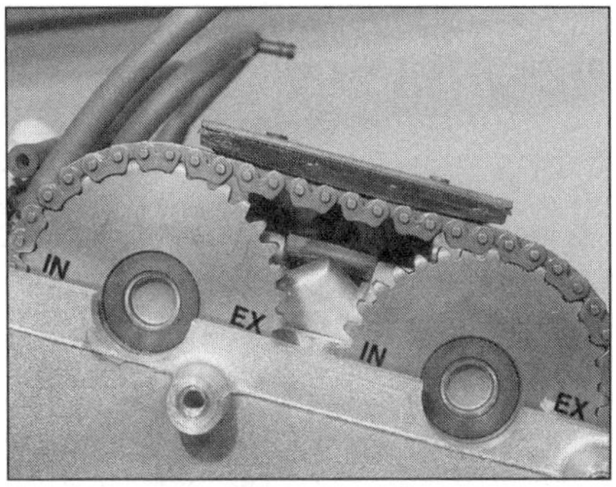

9.21a When installing the camshafts, align the sprocket marks as shown

9.21b Install the exhaust camshaft . . .

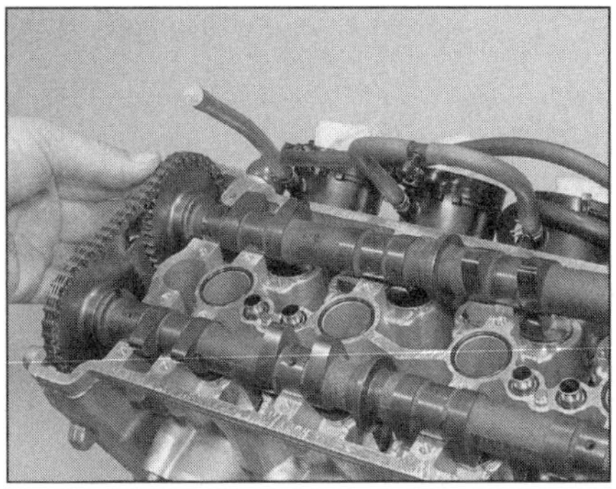

9.21c . . . followed by the inlet camshaft

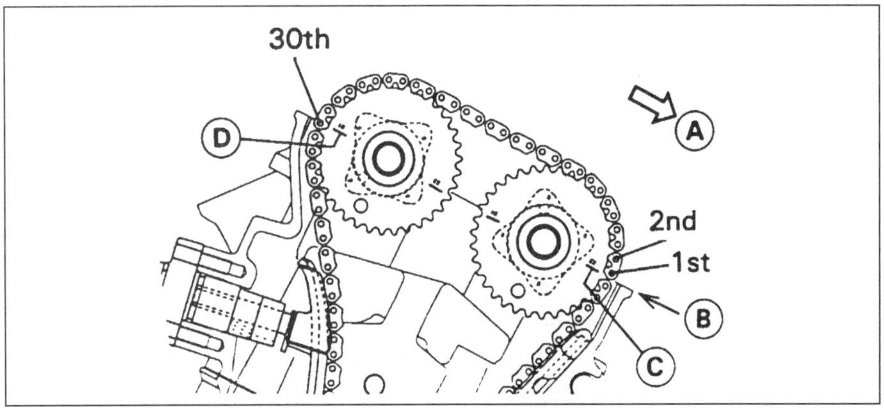

9.22 Check that the cam chain is fitted as described around the sprockets

A Front of engine
B Cylinder head surface
C Front (exhaust) sprocket EX mark
D Rear (inlet) sprocket IN mark

2

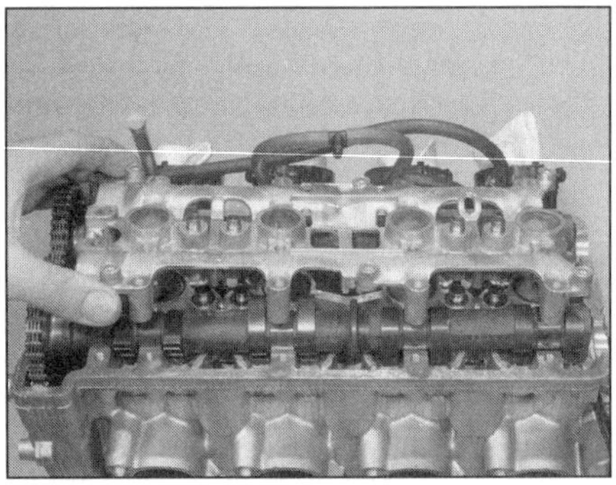

9.23a Install the camshaft holder . . .

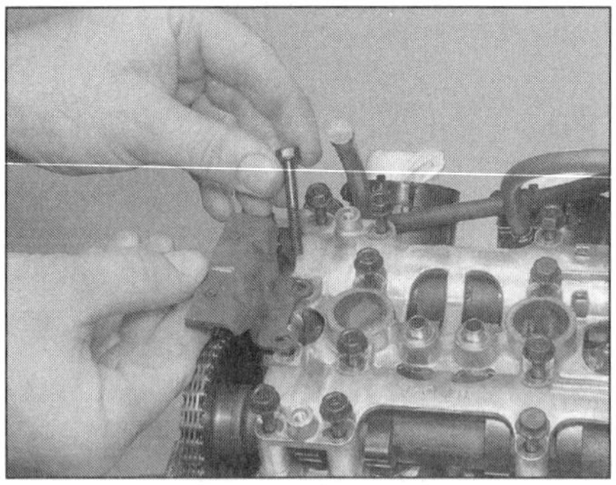

9.23b . . . and the cam chain top guide

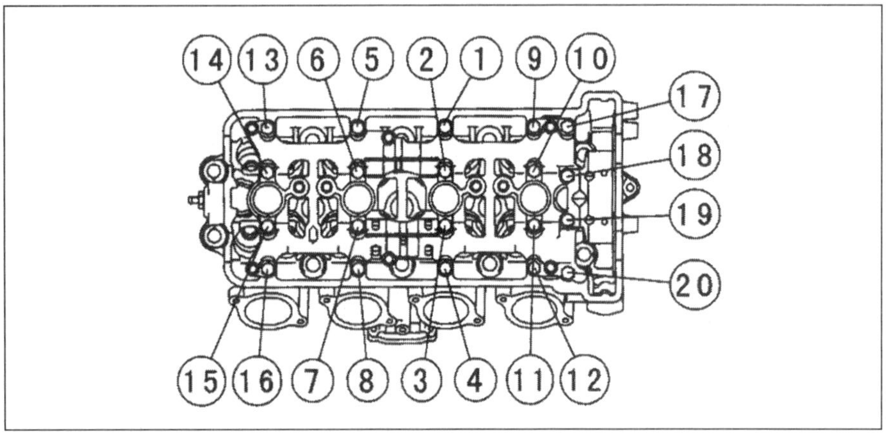

9.23c Camshaft holder bolt tightening sequence – J and A models

9.27a Apply the sealant as described . . .

9.27b . . . then fit a new gasket

10.1 Slacken the clamps and detach the hoses (A), and disconnect the temperature sensor wiring connector (B)

10.4 Unscrew the banjo bolt (arrowed) and detach the oil hose

23 Carefully set the camshaft holder in place and install the cam chain top guide and the holder bolts **(see illustrations)**. On F, G and H models, tighten the bolts evenly and a little at a time in a criss-cross pattern until the specified torque is reached. On J and A models, first tighten the bolts evenly to seat the camshafts, then tighten them to the specified torque in the specified sequence **(see illustration)**.

24 Insert a wood dowel into the cam chain tensioner hole and apply pressure to the cam chain. Check the timing marks to make sure they are still aligned with the pressure applied (see Step 21) and there are still the correct number of link pins between the EX and IN marks on the cam sprockets (see Step 22). If necessary, remove the holder and change the position of the chain on the sprocket(s) to bring all of the marks into alignment.

Caution: If the marks are not aligned exactly as described, the valve timing will be incorrect and the valves may contact the pistons, causing extensive damage to the engine.

25 Install the cam chain tensioner (see Section 8).

26 Check the valve clearances (see Chapter 1).

27 Apply a smear of sealant to the crankcase joints on the mating surface with the pick-up coil cover and to the wiring grommet **(see illustration)**. Apply a suitable non-permanent thread locking compound to the top middle cover bolt. Install the pick-up coil cover using a new gasket and tighten its bolts to the specified torque setting, not forgetting to secure the wiring clamps with the top front and rear cover bolts **(see illustration and 9.2)**.

28 Install the remaining components in the reverse order of removal.

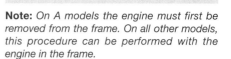

10 Cylinder head – removal and installation

Note: *On A models the engine must first be removed from the frame. On all other models, this procedure can be performed with the engine in the frame.*

Removal

Caution: The engine must be completely cool before beginning this procedure, or the cylinder head may become warped.

1 On F, G, H and J models, remove the exhaust system (see Chapter 4). Drain the cooling system and disconnect the water temperature sensor wiring connector **(see illustration)**.

2 On all models, if not already done, release the clamps securing the coolant hoses to the thermostat housing and pull the hoses off their unions **(see illustration 10.1)**.

3 Remove the camshafts (see Section 9).

4 Remove the external oil hose banjo bolt and washers and detach the hose from the cylinder head **(see illustration)**. Discard the washers as new ones must be used.

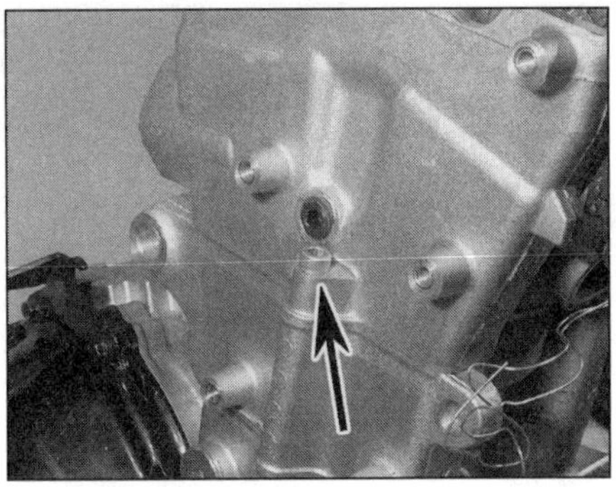

10.5 Unscrew the 6 mm bolt (arrowed)

5 Remove the 6 mm bolt on the right-hand end of the cylinder head **(see illustration)**. Now unscrew the 10 mm bolts (Nos. 1 to 10) evenly and a little at a time in a **reverse** of their numerical tightening sequence **(see illustration 10.14b)**. The bolt numbers are cast into the cylinder head. Remove the bolts, noting which fits where, and remove the washers.

6 Pull the cylinder head off the cylinder block, passing the cam chain down through the tunnel as you do **(see illustration)**. Do not let the chain fall into the block – secure it with a piece of wire or metal bar to prevent it from doing so. If the head is stuck, tap around the side of the head with a rubber mallet to jar it loose.

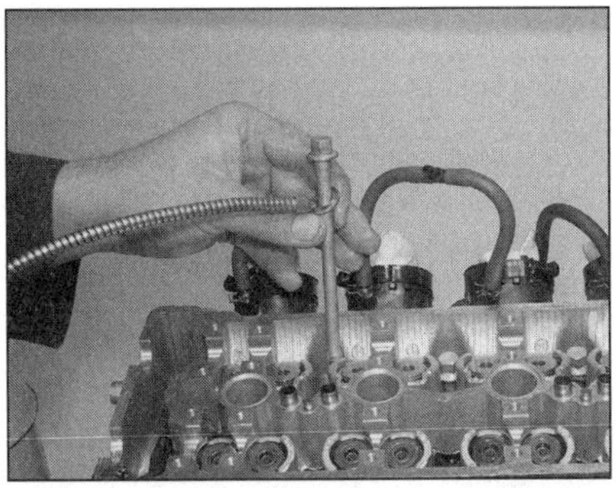

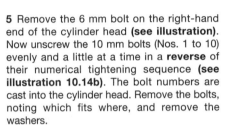

10.14a Apply oil as directed and install the bolts . . .

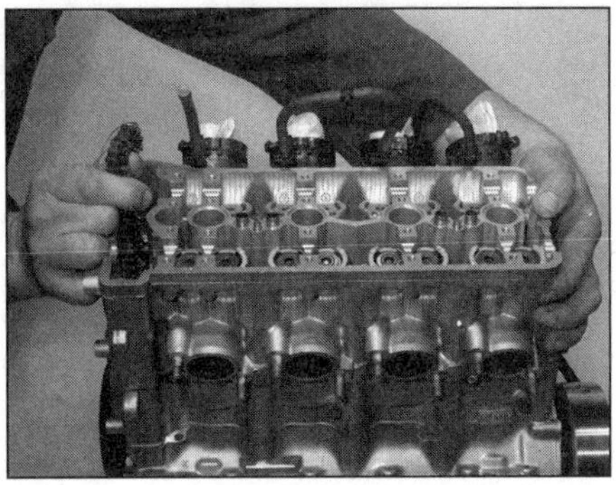

10.6 Lift the cylinder head up off the block

Caution: Don't attempt to prise the head off by inserting a screwdriver between the head and the cylinder block – you'll damage the sealing surfaces.

7 Pull out the cam chain front guide and inspect it (see Section 28). You can't remove the rear cam chain guide without removing the cylinder block, but now is the time to inspect it anyway, just in case it needs to be renewed (see Section 28). Stuff a clean rag into the cam chain tunnel to prevent the entry of debris.

8 Remove the old head gasket and the two dowels from the cylinder block. If the dowels are not in the block, they should be in the underside of the head.

9 Check the cylinder head gasket and the mating surfaces on the cylinder head and block for leakage, which could indicate warpage. Refer to Section 12 and check the flatness of the cylinder head.

10 Clean all traces of old gasket material from the cylinder head and block with a suitable solvent. Take care not to scratch or gouge the soft aluminium. Be careful not to let any of the gasket material fall into the crankcase, the cylinder bores or the water passages.

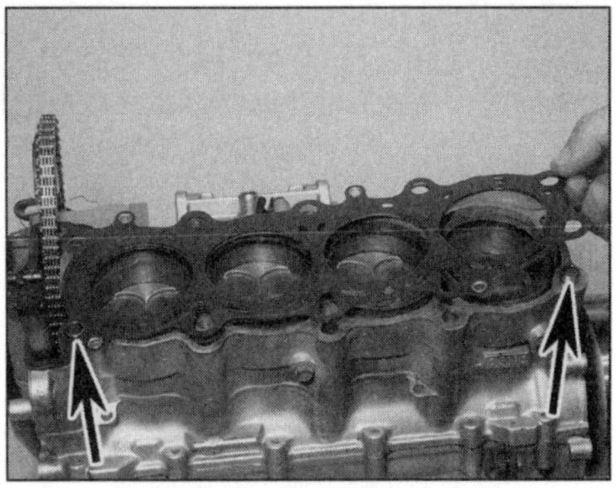

10.12 Fit the dowels (arrowed), then lay a new gasket onto the block

Installation

11 Install the front cam chain guide, with its wider end at the top (see Section 28). Push the guide all the way down and make sure it locates correctly in its cutout – it is visible behind the pick-up rotor on the end of the crankshaft.

12 Install the two dowels, then lay the new gasket in place on the cylinder block, making sure all the holes line up **(see illustration)**. Never reuse the old gasket and don't use any type of gasket sealant.

13 Carefully lower the cylinder head onto the block **(see illustration 10.6)**. It is helpful to have an assistant support the cam chain with a piece of wire so it doesn't fall and become kinked or detached from the crankshaft. When the head is resting against the cylinder block, wire the cam chain to another component to keep tension on it.

14 Apply some clean engine oil to each side of the cylinder head bolt washers **(see illustration)**. Install the cylinder head 10 mm bolts (Nos. 1 to 10) with their washers, noting that the shorter bolts are Nos. 7 and 8 for the left-hand end. Tighten the bolts in the correct numerical sequence to the initial torque setting specified at the beginning of the Chapter, then tighten them in the same sequence to the final torque setting specified **(see illustrations)**. Now install the 6 mm bolt

10.14b . . . and tighten them in the numerical sequence shown . . .

10.14c . . . and as described to the specified torque . . .

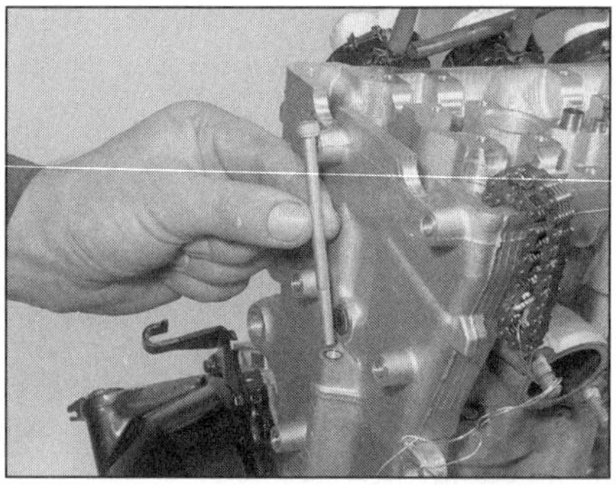

10.14d . . . then install the 6 mm bolt and tighten that to the specified torque

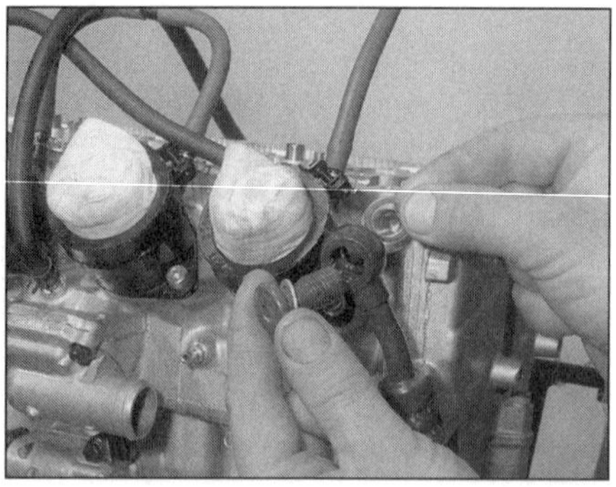

10.15a Use a new sealing washer on each side of the union . . .

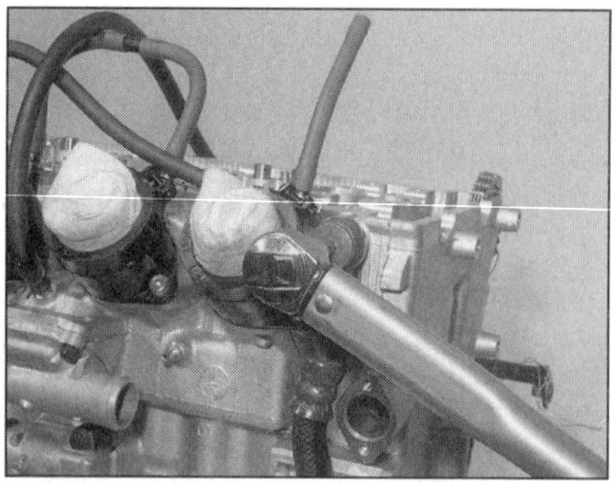

10.15b . . . and tighten the banjo bolt to the specified torque

and tighten it to the specified torque **(see illustration)**.

15 Connect the external oil hose to the cylinder head, using new sealing washers, and tighten the banjo bolt to the specified torque setting **(see illustrations)**.

16 Install the camshafts (see Section 9) and all other removed components.

17 Install the remaining components in the reverse order of removal.

11 Valves/valve seats/valve guides – servicing

1 Because of the complex nature of this job and the special tools and equipment required, most owners leave servicing of the valves, valve seats and valve guides to a professional.

2 The home mechanic can, however, remove the valves from the cylinder head, clean and check the components for wear and assess the extent of the work needed, and, unless a valve service is required, grind in the valves (see Section 12).

3 The dealer will renew the valve guides, recut the valve seats, check the valve springs, spring retainers and collets (as necessary), fit new valve seals and reassemble the valve components.

4 After the valve service has been performed, the head will be in like-new condition. When the head is returned, be sure to clean it again very thoroughly before installation on the engine to remove any metal particles or abrasive grit that may still be present from the valve service operations. Use compressed air, if available, to blow out all the holes and passages.

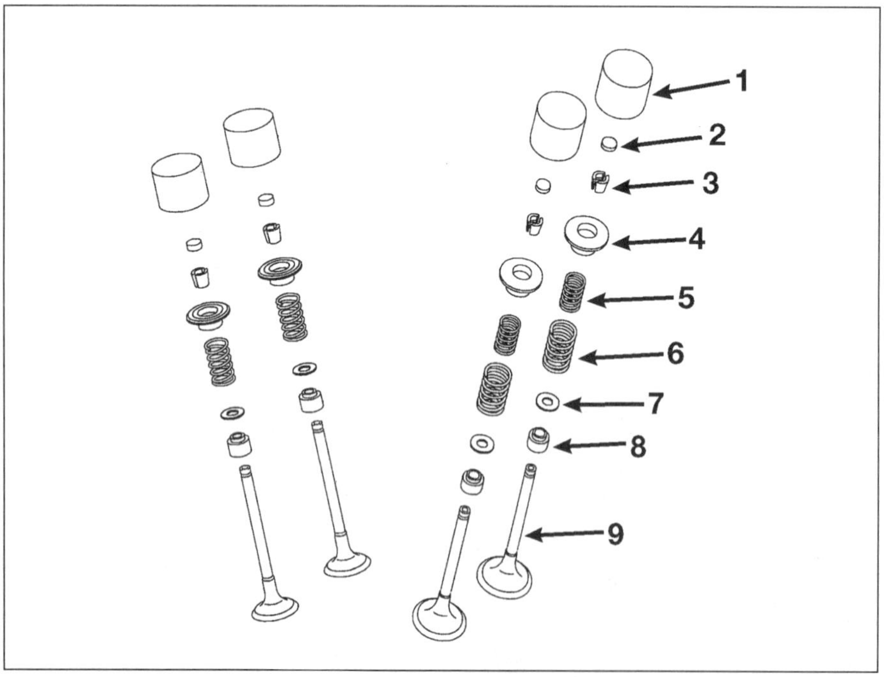

12.3 Valve components – inlet valves (left), exhaust valves (right)

1 Follower (bucket)
2 Shim
3 Collets
4 Spring retainer
5 Inner valve spring
6 Outer valve spring
7 Spring seat
8 Valve stem oil seal
9 Valve

12 Cylinder head and valves – disassembly, inspection and reassembly

1 As mentioned in the previous Section, valve servicing and valve guide renewal should be left to a Kawasaki dealer. However, disassembly, cleaning and inspection of the valves and related components can be done (if the necessary special tools are available) by the home mechanic. This way no expense is incurred if the inspection reveals that service work is not required at this time.

2 To properly disassemble the valve components without the risk of damaging them, a valve spring compressor is absolutely necessary.

Disassembly

3 Before proceeding, arrange to label and store the valves along with their related components in such a way that they can be returned to their original locations without getting mixed up **(see illustration)**. A good way to do this is to use the same container as the followers and shims are stored in (see Section 9) or obtain a separate container and label each compartment accordingly. Alternatively, labelled plastic bags will do just as well.

4 Before the valves are removed, clean any traces of gasket material from the head with a suitable solvent. Take care not to scratch or gouge the soft aluminium.

5 Carefully scrape all carbon deposits out of the combustion chamber area. A hand-held wire brush or a piece of fine emery cloth can be used once the majority of deposits have been scraped away. Do not use a wire brush mounted in a drill motor, or one with extremely stiff bristles, as the head material is soft and may be eroded away or scratched by the wire brush.

6 Compress the valve spring on the first valve with a spring compressor, making sure it is correctly located onto each end of the valve

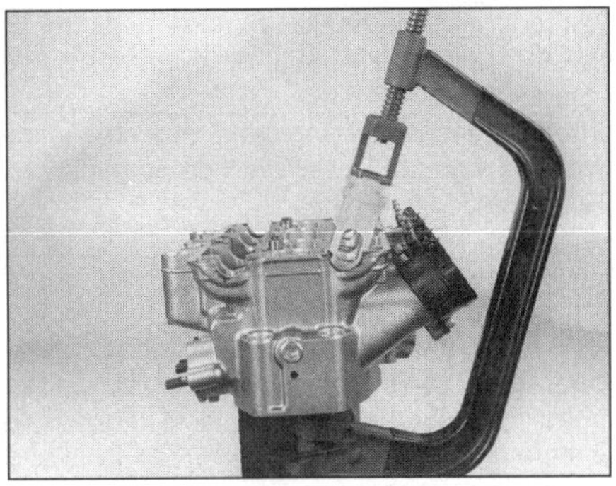

12.6a Compressing the valve springs using a valve spring compressor

12.6b Remove the collets with needle-nose pliers, tweezers, a magnet or a screwdriver with a dab of grease on it

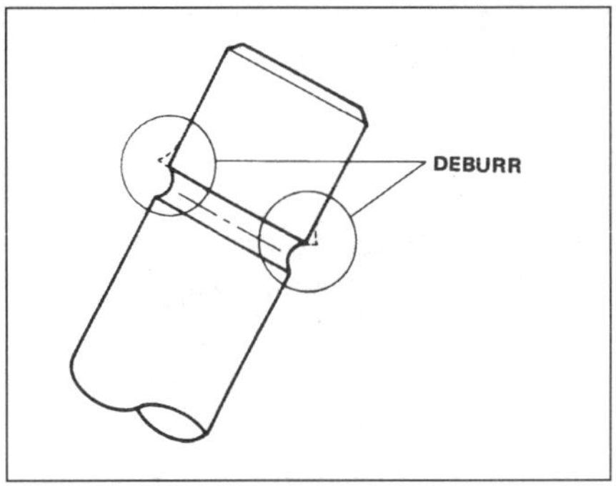

12.6c If the valve stem won't pull through the guide, deburr the area above the collet groove

assembly **(see illustration)**. Do not compress the springs any more than is absolutely necessary. Remove the collets, using either needle-nose pliers, tweezers, a magnet or a screwdriver with a dab of grease on it **(see illustration)**. Carefully release the valve spring compressor and remove the spring retainer, noting which way up it fits, the inner and outer springs, the spring seat, and the valve from the head **(see illustration 12.3)**. **Note:** *Only one spring is fitted to each inlet valve.* If the valve binds in the guide (won't pull through), push it back into the head and deburr the area around the collet groove with a very fine file or whetstone **(see illustration)**.

7 Repeat the procedure for the remaining valves. Remember to keep the parts for each valve together so they can be reinstalled in the same location.

8 Once the valves have been removed and labelled, pull the valve stem seals off the top of the valve guides with pliers and discard them as new seals must be fitted on reassembly.

9 Next, clean the cylinder head with solvent and dry it thoroughly. Compressed air will speed the drying process and ensure that all holes and recessed areas are clean.

10 Clean all the valve springs, collets, retainers and spring seats with solvent and dry them thoroughly. Clean the parts from one valve at a time so that no mixing of parts between valves occurs.

11 Scrape off any deposits that may have formed on the valve, then use a motorised wire brush to remove deposits from the valve heads and stems. Again, make sure the valves do not get mixed up.

Inspection

12 Inspect the cylinder head very carefully for cracks and other damage. If cracks are found, a new head will be required. Check the cam bearing surfaces for wear and evidence of seizure. Check the camshafts for wear as well (see Section 9).

13 Using a precision straight-edge and a feeler gauge, check the head gasket mating surface for warpage. Lay the straight-edge lengthwise, across the head and diagonally (corner-to-corner), intersecting the head bolt holes, and try to slip a 0.05 mm feeler gauge under it, on either side of each combustion chamber **(see illustration)**. If the feeler gauge can be inserted between the head and the straight-edge, the head is warped and must either be machined or, if warpage is excessive, renewed.

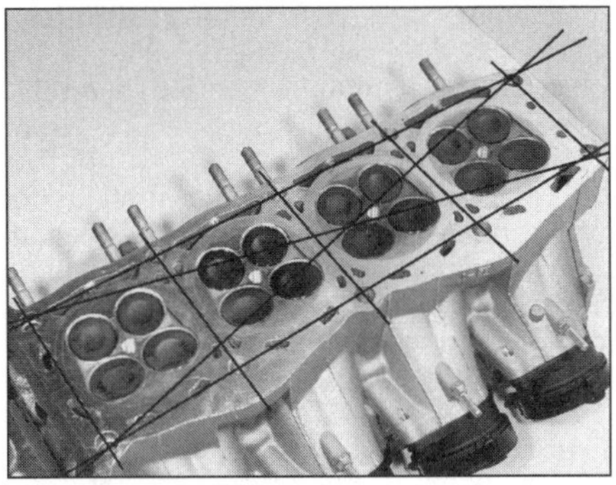

12.13 Checking the cylinder head gasket face for distortion

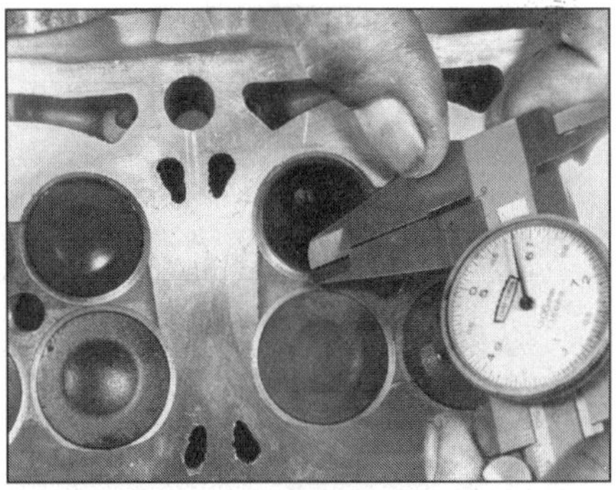

12.14 Measure the valve seat width with a ruler (or for greater precision use a vernier caliper)

14 Examine the valve seats in each of the combustion chambers. If they are pitted, cracked or burned, the head will require valve service that is beyond the scope of the home mechanic. Measure the valve seat width **(see illustration)** and compare it to this Chapter's Specifications. If it is not within the specified range, or if it varies around its circumference, valve service work is required.

15 Clean the valve guides to remove any carbon build-up, then measure the inside diameter of the guides (at both ends and the centre of the guide) with a small hole gauge and a micrometer **(see illustrations)**. Record the measurements for future reference. These measurements, along with the valve stem diameter measurements, will enable you to compute the valve stem-to-guide clearance. This clearance, when compared to the Specifications, will be one factor that will determine the extent of the valve service work required. If the guides are worn more at the ends than in the centre they must be renewed. If the necessary tools are not available, valve guide clearance can be assessed using the

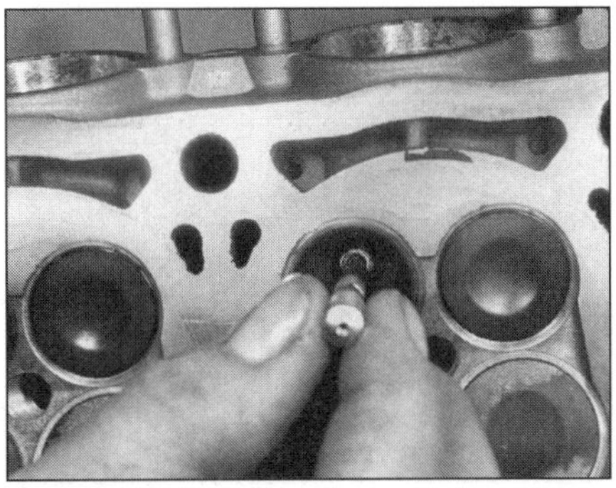

12.15a Insert a small hole gauge into the valve guide and expand it so there's a slight drag when it's pulled out

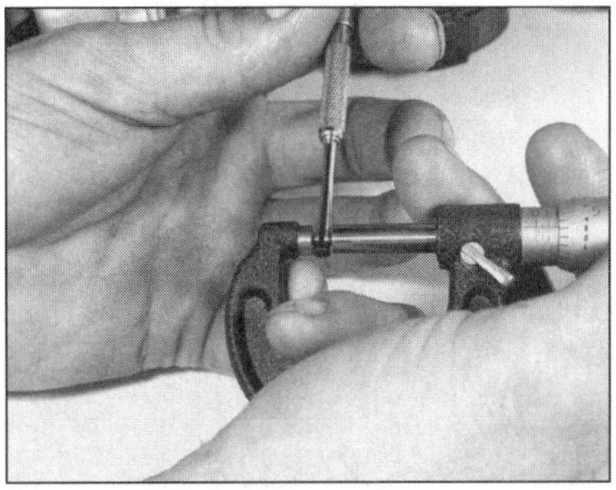

12.15b Measure the small hole gauge with a micrometer

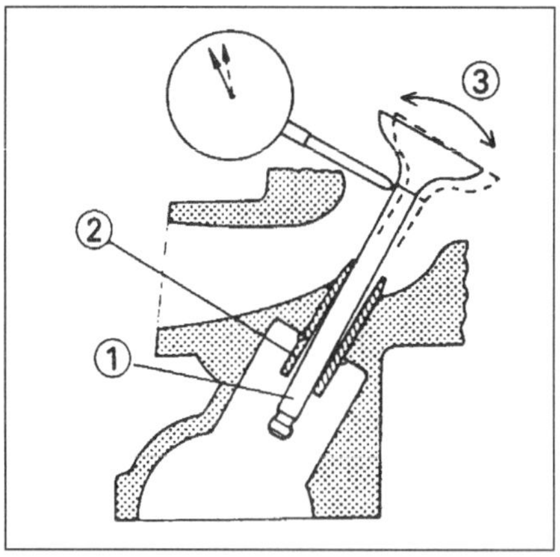

12.15c Measuring valve stem-to-guide clearance using the wobble method

1 Valve 2 Guide 3 Wobble

wobble method **(see illustration)**. Clean the valve guides to remove any carbon build-up, then install the valve in its guide so that its face is 10 mm above the seat. Mount a dial gauge against the valve stem as close to the cylinder head surface as possible and measure the amount of side clearance (wobble) between the valve stem and its guide in two perpendicular directions. If the clearance exceeds the limit specified, the valves and/or guides must be renewed.

16 Carefully inspect each valve face for cracks, pits and burned spots. Check the valve stem and the collet groove area for cracks **(see illustration)**. Check the end of the stem for pitting. The presence of any of the above conditions indicates the need for valve renewal.

17 Measure the valve stem diameter **(see illustration)**. By subtracting the stem diameter from the valve guide internal diameter, the valve stem-to-guide clearance is obtained. If the stem-to-guide clearance is greater than listed in this Chapter's Specifications, new guides and valves will have to be fitted. Also check to see if the valve stem is bent. Set the valve in a V-block with a dial gauge touching the middle of the stem **(see illustration)**. Rotate the valve and note the reading on the gauge. If the stem runout exceeds the value listed in this Chapter's Specifications, renew the valve.

18 Check the end of each valve spring for wear and pitting. Measure the free length and compare it to this Chapter's Specifications **(see illustration)**. Any springs that are shorter than specified have sagged and should not be reused. Stand the spring on a flat surface and check it for squareness **(see illustration)**.

19 Check the spring seats, retainers and collets for obvious wear and damage. Any questionable parts should not be reused, as extensive damage will occur in the event of failure during engine operation.

20 If the inspection indicates that no service work is required, the valve components can be reinstalled in the head.

Reassembly

21 Unless a valve service has been performed, before installing the valves in the head they should be ground in (lapped) to ensure a positive seal between the valves and seats. This procedure requires coarse and fine valve grinding compound and a valve grinding tool. If a grinding tool is not available, a piece of rubber or plastic hose can be slipped over the valve stem (after the valve has been installed in the guide) and used to turn the valve.

22 Apply a small amount of coarse grinding compound to the valve face, then slip the valve into the guide **(see illustration)**. **Note:** *Make sure each valve is installed in its correct guide and be careful not to get any grinding compound on the valve stem.*

23 Attach the grinding tool (or hose) to the valve and rotate the tool between the palms of your hands. Use a back-and-forth motion (as though rubbing your hands together) rather than a circular motion (i.e. so that the valve rotates alternately clockwise and anti-clockwise rather than in one direction only)

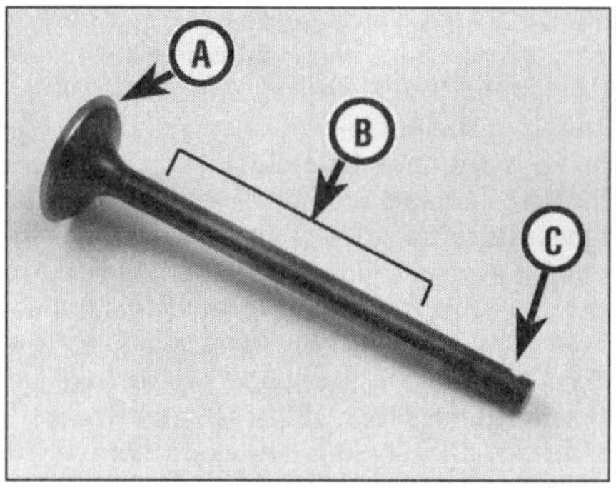

12.16 Check the valve face (A), stem (B) and collet groove (C) for signs of wear and damage

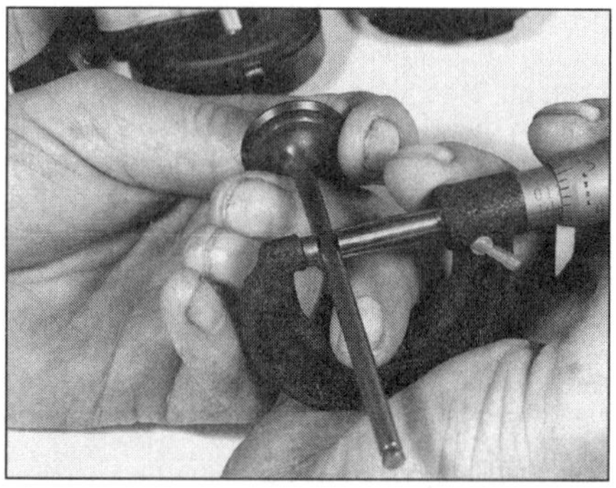

12.17a Measure the valve stem diameter with a micrometer

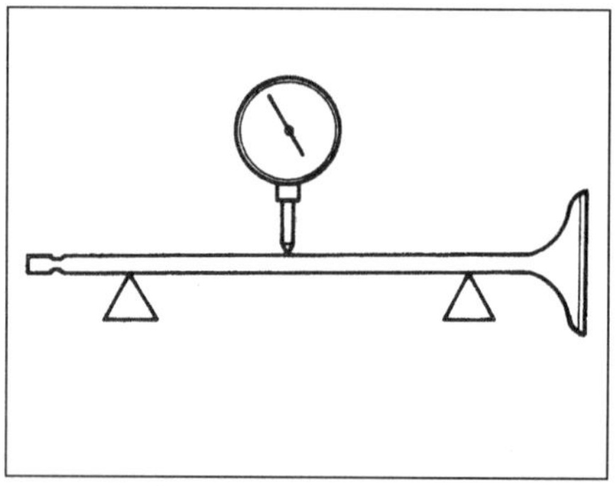

12.17b Check the valve stem for runout using V-blocks and a dial gauge

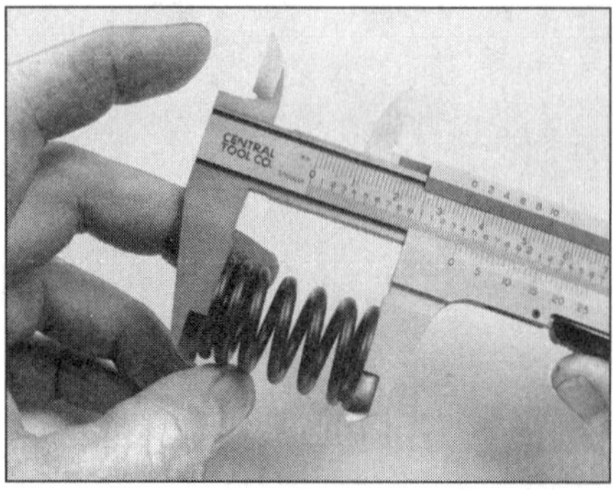

12.18a Measure the free length of the valve springs

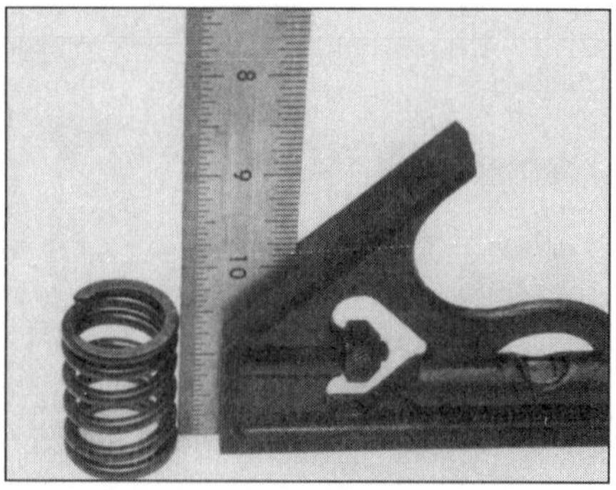

12.18b Check the valve springs for squareness

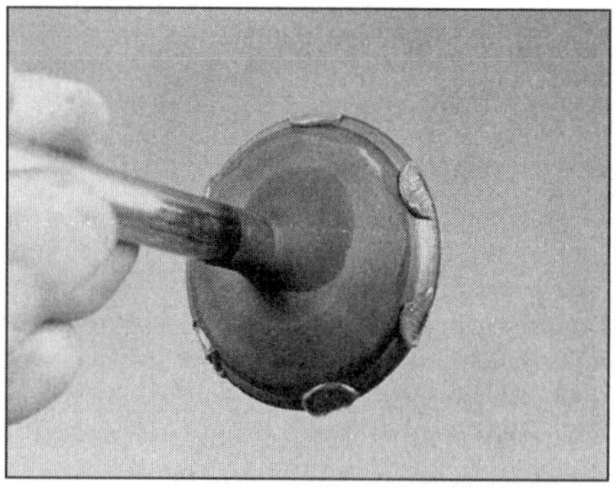

12.22 Apply the lapping compound very sparingly, in small dabs, to the valve face only

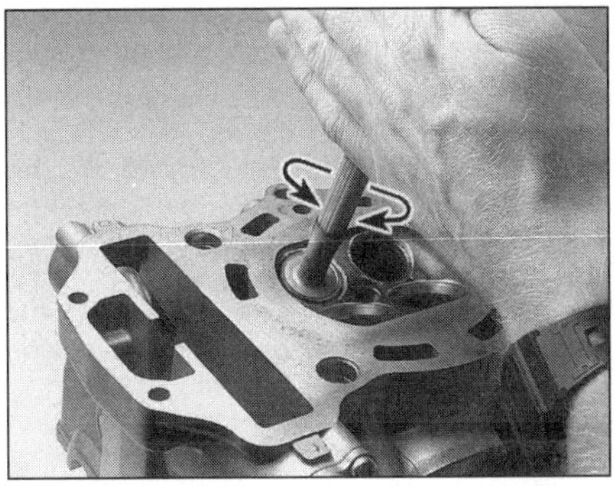
12.23a Rotate the valve grinding tool back and forth between the palms of your hands

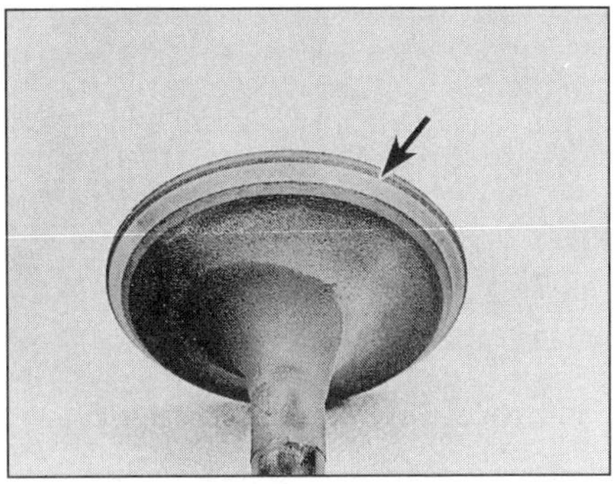
12.23b The valve face and seat should show a uniform unbroken ring . . .

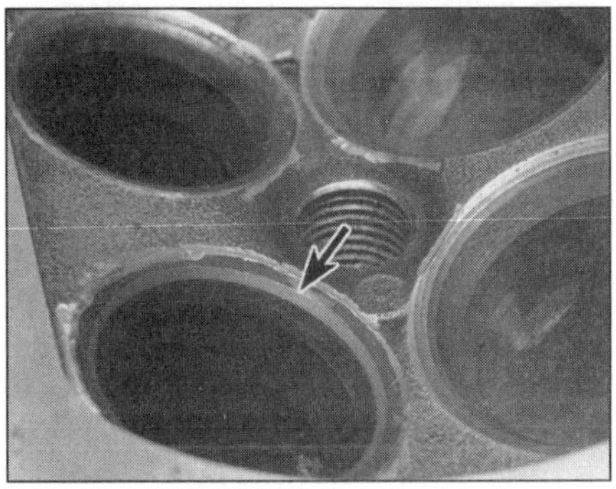
12.23c . . . and the seat (arrowed) should be the specified width all the way round

(see illustration). Lift the valve off the seat and turn it at regular intervals to distribute the grinding compound properly. Continue the grinding procedure until the valve face and seat contact area is of uniform width and unbroken around the entire circumference of the valve face and seat **(see illustrations)**.

24 Carefully remove the valve from the guide and wipe off all traces of grinding compound. Use solvent to clean the valve and wipe the seat area thoroughly with a solvent soaked cloth.

25 Repeat the procedure with fine valve grinding compound, then repeat the entire procedure for the remaining valves.

26 Lay the spring seats in place in the cylinder head, then install new valve stem seals on each of the guides **(see illustration)**. Use an appropriate size deep socket to push the seals into place until they are properly seated **(see illustration)**. Don't twist or cock them, or they will not seal properly against the valve stems. Also, don't remove them again or they will be damaged.

27 Coat one of the valve stems with assembly lube or moly-based grease, then install it into its guide, rotating it slowly to avoid damaging the seal **(see illustration)**. Next, install the spring(s), with the closer-wound coils facing down into the cylinder head, noting that the inlet valves have an inner and outer spring, whilst the exhaust valves have one spring only **(see illustration)**. Install the spring retainer with its shouldered side facing down so that it fits into the top of the spring **(see illustration)**.

28 Apply a small amount of grease to the collets to help hold them in place as the pressure is released from the spring(s) **(see**

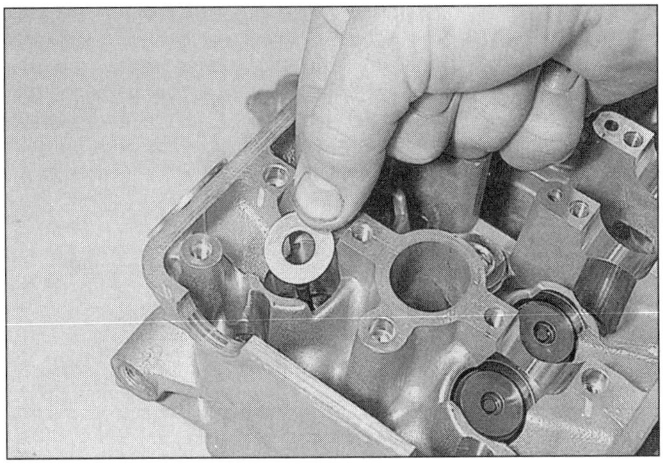
12.26a Fit the spring seat . . .

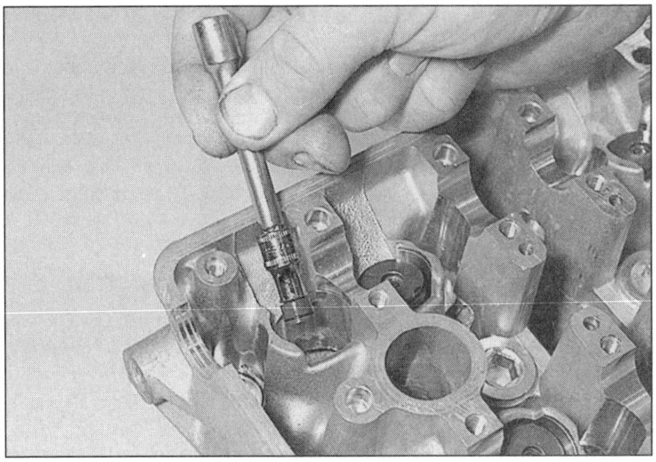
12.26b . . . then press the valve stem seal into position using a suitable deep socket

2

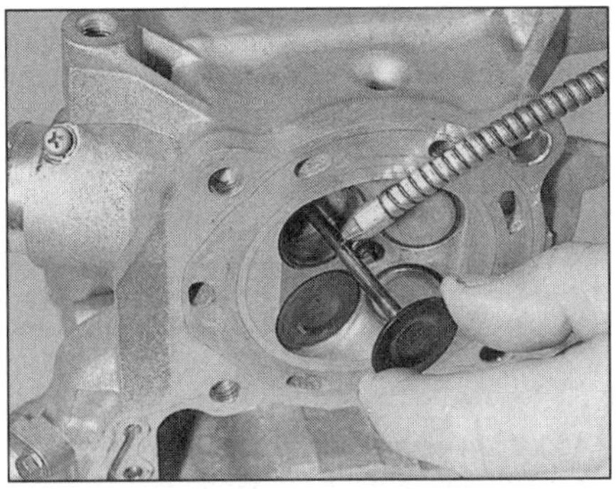
12.27a Lubricate the stem and slide the valve into its correct location

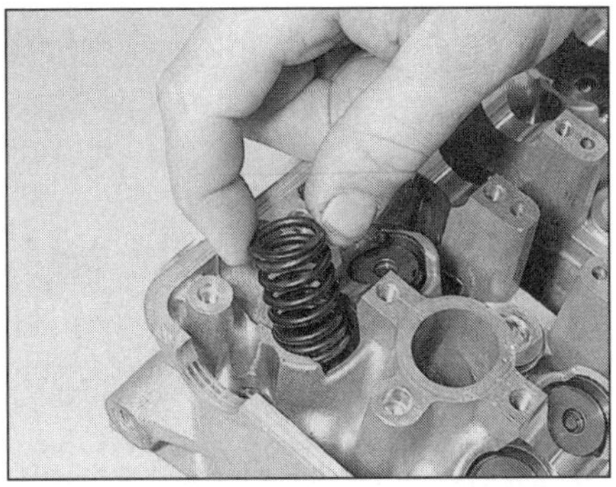
12.27b Fit the valve springs with their closer-wound coils facing down . . .

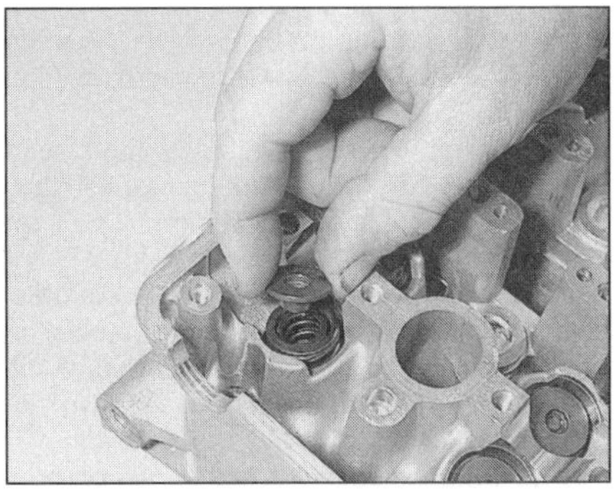
12.27c . . . then fit the spring retainer

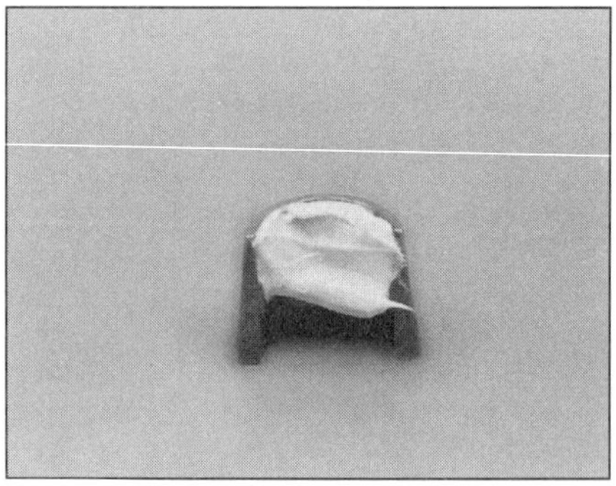

12.28a A small dab of grease will help to keep the collets in place on the valve while the spring is released

illustration). Compress the spring(s) with the valve spring compressor and install the collets **(see illustration)**. When compressing the spring(s), depress them only as far as is absolutely necessary to slip the collets into place. Make certain that the collets are securely locked in the retaining grooves. Repeat the procedure for the remaining valves.

29 Support the cylinder head on blocks so the valves can't contact the workbench, then very gently tap each of the valve stems with a soft-faced hammer. This will help seat the collets in their grooves.

30 Once all of the valves have been installed in the head, check for proper valve sealing by pouring a small amount of solvent into each of the valve ports. If the solvent leaks past the valve(s) into the combustion chamber area, disassemble the valve(s) and repeat the lapping procedure, then reinstall the valve(s) and repeat the check. Repeat the procedure until a satisfactory seal is obtained.

13 Cylinder block – removal, inspection and installation

Note: *On F models, this procedure can be performed with the engine in the frame. On all other models, the engine must be removed from the frame (see Section 5).*

Removal

1 On F models, remove the left-hand front engine mounting bolt and the bolts securing the engine mounting bracket to the frame **(see illustration 5.20a)**.

2 On all models, remove the cylinder head (see Section 10). Make sure the crankshaft is positioned at Top Dead Centre (TDC) for cylinders No. 1 and 4.

3 If not already done, slacken the clamp(s) securing the coolant hose(s) to the union(s) on the back of the cylinder block and detach the hose(s) **(see illustration)**. F models have one hose, all other models have two.

4 Hold the cam chain up and lift the cylinder block up, then pass the cam chain down through the tunnel **(see illustration 13.20)**. Do

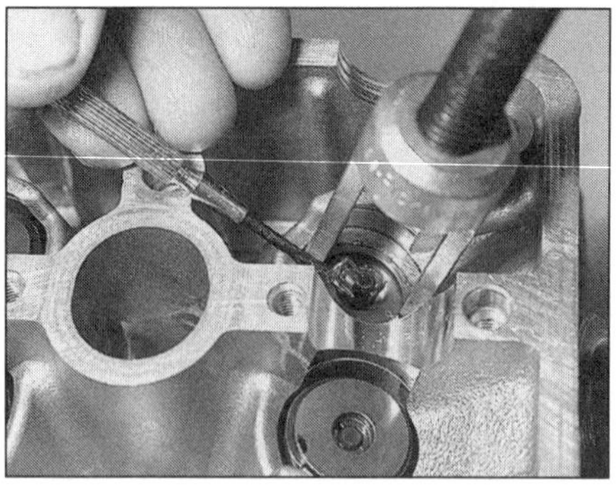

12.28b Compress the springs and install the collets, making sure they locate in the groove

not let the chain fall into the crankcase – secure it with a piece of wire or metal bar to prevent it from doing so. If the block is stuck, tap around the joint face with a soft-faced mallet to free it from the crankcase. Don't attempt to free the block by inserting a screwdriver between it and the crankcase – you'll damage the sealing surfaces. When the block is removed, stuff clean rags around the pistons to prevent anything falling into the crankcase.

5 Remove the dowels from the mating surface of the crankcase or the underside of the block for safekeeping. Be careful not to let the dowels into the engine.

6 If required, remove the cam chain rear guide (see Section 28).

7 Remove the gasket and clean all traces of old gasket material from the cylinder block and crankcase mating surfaces with a suitable solvent. Take care not to scratch or gouge the soft aluminium. Be careful not to let any of the gasket material fall into the crankcase or the oil passages.

Inspection

Caution: On F, G and H models, do not attempt to separate the liners from the cylinder block.

8 Check the cylinder walls carefully for scratches and score marks.

9 Using telescoping gauges and a micrometer (see *Tools and Workshop Tips* in the Reference section), check the dimensions of each cylinder to assess the amount of wear, taper and ovality. Measure near the top (but below the level of the top piston ring at TDC – about 10 mm below the top of the cylinder), centre and bottom (but above the level of the oil ring at BDC – about 20 mm above the bottom of the cylinder) of the bore both parallel to and across the crankshaft axis **(see illustration)**. Calculate any differences between the measurements taken to determine any taper and ovality in the bore. Compare the results to the specifications at the beginning of the Chapter. If the cylinders are tapered, oval, or worn beyond the service limits, or badly scratched, scuffed or scored, they will have to be renewed. Kawasaki list replacement liners for F, G and H models, but fitting them is a specialist task and should only be undertaken by a Kawasaki dealer or engineering workshop. The bores on J and A models are electroplated; this hard surface should last the life of the engine but if it has worn or become damaged a new cylinder block must be fitted. The cylinders cannot be rebored, and accordingly oversize pistons are not available.

10 If the precision measuring tools are not available, take the block to a Kawasaki dealer or specialist motorcycle repair shop for assessment and advice.

11 On F, G and H models, if the cylinders are in good condition and the piston-to-bore clearance is within specifications (see Section 14), the cylinders should be honed (deglazed). To perform this operation you will need the proper size flexible hone with fine stones (see *Tools and Workshop Tips* in the Reference section), or a bottle-brush type hone, plenty of light oil or honing oil, some clean rags and an electric drill motor.

Caution: Do not hone the electroplated bores of J and A models.

12 When honing, hold the block sideways (so that the bores are horizontal rather than vertical) in a vice with soft jaws or cushioned with wooden blocks. Mount the hone in the drill motor, compress the stones and insert the hone into the cylinder. Thoroughly lubricate the cylinder, then turn on the drill

13.3 Slacken the clamp (arrowed) and detach the hose from its union – F models shown

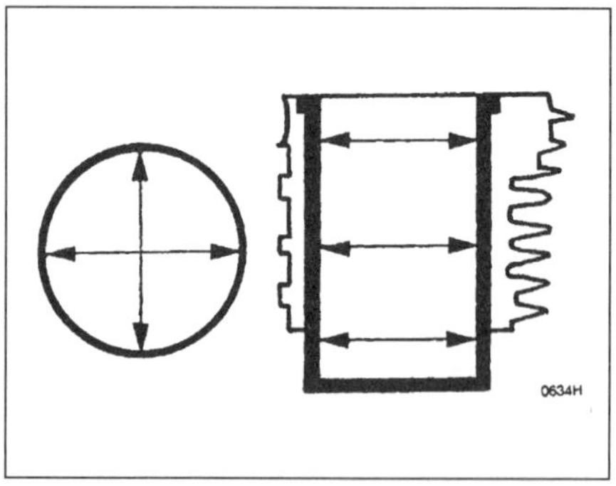

13.9 Measure the cylinder bore in the directions shown with a telescoping gauge, then measure the gauge with a micrometer

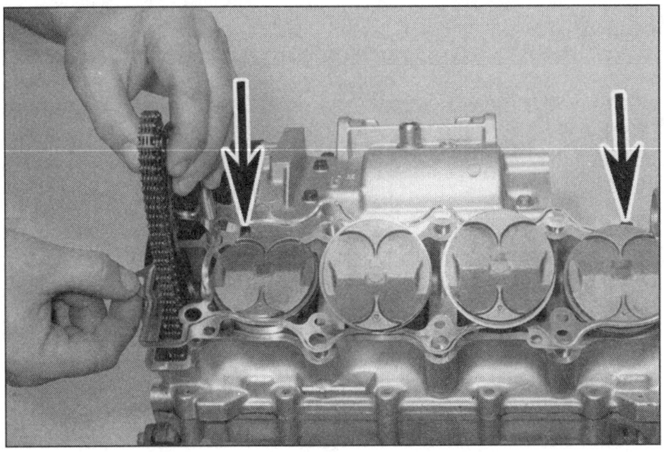

13.17 Make sure the dowels (arrowed) are in place, then lay a new gasket onto the crankcase

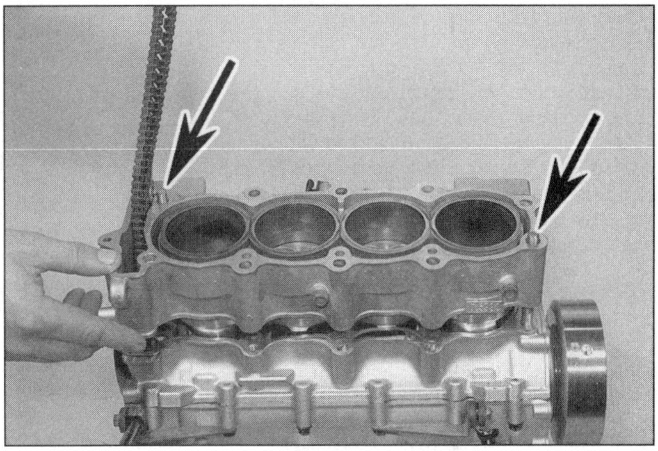

13.20 Fit the cylinder block onto the crankcase. Note the auxiliary bolts (arrowed) used as guides

and move the hone up and down in the cylinder at a pace which produces a fine cross-hatch pattern on the cylinder wall with the lines intersecting at an angle of approximately 60°. Be sure to use plenty of lubricant and do not take off any more material than is necessary to produce the desired effect. Do not withdraw the hone from the cylinder while it is still turning. Switch off the drill and continue to move it up and down in the cylinder until it has stopped turning, then compress the stones and withdraw the hone. Wipe the oil from the cylinder and repeat the procedure on the other cylinder. Remember, do not take too much material from the cylinder wall.

13 Wash the cylinders thoroughly with warm soapy water to remove all traces of the abrasive grit produced during the honing operation. Be sure to run a brush through the bolt holes and flush them with running water. After rinsing, dry the cylinders thoroughly and apply a thin coat of light, rust-preventative oil to all machined surfaces.

14 If you do not have the equipment or desire to perform the honing operation, take the block to a Kawasaki dealer or specialist motorcycle repair shop.

Installation

15 Check that the mating surfaces of the cylinder block and crankcase are free from oil or pieces of old gasket. If removed, fit the dowels into the crankcase **(see illustration 13.17)**.

16 If removed, install the cam chain rear guide (see Section 28).

17 Remove the rags from around the pistons, and lay the new base gasket in place on the crankcase making sure all the holes are correctly aligned **(see illustration)**. Never re-use the old gasket.

18 As there are no studs to keep the block in position while the pistons are fed into the bores, obtain two spare cylinder head bolts (any bolts of a similar length and the same thread will do) and cut off their heads. Thread the bolts into two of the outer holes, diagonal to each other **(see illustration 13.20)**.

19 Check the position of the piston ring end gaps and stagger them correctly **(see illustrations 15.9a and b)**. If required, install piston ring clamps onto the pistons to ease their entry into the bores as the block is lowered. This is not essential as each cylinder has a good lead-in enabling the piston rings to be hand-fed into the bore. If possible, have an assistant to support the block while this is done.

> **HAYNES HiNT** ***Rotate the crankshaft until the inner pistons are uppermost and feed them into the block first. This makes access to the lower pistons easier when compressing the rings and feeding them into the bores as they are on the outside.***

20 Lubricate the cylinder bores, pistons and piston rings, and the connecting rod big- and small-ends, with clean engine oil, then install the block down over the auxiliary bolts until the uppermost piston crowns fit into the bores **(see illustration)**. At this stage feed the cam chain up through the block and secure it in place with a piece of wire to prevent it from falling back down.

21 Gently push down on the cylinder block, making sure the pistons enter the bore squarely and do not get cocked sideways. If piston ring clamps are not being used, carefully compress and feed each ring into the bore as the block is lowered. If necessary, use a soft mallet to gently tap the block down, but do not use force if the block appears to be stuck as the pistons and/or rings will be damaged. If clamps are used, remove them once the pistons are in the bore.

22 When the pistons are correctly installed in the cylinders, press the block down onto the base gasket, making sure it locates correctly onto the dowels. Remove the auxiliary bolts.

23 If required, attach the coolant hose(s) to the union (s) on the back of the cylinder block and tighten the clamp(s) (see Step 3).

24 Install the cylinder head (see Section 10).

25 On F models, install the engine mounting bracket and the left-hand front engine mounting bolt and tighten the bolts to the torque settings specified at the beginning of the Chapter **(see illustration 5.20a)**.

26 Install the remaining components in the reverse order of removal.

14 Pistons – removal, inspection and installation

Note: *On F models, this procedure can be performed with the engine in the frame. On all other models, the engine must be removed from the frame (see Section 5).*

1 Remove the cylinder block (see Section 13).

2 If not already done, stuff clean rag into each crankcase hole, around the connecting rods. This will prevent the circlips from falling into the crankcase if they are inadvertently dropped.

Removal

3 Use a sharp scriber or felt marker pen to write the cylinder identity on the crown of each piston (or on the inside of the skirt if the piston is dirty and going to be cleaned). Each piston should also have an arrow marked on its crown which should face forwards **(see illustration)**.

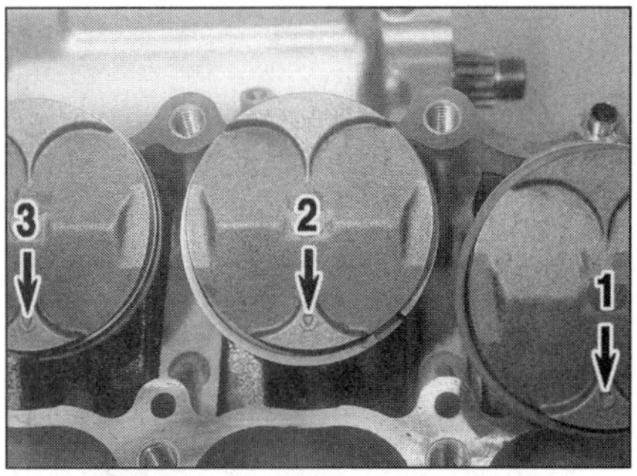

14.3 Scribe or mark the cylinder number onto each piston, and note the arrowhead (arrowed) on each which must face the front

If this is not visible, mark the piston accordingly so that it can be installed the correct way round. Note that on G and H models, two different sizes of piston are fitted (see Specifications). When new, the pistons for cylinders Nos. 1 and 2 are marked with blue paint on the top, and the pistons for cylinders Nos. 3 and 4 are marked with yellow paint and the letter B, though it is doubtful whether after use the paint marks will be visible.

4 Carefully prise out the circlip on one side of the piston using needle-nose pliers or a small flat-bladed screwdriver inserted into the notch **(see illustration)**. Push the piston pin out from the other side to free the piston from the connecting rod **(see illustration)**. Remove the other circlip and discard them both as new ones must be used on reassembly. When the piston has been removed, install its pin back into its bore so that related parts do not get mixed up. Rotate the crankshaft so that the best access is obtained for each piston.

HAYNES HiNT ***To prevent the circlip from dropping into the crankcase, pass a rod or screwdriver, whose diameter is greater than the gap between the circlip ends, through the piston pin. This will trap the circlip if it springs out.***

5 Before the inspection process can be carried out, the pistons must be cleaned and the old piston rings removed.

6 Using your thumbs or a piston ring removal and installation tool, carefully remove the rings from the pistons **(see illustration)**. Do not nick or gouge the pistons in the process. Carefully note which way up each ring fits and in which groove. The top and second compression rings have different profiles and they must be installed in their original positions if being re-used. The upper surface of each ring is marked with a letter at one end. The top ring is identified by the letter R, and the second (middle) ring by the letters RN.

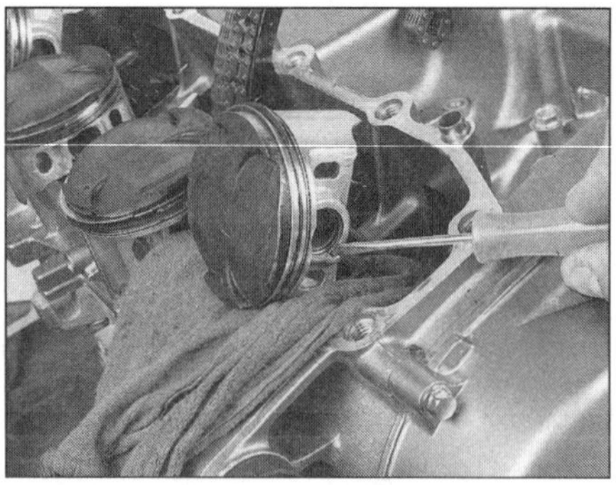

14.4a Remove the circlip using a pair of pliers or a screwdriver inserted in the notch . . .

7 Scrape all traces of carbon from the tops of the pistons. A hand-held wire brush or a piece of fine emery cloth can be used once the majority of the deposits have been scraped away. Do not, under any circumstances, use a wire brush mounted in a drill motor to remove deposits from the pistons; the piston material is soft and will be eroded away by the wire brush.

8 Use a piston ring groove cleaning tool to remove any carbon deposits from the ring grooves. Be very careful to remove only the carbon deposits. Do not remove any metal and do not nick or gouge the sides of the ring grooves.

HAYNES HiNT ***If a ring groove cleaning tool is not available, a piece broken off the old ring will do the job***

TOOL TiP

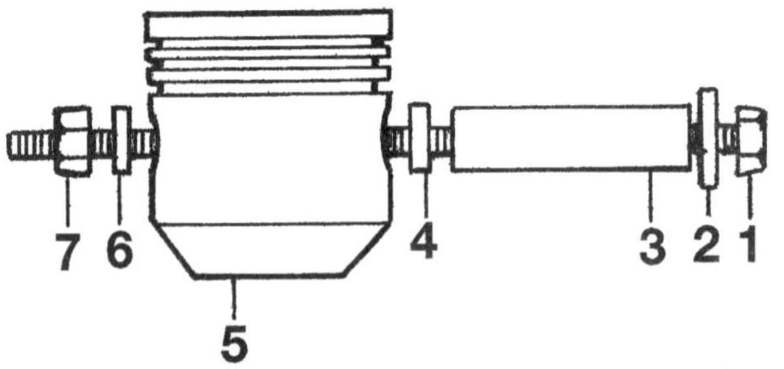

If a piston pin is a tight fit in the piston bosses, soak a rag in boiling water when wring it out and wrap it around the piston – this will expand the alloy piston sufficiently to release its grip on the pin. If the piston pin is particularly stubborn, extract it using a drawbolt tool, but be careful to protect the piston's working surfaces.

1 Bolt	***5 Piston***	***A Large enough for piston pin to fit inside***
2 Washer	***6 Washer (B)***	***B Small enough to fit through piston pin bore***
3 Pipe (A)	***7 Nut (B)***	
4 Padding (A)		

14.4b . . . then push the pin out and withdraw it from the other side of the piston

14.6 Removing the piston rings using a ring removal and installation tool

9 Once the deposits have been removed, clean the pistons with a suitable solvent and dry them thoroughly. Make sure the oil return holes below the oil ring grooves are clear.

Inspection

10 Carefully inspect each piston for cracks around the skirt, at the pin bosses and at the ring lands. Normal piston wear appears as even, vertical wear on the thrust surfaces of the piston and slight looseness of the top ring in its groove. If the skirt is scored or scuffed, the engine may have been suffering from overheating and/or abnormal combustion, which caused excessively high operating temperatures. The oil pump and cooling system should be checked thoroughly.

11 A hole in the top of the piston, in one extreme, or burned areas at the edge of the crown, indicate that pre-ignition or knocking under load have occurred. If you find evidence of any problems the cause must be corrected or the damage will occur again (see *Fault Finding* in the Reference section).

12 Check the piston-to-bore clearance by measuring the bore (see Section 13) and the piston diameter. Make sure that the pistons and cylinders are correctly matched. Measure the piston across the skirt on the thrust faces at 90° to the piston pin, about 5 mm up from

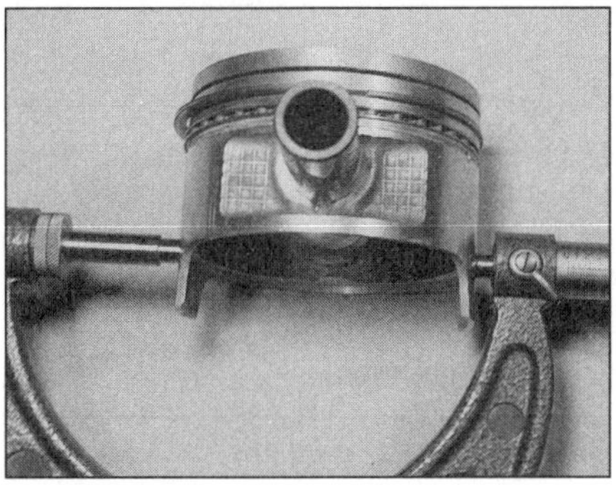

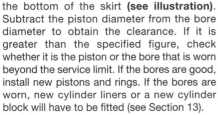

14.12 Measure the piston diameter at the specified distance from the bottom of the skirt using a micrometer

14.13 Measure the piston ring-to-groove clearance using a feeler gauge

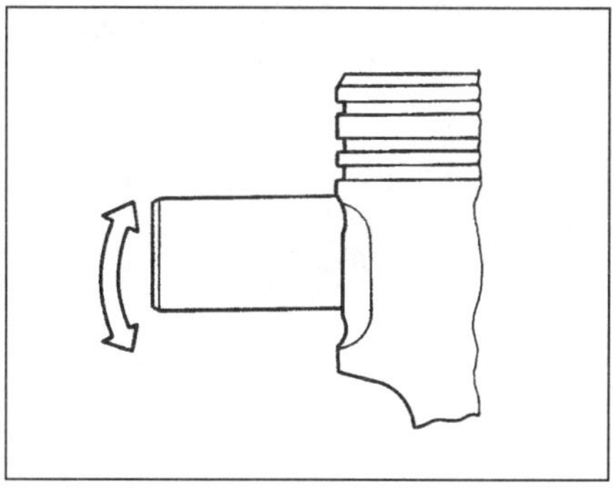

14.14 Slip the pin into the piston and feel for freeplay

the bottom of the skirt **(see illustration)**. Subtract the piston diameter from the bore diameter to obtain the clearance. If it is greater than the specified figure, check whether it is the piston or the bore that is worn beyond the service limit. If the bores are good, install new pistons and rings. If the bores are worn, new cylinder liners or a new cylinder block will have to be fitted (see Section 13).

13 Measure the piston ring-to-groove clearance by laying a new piston ring in the ring groove and slipping a feeler gauge in beside it **(see illustration)**. Check the clearance at three or four locations around the groove. Be sure to use the correct ring for each groove; they are different (see Step 6). If the clearance is greater then specified, new pistons will have to be used when the engine is reassembled.

14 Apply clean engine oil to the pin, insert it into the piston and check for freeplay by rocking the pin back-and-forth **(see illustration)**. If the pin is loose, new pistons and possibly new pins must be installed.

Installation

Note: *Install the pistons for cylinders 2 and 3 first.*

15 Inspect and install the piston rings (see Section 15).

16 Lubricate the piston pin, the piston pin bore and the connecting rod small-end bore with clean engine oil.

17 When installing the pistons onto the connecting rods, make sure that arrow on the piston crown points to the front of the engine (see Step 3). Install a new circlip in one side of the piston (never re-use old circlips). Line up the piston on its correct connecting rod, and insert the piston pin from the other side **(see illustration 14.4b)**. Secure the pin with the other new circlip. When installing the circlips, compress them only just enough to fit them in the piston, and make sure they are properly seated in their grooves with the open end away from the removal notch **(see illustration 14.4a)**.

18 Install the remaining components in the reverse order of removal.

15 Piston rings – installation

1 It is good practice to fit new piston rings when an engine is being overhauled. Before installing the new piston rings, the ring end gaps must be checked with the rings installed in the cylinder.

2 Lay out the pistons and the new ring sets so the rings will be matched with the same piston and cylinder during the end gap measurement procedure and engine assembly. The top and second compression rings have different profiles and the upper surface of each ring is marked with a letter at one end. The top ring is identified by the letter R, and the second (middle) ring by the letters RN.

3 Insert the top ring into the bottom of the first cylinder and square it up with the cylinder walls by pushing it in with the top of the piston. The ring should be about 20 mm above the bottom edge of the cylinder. To measure the end gap, slip a feeler gauge between the ends of the ring **(see illustration)** and compare the measurement to the Specifications.

4 If the gap is larger or smaller than specified, double check to make sure that you have the correct rings before proceeding. Excess end gap is not critical unless it is greater than the specified limit. Again, double check to make sure you have the correct rings for your engine.

5 Repeat the procedure for each ring that will be installed in the first cylinder and for each ring in the remaining cylinder. Remember to keep the rings, pistons and cylinders matched up.

6 Once the ring end gaps have been checked/corrected, the rings can be installed on the pistons. The oil control ring (lowest on the piston) is installed first. It is composed of three separate components. Slip the expander into the groove, making sure its ends butt against each other and do not overlap, then install the lower side rail **(see illustrations)**. Do not use a piston ring

15.3 Measuring piston ring installed end gap

15.6a Install the oil ring expander in its groove, making sure the ends do not overlap . . .

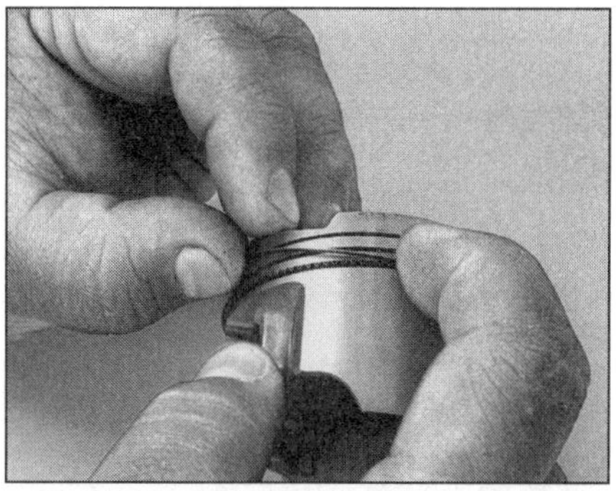

15.6b . . . and fit the side rails each side of it. The oil ring must be installed by hand

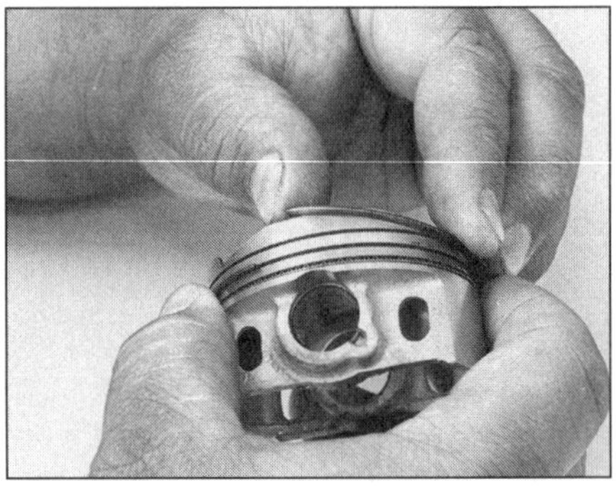

15.7 Fit the second (middle) ring into the middle groove in the piston

installation tool on the oil ring side rails as they may be damaged. Instead, place one end of the side rail into the groove between the spacer expander and the ring land. Hold it firmly in place and slide a finger around the piston while pushing the rail into the groove. Next, install the upper side rail in the same manner. After the three oil ring components have been installed, check to make sure that both the upper and lower side rails can be turned smoothly in the ring groove.

7 Install the second (middle) ring next. Make sure that the identification letters RN near the

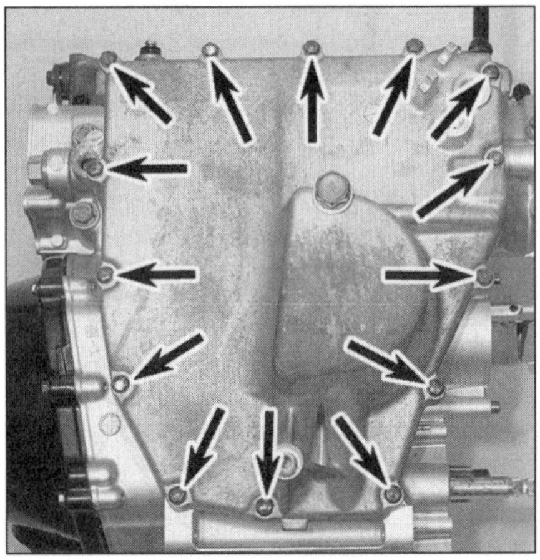

16.4 Unscrew the sump bolts (arrowed) and remove the sump

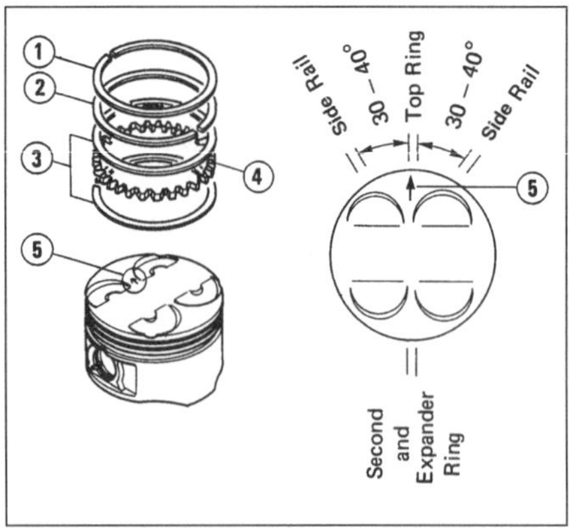

15.9a Ring gap positioning – F models

1 *Top ring*
2 *Second (middle) ring*
3 *Oil ring side rails*
4 *Oil ring expander*
5 *Arrow mark – must point to the front*

end gap are facing up. Fit the ring into the middle groove in the piston **(see illustration)**. Do not expand the ring any more than is necessary to slide it into place. To avoid breaking the ring, use a piston ring installation tool.

8 Finally, install the top ring in the same manner into the top groove in the piston. Make sure the identification letter R near the end gap is facing up.

9 Once the rings are correctly installed, check they move freely without snagging and stagger their end gaps as shown **(see illustrations)**.

16 Oil sump – removal and installation

Removal

Note: *The oil sump can be removed with the engine in the frame.*

1 Drain the engine oil (see Chapter 1).

2 Remove the exhaust system (see Chapter 4).

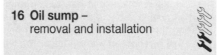

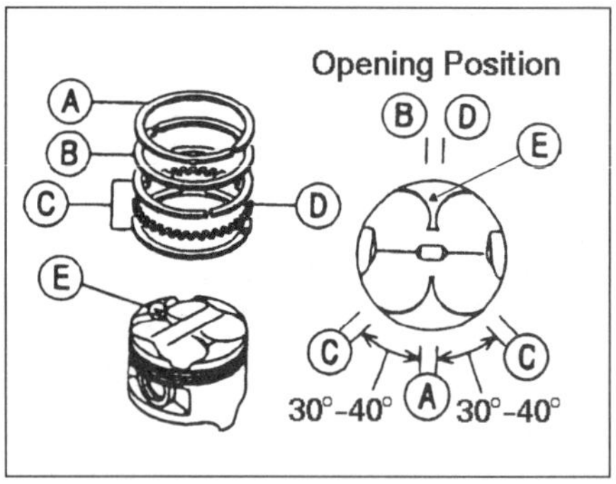

15.9b Ring gap positioning – G, H, J and A models

A *Top ring*
B *Second (middle) ring*
C *Oil ring side rails*
D *Oil ring expander*
E *Arrow mark – must point to the front*

3 On F models, remove the banjo bolts that attach the oil cooler hoses to the sump (see Chapter 3).

4 Remove the oil sump bolts, slackening them evenly in a criss-cross sequence to prevent distortion, and detach the sump from the crankcase **(see illustration)**.

5 If required, remove the oil pick-up tube and its O-ring, noting which way up the O-ring fits, and the oil pipes **(see illustrations)**.

6 Remove all traces of old gasket material from the mating surfaces of the sump and crankcase.

Installation

7 Inspect the screen on the oil pick-up tube. The presence of metal swarf could indicate serious wear or damage in the bottom end or gearbox (pieces of 'casting flash' and gasket look worse than they are; they're typical on a new engine).

8 Inspect the O-rings on the pick-up tube, the oil passages and the oil pipes **(see illustration)**. If they're damaged or have deteriorated, discard them and fit new ones. Be sure to wash the screen before installing the pick-up tube.

9 Apply grease to the oil pipe O-rings, using new ones if necessary, then press the oil

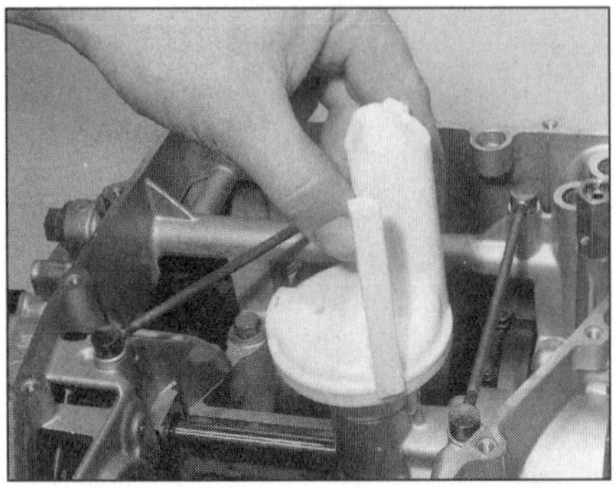

16.5a Remove the pick-up tube . . .

16.5b . . . and the oil pipes (arrowed) if required

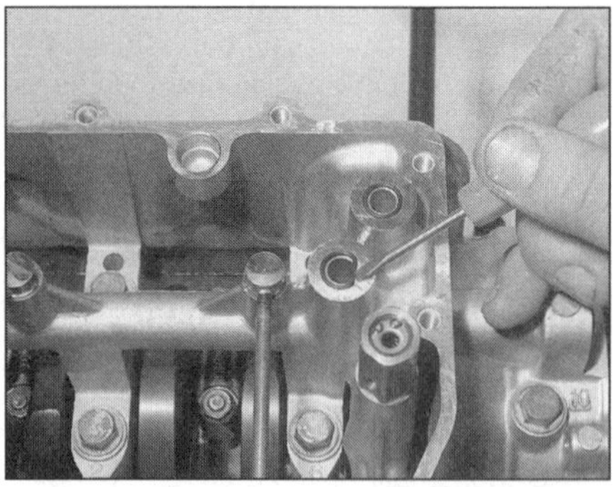

16.8 Check the various O-rings and replace them with new ones if necessary

16.9a Press the oil pipes into their sockets . . .

16.9b . . . then fit the pick-up tube O-ring, making sure it is the correct way round . . .

16.9c . . . the pick-up tube, aligning the slot with the lug (arrowed) . . .

16.9d . . . and the oil passage O-rings

16.10a Lay a new gasket in place . . .

16.10b . . . then install the sump

pipes into their sockets **(see illustration)**. Fit the pick-up tube O-ring with its lipped side facing into the crankcase, then install the tube so that the slot in its base rim locates over the lug on the crankcase **(see illustrations)**. Fit the O-rings into the oil passages, using new ones if necessary **(see illustration)**.

10 Position a new gasket on the oil sump or crankcase **(see illustration)**. A thin film of RTV sealant can be used to hold the gasket in place. Install the sump and bolts, and tighten the bolts to the torque listed in this Chapter's Specifications, using a criss-cross pattern **(see illustration)**.

11 Install the remaining components in the reverse order of removal. On F models, use new sealing washers on each side of the oil cooler hose banjo fittings and tighten the banjo bolts to the specified torque (see Chapter 3). Refill the engine with the correct quantity of oil (see Chapter 1), then run the engine and check for leaks.

17 Oil pump – removal, inspection and installation

Removal

1 Drain the engine oil and the coolant (see Chapter 1).

2 Remove the water pump impeller and seal housing (see Chapter 3).

3 Withdraw the oil pump drum from the housing, followed by the shaft and inner rotor **(see illustrations 17.10b and a)**. Remove the outer rotor **(see illustration)**.

4 If required, slide the inner rotor up the shaft, then remove the drive pin from the shaft, noting how it locates in the slot in the inner rotor, and slide the rotor off, noting which way round it fits **(see illustration)**.

Inspection

5 Wash all the components in solvent, then dry them off. Check the pump cover, drum, housing, rotors and shaft for scoring and wear. Kawasaki provides no specifications for checking the pump, so if any damage or uneven or excessive wear is evident, renew the pump. If you're rebuilding a worn engine, it's a good idea to install a new oil pump anyway. Finally, if you see any sign of wear, be sure to remove the oil sump (see Section 16) and make sure the pick-up screen isn't clogged.

6 The oil pump drive and driven gears can be inspected after removing the clutch (see Section 20). The drive gear is on the back of the clutch housing. Check each gear for cracks, chipped or broken teeth or extreme wear and renew them if necessary. If a new drive gear is needed, the entire clutch housing must be renewed.

7 On F models, the driven gear is secured to the shaft by a bolt – lock the gear using a screwdriver through one of its holes, then

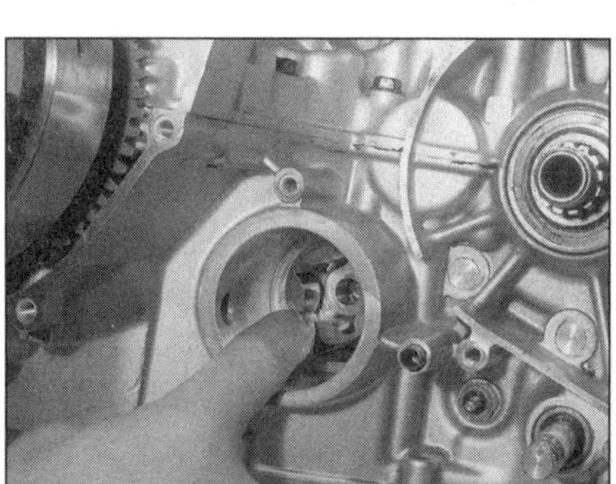

17.3 Remove the outer rotor from the housing

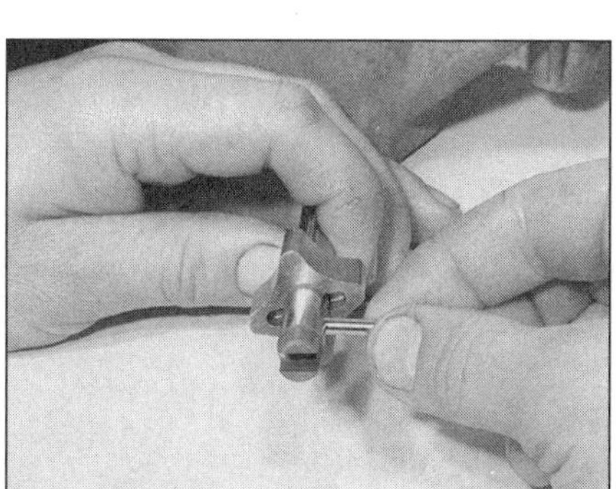

17.4 Withdraw the drive pin and slide the inner rotor off the shaft

17.7a On F models the gear is secured to the shaft by a bolt (arrowed)

17.10a Install the inner rotor and shaft, aligning the slot with the tab

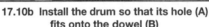

unscrew the bolt and remove the gear **(see illustration)**. To remove the gear and shaft together, remove the sump and oil pick-up tube (see Section 16), then remove the circlip securing the shaft in the crankcase and draw the gear/shaft out **(see illustration)**. On installation, apply clean oil to each side of the bolt washer and tighten the bolt to the torque setting specified at the beginning of the Chapter.

8 On all other models, the driven gear is integral with the shaft – remove the sump (see Section 16), then remove the circlip securing the shaft in the crankcase and draw the gear/shaft out **(see illustration 17.7b)**. Installation is the reverse of removal.

Installation

9 Apply clean engine oil to the outer rotor and

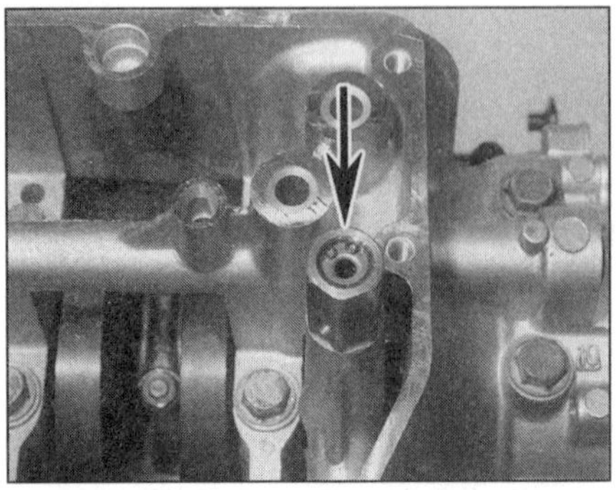

18.2 Oil pressure relief valve (arrowed)

17.7b Remove the circlip (arrowed) and draw the gear and shaft out together

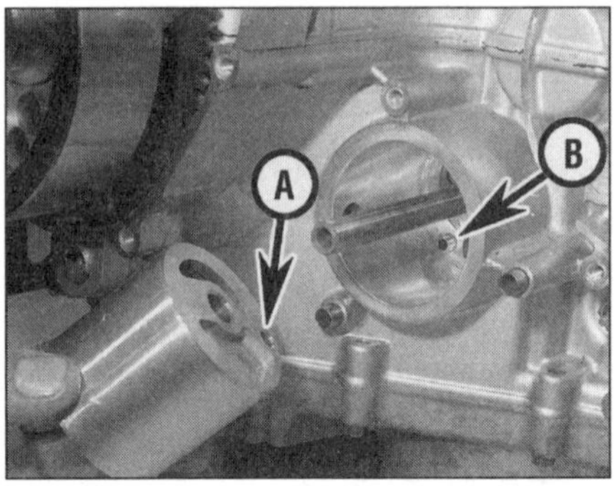

17.10b Install the drum so that its hole (A) fits onto the dowel (B)

fit it into the housing **(see illustration 17.3)**. Check that the drum dowel is in place in the housing **(see illustration)**. If it isn't there, it is probably in the drum itself.

10 Fit the inner rotor onto the pump shaft and fit the drive pin, making sure it locates correctly in the slots in the rotor **(see illustration 17.4)**. Slide the inner rotor and shaft into the housing, aligning the slot in the pump shaft with the tab on the end of the drive shaft **(see illustration)**. Fit the drum onto the shaft and into the housing, aligning the hole in the drum with the dowel in the housing **(see illustration)**.

11 Install the water pump seal housing and impeller (see Chapter 3).

12 Fill the engine with the specified quantities of oil and coolant (see Chapter 1). Run the engine and check for leaks.

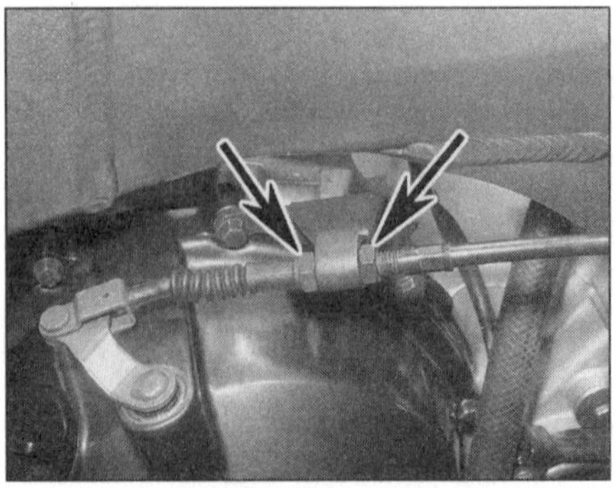

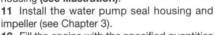

19.3 Fully slacken both locknuts (arrowed) . . .

17.9 Make sure the dowel (arrowed) is in place

18 Oil pressure relief valve – removal, inspection and installation

Removal

1 Remove the oil sump (see Section 16).

2 The oil pressure relief valve is screwed into the crankcase **(see illustration)** The valve is normally trouble-free; its only function is to prevent excessive oil pressure (which can cause seals to leak) in the event an oil passage becomes clogged.

Inspection

3 Clean the valve with a suitable solvent and dry it, using compressed air if available.

4 Using a wood or plastic tool, depress the steel ball inside the valve and see if it moves smoothly. Make sure it returns to its seat completely. If it doesn't, fit a new valve.

Installation

5 Apply a non-permanent thread locking compound to the threads of the valve, install it into the crankcase, and tighten it to the torque listed in this Chapter's Specifications.

6 Install the oil sump (see Section 16).

19 Clutch cable – removal and installation

1 Remove the right-hand lower fairing panel (see Chapter 8).

2 On F, G and H models, push the clutch lever forward (away from the handlebar) and set the span adjuster to position 5 on the dial, then loosen the knurled lock wheel on the handlebar lever adjuster.

3 Pull back the dust boot on the lower (clutch) end of the cable and fully loosen the adjuster nuts at the bracket on the clutch cover **(see illustration)**.

4 Fully back off the lockwheel on the adjuster

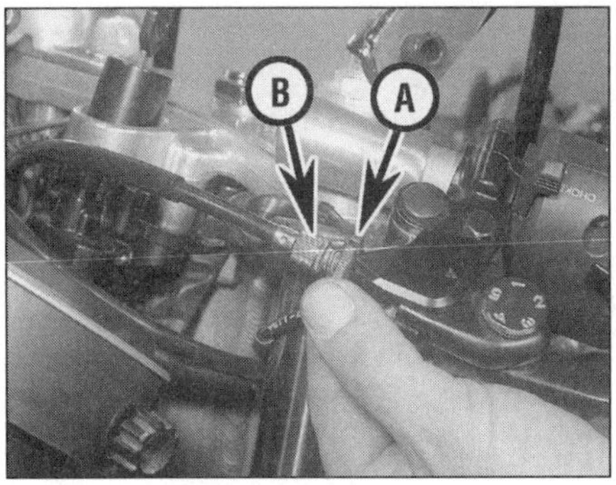

19.4 . . . then slacken the lockwheel (A) and turn the adjuster (B) fully in

19.5a Align the slots and slip the cable out . . .

19.5b . . . and detach the nipple from the lever

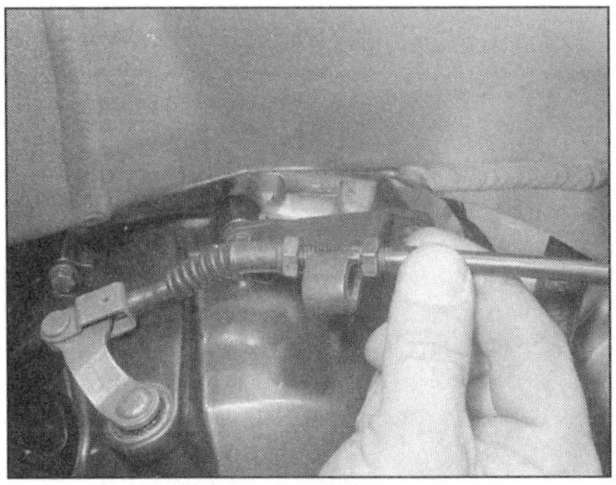

19.6a Slip the adjuster out of the bracket . . .

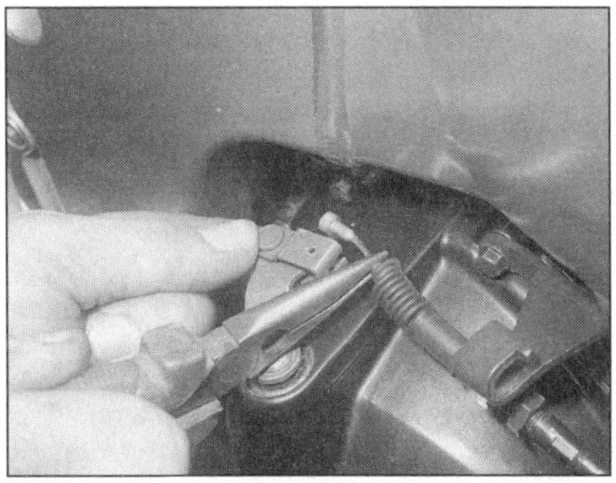

19.6b . . . and detach the cable end from the lever

at the clutch lever, then screw the adjuster all the way in until it stops **(see illustration)**.

5 To disconnect the clutch cable from the handlebar lever, align the slots in the adjuster, the lock wheel (where fitted) and the lever, then slip the cable out and disengage the cable end from its socket in the underside of the lever **(see illustrations)**.

6 Slip the adjuster on the lower end of the cable out of the bracket on the cover and disengage the cable from the release lever **(see illustrations)**.

7 Before removing the cable from the bike, tape the lower end of the new cable to the upper end of the old cable. Slowly pull the lower end of the old cable out, guiding the new cable down into position. Using this method will ensure the cable is routed correctly.

8 Lubricate the cable (see Chapter 1).

9 Install the cable in the reverse of removal, then adjust the cable freeplay (see Chapter 1). On F, G and H models, reset the clutch lever span adjuster to the desired position.

20 Clutch – removal, inspection and installation

Note: *The clutch can be removed with the engine in the frame.*

Removal

1 Remove the fairing right-hand lower panel (see Chapter 8).

2 Drain the engine oil (see Chapter 1).

3 Completely loosen the adjustment nuts on the lower end of the clutch cable at the bracket on the clutch cover. Slip the cable out of the bracket, then detach the cable end from the release lever **(see illustrations 19.3, 19.6a and b)**.

4 Unscrew the clutch cover bolts, noting how the cable bracket fits, and remove the cover, turning the release lever approximately 90° to the rear as you do **(see illustration)**. If the cover is stuck, tap around its perimeter with a soft-faced hammer. Be prepared to catch any residual oil as you remove the cover. Discard the gasket as a new one must be used. Note the two locating dowels fitted to the crankcase and remove them for safe-keeping if they are loose.

5 Working in a criss-cross pattern, gradually slacken the clutch spring retaining bolts until spring pressure is released **(see illustration)**. To prevent the assembly from turning, cover it with a rag and hold it securely – the bolts are not very tight. If available, have an assistant to hold the clutch while you unscrew the bolts. Unscrew the bolts and remove them along with their washers and the springs.

6 Grasp the pressure plate and the complete set of clutch plates and remove them as a pack **(see illustration)**. Withdraw the release rod, and on G, H, J and A models the spring and washer, from either the pressure plate or the transmission input shaft **(see illustration 20.22)**. Remove the bearing from the back of the pressure plate for safekeeping if it is

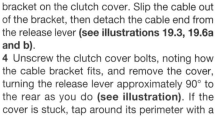

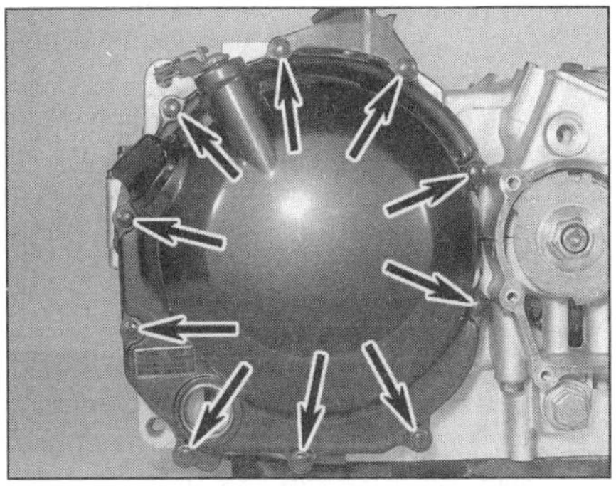

20.4 Clutch cover bolts (arrowed)

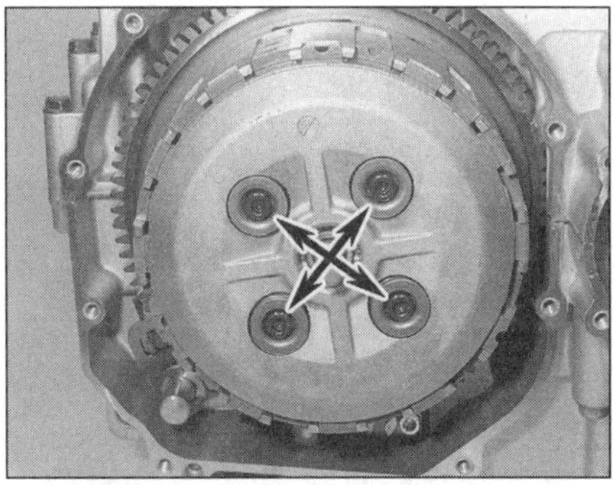

20.5 Clutch spring bolts (arrowed)

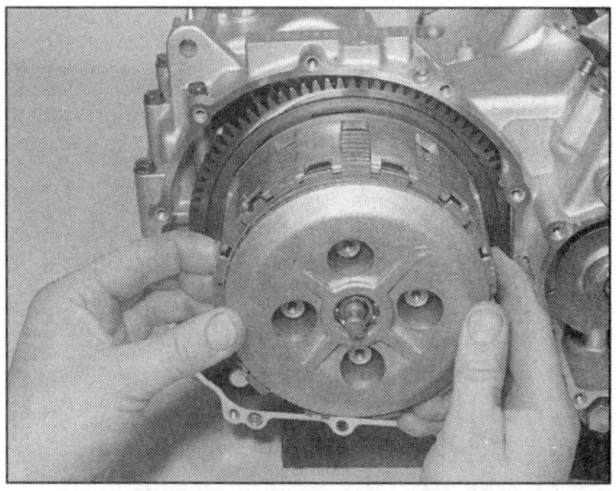

20.6 Remove the pressure plate and clutch plates

20.7 With the holding tool in place, unscrew the clutch nut (arrowed)

loose. Unless the plates are being renewed, keep them in their original order. Also remove the anti-judder spring and spring seat, from the clutch centre, noting which way round they fit **(see illustration 20.20a)**.

7 To remove the clutch nut the input shaft must be locked. This can be done in several ways. If the engine is in the frame, engage 1st gear and have an assistant hold the rear brake on hard with the rear tyre in firm contact with the ground. Alternatively, the Kawasaki service tool (Pt. No. 57001-1243), a commercial equivalent, or a similar home-made tool (see **Tool tip)**, can be used to stop the clutch centre from turning whilst the nut is slackened **(see illustration)**. Unscrew the nut and remove the washer from the input shaft, noting which way round it fits. Discard the nut as a new one must be used.

20.8 Withdraw the bearing and sleeve from the centre of the housing

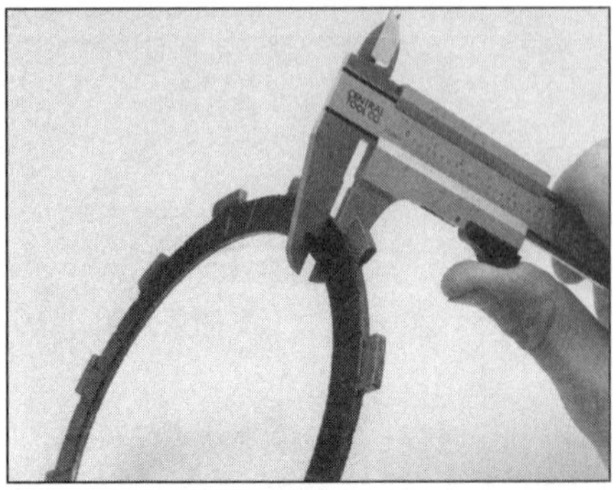

20.11 Measure the thickness of the friction plates

TOOL TIP

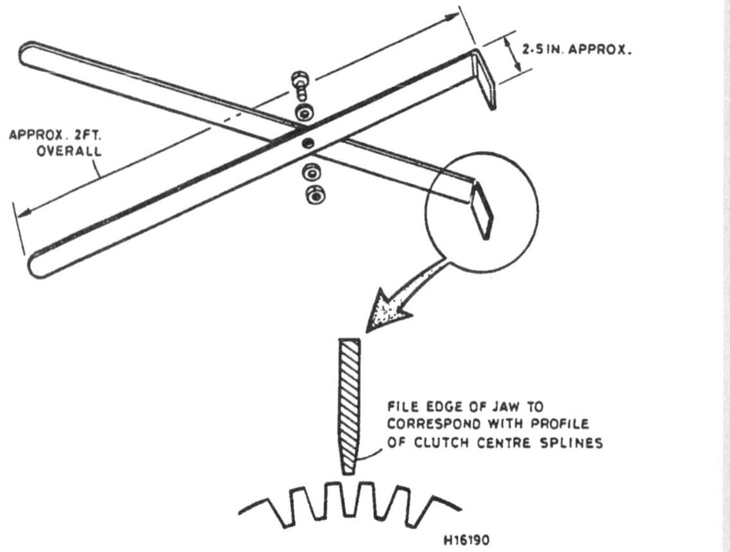

An alternative to the Kawasaki tool can be fabricated from some steel strap, bent at the ends and bolted together in the middle.

8 Slide the clutch centre off the shaft, then remove the outer thrust washer, noting which way round it fits **(see illustrations 20.19b and a)**. Withdraw the needle roller bearing and its sleeve from the centre of the clutch housing **(see illustration)**, then remove the housing and the inner thrust washer, noting which way round it fits **(see illustrations 20.18 and 17)**. To gain a hold on the needle bearing and its sleeve, draw the clutch housing off the shaft as far as it will go, then push it back – the bearing and sleeve should become accessible as the housing is slid back. Alternatively, thread two suitable bolts into the holes in the sleeve, then support the housing and use the bolts to pull out the sleeve.

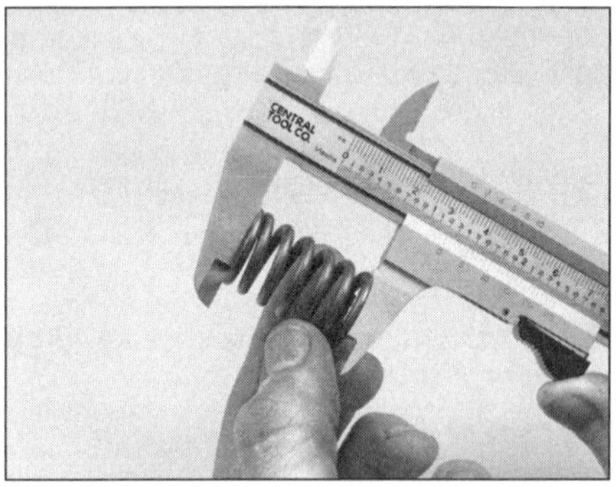

20.10 Measure the clutch spring free length

20.12 Check the plates for warpage by trying to slide the feeler gauge between each plate and a flat surface

Inspection

9 Check the edges of the slots in the clutch housing for indentations made by the friction plate tabs. Similarly check for wear between the inner tongues of the plain plates and the slots in the clutch centre. Wear of this nature will cause clutch drag and slow disengagement during gear changes, since the plates will snag when the pressure plate is lifted. With care a small amount of wear can be corrected by dressing with a fine file, but if wear is excessive the worn components should be renewed.

10 Measure the free length of the clutch springs **(see illustration)** and compare the results to this Chapter's Specifications. If the springs have sagged or are damaged, fit a new set of springs. Check the clutch pressure plate for wear and damage.

11 If the lining material of the friction plates smells burnt or if it is glazed, new parts are required. If the metal clutch plates are scored or discoloured, they must be renewed. Measure the thickness of each friction plate **(see illustration)** and compare the results to this Chapter's Specifications. Renew any friction plates that are near the wear limit.

12 Lay the plain plates, one at a time, on a perfectly flat surface (such as a piece of plate glass) and check for warpage by trying to slip a 0.3 mm feeler gauge between the flat surface and the plate **(see illustration)**. Do

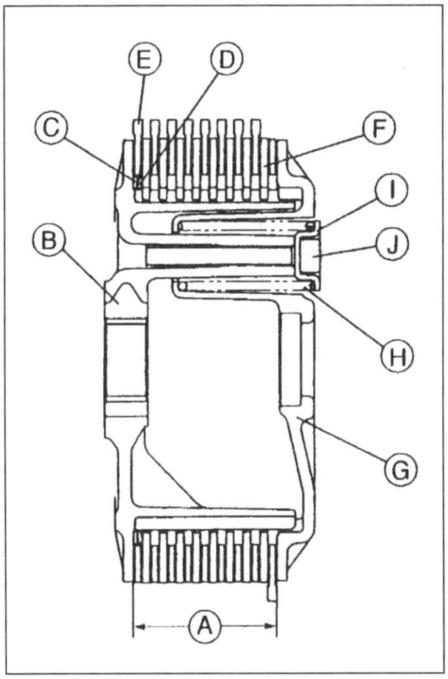

20.13 Clutch plate pack width check

A Pack width
B Clutch centre
C Spring seat
D Anti-judder spring
E Friction plate
F Plain plate
G Pressure plate
H Springs
I Washers
J Bolts

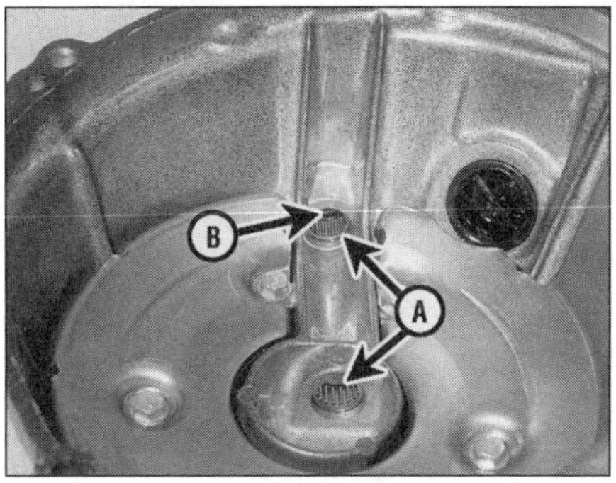

20.16 Check the shaft bearings (A) and the seal (B) in the cover

20.17 Fit the inner thrust washer . . .

this at several places around the plate's circumference. If the feeler gauge can be slipped under the plate, it is warped and should be renewed with a new one. Similarly check the friction plates.

13 Kawasaki advise that the following parts are built up on the bench and the assembled width of the clutch plate pack measured to determine whether it is within specification. Assemble the anti-judder spring seat and anti-judder spring on the clutch centre, followed by the friction and plain plates (as described in Steps 20 and 21). Fit the pressure plate and secure it with the springs, washers and bolts, then tighten the bolts to the specified torque. Now measure the width of the assembled clutch pack **(see illustration)**. If the measurement is outside that specified, use either thin or thick plain plates to bring it to within tolerance (see Specifications at the beginning of this Chapter). Do not mix thin and thick plain plates in the same clutch pack. Disassemble the clutch components once this check has been made.

14 Check the tabs on the friction plates for excessive wear and burrs. They can be cleaned up with a file if the damage is not severe. Examine the splines on the inside of the clutch centre. Also, check the teeth on the primary driven gear (on the back of the clutch housing) for cracks, chips and excessive wear. If the gear is worn or damaged, the clutch housing must be renewed and the primary drive gear on the end of the crankshaft should also be checked.

15 Check the needle bearing and its sleeve and the bearing journal on the transmission input shaft for score marks, heat discoloration and excessive wear.

16 Clean all traces of old gasket material from the clutch cover and crankcase. If the seal for the oil level window has been leaking, pry out the old seal and install a new one. If the release shaft seal in the top of the clutch cover has been leaking, pull out the release shaft, pry out the seal and drive in a new seal with a hammer and a small socket with an outside diameter slightly smaller than that of the seal. While the release shaft is removed, inspect the two small needle bearings that support the shaft at each end **(see illustration)**. It's unlikely that either of these bearings will ever need renewal; if either one is worn or damaged, take the cover to an automotive or motorcycle machine shop and have them pressed out and new ones installed. Also check the contact areas between the release shaft and the release rod for wear and damage. Before fitting the shaft back into the cover, apply some oil to the bearings and some grease to the lips of the seal. Finally, if you're planning to install a new cover, remove the noise damper from the old cover and install it on the new cover.

Installation

17 Slide the inner thrust washer, with its flat surface facing out, onto the end of the input shaft **(see illustration)**.

18 Lubricate the spacer and needle roller bearing with clean engine oil. Slide the clutch housing over the shaft, making sure it engages correctly with the teeth on the primary drive gear, then slide the needle bearing and its sleeve onto the shaft and into the centre of the housing **(see illustration)**.

19 Slide the outer thrust washer onto the shaft, then install the clutch centre, making sure it locates correctly onto the shaft splines **(see illustrations)**. Slide the clutch nut washer onto the shaft splines with the

2

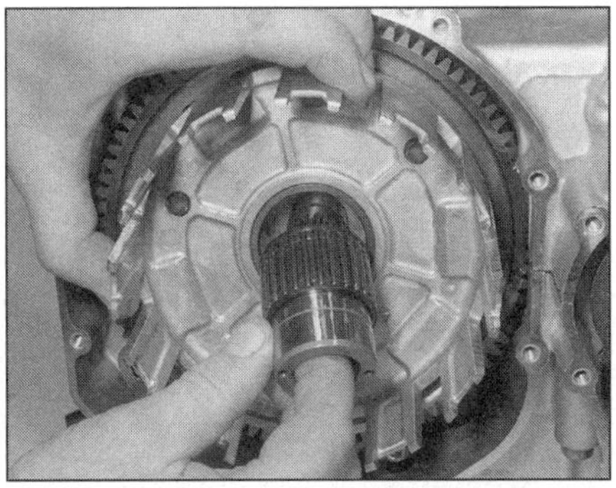

20.18 . . . then fit the clutch housing, bearing and sleeve

20.19a Fit the outer thrust washer . . .

20.19b . . . followed by the clutch centre

20.19c Fit the washer with the mark facing out . . .

20.19d . . . and the new nut . . .

20.19e . . . and tighten it to the specified torque

20.20a Fit the spring seat and spring . . .

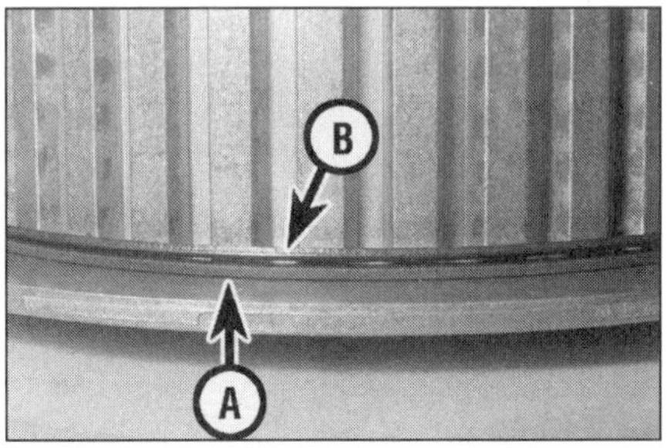

20.20b . . . making sure they are positioned as shown

A Anti-judder spring seat
B Anti-judder spring

20.21a Fit a friction plate first . . .

20.21b . . . then a plain plate

OUTSIDE mark facing out **(see illustration)**. Install a new clutch nut and, using the method employed on removal to prevent the input shaft turning, tighten the nut to the torque setting specified at the beginning of the Chapter **(see illustrations)**. **Note:** *Check that the clutch centre rotates freely after tightening.*

20 Fit the anti-judder spring seat and spring onto the clutch centre, making sure the inner edge of the spring contacts the spring seat and the outer edge is raised off it **(see illustrations)**.

21 Coat each clutch plate with clean engine oil, then build up the plates in the clutch housing, starting with a friction plate, then a plain plate and alternating friction and plain plates until all are installed **(see illustrations)**. Note that the tabs of the outer friction plate must be fitted into the shallow slots in the housing, not in the deep slots with the other plates **(see illustration)**.

22 If removed, fit the bearing into the back of the pressure plate. Lubricate the release rod with molybdenum disulphide grease. Install the release rod, on G, H, J and A models with its spring and washer, into the transmission input shaft so that the mushroomed end protrudes from the front **(see illustration)**.

23 Install the pressure plate onto the clutch

20.21c The tabs on the outer friction plate locate in the shallow slots in the housing

20.22 Fit the release rod into the shaft (F models shown)

20.23a Fit the pressure plate . . .

20.23b . . . and the springs, washers and bolts

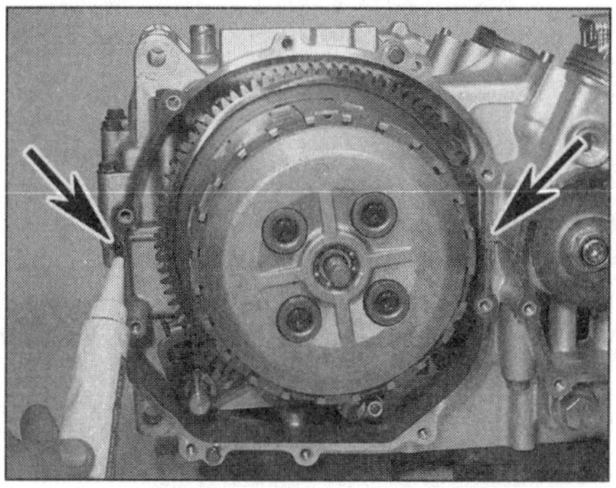

20.24a Apply the sealant to the crankcase joints (arrowed) . . .

20.24b . . . then position the new gasket, locating it onto the dowels (arrowed)

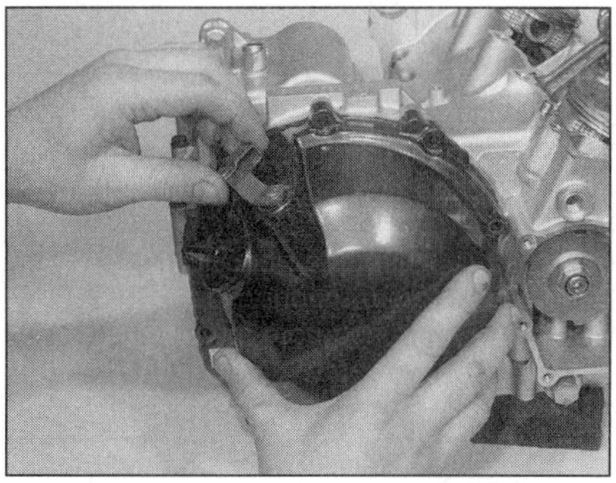

20.24c Fit the cover as described . . .

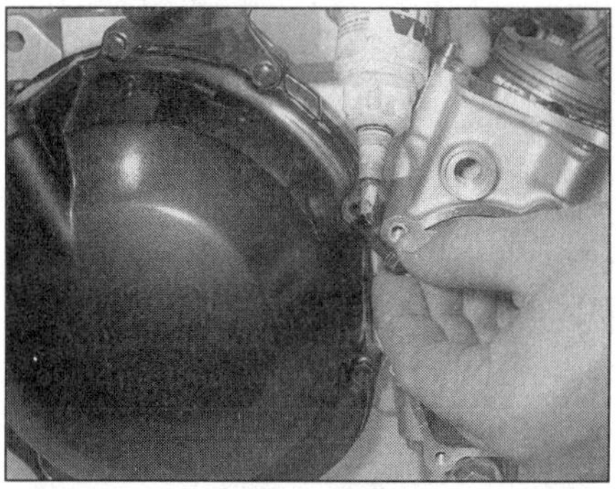

20.24d . . . applying the threadlock to the specified bolts

(see illustration). Install the springs and the spring bolts, with the shouldered side of the washers fitting into the tops of the springs, and tighten the bolts evenly in a criss-cross sequence to the specified torque setting **(see illustration)**.

24 Apply a smear of silicone sealant to the area around the crankcase joints **(see illustration)**. Check that the dowels are in place, then place a new gasket onto the crankcase **(see illustration)**. Fit the clutch cover with the release lever pushed back, then install the cover bolts, applying a suitable non-permanent thread locking compound to the two front bolts on either side of the crankcase joint, and not forgetting the clutch cable bracket **(see illustrations)**. Tighten the bolts evenly in a criss-cross sequence to the specified torque.

25 Move the release lever forward so that the cutout in the shaft end engages with the release rod. If the shaft is difficult to engage with the rod, pull up on the lever so that there is a small clearance between it and the clutch cover, and again move it forward to engage it. Ensure the pick-up and oil pressure switch wiring is correctly routed and secured by its clamps.

26 Connect the clutch cable (see Section 19) and adjust the freeplay (see Chapter 1).

27 Refill the engine with the correct quantity of oil (see Chapter 1) and install the fairing right-hand lower panel (see Chapter 8).

21 Gearchange mechanism (external parts) – removal, inspection and installation

Note: *The gearchange mechanism (external components) can be removed with the engine in the frame.*

Removal

1 Make sure the transmission is in neutral. Make an alignment mark between the gearchange linkage arm and the shaft so that they can be correctly aligned on installation (a small dot of paint on the shaft aligned with the split in the arm is best). Unscrew the linkage arm pinch bolt and slide the arm off the shaft **(see illustration)**.

2 Remove the clutch (see Section 20).

3 Unscrew the two bolts securing the oil pipe and remove the holders **(see illustration)**. Pull each end of the pipe out of its bore and remove the pipe. Discard the O-rings as new ones must be fitted on reassembly.

4 Note how the gearchange shaft centralising spring ends fit on each side of the locating pin in the crankcase and how the selector arm locates onto the pins on the stopper plate on the end of the selector drum. Grasp the end of

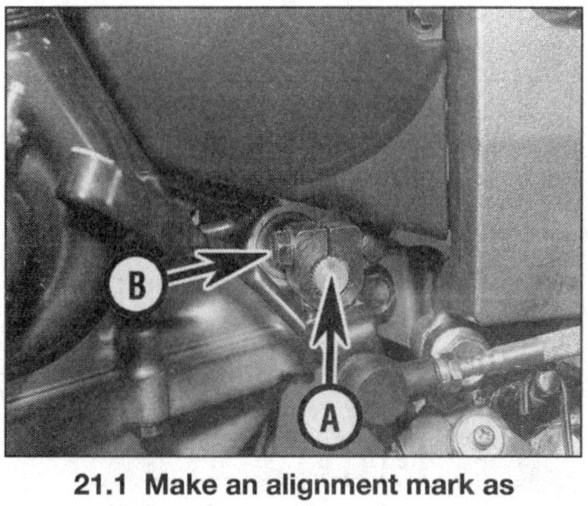

21.1 Make an alignment mark as shown (A), then unscrew the bolt (B) and slide the arm off the shaft

21.3 Unscrew the bolts (arrowed) and remove the holders, then pull the pipe out of its sockets

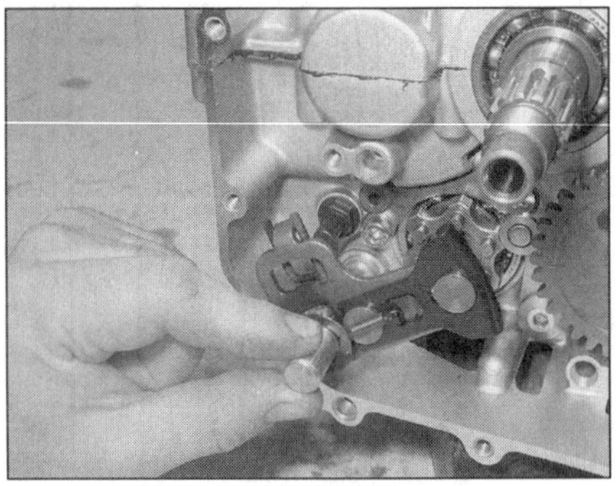

21.4 Withdraw the shaft/arm assembly, noting how it fits

21.5 Unscrew the bolt (arrowed) and remove the stopper arm, noting how it fits

21.7a The stopper plate is secured by a bolt (arrowed)

21.7b On installation, align the cutout (A) with the pin (B) . . .

21.7c . . . and tighten the bolt to the specified torque

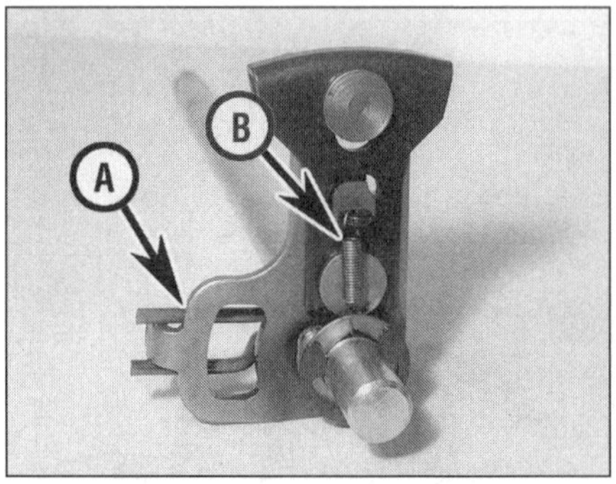

21.8 Check the centralising spring (A) and the return spring (B)

the shaft and withdraw the shaft/arm assembly **(see illustration)**.

5 Note how the stopper arm spring ends locate and how the arm itself locates in the neutral detent on the stopper plate, then unscrew the stopper arm bolt and remove the arm, spring and collar **(see illustration)**.

Inspection

6 Check the condition of the selector arm and stopper arm return springs and renew them if they are cracked, weakened or distorted.

7 Check the selector arm for cracks, distortion and wear of its pawls, and check for any corresponding wear on the selector pins on the stopper plate. Also check the stopper arm roller and the stopper plate for any wear or damage, and make sure the roller turns freely. Renew any components that are worn or damaged. The stopper plate is secured by a bolt and has a locating pin between it and the selector drum **(see illustration)**. On installation, align the cutout in the back of the plate with the locating pin, then apply a suitable non-permanent thread locking compound to the bolt and tighten it to the specified torque **(see illustrations)**.

8 Inspect the shaft centralising spring and the selector arm return spring for fatigue, wear or damage and renew them if necessary **(see illustration)**. Also check that the centralising spring locating pin in the crankcase is securely tightened. If it is loose, remove it and apply a non-permanent thread locking compound to its threads, then tighten it to the torque setting specified at the beginning of the Chapter.

9 Check the gearchange shaft for straightness and damage to the splines. If the shaft is bent you can attempt to straighten it, but if the splines are damaged a new shaft must be fitted. Also check the condition of the shaft oil seal in the left-hand side of the lower crankcase. If it is damaged, deteriorated or shows signs of leaking, fit a new seal. Lever out the old seal and drive the new one squarely into place, with its lip facing inward, using a seal driver or suitable socket **(see illustrations)**.

Installation

10 Assemble the stopper arm components in order, return spring, collar, stopper arm and bolt, then locate the arm on the neutral detent on the stopper plate and tighten the bolt to the specified torque **(see illustration 21.5)**. Make sure the spring is positioned correctly **(see illustration)**.

21.9a Lever out the old seal . . .

21.9b . . . and drive a new one in as described

21.10 Make sure the spring ends (arrowed) are correctly located

21.11 Make sure the spring ends (arrowed) are correctly located

21.12a Fit new O-rings . . .

21.12b . . . then install the pipe, holders and bolts

11 Slide the shaft into place and push it all the way through the case until the splined end comes out the other side, lifting the selector arm slightly as you do and engaging it with the pins on the stopper plate **(see illustration 21.4)**. Make sure the centralising spring ends locate correctly on each side of the locating pin **(see illustration)**.

12 Fit a new O-ring onto each end of the oil pipe and press the ends into their bores **(see illustration)**. Fit the holders and tighten the bolts to the specified torque **(see illustration)**.

13 Install the clutch (see Section 20).

14 Align the split in the gearchange linkage arm with the mark previously made on the shaft, then fit the arm on the shaft and tighten the pinch bolt securely **(see illustration 21.1)**.

22 Starter clutch, idle/reduction gear assembly – removal, inspection and installation

Note: *The starter clutch and idle gear assembly can be removed with the engine in the frame.*

Removal

1 To check the operation of the starter clutch, remove the alternator cover (see Chapter 9), then turn the starter driven gear by hand. It should turn freely in a clockwise direction (when viewed straight on), but should lock against the alternator rotor when turned in an anti-clockwise direction **(see illustration)**. If not, remove and inspect the components as described below.

2 Remove the alternator rotor (see Chapter 9). The starter driven gear should come away with the rotor. If it doesn't, remove it from the crankshaft. The starter clutch is secured to the back of the rotor by three Allen bolts **(see illustration)**.

Inspection

3 To check the operation of the starter clutch, place the alternator rotor face down on the workbench and install the starter driven gear. The gear should rotate freely in an anti-clockwise direction and lock against the rotor in a clockwise direction. If it doesn't, renew the starter clutch – it is secured to the rotor by three Allen bolts. When installing a new one, apply a suitable non-permanent thread locking compound to the bolt threads and tighten them to the torque setting specified at the beginning of the Chapter, using a strap wrench to hold the rotor.

4 Withdraw the starter driven gear from the starter clutch. If it appears stuck, rotate it anti-clockwise as you withdraw it to free it from the starter clutch.

5 Check the bearing surface of the starter driven gear hub and the condition of the sprags inside the clutch body. If the bearing surface shows signs of excessive wear or the sprags are damaged, the gear or the clutch body should be renewed.

6 If required, remove the sprags and check the plungers and springs for signs of deformation or damage. Make sure the plungers move freely in their sockets.

7 Check that the three Allen bolts securing the starter clutch to the alternator rotor are tight. If any are loose, unscrew all the bolts, then apply a suitable non-permanent thread locking compound to their threads and tighten them to the torque setting specified at the beginning of the Chapter, using a strap wrench to hold the rotor. Lubricate the starter clutch sprags with clean engine oil.

8 Examine the teeth of the starter idle/reduction gear and the corresponding teeth of the starter driven gear and starter motor drive shaft. Fit new gears and/or starter motor if any of the teeth are worn or chipped.

Installation

9 Lubricate the hub of the starter driven gear with clean engine oil, then install the starter driven gear into the starter clutch, rotating it anti-clockwise as you do so to spread the sprags and allow the hub of the gear to enter.

10 Install the alternator rotor (see Chapter 9).

23 Crankcase – separation and reassembly

1 To examine and repair or renew the crankshaft, connecting rods, bearings, and/or

22.1 Check that the starter clutch won't turn anticlockwise (A), but turns freely clockwise (B)

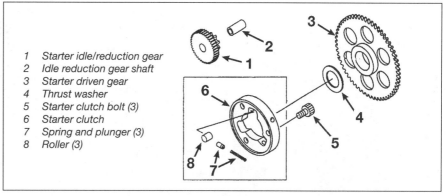

1 Starter idle/reduction gear
2 Idle reduction gear shaft
3 Starter driven gear
4 Thrust washer
5 Starter clutch bolt (3)
6 Starter clutch
7 Spring and plunger (3)
8 Roller (3)

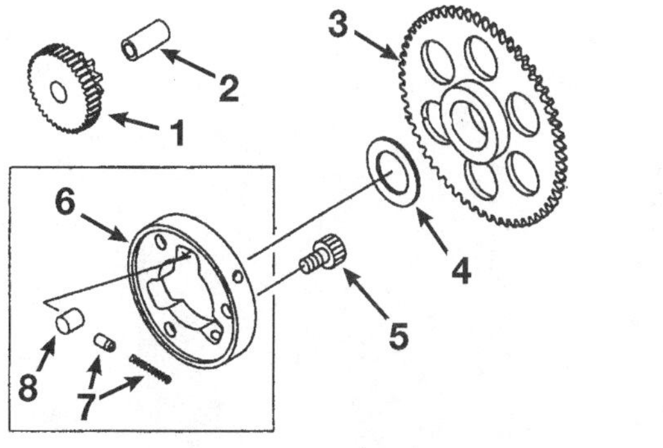

22.2 Starter clutch components

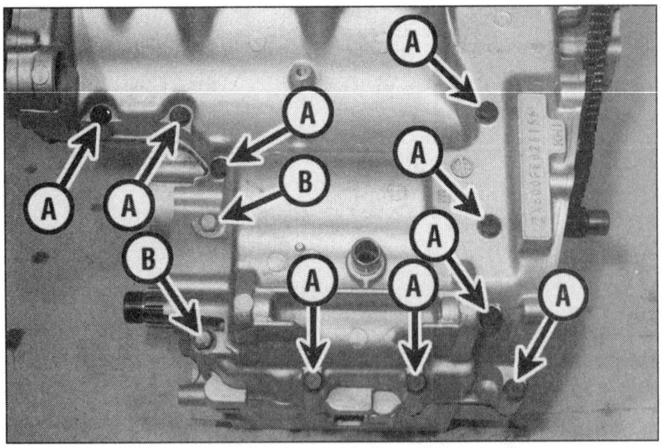

23.4 Upper crankcase 6 mm bolts (A) and 7 mm bolts (B)

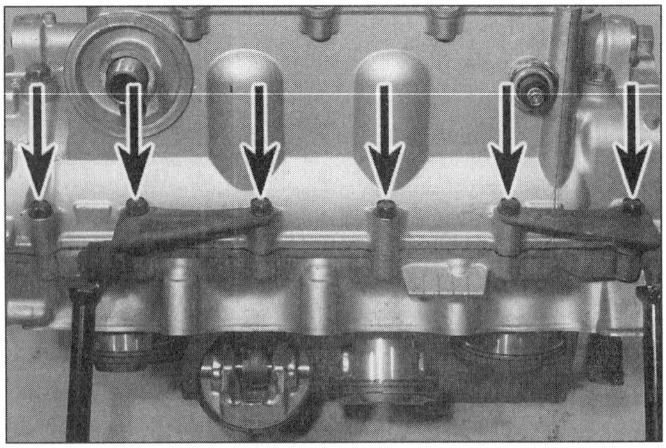

23.6 Lower crankcase 6 mm bolts – F models shown

23.7 Lower crankcase 8 mm bolts tightening sequence

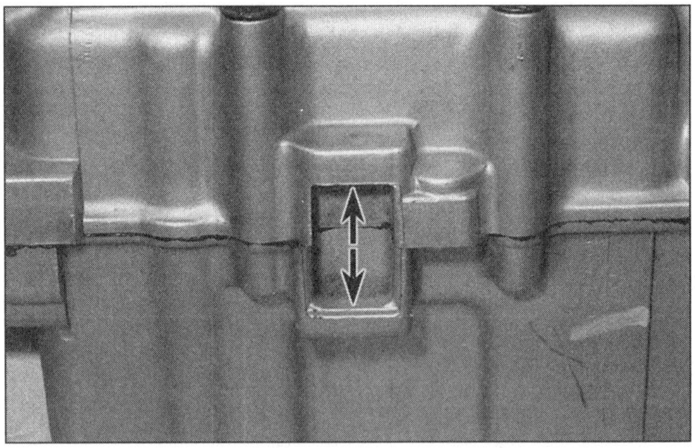

23.8a Using the leverage point (arrowed) if required . . .

transmission components, the engine must be removed (see Section 5) and the crankcase must be split into two parts. **Note:** *The transmission selector drum and forks can be removed without splitting the crankcases (see Section 30).*

2 If the crankcase is being separated to remove the crankshaft, first remove the cylinder head, cylinder block and pistons (see Sections 10, 13 and 14).

3 Before splitting the cases, remove the following components:

- Coolant hoses and oil pipe (see Chapter 3). **Note:** *If the cylinder head and block are not being removed, the oil pipe can be left in place.*
- Alternator cover and alternator rotor (see Chapter 9). **Note:** *The cover has to come off for everything, but the alternator rotor can remain installed on the crankshaft if you're only servicing the transmission.*
- Starter motor (see Chapter 9).
- Timing rotor and pick-up coil (see Chapter 5). **Note:** *The timing rotor must come off if you're servicing the crank, but can remain on the crank if you're only servicing the transmission.*
- Clutch cover and clutch (see Section 20). **Note:** *The cover has to come off for everything, but the clutch can remain on the transmission input shaft if you're only servicing the crankshaft.*
- Gearchange mechanism - external parts (see Section 21).
- Oil filter (see Chapter 1), oil cooler (see Chapter 3), oil sump, strainer and pipes, and oil pump (see Sections 16 and 17). **Note:** *If required, the oil pump can be left in place.*
- Cam chain guides (see Section 28).

23.8b . . . separate the crankcase halves

Separation

4 Unscrew the nine 6 mm upper crankcase bolts, followed by the two 7 mm bolts **(see illustration)**. **Note:** *As each bolt is removed, store it in its relative position in a cardboard template of the crankcase halves. This will ensure all bolts are installed in the correct location on reassembly.*

5 Turn the engine upside down and support it on wooden blocks as required.

6 Unscrew the six (F models) or eight (G, H, J and A models) 6 mm lower crankcase bolts as shown and remove them along with the mounting brackets, noting how they fit **(see illustration)**. On G, H, J and A models, note the different pattern of the two extra bolts located inside the crankcase.

7 Working in a **reverse** of the tightening sequence shown **(see illustration)** (the numbers are cast into the crankcase), slacken the ten 8 mm lower crankcase bolts evenly and a little a time until they are all finger-tight, then remove the bolts.

8 Carefully lift the lower crankcase half off the upper half, using either a soft-faced hammer to tap around the joint or a screwdriver inserted into the leverage point cast into the back of the crankcase, to initially separate the halves if necessary **(see illustrations)**. **Note:** *If the halves do not separate easily, make sure all fasteners have been removed.*

23.12 Check that all components are correctly installed and the dowels (arrowed) are fitted

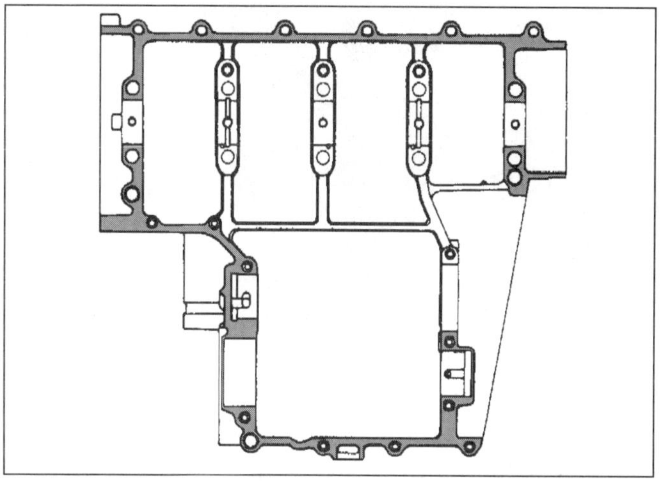

23.15 Apply the sealant to the shaded areas as shown

Caution: Do not try and separate the halves by levering against the crankcase mating surfaces as they are easily scored and will leak oil. Use only the leverage point.
The lower crankcase half will come away with the selector drum and forks, leaving the crankshaft and transmission shafts in the upper crankcase half.

9 Remove the three locating dowels from the crankcase if they are loose (they could be in either crankcase half), noting their locations **(see illustration 23.12)**.

10 Refer to the relevant Sections for the removal and installation of the components housed within the crankcases.

Reassembly

11 Remove all traces of sealant from the crankcase mating surfaces. Be careful not to let any old sealant fall into the case.

12 Ensure that all components and their bearings are in place in the upper and lower crankcase halves. Check that the cam chain is correctly engaged with the sprocket on the crankshaft. Check that the transmission bearing locating pins and half-ring retainers are all correctly located. Check that the three dowel pins are in place in their holes in the mating surfaces of the crankcase halves **(see illustration)**.

23.16 Make sure the hose passes through its bracket (arrowed)

13 Generously lubricate the transmission shafts, selector drum and forks (if installed), and the crankshaft, particularly around the bearings, with clean engine oil, then use a rag soaked in high flash-point solvent to wipe over the mating surfaces of both crankcase halves to remove all traces of oil.

14 Check the position of the selector drum and transmission gears – make sure they are in the neutral position (see Section 30). Check that the transmission shafts rotate freely and independently in neutral.

15 Apply a small amount of suitable silicone sealant (Kawasaki-Bond 56019-120 or equivalent) to the mating surfaces of the crankcase halves as shown **(see illustration)**. ***Caution: Do not apply an excessive amount of sealant as it will ooze out when the case halves are assembled and may obstruct oil passages. Do not apply the sealant on or too close to any of the oil passages, bearing inserts or bearing surfaces.***

16 Check again that all components are in position, particularly that the bearing inserts are still correctly located in the lower crankcase half. Carefully install the lower crankcase half down onto the upper crankcase half, making sure that the gear selector forks locate correctly into their grooves in the gears, and the oil return hose is properly routed through its bracket in the lower crankcase half **(see illustration)**. Make sure the dowels locate correctly into the lower crankcase half.

17 Check that the lower crankcase half is correctly seated. **Note:** *The crankcase halves should fit together without being forced. If the casings are not correctly seated, remove the lower crankcase half and investigate the problem. Do not attempt to pull them together using the crankcase bolts as the casing will crack and be ruined.*

18 Clean the threads of the ten 8 mm lower crankcase bolts and insert them in their original locations. Tighten them finger-tight. The four longer bolts go into the number 7, 8, 9 and 10 holes. Tighten the bolts a little at a time and in the numerical sequence shown (as cast into the crankcase) to the torque setting specified at the beginning of the Chapter **(see illustration 23.7)**.

19 Clean the threads of the six (F models) or eight (G, H, J and A models) 6 mm lower crankcase bolts and insert them in their original locations, not forgetting to fit the two brackets **(see illustration 23.6)**. Tighten all the bolts evenly and a little at a time to the specified torque setting. **Note:** *On G, H, J and A models, the two bolts located inside the crankcase have a different torque setting to the rest.*

20 Turn the engine over. Install the two 7 mm upper crankcase bolts, followed by the nine 6 mm bolts and tighten them finger-tight **(see illustration 23.4)**. Tighten the bolts evenly and a little at a time to the specified torque setting, noting that the setting for the 7 mm bolts is different to the 6 mm bolts.

21 With all crankcase fasteners tightened, check that the crankshaft and transmission shafts rotate smoothly and easily. Turn the input shaft and the output shaft to make sure they turn freely. Install the gearchange lever on the shaft and, while turning the output shaft as fast as possible, shift the transmission through the gears, first through to sixth, then back to first. **Note:** *Due to the positive neutral selector mechanism, it is not possible to select each gear in turn and check the shafts unless the output shaft is turning, however spinning the shaft by hand will be sufficient to disengage the mechanism.* If the transmission doesn't shift properly, and this is not due to insufficient speed of the output shaft, the crankcase will have to be separated again to correct the problem. Also make sure the crankshaft turns freely. If there are any signs of undue stiffness, tight or rough spots in either the transmission or the crankshaft, or of any other problem, the fault must be rectified before proceeding further.

22 Install the remaining components in the reverse order of removal (see Steps 2 and 3).

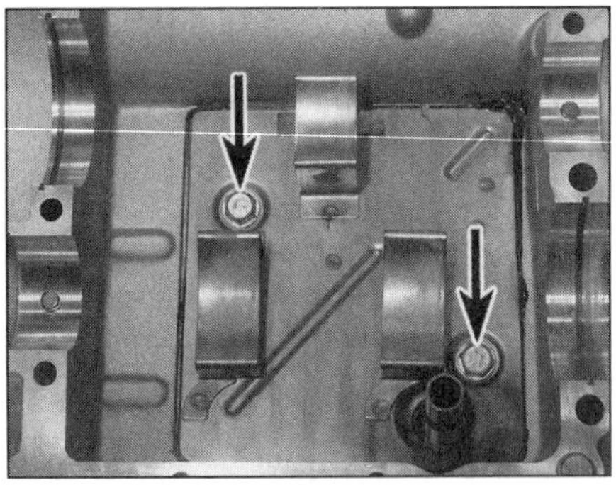

24.2 The breather plate is secured by two bolts (arrowed)

24 Crankcase - inspection and servicing

1 After the crankcases have been separated, remove the crankshaft, bearings, oil pressure switch, neutral switch and transmission components referring to the relevant Sections of this Chapter and to Chapter 9 for the oil pressure and neutral switches.

2 If required, unscrew the two bolts securing the breather plate in the upper crankcase half and remove the plate **(see illustration)**. **Note:** *The breather plate mating surfaces are coated with sealant – lift the plate off carefully to avoid damaging it.*

3 The crankcases should be cleaned thoroughly with a suitable solvent and dried with compressed air. All oil passages should be blown out with compressed air.

4 All traces of old gasket sealant should be removed from the mating surfaces. Minor damage to the surfaces can be cleaned up with a fine sharpening stone or grindstone. ***Caution: Be very careful not to nick or gouge the crankcase mating surfaces or oil leaks will result. Check both crankcase halves very carefully for cracks and other damage.***

5 Small cracks or holes in aluminium castings may be repaired with an epoxy resin adhesive as a temporary measure. Permanent repairs can only be effected by argon-arc welding, and only a specialist in this process is in a position to advise on the economy or practical aspect of such a repair. If any damage is found that can't be repaired, renew the crankcase halves as a set.

6 Damaged threads can be economically reclaimed by using a diamond section wire insert, of the Helicoil type, which is easily fitted after drilling and re-tapping the affected thread. Most motorcycle dealers and small engineering firms offer a service of this kind.

> **HAYNES HINT** ***Refer to Tools and Workshop Tips for details of installing a thread insert and using screw extractors.***

7 Sheared studs or screws can usually be removed with screw extractors, which consist of a tapered, left-thread screw of very hard steel. These are inserted into a pre-drilled hole in the stud, and usually succeed in dislodging the most stubborn stud or screw. If a problem arises which seems beyond your scope, it is worth consulting a professional engineering firm before condemning an otherwise sound casing. Many of these firms advertise regularly in the motorcycle press.

8 Install all components and assemblies, referring to the relevant Sections of this Chapter and to Chapter 9, before reassembling the crankcase halves. If the crankcase breather plate was removed, apply a 1 to 1.5 mm thick layer of a suitable silicone sealant (Kawasaki-Bond 56019-120 or equivalent) to its mating surface on the crankcase, then allow the sealant to dry before fitting the plate. Apply a suitable non-permanent thread-locking compound to the plate bolts and tighten them to the torque setting specified at the beginning of the Chapter **(see illustration 24.2)**.

25 Main and connecting rod bearings - general note

1 Even though main and connecting rod bearings are generally renewed during engine overhaul, the old bearing inserts should be retained for close examination as they may reveal valuable information about the condition of the engine.

2 Bearing failure occurs mainly because of lack of lubrication, the presence of dirt or other foreign particles, overloading the engine and/or corrosion. Regardless of the cause of bearing failure, it must be corrected before the engine is reassembled to prevent it from happening again.

3 When examining the connecting rod bearings, remove them from the connecting rods and caps and lay them out on a clean surface in the same general position as their location on the crankshaft journals. This will enable you to match any noted bearing problems with the corresponding crankshaft journal.

4 Dirt and other foreign particles get into the engine in a variety of ways. It may be left in the engine during assembly or it may pass through filters or breathers. It may get into the oil and from there into the bearings. Metal chips from machining operations and normal engine wear are often present. Abrasives are sometimes left in engine components after reconditioning operations, especially when parts are not thoroughly cleaned using the proper cleaning methods. Whatever the source, these foreign objects often end up imbedded in the soft bearing material and are easily recognised. Large particles will not imbed in the bearing and will score or gouge the bearing and journal. The best prevention for this cause of bearing failure is to clean all parts thoroughly and keep everything spotlessly clean during engine reassembly. Frequent and regular oil and filter changes are also recommended.

5 Lack of lubrication or lubrication breakdown has a number of interrelated causes. Excessive heat (which thins the oil), overloading (which squeezes the oil from the bearing face) and oil leakage or throw off (from excessive bearing clearances, worn oil pump or high engine speeds) all contribute to lubrication breakdown. Blocked oil passages will also starve a bearing and destroy it. When lack of lubrication is the cause of bearing failure, the bearing material is wiped or extruded from the steel backing of the bearing. Temperatures may increase to the point where the steel backing and the journal turn blue from overheating.

> **HAYNES HINT** ***Refer to Tools and Workshop Tips for bearing fault finding.***

6 Riding habits can have a definite effect on bearing life. Full throttle low speed operation, or labouring the engine, puts very high loads on bearings, which tend to squeeze out the oil film. These loads cause the bearings to flex, which produces fine cracks in the bearing face (fatigue failure). Eventually the bearing material will loosen in pieces and tear away from the steel backing. Short trip riding leads to corrosion of bearings, as insufficient engine heat is produced to drive off the condensed water and corrosive gases produced. These products collect in the engine oil, forming acid and sludge. As the oil is carried to the engine bearings, the acid attacks and corrodes the bearing material.

7 Incorrect bearing installation during engine assembly will lead to bearing failure as well. Tight fitting bearings which leave insufficient bearing oil clearances result in oil starvation. Dirt or foreign particles trapped behind a bearing insert result in high spots on the bearing which lead to failure.

8 To avoid bearing problems, clean all parts thoroughly before reassembly, double check all bearing clearance measurements and lubricate the new bearings with clean engine oil during installation.

26 Crankshaft and main bearings - removal, inspection and installation

Note: *To remove the crankshaft the engine must be removed from the frame and the crankcases separated.*

Removal

1 Separate the crankcase halves (see Section 23).

2 Before removing the crankshaft check the

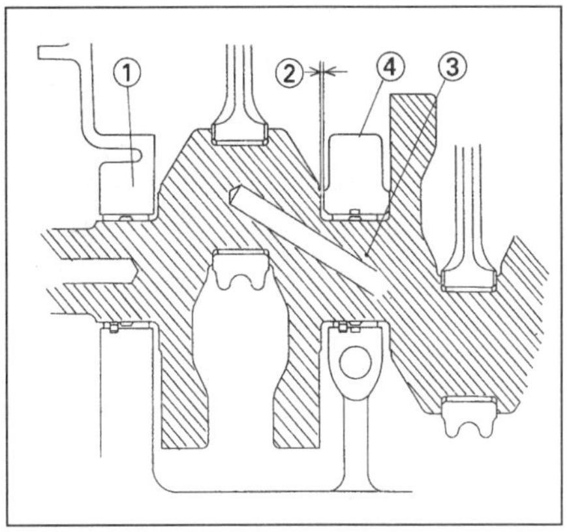

26.2 Check the crankshaft side clearance

1 Crankcase
2 Measure here
3 Crankshaft
4 No. 2 journal

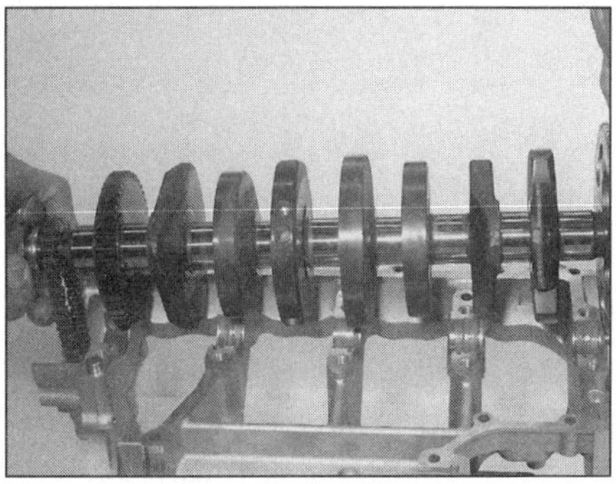

26.3 Lift the crankshaft out of the case

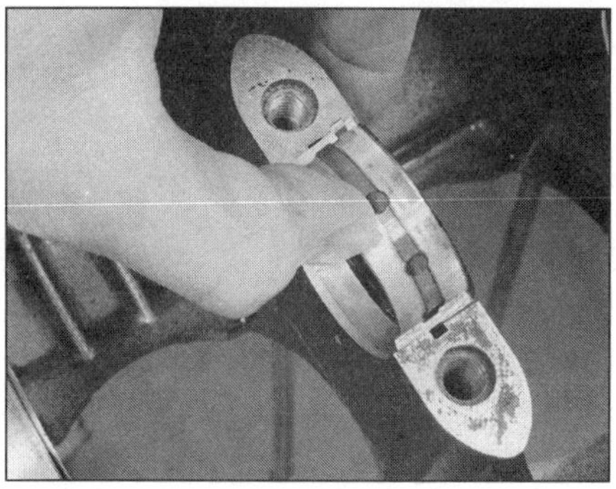

26.4 To remove a main bearing insert, push it sideways and lift it out

side clearance. Insert a feeler gauge between the crankshaft web and the No. 2 main bearing journal and record the clearance **(see illustration)**. Compare the measurement with this Chapter's Specifications. If the clearance is excessive, renew the crankcase halves as a set.

3 Lift the crankshaft together with the connecting rods and cam chain out of the upper crankcase half **(see illustration)**. If the crankshaft appears stuck, tap it gently using a soft-faced mallet.

4 The main bearing inserts can be removed from their cut-outs by pushing their centres to the side, then lifting them out **(see illustration)**. Keep the bearing inserts in order, as they must be installed in their original location if they are being reused.

5 If required, remove the connecting rods from the crankshaft (see Section 27), and disengage the cam chain from the sprockets.

Inspection

6 Clean the crankshaft with solvent. If available, blow the crank dry with compressed air, and also blow through the oil passages. Check the cam chain sprocket for wear or damage. If any of the sprocket teeth are excessively worn, chipped or broken, a new crankshaft must be fitted. Similarly check the primary drive gear.

7 Refer to Section 25 and examine the main bearings. If they are scored, badly scuffed or appear to have been seized, new inserts must be installed. Always renew the bearing inserts as a set. If they are badly damaged, check the corresponding crankshaft journal. Evidence of extreme heat, such as discoloration, indicates that lubrication failure has occurred. Be sure to thoroughly check the oil pump and pressure regulator as well as all oil holes and passages before reassembling the engine.

8 The crankshaft journals should be given a close visual examination, paying particular attention where damaged bearings have been discovered. If the journals are scored or pitted in any way a new crankshaft will be required. Note that undersize bearing inserts are not available, precluding the option of re-grinding the crankshaft.

9 Place the crankshaft on V-blocks and check the runout at the main bearing journals using a dial gauge. Compare the reading to the maximum specified at the beginning of the Chapter. If the runout exceeds the limit, the crankshaft must be renewed.

Oil clearance check and main bearing selection

10 To check the main bearing oil clearance, clean off the bearing inserts (and reinstall them, if they've been removed from the case, making sure they are in their original locations) and lower the crankshaft into the upper half of the case. Cut five pieces of Plastigauge and lay them on the crankshaft main journals, along with journal centreline **(see illustration)**.

11 Very carefully, guide the lower crankcase half down onto the upper half **(see illustration 23.8b)**. Install the large (8 mm) bolts and tighten them evenly and a little at a time, using the specified numerical sequence, to the torque listed in this Chapter's Specifications (see Section 23) **(see illustration 23.7)**. Don't rotate the crankshaft!

12 In a reverse of the tightening sequence, unscrew the bolts evenly and a little at a time and carefully lift the lower crankcase half off. Compare the width of the crushed Plastigauge on each journal to the scale printed on the Plastigauge envelope to obtain the main bearing oil clearance **(see illustration)**. Write down your findings, then remove all traces of Plastigauge from the journals, using your fingernail or other object which will not score the bearing surface.

13 If the oil clearance falls within the range specified at the beginning of the Chapter, and the bearing inserts are in perfect condition, they can be reused. If the clearance is between the maximum standard measurement and the service limit, fit new inserts that have blue paint marks **(see illustration)**, then check the oil clearance again. The clearance can slightly exceed the standard clearance, but it must not be less than the minimum clearance otherwise bearing seizure will result. Always renew all of the inserts at the same time.

26.10 Lay the Plastigauge strip (arrowed) along the journal centreline

26.12 Measure the width of the crushed Plastigauge

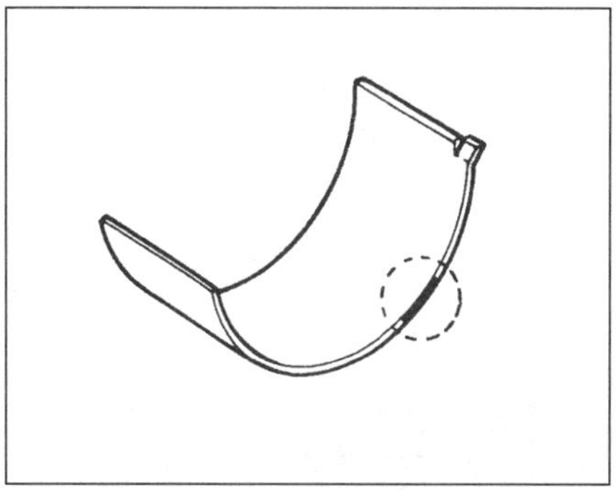

26.13 Location of the bearing insert colour code

26.14 Measure the diameter of each crankshaft journal

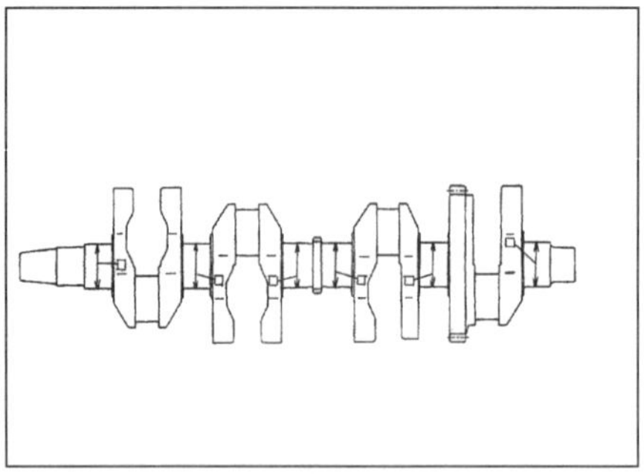

26.16 Crankshaft main journal size marking locations ('1' mark or no mark); use them in conjunction with . . .

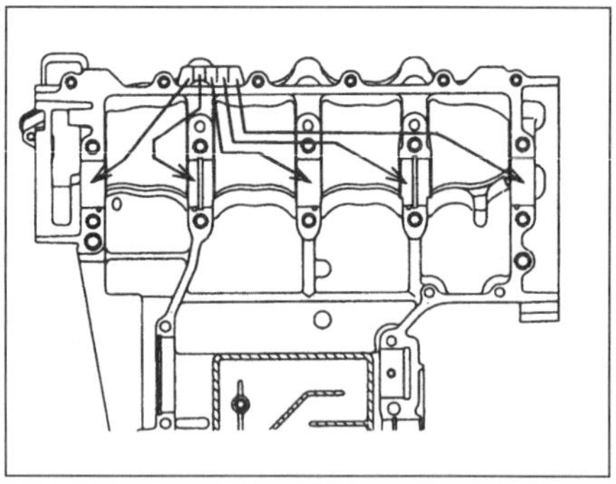

26.17 . . . the crankcase markings to determine insert size

Crankcase Main Bearing Bore Diameter Marking	Crankshaft Main Journal Diameter Marking	Bearing Insert*		
		Size Color	Part Number	Journal Nos.
O	1	Brown	92028-1418	3, 5
			92028-1421	1, 2, 4
None	1	Black	92028-1417	3, 5
O	None		92028-1420	1, 2, 4
None	None	Blue	92028-1416	3, 5
			92028-1419	1, 2, 4

*The bearing inserts for Nos. 1, 2 and 4 journals have an oil groove, respectively.

26.18a Main bearing selection chart – F models

Crankcase Main Bearing Bore Diameter Marking	Crankshaft Main Journal Diameter Marking	Bearing Insert*		
		Size Color	Part Number	Journal Nos.
O	1	Brown	92028-1883	3, 5
			92028-1886	1, 2, 4
None	1	Black	92028-1882	3, 5
O	None		92028-1885	1, 2, 4
None	None	Blue	92028-1881	3, 5
			92028-1884	1, 2, 4

*The bearing inserts for Nos. 1, 2 and 4 journals have an oil groove, respectively.

26.18b Main bearing selection chart – G, H, J and A models

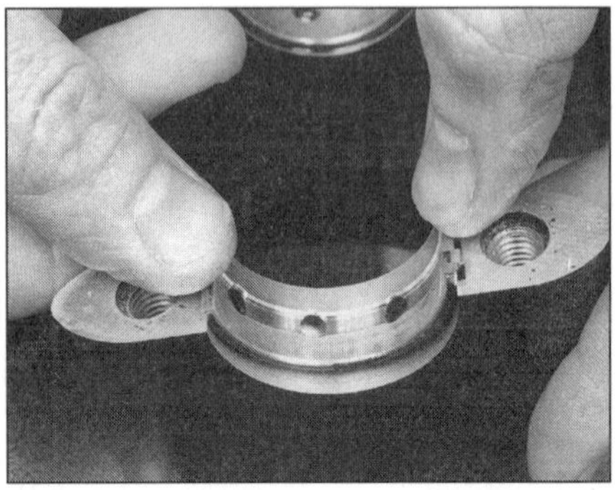

26.19a Make sure the tabs on the bearing inserts fit into the notches in the housings

26.19b Make sure the inserts with the oil grooves (arrowed) are correctly positioned

14 If the clearance is greater than the service limit listed in this Chapter's Specifications, measure the diameter of the crankshaft journals with a micrometer and compare your findings with this Chapter's Specifications **(see illustration)**. Also, by measuring the diameter at a number of points around each journal's circumference, you'll be able to determine whether or not the journal is out-of-round. Take the measurement at each end of the journal, near the crank throws, to determine if the journal is tapered.

15 If any crank journal has worn down past the service limit, renew the crankshaft.

16 If the diameters of the journals aren't less than the service limit, but differ from their original specification as indicated by the markings on the crankshaft **(see illustration)**, apply new marks with a hammer and punch.

- If the journal measures between 29.984 to 29.994 mm don't make any mark on the crank (if there is a '1' mark, erase it).
- If the journal measures between 29.995 to 30.000 mm, make a '1' mark on the crank in the area indicated (if it's not already there).

17 Next remove the main bearing inserts and assemble the case halves (see Section 23). Using a telescoping gauge and a micrometer, measure the diameters of the main bearing bores, then compare the measurements with the marks on the upper case half **(see illustration)**.

- If the bores measure between 33.000 to 33.008 mm, there should be an 'O' mark in the indicated areas. If not, make one.
- If the bores measure between 33.009 to 33.016 mm, there shouldn't be any marks in the indicated areas.

18 Using the appropriate marks on the crank and the marks on the case, determine the bearing sizes required by referring to the accompanying bearing selection charts **(see illustrations)**.

Installation

19 Clean the backs of the bearing inserts and the bearing housings in the case halves with solvent. Install the bearing inserts, making sure the tabs locate in the notches **(see illustration)**. The inserts for Nos. 1, 2 and 4 journals have oil grooves **(see illustration)**. When installing the inserts, press them in

27.2 Measure the big-end side clearance

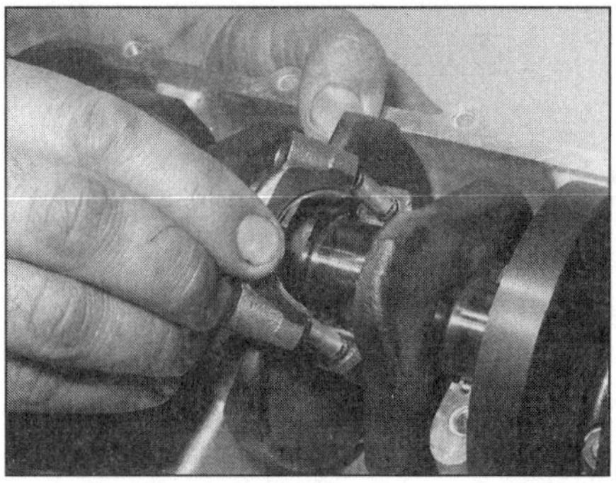
27.4 Unscrew the nuts and separate the cap from the rod

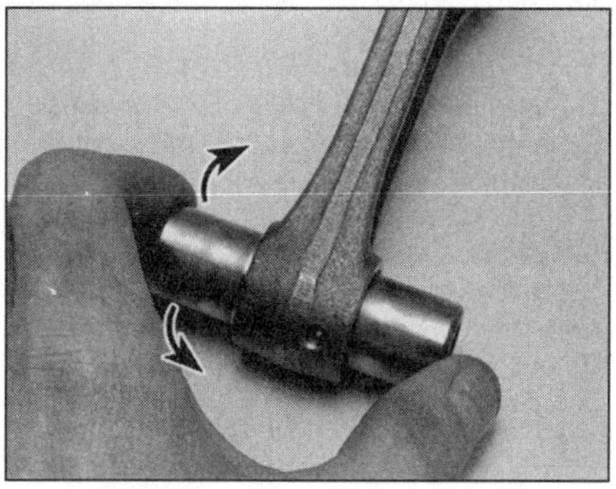
27.6 Check the piston pin and connecting rod small-end for excessive wear by rocking the pin back and forth

firmly by hand, don't tap them into place with a hammer, and take care not to touch the bearing surfaces with your fingers.

20 Lubricate the bearing inserts with clean engine oil, engine assembly lube or moly-based grease.

21 If removed, install the connecting rods (see Section 27).

22 Loop the cam chain over the crankshaft sprocket.

23 Carefully lower the crankshaft into place **(see illustration 26.3)**.

24 Assemble the crankcase halves (see Section 23).

27 Connecting rods and bearings – removal, inspection and installation

Removal

1 Remove the crankshaft (see Section 26).

2 Before removing the connecting rods from the crankshaft, measure the side clearance of each rod with a feeler gauge **(see illustration)**. If the clearance on any rod is greater than the service limit listed in this Chapter's Specifications, that rod will have to be renewed.

3 Using paint or a felt marker pen, mark the relevant cylinder identity on each connecting rod and bearing. Mark across the cap-to-connecting rod join and note which side of the rod faces the front of the engine to ensure that the cap and rod are fitted the correct way around on reassembly. Note that the letter already across the rod and cap indicates rod weight – each left-hand or right-hand pair of rods should have the same letter for proper balance **(see illustration 27.21)**.

4 Unscrew the bearing cap nuts, separate the cap from the rod, then detach the rod from the crankshaft **(see illustration)**. If the cap is stuck, tap on the ends of the rod bolts with a soft-faced hammer to free them. Leave the bolts in the rod until the big-end oil clearance has been checked, then discard them. New bolts and nuts must be used for final assembly.

5 Separate the bearing inserts from the rods and caps, keeping them in order as they must be reinstalled in their original locations. Wash the parts in solvent and dry them with compressed air, if available.

Inspection

6 Check the connecting rods for cracks and other obvious damage. Lubricate the piston pin for each rod, install it in the correct rod and check for play **(see illustration)**. If it is loose, renew the connecting rod and/or the pin.

7 Refer to Section 25 and examine the connecting rod bearing inserts. If they are scored, badly scuffed or appear to have been seized, new bearings must be installed. Always renew the bearings in the connecting rods as a set. If they are badly damaged, check the corresponding crankshaft journal.

HAYNES HiNT

Evidence of extreme heat, such as discoloration of the bearing inserts, indicates that lubrication failure has occurred. Be sure to thoroughly check the oil pump and pressure relief valve as well as all oil holes and passages before reassembling the engine.

8 Have the rods checked for twist and bending by a Kawasaki dealer or engineer.

Oil clearance check and bearing selection

9 If the bearings and journals appear to be in good condition, check the oil clearances as follows. **Note:** *Support the crankshaft so that it cannot rotate during the check. During the procedure, the connecting rod must not rotate around the crankshaft.*

10 Start with the rod for No. 1 cylinder. Clean the bearing inserts and the connecting rod and cap using solvent and a lint-free cloth.

11 Install the bearing inserts in the connecting rod and cap. Make sure the tab on the insert engages with the notch in the rod or cap **(see illustration 27.24b)**.

12 Clean the connecting rod journal with solvent and a lint-free cloth. Lay a strip of Plastigauge across the journal, parallel with the journal centreline **(see illustration 26.10)**.

13 Position the connecting rod on the journal, then install the rod cap **(see illustration 27.4)**. Refer to Step 26 and tighten the nuts to the torque setting listed in this Chapter's Specifications.

14 Unscrew the nuts and remove the connecting rod and cap from the journal, being very careful not to disturb the Plastigauge. Compare the width of the crushed Plastigauge to the scale printed in the Plastigauge envelope **(see illustration 26.12)**

HAYNES HiNT

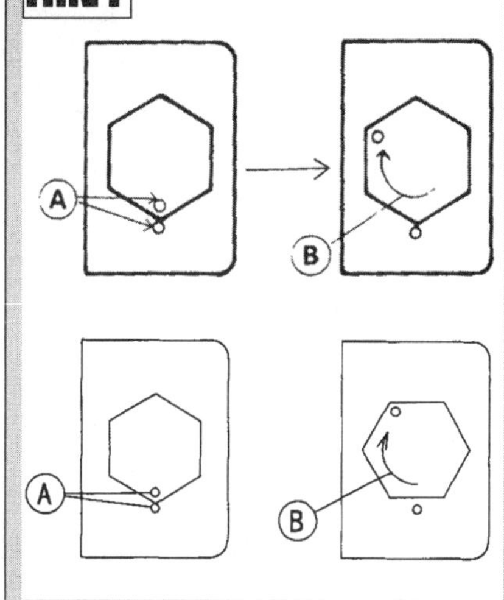

If a degree disc is not available, the angle for the final torque setting can be determined by using the points on the connecting rod cap nut. Select one point on the nut as a reference and mark it with paint or a marker (A). Now select the second point clockwise from it and mark its position on the connecting rod cap. Tighten the nut – when the mark on the first point aligns with the mark made on the connecting rod cap, it will have turned through the requisite number of degrees (B). Upper illustration F, G and H models, lower illustration J models.

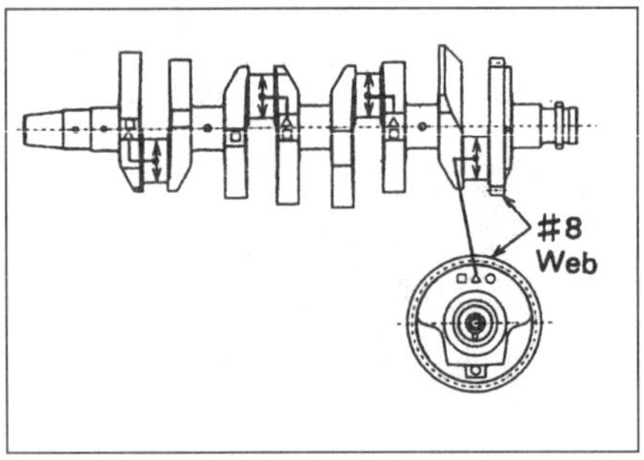

27.19 Crankshaft big-end journal size marking locations; use in conjunction with . . .

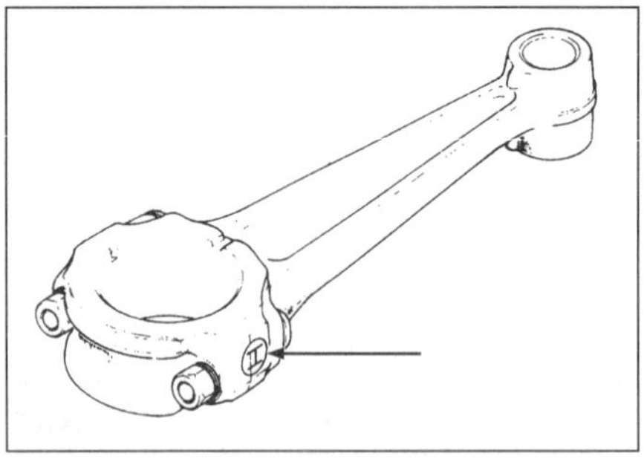

27.21 . . . the mark 'O' (or no mark) around the weight letter on the connecting rod to determine bearing insert size

Con-rod Big End Bore Diameter Marking	Crankpin Diameter Marking	Bearing Insert	
		Size Color	Part Number
None	O	Pink	92028-1709
None	None	Brown	92028-1494
O	O		
O	None	Black	92028-1493

27.22a Connecting rod big-end bearing selection chart – F models

Con-rod Big End Bore Diameter Marking	Crankpin Diameter Marking	Bearing Insert	
		Size Color	Part Number
None	O	Pink	92028-1880
None	None	Brown	92028-1879
O	O		
O	None	Black	92028-1878

27.22b Connecting rod big-end bearing selection chart – G, H, J and A models

to determine the bearing oil clearance. Write down your findings, then remove all traces of Plastigauge from the journal, using your fingernail or other object which will not score the bearing surface.

15 If the clearance falls within the range specified at the beginning of the Chapter, and the bearing inserts are in perfect condition, they can be reused.

16 If the clearance is between the maximum standard measurement and the service limit, fit new inserts that have black paint marks, then check the oil clearance once again **(see illustration 26.13)**. The clearance can slightly exceed the standard clearance, but it must not be less than the minimum clearance otherwise bearing seizure will result. Always renew all of the inserts at the same time.

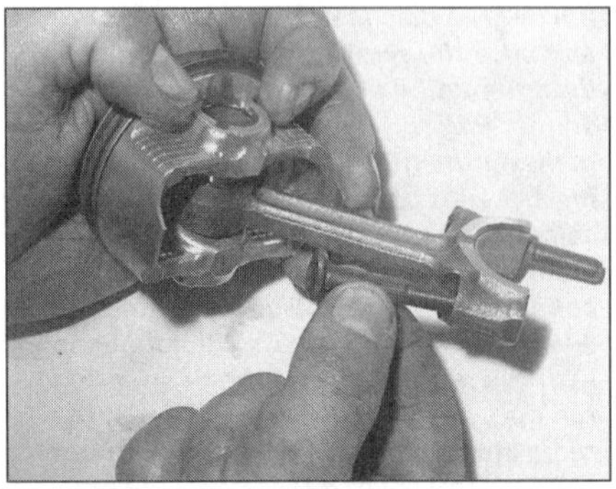

27.24a Fit the new bolts into the rod

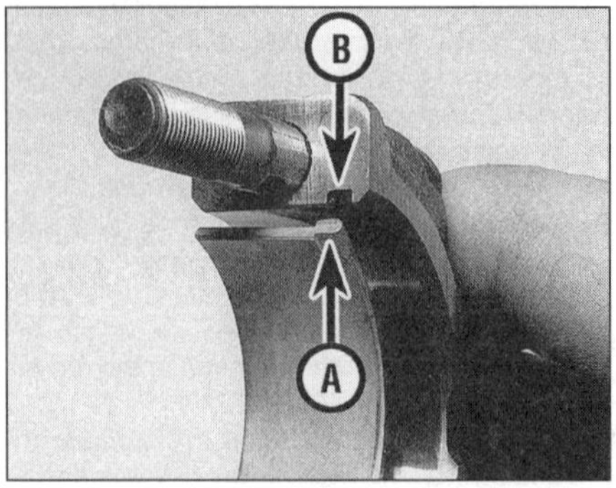

27.24b Make sure the tab (A) locates in the notch (B)

17 If the clearance is greater than the service limit listed in this Chapter's Specifications, measure the diameter of the connecting rod journal on the crankshaft with a micrometer and compare your findings with this Chapter's Specifications. Also, by measuring the diameter at a number of points around the journal's circumference, you'll be able to determine whether or not the journal is out-of-round. Take the measurement at each end of the journal to determine if the journal is tapered.

18 If any journal has worn down past the service limit, fit a new crankshaft.

19 If the diameter of the journal isn't less than the service limit but differs from the original markings on the crankshaft **(see illustration)**, apply new marks with a hammer and punch.

- If the journal measures between 29.984 to 29.994 mm, don't make any marks on the crank (if there is a 'O' mark, erase it).
- If the journal measures between 29.995 to 33.000 mm, make a 'O' mark on the crank in the area indicated (if not already there).

20 Remove the bearing inserts from the connecting rod and cap, then assemble the cap to the rod. Tighten the nuts to the torque listed in this Chapter's Specifications.

21 Using a telescoping gauge and a micrometer, measure the inside diameter of the connecting rod. The mark on the connecting rod (if any) should coincide with the measurement, but if it doesn't, make a new mark **(see illustration)**.

- If the inside diameter measures between 33.000 to 33.008 mm, there should be no 'O' mark around the weight letter on the rod (if there is a 'O' mark, erase it).
- If the inside diameter measures between 33.009 to 33.016 mm, there should be a 'O' mark around the weight code letter. If there isn't, make one.

22 Using the appropriate mark on the crank and the mark on the rod, determine the bearing size required by referring to the accompanying bearing selection charts **(see illustrations)**.

23 Repeat the bearing selection procedure for the remaining connecting rods.

Installation

24 Clean the new connecting rod nuts and bolts with solvent to remove the anti-rust coating then dry them using compressed air. Fit the bolts into the rods, tapping them lightly with a hammer if necessary to make sure they are correctly seated **(see illustration)**. ***Caution: The connecting rod bolts are designed to stretch when they are tightened. NEVER reuse the old bolts.*** Clean the backs of the bearing inserts and the connecting rods and caps with solvent. Install the inserts into the rods and caps, making sure the tabs on the inserts engage with the notches in the rods and caps **(see illustration)**. When

27.26a Apply the oil as described . . .

27.26b . . . then tighten the nuts to the specified torque . . .

27.26c . . . and, on F, G, H and J models, to the specified angle

installing the inserts, press them in firmly by hand, don't tap them into place with a hammer, and take care not to touch the bearing surfaces with your fingers. When all the inserts are installed, lubricate them with engine assembly lube or moly-based grease. Don't get any lubricant on the mating surfaces of the rod or cap.

25 Assemble each connecting rod to its proper journal, making sure the previously applied matchmarks correspond to each other (see Step 3) **(see illustration 27.4)**. **Note:** *The letter present at the rod/cap seam on one side of the connecting rod is a weight mark* ***(see illustration 27.21)****. Kawasaki advise that a pair of rods (the left two rods or the right two rods) should have the same weight mark to minimise vibration.*

26 When you're sure the rods are positioned correctly, apply a small amount of engine oil to the threads of the bolts and the seating surface of the nuts **(see illustration)**. On F, G, H and J models, tighten the nuts to the initial torque setting listed in this Chapter's Specifications, then tighten them in one continuous movement to the final torque setting using a torque angle gauge **(see illustrations)**. **Note:** *If a torque angle gauge is not available see* ***Haynes Hint****.* On A models, tighten the nuts evenly, in two or three stages, to the torque setting specified.

27 Turn the rods on the crankshaft. If any of them feel tight, tap on the bottom of the connecting rod caps with a hammer – this should relieve stress and free them up. If it doesn't, recheck the bearing clearance.

28 As a final step, recheck the connecting rod side clearances (see Step 2). If the clearances aren't correct, find out why before proceeding with engine assembly.

28.3 Note how the guide seats at the bottom (arrowed)

28.4 The rear guide is secured by a pivot bolt (arrowed)

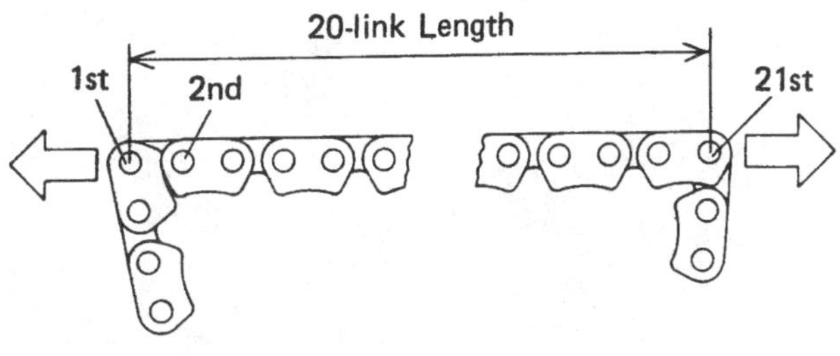

28.5 Cam chain stretch measurement

28 Cam chain and guides – removal, inspection and installation

Removal

Cam chain

1 Remove the crankshaft (see Section 26).

2 Remove the chain from the crankshaft.

Chain guides

3 The front guide can be lifted from the cylinder block after the head has been removed (see Section 10) **(see illustration)**. Note which way up the guide fits and how it locates in its seat behind the timing rotor.

4 The rear guide is secured to the crankcase by a pivot bolt, and can be removed after removing the cylinder block (see Section 13) **(see illustration)**. Unscrew the bolt and withdraw the guide from the case. Discard the O-ring as a new one must be used.

Inspection

Camshaft chain

5 Pull the chain tight to remove any slack, then measure the length of 20 links (from the centre of the 1st pin to the centre of the 21st pin) and compare the result with the service limit specified at the beginning of the Chapter **(see illustration)**. Take several measurements at different places in case the chain has worn unevenly. If any measurement exceeds the service limit, a new chain must be fitted.

6 Also check the chain for binding and obvious damage.

Chain guides

7 Check the guides for excessive wear, deep grooves, cracking and other obvious damage, replacing them if necessary. Check the condition of the pivot hardware on the rear guide and renew any components that are damaged or deteriorated.

Installation

8 Installation of the chain and guides is the reverse of removal. Make sure the wider end of the camshaft front chain guide is at the top

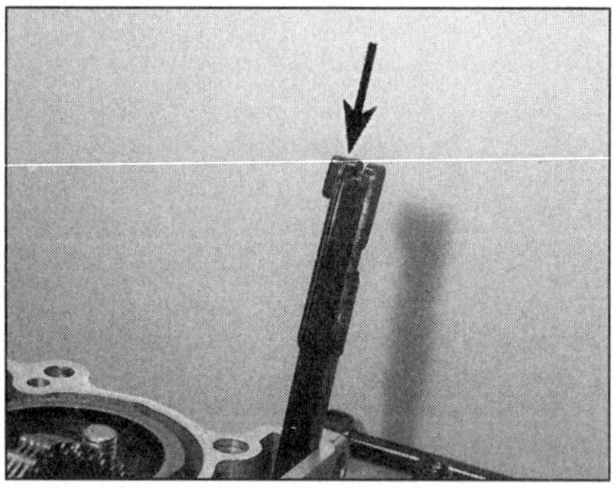

28.8a Make sure the wider end (arrowed) is at the top

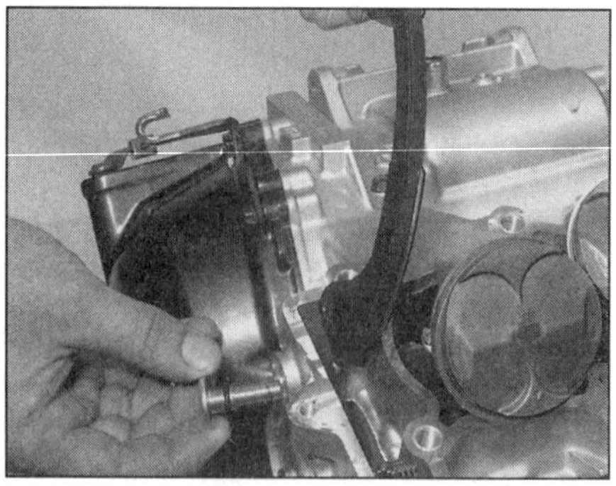

28.8b Use a new O-ring on the rear guide pivot bolt

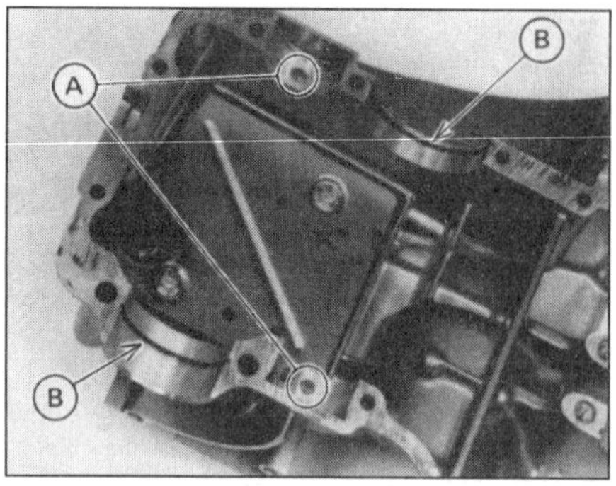

29.3 Remove the needle bearing pins (A) and the caged bearing half-ring retainers (B) if required, noting how they fit

(see illustration). Push the guide all the way down and make sure it locates correctly in its cutout – it is visible behind the timing rotor on the end of the crankshaft **(see illustration 28.3)**. When installing the pivot bolt for the cam chain rear guide, use a new O-ring and tighten the bolt to the torque listed in this Chapter's Specifications **(see illustration)**. Apply engine oil to the faces of the guides and to the chains.

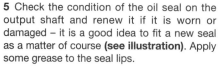

29 Transmission shafts – removal and installation

Note: *To remove the transmission shafts the engine must be removed from the frame and the crankcases separated.*

Removal

1 Remove the engine and clutch, then separate the crankcase halves (see Sections 5, 20 and 23).

2 Lift the input shaft and output shaft out of the crankcase, noting their relative positions in the crankcase and how they fit together **(see illustration 29.7)**. If they are stuck, use a soft-faced hammer and gently tap on the ends of the shafts to free them.

3 If required, remove the caged-ball bearing half-ring retainers and the needle bearing dowel pins from the upper crankcase half, noting how they fit **(see illustration)**. If they are not in their slots or holes in the crankcase, remove them from the bearings themselves on the shafts.

4 If necessary, the input shaft and output shaft can be disassembled and inspected for wear or damage (see Section 30).

Installation

5 Check the condition of the oil seal on the output shaft and renew it if it is worn or damaged – it is a good idea to fit a new seal as a matter of course **(see illustration)**. Apply some grease to the seal lips.

6 If removed, install the caged-ball bearing half-ring retainers into their slots in the upper crankcase half, and install the needle bearing dowels into their holes **(see illustration 29.3)**.

7 Lower each shaft into position in the crankcase half, making sure the hole in the needle bearing engages correctly with the dowel, and the groove in the caged-ball bearing engages correctly with the bearing half-ring retainer **(see illustration)**.

8 Make sure both transmission shafts are correctly seated and their related pinions are correctly engaged.

Caution: If the caged-ball bearing half-ring retainers or needle bearing dowel pins are not correctly engaged, the crankcase halves will not seat correctly.

9 Position the gears in the neutral position and check the shafts are free to rotate easily and independently (i.e. the input shaft can turn whilst the output shaft is held stationary) before proceeding further.

10 Reassemble the crankcase halves (see Section 23).

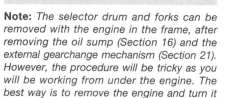

30 Selector drum and forks – removal, inspection and installation

Note: *The selector drum and forks can be removed with the engine in the frame, after removing the oil sump (Section 16) and the external gearchange mechanism (Section 21). However, the procedure will be tricky as you will be working from under the engine. The best way is to remove the engine and turn it upside down, then remove the oil sump.*

Removal

1 Either remove the engine and separate the crankcase halves, or remove the engine and the oil sump, or simply leave the engine in place and just remove the oil sump (see **Note** above) (see Sections 5, 16 and 23 as required).

2 Remove the gearchange mechanism (external components), and remove the stopper plate from the selector drum (see Section 21).

3 Unscrew the bolt and screw securing the selector drum/fork shaft retainer plate and remove the plate **(see illustration)**.

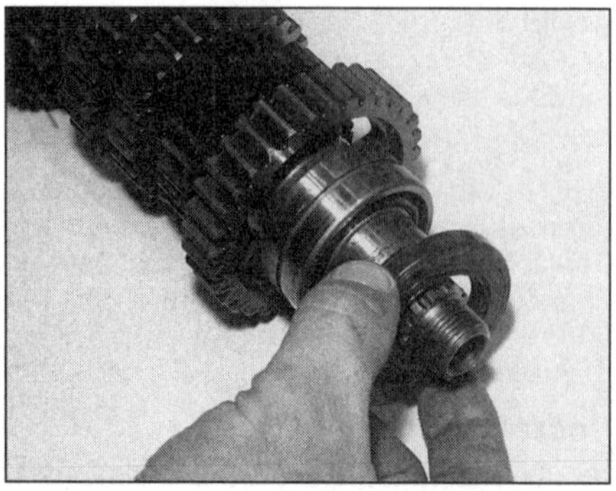

29.5 Replace the output shaft oil seal if required

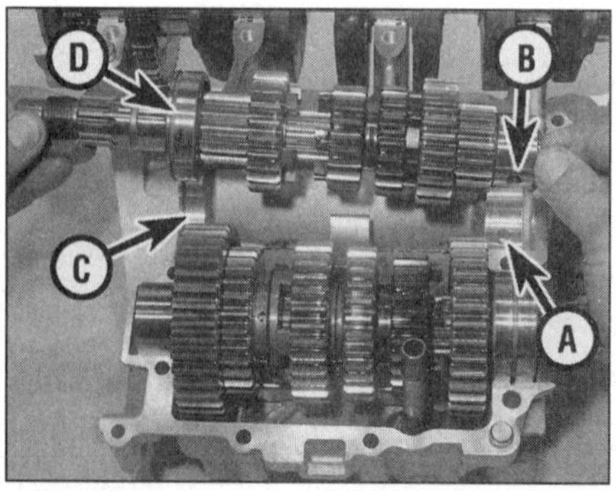

29.7 Make sure the pin (A) enters the hole (B) and the half-ring (C) enters the groove (D)

30.3 Unscrew the bolt and screw (arrowed) and remove the plate . . .

30.4 . . . then withdraw the shafts and remove the forks . . .

30.5 . . . and slide the drum out

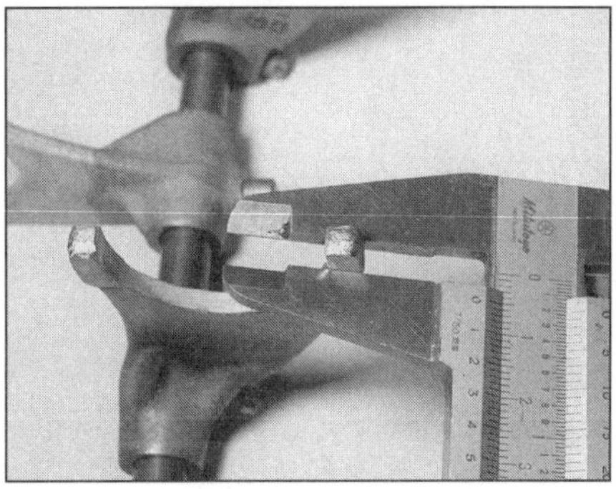

30.7a Measure the fork end thickness as shown . . .

4 Mark each fork according to its fitted location and note which way round they fit. Support the selector forks and pull the shafts out **(see illustration)**.

5 Swing each fork away from the selector drum, noting how the guide pins locate in the selector drum grooves. Slide the selector drum out of the crankcase **(see illustration)**. Lift the forks out of the casing and reassemble them on the shafts as soon as they're removed so they can be returned to their original positions.

Inspection

6 Inspect the selector forks for any signs of wear or damage, especially around the fork ends where they engage with the groove in the pinion. Check that each fork fits correctly in its pinion groove. Check closely to see if the forks are bent. If the forks are in any way damaged they must be renewed.

7 Measure the thickness of the fork ends and the width of its groove in the relevant pinion and compare the readings to the specifications **(see illustrations)**. Renew whichever components are worn beyond their specifications.

8 Check that the forks fit correctly on their shaft. They should move freely with a light fit but no appreciable freeplay. Check that the fork shaft holes in the crankcases are not worn or damaged.

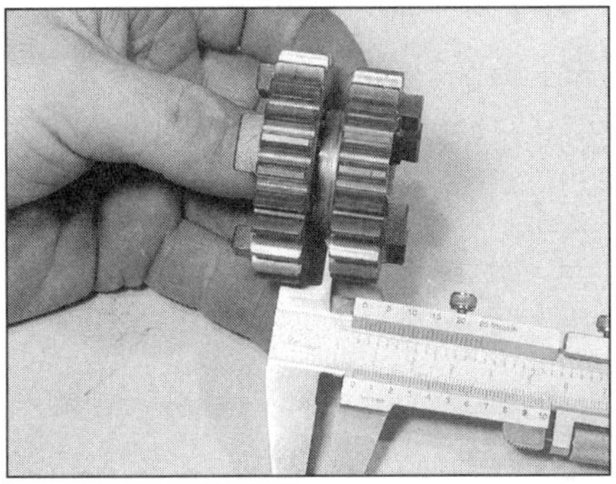

30.7b . . . and the width of its pinion groove

9 The selector fork shaft can be checked for trueness by rolling it along a flat surface. A bent rod will cause difficulty in selecting gears and make the gearshift action heavy. Renew the shaft if it is bent.

10 Inspect the selector drum grooves and selector fork guide pins for signs of wear or damage. Measure the width of each groove and the diameter of the corresponding fork guide pin and compare the results to the specifications. If any component is worn beyond its service limit or is damaged, it must be renewed.

11 Check that the selector drum bearing rotates freely and has no rough spots. There should be no excessive freeplay between the bearing, the drum and the crankcase. Renew the bearing if necessary.

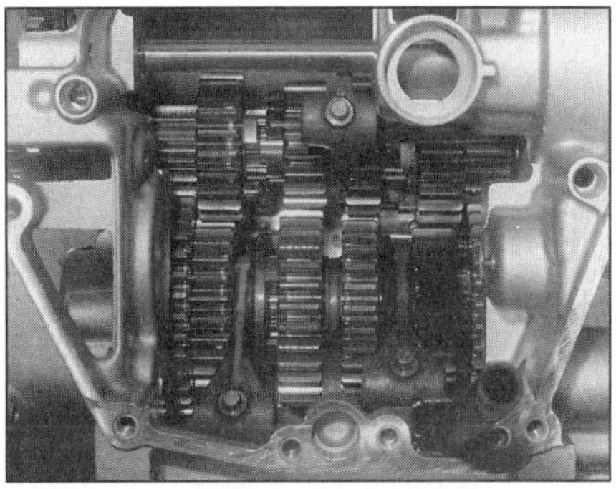

30.12 Locate each fork into its pinion groove as shown

Installation

12 Lubricate all parts with engine oil before installing them. Locate each fork into its correct pinion groove, making sure they are the correct way round **(see illustration)**. Swing the forks clear so they do not impede the selector drum as it is installed.

13 Slide the selector drum into the casing, making sure the shaft end enters its bore, and aligning the small hole with the neutral switch contact plunger **(see illustrations)**.

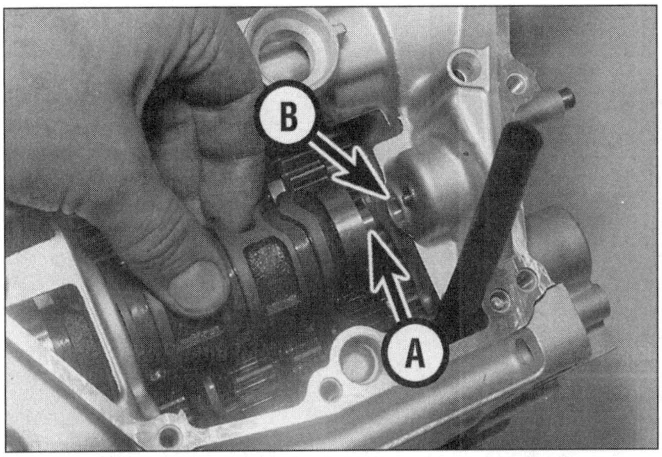

30.13a Fit the end of the selector drum (A) into the bore (B) . . .

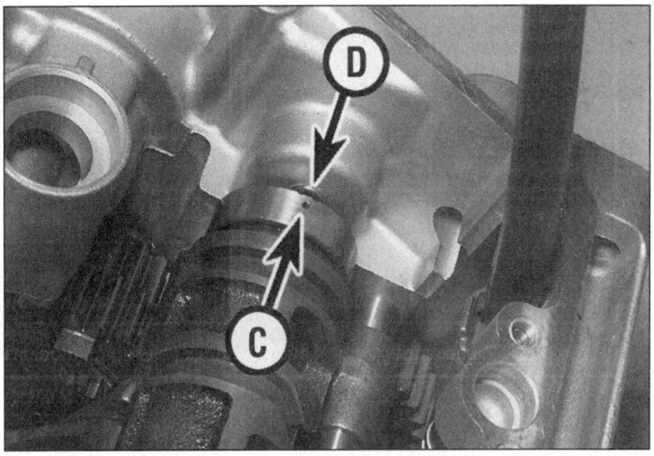

30.13b . . . and align the hole (C) with the neutral contact (D)

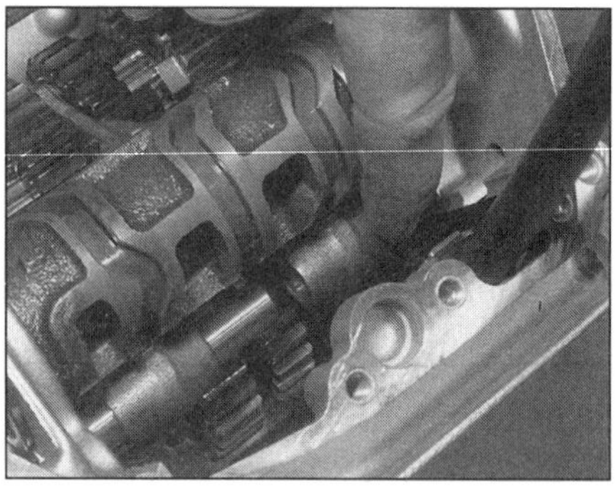

30.14a Slide the shafts through the forks . . .

30.14b . . . then fit the retainer plate into the slots in the shaft ends

14 Locate the fork guide pins in the tracks in the selector drum, then slide the fork shafts, with the slotted end outermost, into the casing, through the forks, and into their bores **(see illustration)**. Fit the retainer plate into the groove in each shaft end **(see illustration)**. Use a non-permanent thread locking compound on the threads of the retainer plate bolt and screw and tighten them to the torque setting specified at the beginning of the Chapter.

15 The remainder of installation is the reverse of removal.

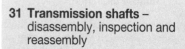

31 Transmission shafts – disassembly, inspection and reassembly

31.2a Slide off the needle bearing outer race . . .

31.2b . . . then remove the circlip and bearing

1 Remove the shafts from the crankcase (see Section 29).

Input shaft

Disassembly

2 Remove the needle bearing outer race, then remove the circlip from the end of the shaft and slide the needle bearing off **(see illustrations)**.

3 Remove the thrust washer and slide the second gear off the shaft **(see illustration)**.

4 Remove sixth gear and bushing **(see illustrations)**.

31.3 Remove the thrust washer and 2nd gear

31.4a Slide off 6th gear . . .

> **HAYNES HiNT** *When disassembling the transmission shafts, place the parts on a long rod or thread a wire through them to keep them in order and facing the proper direction. A large rubber band will keep them from being disturbed*

5 Slide the toothed washer off and remove the circlip **(see illustration)**. To keep the circlip from bending as it's expanded, hold the back of it with pliers **(see illustration)**.

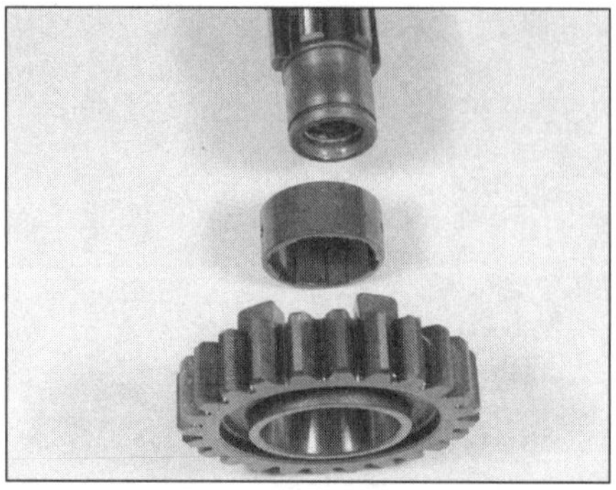

31.4b . . . and its bushing

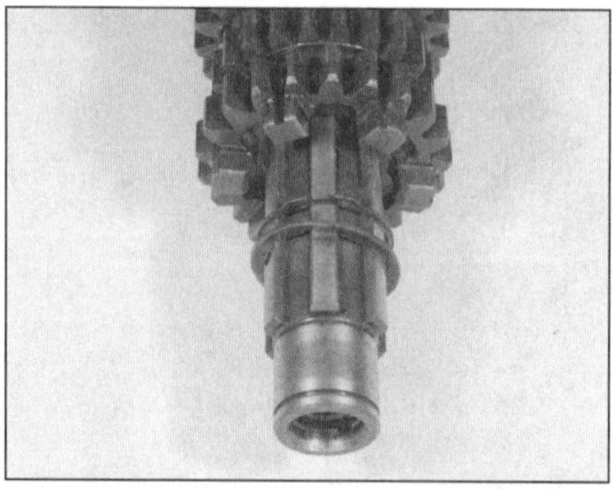

31.5a Remove the toothed washer and circlip . . .

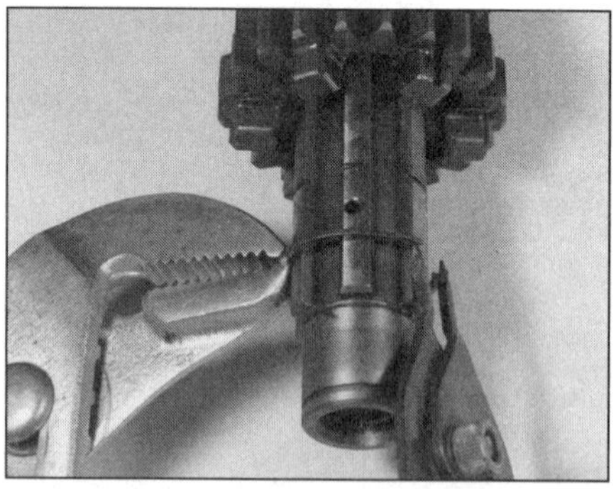

31.5b . . . holding the back of the circlip with pliers to prevent it twisting

31.6 Slide the 3rd/4th gear off the shaft

31.7a Remove the circlip . . .

31.7b . . . the toothed washer and 5th gear . . .

31.7c . . . and its bushing

6 Remove the third/fourth gear cluster from the shaft **(see illustration)**.
7 Remove the next circlip, then slide the washer, fifth gear and its bushing off the shaft **(see illustrations)**. First gear is integral with the shaft.

Inspection

8 Wash all of the components in clean solvent and dry them off. Rotate the ball bearing on the shaft, checking for tightness, rough spots or excessive wear. If any of these conditions are found, fit a new bearing. This will require the use of a hydraulic press or a bearing puller. If you don't have access to these tools, take the shaft to a Kawasaki dealer or other motorcycle repair shop and have them press the old bearing off the shaft and install the new one.
9 Measure the shift fork groove in each pinion **(see illustration)**. If the groove width exceeds the figure listed in this Chapter's Specifications, fit a new pinion assembly, and also check the shift fork (see Section 30).
10 Check the gear teeth for cracking and other obvious damage. Check the bushing and surface in the inner diameter of the fifth and sixth gears for scoring or heat discoloration. If either one is damaged, renew it.
11 Inspect the dogs and the dog holes in the gears for excessive wear **(see illustration and illustration 31.9)**. Always renew the paired gears as a set.
12 Check the needle bearing and race for wear or heat discoloration and renew them if necessary.

Reassembly

13 Reassembly is the basically the reverse of the disassembly procedure, but take note of the following points **(see illustration)**:

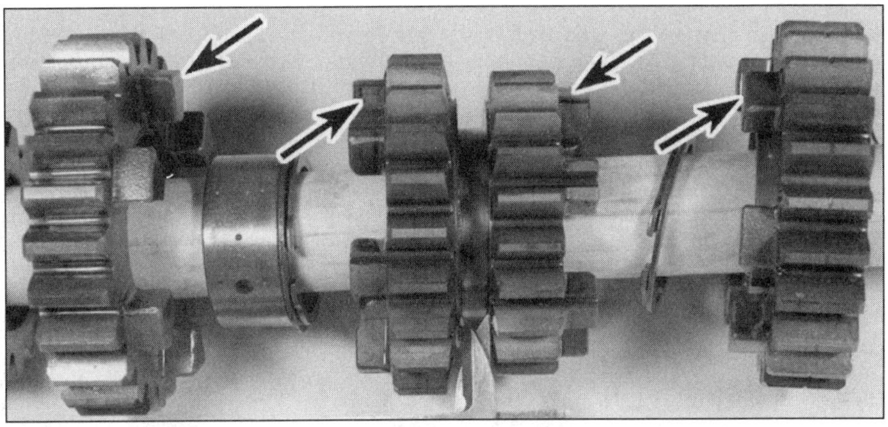

31.9 If the fork grooves are too wide, or if the dogs (arrowed) are worn, replace the gear

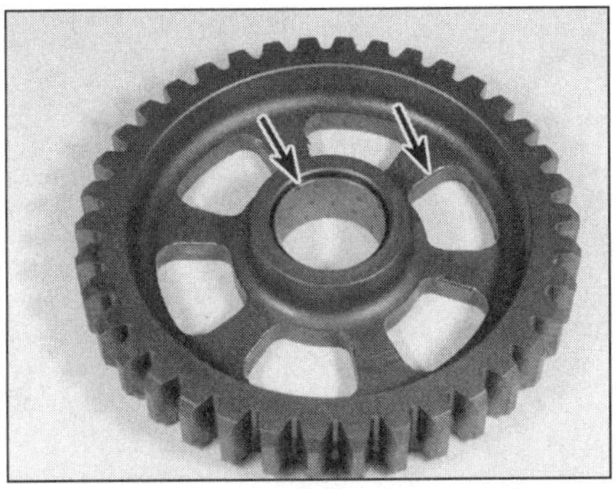

31.11 Replace the gear if the bushing is worn or the slot edges are rounded

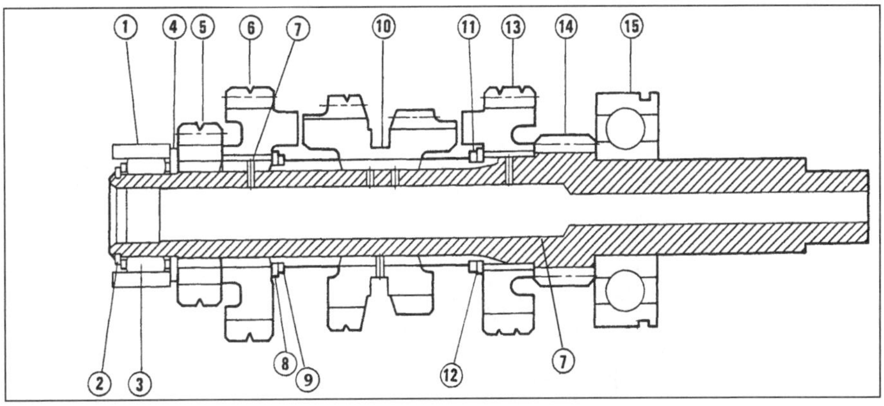

31.13a Input shaft assembly

1 Needle bearing outer race
2 Circlip
3 Needle bearing
4 Thrust washer
5 2nd gear
6 6th gear
7 Bushing
8 Toothed washer
9 Circlip
10 3rd/4th gear
11 Circlip
12 Toothed washer
13 5th gear
14 1st gear
15 Ball bearing

2

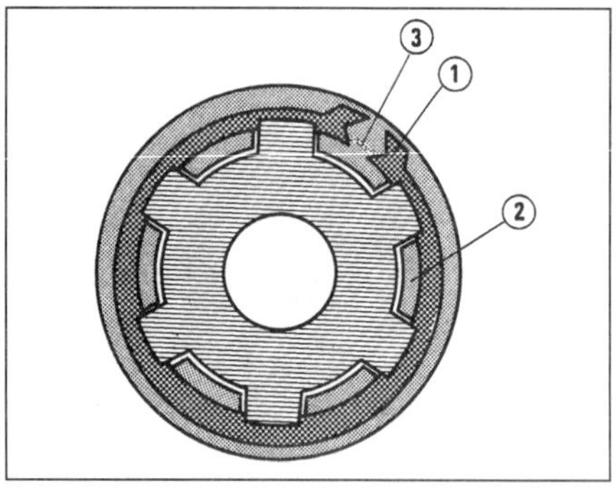

31.13b When installing circlips (1), align the opening (3) with a spline groove (2)

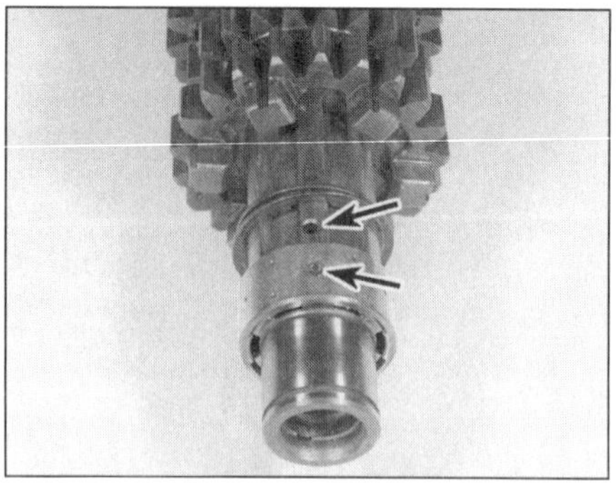
31.13c Be sure to align the bushing oil hole with the shaft oil hole (arrows)

31.14a Slide off the bearing outer race . . .

- Always use new circlips and align the opening of the ring with a spline groove **(see illustration)**.
- When installing the gear bushings on the shaft, align the oil hole in the shaft with the oil hole in the bushing **(see illustration)**.
- Lubricate the components with engine oil before assembling them.

Output shaft

Disassembly

14 Remove the needle bearing outer race, then remove the circlip from the end of the shaft and slide the needle bearing off **(see illustrations)**.

15 Remove the thrust washer and first gear from the shaft **(see illustration)**.

16 Remove fifth gear from the shaft. Fifth gear has three steel balls in it for the positive neutral finder mechanism. These lock fifth gear to the shaft unless it is spun rapidly enough to fling the balls outward. To remove fifth gear, grasp third gear and hold the shaft in a vertical position with one hand, and with the other hand, spin the shaft back and forth, holding onto fifth gear and pulling up **(see illustration)**; it may take several tries to disengage fifth gear from the shaft, but it will slide off easily once it is disengaged. After fifth gear is removed, collect the three steel balls **(see illustration)**.

Caution: Don't pull the gear up too hard or fast – the balls will fly out of the gear.

17 Remove the circlip, toothed washer, third

31.14b . . . and the bearing

31.15 Remove the thrust washer (arrowed) and 1st gear

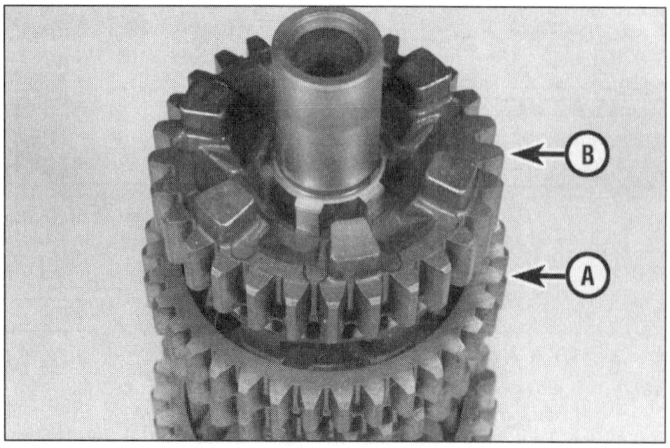

31.16a Hold 3rd gear (A) with one hand and spin the transmission shaft while lifting up on 5th gear (B)

31.16b These balls ride in slots in the shaft – they must be flung outwards by centrifugal force to remove 5th gear

31.17a Remove the circlip . . .

31.17b . . . the toothed washer . . .

31.17c . . . 3rd gear . . .

gear, bushing and fourth gear from the shaft **(see illustrations)**.

18 Remove the toothed washer, circlip and sixth gear **(see illustrations)**.

19 Remove the next circlip, toothed washer, second gear and its bushing **(see illustrations)**.

20 The ball bearing and collar can remain on the shaft unless new ones need to be fitted **(see illustration)**.

Inspection

21 Refer to Steps 8 through 12 for the inspection procedures. They are the same, except when checking the selector fork groove width you'll be checking it on fifth and sixth gears.

31.17d . . . its bushing, and 4th gear

31.18a Remove the toothed washer . . .

31.18b . . . the circlip . . .

31.18c . . . and 6th gear

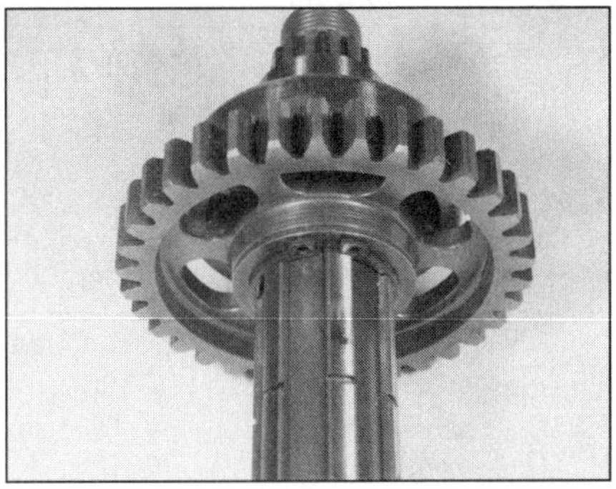

31.19a Remove the circlip . . .

31.19b . . . the toothed washer and 2nd gear . . .

31.19c . . . and its bushing

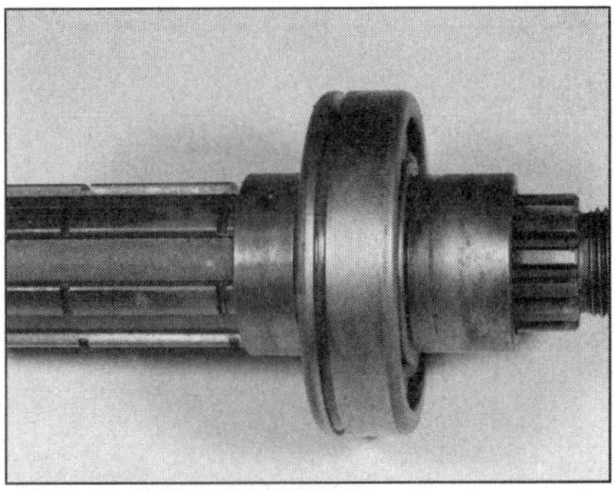

31.20 The bearing and collar can remain on the shaft unless they are worn or damaged

Reassembly

22 Reassembly is the basically the reverse of the disassembly procedure, but take note of the following points **(see illustration)**:

- Always use new circlips and align the opening of the ring with a spline groove **(see illustration 31.13b)**.
- When installing the bushing for third and fourth gear and second gear, align the oil hole in the bushing with the hole in the shaft.
- When installing fifth gear, don't use grease to hold the balls in place – to do so would impair the positive neutral finder mechanism. Just set the balls in their holes (the holes that they can't pass through), keep the gear in a vertical position and carefully set it on the shaft (engine oil will help keep them in place). The spline grooves that contain the holes with the balls must be aligned with the slots in the shaft spline grooves. Lubricate the components with engine oil before assembling them.

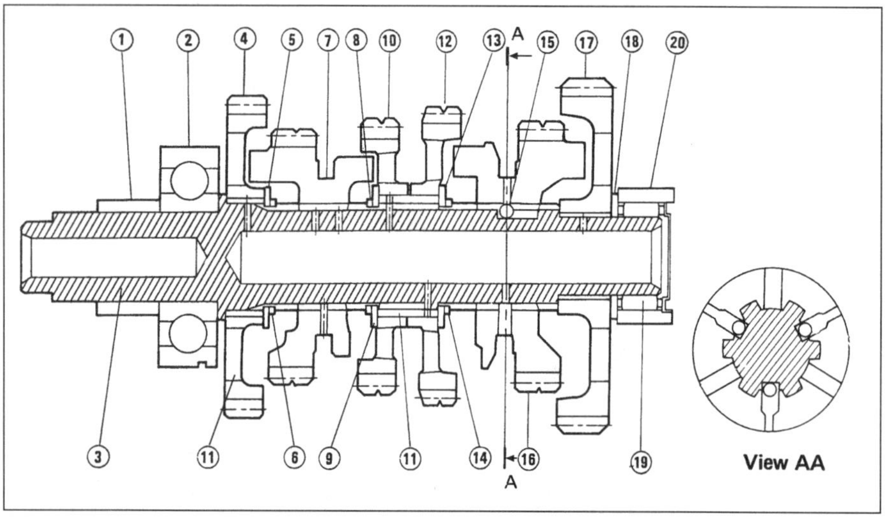

31.22 Output shaft assembly

1 *Collar*
2 *Ball bearing*
3 *Output shaft*
4 *2nd gear*
5 *Toothed washer*
6 *Circlip*
7 *6th gear*
8 *Circlip*
9 *Toothed washer*
10 *4th gear*
11 *Bushing*
12 *3rd gear*
13 *Toothed washer*
14 *Circlip*
15 *Steel ball*
16 *5th gear*
17 *1st gear*
18 *Thrust washer*
19 *Needle bearing*
20 *Needle bearing outer race*

32 Initial start-up after overhaul

1 Make sure the engine oil level and coolant level are correct (see *Daily (pre-ride) checks*). Turn the fuel tap to the 'OFF' position.

2 Pull the plug caps off the spark plugs and insert a spare spark plug into each cap. Position the spare plugs so that their bodies are earthed (grounded) against the engine. Turn on the ignition switch and crank the engine over with the starter until the oil pressure warning light goes off (which indicates that oil pressure exists). Turn off the ignition. Remove the spare spark plugs and reconnect the plug caps.

3 Make sure there is fuel in the tank, then turn the fuel tap to the 'ON' or 'RES' position as required, and set the choke.

4 Start the engine and allow it to run at a moderately fast idle until it reaches operating temperature.

Warning: If the oil pressure warning light doesn't go off, or it comes on while the engine is running, stop the engine immediately.

5 Check carefully for oil and coolant leaks and make sure the transmission and controls, especially the brakes, function properly before road testing the machine. Refer to Section 33 for the recommended running-in procedure.

6 Upon completion of the road test, and after the engine has cooled down completely, recheck the valve clearances (see Chapter 1) and check the engine oil and coolant levels (see *Daily (pre-ride) checks*).

33 Recommended break-in procedure

1 Any rebuilt engine needs time to break-in, even if parts have been installed in their original locations. For this reason, treat the machine gently for the first few miles to make sure oil has circulated throughout the engine and any new parts installed have started to seat.

2 Even greater care is necessary if the engine has been rebored or a new crankshaft has been installed. In the case of a rebore, the engine will have to be broken in as if the machine were new. This means greater use of the transmission and a restraining hand on the throttle (max. 4000 rpm) until at least 500 miles (800 km) have been covered. There's no point in keeping to any set speed limit – the main idea is to keep from lugging the engine and to gradually increase performance. Between 500 miles (800 km) and 1000 miles (1600 km) the same principles apply but the revs can be increased (max 6000 rpm). These recommendations can be lessened to an extent when only a new crankshaft is installed. Experience is the best guide, since it's easy to tell when an engine is running freely.

3 If a lubrication failure is suspected, stop the engine immediately and try to find the cause. If an engine is run without oil, even for a short period of time, irreparable damage will occur.

Chapter 3
Cooling system

Contents

Degrees of difficulty

Easy, suitable for novice with little experience	**Fairly easy,** suitable for beginner with some experience	**Fairly difficult,** suitable for competent DIY mechanic	**Difficult,** suitable for experienced DIY mechanic	**Very difficult,** suitable for expert DIY or professional

Specifications

General

Coolant type and mixture ratio	see Chapter 1
Radiator cap pressure rating	14 to 18 psi (0.95 to 1.25 bars)

Thermostatic fan switch rating

Rising temperature	
F, G and H models	from Off to On at 93 to 103°C (199 to 217°F)
J and A models	from Off to On at 96 to 100°C (204 to 212°F)
Falling temperature	from On to Off above 91°C (196°F)
Resistance	
On	less than 0.5 ohms
Off	more than 1 M-ohm

Coolant temperature sensor resistance

F models	
At 80°C (176°F)	47 to 57 ohms
At 100°C (212°F)	25 to 30 ohms
G, H, J and A models	
At 50°C (122°F)	9.18 to 9.94 K-ohms
At 80°C (176°F)	2.50 to 3.06 K-ohms
At 120°C (248°F)	0.65 to 0.73 K-ohms

Thermostat rating

F, G and H models	
Valve opening temperature	58 to 62°C (136 to 144°F)
Valve fully open at	95°C (203°F)
J and A models	
Models without catalytic converter	
Valve opening temperature	58 to 62°C (136 to 144°F)
Valve fully open at	75°C (167°F)
Models with catalytic converter	
Valve opening temperature	80 to 84°C (176 to 183°F)
Valve fully open at	95°C (203°F)
Valve travel (when fully open)	not less than 8 mm

3

Torque specifications

Coolant temperature sensor	7.8 Nm
Inlet hose union bolts	
F models	12 Nm
G, H, J and A models	11 Nm
Oil cooler bolt (G, H, J and A models)	78 Nm
Oil cooler hose banjo bolts (F models)	25 Nm
Thermostat cover bolts	
F models	7 Nm
G and H models	6 Nm
J and A models	9.8 Nm
Thermostatic fan switch	18 Nm
Water pump cover bolts	12 Nm
Water pump impeller bolt	
F, G and H models	10 Nm
J and A models	9.8 Nm

1 General information

The models covered by this manual are equipped with a liquid cooling system which utilises a water/antifreeze mixture to carry away excess heat produced during the combustion process. The cylinders are surrounded by water jackets, through which the coolant is circulated by the water pump. The pump is mounted on the left-hand side of the crankcase and is driven by a shaft from the oil pump. The coolant passes from the pump up through a flexible hose and around the four cylinders. The hot coolant then flows past the thermostat, which controls the flow according to engine temperature, and down into the radiator. The coolant is cooled by air passing through the radiator, which is mounted in front of the engine to take advantage of maximum air flow. The coolant then flows out of the radiator, through another hose and back to the water pump, where the cycle is repeated.

An electric fan, mounted behind the radiator and automatically controlled by a thermostatic switch, provides a flow of cooling air through the radiator when the motorcycle is not moving. Under certain conditions, the fan may come on even after the engine is stopped, and the ignition switch is off, and may run for several minutes.

The coolant temperature sensor, threaded into the cylinder head, senses the temperature of the coolant and controls the coolant temperature gauge on the instrument cluster.

The entire system is sealed and pressurised. The pressure is controlled by a valve which is part of the radiator cap. By pressurising the coolant, the boiling point is raised, which prevents premature boiling of the coolant. An overflow hose, connected between the radiator and reservoir tank, directs coolant to the tank when the radiator cap valve is opened by excessive pressure. The coolant is automatically siphoned back to the radiator as the engine cools.

Many cooling system inspection and service procedures are considered part of routine maintenance and are included in *Daily (pre-ride) checks* at the beginning of this Manual and in Chapter 1.

The coolant is also used to warm the carburettor bodies via an arrangement of small hoses. The coolant travels from the rear of the cylinder block, through a filter, through the carburettor castings and then rejoins the main cooling system at the water pump. A check valve is fitted to ensure the correct flow of coolant.

On F models the oil is cooled by routing it through an oil cooler radiator mounted below the main cooling system radiator. On all other models the oil is cooled by coolant which is distributed through a cooler unit mounted between the oil filter and crankcase.

Warning: Do not allow antifreeze to come in contact with your skin or painted surfaces of the vehicle. Rinse off spills immediately with plenty of water. Antifreeze is highly toxic if ingested. Never leave antifreeze lying around in an open container or in puddles on the floor; children and pets are attracted by it's sweet smell and may drink it. Check with local authorities about disposing of used antifreeze. Many communities have collection centres which will see that antifreeze is disposed of safely.

Warning: Do not remove the radiator cap when the engine and radiator are hot. Scalding hot coolant and steam may be blown out under pressure, which could cause serious injury. To open the radiator cap, remove the rear screw from the right side panel on the inside of the fairing (if equipped). When the engine has cooled, lift up the panel and place a thick rag, like a towel, over the radiator cap; slowly rotate the cap anti-clockwise to the first stop. This procedure allows any residual pressure to escape. When the steam has stopped escaping, press down on the cap while turning anti-clockwise and remove it.

2 Radiator cap - check

If problems such as overheating and loss of coolant occur, check the entire system as described in Chapter 1. The radiator cap opening pressure should be checked by a dealer service department or service station equipped with the special tester required to do the job. If the cap is defective, fit a new one.

3 Coolant reservoir - removal and installation

Removal

1 Remove the right-hand lower fairing panel (see Chapter 8).

2 Remove the reservoir cap, then position a suitable container below the reservoir. Detach the feed and return hose from the base of the reservoir and allow the coolant to drain **(see illustration)**. Disconnect the overflow hose from the top of the reservoir. It is a good idea to mark the positions of the hoses so they aren't attached to the wrong fitting when the reservoir is installed.

3 Remove the reservoir retaining screws,

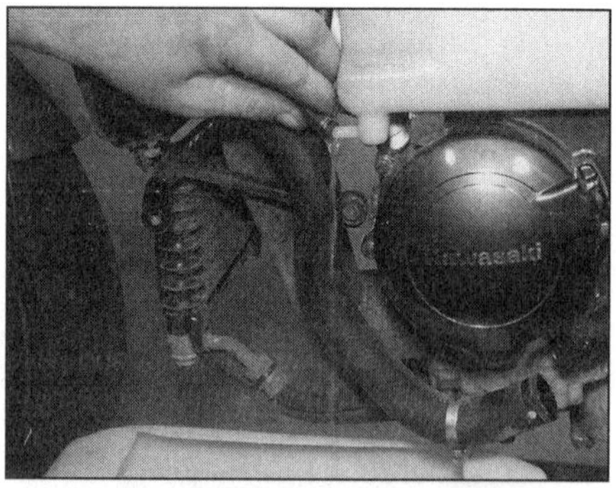

3.2 Detach the hose and allow the reservoir to drain

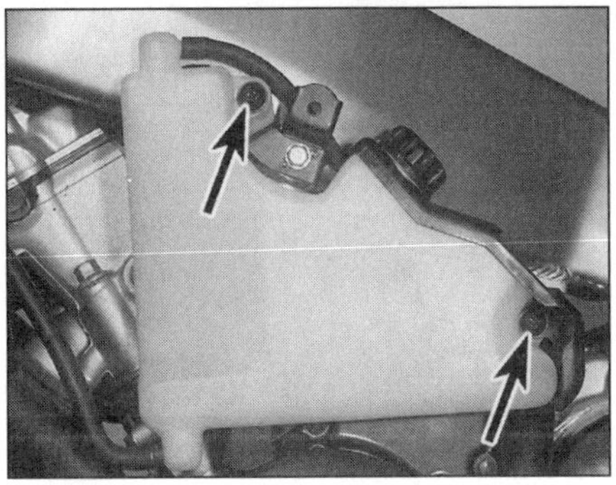

3.3a Remove the reservoir mounting screws (arrowed) . . .

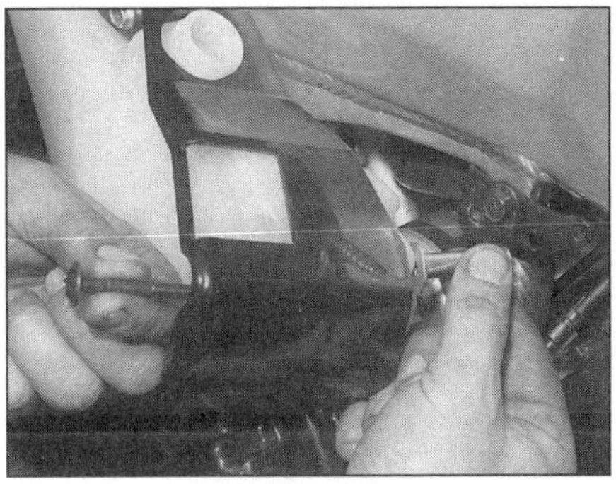

3.3b . . . noting how the cover and collar fit on F models . . .

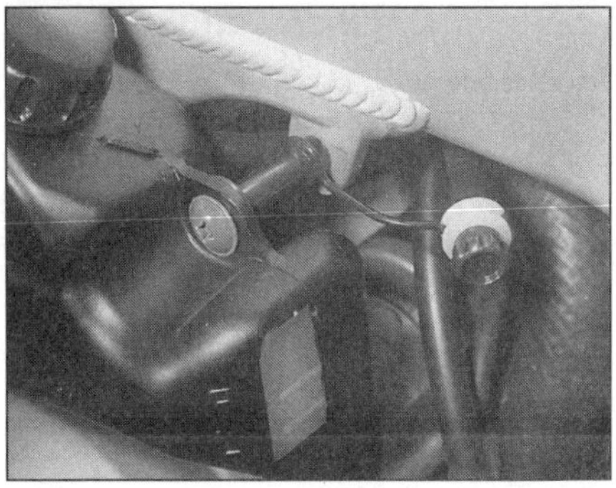

3.3c . . . and how the collar with the idle speed adjuster bracket fits on G, H, J and A models

noting how the spacer on the rear screw fits, and on F models how the cover fits, and detach the reservoir from the frame **(see illustrations)**.

Installation

4 Installation is the reverse of removal.

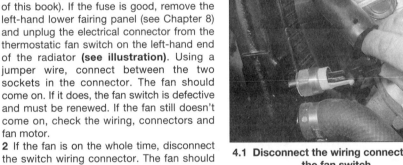

4 Cooling fan and thermostatic fan switch – check, removal and installation

Check

1 If the engine is overheating and the cooling fan isn't coming on, remove the seat and check the (10A) fan fuse (see Chapter 9). If the fuse is blown, check the fan circuit for a short to ground (see the *Wiring diagrams* at the end of this book). If the fuse is good, remove the left-hand lower fairing panel (see Chapter 8) and unplug the electrical connector from the thermostatic fan switch on the left-hand end of the radiator **(see illustration)**. Using a jumper wire, connect between the two sockets in the connector. The fan should come on. If it does, the fan switch is defective and must be renewed. If the fan still doesn't come on, check the wiring, connectors and fan motor.

2 If the fan is on the whole time, disconnect the switch wiring connector. The fan should stop. If it does, the switch is defective and must be renewed. If it doesn't, check the wiring between the switch and the fan.

3 To check the motor, on F, G and H models, remove the fuel tank and trace the wiring from the fan motor to its electrical connector, located behind the steering head **(see illustration)**. On J and A models, trace the wiring from the fan motor to its electrical connector behind the radiator **(see illustration)**. Unplug the connector and, using two jumper wires connected to the battery terminals, apply battery voltage to the fan side of the electrical connector. If the fan doesn't rotate, renew the fan motor. If it does rotate, the problem is either in the wiring, connectors or the thermostatic fan switch

4 If the fan works but is suspected of cutting in at the wrong temperature, a more comprehensive test of the switch can be made as follows.

5 Remove the switch (see Steps 10 to 13). Fill a small heatproof container with coolant and place it on a stove. Connect the positive (+ve) probe of an ohmmeter to the terminal of the switch and the negative (-ve) probe to the switch body, and using some wire or other support suspend the switch in the coolant so that just the sensing portion and the threads are submerged **(see illustration)**. Also place a thermometer capable of reading temperatures up to 110°C in the coolant so that its bulb is close to the switch. **Note:** *None of the components should be allowed to directly touch the container.*

6 Initially the ohmmeter reading should be very high indicating that the switch is open (OFF). Heat the coolant, stirring it gently.

Warning: This must be done very carefully to avoid the risk of personal injury.

When the temperature reaches around 93 to 103°C (F, G and H models) or 96 to 100°C (J and A models) the meter reading should drop to around zero ohms, indicating that the switch has closed (ON). Now turn the heat off. As the temperature falls to 91°C the meter reading should show infinite (very high) resistance, indicating that the switch has opened (OFF). If the meter readings obtained are different, or they are obtained at different temperatures, then the switch is faulty and must be renewed.

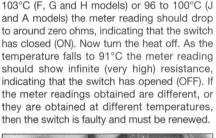

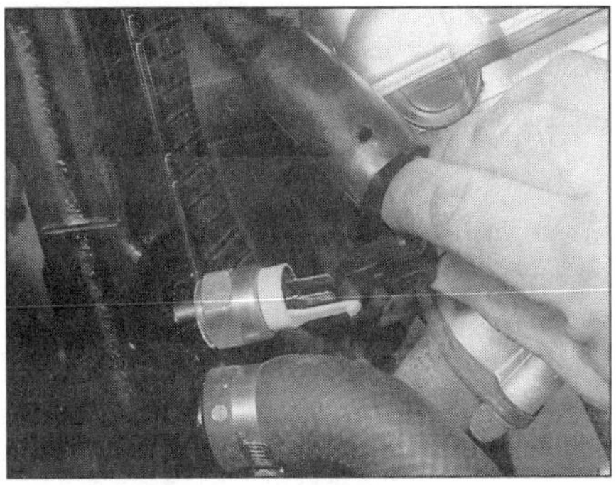

4.1 Disconnect the wiring connector from the fan switch

4.3a Fan motor wiring connector (arrowed) – F, G and H models

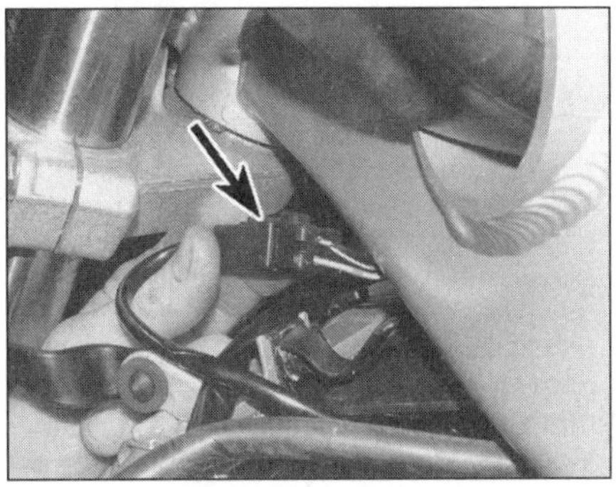

4.3b Fan motor wiring connector (arrowed) – J and A models

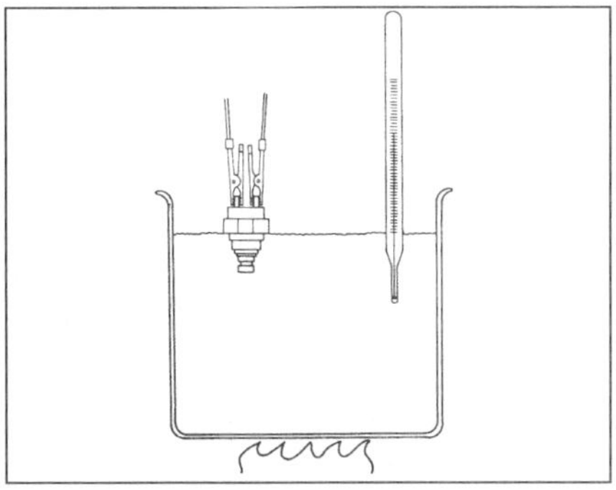

4.5 Connect an ohmmeter, heat the water and note the temperature at which the switch closes the circuit

Removal and installation

Fan motor

Warning: The engine must be completely cool before beginning this procedure.

7 Remove the radiator (see Section 7).

8 Remove the three bolts securing the fan assembly to the radiator and remove the assembly **(see illustration)**. The fan assembly comes as a unit for which individual components are not available. If the motor is faulty, the entire assembly must be renewed.

9 Installation is the reverse of the removal procedure.

Thermostatic fan switch

Warning: The engine must be completely cool before beginning this procedure.

10 Drain the cooling system (see Chapter 1).

11 Remove the left-hand lower fairing panel (see Chapter 8), and disconnect the wiring connectors from the fan switch on the left-hand end of the radiator **(see illustration 4.1)**. Unscrew the switch and withdraw it from the radiator.

12 Apply a suitable silicone sealant (Kawasaki-Bond 56019-120 or equivalent) to the switch threads, then install the switch and tighten it to the torque setting specified at the beginning of the Chapter. Take care not to overtighten the switch as the radiator could be damaged.

13 Reconnect the switch wiring and refill the cooling system (see Chapter 1).

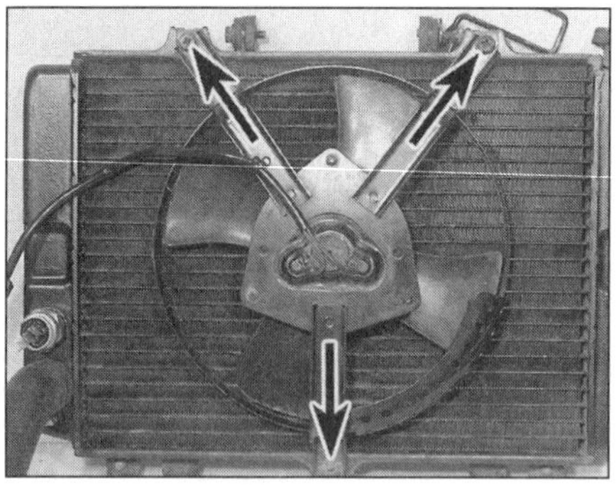

4.8 Fan assembly mounting bolts (arrowed) – F models shown

5 Coolant temperature sensor and gauge – check, removal and installation

Check

1 If the engine has been overheating but the coolant temperature gauge hasn't been indicating a hotter than normal condition, begin with a check of the coolant level (see *Daily (pre-ride) checks*). If it's low, add the recommended type of coolant and be sure to locate the source of the leak. Also check that the battery is fully charged and that the fuses are all good.

2 To check the gauge on F models, remove the fuel tank (see Chapter 4). Locate the coolant temperature sensor, which is screwed into the cylinder head **(see illustration)**. Disconnect the wire from the sensor and turn the ignition switch ON. The temperature gauge needle should be on the C on the gauge. Now earth the sensor wire on the engine. The needle should swing immediately over to the H on the gauge.

Caution: Don't earth the wire any longer than necessary or the gauge may be damaged.

3 To check the gauge on G and H models, a variable resistor with a zero to 25 K ohm range is needed. If this is not available, the gauge should be checked by a Kawasaki dealer. If the resistor is available, remove the instrument cluster (see Chapter 9). Using a 12 V battery, connect the battery positive terminal to the No. 1 terminal on the cluster wiring connector, and the battery negative terminal to the No. 2 terminal **(see illustration)**. Use a jumper wire to connect

5.2 Coolant temperature sensor (arrowed) – the wiring connector is a push fit

Resistance Value (Ω)	Display Segment
24400	1
9560	2
6180	3
2780	4
1340	5
950	6
810	7
690	8
less than 690	Warning light [A] and segments flash.

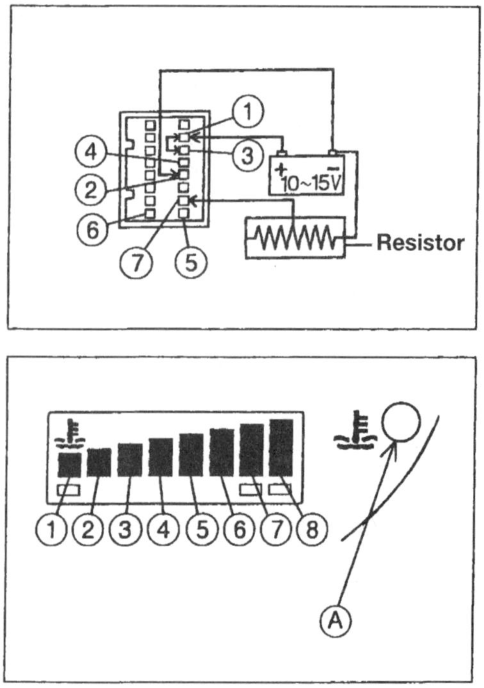

5.3 Temperature gauge test set-up – G and H models

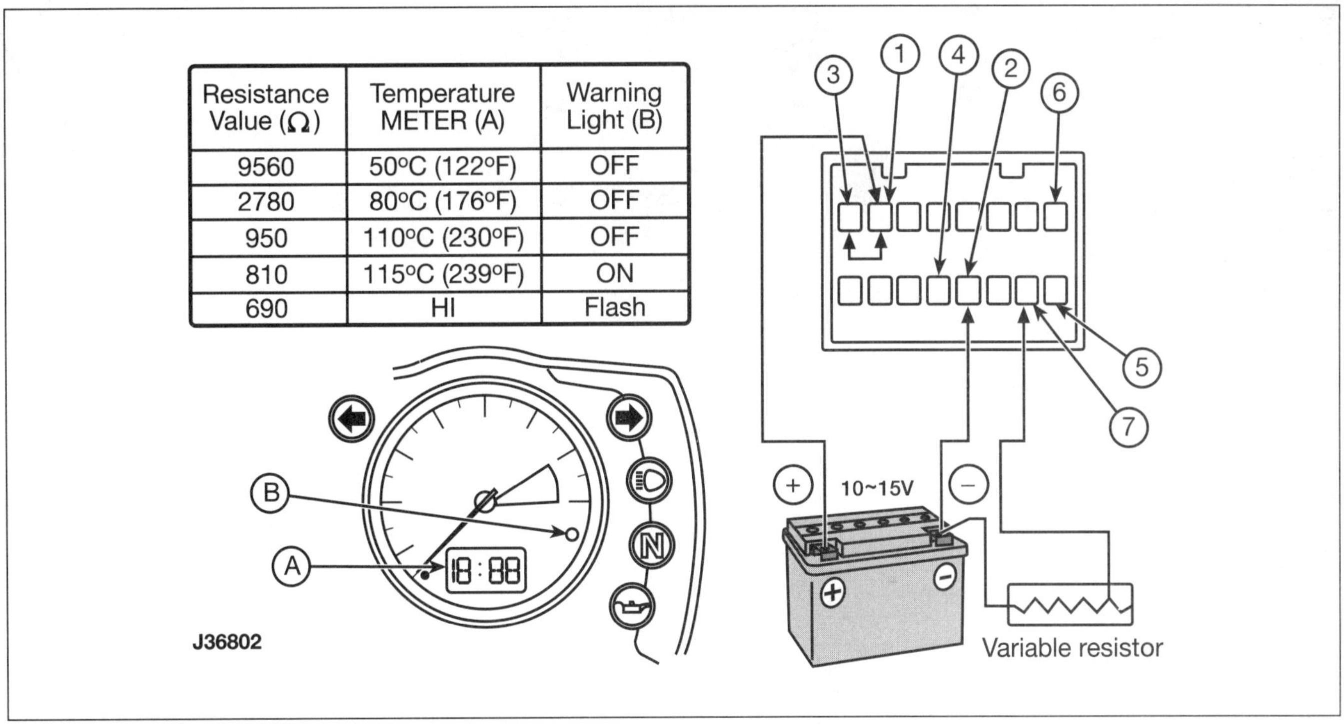

Resistance Value (Ω)	Temperature METER (A)	Warning Light (B)
9560	50°C (122°F)	OFF
2780	80°C (176°F)	OFF
950	110°C (230°F)	OFF
810	115°C (239°F)	ON
690	HI	Flash

5.4 Temperature gauge test set-up – J and A models

between the No 1 and No 3 terminals on the connector. Connect the resistor between the No. 7 terminal on the connector and the battery negative terminal. Starting with the resistor at the 25 K ohm setting, slowly reduce the resistance to zero. As the resistance drops, the display segments of the temperature gauge should illuminate at the appropriate values in the table. If the segments do not illuminate, or they do so at resistance values different to those specified, the gauge is faulty and must be renewed. **Note:** *The connector terminals on the instrument cluster are very closely spaced – take great care when connecting test wires to them.*

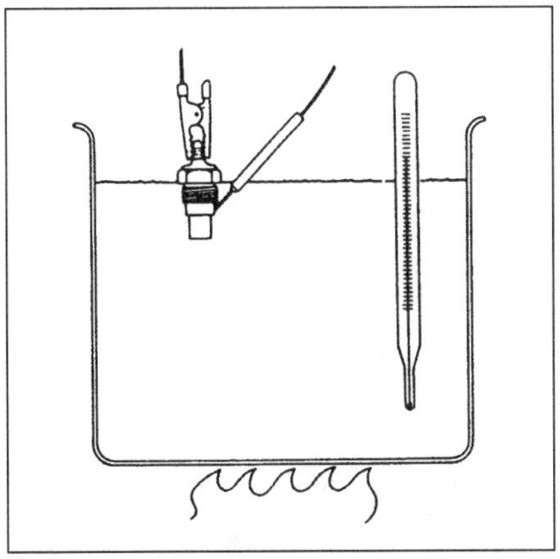

5.5 Suspend the sensing and threaded portion in the water and measure the resistance as the water heats up

4 To check the gauge on J and A models, first remove the instrument cluster and test the start-up and display button operations (see Chapter 9). If the test is good, check the operation of the gauge with a variable resistor with a zero to 96 K ohm range. If this is not available, the gauge should be checked by a Kawasaki dealer. If the resistor is available, connect the positive terminal of a 12 V battery to the No. 1 terminal on the cluster wiring connector, and the battery negative terminal to the No. 2 terminal **(see illustration)**. Use a jumper wire to connect between the Nos. 1 and 3 terminals. Connect the resistor between the No. 7 terminal and the battery negative terminal. Starting with the resistor at the 96 K ohm setting, slowly reduce the resistance to zero. As the resistance drops, the temperature gauge should display the corresponding temperatures shown in the table. If the temperatures are not displayed, or they are displayed at resistance values different to those specified, the gauge is faulty and must be renewed. **Note:** *The connector terminals on the instrument cluster are very closely spaced – take great care when connecting test wires to them.*

5 On all models, if the gauge passes these tests, but doesn't operate correctly under normal riding conditions, the temperature sensor is probably defective. Remove the sensor (see Steps 7 and 8 below). Fill a small heatproof container with coolant and place it on a stove. Using an ohmmeter, connect the positive (+ve) probe of the meter to the terminal on the sensor, and the negative (-ve) probe to the body of the sensor. Using some wire or other support suspend the sensor in the coolant so that just the sensing portion and the threads are submerged. Also place a thermometer capable of reading temperatures up to 120°C in the water so that its bulb is close to the sensor **(see illustration)**. **Note:** *None of the components should be allowed to directly touch the container.*

6 Heat the coolant, stirring it gently.

Warning: This must be done very carefully to avoid the risk of personal injury.

As the temperature of the coolant rises, compare the resistance readings on the ohmmeter at the temperatures specified at the beginning of the Chapter. If the meter readings obtained are different, or they are obtained at different temperatures, then the sensor is faulty and must be renewed.

7 If the sensor is proven good, the fault lies in the wiring or and intermittent fault in the gauge itself. Check all the relevant wiring and wiring connectors (see Chapter 9). If all appears to be well, have the gauge checked by a Kawasaki dealer.

Removal and installation

Coolant temperature sensor

Warning: The engine must be completely cool before beginning this procedure.

8 Drain the cooling system (see Chapter 1) and remove the fuel tank (see Chapter 4). The sensor is screwed into the back of the cylinder head **(see illustration 5.2)**. Disconnect the sensor wiring connector and unscrew the sensor.

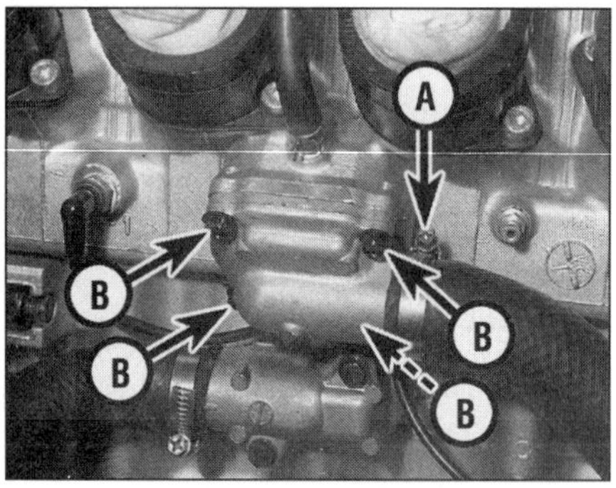

6.3a Slacken the clamp (A) and detach the hose if required, then unscrew the housing mounting bolts (B) . . .

9 Apply a smear of silicone sealant (Kawasaki Bond 56019-120 or equivalent) to the sensor threads, then install it into the cylinder head and tighten it to the torque setting specified at the beginning of the Chapter. Connect the sensor wiring.

10 Refill the cooling system (see Chapter 1) and install the fuel tank (see Chapter 4).

Coolant temperature gauge

11 The gauge can only be renewed as an individual item on F models; on all other models it is an integral part of the instrument cluster (see Chapter 9).

6 Thermostat – removal, check and installation

Removal

Warning: The engine must be completely cool before carrying out this procedure.

1 The thermostat is automatic in operation and should give many years service without requiring attention. In the event of a failure, the valve will probably jam open, in which case the engine will take much longer than normal to warm up. Conversely, if the valve jams shut, the coolant will be unable to circulate and the engine will overheat. Neither condition is acceptable, and the fault must be investigated promptly.

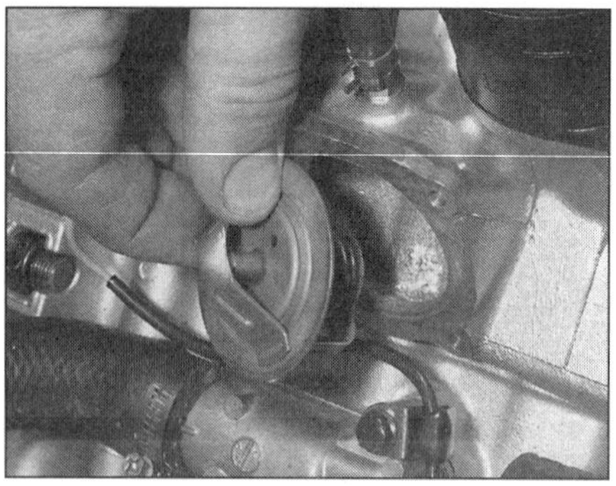

6.3b . . . and remove the thermostat

2 Drain the cooling system (see Chapter 1) and remove the fuel tank (see Chapter 4).

3 The thermostat is located in the thermostat housing on the back of the cylinder head. Slacken the hose clamp and detach the hose from the housing if required, then unscrew the four bolts securing the cover and separate it from the housing **(see illustration)**. Withdraw the thermostat, noting how it fits **(see illustration)**. Discard the cover O-ring as a new one must be used.

Check

4 Examine the thermostat visually before carrying out the test. If it remains in the open position at room temperature, it should be renewed.

5 Suspend the thermostat by a piece of wire in a container of cold water. Place a thermometer in the water so that the bulb is close to the thermostat **(see illustration)**. Heat the water, noting the temperature when the thermostat opens, and compare the result with the specifications given at the beginning of the Chapter. Also check the amount the valve opens after it has been heated at the specified fully open temperature for a few minutes and compare the measurement to the specifications. If the readings obtained differ from those given, the thermostat is faulty and must be renewed.

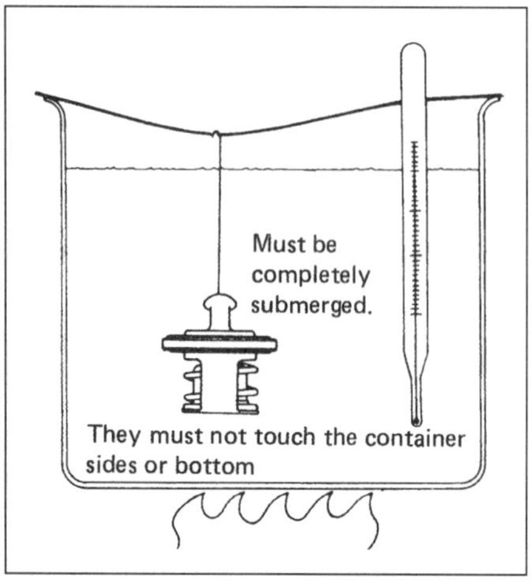

6.5 Submerge the thermostat in water and gradually heat the water

6 In the event of thermostat failure, as an emergency measure only, it can be removed and the machine used without it. **Note:** *Take care when starting the engine from cold as it will take much longer than usual to warm up.* Ensure that a new unit is installed as soon as possible.

Installation

7 Fit the thermostat into the housing, making sure that it seats correctly and that the hole is at the top **(see illustration 6.3b)**.

8 Fit a new O-ring onto the cover, using a dab of grease to keep it in place if required **(see illustration)**. Fit the cover onto the housing, then install the bolts and tighten them to the torque setting specified at the beginning of the Chapter **(see illustration)**. If detached, fit the hose onto its union and tighten the clamp **(see illustration 6.3a)**.

9 Refill the cooling system (see Chapter 1) and install the fuel tank (see Chapter 4).

7 Radiator – removal, inspection and installation

Removal

Warning: The engine must be completely cool before beginning this procedure.

1 Disconnect the battery negative lead (see Chapter 9).

2 Remove the upper and lower fairings (see Chapter 8).

3 Drain the coolant (see Chapter 1).

4 On F, G and H models, remove the air filter housing (see Chapter 4). Follow the wiring from the fan motor to the electrical connector, then unplug the connector **(see illustration 4.3a)**. On J and A models, trace the wiring from the fan motor and disconnect it at the connector **(see illustration 4.3b)**. On all models, disconnect the wiring connector from the fan switch in the radiator **(see illustration 4.1)**.

5 Loosen the hose clamps on both large-bore radiator hoses (one at the lower left corner and one at the upper right corner of the radiator) and detach the hoses (it may be

6.8a Fit a new O-ring into the cover . . .

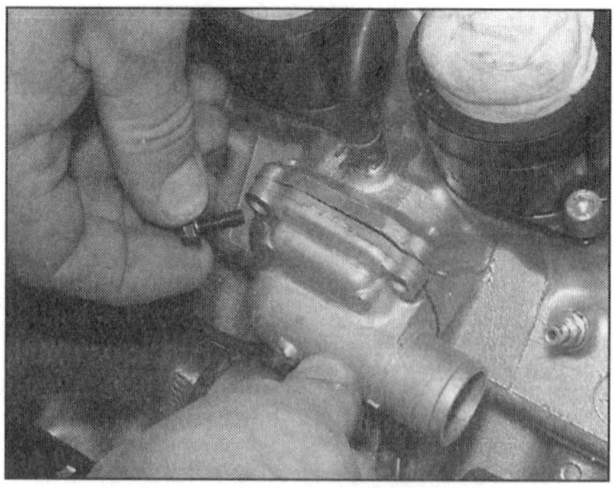

6.8b . . . and install the cover

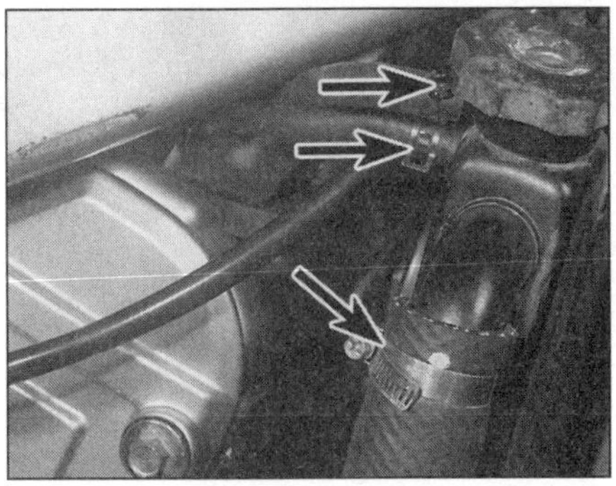

7.5a Radiator hose connections (arrowed) on right side . . .

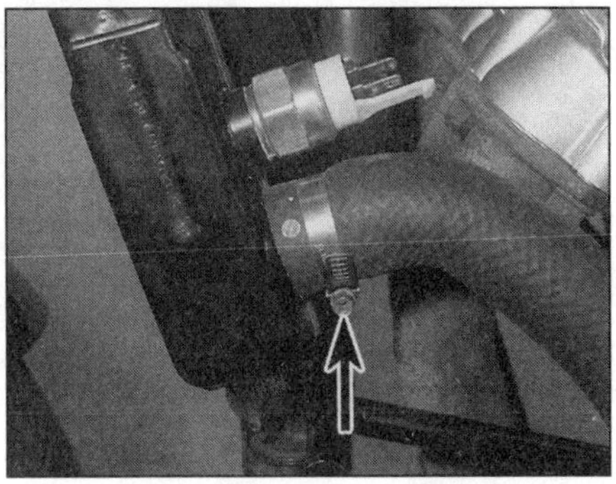

7.5b . . . and left side (arrowed) . . .

7.5c . . . plus this small-bore hose on G, H J and A models

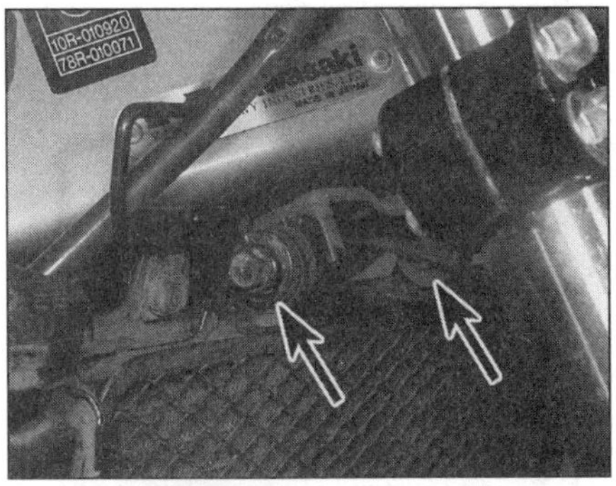

7.6a Radiator upper mounting bolts (arrowed) . . .

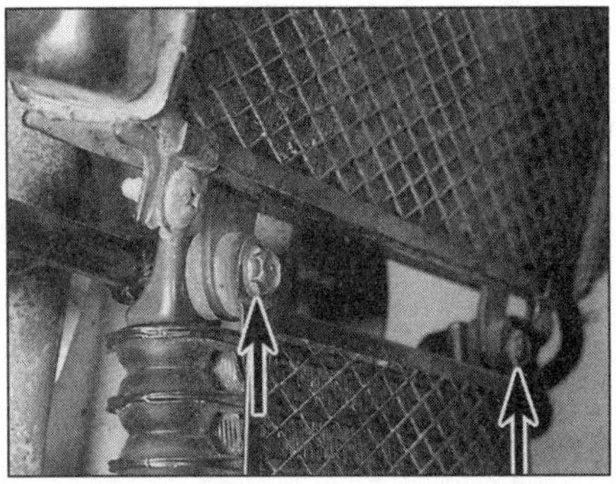

7.6b . . . and lower mounting bolts (arrowed) – F models

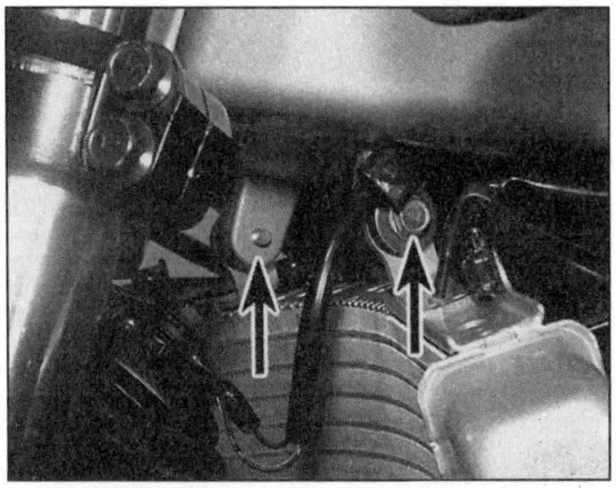

7.6c Radiator upper mounting bolts (arrowed) . . .

easier to detach the left side hose at the water pump, instead of the radiator). Also disconnect the two small-bore hoses from the radiator filler neck, noting which fits where, and on G, H, J and A models, the small-bore hose from the right-hand side of the radiator **(see illustrations)**.

6 Unscrew the radiator mounting bolts, noting any cable or wiring guides or clamps, and remove the radiator, noting how it fits **(see illustrations)**.

Inspection

7 If the radiator is to be repaired or renewed, remove the cooling fan (see Section 4).

8 Carefully examine the radiator for evidence of leaks and damage. It is recommended that any necessary repairs be performed by a professional.

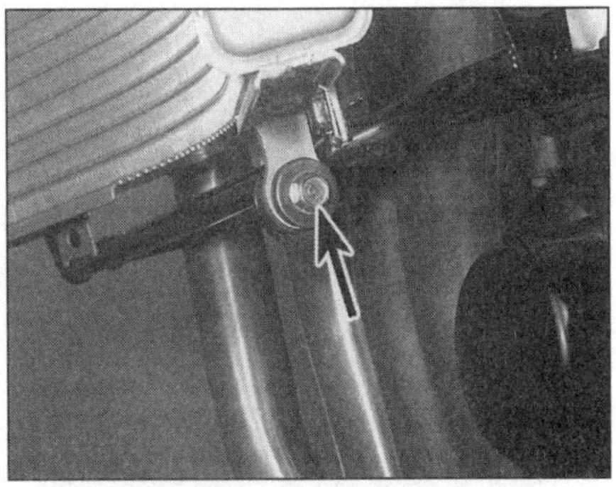

7.6d . . . and lower mounting bolt (arrowed) – G, H, J and A models

9 If the radiator is clogged, or if large amounts of rust or scale have formed, it can be flushed through using a proprietary flushing compound.

10 Make sure the spaces between the cooling tubes and fins are clear. If necessary, use compressed air or running water to remove anything that may be clogging them. If the radiator fins are bent or flattened, straighten them very carefully with a small screwdriver.

Installation

11 Installation is the reverse of the removal procedure. Check the condition of the rubber mounting grommets and renew them if they are damaged or deteriorated. Be sure to renew the hoses if they are deteriorated, and make sure they are securely and correctly connected. Of the two small-bore hoses attached to the radiator filler neck, the hose from the coolant reservoir attaches to the upper union, and the hose from the bleed valve on the rear of the cylinder head attaches to the lower union.

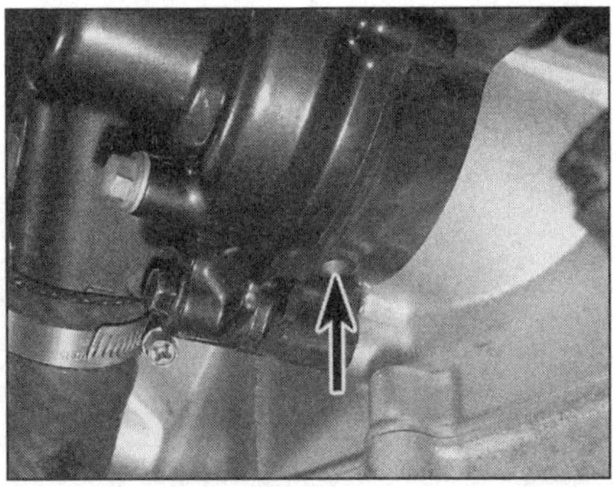

8.2 Check the drainage hole (arrowed) for leakage

12 Refill the cooling system with the recommended coolant (see Chapter 1).

8 Water pump – check, removal and installation

Check

1 Visually check around the area of the water pump for coolant leaks. Try to determine if the leak is simply the result of a loose hose clamp or deteriorated hose.

2 To prevent leakage of water from the cooling system to the lubrication system and vice versa, two seals are fitted on the pump shaft. On the underside of the pump body there is also a drainage hole **(see illustration)**. If either seal fails, this hole should allow the coolant or oil to escape and prevent the oil and coolant mixing.

3 If there is any leakage from the drainage hole, both seals must be renewed. The seal on the water pump side is of the mechanical type which bears on the rear face of the impeller. The second seal, which is mounted behind the mechanical seal is of the normal feathered lip type.

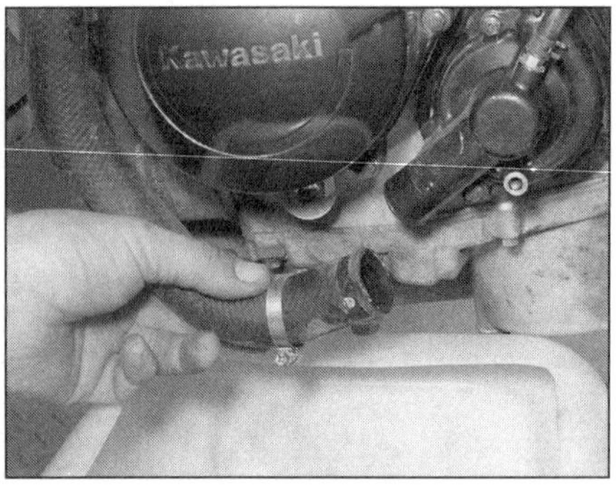

8.5 Slacken or release the clamps and detach the hoses from the cover

8.6 Unscrew the bolts (arrowed) and remove the cover

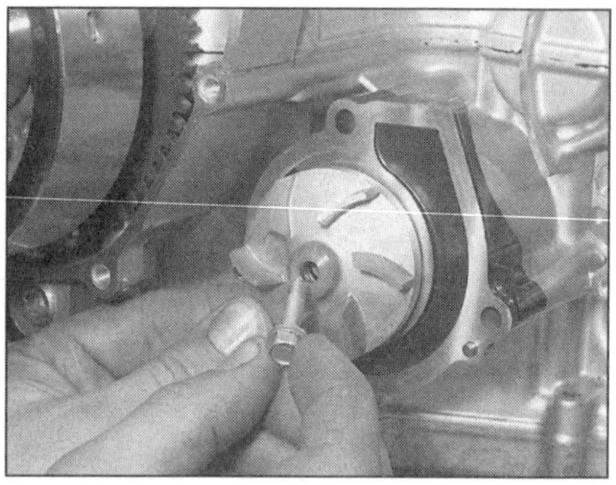
8.7 Unscrew the bolt and remove the impeller

Removal

Warning: The engine must be completely cool before beginning this procedure.

4 Remove the fairing left-hand lower panel (see Chapter 8). Drain the engine oil and the coolant (see Chapter 1).

5 Loosen the hose clamps and detach the hoses from the water pump cover **(see illustration)**.

6 Remove the cover bolts, noting the wiring clamp, and separate the cover from the water pump body **(see illustration)**. Discard the O-ring as a new one must be fitted.

7 Hold the impeller to prevent it from turning, then unscrew the bolt and remove the impeller **(see illustration)**.

8 Keeping a finger pressed onto the end of the pump drive shaft to prevent withdrawing the oil pump as well, remove the pump seal housing **(see illustration)**. Discard the O-ring on the back of the housing and discard it as a new one must be used.

9 If required, remove the seals from the housing, noting how they fit, and renew them.

10 Check the impeller blades for corrosion. If they are heavily corroded, fit a new impeller and flush the system thoroughly (it would also be a good idea to check the internal condition of the radiator).

Installation

11 Fit a new O-ring onto the back of the seal housing, then fit the housing over the shaft and locate it onto the dowels in the crankcase **(see illustration)**.

12 Fit the impeller onto the shaft, then install the bolt with its washer and tighten it to the torque setting specified at the beginning of the Chapter **(see illustrations)**. Hold the impeller to prevent it from turning.

13 Fit a new O-ring into the cover, then locate the cover onto the pins in the seal housing **(see illustrations)**. Apply a suitable non-permanent thread locking compound to the cover bolts and tighten them to the specified torque.

14 Attach the hoses to the pump cover and secure them with their clamps **(see illustration 8.5)**.

15 Install the fairing left-hand lower panel

8.8 Remove the seal housing, noting how it locates on the dowels

8.11 Fit the new O-ring into the groove in the back of the housing

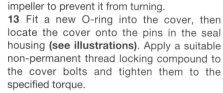

8.12a Fit the impeller onto the shaft . . .

8.12b . . . and tighten the bolt to the specified torque

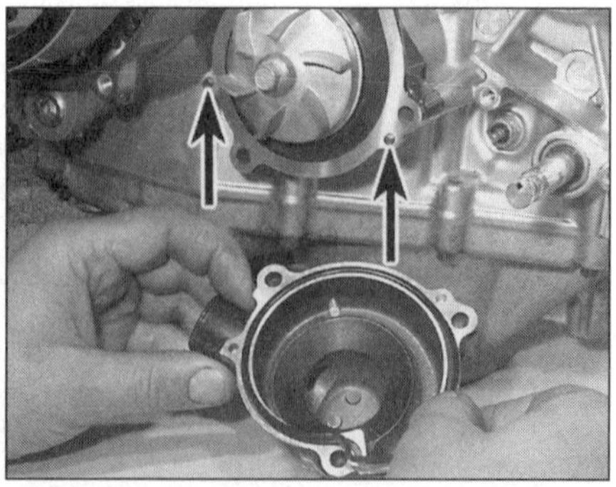
8.13a Fit the new O-ring into the groove in the cover. Note the two locating pins (arrowed) . . .

8.13b . . . and fit the cover onto them

(see Chapter 8). Fill the engine with the recommended type and amount of oil and coolant (see Chapter 1).

9 Coolant hoses – removal and installation

Warning: The engine must be completely cool before beginning this procedure.

Removal

1 Before removing a hose, drain the coolant (see Chapter 1).

2 Use a screwdriver to slacken the larger-bore hose clamps, then slide them back along the hose and clear of the union spigot **(see illustrations 7.5a and 8.5)**. The small-bore hoses are secured by spring clamps which can be expanded by squeezing their ears together with pliers.

Caution: The radiator unions are fragile. Do not use excessive force when attempting to remove the hoses.

3 If a hose proves stubborn, release it by rotating it on its union before working it off. If all else fails, cut the hose with a sharp knife then slit it at each union so that it can be peeled off in two pieces. Whilst this means replacing the hose, it is preferable to buying a new radiator (see the section on freeing and fitting hoses in *Tools and Workshop Tips* at the end of this manual).

4 The water pipe inlet union on the cylinder block can be removed by unscrewing the retaining bolts **(see illustration)**. If it is removed, the O-ring must be renewed.

Installation

5 Slide the clips onto the hose and then work the hose onto its respective union.

HAYNES HiNT ***If the hose is difficult to push on its union, it can be softened by soaking it in very hot water, or alternatively a little soapy water can be used as a lubricant.***

9.4 The inlet union on the cylinder block is secured by two bolts (arrowed)

6 Rotate the hose on its unions to settle it in position before sliding the clamps into place and tightening them securely.

7 If the inlet union on the cylinder block has been removed, fit a new O-ring, then install the union and tighten the mounting bolts to the torque setting specified at the beginning of the Chapter.

10 Oil cooler – removal and installation

Note: *Wait until the engine is cool before beginning this procedure.*

F models

1 Drain the engine oil (see Chapter 1).

2 Remove the fairing lower panels (see Chapter 8).

3 The cooler can be removed either with or without its hoses, though due to the flexible mountings of the cooler it is better to remove it with the hoses to prevent straining the mountings if the hose banjo bolts are unscrewed from the cooler. Place a drain pan under the engine and unscrew the banjo bolts from the engine, noting their alignment and which hose fits on which union **(see illustration)**. Discard the sealing washers as new ones must be used.

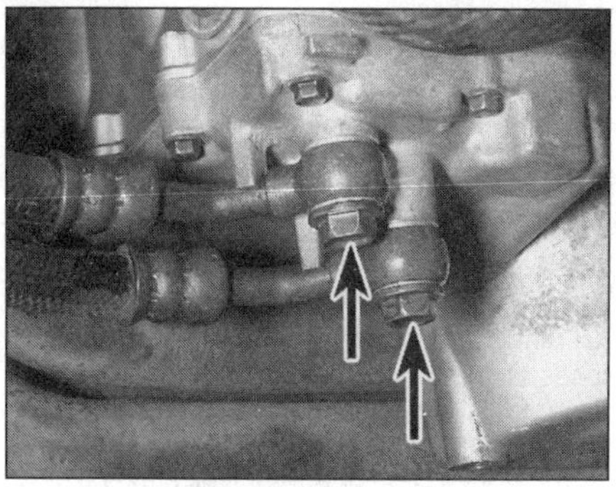

10.3 Oil cooler hose unions with crankcase (arrowed)

4 Remove the oil cooler mounting bolts and remove the cooler **(see illustration)**.

5 Remove the two screws retaining the stone guard to the cooler and detach the guard to enable access for cleaning and examination. Carefully examine the cooler for evidence of leaks and damage. It is recommended that any necessary repairs be performed by a reputable engineer.

6 Make sure the spaces between the cooling tubes and fins are clear. If necessary, use compressed air or running water to remove anything that may be clogging them, taking care not to damage any of the fins.

HAYNES HiNT ***If the radiator fins are bent or flattened, straighten them very carefully with a small screwdriver.***

7 Inspect both oil cooler hoses for cracks and tears. If either hose is damaged or otherwise deteriorated, fit a new one. To detach the hoses from the cooler, unscrew the banjo bolts and remove the hoses, noting their alignment. Discard the sealing washers as new ones must be used.

8 Installation of the oil cooler is the reverse of removal. Check the condition of the cooler rubber mounting grommets and renew them if they are damaged or deteriorated. Be sure to use new sealing washers on each side of the hose union connections **(see illustration)**.

3

10.4 Oil cooler mounting bolts (arrowed)

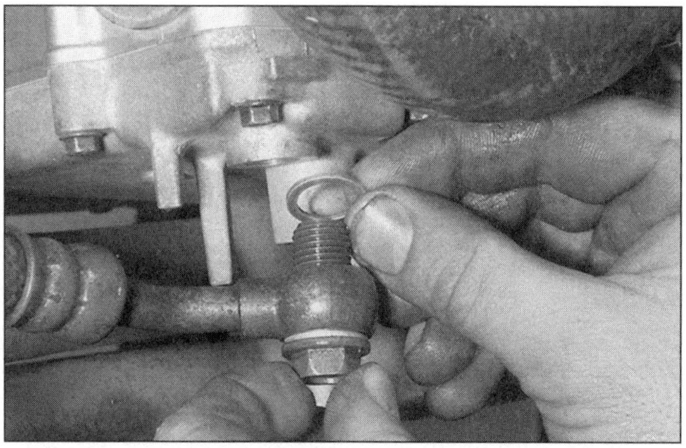

10.8 Fit a new sealing washer on each side of the unions

Tighten the banjo bolts to the torque listed in this Chapter's Specifications. Fill the crankcase with the recommended type and amount of oil (see Chapter 1).

G, H, J and A models

9 Drain the engine oil and remove the oil filter (see Chapter 1). Also drain the coolant (see Chapter 1).

10 Slacken the clamps securing the coolant hoses to the oil cooler and detach the hoses, noting which fits where **(see illustration)**.

11 The cooler is secured to the crankcase by a large bolt, the outer end of which the oil filter threads onto. Using the large hex at the base of the filter threads, unscrew the bolt and remove the cooler, noting how it fits.

12 Remove the O-ring from the cooler and discard it as a new one must be used.

13 Check that the coolant passage is not clogged by flushing the cooler with water. If it appears clogged, use a flushing agent. If this does not clear it, the cooler must be renewed.

10.10 Slacken the clamps (arrowed) and detach the hoses

14 Smear some grease onto the new cooler O-ring and fit it onto the cooler. Install the cooler, aligning the slotted bracket on the outside of the cooler with the notch in the crankcase, then install the bolt and tighten it to the torque setting specified at the beginning of the Chapter **(see illustration)**.

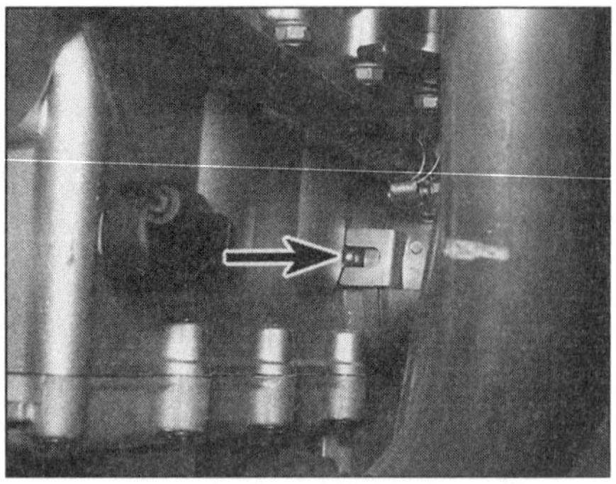

10.14 Make sure the slotted bracket on the cooler fits over the notch on the crankcase (arrowed)

15 Fit a new oil filter, then fill the engine with the recommended type and amount of oil (see Chapter 1). Also fill the cooling system with the correct coolant (see Chapter 1).

Chapter 4
Fuel and exhaust systems

Contents

Degrees of difficulty

Easy, suitable for novice with little experience	**Fairly easy,** suitable for beginner with some experience	**Fairly difficult,** suitable for competent DIY mechanic	**Difficult,** suitable for experienced DIY mechanic	**Very difficult,** suitable for expert DIY or professional

Specifications

General

Carburettor type	
F models	Keihin CVK-D36
G, H and J models	Mikuni BDSR 36R
A models	Mikuni BDSR 37

Fuel pump

Fuel pump cut-off pressure	1.6 to 2.3 psi (0.11 to 0.16 bars)
Fuel pump relay internal resistance	see text
Fuel cut-off valve protrusion (California and H models)	
Battery connected	18.6 to 19.1 mm
Battery disconnected	16.6 mm

Jet sizes – F models

Main jet	
Cylinders 1 and 4	145
Cylinders 2 and 3	150
Main air jet	60
Jet needle	N1VV
Pilot jet	35
Pilot air jet	100
Starter jet	50

Jet sizes – G and H models

Main jet	
Cylinders 1 and 4	137.5
Cylinders 2 and 3	140
Main air jet	
Cylinders 1 and 4	70
Cylinders 2 and 3	45
Jet needle	
UK models	
Cylinders 1 and 4	5EI1
Cylinders 2 and 3	5EI2
US models	5EI6-55
Pilot jet	12.5
Pilot air jet	120
Starter jet	35

Jet sizes – J models

Main jet	
Cylinders 1 and 4	155
Cylinders 2 and 3	157.5
Main air jet	45
Jet needle	
UK models	
Cylinders 1 and 4	5E18-3
Cylinders 2 and 3	5E19-3
US models	5E110-54-1
Pilot jet	12.5
Pilot air jet	125
Starter jet	35

Jet sizes – A models

Main jet	157.5
Main air jet	50
Jet needle	5E112-3
Pilot jet	12.5
Pilot air jet	125
Starter jet	35

Carburettor adjustments

Float height	
F models	15 to 19 mm
G, H, J and A models	5 to 9 mm
Fuel level	
F models	8 to 10 mm below the level mark
G and H models	21.2 to 23.2 mm below the level mark
J and A models	19.2 to 21.2 mm below the level mark
Pilot screw (turns out)	
F models	
UK models	2
US models	n/a
G, H and J models	3
A models	2¼
Carburettor synchronisation	see Chapter 1
Throttle and choke cable freeplay	see Chapter 1

Torque specifications

Exhaust system nuts and bolts	
Downpipe assembly to sump	34 Nm
Silencer to downpipe assembly	
F, G and H models	34 Nm
J and A models	45 Nm
Silencer to footrest bracket	
F, G and H models	34 Nm
J and A models	45 Nm
Fuel tap mounting bolts (G, H, J and A models)	2.5 Nm

1 General information

The fuel system consists of the fuel tank, fuel tap, fuel pump, filters, carburettors and the connecting hoses and control cables. The carburettors used are four constant vacuum Keihin (F models) or Mikuni (G, H, J and A models) with butterfly-type throttle valves. For cold starting, an enrichment circuit is actuated by a cable from the choke lever mounted on the left handlebar.

The exhaust system is a four-into-one design. An open-loop catalytic converter is fitted in the exhaust system of California market G models, H models for Germany and Switzerland, and all J and A models except for the Australian market. The catalytic converters are protected from the intake of excess unburnt fuel by the carburettor-mounted fuel cut-off valves.

Many of the fuel system service procedures are considered routine maintenance items and for that reason are included in Chapter 1.

Warning: Gasoline (petrol) is extremely flammable, so take extra precautions when you work on any part of the fuel system. Don't smoke or allow open flames or bare light bulbs near the work area, and don't work in a garage where a natural gas-type appliance (such as a water heater or clothes dryer) with a pilot light is present. Since gasoline is carcinogenic, wear latex gloves when there's a possibility of being exposed to fuel, and, if you spill any fuel on your skin, rinse it off immediately with soap and water. Mop up any fuel spills immediately and do not store fuel-soaked rags where they could ignite. When you perform any kind of work on the fuel system, wear safety glasses and have a fire extinguisher suitable for a class B type fire (flammable liquids) on hand.

2 Fuel tank and tap – removal, cleaning, repair and installation

Warning: Refer to the warning in Section 1 concerning contact with fuel.

Removal

1 Turn the fuel tap to the OFF position

2 Remove the seats (see Chapter 8).

3 On California models, mark and disconnect the evaporative emission hoses.

4 On F models, remove the two screws securing the tap to the bracket and detach the tap **(see illustration)**. Release the clamp securing the fuel hose to the union on the side of the fuel tap and detach the hose **(see illustration)**.

5 On G, H, J and A models, remove the screw from the centre of the fuel tap knob using a small Phillips screwdriver, then detach the knob from the tap **(see illustration)**. Release the clamp securing the fuel hose to the union on the side of the fuel tap and detach the hose **(see illustration)**.

6 On F models, remove the front screw from each side panel **(see illustration 2.7a)**, then carefully pull the front of each panel away from the tank until the peg is released from the rubber grommet (see Chapter 8).

7 Remove the two bolts that secure the rear of the tank, noting the earth lead secured by the left-hand bolt on F models, and remove the bolts along with the bracket, noting how it fits **(see illustrations)**. On G, H, J and A models, release the clip securing the breather/drain hose at the back of the tank and detach the hose.

8 Remove the two bolts that attach the front of the tank to the frame **(see illustration)**.

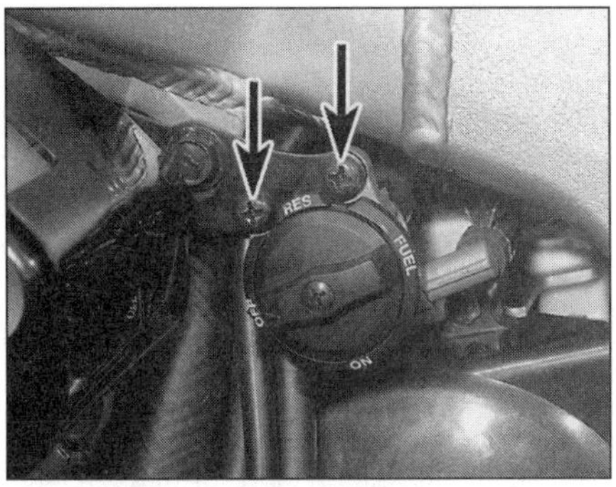

2.4a On F models, remove the screws (arrowed) and detach the tap . . .

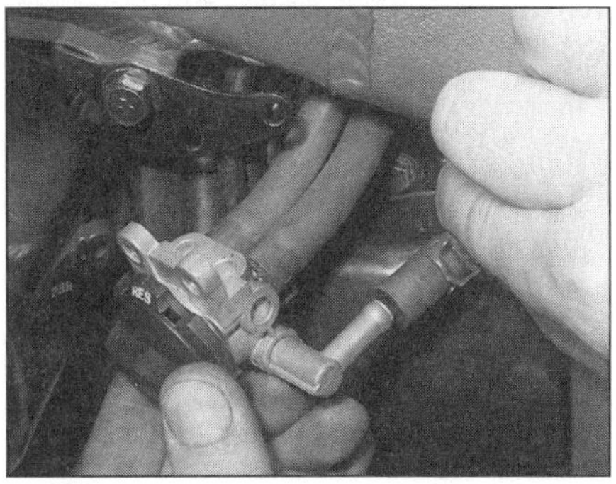
2.4b . . . then release the clamp and pull the hose off its union

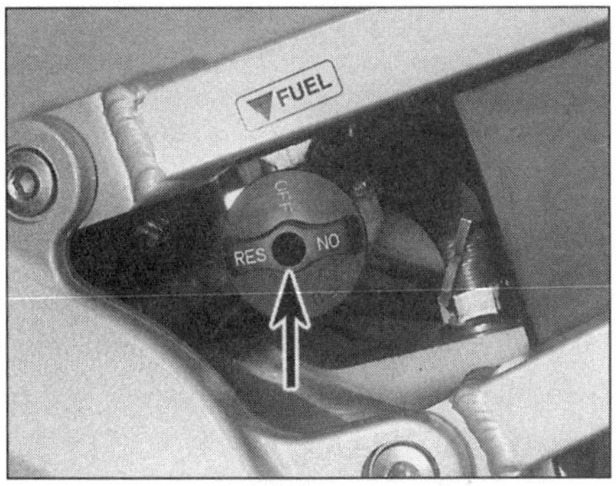

2.5a Remove the screw from the centre of the knob (arrowed) and pull off the knob . . .

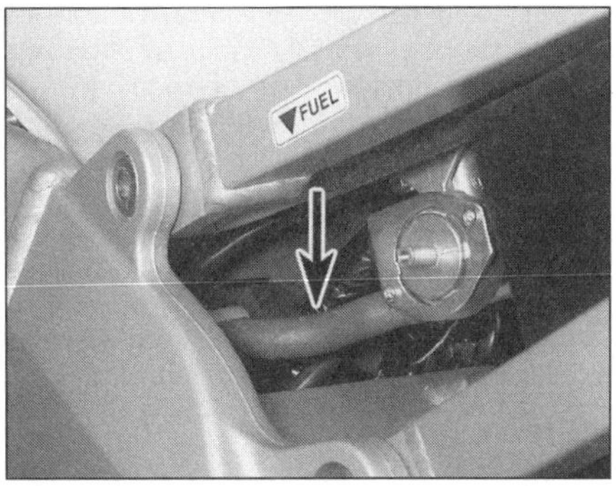

2.5b . . . then release the clamp and pull the hose (arrowed) off the union – G, H, J and A models

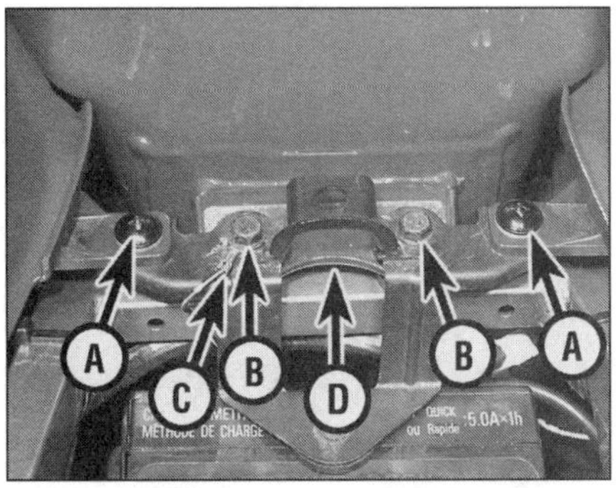

2.7a Side panel screws (A), fuel tank bolts (B), earth lead (C), bracket (D) – F models

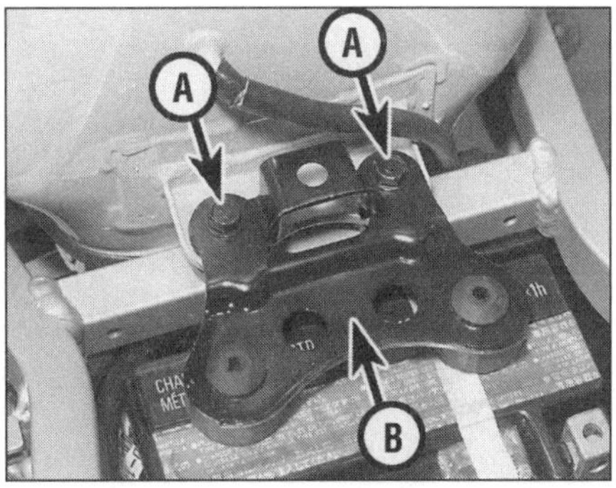

2.7b Fuel tank bolts (A), bracket (B) – G, H, J and A models

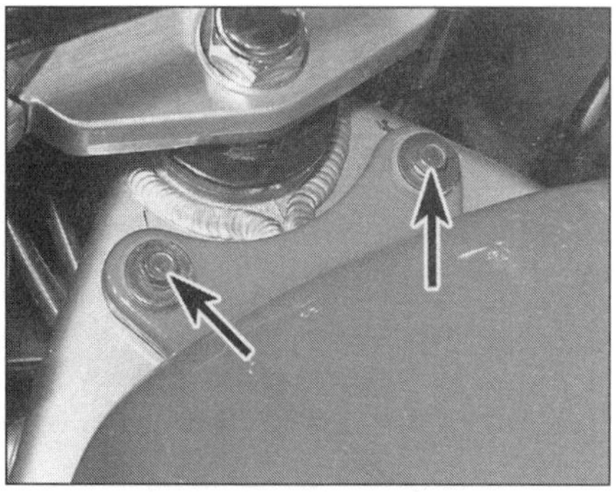
2.8 Front mounting bolts (arrowed)

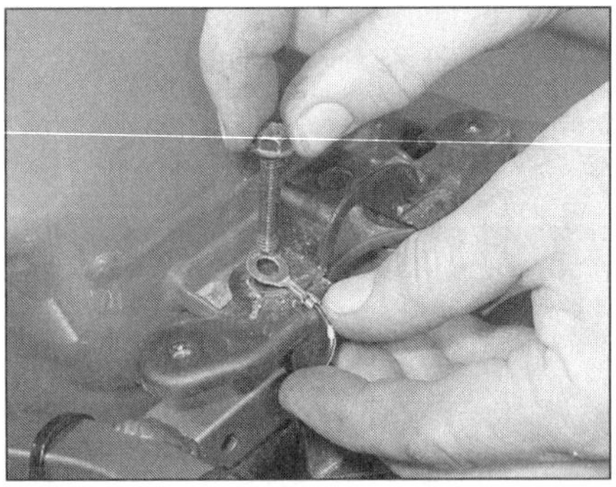

2.16 Do not forget to secure the earth wire - F models

9 Carefully lift the tank away from the machine. On F models, make sure the side panels are clear of the tank and take care not to damage them. On G, H, J and A models, draw the rear of the tank to the right so that the fuel tap clears the frame.

10 If the tap is to be removed or disassembled, first turn it to the RES position and drain the fuel into a container marked as being suitable for the storage of petrol (gasoline).

11 On G, H, J and A models, the tap should not be removed unnecessarily from the tank to prevent the possibility of damaging the O-ring or the filter. To remove the tap, unscrew the two bolts securing the tap and withdraw it from the tank. Check the condition of the O-ring. If it is in good condition it can be re-used, though it is better to use a new one. If it is in any way deteriorated or damaged it must be renewed. Similarly check the nylon washers fitted with the mounting bolts and renew them if necessary. Do not use steel washers as they will not seal properly.

Cleaning and repair

12 Remove the fuel tank as described above, then turn the tap to the RES position and drain the fuel into a container marked as being suitable for the storage of petrol (gasoline). Flush the tank and the tap with a high flash-point solvent, turning the tap through all its positions, then pour the solvent out of the tank. Refer to Chapter 1 for cleaning of the fuel filters.

3.3 Disconnect the wiring connector

13 All repairs to the fuel tank should be carried out by a professional who has experience in this critical and potentially dangerous work. Even after cleaning and flushing of the fuel system, explosive fumes can remain and ignite during repair of the tank.

14 If the fuel tank is removed from the vehicle, it should not be placed in an area where sparks or open flames could ignite the fumes coming out of the tank. Be especially careful inside garages where a natural gas-type appliance is located, because the pilot light could cause an explosion.

15 If the fuel tap has been leaking, tightening the assembly screws may help. On F models, remove the screw in the centre of the knob and remove the knob to access the assembly screws. Slacken all the screws a little first, then tighten them evenly a little at a time to ensure the cover seats properly on the tap body. If leakage persists, the tap should be renewed, however nothing is lost by dismantling the tap for further inspection. Unscrew the screws and disassemble the tap, noting how the components fit. Inspect all components for wear or damage, and renew them as necessary, if available. If any of the components are worn or damaged beyond repair and are not available individually, a new tap must be fitted.

Installation

16 Installation is the reverse of removal. Make sure the tank seats properly and does not pinch any control cables or wires. If it is difficult to align the holes in the tank brackets with the holes in the frame, stop and check to see if a hose or cable is in the way. On F models, do not forget to secure the earth (ground) wire with the left rear mounting bolt **(see illustration)**.

3 Fuel pump, relay and cut-off valves – removal, check and installation

Warning: Refer to the warning in Section 1 concerning contact with fuel.

Fuel pump and relay

Removal

1 The fuel pump operates when the starter button is depressed and as required when the engine is running. The fuel pump supplies fuel to the carburettors when the fuel level in the float chambers is low; when the fuel reaches the predetermined level, the fuel pressure rises and the fuel pump shuts off. The fuel pressure sensor is integral with the pump.

2 Remove the fuel tank (see Section 2).

3 Disconnect the fuel pump electrical connector **(see illustration)**.

4 Release the clamp and detach the fuel outlet hose from the carburettors **(see illustration 5.4a)**. Lift the pump and the filter in their rubber sleeves off the mounting pegs and remove the pump and filter as a linked assembly **(see illustration)**. The filter can be separated from the pump if required, though for testing the pump it must be left connected.

5 The fuel pump relay is also mounted in a rubber sleeve which fits onto mounting pegs on the frame **(see illustrations)**. Disconnect the wiring connector and either lift the relay in its sleeve off the mounting pegs, or slip the relay out of its sleeve.

Check – fuel pump relay

6 Remove the relay (see Step 5).

7 Using the Kawasaki tester, part no. 57001-983, set the ohmmeter scale to the 1 x K-ohms range and measure the resistance

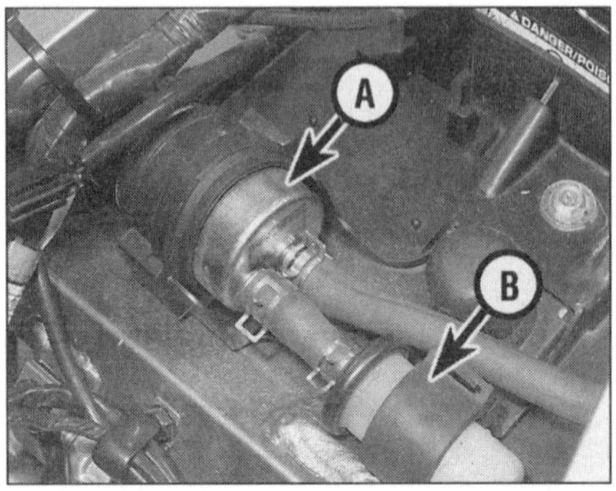

3.4 Remove the pump (A) and filter (B) as an assembly

3.5a Fuel pump relay - F models

3.5b Fuel pump relay - G, H, J and A models

Fuel Pump Relay Internal Resistance

Range x 1 kΩ		Tester (+) Lead Connection 1	2	3	4
*	1	–	∞	∞	∞
	2	∞	–	∞	∞
	3	∞	10-100	–	∞
	4	∞	20-200	1 - 5	–

*: Tester (–) Lead Connection

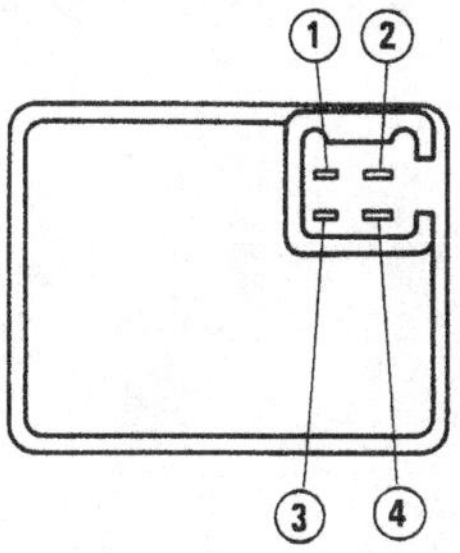

3.7 Terminal identification and resistance table for testing the fuel pump relay

at the indicated terminals **(see illustration)**. If your readings are not as specified in the table, fit a new fuel pump relay. If your readings are okay, check the fuel pump itself.

Caution: Using a meter other than that specified may produce inaccurate results and could damage the fuel pump relay. If the meter is not available, have the relay checked by a Kawasaki dealer.

Check – fuel pump

Warning: To protect your eyes from spilled or splashed paraffin (kerosene), wear safety goggles during the following test procedure.

Note: *If you don't have a suitable automotive-type fuel pressure gauge for this procedure, take the pump to a Kawasaki dealer and have it tested there.*

8 Remove the fuel pump with the fuel filter (see Steps 2 to 4 above).

9 Fill a container with paraffin (kerosene) and hook up the fuel pump, hoses and filter as shown **(see illustration)**. Connect a fuel pressure gauge to the high pressure side with a T-fitting as shown.

Warning: Do NOT use petrol (gasoline) for this test! It is unnecessary and dangerous.

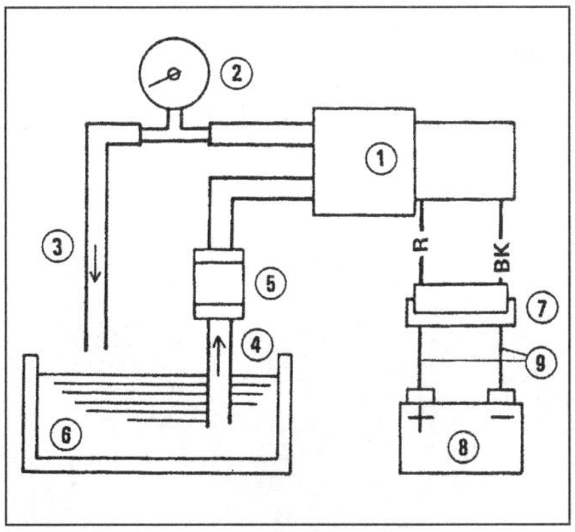

3.9 Fuel pump test set-up

1 Fuel pump
2 Pressure gauge
3 Outlet hose
4 Inlet hose
5 Fuel filter
6 Paraffin (kerosene)
7 2-pin connector
8 12V battery
9 Jumper leads

10 Hook up the pump wiring connector to a 12-volt battery as shown **(see illustration 3.9)** and note whether the pump comes on:

- If the pump operates, check the pump relay.
- If the pump does not operate, fit a new pump.
- If the pump operates AND the fuel pump relay is also okay, close the outlet hose momentarily while the pump is running – when the pump stops, note the indicated pressure on the fuel pressure gauge and compare this reading to the fuel pressure listed in this Chapter's Specifications. If the gauge reading is outside that spec, the pump is defective.

Installation

11 Installation is the reverse of removal **(see illustration 3.4)**. Make sure all the hose clamps are a tight fit.

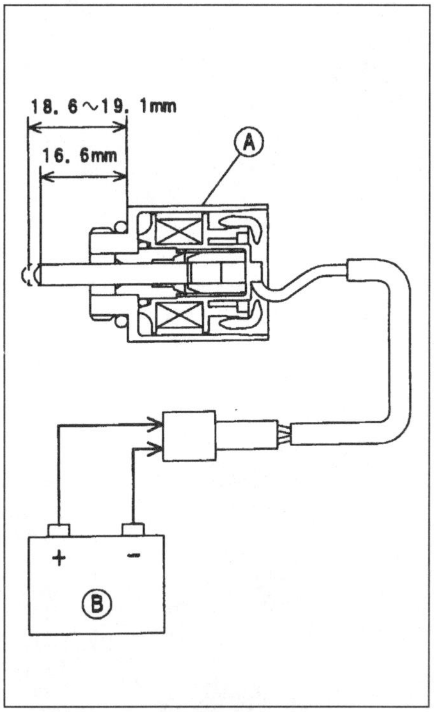

3.15 Fuel cut-off valve test set-up

A Cut-off valve B 12V battery

Fuel pump cut-off valves (catalytic converter models)

Removal

12 The valves are installed to protect the catalytic converter fitted to these models. Remove the fuel tank (see Section 2).

13 Connect a suitable drain hose to the union on the bottom of the float chamber on each carburettor and place the end in a suitable container. Slacken each drain screw in turn and drain the carburettors. Tighten the drain screws on completion.

14 Disconnect each cut-off valve wiring connector, then unscrew each valve from the carburettors, noting which fits where.

Check

15 To test the valve, first measure the amount of protrusion of the plunger as shown **(see illustration)**. Now connect a 12V battery to the terminals of the wiring connector and measure the protrusion. If the valve plunger does not move when the battery is connected, or if the amount of protrusion differs from that specified, fit a new valve.

Installation

16 On installation, the valves with the grey wiring connectors must be fitted to Nos. 1 and 4 carburettors, and the valves with the brown connectors must be fitted to Nos. 2 and 3 carburettors.

4 Air filter housing – removal and installation

Removal

1 Remove the fuel tank (see Section 2).

2 Release the clamp and detach the crankcase breather hose from the air filter over. On F models, also detach the vacuum valve hose from the cover and the drain hose from the housing on the left-hand side **(see illustration)**.

3 Remove the air filter (see Chapter 1). Unscrew the two bolts securing the housing to the carburettors and remove the housing, lifting it up at the rear and drawing it out of the

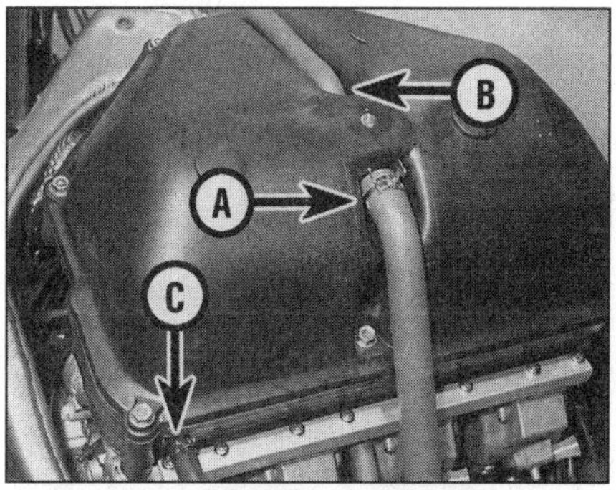

4.2 Detach the breather hose (A), and on F models the vacuum valve hose (B) and the drain hose (C)

4.3a Unscrew the two bolts (arrowed) . . .

4.3b . . . and remove the housing

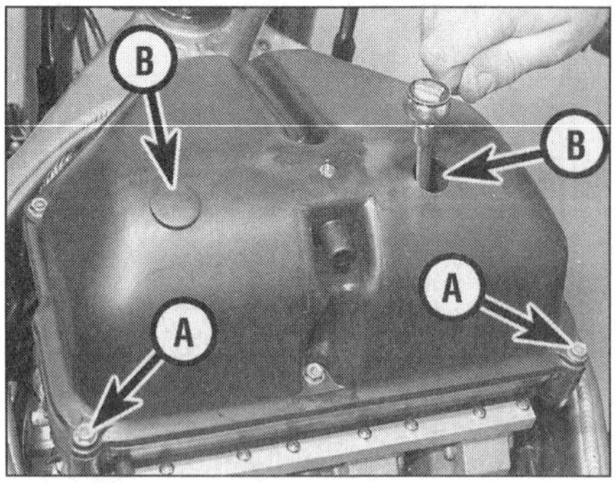

4.3c To remove the housing complete, remove the two bolts (A), and the bolts (B) accessed via the blanking plug using a socket extension

air ducts at the front **(see illustrations)**. **Note:** *Kawasaki provide a pair of removable plugs on the cover to allow access to the mounting bolts without having to remove the cover* ***(see illustration)****; this is the faster removal method, but you may still have to separate the cover from the housing when installing the bolts.*

Installation

4 Installation is the reverse of removal. Make sure the housing locates correctly into the air ducts at the front. Make sure all hoses are securely and correctly connected.

5 Carburettors – removal and installation

Warning: Refer to the warning in Section 1 concerning contact with fuel.

Removal

1 Remove the fuel tank (see Section 2).

2 Remove the air filter housing (see Section 4).

3 Disconnect the choke cable from the carburettor assembly (see Section 11).

4 Mark and disconnect the fuel hose, the vent hose and the vacuum valve switch and valve hoses from the carburettors **(see illustrations)**.

5 On UK models, drain the cooling system (see Chapter 1), then detach the hoses for the carburettor heating system from the cylinder head and the water pump cover **(see illustrations)**.

6 On G, H, J and A models, disconnect the throttle position sensor wiring connector **(see illustration)**. Where fitted, disconnect the fuel cut-off valve wiring connectors.

7 Loosen the clamp screws on the intake

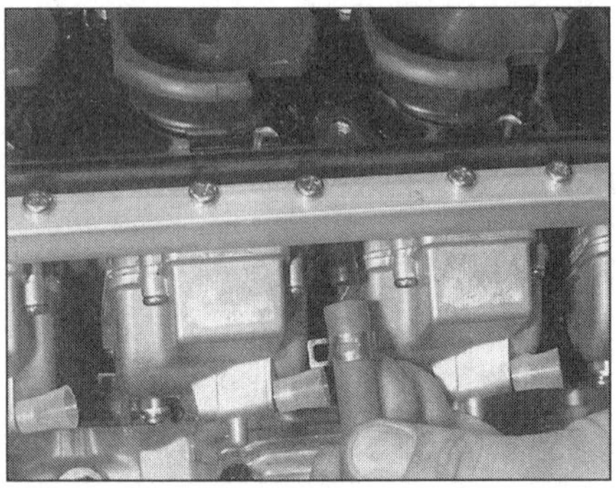

5.4a Disconnect the fuel hose . . .

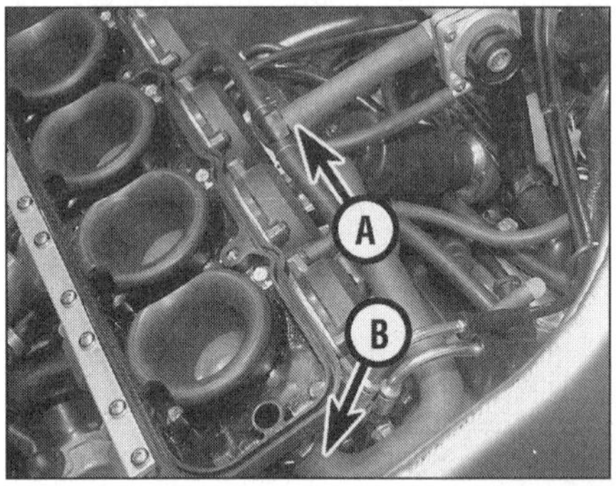

5.4b . . . the vacuum valve switch hose (A) and the vacuum valve hose (B)

5.5a Detach the carburettor heater system hoses from the back of the cylinder head on F models (arrowed) . . .

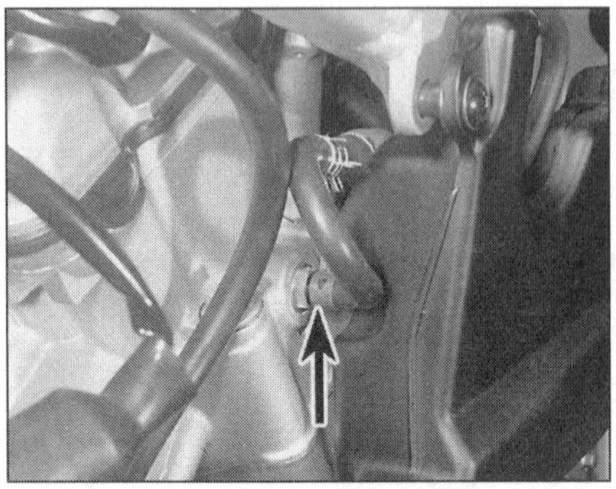

5.5b . . . and from the left-hand side of it on G, H, J and A models (arrowed) . . .

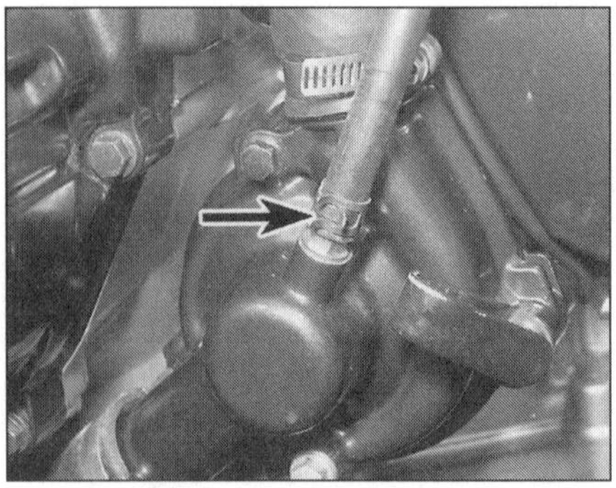

5.5c . . . also from the water pump cover (arrowed)

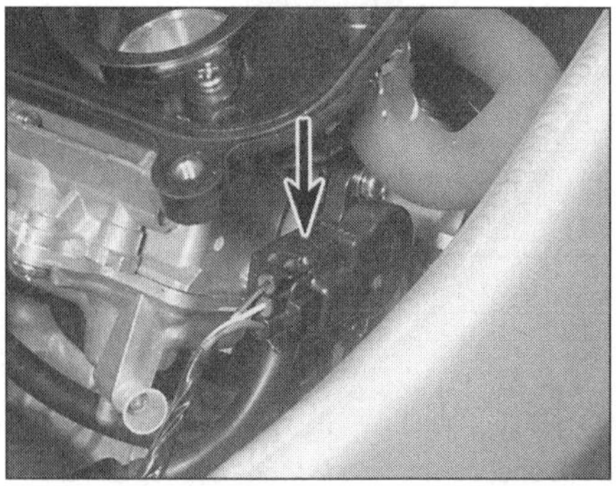

5.6 Disconnect the throttle position sensor wiring connector (arrowed)

5.7a Slacken the four clamp screws (two shown – arrowed) . . .

manifolds (the rubber tubes that connect the carburettors to the engine), then pull the carburettor assembly back until it is free of the manifolds **(see illustrations)**.

8 Raise the carburettor assembly up far enough to disconnect the throttle cables from the throttle pulley (see Section 10), then remove the carburettors.

9 Stuff clean rags into the intake manifold tubes to prevent the entry of dirt or other objects.

Installation

10 Installation is the reverse of removal, noting the following.

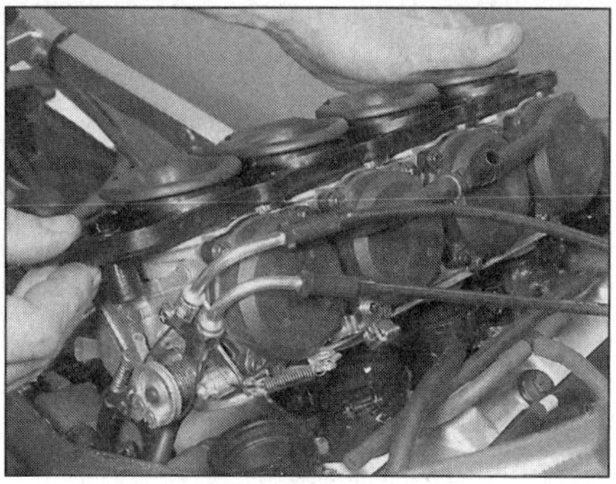

5.7b . . . and lift the carburettors up off the manifolds

- Check for cracks or splits in the cylinder head intake manifold rubbers, and renew them if necessary.
- Make sure the carburettors are fully engaged with the intake rubbers and the clamps are securely tightened.
- Make sure all hoses are correctly routed and secured and not trapped or kinked.
- Refer to Section 10 for installation of the throttle cables and to Section 11 for the choke cable. Check the operation of the cables and adjust them as necessary (see Chapter 1).
- Check idle speed and carburettor synchronisation and adjust as necessary (see Chapter 1).
- Check the entire fuel system for leaks.

6 Carburettor overhaul – general information

1 Poor engine performance, hesitation, hard starting, stalling, flooding and backfiring are all signs that major carburettor maintenance may be required.

2 Keep in mind that many so-called carburettor problems are really not carburettor problems at all, but mechanical problems within the engine or ignition system malfunctions. Try to establish for certain that the carburettors are in need of maintenance before beginning a major overhaul.

3 Check the fuel tap, fuel pump, fuel filters, fuel hoses, the tank filler cap vent, the intake manifold clamps, the breather and vacuum hoses, air filter element, cylinder compression, spark plugs and carburettor synchronisation before assuming that a carburettor overhaul is required.

4 Most carburettor problems are caused by dirt particles, varnish and other deposits which build up in and block the fuel and air passages. Also, in time, gaskets and O-rings

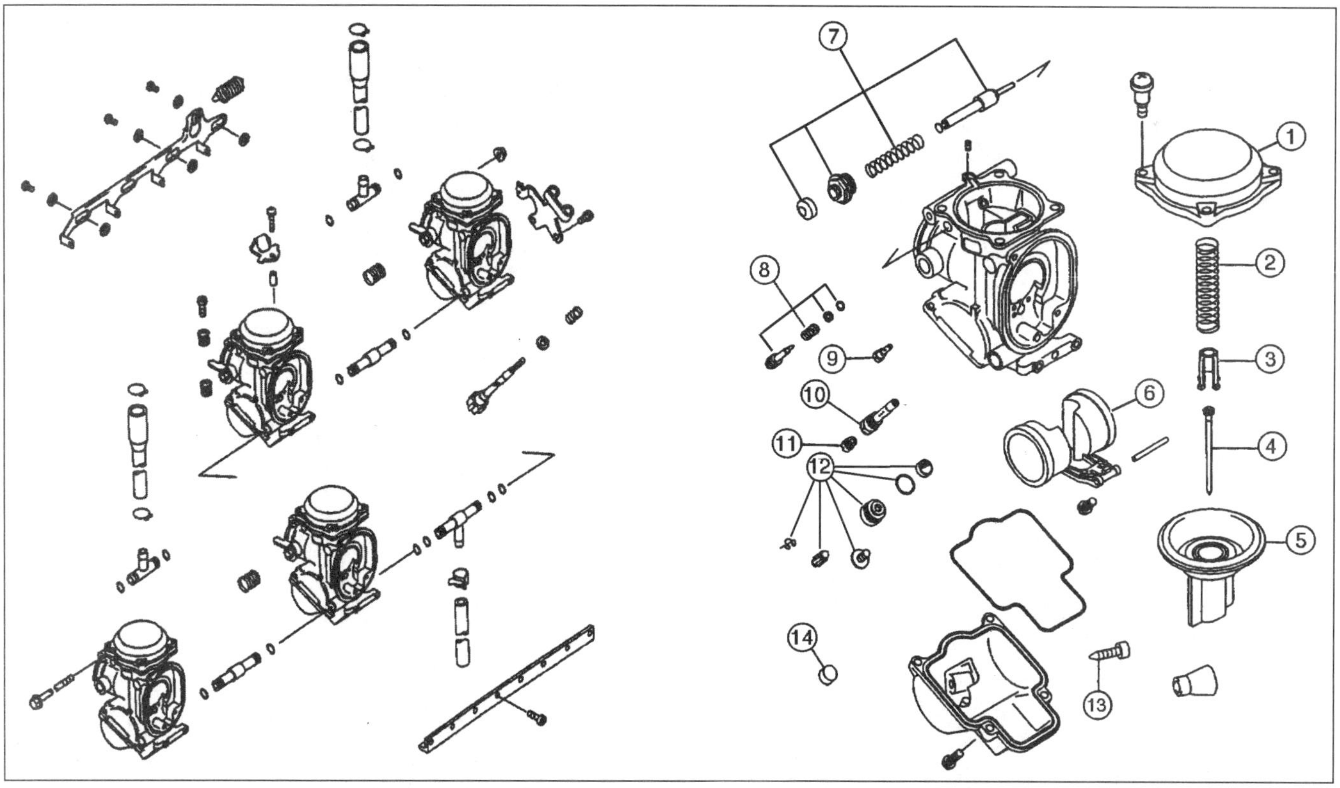

7.2a Carburettor components – F models

1 Top cover
2 Spring
3 Spring seat
4 Needle
5 Diaphragm/piston assembly
6 Float
7 Choke plunger assembly
8 Pilot screw assembly
9 Pilot jet
10 Needle jet holder
11 Main jet
12 Valve needle seat assembly
13 Drain screw
14 Pilot screw blanking plug (US models)

shrink or deteriorate and cause fuel and air leaks which lead to poor performance.

5 When a carburettor is overhauled, it is generally disassembled completely and the parts are cleaned thoroughly with a carburettor cleaning solvent and dried with filtered, unlubricated compressed air. The fuel and air passages are also blown through with compressed air to force out any dirt that may have been loosened but not removed by the solvent. Once the cleaning process is complete, the carburettor is reassembled using new gaskets, O-rings and, generally, a new fuel inlet needle valve and seat assembly.

6 Before disassembling the carburettors, make sure you have a carburettor rebuild kit (which will include all necessary O-rings and other parts), some carburettor cleaner, a supply or rags, some means of blowing out the carburettor passages and a clean place to work.

Caution: It is recommended that only one carburettor be overhauled at a time to avoid mixing up parts.

7 Carburettors - disassembly, cleaning and inspection

Warning: Refer to the warning in Section 1 concerning contact with fuel.

Caution: On G, H, J and A models, do not remove the throttle position sensor from the carburettors. Refer to Chapter 5 for checking and adjusting the sensor.

Disassembly

1 Remove the carburettors from the machine as described in Section 5. Set the assembly on a clean working surface. **Note:** *Unless the O-rings on the fuel and vent fittings between the carburettors are leaking, don't detach the carburettors from their mounting brackets. Also, work on one carburettor at a time to avoid getting parts mixed up.*

2 If the carburettors must be separated from each other, remove the choke lever return spring, then remove the choke lever by removing the three screws and their washers. **Note:** *There is no screw on the No. 2 carburettor.* On F models there are two washers per screw, one on each side of the lever; on G, H, J and A models there is one washer per screw on the outside of the lever **(see illustrations on previous page and below)**. On UK models, release the clamps securing the heater system hoses and detach the hoses. On F models, unscrew the nut on the end of the long through-bolt and withdraw the bolt, then remove the screws securing the mounting plate and remove the plate, noting how it fits. On G, H, J and A models, unscrew and withdraw the two long through-bolts. Mark the position of each carburettor and gently separate them, noting how the throttle linkage is connected and

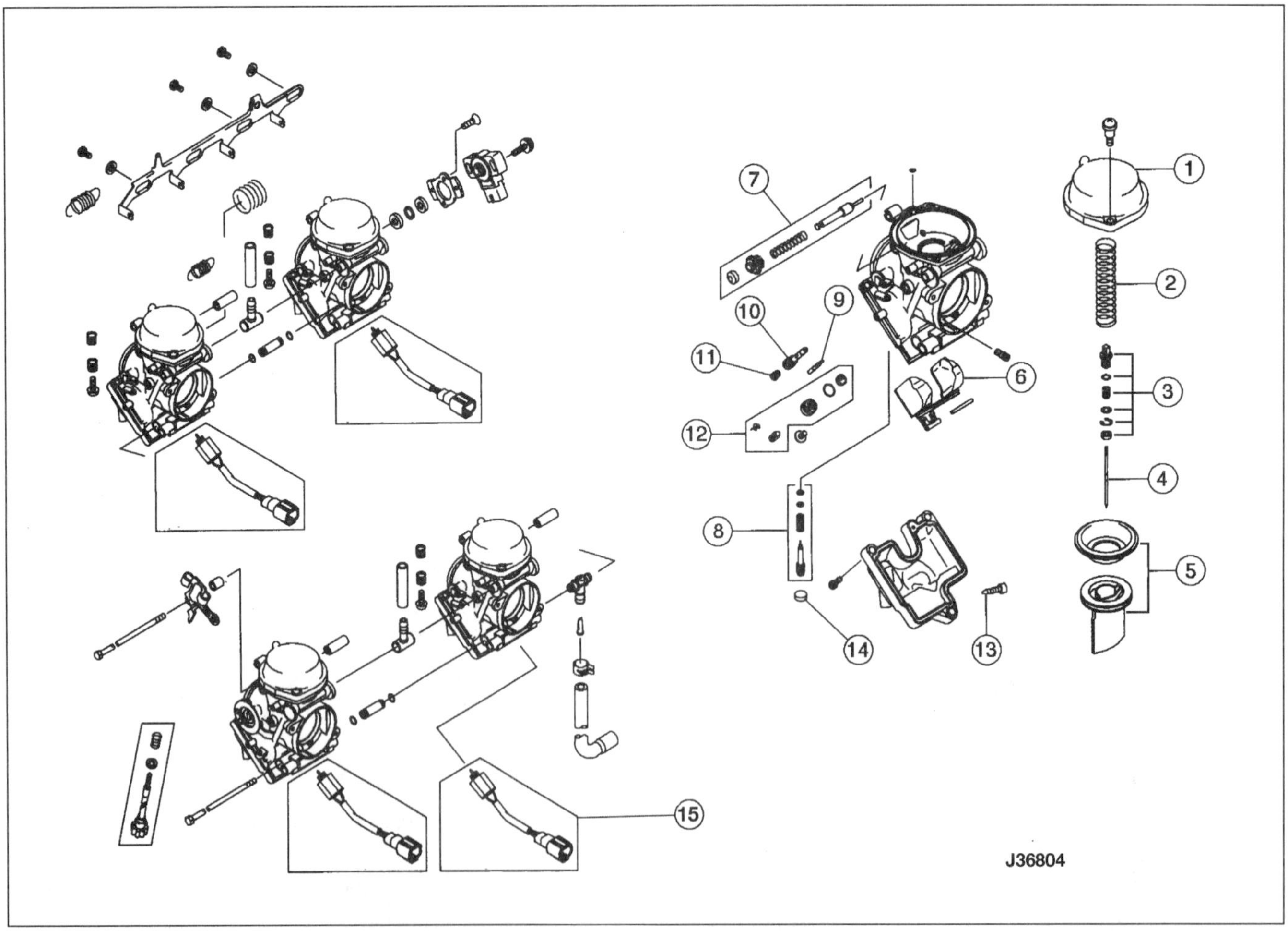

7.2b Carburettor components - G, H, J and A models

1 Top cover
2 Spring
3 Spring seat
4 Needle
5 Diaphragm/piston assembly
6 Float
7 Choke plunger assembly
8 Pilot screw assembly
9 Pilot jet
10 Needle jet holder
11 Main jet
12 Valve needle seat assembly
13 Drain screw
14 Pilot screw blanking plug (US models)
15 Fuel cut-off valve (where fitted)

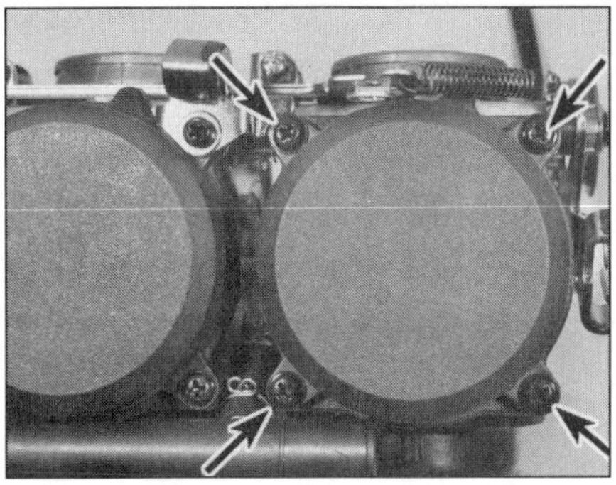

7.3a Remove the vacuum chamber cover screws (arrowed)

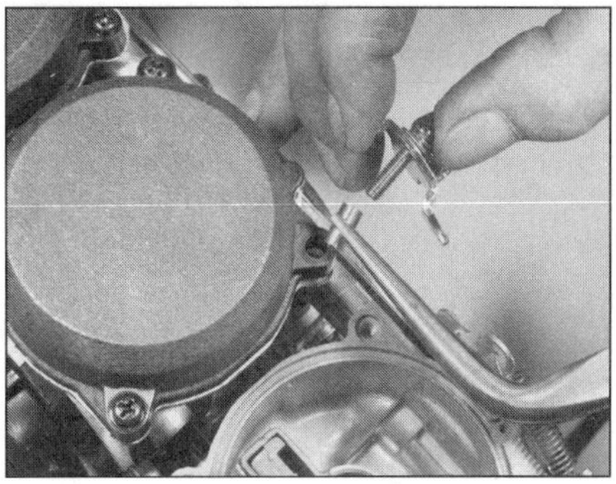

7.3b The screw that secures the choke cable bracket has a locating dowel – F models

7.3c Lift off the cover and spring . . .

7.3d . . . and separate the diaphragm from its groove and the locating tab (arrowed) from its notch

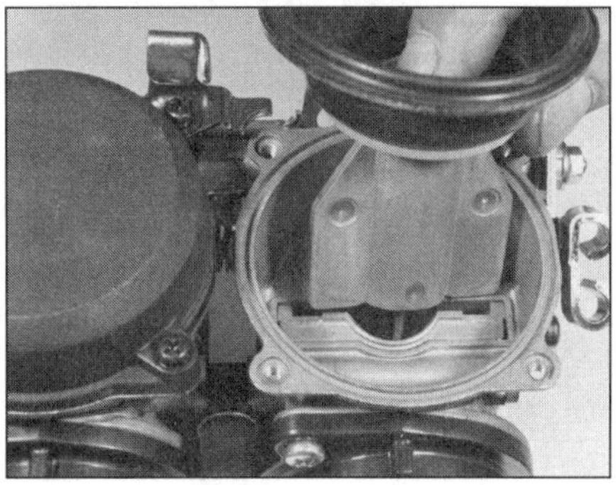

7.3e Lift the piston out

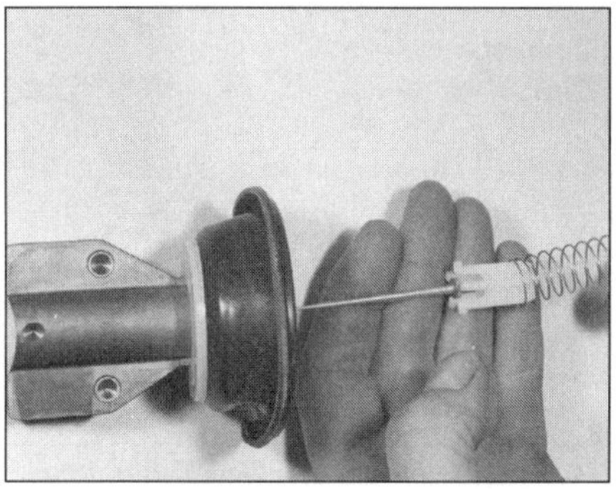

7.4 Separate the jet needle from the piston

being careful not to lose any springs or fuel and vent fittings that are fitted between the carburettors.

3 Remove the four screws securing the vacuum chamber cover to the carburettor body; on F models, note the locating dowel on the screw that secures the choke cable bracket on the No. 3 carburettor **(see illustrations)**. Lift the cover off and remove the piston spring **(see illustration)**. Peel the diaphragm away from its groove in the carburettor body, being careful not to tear it **(see illustration)**. Lift out the diaphragm/ piston assembly **(see illustration)**.

4 On F models, remove the piston spring seat (if it wasn't in the end of the spring) and withdraw the needle from the piston **(see illustration)**. On G, H, J and A models, carefully draw the needle holder and needle from the piston using a pair of long-nose pliers.

5 Remove the four screws securing the float chamber to the carburettor body, then detach the chamber **(see illustrations)**.

6 Push the float pivot pin out and detach the float (and fuel inlet valve needle) from the

7.5a Remove the float chamber screws . . .

7.5b . . . and lift off the chamber

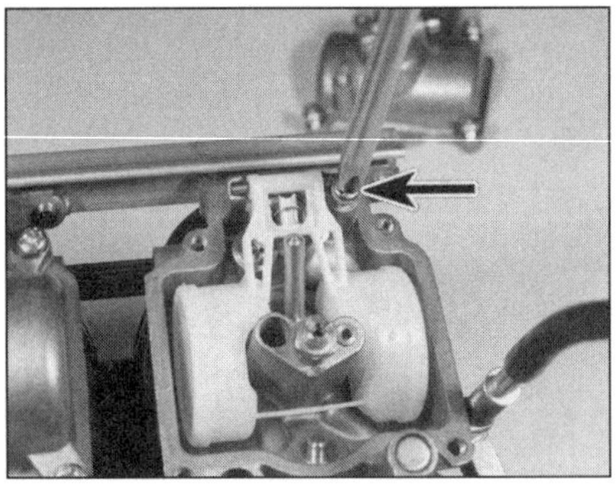

7.6a Loosen the screw (arrowed) . . .

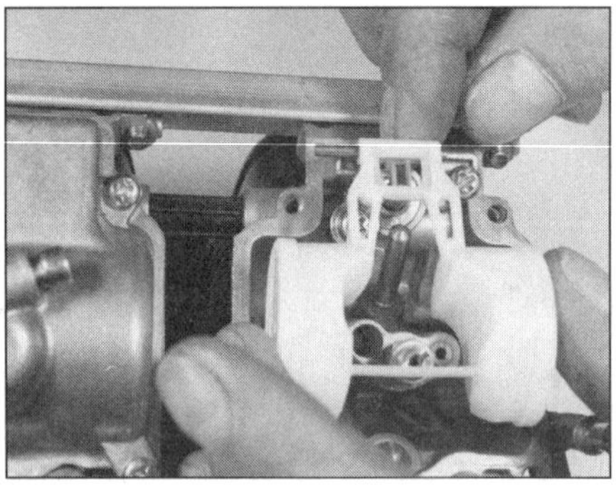

7.6b . . . then push out the float pivot pin . . .

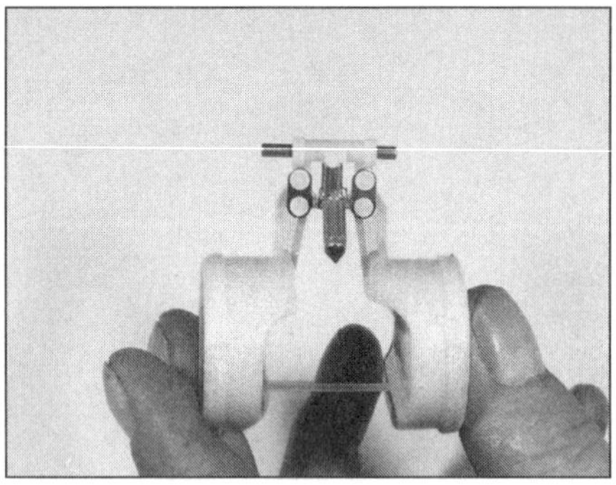

7.6c . . . and lift out the float together with the needle valve

7.6d Remove the screw and lift out the needle valve seat

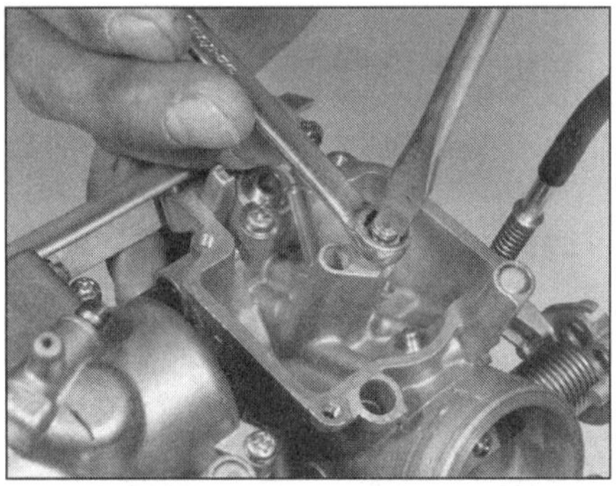

7.7 Prevent the needle jet holder from turning and unscrew the main jet using a screwdriver

7.8 Unscrew the needle jet holder

7.9a Unscrew the pilot jet . . .

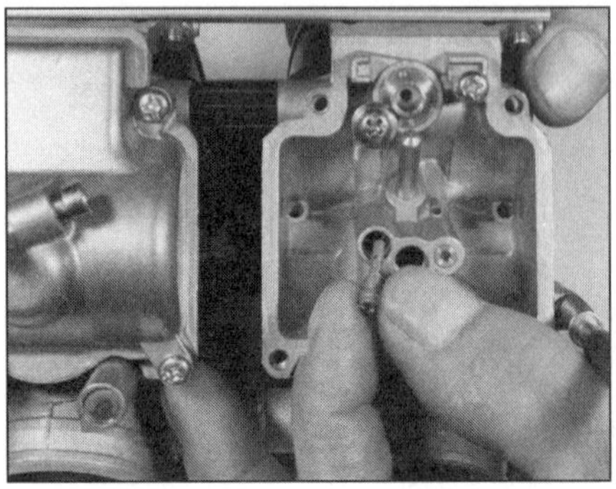

7.9b . . . and lift it out

7.10a The pilot screw on US models is beneath a blanking plug (arrowed)

carburettor body **(see illustrations)**. Detach the valve needle from the float. Remove the retaining screw and remove the valve needle seat **(see illustration)**.

7 Hold the needle jet holder to prevent it turning and unscrew the main jet **(see illustration)**.

8 Unscrew the needle jet holder/air bleed pipe **(see illustration)**.

9 Using a small, flat-bladed screwdriver, remove the pilot jet **(see illustrations)**.

10 The pilot (idle mixture) screw is located in the bottom of the carburettor body **(see illustration)**. On US models, this screw is hidden behind a plug which will have to be removed if the screw is to be taken out **(see illustration)**. To do this, punch a hole in the plug with an awl or a scribe, then prise it out. On all models, turn the pilot screw in, counting the number of turns until it bottoms lightly. Record that number for use when installing the screw. Now remove the pilot screw along with its spring, washer and O-ring.

11 The choke plunger can be removed after the choke shaft has been removed (see Step 2). Unscrew the nut that retains the

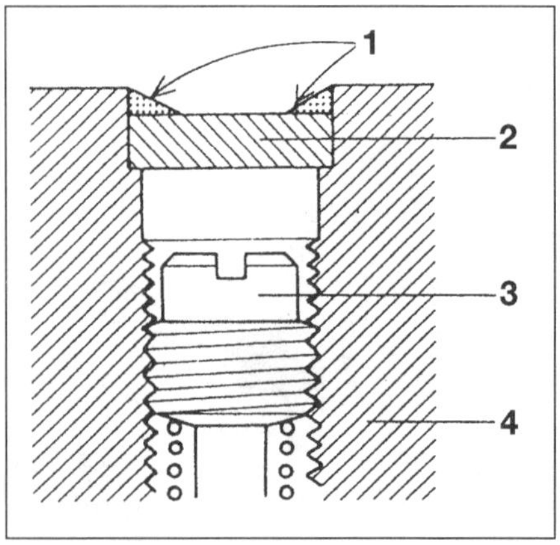

7.10b Pilot screw detail showing plug on US models

1 Bonding agent
2 Plug
3 Pilot screw
4 Carburettor body

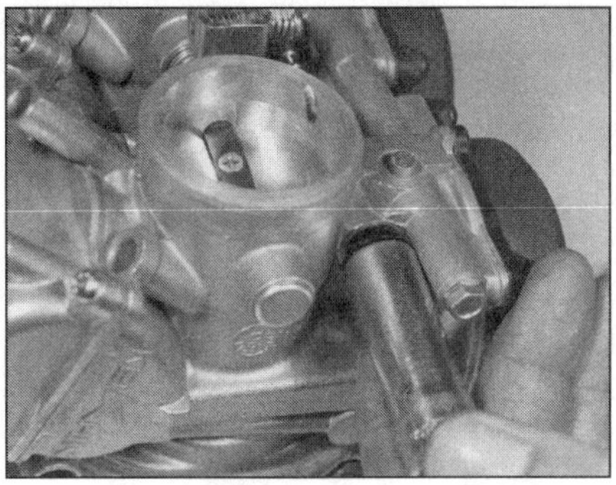

7.11a Unscrew the choke plunger nut with a socket . . .

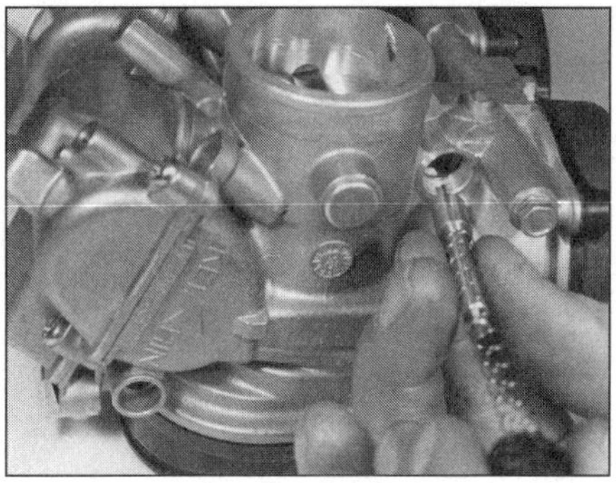

7.11b . . . and withdraw the spring and plunger

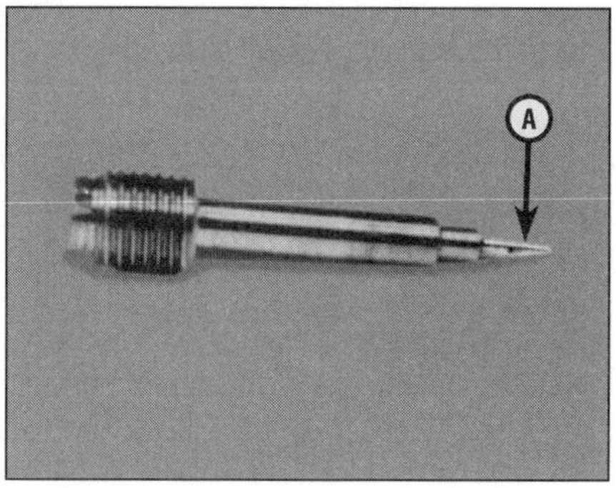

7.15 Check the tapered portion (A) of the pilot screw for wear or damage

plunger to the carburettor body and withdraw the plunger and spring **(see illustrations)**.

Cleaning

Caution: Use only a carburettor cleaning solution that is safe for use with plastic parts (be sure to read the label on the container).

12 Submerge the metal components in the carburettor cleaner for approximately thirty minutes (or as the directions recommend).

13 After the carburettor has soaked long enough for the cleaner to loosen and dissolve most of the varnish and other deposits, use a brush to remove the stubborn deposits. Rinse it again, then dry it with compressed air. Blow out all of the fuel and air passages in the main and upper body.

Caution: Never clean the jets or passages with a piece of wire or a drill bit, as they will be enlarged, causing the fuel and air metering rates to be upset.

Inspection

14 Check the operation of the choke plunger. If it doesn't move smoothly, fit a new plunger and return spring.

15 Check the tapered portion of the pilot screw for wear or damage **(see illustration)**. Renew the pilot screw if necessary.

16 Check the carburettor body, float chamber and vacuum chamber cover for cracks, distorted sealing surfaces and other damage. If any defects are found, renew the faulty component or fit a new carburettor.

7.18 Check the piston insert for wear or damage

17 Check the jet needle for straightness by rolling it on a flat surface (such as a piece of glass). Renew the needle if it's bent or if the tip is worn.

18 Check the piston insert in the carburettor body for wear and fit a new carburettor if it's worn or damaged **(see illustration)**.

19 Check the tip of the fuel inlet valve needle for grooves or scratches, then push in the rod on the other end of the needle and release it **(see illustration)**. If the rod doesn't spring back, or if the needle tip is damaged, fit a new valve needle and seat assembly.

20 Check the O-rings on the float chamber, the pilot screw and the needle valve seat. Renew them if they're damaged.

21 Operate the throttle shaft to make sure the throttle butterfly valve opens and closes smoothly. If it doesn't, and the problem is not due to dirt or any other obstruction, fit a new carburettor.

22 Check the floats for damage. This will usually be apparent by the presence of fuel inside the float. If a float is damaged, fit a new one.

23 Check the diaphragm for splits, holes and general deterioration and fit a new one if any are found. Holding the diaphragm up to a light will help to reveal problems of this nature.

24 Insert the vacuum piston in the carburettor body and see that it moves up-and-down smoothly. Check the surface of the piston for wear. If it's worn excessively or doesn't move smoothly in the bore, fit a new piston.

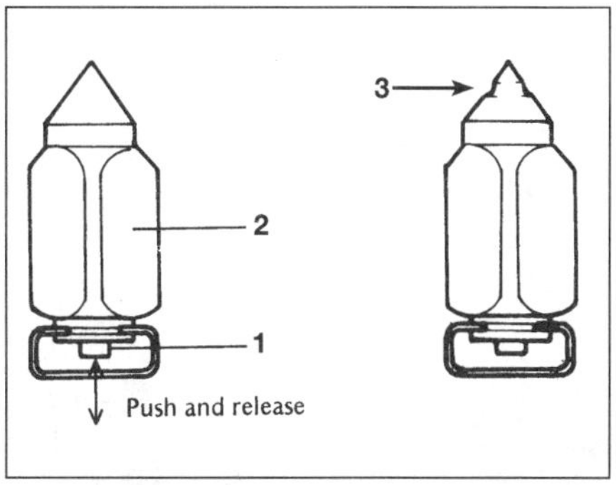

7.19 Check the tip of the fuel inlet valve needle for grooves and scratches

1 Rod 2 Valve needle 3 Groove in tip

8 Carburettors – reassembly and float height adjustment

Caution: When installing the jets, be careful not to overtighten them – they're made of soft material and can distort, strip or shear easily.

Note: *When reassembling the carburettors, be sure to use the new O-rings, gaskets and other parts supplied in the rebuild kit.*

1 If the choke plunger was removed, install it in its bore, followed by its spring and nut **(see illustration 7.11b)**. Tighten the nut securely and install the cap.

2 Install the pilot screw (if removed) along with its spring, washer and O-ring, turning it in until it seats lightly. Now, turn the screw out the number of turns that was previously recorded. If you're working on a US model, install a new metal plug in the hole over the screw. Apply a little bonding agent around the circumference of the plug after it has been seated **(see illustration 7.10b)**. **Note:** *If installing a new pilot screw, set it to the number of turns out given in the Specifications at the beginning of this Chapter.*

3 Install the pilot jet, tightening it securely **(see illustration 7.9b)**.

4 Install the needle jet holder/air bleed pipe, tightening it securely **(see illustration 7.8)**.

5 Install the main jet into the needle jet holder/air bleed pipe, tightening it securely **(see illustration 7.7)**.

6 On F models, drop the jet needle down into its hole in the vacuum piston and install the spring seat over the needle **(see illustration 7.4)**. Make sure the spring seat doesn't cover the hole in the bottom of the vacuum piston – reposition it if necessary. On G, H, J and A models, fit the jet needle assembly into the piston and press down on the holder to make sure it is properly seated.

7 Install the diaphragm/vacuum piston assembly into the carburettor body **(see illustration 7.3e)**. Fit the spring into the piston, making sure it locates correctly onto the spring seat (F models) or needle holder (G, H, J and A models). Seat the bead of the diaphragm into the groove in the top of the carburettor body,

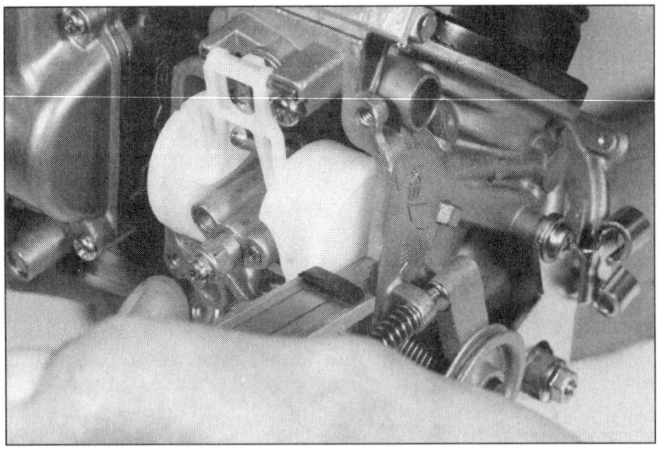

8.9 Measure the float height using a vernier caliper or similar

8.14a Make sure the choke shaft engages all four plungers (arrowed)

making sure the diaphragm isn't distorted or kinked **(see illustration 7.3d)**.

> HAYNES HiNT ***Seating the diaphragm bead is not always an easy task. If the diaphragm seems too large in diameter and doesn't want to seat in the groove, place the vacuum chamber cover over the carburettor diaphragm, insert your finger into the throat of the carburettor and push up on the vacuum piston. Push down gently on the vacuum chamber cover – it should drop into place, indicating the diaphragm has seated in its groove.***

8 Install the vacuum chamber cover, tightening the screws securely **(see illustration 7.3c)**. On F models, if you're working on the No. 3 carburettor, don't forget to install the dowel and choke cable bracket **(see illustration 7.3b)**.

9 Invert the carburettor. Install the fuel inlet valve needle seat and secure it with the screw **(see illustration 7.6d)**. Attach the valve needle to the float. Attach the valve needle to the tab on the float **(see illustration 7.6c)**. Set the float into position in the carburettor, making sure the valve needle seats correctly. Install the float pivot pin and tighten the screw **(see illustrations 7.6b and a)**. To check the float height, hold the carburettor so the float hangs down, then tilt it back until the valve needle is just seated (the rod in the end of the valve shouldn't be compressed). Measure the distance from the float chamber gasket surface to the top of the float **(see illustration and 9.5)** and compare your measurement to the float height listed in this Chapter's Specifications. If it isn't as specified, carefully bend the tang that contacts the valve needle up or down until the float height is correct.

10 Install the O-ring into the groove in the float chamber. Place the float chamber on the carburettor and install the screws, tightening them securely.

11 If the carburettors were separated, install new O-rings on the fuel and vent fittings. Lubricate the O-rings on the fittings with a light film of oil and install them into their respective holes, making sure they seat completely **(see illustrations 7.2a or b)**.

12 Position the coil springs between the carburettors, gently push the carburettors together, then make sure the throttle linkages are correctly engaged. Check the fuel and vent fittings to make sure they have engage properly.

13 On F models, install the lower mounting plate and its screws, and the long through-bolt and its nut, but don't tighten them completely yet. On G, H, J and A models, install the two long through-bolts but do not yet tighten them. Set the carburettors on a surface plate or sheet of glass, then align them with a straight-edge placed along the edges of the bores. When the centrelines of the carburettors are all in horizontal and vertical alignment, tighten the screws and nut or bolts securely.

14 On F models, fit a plastic washer on each choke lever mounting, with the exception of No. 2 carburettor. On all models, install the choke lever, making sure it engages correctly with all the choke plungers **(see illustration)**. Fit the outer plastic washers, again with the exception of No. 2 carburettor, and install the screws, tightening them securely **(see illustration)**. Install the lever return spring, then make sure the choke mechanism operates smoothly.

15 Install the throttle synchronising screw springs **(see illustration)**. Visually

8.14b Be sure to reinstall the plastic washers as described

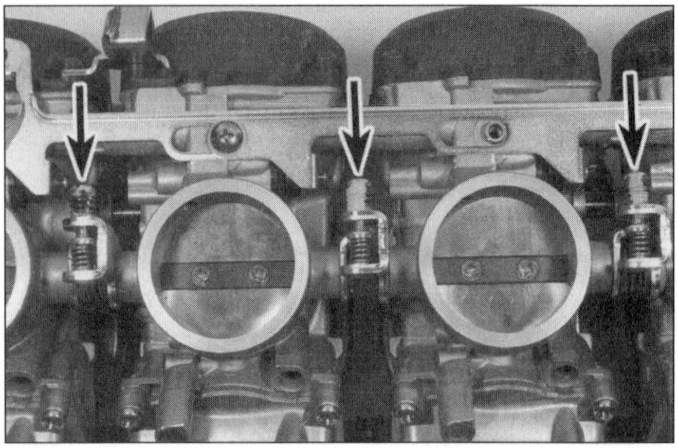

8.15 The synchronising screws and springs (arrowed) should be as shown

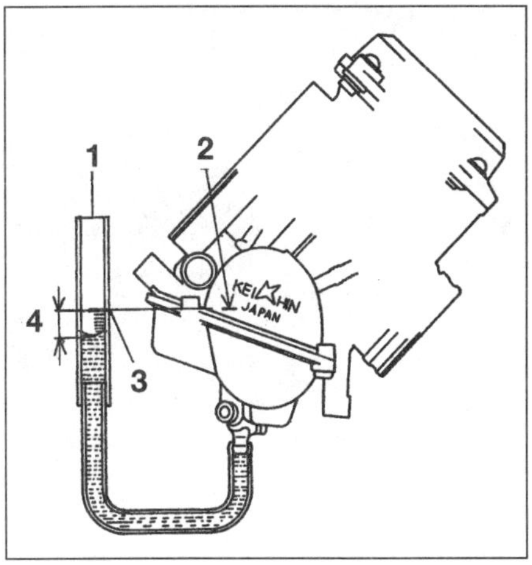

9.2a Fuel level measuring tool – F models

1 Fuel level gauge
2 Fuel level mark
3 Zero line
4 Fuel level

synchronise the throttle butterfly valves, turning the adjusting screws on the throttle linkage, if necessary, to equalise the clearance between the butterfly valve and throttle bore of each carburettor. Check to ensure the throttle operates smoothly.

16 If they were removed, install the throttle stop screw, throttle cable bracket and the air cleaner housing intake fittings. On UK models, connect the heater system hoses and secure them with their clamps.

9 Carburettors – fuel level adjustment

Warning: Refer to the warning in Section 1 concerning contact with fuel.

1 Remove the fuel tank (see Section 2) and the air filter housing (see Section 4). Connect an auxiliary fuel tank to the carburettors with a suitable length of hose, then support the motorcycle in an upright position using an auxiliary stand.

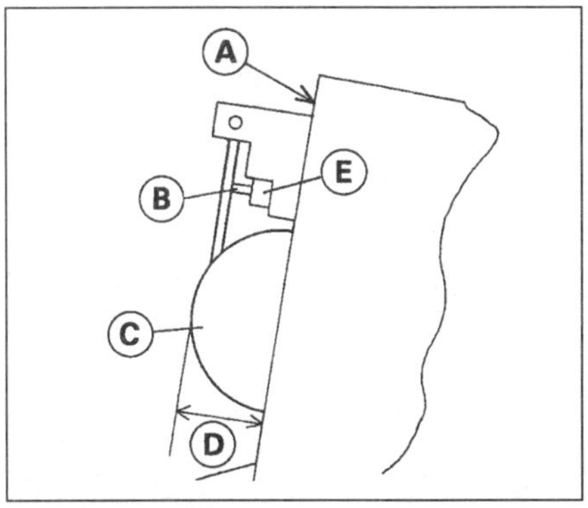

9.5 Measure the float height with the carburettor tilted so that the tang is just touching the needle rod

A Float chamber mating surface
B Needle rod
C Float
D Float height
E Float valve

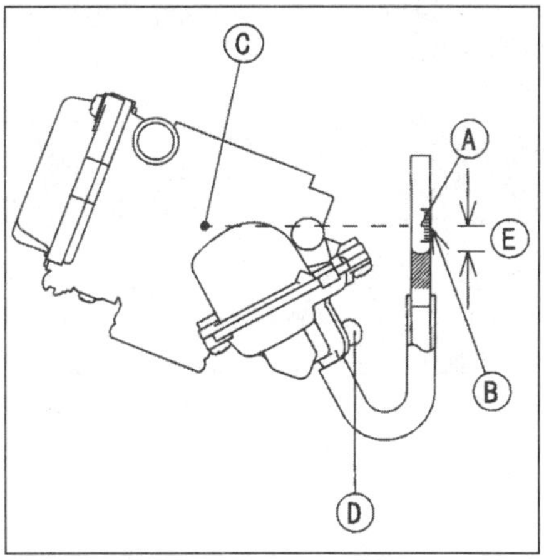

9.2b Fuel level measuring tool – G, H, J and A models

A Fuel level gauge
B Zero line
C Fuel level mark
D Drain screw
E Fuel level

2 Attach Kawasaki service tool no. 57001-1017 to the drain fitting on the bottom of one of the carburettor float chambers (all four will be checked) **(see illustrations)**. This is a clear plastic tube graduated in millimetres. An alternative is to use a length of clear plastic tubing and an accurate ruler. Hold the graduated tube (or the free end of the clear plastic tube) against the carburettor body, as shown in the accompanying illustration. If the Kawasaki tool is being used, raise the zero line to a point several millimetres above the float level mark on the carburettor main body. If a piece of clear plastic tubing is being used, make a line on the tubing at a point several millimetres above the float level mark.

3 Unscrew the drain screw at the bottom of the float chamber a couple of turns, then let fuel flow into the tube **(see illustration)**. Wait for the fuel level to stabilise, then slowly lower the tube until the zero line is level with the fuel level mark on the carburettor body. **Note:** *Don't lower the zero line below the fuel level mark then bring it back up – the reading will be inaccurate. If you do, drain the fuel from the tube and start again.*

10.2a Cable adjuster lockwheel (A) and adjuster (B) – F models

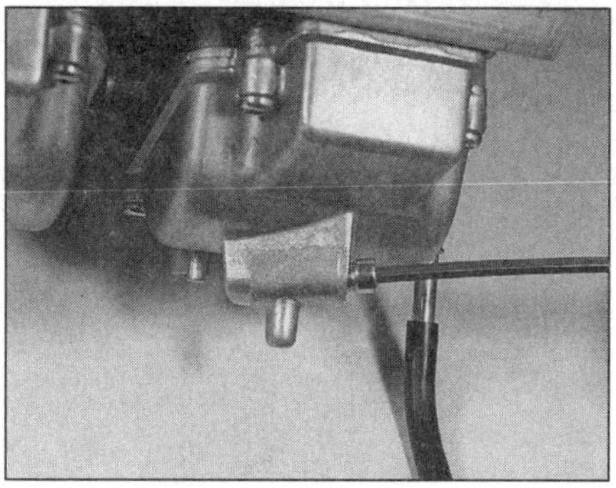

9.3 Loosen the float chamber drain screw

4 Measure the distance between the zero line and the top of the fuel level in the tube or gauge. This distance is the fuel level – write it down on a piece of paper, screw in the drain screw, shut off the fuel flow, then move on to the next carburettor and check it the same way.

5 Compare your fuel level readings to the value listed in this Chapter's Specifications. If the fuel level in any carburettor is not correct, remove the float chamber and bend the tang on the float up or down (see Section 8), as necessary, then measure the float height with the carburettor tilted so that the tang on the float just touches the needle rod in the float valve **(see illustration)**. **Note:** *Bending the tang up increases the float height and lowers the fuel level – bending it down decreases the float height and raises the fuel level.*

10 Throttle cables and grip – removal and installation

Throttle cables

Removal

1 Remove the fuel tank (see Section 2) and the air filter housing (see Section 4). Access to the cables at the carburettor end is restricted – if required, slacken the carburettor clamp screws and lift the carburettors off the intake manifolds to improve access (see Section 5).

2 Loosen the accelerator cable adjuster lockwheel at the handlebar and screw the cable adjuster in **(see illustrations)**.

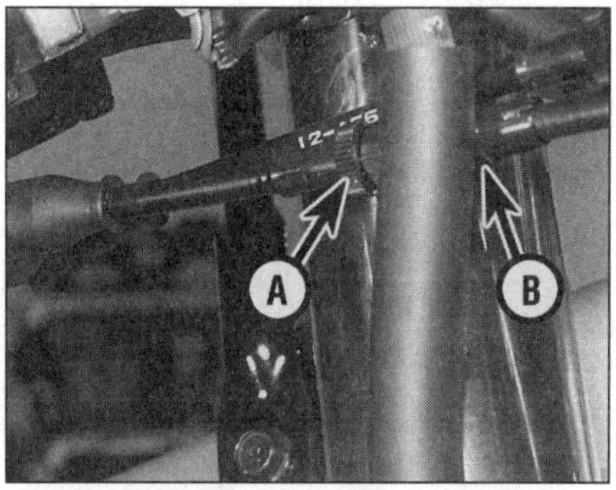

10.2b Cable adjuster lockwheel (A) and adjuster (B) – G, H, J and A models

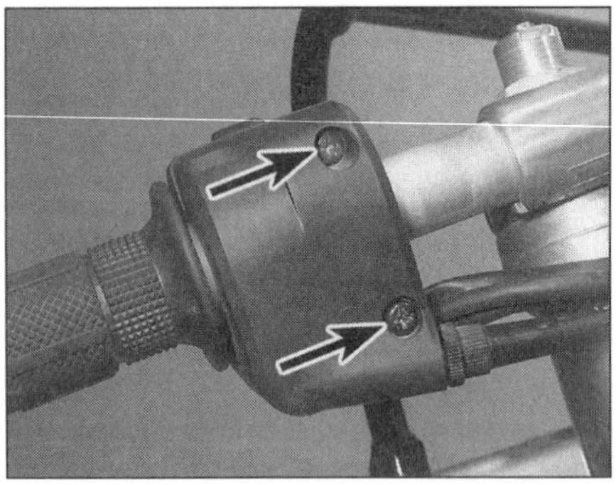

10.3a Throttle housing screws (arrowed) – F models

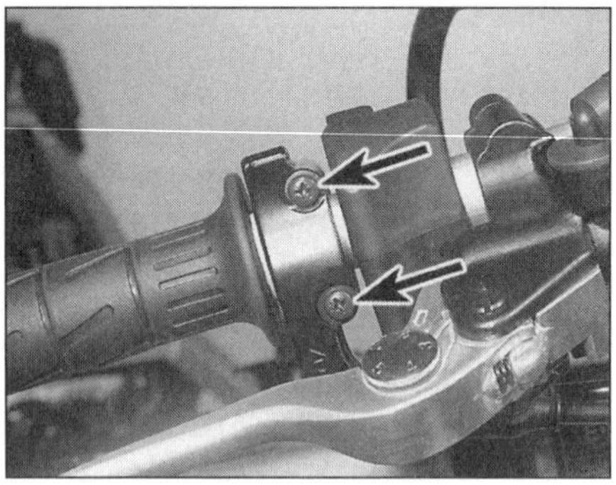

10.3b Throttle housing screws – G, H, J and A models

10.3c Separate the housing halves . . .

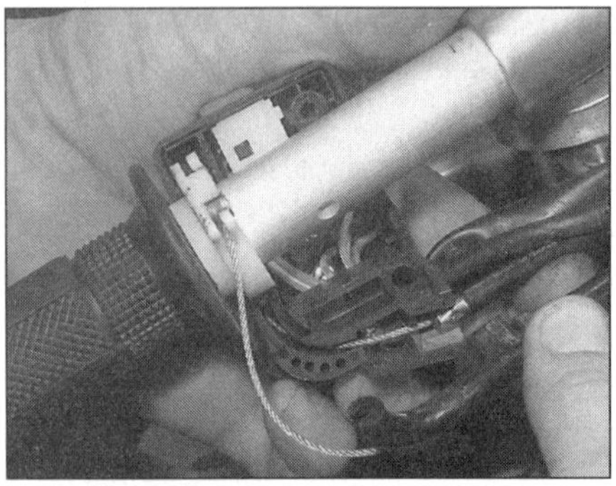

10.4 . . . then remove the cable elbows from the housing . . .

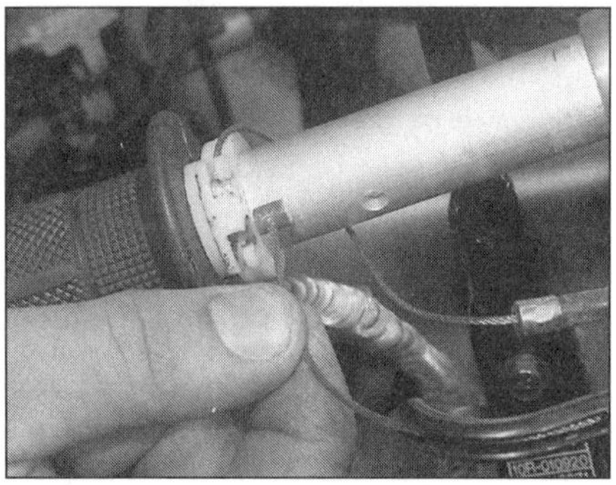

10.5 . . . and detach the cable ends from the pulley

10.6a On F models the bracket and pulley are on the right-hand end of the carburettors . . .

10.6b . . . on G, H, J and A models they are on the left-hand end

3 Remove the throttle housing screws **(see illustrations)** and separate the front and rear halves of the housing **(see illustration)**.

4 Detach the cables from the housing, noting how they fit **(see illustration)**.

5 Rotate the ends of the cables to align with the slots in the throttle grip pulley, then detach the cables from the pulley **(see illustration)**.

6 Detach the cables from the bracket and throttle pulley on the carburettor, noting which cable fits where **(see illustrations)**.

7 Remove the cables, noting how they are routed.

Installation

8 Installation is basically the reverse of removal. Make sure the cables are routed properly. Also ensure they don't interfere with any other components and aren't kinked or bent sharply. Lubricate the ends of the cables with multi-purpose grease. Make sure the locating pin in the housing engages with the hole in the handlebar **(see illustration)**.

Adjustment

9 Follow the procedure outlined in Chapter 1, Section 18, to adjust the cables.

10 Turn the handlebars back and forth to make sure the cables don't cause the steering to bind.

11 Install the carburettors if displaced, the air filter housing and fuel tank.

12 With the engine idling, turn the handlebars through their full travel (full left lock to full right

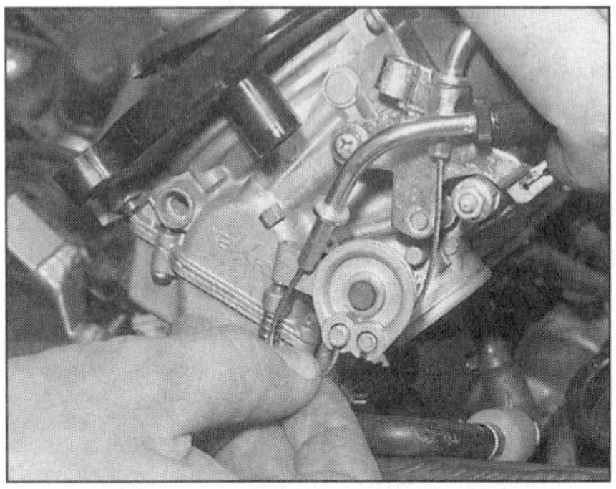

10.6c Lift the elbow out of the bracket and detach the cable end from the pulley

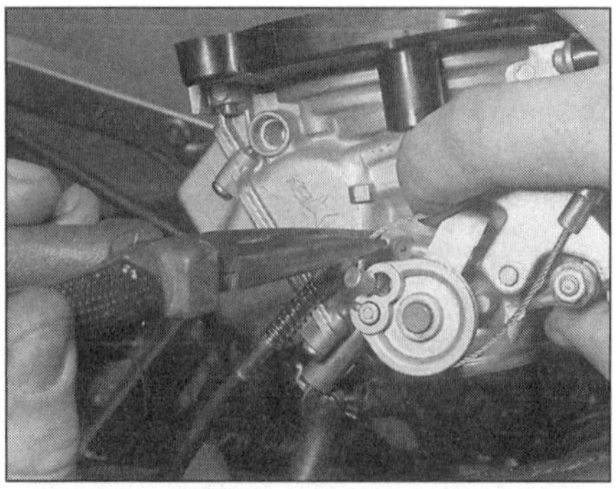

10.6d If the cables are still attached at the handlebar, rotate the pulley by hand to create slack

10.8 Make sure the pin (A) locates in the hole (B) in the handlebar

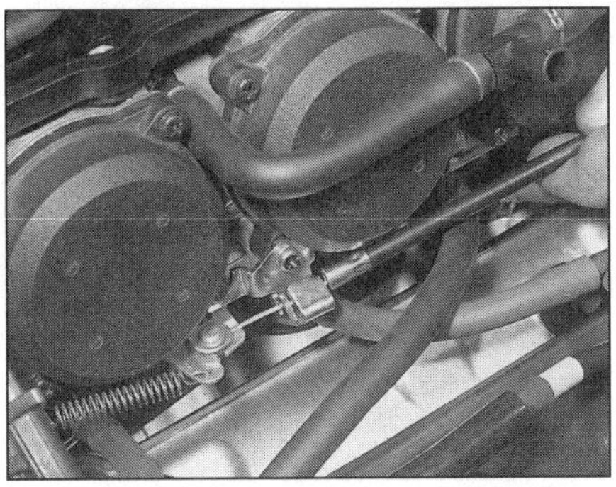

11.2a Pull the outer cable from the bracket . . .

11.2b . . . and detach the cable end from the lever

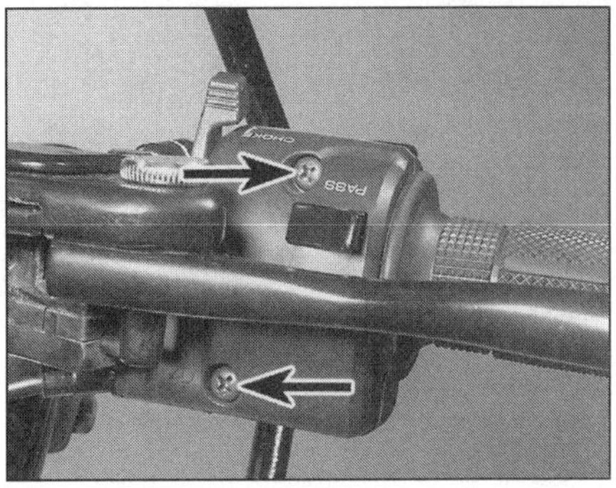

11.3a Remove the screws (arrowed) . . .

11.3b . . . and separate the halves

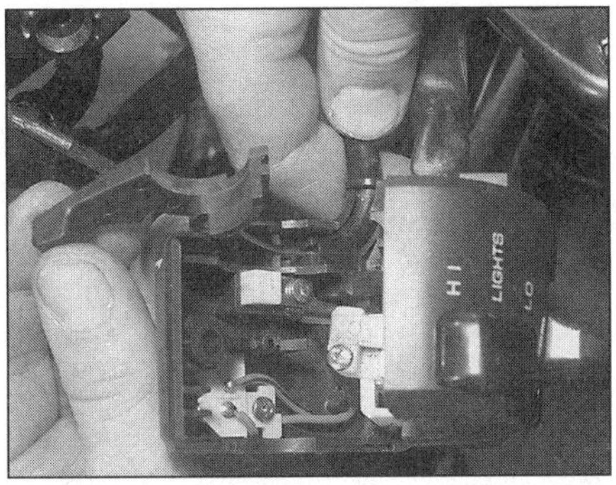

11.3c Remove the lever and elbow . . .

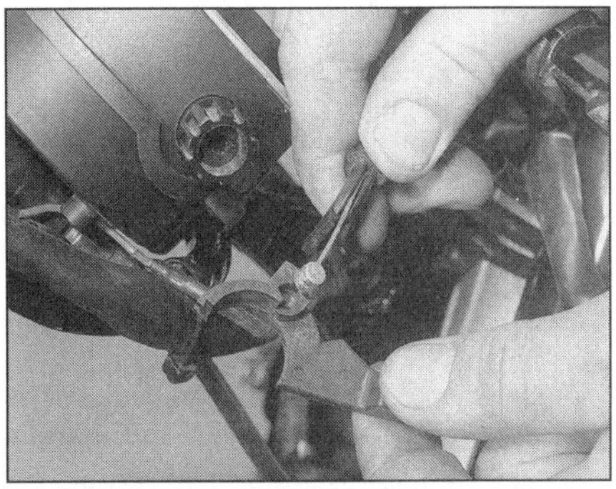

11.3d . . . and detach the cable

lock) and note whether idle speed increases. If it does, the cables are routed incorrectly. Correct this dangerous condition before riding the bike.

Throttle grip

Removal

13 Follow Steps 2 through 5 to detach the upper ends of the throttle cables from the throttle grip pulley.

14 Remove the grip end weight and slide the throttle grip off the handlebar.

Installation

15 Clean the handlebar and apply a light coat of multi-purpose grease.

16 Push the throttle grip on. Install the grip end weight and tighten the screw securely.

17 Reconnect the cables in a reverse of the dismantling order, then adjust them following the procedure outlined in Chapter 1, Section 18.

11 Choke cable – removal, installation and adjustment

Removal

1 Remove the fuel tank (see Section 2) and the air filter housing (see Section 4).

2 Pull the choke cable out of its mounting bracket at the carburettor assembly, then pass the inner cable through the opening in the bracket and detach the cable end from the choke lever **(see illustrations)**.

3 Remove the two screws securing the choke cable/switch housing halves to the left handlebar and separate the halves **(see illustrations)**. Remove the choke lever and cable elbow from the housing, noting how they fit, and detach the cable end from the lever **(see illustrations)**.

4 Remove the cable, noting how it's routed.

Installation

5 Route the cable into position. Connect the upper end of the cable to the choke lever **(see illustration 11.3d)**. Make sure the cable guide and lever seat properly in the housing **(see illustration 11.3c)**. Place the housing up against the handlebar, making sure the pin in the housing fits into the hole in the handlebar **(see illustration 11.3b)**. Install the screws, tightening them securely.

6 Connect the lower end of the cable to the choke lever **(see illustration 11.2b)**. Pull back on the cable and feed it into the bracket, making sure it seats correctly **(see illustration 11.2a)**.

7 Install the air filter housing (see Section 4) and the fuel tank (see Section 2).

Adjustment

8 Follow the procedure outlined in Chapter 1, Section 18, to adjust the cables.

12 Air/fuel mixture adjustment – general information

Note: *Due to the increased emphasis on controlling exhaust emissions in certain world markets, regulations have been formulated which prevent adjustment of the air/fuel mixture. On such models the pilot screw positions are pre-set at the factory and in some cases have a metal sealing plug pressed into the hole over the pilot screw to prevent tampering. Where adjustment is possible, it can only be made in conjunction with an exhaust gas analyser to ensure that the machine does not exceed emissions regulations.*

1 If the engine runs extremely rough at idle or continually stalls, and if a carburettor overhaul does not cure the problem (and it definitely is a carburation problem – see Section 6), the pilot screws may require adjustment. It is worth noting at this point that unless you have the experience to carry this out it is best to entrust the task to a motorcycle dealer, tuner or fuel systems specialist. The pilot screws are located underneath the carburettors and are best accessed using a purpose-made angled screwdriver, available from any good accessory dealer. Make sure the valve clearances are correct and the carburettors are synchronised before adjusting the pilot screws (see Chapter 1).

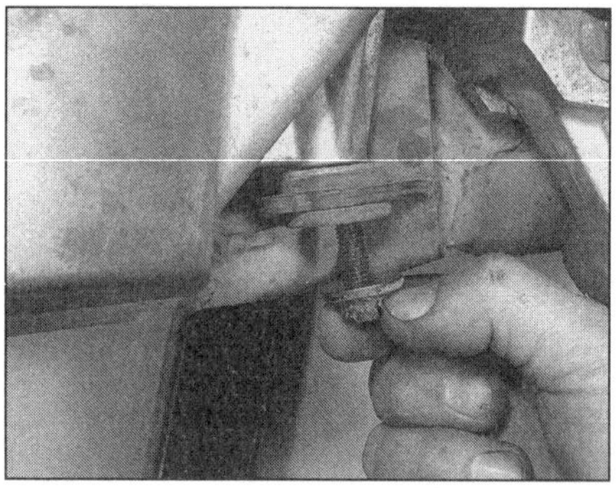

13.3 Remove the bolt securing the system to the sump

2 Before adjusting the pilot screws, warm the engine up to normal working temperature, then stop it. Screw in the pilot screw on all carburettors until they seat lightly, counting the number of turns as an analysis check, then back them out to the number of turns specified (see this Chapter's Specifications). This is the base position for adjustment.

3 Start the engine and reset the idle speed to the correct level (see Chapter 1). Working on one carburettor at a time, turn the pilot screw by a small amount either side of this position to find the point at which the highest consistent idle speed is obtained. When you've reached this position, reset the idle speed to the specified amount (see Chapter 1). Repeat on the other carburettors.

13.5b . . . and remove the exhaust

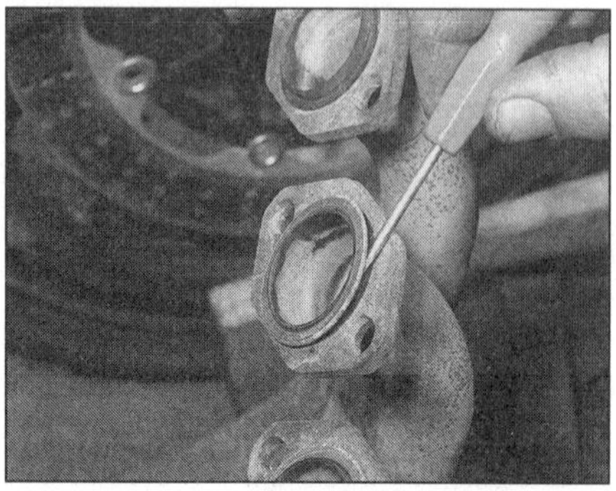

13.7a Remove the old gaskets . . .

13.4 Unscrew the nut securing the silencer bracket bolt

13 Exhaust system – removal and installation

Warning: Always allow the exhaust system time to cool down before attempting removal. This is especially important in the case of catalytic converter equipped models due to the high operating temperature of the converter elements.

Removal

1 Remove the lower fairing panels (see Chapter 8).

13.6 Remove the three bolts (arrowed) or nuts (G, H, J and A models) securing the silencer to the downpipe assembly

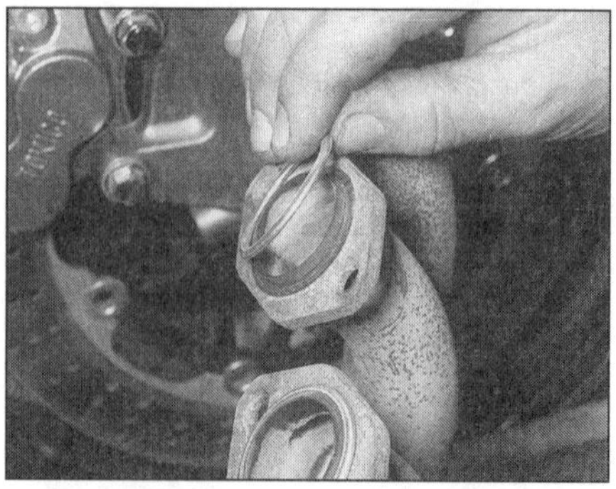

13.7b . . . and fit new ones

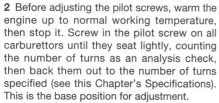

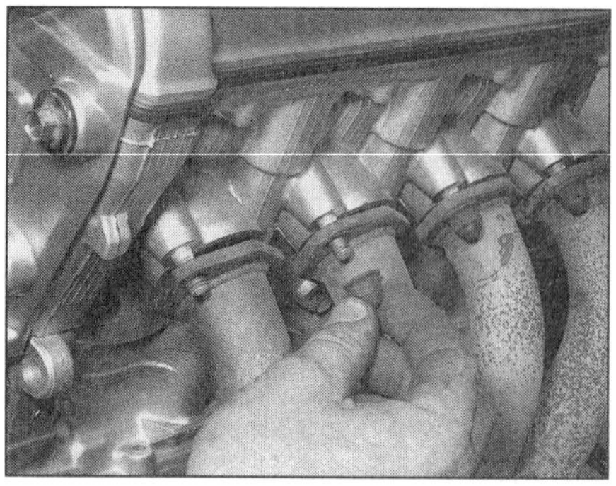

13.5a Unscrew the downpipe nuts . . .

2 On F models, first detach the oil cooler from the bottom of the radiator (see Chapter 3), then loosen the upper radiator mounting bolts and swing the radiator forward to provide clearance. On G and H models, remove the radiator (see Chapter 3). On J and A models, remove the bottom radiator mounting bolt, then loosen the upper mounting bolts and swing the radiator forward to provide clearance.

3 Unscrew the bolt that secures the exhaust system to the oil sump **(see illustration)**.

4 Unscrew the nut on the bolt securing the silencer to the footrest bracket, but leave the bolt loosely in place **(see illustration)**.

5 Unscrew the nuts securing the downpipes to the cylinder head **(see illustration)**. Support the system, then withdraw the silencer mounting bolt and manoeuvre the exhaust away from the bike **(see illustration)**.

6 If required, the silencer can be separated from the downpipe assembly by unscrewing the three nuts or bolts that join them **(see illustration)**. Also, the silencer can be removed leaving the downpipe assembly installed on the machine, if required. Unscrew the three joining nuts or bolts and the silencer mounting bolt and remove the silencer.

Installation

7 Installation is the reverse of removal. Always use new gaskets between the downpipes and the cylinder head, and between the downpipe assembly and the silencer, if separated **(see illustrations)**. Check the condition of the rubber mountings on the footrest bracket and the sump and renew them if they are damaged or deteriorated.

8 Tighten the mounting nuts and bolts to the torque settings specified at the beginning of the Chapter. **Note:** *Kawasaki do not specify a torque setting for the exhaust downpipe to cylinder head nuts.* Before installing the lower fairing panels, run the engine until it reaches normal operating temperature, then allow it to cool and recheck the mounting nuts and bolts.

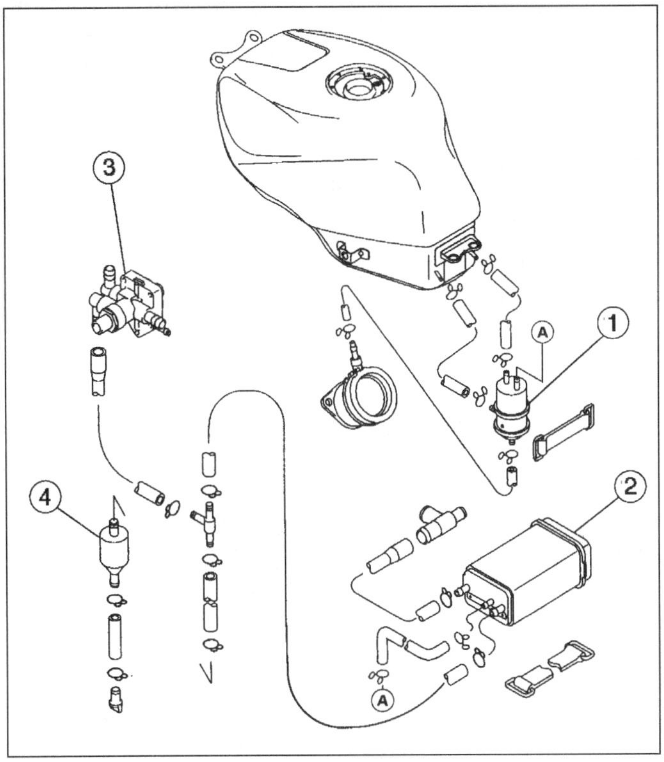

14.1a Evaporative loss system (EVAP) – California F models

1 Vapour separator
2 Charcoal canister
3 Vacuum valve
4 Catch tank

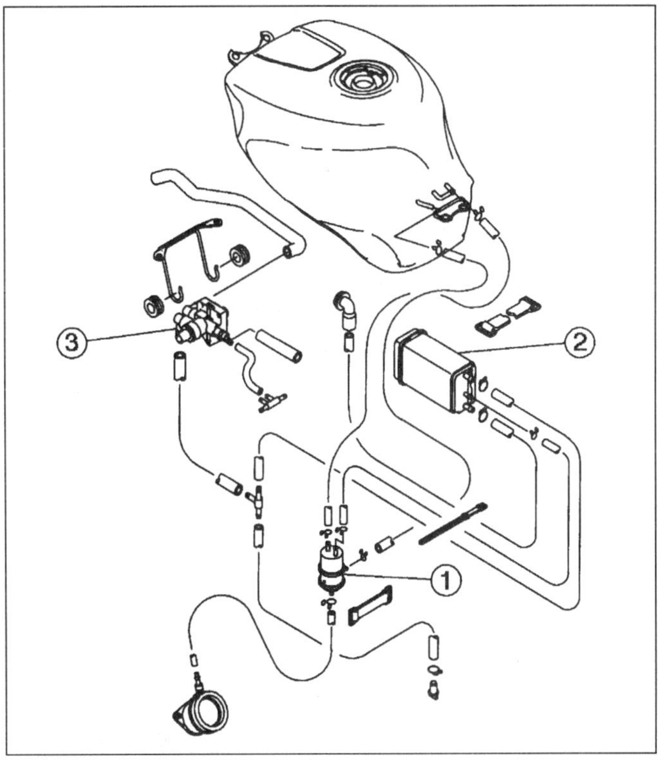

14.1b Evaporative loss system (EVAP) – California G and J models

1 Vapour separator 2 Charcoal canister 3 Vacuum valve

14 Evaporative loss system (US California models only) – general information

1 On all California models, an evaporative loss system is fitted **(see illustrations)**. This system prevents the escape of fuel vapours into the atmosphere and functions as follows.

2 When the engine is stopped, fuel vapour from the tank and the carburettor float chambers is directed into a charcoal canister where it is absorbed and stored whilst the motorcycle is standing. When the engine is started, inlet manifold depression draws the stored vapours into the engine to be burned during the normal combustion process.

3 The fuel tank fitted to California models incorporates a special vapour collection chamber which allows the vapours to pass into the canister. The tank filler cap has a one way valve which allows air into the tank as the volume of fuel decreases, but prevents any fuel vapour from escaping.

4 The system is not adjustable and can be tested only by a Kawasaki dealer. Checks which can be performed by the owner are given in Chapter 1.

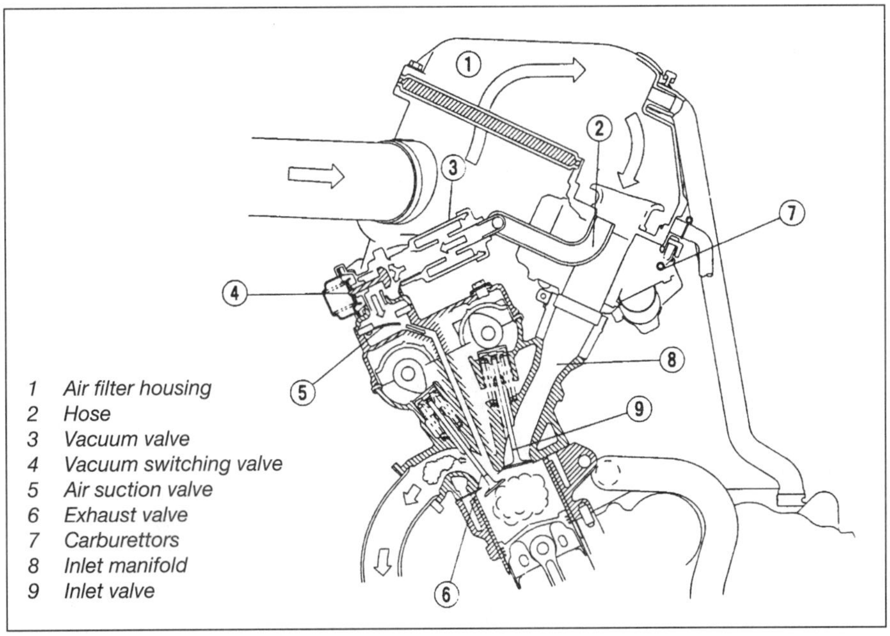

15.1 Secondary air injection system

15 Secondary air injection system

1 This system aids the burning of fuel/air mixture, preventing unburnt fuel from passing into the exhaust system and thus into the atmosphere. When the exhaust valves open to allow spent gases to escape into the exhaust system, fresh air is drawn from the air filter into the exhaust valve tracts via the air suction valves **(see illustration)**. This fresh air aids the burning of any unburnt fuel/air mixture present, so converting the harmful carbon monoxide (CO) and hydrocarbons (HC) into carbon dioxide (CO_2) and water (H_2O).

2 The air suction valves are situated on the

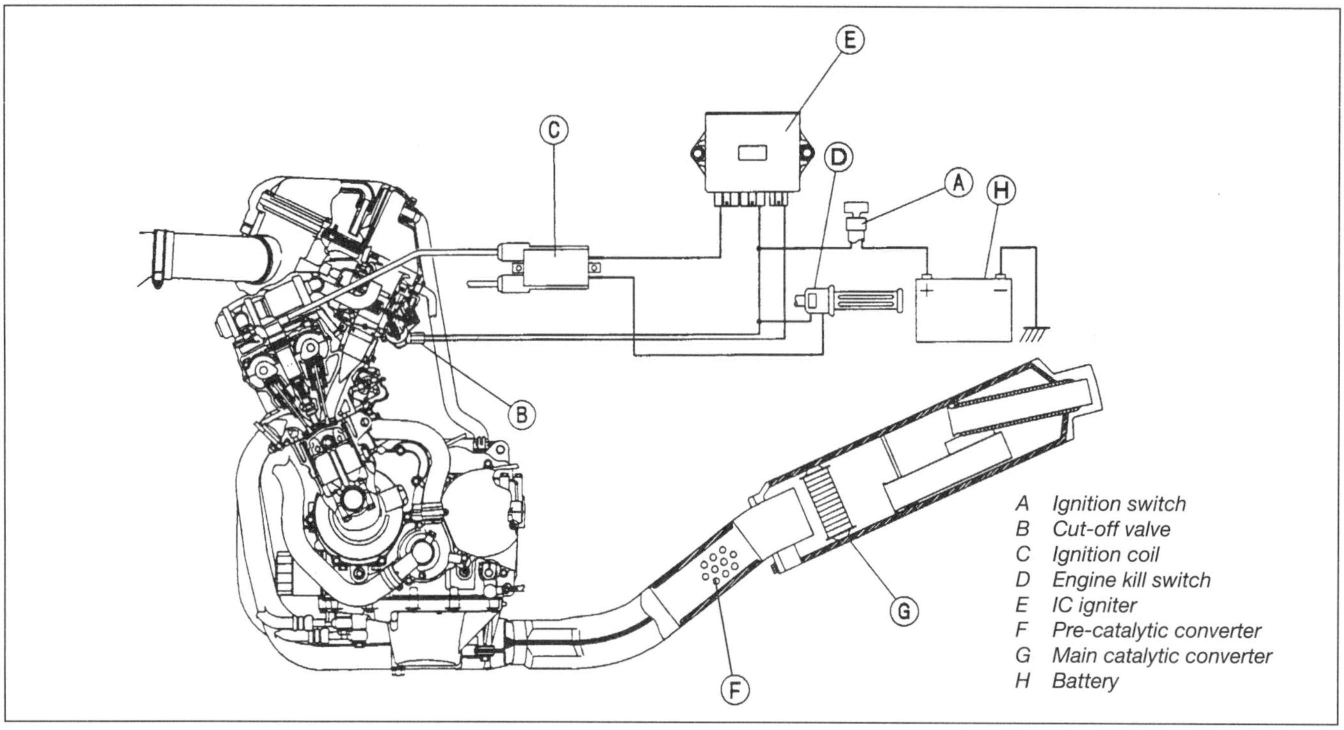

16.1 Catalytic converter and fuel cut-off circuit

valve cover and operate by the vacuum generated by the exhaust pulses. The valves are automatic in operation and should be checked according the maintenance schedule (see Chapter 1). A vacuum switching valve is fitted to shut off air flow to the air suction valves under engine braking conditions when inlet manifold vacuum is high, and prevents explosions or backfiring in the exhaust system.

16 Catalytic converter

1 An open-loop catalytic converter is fitted in the exhaust system of California market G models, H models for Germany and Switzerland, and all J and A models except for the Australian market **(see illustration)**.

2 The Kawasaki system uses two converter elements, one located in the exhaust pipe, just ahead of the silencer, and the other located in the front section of the silencer. The catalytic converter reduces the harmful elements of the exhaust gases by converting carbon monoxide (CO), hydrocarbons (HC) and nitrogen oxides (NO_x) into carbon dioxide (CO_2), water (H_2O) and nitrogen (N_2).

3 Fuel cut-off valves installed on the carburettor float chambers provide protection for the catalytic converters by preventing excess fuel being passed into the exhaust system. If a high level of unburnt fuel enters the exhaust system the catalysts will overheat and may eventually meltdown. The cut-off valves are controlled by the IC igniter and close if the ignition is cut by the speed limiter, if the engine kill switch is turned OFF when the engine is running, or if a misfire or interruption in the ignition coil primary circuit occurs. Since the fuel cut-off valves are unlikely to operate under normal running conditions, the IC igniter is programmed to operate the valves for an instant every time the engine is started; in this way the valves are less likely to become gummed up with fuel deposits.

4 The following precautions should be noted:

- Always use unleaded fuel only. Leaded fuel will poison the catalytic converter and reduce its efficiency.
- Always use the specified engine oil . Do not use engine oil which has phosphorus (P), lead (Pb) or sulphur (S) ingredients.
- Do not coast the motorcycle at any time with the ignition main switch OFF or engine kill switch OFF. With the switches OFF, the fuel cut-off valves are disabled and will allow unburnt fuel to pass into the exhaust system leading to overheating of the catalytic converters and their eventual failure due to meltdown.
- In the case of a flat battery, do not push-start the engine. Recharge the battery or connect up an auxiliary battery using jumper leads.
- Do not continue to use the motorcycle if it develops a misfire or ignition system fault. Correct the fault at the earliest opportunity.
- Keep the fuel and ignition systems in good order – if the fuel/air mixture is suspected of being incorrect have it checked by a dealer equipped with an exhaust gas analyser.
- Take care to avoid burns when handling the silencer and exhaust pipe; these components can become extremely hot.
- Check the air suction valves at the specified interval (see Chapter 1).

Chapter 5
Ignition system

Contents

Degrees of difficulty

Easy, suitable for novice with little experience	**Fairly easy,** suitable for beginner with some experience	**Fairly difficult,** suitable for competent DIY mechanic	**Difficult,** suitable for experienced DIY mechanic	**Very difficult,** suitable for expert DIY or professional

Specifications

General

Cylinder identification	from left to right, numbered 1, 2, 3 and 4
Firing order	1-2-4-3

Spark plugs

Plug type and gap	see Chapter 1
Spark plug cap resistance (F, G and H models)	3.75 to 6.25 K-ohms

Ignition coil

Primary resistance	
F, G and H models	2.6 to 3.2 ohms
J and A models	1.2 to 1.6 ohms
Secondary resistance	
F models	13.0 to 17.0 K-ohms
G and H models	13.5 to 16.5 K-ohms
J and A models	8.5 to 11.5 K-ohms
Arcing distance	
F models	6 mm or more
G and H models	8 mm or more
J and A models	not available

Pick-up coil

Resistance	
F, G and H models	380 to 570 ohms
J and A models	452 to 462 ohms

Ignition timing

F models	
Californian models	from 5° BTDC @ 1300 rpm to 35° BTDC @ 5000 rpm
All other models	from 12.5° BTDC @ 1050 rpm to 35° BTDC @ 3000 rpm
G and H models	from 12.5° BTDC @ 1300 rpm to 35° BTDC @ 5000 rpm
J and A models	from 12.5° BTDC @ 1300 rpm to 42.5° BTDC @ 5000 rpm

Throttle position sensor (G, H, J and A models)

Output voltage	
At idle (all models)	0.95 to 1.05 volts
Engine OFF, throttle fully open (J and A models)	3.95 to 4.15 volts

Torque specifications

Pick-up coil cover bolts	12 Nm
Pick-up coil mounting bolts	6 Nm
Timing rotor Allen bolt (F models)	25 Nm
Timing rotor bolt	
G and H models	39 Nm
J and A models	40 Nm
Throttle position sensor screws (G, H, J and A models)	3.4 Nm

1 General information

All models are fitted with a fully transistorised electronic ignition system, which due to its lack of mechanical parts is totally maintenance free. The system consists of the following components:

Pick-up coil
IC igniter unit
Battery and fuse
Ignition coils
Spark plugs
Stop and main (key) switches
Primary and secondary circuit wiring

The ignition triggers, which are on the rotor on the right-hand end of the crankshaft, magnetically operate the pick-up coil as the crankshaft rotates. The pick-up coil sends a signal to the ignition control igniter unit which then supplies the ignition HT coils with the power necessary to produce a spark at the plugs. The system incorporates an electronic advance system controlled by signals generated by the ignition triggers and the pick-up coil.

On F, G and H models, there are two HT coils, one supplying Nos. 1 and 4 cylinder spark plugs and the other supplying Nos. 2 and 3 cylinder plugs. On J and A models, a combined ignition coil/plug caps is used for each cylinder.

The system incorporates a safety interlock circuit which will cut the ignition if the sidestand is put down whilst the engine is running and in gear, or if a gear is selected whilst the engine is running and the sidestand is down. It also prevents the engine from being started if the sidestand is down and the engine is in gear unless the clutch lever is pulled in.

Because of their nature, the individual ignition system components can be checked but not repaired. If ignition system troubles occur, and the faulty component can be isolated, the only cure for the problem is to replace the part with a new one. Keep in mind that most electrical parts, once purchased, cannot be returned. To avoid unnecessary expense, make very sure the faulty component has been positively identified before buying a replacement part.

Note that there is no provision for adjusting the ignition timing on these models.

2.3 Ground (earth) the spark plug and operate the starter – bright blue sparks should be visible

2 Ignition system – check

Warning: Because of the very high voltage generated by the ignition system, extreme care should be taken when these checks are performed. On no account should the ignition be switched on whilst the plugs or plug caps are being held. Shocks from the HT circuit can be most unpleasant. Secondly, it is vital that the engine is not turned over or run with any of the plug caps removed, and that the plugs are soundly earthed (grounded) when the system is checked for sparking. The ignition system components can be seriously damaged if the HT circuit becomes isolated.

1 If the ignition system is the suspected cause of poor engine performance or failure to start, a number of checks can be made to isolate the problem.

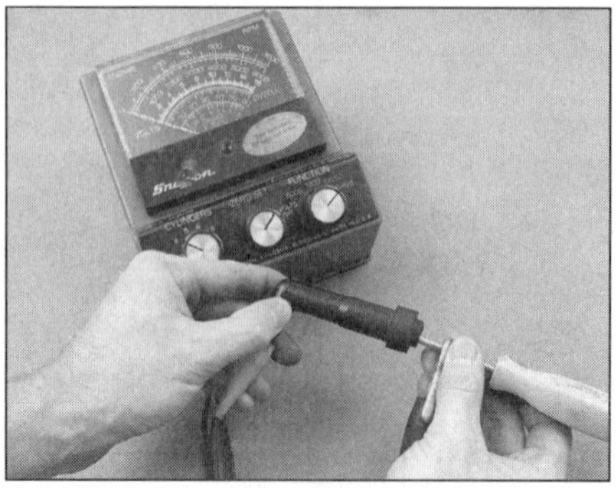

2.5 Unscrew the spark plug caps from the leads and measure their resistance with an ohmmeter

2 Make sure the ignition stop switch is in the RUN or ON position.

Engine will not start

3 Remove the air filter housing (see Chapter 4). On F, G and H models, check that the cylinder location is marked on each spark plug cap, then disconnect one of the caps, connect it to a known good spark plug and lay the plug on the engine with the threads earthed (grounded). On J and A models, check that the cylinder location is marked on each ignition coil/plug cap, then disconnect one of the coil/cap connectors and pull the coil/cap off the spark plug. **Note:** *To avoid damaging the wiring, always disconnect the connectors before removing the coil/caps. Do not attempt to lever the coil/caps off the plugs or pull them off with pliers. Do not drop the coils.* Reconnect the wiring connector, then connect the coil/cap to a known good spark plug and lay the plug on the engine with the threads earthed (grounded).

Caution: Do not lay the plug against the magnesium engine covers (such as the valve cover on J and A models) as they could be damaged. If necessary, hold the spark plug with an insulated tool (see illustration).

Warning: Don't remove one of the spark plugs from the engine to perform this check – atomised fuel being pumped out of the open spark plug hole could ignite, causing severe injury!

4 Crank the engine over and make sure a well-defined, blue spark occurs between the spark plug electrodes. If no spark occurs, the following checks should be made:

5 On F, G and H models, unscrew the spark plug cap from the HT lead and check the cap resistance with an ohmmeter **(see illustration)**. If the resistance is infinite, or is outside the specified range, fit a new cap. Repeat this check on the remaining plug caps. On J and A models, check the coil/cap primary and secondary resistance (see Section 3).

6 Make sure all electrical connectors are clean and tight. Check all wires for short circuits, open circuits and correct installation.

7 Check the battery voltage with a voltmeter. If the voltage is less than 12V, recharge the battery.

TOOL TiP

A simple spark gap testing tool can be made from a block of wood, a large alligator clip and two nails, one of which is fashioned so that a spark plug cap or bare HT lead end can be connected to its end. Make sure the gap between the two nail ends is the same as specified.

8 Check the ignition fuse and the fuse connections. If the fuse is blown, fit a new one; if the connections are loose or corroded, clean or repair them.

9 On F, G and H models, check the ignition coil primary and secondary resistance (see Section 3).

10 Refer to Section 4 and check the pick-up coil resistance.

11 If the preceding checks produce positive results but there is still no spark at the plug, remove the IC igniter and have it checked by a Kawasaki dealer service department or other repair shop equipped with the special tester required.

Engine starts but misfires

12 If the engine starts but misfires, make the following checks before deciding that the ignition system is at fault.

13 The ignition system must be able to produce a spark across a minimum gap of 6 mm (F models) or 8 mm (G and H models). **Note:** *Kawasaki do not specify a minimum spark gap for J and A models, but the spark generated should jump a similar gap.* A simple test tool can be constructed to make sure the minimum spark gap can be jumped (see **Tool Tip**). Alternatively, it is possible to buy an ignition spark gap tester tool. Make sure the test tool electrodes are positioned the correct distance apart.

2.14 Connect the tester as shown – when the engine is cranked sparks should jump the gap between the nails

14 On F, G and H models, pull one of the spark plug caps off its plug and connect it to the protruding electrode on the test tool, then clip the tool to a good earth (ground) on the engine or frame **(see illustration)**. Turn the ignition switch ON and crank the engine over and see if well-defined, blue sparks occur between the test tool electrodes. If the minimum spark gap test is positive, the ignition coil for that cylinder (and its companion cylinder) is functioning properly. If the spark will not jump the gap, or if it is weak (orange coloured), refer to Steps 5 to 11 of this Section and perform the component checks described. Repeat the check with one of the spark plug caps that is connected to the other coil.

15 On J and A models, pull one of the coil/caps off its plug, reconnect the wiring connector then connect the coil/cap to the test tool. Ensure the tool is clipped to a good earth (ground) on the engine or frame, then follow the procedure described in Step 14 to test the minimum spark gap **(see illustration)**. If the spark will not jump the gap, or if it is weak (orange coloured), check the coil/cap primary and secondary resistance (see Section 3). Repeat the test on the other coil/caps.

3 Ignition coils – check, removal and installation

1 In order to determine conclusively that the ignition coils are defective they should be tested by a Kawasaki dealer.

2 However, the coils can be checked visually (for cracks and other damage) and the primary and secondary coil resistances can be measured with an ohmmeter. If the coils are undamaged, and if the resistances are as specified, they are probably capable of proper operation.

Check – F, G and H models

3 To check the resistances, first remove the air filter housing (see Chapter 4), then unplug the primary circuit electrical connectors from the coil(s) **(see illustration 3.9a)** and pull the spark plug caps off the plugs that are connected to the coil being checked. Mark the locations of all wires before disconnecting them.

4 Place the ohmmeter selector switch in the ohms x 1 position. To check the coil primary resistance, attach one ohmmeter lead to one of the primary terminals and the other ohmmeter lead to the other primary terminal **(see illustration)**.

5 Compare the measured resistance to the value listed in this Chapter's Specifications. If required, check the primary resistance of the other coil.

6 Place the ohmmeter selector switch in the K-ohms position. To check the coil secondary resistance, unscrew the spark plug caps from the leads, then insert the ohmmeter leads into

2.15 Using a test tool to check the spark gap – J and A models

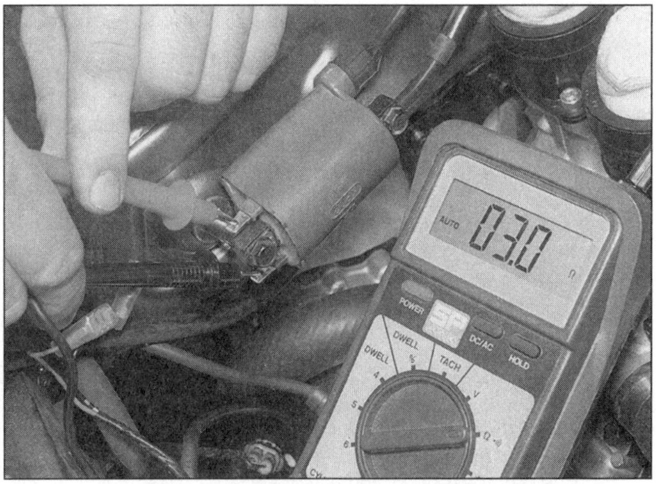

3.4 Checking the coil primary circuit resistance

5

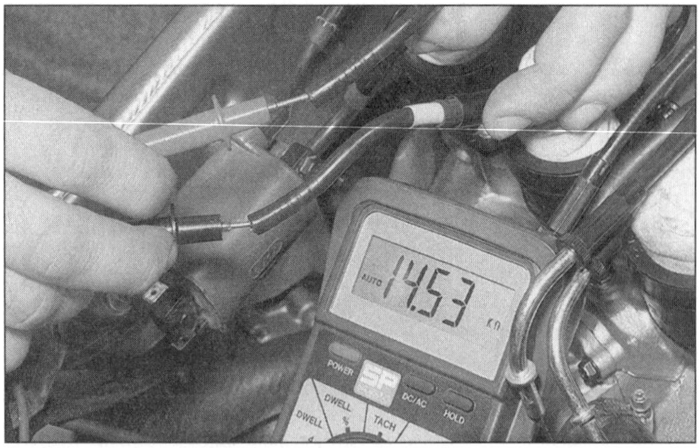

3.6 Checking the coil secondary circuit resistance

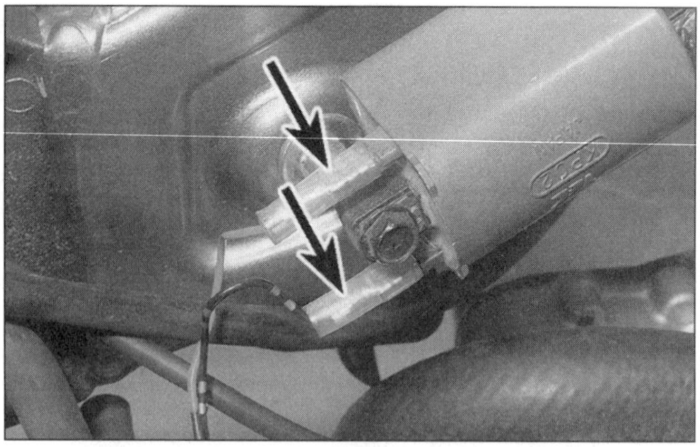

3.9a Coil primary circuit connectors (arrowed)

3.9b On G and H models, the coils (arrowed) are mounted between the frame spars

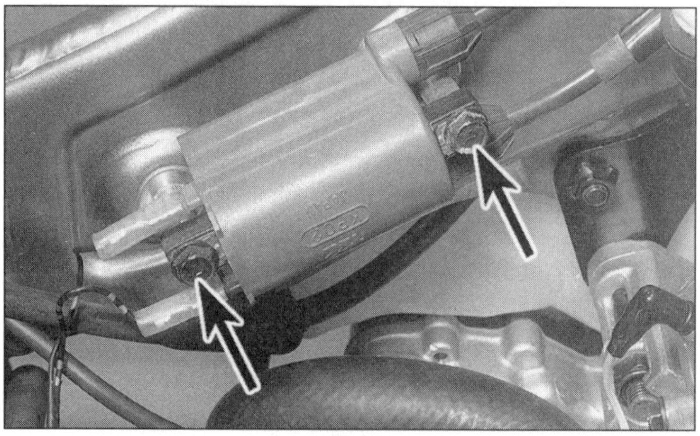

3.10 Coil mounting bolts (arrowed)

the ends of the spark plug leads **(see illustration)**.

7 Compare the measured resistance to the values listed in this Chapter's Specifications. If required, check the secondary resistance of the other coil.

8 If the resistances are not as specified, unscrew the spark plug lead retainers from the coil, detach the leads and check the resistance again. If it is now within specifications, one or both of the leads is bad. If it's still not as specified, the coil is probably defective and should be renewed.

Removal and installation – F, G and H models

9 Remove the air filter housing (see Chapter 4). On F, G and H models, make a note of which colour wire fits on which terminal, then disconnect the primary circuit electrical connectors from the coil and the spark plug leads from the plugs **(see illustrations)**. Label them with tape to aid installation.

10 Support the coil with one hand, then unscrew the coil mounting bolts and remove the coil from its bracket **(see illustration)**.

HAYNES HiNT *If you're removing both coils, it's a good idea to label the coils with the cylinder numbers to which they're connected.*

11 Installation is the reverse of removal. If a new coil is being installed and the old leads are being used, unscrew the spark plug lead terminals from the old coil, pull the leads out and transfer them to the new coil. Make sure the primary circuit electrical connectors are attached to the proper terminals – the black and red wires connect to the Nos.1 and 4 ignition coil (red to positive, black to negative) and the red and green wires attach to the Nos.2 and 3 coil (red to positive, green to negative).

Check – J and A models

12 Remove the air filter housing (see Chapter 4). Check that the cylinder location is marked on each ignition coil/plug cap wiring connector and mark them accordingly if not, then disconnect the connectors **(see illustration)**. Pull the coil/caps off the spark plugs and mark their cylinder location also **(see illustration)**. **Note:** *To avoid damaging the wiring, always disconnect the connectors before removing the coil/caps. Do not attempt to lever the coil/caps off the plugs or pull them off with pliers. Do not drop the coils.*

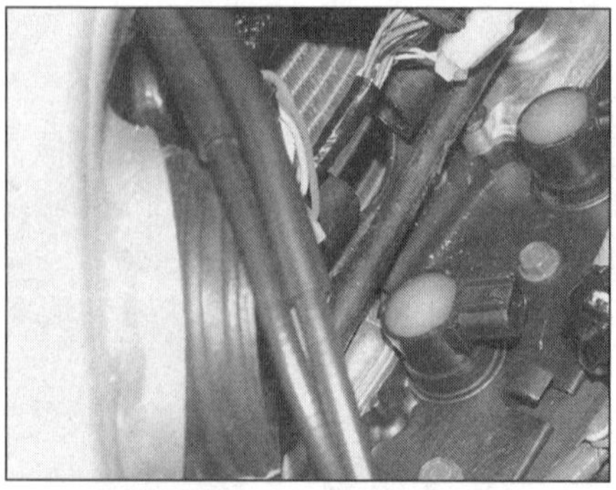

3.12a On J and A models, disconnect the coil/cap wiring connectors . . .

3.12b . . . then pull the coil/caps off the spark plugs

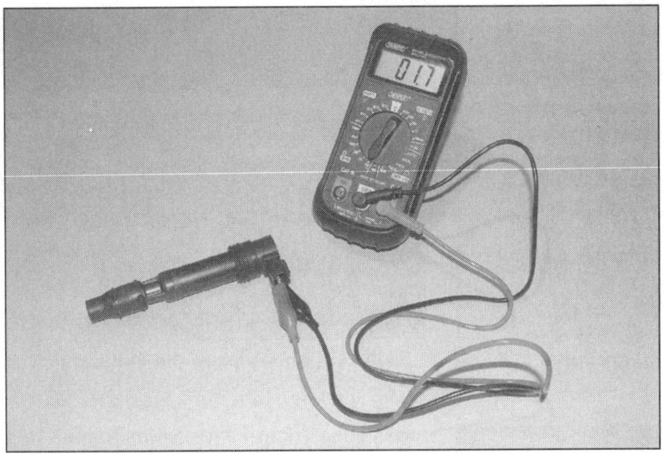

3.13 Measuring the coil/cap primary resistance

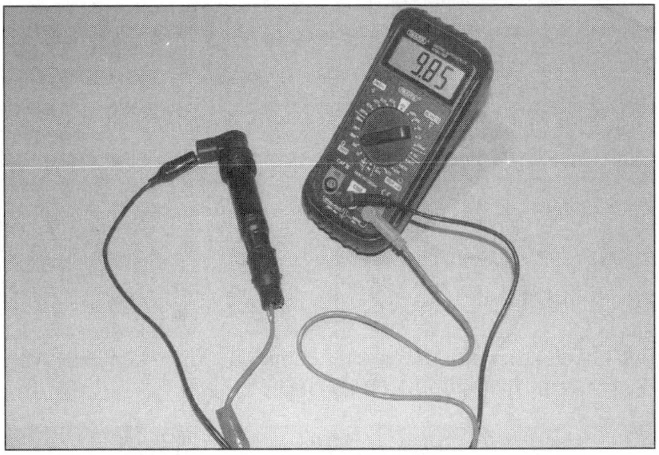

3.14 Measuring the coil/cap secondary resistance

13 Using an ohmmeter or multimeter set to the ohms scale, measure the coil/cap primary resistance between the primary circuit terminals **(see illustration)**. Compare the result with the specifications at the beginning of this Chapter.

14 Now set the meter to the K-ohms scale and measure the coil/cap secondary resistance between the negative (-ve) (red wire) primary circuit terminal and the spark plug terminal **(see illustration)**. Compare the result with the specifications at the beginning of this Chapter.

15 If either of the results are not as specified the coil/cap is probably faulty. Have the coil/cap peak voltage tested by a Kawasaki dealer.

Removal and installation – J and A models

16 Remove the air filter housing (see Chapter 4). Follow Step 12 and disconnect each coil/ cap wiring connector, then pull the coil/caps off the spark plugs.

17 Ensure the primary circuit terminals in the top of the coil/cap and the spark plug terminal inside the cap are undamaged and free from corrosion.

18 Press the coil/caps fully home onto the spark plugs. Ensure the connectors are reconnected in the correct order.

4 Pick-up coil – check, removal and installation

Check

1 Remove the fuel tank (see Chapter 4).

2 Trace the pick-up coil wiring from the cover on the right-hand side of the engine and disconnect it at the connector **(see illustration)**.

3 Connect the probes of an ohmmeter between the black/yellow and black terminals on the pick-up coil side of the wiring connector **(see illustration)** and compare the resistance reading with the range of resistance listed in this Chapter's Specifications.

4 Set the ohmmeter on the highest resistance range. Measure the resistance between a good earth (ground) and each terminal in the pick-up coil connector. The meter should indicate infinite resistance.

5 If the pick-up coil fails either of the above tests, it must be renewed.

Removal

6 Remove the fuel tank (see Chapter 4) and the fairing right-hand lower panel (see Chapter 8).

7 Trace the pick-up coil wiring from the cover on the right-hand side of the engine and disconnect it at the connector **(see illustration 4.2)**. On F, G and H models, also disconnect the wiring connectors from the coolant temperature sensor on the back of the cylinder head and the oil pressure switch on the front of the crankcase (they are wired into the same connector as the pick-up coil) **(see illustrations)**. On J and A models, also disconnect the connectors from the sidestand switch, neutral switch, coolant temperature sensor and the oil pressure switch.

8 Release the wiring from the two clips on the pick-up coil cover, then unscrew the bolts that secure the cover to the right-hand side of the

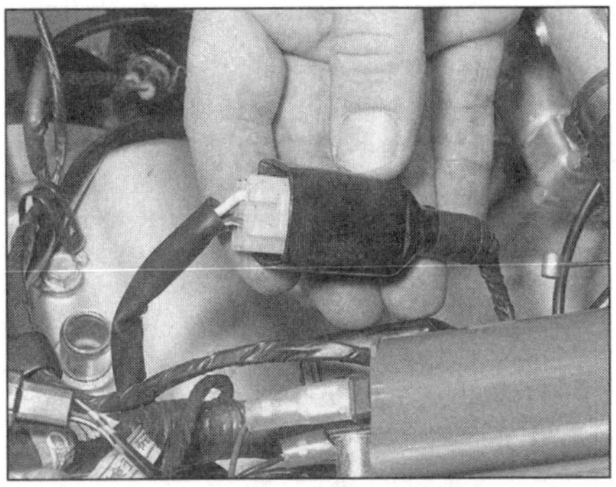

4.2 Disconnect the pick-up coil wiring connector . . .

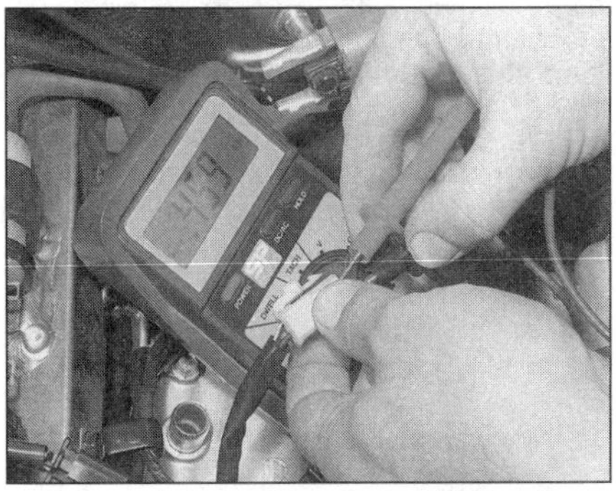

4.3 . . . and test the coil as described

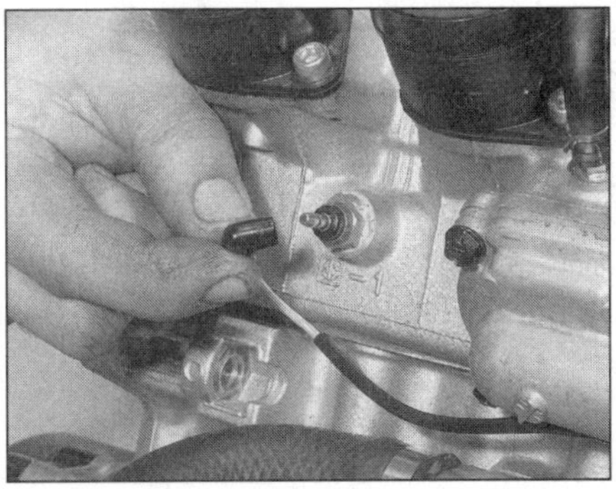

4.7a Disconnect the coolant temperature sensor wiring connector . . .

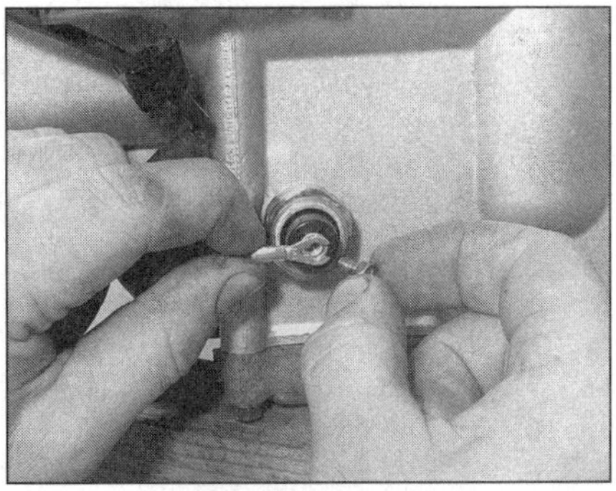

4.7b . . . and the oil pressure switch wiring connector

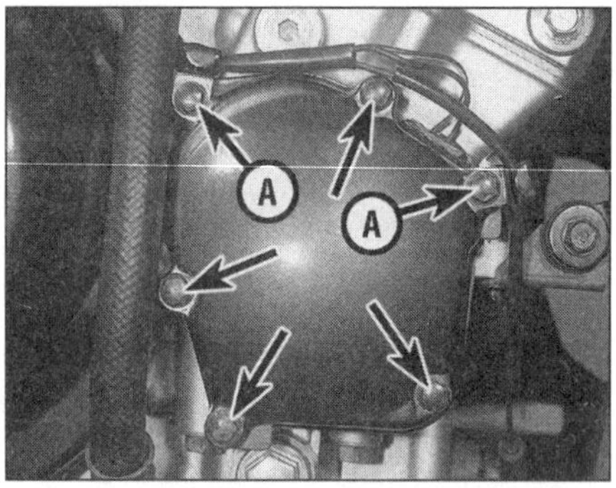

4.8 Unscrew the bolts (arrowed) and remove the cover, noting the wiring clamps (A)

4.9a Free the wiring grommet . . .

4.9b . . . and remove the pick-up coil

4.11a Apply the sealant as shown (arrowed) . . .

engine and remove the cover **(see illustration)**.

9 Pull the rubber wiring grommet from its recess, then unscrew the pick-up coil mounting bolts and remove the pick-up coil **(see illustrations)**. Note the routing of the wiring.

Installation

10 Install the new pick-up coil unit and tighten the bolts to the torque setting specified at the beginning of the Chapter. Apply silicone sealant to the grommet for the electrical leads and push the grommet into its notch in the crankcase.

11 Apply silicone sealant to the 'split-line' of

4.11b . . . then fit the cover using a new gasket

the crankcase halves, then install the pick-up coil cover using a new gasket, not forgetting the wiring clips with the upper front and rear bolts **(see illustrations and 4.8)**. Apply a suitable non-permanent thread locking compound to the upper central bolt and tighten the bolts to the specified torque.

12 Route the wiring exactly the same way it was routed before and connect the wiring connectors to the coolant temperature sensor and oil pressure switch **(see illustrations 4.7a and b)**, and on J and A models, plus the neutral switch and sidestand switch. Also connect the four-pin connector to the wiring loom **(see illustration 4.2)**.

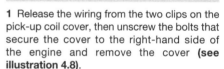

13 Install the fuel tank (see Chapter 4) and the fairing right-hand lower panel (see Chapter 8).

5 Timing rotor – removal and installation

1 Release the wiring from the two clips on the pick-up coil cover, then unscrew the bolts that secure the cover to the right-hand side of the engine and remove the cover **(see illustration 4.8)**.

2 On F models, counter-hold the timing rotor with a wrench on its hex and remove the Allen bolt from its centre **(see illustration 5.5a)**.

3 On G, H, J and A models, counter-hold the timing rotor using a suitable tool inserted into one or both holes in the rotor (Kawasaki provide a service tool, pt. no. 57001-1343) and remove the bolt from the centre of the rotor **(see illustration 5.5b)**.

4 Take the timing rotor off the crankshaft, noting how it locates.

5 Installation is the reverse of removal, noting the following:

- Align the timing rotor notch with the pin on the end of the crankshaft.
- Counter-hold the timing rotor in the same way used during removal and tighten the bolt to the torque listed in this Chapter's Specifications **(see illustrations)**.

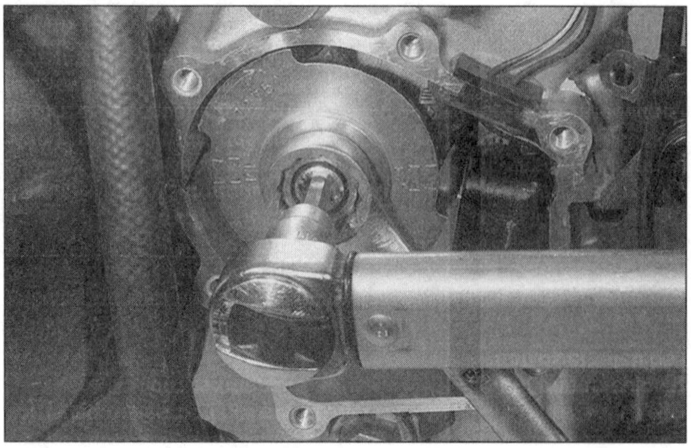

5.5a Counter-hold the hex and tighten the Allen bolt – F models

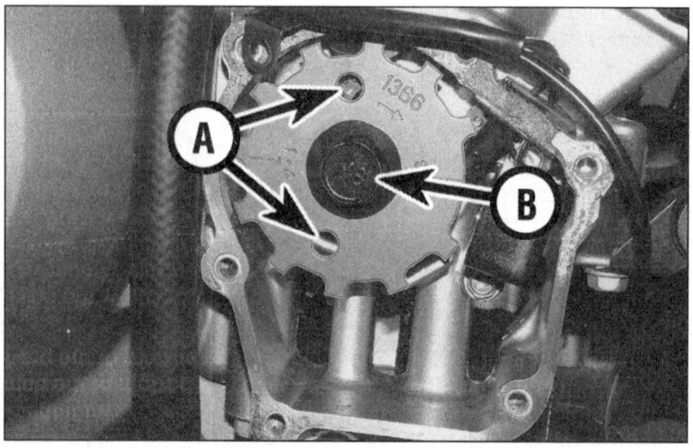

5.5b Hold the rotor by the holes (A) and tighten the bolt (B) – G, H, J and A models

6.2a IC igniter - F models

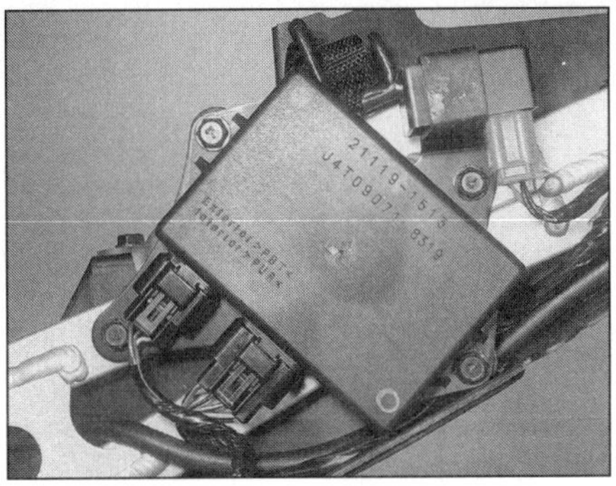

6.2b IC igniter - G and H models

6.2c IC igniter - J and A models

6 IC igniter - removal, check and installation

Removal

1 Remove the side panels (see Chapter 8). Make sure the ignition is switched OFF.

2 Unbolt the igniter and unplug the electrical connectors **(see illustrations)**.

Check

3 The igniter is a delicate and expensive component requiring the use of a specific tester to check its condition. Take the machine to a Kawasaki dealer if the igniter is suspected of being faulty.

Installation

4 Plug in the electrical connectors, place the igniter in position, install the mounting bolts and tighten them securely.

5 Install the side panels (see Chapter 8).

7 Throttle position sensor (G, H, J and A models) - check and adjustment

Check

1 Before checking the sensor itself, check the idle speed and carburettor synchronisation (see Chapter 1).

2 Remove the fuel tank (see Chapter 4). Arrange a temporary fuel supply, either by using a small temporary tank or by using extra long fuel pipes to the now remote fuel tank, or position the tank on a suitable base on the motorcycle, taking care not to scratch any paintwork, and making sure that the tank is safely and securely supported.

3 The throttle sensor is mounted on the outside of the right-hand carburettor **(see illustration)**. Using a voltmeter, insert the positive probe into the back of the sensor wiring connector yellow/white wire terminal, and the negative probe into the black/blue wire terminal. If the probes cannot be inserted into the connector, disconnect it and prepare some auxiliary wires to run between the terminals of the connector and the sensor itself, with a small portion of the insulation cut away so that the meter probes can be connected to them using crocodile clips. Alternatively, and preferably, prepare two insulated terminals midway along each wire to accept the meter probes.

Caution: Do not allow the bare sections of wire to contact each other or any other part of the motorcycle. Make sure the wires connect between the correct terminals - do not get them crossed.

4 Start the engine and allow it to idle. Check the voltage output of the sensor and compare it to the output specified at the beginning of the Chapter, then stop the engine. If the recorded output differs from that specified, adjust the sensor position (see Step 6).

5 For a further test on J and A models, with the voltmeter connected as before, turn the ignition ON but *do not* start the engine. Open the throttle fully. If the output voltage is not as specified, fit a new sensor.

Adjustment

6 Unless an angled screwdriver is available, it will be necessary to displace the carburettors to access the screws (see Chapter 4). Slacken the sensor mounting screws and turn the ignition ON **(see illustration 7.3)**. Rotate the sensor until the output is within the specified range, then tighten the screws evenly and a little at a time to the torque specified at the beginning of the Chapter. If it cannot be adjusted to within the range, see Step 8.

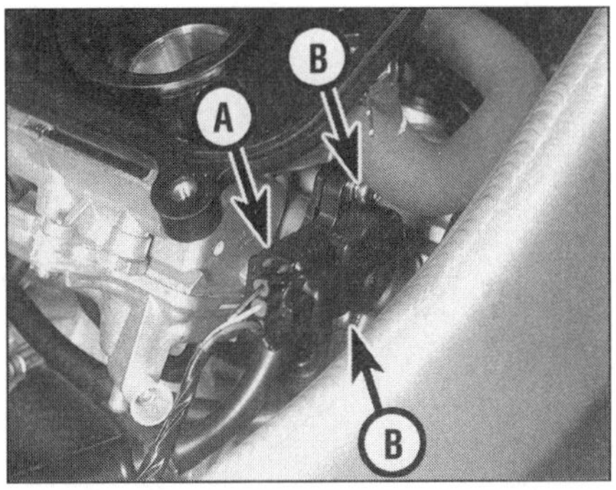

7.3 Throttle position sensor wiring connector (A) and mounting screws (B)

7 If no reading is obtained, disconnect the relevant ignition control module wiring connector and check the connectors for loose or corroded terminals. Test the wiring between the terminals of the sensor wiring connector and the corresponding terminals on the IC igniter connector for continuity. There should be continuity between each terminal. If not, this is probably due to a damaged or broken wire between the connectors; pinched or broken wires can usually be repaired. Also check the sensor for cracks and other damage.

8 If the sensor is suspected of being faulty, take the bike to a Kawasaki dealer for testing. If it is confirmed to be faulty, it must be renewed; the sensor is a sealed unit and cannot therefore be repaired. If the sensor is good, have the IC igniter checked by a Kawasaki dealer.

Chapter 6
Frame, suspension and final drive

Contents

Degrees of difficulty

Easy, suitable for novice with little experience

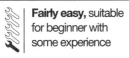

Fairly easy, suitable for beginner with some experience

Fairly difficult, suitable for competent DIY mechanic

Difficult, suitable for experienced DIY mechanic

Very difficult, suitable for expert DIY or professional

Specifications

Front fork

Spring free length	
F models	
Standard	389.9 mm
Minimum	382 mm
G and H models	
Standard	269.3 mm
Minimum	264 mm
J and A models	
Standard	234.6 mm
Minimum	230 mm
Fork oil type (all models)	SAE 10W
Fork oil quantity	
F models	
Oil change	approx. 325 cc
After disassembly	379 to 383 cc
G and H models	
Oil change	approx. 500 cc
After disassembly	584 to 592 cc
J models	
Oil change	approx. 455 cc
After disassembly	533 to 541 cc
A models	
Oil change	approx. 457 cc
After disassembly	537 to 545 cc
Fork oil level*	
F models	148 to 152 mm
G and H models	103 to 107 mm
J models	114 to 118 mm
A models	111 to 115 mm

**Oil level is measured from the top of the tube with the fork spring removed and the leg fully compressed.*

Rear shock absorber

Gas pressure	142 psi (10 bars)
Spring pre-load setting	
F models	
Standard	spring free length minus 14.5 mm
Usable range	spring free length minus 12.5 to 22.5 mm
G and H models	
Standard	spring length 186 mm
Usable range	spring length 188 to 178.5 mm
J and A models	
Standard	spring length 180 mm
Usable range	spring length 182 to 170 mm

Final drive

Chain	
Size	525 sealed
No. of links	108
Sprocket sizes	
Front	15T
Rear	40T

Torque specifications

Bottom yoke fork clamp bolts	20 Nm
Handlebar end bolts	34 Nm
Handlebar holder clamp bolts	
F, G, H and J models	23 Nm
A models	25 Nm
Handlebar positioning bolts	10 Nm
Footrest bolt	34 Nm
Footrest bracket bolt	25 Nm
Fork damper cartridge bolt	39 Nm
Fork pre-load adjuster against locknut	
F models	15 Nm
G, H, J and A models	28 Nm
Fork top bolts	23 Nm
Front brake lever pivot bolt	1 Nm
Front brake lever pivot bolt locknut	5.9 Nm
Front brake master cylinder clamp bolts	11 Nm
Front sprocket cover bolts (G and H models)	12 Nm
Front sprocket cover bolts (J and A models)	11 Nm
Front sprocket nut	
F, G, H and J models	125 Nm
A models	127 Nm
Rear shock absorber mountings	
F models	59 Nm
G, H, J and A models	34 Nm
Rear shock absorber upper bracket nut	59 Nm
Rear sprocket nuts	
F models	74 Nm
G, H, J and A models	59 Nm
Sidestand bracket bolts	49 Nm
Speedometer sensor mounting bolt	
G, H and J models	6.9 Nm
A models	5 Nm
Steering stem bearing adjuster locknut (J and A models)	15 Nm
Steering stem bearing adjuster nut	
F, G and H models	
Initial setting	39 Nm
Final setting	5 Nm
J and A models	15 Nm
Steering stem nut	49 Nm
Suspension linkage arm to frame	
Suspension linkage rods to linkage arm	59 Nm
Suspension linkage rods to swingarm	59 Nm
F models	59 Nm
G, H, J and A models	34 Nm
Swingarm pivot bolt nut	110 Nm
Top yoke fork clamp bolts	20 Nm

1 General information

Front suspension is by a pair of oil-damped telescopic forks with a cartridge damper. The forks are adjustable for pre-load and both rebound and compression damping.

At the rear, an alloy swingarm acts on a single shock absorber via a three-way linkage. The shock absorber is adjustable for spring pre-load and both rebound and compression damping. The shock absorber has a remote reservoir.

The drive to the rear wheel is by endless chain. A rubber damper system (often called a 'cush drive') is fitted between the rear sprocket coupling and the wheel.

2 Frame – inspection and repair

1 The frame should not require attention unless accident damage has occurred. In most cases, frame renewal is the only satisfactory remedy for such damage. A few frame specialists have the jigs and other equipment necessary for straightening the frame to the required standard of accuracy, but even then there is no simple way of assessing to what extent the frame may have been over stressed.

2 After the machine has accumulated a lot of miles, the frame should be examined closely for signs of cracking or splitting at the welded joints. Loose engine mount bolts can cause ovaling or fracturing of the mounting tabs. Minor damage can often be repaired by welding, depending on the extent and nature of the damage.

3 Remember that a frame which is out of alignment will cause handling problems. If misalignment is suspected as the result of an accident, it will be necessary to strip the machine completely so the frame can be thoroughly checked.

3 Footrests, brake pedal and gearchange lever – removal and installation

Footrests

Removal

1 Remove the E-clip from the bottom of the footrest pivot pin, then withdraw the pivot pin and remove the footrest. On the front footrests, note the fitting of the return spring **(see illustration)**. On the rear footrests, note the fitting of the detent plates and spring, and take care that they do not spring out when removing the footrest **(see illustration)**.

Installation

2 Installation is the reverse of removal.

Brake pedal

Removal

3 Unscrew the two bolts securing the rider's right-hand footrest bracket to the frame and swivel the bracket to access the components on the inside **(see illustration)**. Unhook the brake pedal return spring and the brake light switch spring from the bolt on the pedal **(see illustration)**.

4 Remove the split pin from the clevis pin securing the brake pedal to the master cylinder pushrod **(see illustration 3.3b)**. Remove the clevis pin and separate the pedal from the pushrod.

5 The pedal pivots on the footrest holder. Remove the bolt on the inside of the footrest bracket and remove the footrest and its holder **(see illustration 3.3b)**. Slide the pedal off the holder. Check the condition of the pedal bush and renew it if necessary.

Installation

6 Installation is the reverse of removal, noting the following:

- Apply molybdenum disulphide grease to the brake pedal pivot.
- Align the flat on the footrest holder with that in the bracket.
- Apply a suitable non-permanent threadlocking compound to the footrest holder bolt and tighten it to the torque setting specified at the beginning of the Chapter.
- Use a new split pin on the clevis pin securing the brake pedal to the master cylinder pushrod.
- Check the operation of the rear brake light switch and adjust the brake pedal height, if required (see Chapter 1).
- Tighten the footrest bracket bolts securely.

Gearchange lever

Removal

7 Slacken the gearchange lever linkage rod locknuts, then unscrew the rod and separate it from the lever and the arm (the rod is reverse-threaded on one end and so will simultaneously unscrew from both lever and arm when turned in the one direction) **(see illustration)**. Note the how far the rod is

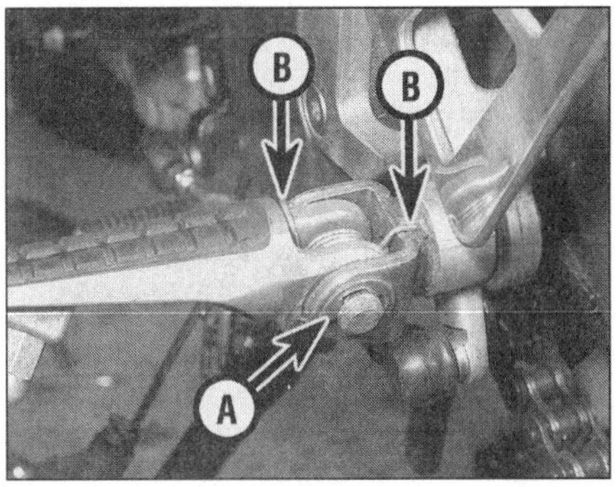

3.1a Remove the E-clip (A) and withdraw the pivot pin. Note how the spring ends (B) locate

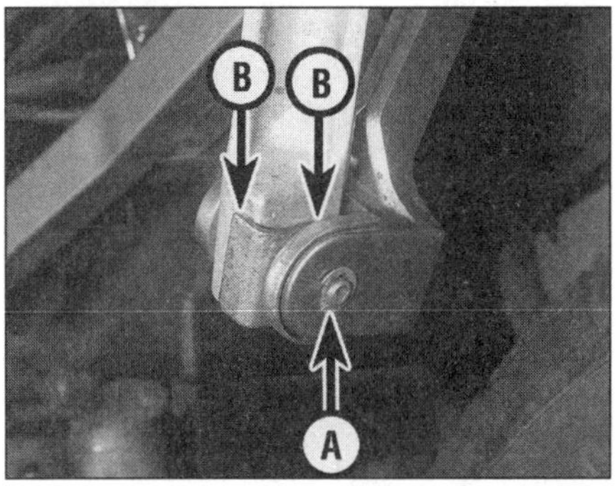

3.1b Remove the E-clip (A) and withdraw the pivot pin. Note how the detent plates (B) locate

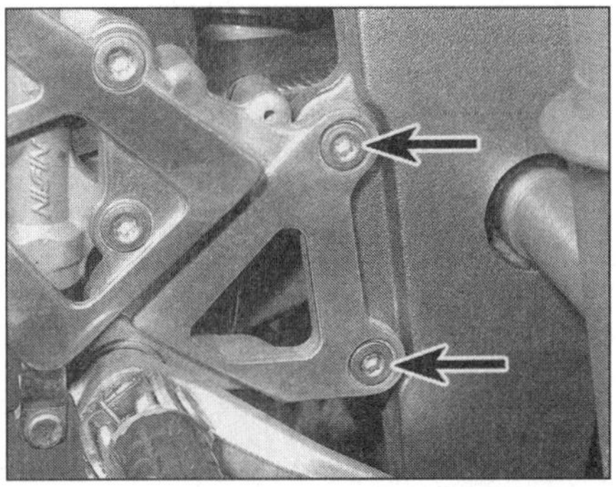

3.3a Unscrew the two bolts (arrowed) and swivel the bracket to access the back

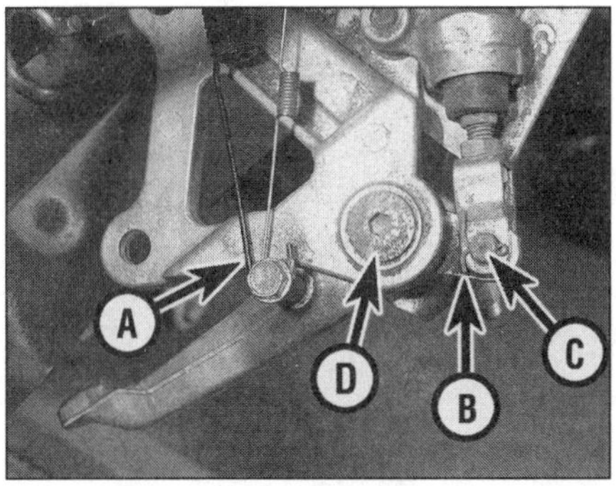

3.3b Unhook the springs (A), remove the split pin (B) and withdraw the clevis pin (C), then unscrew the bolt (D)

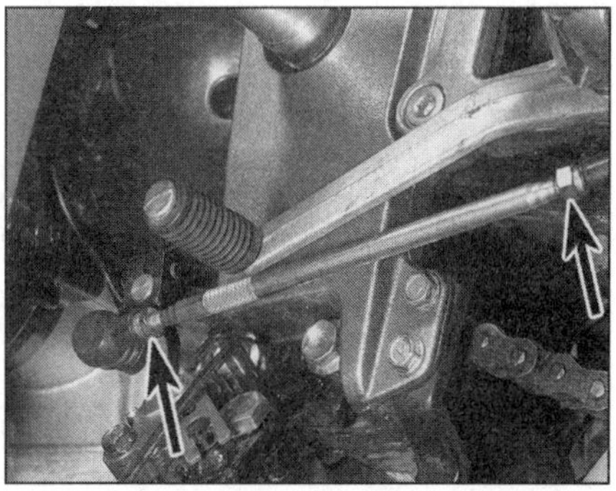

3.7 Slacken the locknuts (arrowed) and thread the rod out of the lever and arm

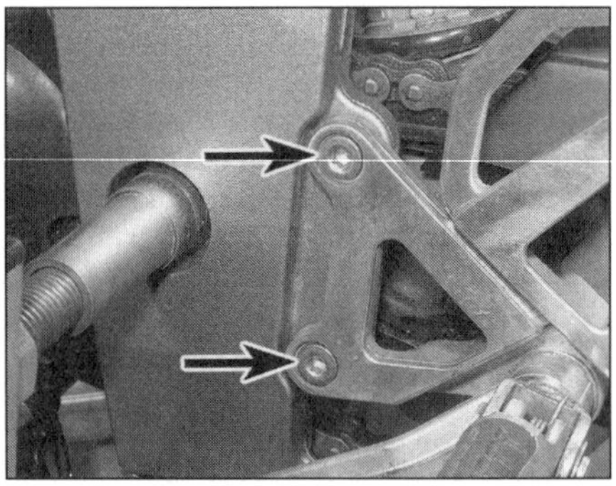

3.8a Unscrew the two bolts (arrowed) and swivel the bracket to access the back

threaded into the lever and arm as this determines the height of the lever relative to the footrest.

8 Unscrew the two bolts securing the rider's left-hand footrest bracket to the frame and swivel the bracket to access the inside **(see illustration)**. The lever pivots on the footrest holder. Remove the bolt on the inside of the footrest bracket and remove the footrest and its holder **(see illustration)**. Slide the lever off the holder.

Installation

9 Installation is the reverse of removal, noting the following:

- Apply molybdenum disulphide grease to the gear lever pivot.
- Align the flat on the footrest holder with that in the bracket.
- Apply a suitable non-permanent threadlocking compound to the footrest holder bolt and tighten it to the torque setting specified at the beginning of the Chapter.
- Adjust the gear lever height as required by screwing the rod in or out of the lever and arm. Tighten the locknuts securely.
- Tighten the footrest bracket bolts securely.

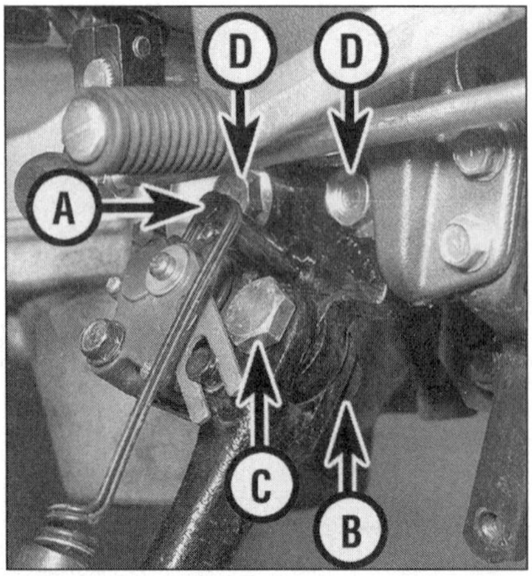

4.3 Unhook the spring (A), unscrew the nut (B) and remove the pivot bolt (C). The bracket is secured by two bolts (D)

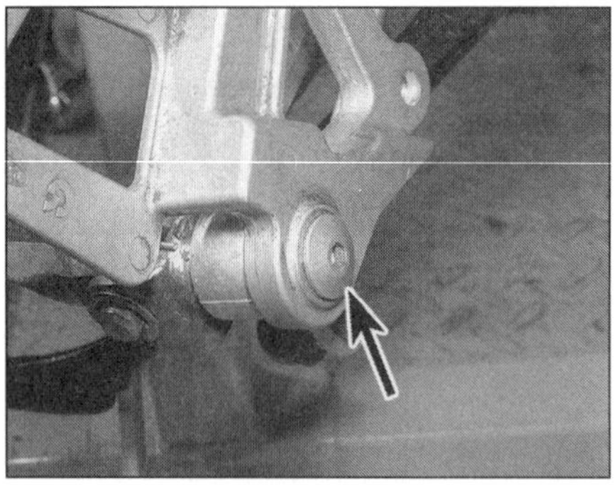

3.8b Unscrew the bolt to free the footrest and lever

4 Sidestand – removal and installation

Removal

1 The sidestand is attached to a bracket on the frame. A spring anchored to the stand ensures that it is held in the retracted or extended position.

2 Support the bike using an auxiliary stand. Remove the sidestand switch (see Chapter 9).

3 Unhook the stand spring, then unscrew the nut on the back of the pivot bolt **(see illustration)**. Withdraw the pivot bolt and remove the stand.

4 If required, unscrew the gearchange linkage arm pinch bolt and slide the arm off the shaft, then unscrew the bolts securing the sidestand bracket to the frame and remove the bracket **(see illustration 4.3)**.

Installation

5 On installation, if removed tighten the sidestand bracket bolts to the torque setting specified at the beginning of the Chapter. Apply grease to the pivot bolt shank and tighten the nut securely. Reconnect the sidestand spring and check that it holds the stand securely up when not in use – an accident is almost certain to occur if the stand extends while the machine is in motion.

6 Install the sidestand switch (see Chapter 9).

5.1a Slacken the clamp bolt (arrowed) . . .

5 Handlebars and levers – removal and installation

Right handlebar removal

Note: *If required, the handlebars can be removed from the handlebar holders which clamp around the top of the forks, leaving the holders in place.*

1 On F models, to displace the handlebar assembly for access to other components, such as the steering head, simply slacken the handlebar holder clamp bolt and unscrew the positioning bolt, then ease the handlebar holder up and off the fork **(see illustrations)**. It isn't necessary to disconnect the cables, wires or brake hose, but support the assembly with a piece of wire or cable tie to avoid straining them. On G and H models, undo the bolt securing the master cylinder reservoir bracket to the top yoke before displacing the handlebar assembly (see Chapter 7). Keep the reservoir upright to avoid air entering the hydraulic system. On J and A models, the handlebar assembly must be detached from the handlebar holder before it can be displaced (see Step 4). Note that the master cylinder reservoir must be detached from the bracket on the top yoke as on G and H models.

2 To remove the handlebar completely, detach the throttle cables from the twistgrip and, if required, remove the twistgrip itself (see Chapter 4). On G, H, J and A models, unscrew the two handlebar switch screws and free the switch from the handlebar. Position the switch housing and on G, H, J and A models the throttle housing away from the handlebar.

3 Disconnect the brake light switch wires from the master cylinder assembly **(see**

5.1b . . . and remove the positioning bolt (arrowed) to free the handlebar – F, G and H models shown

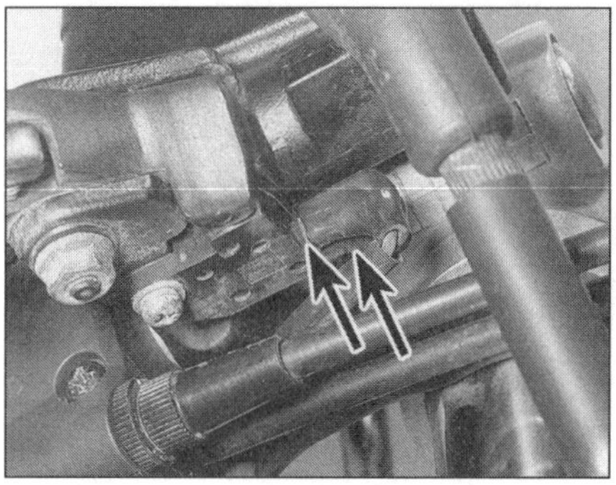

5.3a Disconnect the brake light switch wiring connectors (arrowed)

5.3b Unscrew the clamp bolts and detach the master cylinder assembly

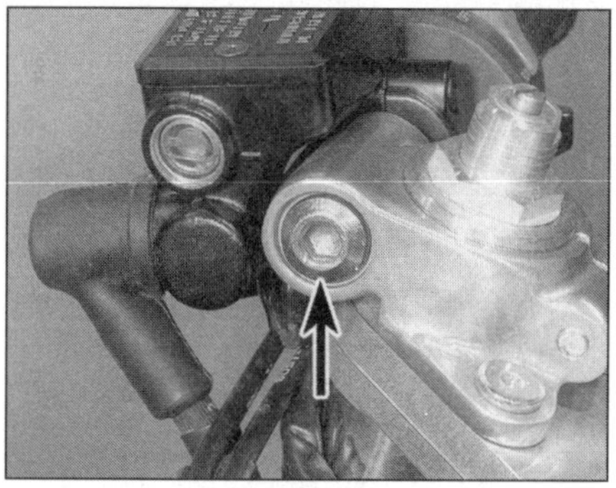

5.4 Unscrew the bolt (arrowed) and draw the bar out of the holder

illustration). On G, H, J and A models, undo the bolt securing the master cylinder reservoir bracket to the top yoke. Unscrew the two master cylinder assembly clamp bolts and position the assembly clear of the handlebar, making sure no strain is placed on the hydraulic hose **(see illustration)**. Keep the master cylinder reservoir upright to prevent air entering the hydraulic system.

4 If removing the handlebar leaving the holder in place, unscrew and remove the bolt in the inner end of the handlebar and slide the handlebar out of the holder, noting how the peg on the underside locates in the cutout in the holder **(see illustration)**.

5 On F, G and H models, to remove the handlebar and holder together, slacken the handlebar holder clamp bolt and unscrew the positioning bolt, then ease the handlebar holder up and off the fork **(see illustrations 5.1a and b)**. On J and A models, both handlebars, handlebar holders and top yoke must be removed as an assembly (see Section 8).

Left handlebar removal

Note: *If required, the handlebars can be removed from the handlebar holders which clamp around the top of the forks, leaving the holders in place.*

6 On F, G and H models, to displace the handlebar for access to other components, such as the steering head, simply slacken the handlebar holder clamp bolt and unscrew the positioning bolt, then ease the handlebar holder up and off the fork **(see illustrations 5.1a and b)**. It isn't necessary to disconnect the cables or wires, but support the assembly with a piece of wire or cable tie to avoid straining them. On J and A models, the handlebar assembly must be detached from the handlebar holder before it can be displaced (see Step 9). the top yoke must be removed before the handlebar is displaced (see Section 8).

7 To remove the handlebar completely, unscrew the two handlebar switch screws and free the switch from the handlebar **(see illustration)**. Position the switch housing away from the handlebar.

8 Disconnect the clutch switch wiring connector from the switch in the clutch lever bracket **(see illustration)**. Unscrew the two lever assembly clamp bolts and position the assembly clear of the handlebar, making sure the cable is not unduly bent or kinked **(see illustration)**.

9 If removing the handlebar leaving the holder in place, unscrew and remove the bolt in the inner end of the handlebar **(see illustration 5.4)** and slide the handlebar out of the holder, noting how the peg on the underside locates in the cutout in the holder **(see illustration 5.11)**.

10 On F, G and H models, to remove the handlebar and holder together, slacken the handlebar holder clamp bolt and unscrew the positioning bolt, then ease the handlebar holder up and off the fork **(see illustrations 5.1a and b)**. On J and A models, both handlebars, handlebar holders and top yoke must be removed as an assembly (see Section 8).

Handlebar installation

11 Installation is the reverse of removal, noting the following.

- When installing the handlebar into the holder, align the peg in the bar with the cutout in the holder **(see illustration)**.
- Refer to the Specifications at the beginning of the Chapter and tighten the handlebar end bolts, holder clamp bolts and the positioning bolts to the specified torque settings.
- Make sure the pin in each switch housing locates in the hole in the front of the handlebar.
- Make sure the front brake master cylinder assembly clamp is installed with the UP mark facing up, and that the clamp mating

5.7 Remove the two screws and separate the switch halves

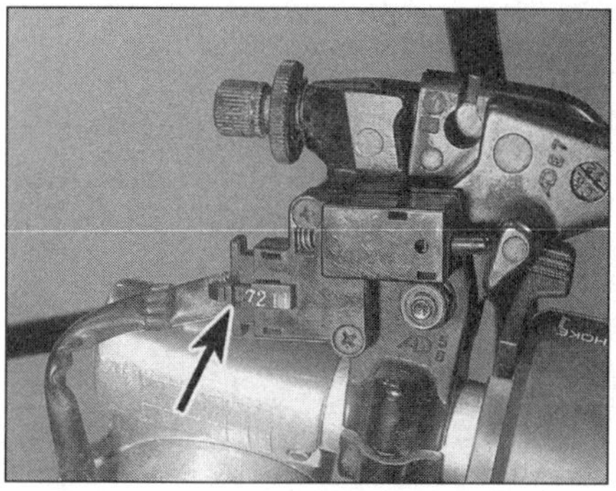

5.8a Disconnect the clutch switch wiring connectors (arrowed) . . .

5.8b . . . then unscrew the clamp bolts and displace the bracket

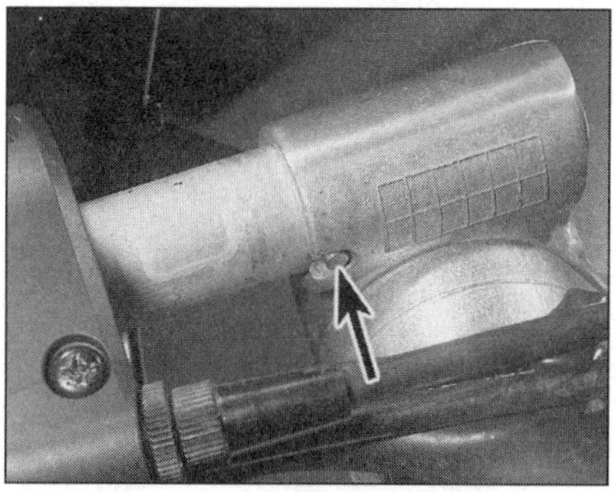

5.11 Make sure the peg locates in the cutout in the holder (arrowed)

6

surfaces align with those of the switch housing on F models, and with the punch mark on the handlebar on all other models **(see illustration 5.3b)**. Tighten the upper bolt first, then the lower bolt, to the torque setting specified at the beginning of the Chapter.

- Align the clutch lever assembly clamp mating surfaces with those of the handlebar switch housing.
- If removed, apply a suitable non-permanent locking compound to the handlebar end-weight retaining screws. If new grips are being fitted, the old ones will probably have to be slit with a knife to remove them from either the throttle twist or the handlebar. Secure the new ones using a suitable adhesive.
- Do not forget to reconnect the front brake light switch and clutch switch wiring connectors.

Front brake lever

Removal

12 Unscrew the lever pivot bolt locknut, then unscrew the pivot bolt and remove the lever **(see illustrations)**.

Installation

13 Installation is the reverse of removal. Apply grease to the pivot bolt shaft, the contact areas between the lever and its bracket, and to the contact point between the brake lever and the master cylinder pushrod. Tighten the brake lever pivot bolt and its locknut to the torque settings specified at the beginning of the Chapter.

5.12a Unscrew the locknut (arrowed) . . .

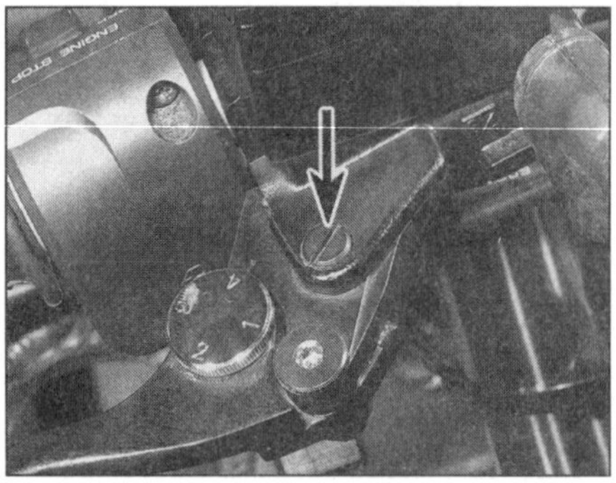

5.12b . . . then unscrew the pivot bolt (arrowed) and remove the lever

Clutch lever

Removal

14 Where fitted, slacken the clutch cable adjuster lockring, then thread the adjuster fully into the bracket to provide maximum freeplay in the cable. Unscrew the lever pivot bolt locknut, then withdraw the pivot bolt and remove the lever, detaching the cable nipple as you do. To access the locknut, depending on the tools available it may be necessary to slacken the clutch lever bracket clamp bolts and swivel the bracket on the handlebar – if doing this it is advisable to first detach the cable from the lever (see Chapter 2).

Installation

15 Installation is the reverse of removal. Apply grease to the pivot bolt shaft, the contact areas between the lever and its bracket, and to the clutch cable end. Adjust the clutch cable freeplay (see Chapter 1).

6 Forks – removal and installation

Removal

1 Remove the upper fairing and the lower fairing panels (see Chapter 8).
2 Remove the front wheel (see Chapter 7).
3 Remove the front mudguard (see Chapter 8).
4 Slacken the handlebar holder clamp bolts **(see illustration 5.1a)**. **Note:** *On J and A models, the handlebar holders are located below the top yoke.* Slacken the fork clamp bolts in the top yoke **(see illustration)**. If the forks are to be disassembled, or if the fork oil is being changed, it is advisable to slacken the fork top bolts at this stage.

> **HAYNES HiNT** ***Slackening the fork clamp bolts in the top yoke before slackening the fork top bolts releases pressure on the top bolt. This makes it much easier to remove and helps to preserve the threads.***

5 Slacken the fork clamp bolts in the bottom yoke, and remove the forks by twisting them and pulling them downwards **(see illustration)**.

> **HAYNES HiNT** ***If the fork legs are seized in the yokes, spray the area with penetrating oil and allow time for it to soak in before trying again.***

Installation

6 Remove all traces of corrosion from the fork tubes and the yokes. Slide the forks up through the bottom yoke then up into the top yoke **(see illustration)**. On F, G and H models, align the top edge of the fork tube with the top of the handlebar holder. On J and A models, align the top edge of the fork tube with the upper surface of the top yoke **(see illustration)**.

6.4 Slacken the top yoke clamp bolt (arrowed) – F, G and H models shown . . .

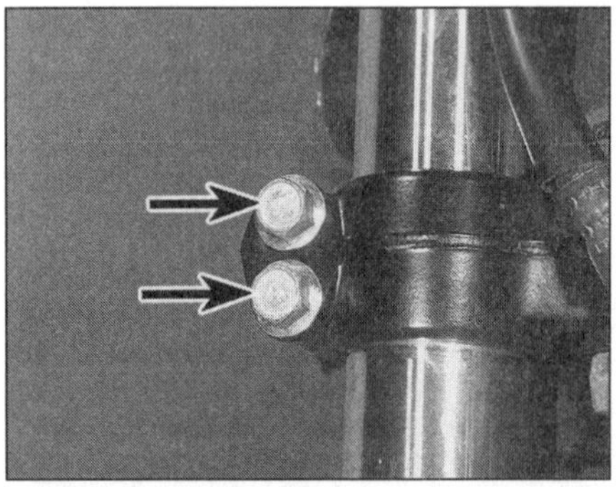

6.5 . . . and the bottom yoke clamp bolts

6.6a Slide the forks up through the yokes . . .

6.6b . . . and align the top edge of the fork tubes (arrowed) as described – J and A models shown

6.7 Tighten the clamp bolts to the specified torque

Caution: Setting the forks unevenly or higher or lower in the yokes than specified will affect the handling of the machine.

7 Tighten the fork clamp bolts in the bottom yoke to the torque setting specified at the beginning of the Chapter **(see illustration)**. If the fork legs have been dismantled or if the fork oil has been changed, the fork top bolts should now be tightened to the specified torque setting. Now tighten the fork clamp bolts in the top yoke and the handlebar holder clamp bolts to the specified torque setting.

8 Install the front mudguard (see Chapter 8), the front wheel (see Chapter 7), and the upper and lower fairing panels (see Chapter 8).

9 Check the operation of the front forks and brakes before taking the machine out on the road.

7 **Forks** – disassembly, inspection and reassembly

Disassembly

1 Always dismantle the fork legs separately to avoid interchanging parts and thus causing an accelerated rate of wear. Store all components in separate, clearly marked containers **(see illustration)**.

2 Before dismantling the fork, it is advised that the damper cartridge bolt be slackened at this stage. If the left-hand fork is being worked, first slacken the axle nut clamp bolts and remove the axle nut **(see illustration)**. Compress the fork tube in the slider so that the spring exerts maximum pressure on the damper head, then have an assistant slacken the damper cartridge bolt in the base of the fork slider **(see illustration)**.

3 Set the spring pre-load adjuster to its minimum setting (see Section 12). If the fork top bolt was not slackened with the fork in situ, carefully clamp the fork tube in a vice equipped with soft jaws, taking care not to overtighten the vice or score the tube surface, and slacken the top bolt.

4 Unscrew the fork top bolt from the top of

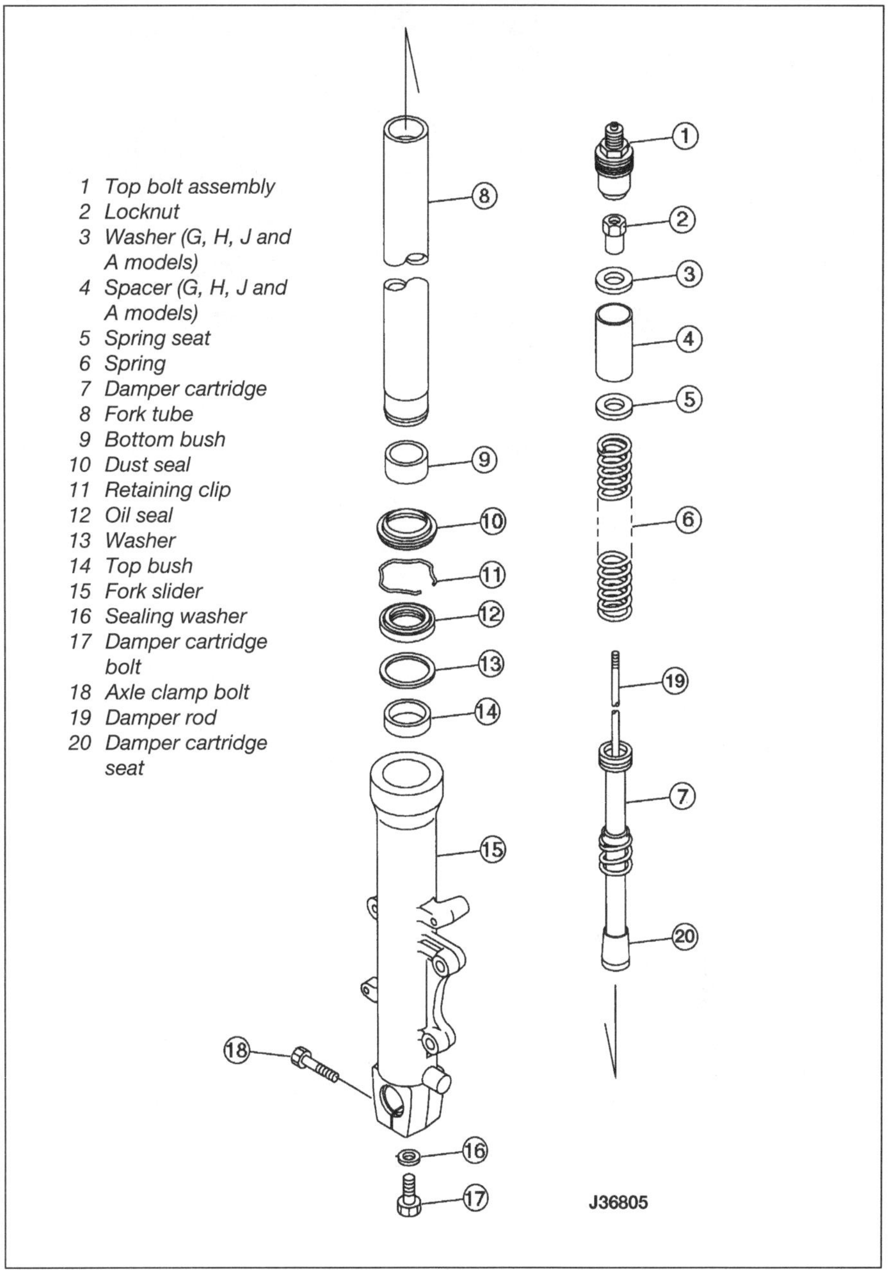

7.1 Front fork components

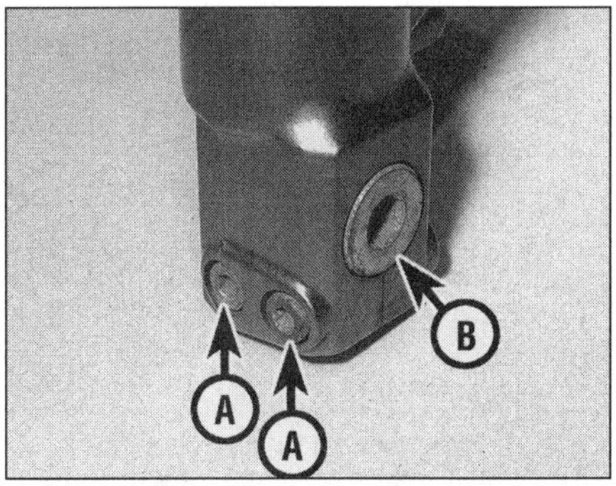

7.2a Slacken the clamp bolts (A) and remove the axle nut (B)

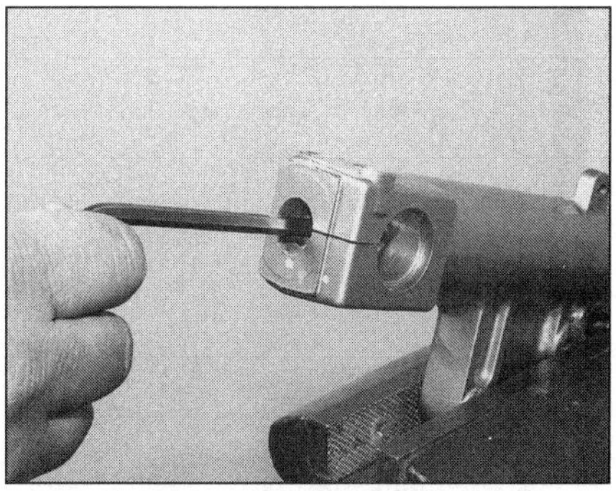

7.2b Slacken the damper cartridge Allen bolt

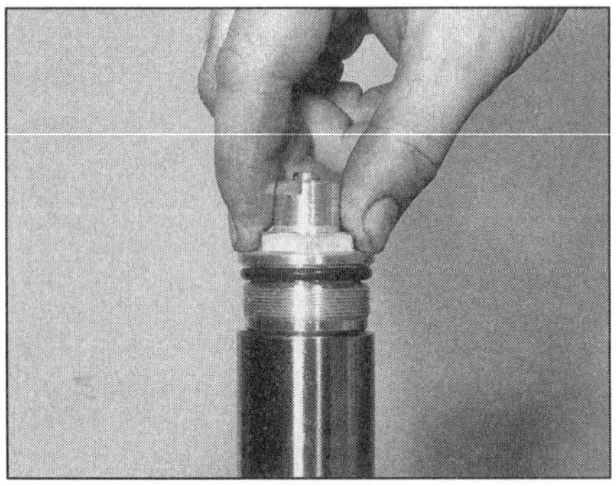

7.4 Unscrew the top bolt from the fork tube

the fork tube **(see illustration)**. The bolt will remain threaded on the damper cartridge rod.

5 Clamp the fork slider upright in a vice and slide the fork tube down into the slider; wrap a rag around the top of the tube to minimise oil spillage. With the aid of an assistant to keep the damper cartridge rod fully extended, counter-hold the locknut at the top of the damper rod and unscrew the top bolt assembly using a spanner on the flats of the pre-load adjuster **(see illustration)**.

6 On F models, remove the spring seat. On all other models, remove the washer, spacer and spring seat **(see illustrations 7.28d, c and b)**.

7 Withdraw the spring from the tube, noting which way up it fits **(see illustration 7.28a)**.

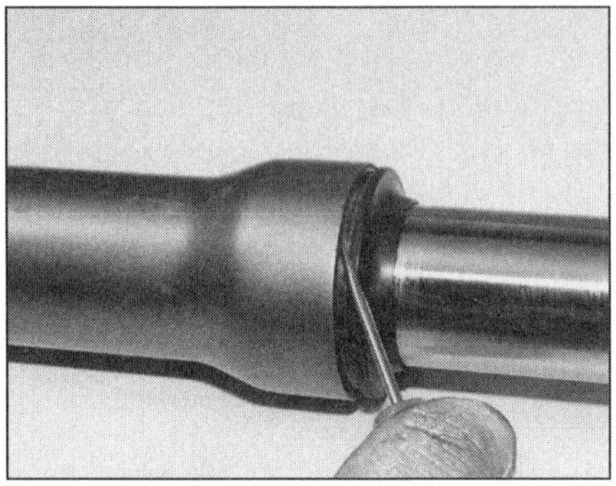

7.10 Prise out the dust seal using a flat-bladed screwdriver

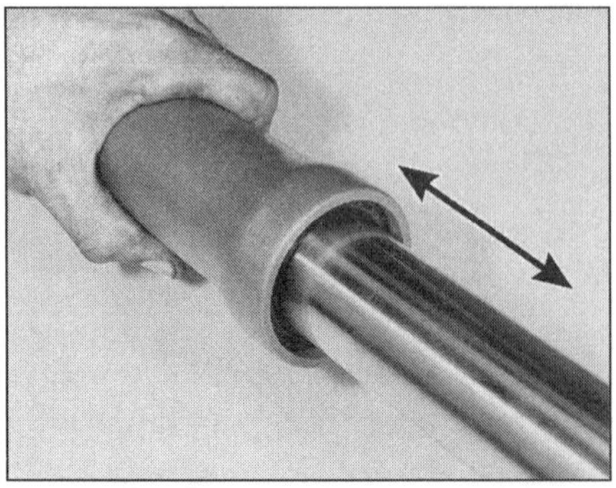

7.12 To separate the inner and outer fork tubes, pull them apart firmly several times – the slide-hammer effect will pull the tubes apart

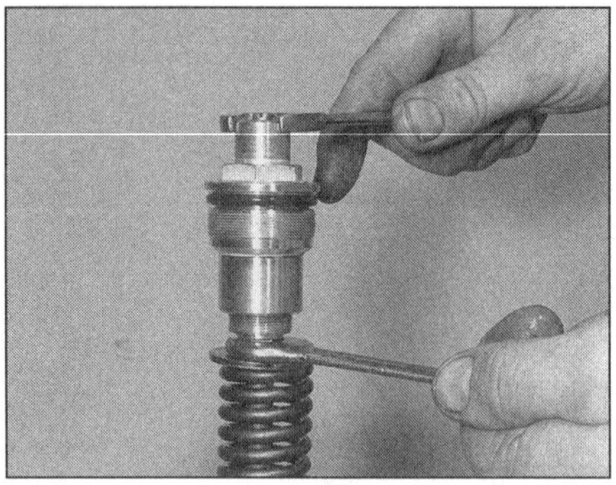

7.5 Counter-hold the locknut and unscrew the top bolt assembly using a spanner on the flats of the pre-load adjuster

Withdraw the rebound damping adjuster rod from the centre of the damper rod **(see illustration 7.29a)**. Invert the fork leg over a suitable container and pump the damper rod vigorously at least ten times to expel as much fork oil as possible.

8 Remove the previously slackened damper cartridge bolt and its sealing washer from the bottom of the slider **(see illustration 7.21)**. Discard the sealing washer as a new one must be used on reassembly. If the damper cartridge bolt was not slackened before dismantling the fork, it may be necessary to re-install the spring, spring seat, spacer and top bolt to prevent the damper rod from turning. Alternatively, an air gun, if available,

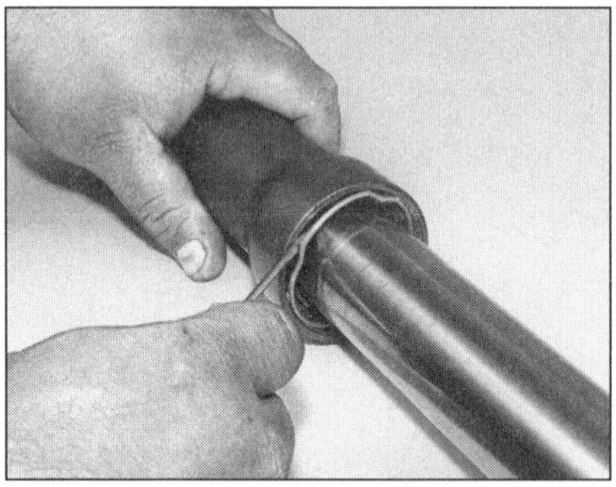

7.11 Prise out the retaining clip using a flat-bladed screwdriver

7.13 The oil seal (1), washer (2), top bush (3) and bottom bush (4) will come out with the fork tube

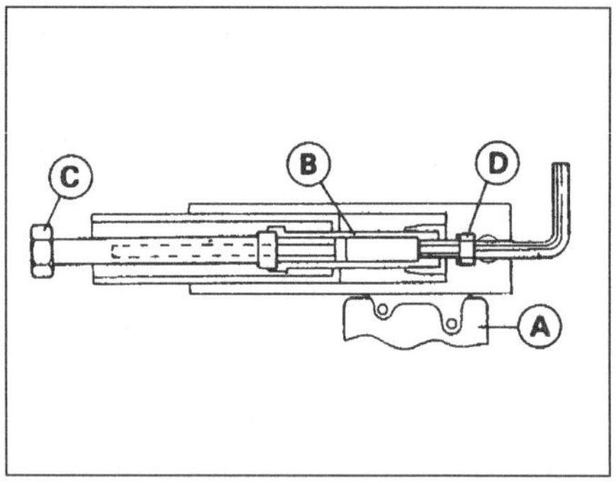

7.8 Using the Kawasaki tool to hold the damper cartridge whilst the retaining bolt is unscrewed

A Fork slider held in vice
B Damper cartridge body
C Service tool passed over damper rod tube and engaged in cartridge body
D Retaining bolt head with Allen key engaged

should do the trick. Kawasaki produce a service tool for the purpose (pt. no. 57001-1297 for F models, or 57001-1406 for G, H, J and A models) **(see illustration)**.

9 Invert the fork and withdraw the damper cartridge from inside the fork tube **(see illustration 7.20a)**.

10 Carefully prise out the dust seal from the top of the slider to gain access to the oil seal retaining clip **(see illustration)**. Discard the dust seal as a new one must be used.

11 Carefully remove the retaining clip, taking care not to scratch the surface of the tube **(see illustration)**.

12 To separate the tube from the slider it is necessary to displace the top bush and oil seal. The bottom bush should not pass through the top bush, and this can be used to good effect. Push the tube gently inwards until it stops against the damper cartridge seat. Take care not to do this forcibly or the seat may be damaged. Then pull the tube sharply outwards until the bottom bush strikes the top bush **(see illustration)**. Repeat this operation until the top bush and seal are tapped out of the slider.

13 With the tube removed, slide off the oil seal, washer and top bush, noting which way up they fit **(see illustration)**. Discard the oil seal as a new one must be used.

Caution: Do not remove the bottom bush from the tube unless it is to be renewed.

14 Tip the damper cartridge seat out of the slider, noting which way up it fits.

Inspection

15 Clean all parts in solvent and blow them dry with compressed air, if available. Check the fork tube for score marks, scratches, flaking of the chrome finish and excessive or abnormal wear. Look for dents in the tube and fit new tube if any are found. Check the fork seal seat for nicks, gouges and scratches. If damage is evident, leaks will occur. Also

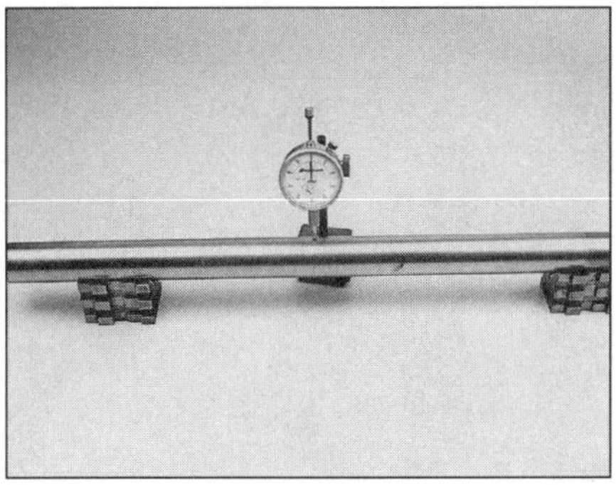

7.16 Check the fork tube for runout using V-blocks and a dial gauge

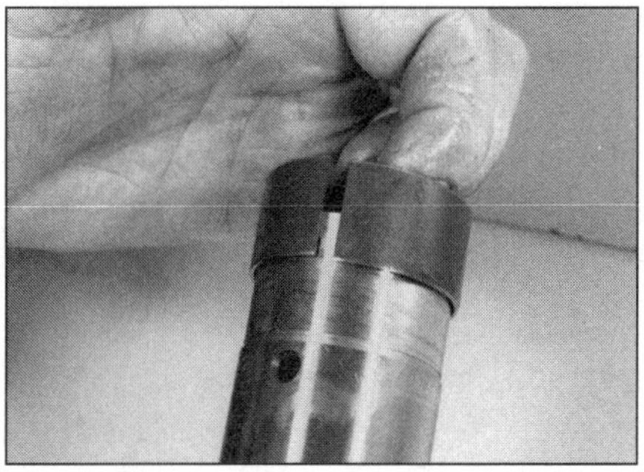

7.18 Part the bottom bush at the slit using a flat-bladed screwdriver and slide it off the tube

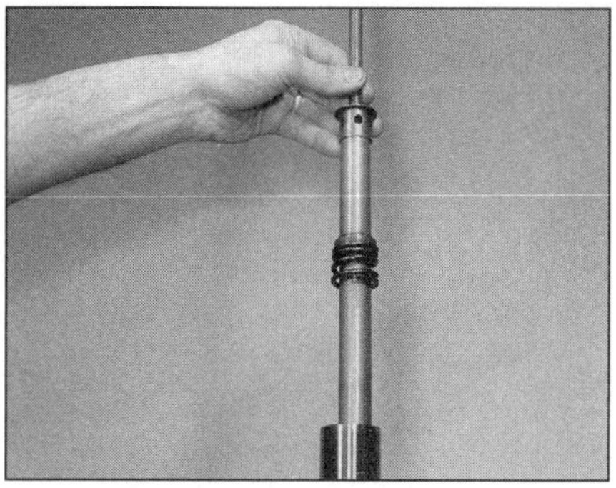

7.20a Slide the damper cartridge into the tube . . .

check the oil seal washer for damage or distortion and renew it if necessary.

16 Check the fork tube for runout using V-blocks and a dial gauge, or have it done at a dealer service department or other repair shop **(see illustration)**. If the amount of runout is excessive (Kawasaki provide no specifications), the tube should be renewed.

Warning: If the tube is bent or the runout is excessive, it should not be straightened; fit a new one.

17 Check the spring for cracks and other damage. Measure the spring free length and compare the measurement to the specifications at the beginning of the Chapter. If it is defective or sagged below the service limit, fit new springs in both forks. Never renew only one spring.

18 Examine the working surfaces of the two bushes; if worn or scuffed they must be renewed. To remove the bottom bush from the fork tube, prise it apart at the slit using a flat-bladed screwdriver and slide it off **(see illustration)**. Make sure the new one seats properly.

19 Check the damper cartridge assembly for damage and wear. Hold the outside of the cartridge and pump the rod in and out. If the rod does not move smoothly in the cartridge renew the assembly.

Reassembly

20 Insert the damper cartridge into the fork tube so that it projects from the bottom of the tube, then install the seat on the bottom of the cartridge **(see illustrations)**.

21 Oil the fork tube and bottom bush with the specified fork oil and insert the assembly into the slider. Fit a new sealing washer to the damper cartridge bolt and apply a few drops of a suitable non-permanent thread locking compound, then install the bolt into the bottom of the slider **(see illustration)**. Tighten the bolt to the specified torque setting. If the damper cartridge rotates inside the tube, and the Kawasaki service tool is not available, temporarily install the spring, spring seat, spacer (G, H, J and A models) and top bolt to hold it.

22 Push the fork tube fully into the slider, then oil the top bush and slide it down over the tube **(see illustration)**. Press the bush squarely into its recess in the slider as far as possible, then install the oil seal washer **(see illustration)**. Either use the Kawasaki service tool (pt. no. 57001-1219) or a suitable piece of tubing to tap the bush fully into place; the tubing must be slightly larger in diameter than the fork tube and slightly smaller in diameter than the bush recess in the slider. Take care not to scratch the fork tube during this operation; it is best to make sure that the fork tube is pushed fully into the slider so that any accidental scratching is confined to the area above the oil seal.

23 When the bush is seated fully and squarely in its recess in the slider, (remove the washer to check, wipe the recess clean, then reinstall the washer), install the new oil seal. Smear the seal's lips with fork oil and slide it over the tube so that its markings face upwards and drive the seal into place as described in Step 22 until the retaining clip groove is visible above the seal **(see illustration)**.

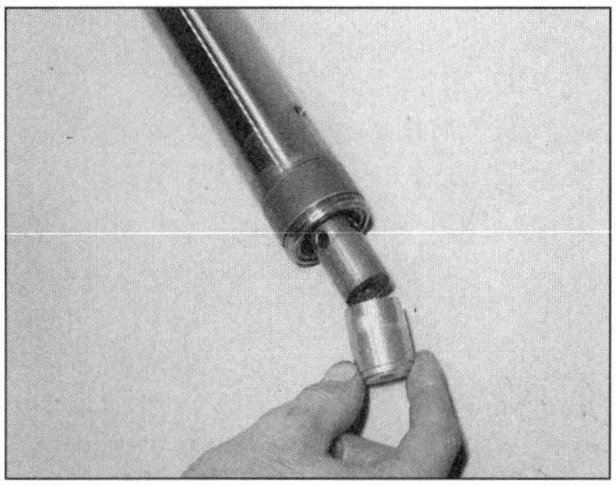

7.20b . . . and fit the seat onto its bottom end

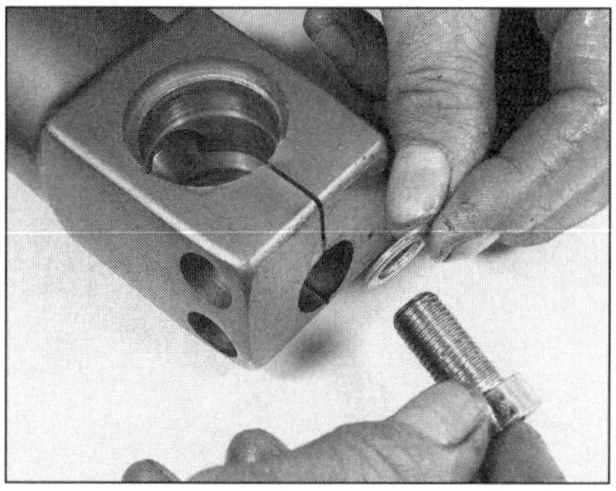

7.21 Use a new sealing washer on the damper cartridge Allen bolt

7.22a Install the top bush . . .

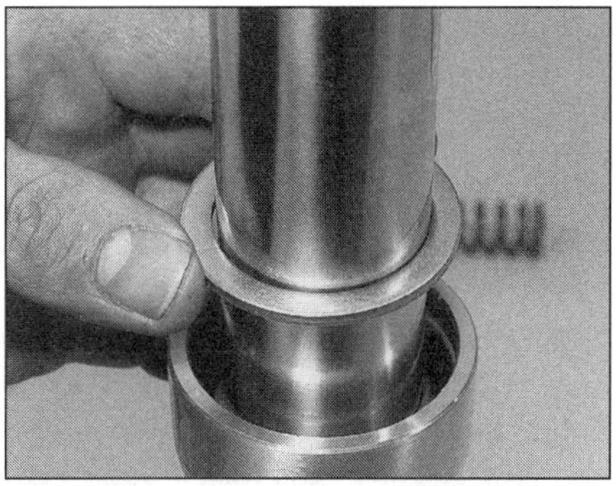

7.22b . . . followed by the washer

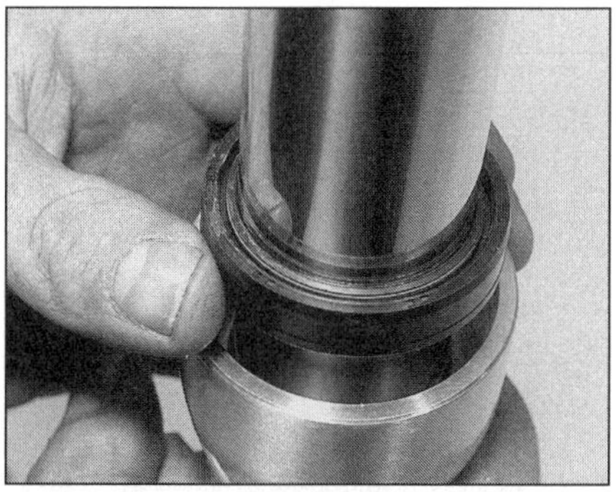

7.23 Make sure the oil seal is the correct way up

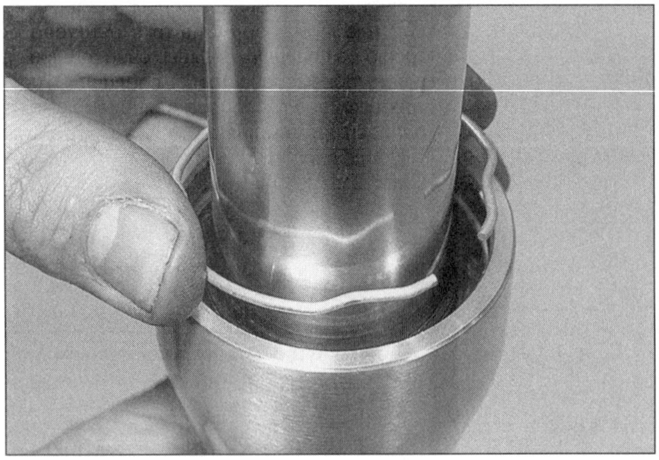

7.24 Install the retaining clip . . .

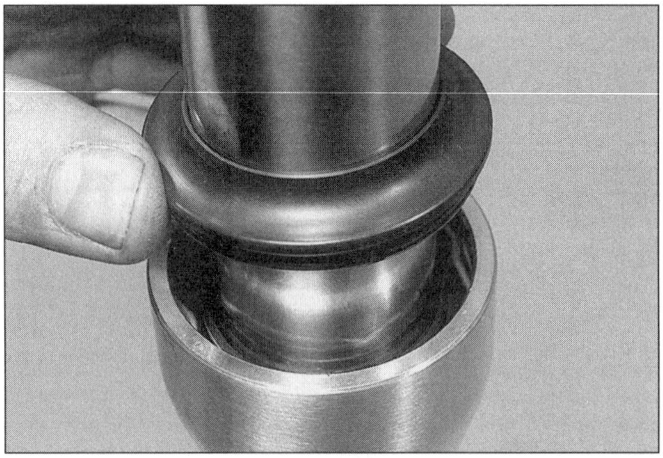

7.25 . . . followed by the dust seal

HAYNES HiNT *Place the old oil seal on top of the new one to protect it when driving the seal into place.*

24 Once the seal is correctly seated, fit the retaining clip, making sure it is correctly located in its groove **(see illustration)**.

25 Lubricate the lips of the new dust seal then slide it down the fork tube and press it into position **(see illustration)**.

26 Clamp the fork slider upright in a vice. Slowly pour in the specified quantity and grade of fork oil and pump the fork and damper cartridge rod at least ten times each to distribute it evenly **(see illustration)**; the oil level should also be measured and adjustment made by adding or subtracting oil. Fully compress the fork tube and damper cartridge rod into the slider and measure the fork oil level from the top of the tube **(see illustration)**. Add or subtract fork oil until it is at the level specified at the beginning of the Chapter.

27 Pull the fork tube and damper rod out of the slider as far as possible. If it was removed, thread the locknut onto the damper rod, making sure the chamfered side of the nut is at the bottom. Set the nut so that on F models there is 12 mm of damper rod thread visible above the top of the nut, and on all other models so that there is 11 mm of thread visible.

28 Install the spring with its narrower end or closer-wound coils at the top on F models, and at the bottom on all other models **(see illustration)**. Install the spring seat. On G, H, J and A models, install the spacer and the washer **(see illustrations)**.

29 Insert the rebound damping adjuster rod into the centre of the damper cartridge rod

7.26a Pour the oil into the top of the tube

7.26b Measure the oil level with the fork held vertical

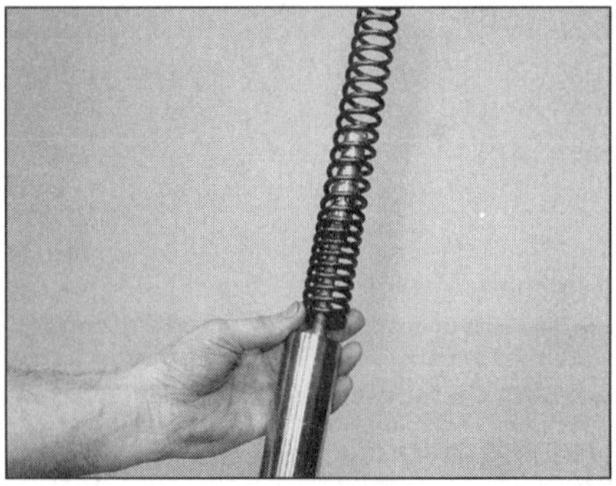

7.28a Install the spring . . .

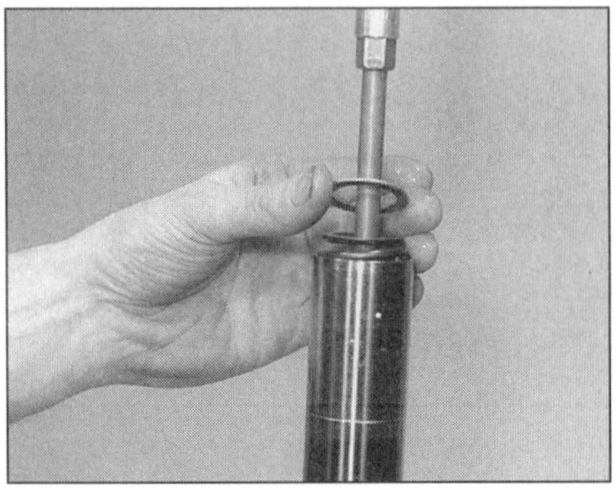

7.28b . . . followed by the spring seat . . .

7.28c . . . and on G, H, J and A models the spacer . . .

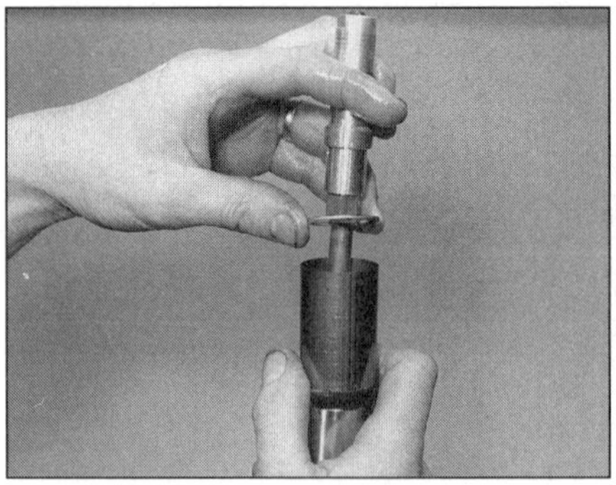

7.28d . . . and the washer

(see illustration). Check the condition of the O-ring on the fork top bolt and renew it if it is damaged or deteriorated. Screw the rebound damping adjuster into the pre-load adjuster until the distance between the bottom of the damping adjuster (inside the pre-load adjuster) and the bottom of the pre-load adjuster is 25 mm **(see illustrations)**. Thread the top bolt assembly fully onto the damper rod **(see illustration)**. Counter-hold the locknut and tighten the pre-load adjuster against it to the torque setting specified at the beginning of the Chapter **(see illustration 7.5)**.

30 Withdraw the tube fully from the slider and carefully screw the top bolt into the fork tube making sure it is not cross-threaded **(see illustration 7.4)**. **Note:** *The top bolt can be tightened to the specified torque setting at this stage if the tube is held between the padded jaws of a vice, but do not risk distorting the tube by doing so. A better method is to tighten the top bolt when the fork has been installed and is securely held in the yokes*

31 Install the forks (see Section 6). Set the spring pre-load adjuster as required (see Section 12).

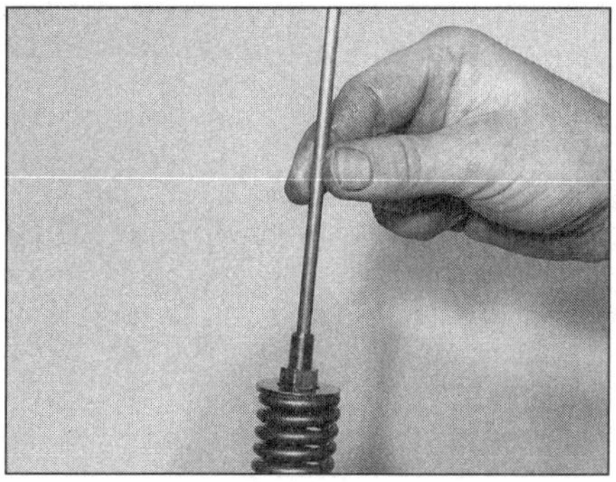

7.29a Insert the damping adjuster rod

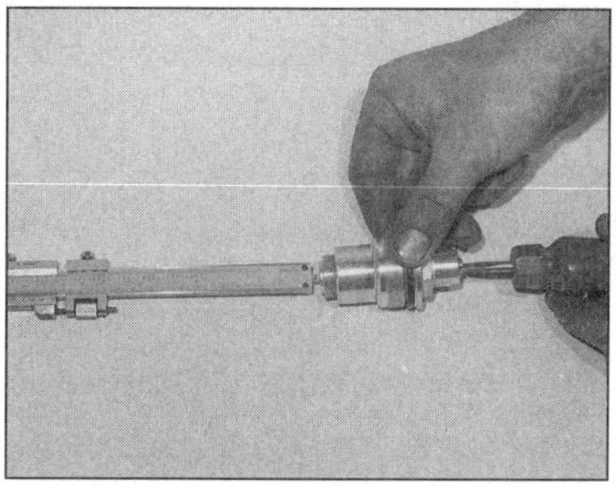

7.29b Screw in the rebound damping adjuster . . .

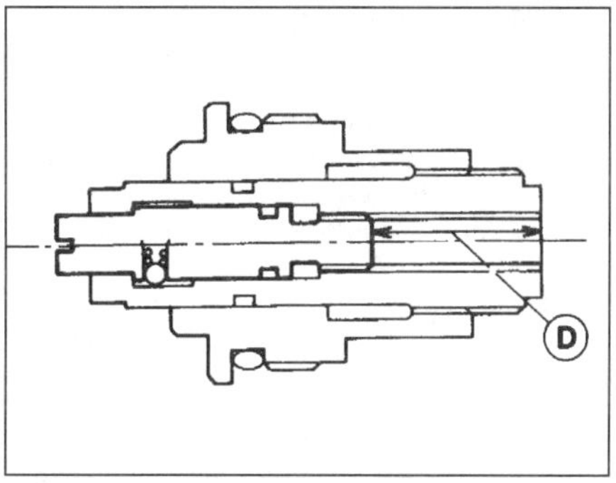

7.29c . . . until the distance (D) between the bottom of the damping adjuster and the bottom of the pre-load adjuster is 25 mm

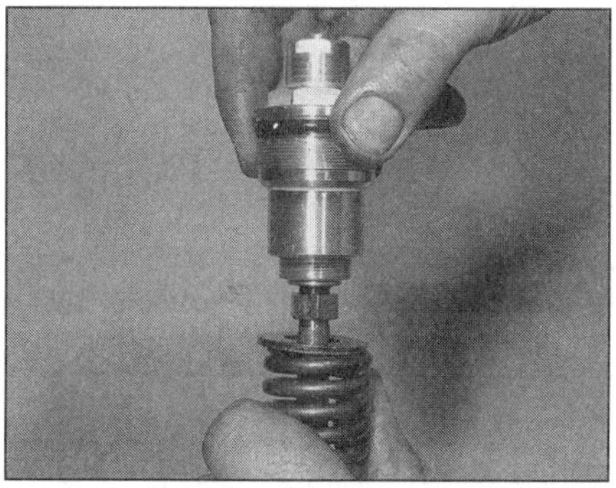

7.29d Thread the top bolt assembly onto the damper rod

8 Steering stem - removal and installation

Removal

1 Remove the front forks (see Section 6).

2 On F, G and H models, disconnect the horn wiring connectors. On all models, unscrew the bolts securing the front brake hose union to the bottom yoke and displace the union – there is no need to disconnect the hoses **(see illustration)**. On F, G and H models, remove the horn. Take care not to strain the brake hoses when removing the steering stem.

3 Remove the fuel tank and air filter housing (see Chapter 4).

4 Unscrew the bolts securing the fairing/rear view mirror mounting bracket to the frame and remove the bracket.

5 Unscrew the steering stem nut and remove the washer **(see illustration)**. Lift the top yoke off the steering stem. If required, undo the handlebar positioning bolts and detach the handlebars from the yoke to remove it. Secure the handlebars with a piece of wire or cable tie to avoid straining the wiring, cables and hydraulic hose. Keep the master cylinder reservoir upright to prevent air entering the system. Otherwise ensure the yoke/handlebar assembly is secure.

6 Unscrew and remove the bearing adjuster locknut using a suitable C-spanner, peg spanner or a drift located in one of the notches **(see illustration 8.5)**.

7 Supporting the bottom yoke, unscrew the bearing adjuster nut, then remove the adjuster nut and the bearing cover from the steering stem **(see illustration)**. On F, G and H models, remove the O-ring and discard it as a new one must be used.

8 Gently lower the bottom yoke and steering stem out of the frame.

9 On F, G and H models, remove the upper bearing inner race from the top of the steering

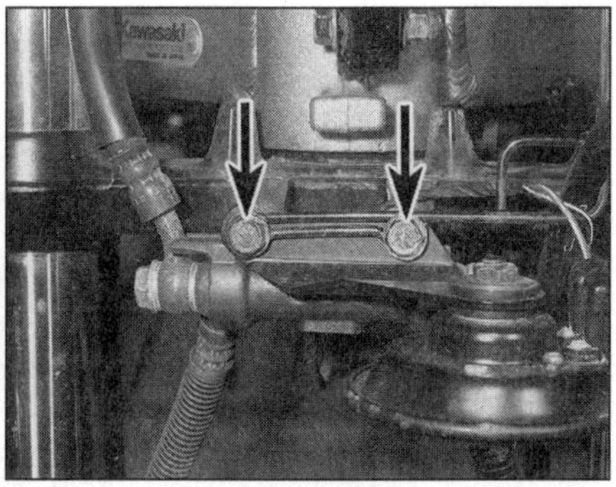

8.2 Unscrew the two bolts (arrowed) and displace the brake hose union. On F, G and H models remove the horn

8.5 Steering stem nut (A), washer (B), locknut (C), adjuster nut (D)

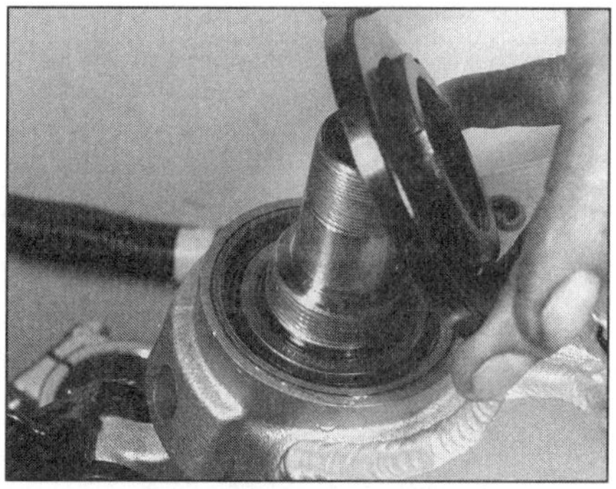

8.7 Remove the bearing cover

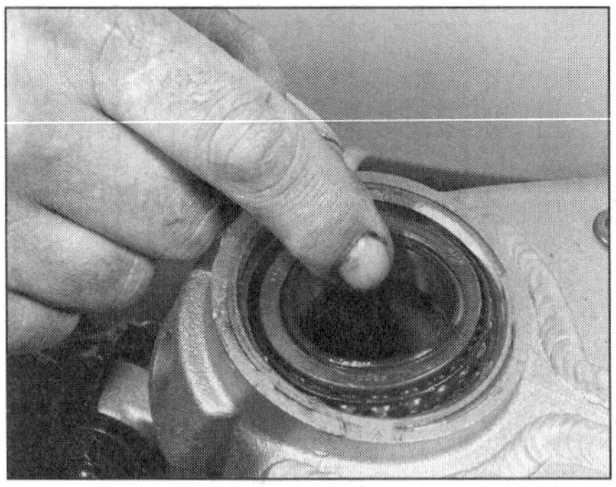

8.9 Remove the upper bearing

head **(see illustration)**. On J and A models, remove the upper bearing inner race and the upper bearing. **Note:** *F, G and H models are fitted with tapered roller bearings, J and A models are fitted with caged ball bearings.* Remove all traces of old grease from the bearings and races and check them for wear or damage as described in Section 9. **Note:** *Do not attempt to remove the outer races from the frame or the lower bearing from the steering stem unless they are to be renewed (see Section 9).*

Installation

10 Smear a liberal quantity of grease on the bearing outer races in the frame and work grease well into both the upper and lower bearings.

11 Carefully lift the steering stem/bottom yoke up through the frame. On F, G and H models, install the upper bearing inner race in the top of the steering head, then push up on the bottom yoke and fit the new O-ring around the stem **(see illustration)**. On J and A models install the upper bearing and its inner race. On all models, install the bearing cover **(see illustration 8.7)**, then thread the adjuster nut, with its stepped side facing down, onto the steering stem and tighten it hand-tight against the bearing.

12 On F, G and H models, tighten the adjuster nut to the ***initial*** torque setting specified at the beginning of the Chapter to settle the bearings, then turn the steering stem through its full lock four or five times.

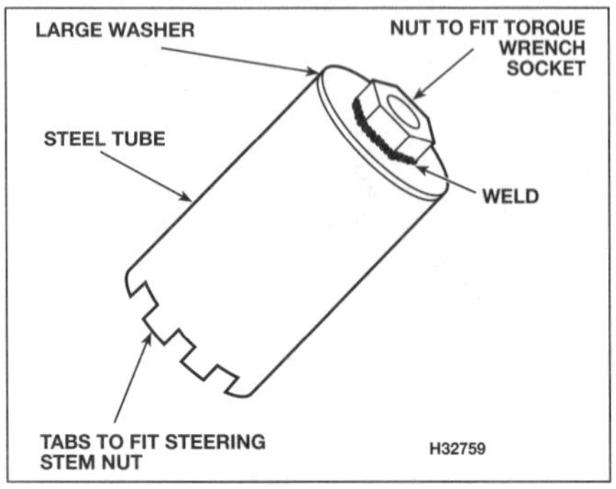

8.12b Tool to tighten the steering head bearing adjuster nut

8.11 Install the upper bearing and the O-ring – F, G and H models

Now slacken and then re-tighten the adjuster nut to the ***final*** specified setting, or until it just becomes tight. The torque settings can be achieved by applying a measured pull to the Kawasaki steering stem wrench (pt. no. 57001-1100) **(see illustration)**. Alternatively, a suitable peg spanner can be made and used in conjunction with a torque wrench **(see illustration)**.

13 On J and A models, tighten the adjuster nut to the specified torque setting to settle the bearings, using either the Kawasaki steering stem wrench (pt. no. 57001-1100) and applying the measured pull **(see illustration 8.12a)**. Alternatively, a suitable peg spanner can be made and used in conjunction with a torque wrench **(see illustration 8.12b)**. Then slacken the nut slightly and turn the steering stem through its full lock four or five times. Now re-tighten the adjuster nut to the specified setting.

14 As an alternative to using the Kawasaki tool or a peg spanner, tighten the nut and adjust the bearings as described in Chapter 1 after the installation procedure is complete.

Caution: Take great care not to apply excessive pressure because this will cause premature failure of the bearings.

15 Thread on the locknut; on F, G and H models tighten it lightly against the adjuster nut, on J and A models tighten the locknut to the specified torque. **Note:** *Hold the adjuster nut in position as the locknut is secured against it.*

16 Fit the top yoke onto the steering stem,

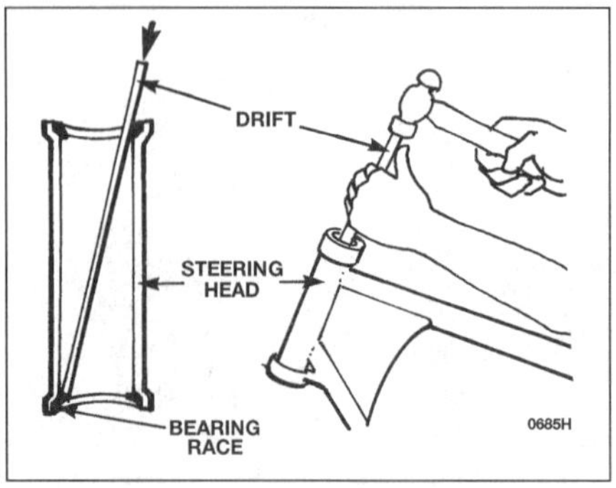

9.4 Drive the bearing races out with a brass drift as shown

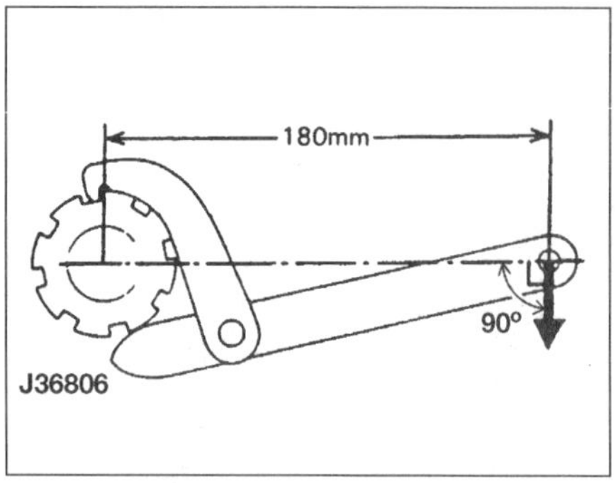

8.12a Using the Kawasaki service tool to settle the bearings

Use a spring balance to apply a force of 22.2 kg (F, G and H models) or 8.3 kg (J and A models) in the direction shown

then install the washer and the steering stem nut and tighten it hand-tight **(see illustration 8.5)**.

17 Install the front forks (see Section 6), tightening the clamp bolts in the top yoke first, followed by the steering stem nut, and finally the clamp bolts in the bottom yoke, all to the specified torque settings.

18 Install the remaining components, referring the relevant Chapters.

19 Carry out a check of the steering head bearing freeplay as described in Chapter 1, and if necessary re-adjust.

9 Steering head bearings – inspection and renewal

***Note:** F, G and H models are fitted with tapered roller bearings, J and A models are fitted with caged ball bearings.*

Inspection

1 Remove the steering stem (see Section 8).

2 Remove all traces of old grease from the bearings and races and check them for wear or damage. **Note:** *On F, G and H models the bearing rollers are integral with the inner races; on J and A models the caged ball bearings are separate from the inner races.*

3 The races should be polished and free from indentations. Inspect the bearing rollers for signs of wear, damage or discoloration, and examine the bearing cages for signs of cracks or splits. Spin the bearings by hand. They should spin freely and smoothly. If there are any signs of wear on any of the above components both upper and lower bearing assemblies must be renewed as a set. Only remove the outer races from the frame or the lower bearing from the steering stem if they need to be renewed – do not re-use them once they have been removed.

Renewal

4 The outer races are an interference fit in the steering head and can be tapped out with a suitable drift **(see illustration)**. Tap firmly and

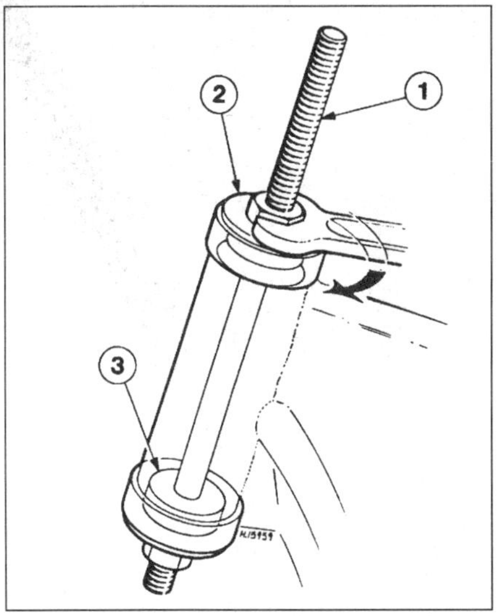

9.6 Drawbolt arrangement for fitting steering stem bearing races

1 Long bolt or threaded bar
2 Thick washer
3 Guide for lower race

evenly around each race to ensure that it is driven out squarely. It may prove advantageous to curve the end of the drift slightly to improve access.

5 Alternatively, the races can be removed using a slide-hammer type bearing extractor; these can often be hired from tool shops.

6 The new outer races can be pressed into the head using a drawbolt arrangement **(see illustration)**, or by using a large diameter tubular drift which bears only on the outer edge of the race. Ensure that the drawbolt washer or drift (as applicable) bears only on the outer edge of the race and does not contact the working surface. Alternatively, have the races installed by a Kawasaki dealer equipped with the bearing race installing tools.

HAYNES HiNT ***Installation of new bearing outer races is made much easier if the races are left overnight in the freezer. This causes them to contract slightly making them a looser fit.***

7 To remove the lower bearing from the steering stem, use two screwdrivers placed on opposite sides of the race to work it free **(see illustration)**. If the race is firmly in place it will be necessary to use a bearing puller **(see illustration)**, or a hammer and chisel – take care not to damage the bearing seat or the steering stem. Check the condition of the grease seal that fits under the lower bearing and fit a new one if it is worn, damaged or deteriorated.

8 Fit the new lower bearing onto the steering stem. A length of tubing with an internal diameter slightly larger than the steering stem will be needed to tap the new bearing into

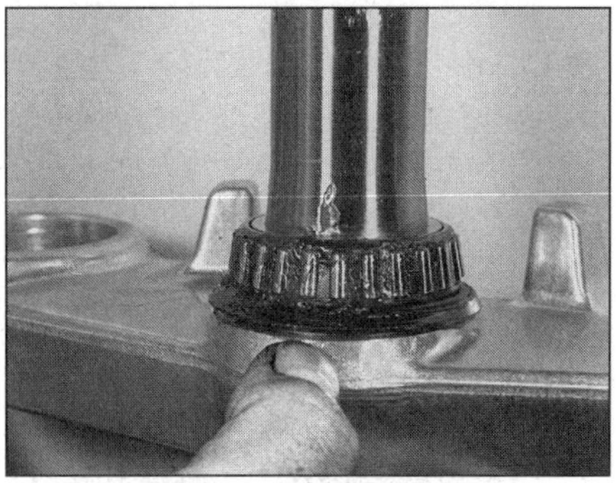

9.7a Remove the lower bearing and grease seal only if they are being replaced – F, G and H models shown

position **(see illustration)**. Ensure that the drift bears only on the inner edge of the race and does not contact the rollers on F, G and H models or working surface of the inner race on J and A models.

9 Install the steering stem (see Section 8).

10 Rear shock absorber – removal, inspection and installation

Warning: Do not attempt to disassemble this shock absorber. It is nitrogen-charged under high pressure. Improper disassembly could result in serious injury. Instead, take the shock to a Kawasaki dealer or suspension specialist with the proper equipment to do the job.

Removal

1 Place the machine on an auxiliary stand. Position a support under the rear wheel so that it does not drop when the shock absorber is removed, but also making sure that the weight of the machine is off the rear suspension so that the shock is not compressed.

2 On F models, remove the seats, the side panels and the lower fairing panels (see Chapter 8). If required for improved clearance, also unscrew the two bolts securing the rider's right-hand footrest bracket assembly, then detach the assembly from the frame and position it aside, making sure no strain is

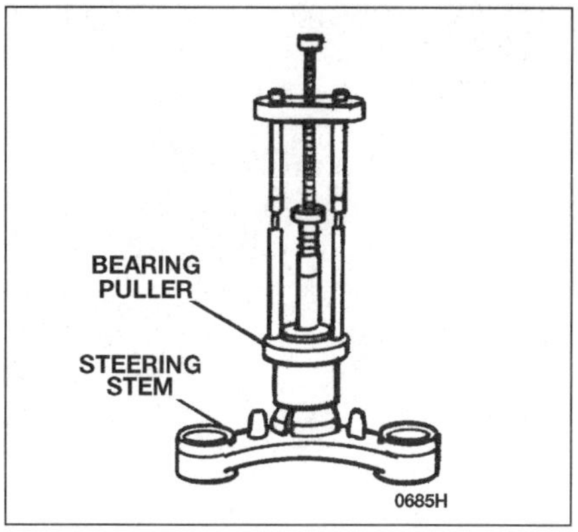

9.7b It is best to remove the lower bearing using a puller

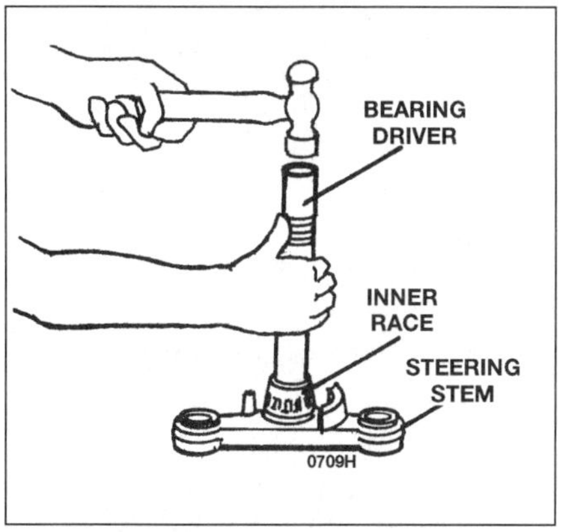

9.8 Drive the new bearing (F, G and H models) or inner race (J and A models) on using a suitable bearing driver or a length of pipe that bears only against the top edge of the inner race and not against the bearing/race

placed on the brake hose. This makes it easier to manoeuvre the reservoir through the frame.

3 On G, H, J and A models, remove the lower fairing panels (see Chapter 8).

4 Unscrew the nut and withdraw the bolt securing the linkage rods to the linkage arm **(see illustration)**. Unscrew the nut and withdraw the bolt securing the bottom of the shock absorber to the linkage arm **(see illustration)**. Swing the linkage rods rearwards and the linkage arm down.

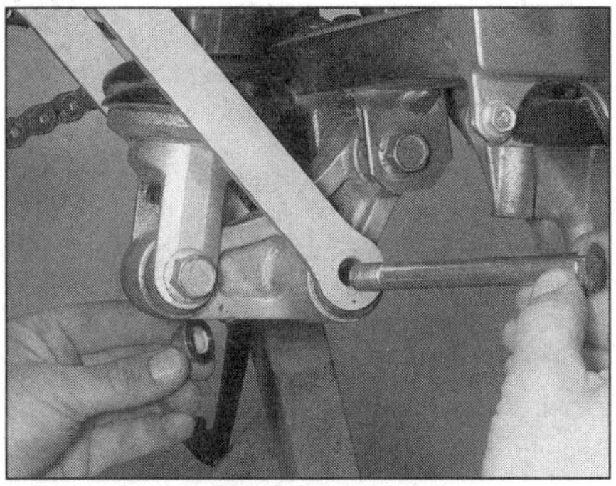

10.4a Remove the bolt securing the linkage rods to the arm . . .

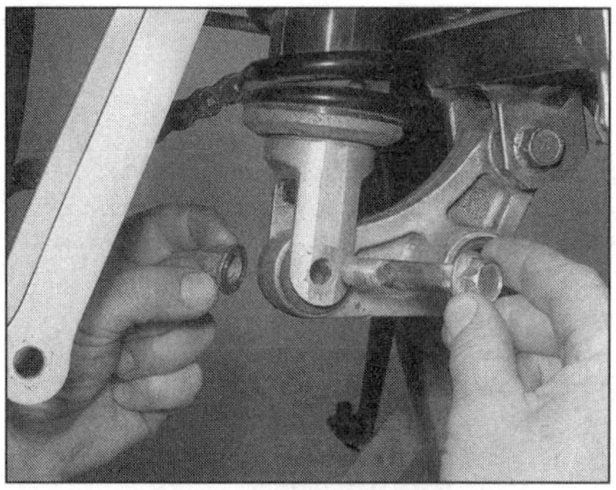

10.4b . . . and the bolt securing the bottom of the shock to the arm

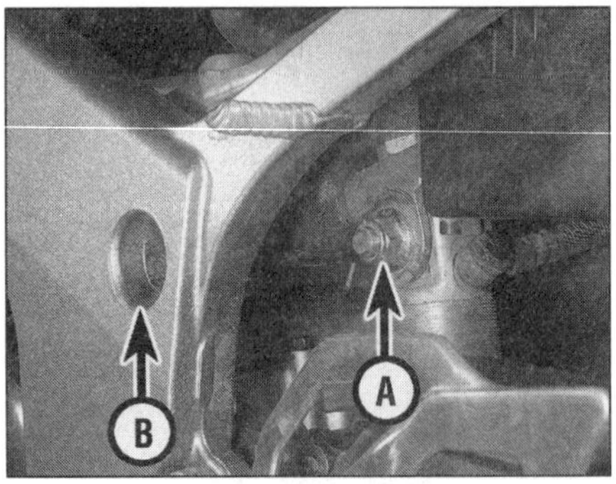

10.5 Unscrew the nut (A) – on F models access it via the hole in the frame (B)

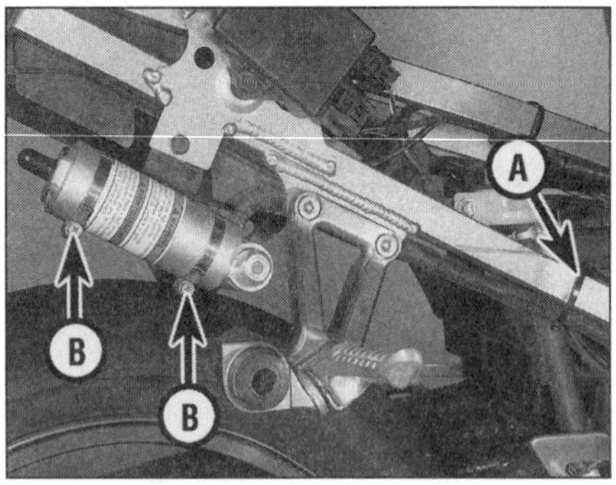

10.6 Cut the cable tie (A) and slacken the reservoir clamp screws (B)

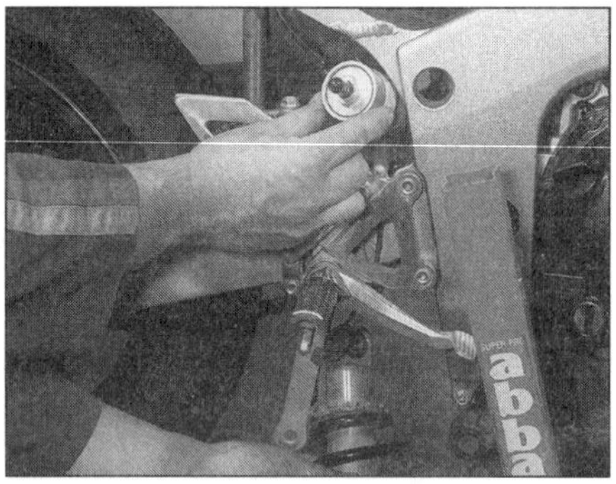
10.7 Remove the upper mounting bolt and manoeuvre the shock, and on F models the reservoir, out

10.9 Look for pitting and oil leakage on the rod (arrowed)

10.11 Tightening the shock upper mounting bolt on F models

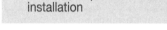

5 Unscrew the nut on the shock absorber upper mounting bolt **(see illustration)**. On F models, access to the upper mounting is best achieved using a socket extension inserted through the hole in each side of the frame **(see illustration 10.11)**.

6 On F models, cut the cable tie securing the reservoir hose to the frame, then slacken the clamps screws securing the reservoir to its holder **(see illustration)**. Slip the reservoir out and feed it through to the shock absorber.

7 Support the shock absorber and withdraw the upper mounting bolt, then manoeuvre the shock down and out of the bottom of the machine, on F models feeding the reservoir and hose through as you do **(see illustration)**.

Inspection

8 Inspect the shock absorber for obvious physical damage and the coil spring for looseness, cracks or signs of fatigue.

9 Inspect the shock damper rod for signs of bending, pitting and oil leakage **(see illustration)**.

10 Inspect the pivot hardware at the top and bottom of the shock for wear or damage. Check that the shock upper mounting is tight and if necessary tighten the mounting nut to the specified torque setting.

Installation

11 Installation is the reverse of removal. Apply grease to the shock absorber and linkage rod pivot points. Install the bolts and nuts finger-tight only until all components are in position, then tighten the nuts to the torque settings specified at the beginning of the Chapter **(see illustration)**.

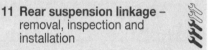

11 Rear suspension linkage – removal, inspection and installation

Removal

1 Place the machine on an auxiliary stand. Position a support under the rear wheel so that it does not drop when the shock absorber lower mounting bolt is removed, but also making sure that the weight of the machine is off the rear suspension so that the shock is not compressed.

2 Remove the exhaust system (see Chapter 4).

3 Unscrew the nuts and withdraw the bolts securing the shock absorber and the linkage rods to the linkage arm **(see illustrations 10.4a and b)**.

4 Unscrew the nut and withdraw the bolt securing the linkage rods to the swingarm and remove the rods.

5 Unscrew the nut and withdraw bolt securing the linkage arm to the frame and remove the linkage arm, noting which way round it fits **(see illustration)**.

Inspection

6 Withdraw the spacers and lever out the grease seals from the linkage arm and swingarm, noting their different sizes **(see illustrations)**. Thoroughly clean all components, removing all traces of dirt, corrosion and grease.

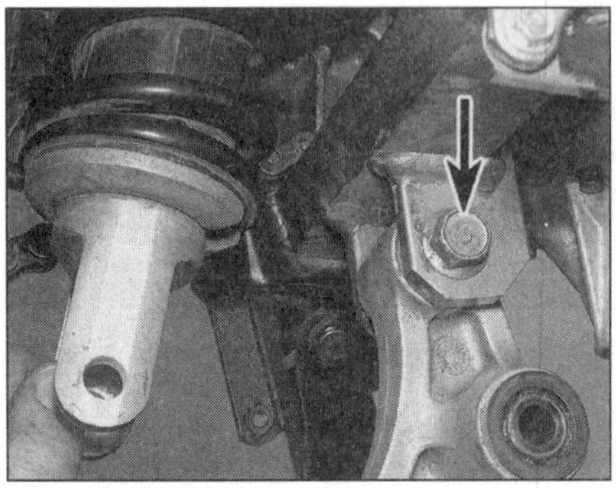
11.5 Unscrew the bolt (arrowed) and remove the linkage arm

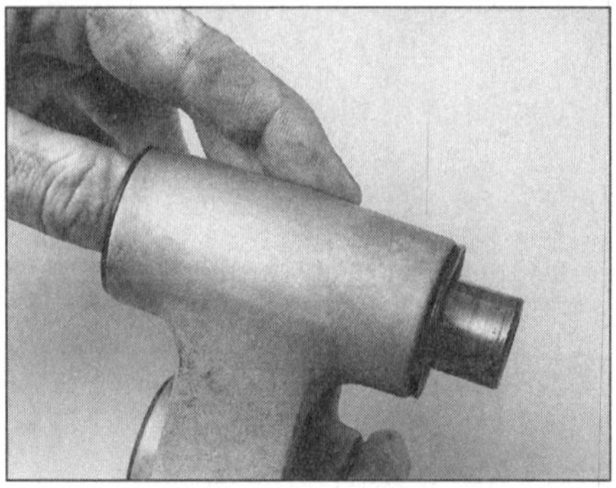
11.6a Withdraw the spacers . . .

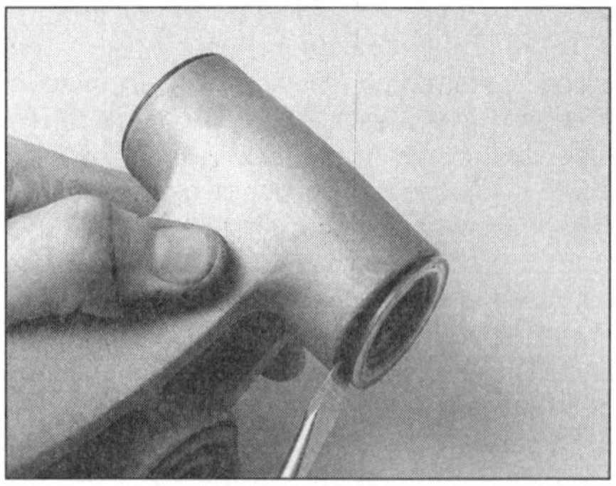
11.6b . . . and lever out the grease seals

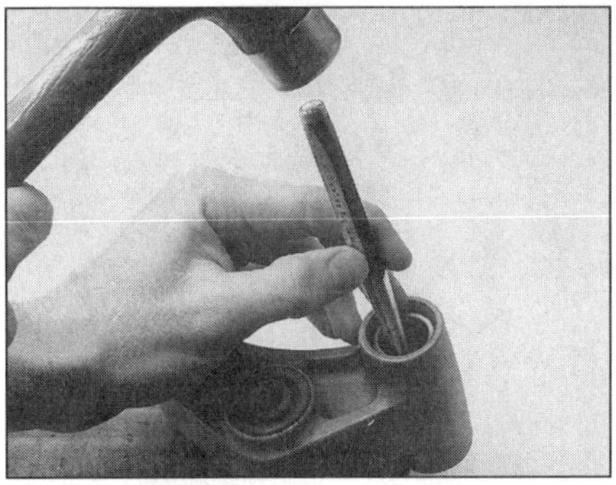

11.9 Knock out the old bearings with a hammer and punch

7 Inspect all components closely, looking for obvious signs of wear such as heavy scoring, or for damage such as cracks or distortion. Check the condition of the needle roller bearings in the linkage arm and swingarm.

8 On J and A models, clean the grease nipples on the linkage arm and swingarm and pump some grease through them to ensure that they are not blocked. Fit new grease nipples if necessary.

9 Worn bearings can be drifted out of their bores, but note that removal will destroy them **(see illustration)**; new components should be obtained before work commences. The new ones should be pressed or drawn into their bores rather than driven into position. In the absence of a press, a suitable drawbolt arrangement can be made up as described below.

10 Obtain a long bolt or a length of threaded rod from a local engineering works or some other supplier. The bolt or rod should be about one inch longer than the combined width of the linkage piece and one bearing. Also required are suitable nuts and two large and robust washers having a larger outside diameter than the bearing housing. In the case of the threaded rod, fit one nut to one end of the rod and stake it in place for convenience.

11 Fit one of the washers over the bolt or rod so that it rests against the head or staked nut, then pass the assembly through the relevant bore. Over the projecting end place the bearing, which should be greased to ease installation, followed by the remaining washer and nut.

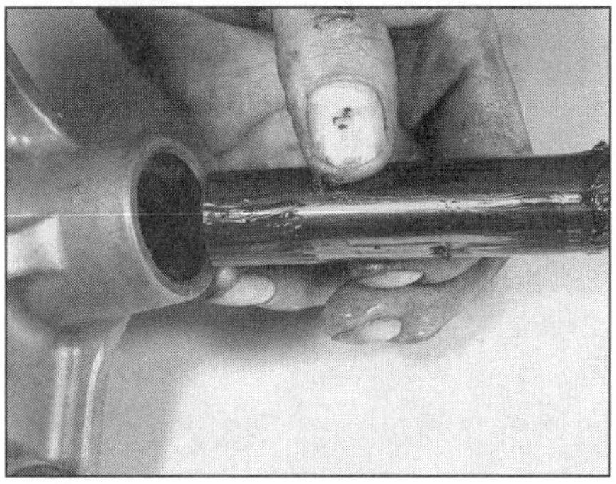

11.14 Coat the spacers with moly-grease before installing them

12 Holding the bearing to ensure that it is kept square, slowly tighten the nut so that the bearing is drawn into its bore.

13 Once it is fully home, remove the drawbolt arrangement and, if necessary, repeat the procedure to fit the other bearings.

14 Lubricate the needle roller bearings and the spacers with molybdenum disulphide grease and install the spacers **(see illustration)**.

15 Check the condition of the grease seals and renew them if they are damaged or deteriorated. Press the seals squarely into place.

Installation

16 Installation is the reverse of removal. Apply grease to the pivot points. Install the bolts and nuts finger-tight only until all components are in position, then tighten the nuts to the torque settings specified at the beginning of the Chapter.

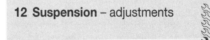

12 Suspension - adjustments

Front forks

1 The front forks are adjustable for spring pre-load and both rebound and compression damping.

2 Spring pre-load is adjusted using a suitable spanner on the adjuster flats on the top of the forks **(see illustration)**. The amount of pre-load is indicated by lines on the adjuster. There are eight lines. The standard position is with the sixth line just visible above the top bolt hex. Turn the adjuster clockwise to increase pre-load and anti-clockwise to decrease it. Always make sure both adjusters are set equally.

3 Rebound damping is adjusted using a screwdriver in the slot in the adjuster protruding from the pre-load adjuster **(see illustration 12.2)**. The amount of damping is indicated by the number of clicks when turned anti-clockwise from the fully screwed-in position. There are twelve positions. The standard position is seven clicks out on F models, eight clicks on G and H models, seven clicks on J models and six clicks ($1\frac{1}{2}$ turns out) on A models. Turn the adjuster clockwise to increase damping and anti-clockwise to decrease it. To establish the current setting, turn the adjuster in (clockwise) counting the number of clicks, then reset it as required. Always make sure both adjusters are set equally.

4 Compression damping is adjusted using a screwdriver in the slot in the adjuster in the bottom of the fork slider **(see illustration)**. The amount of damping is indicated by the number of clicks when turned anti-clockwise from the fully screwed-in position. There are twelve positions on F models, ten on G and H models and twelve on J and A models. The standard position is seven clicks out on F models, nine clicks on G, H and J models and eight clicks on A models. Turn the adjuster clockwise to increase damping and anti-clockwise to decrease it. To establish the current setting, turn the adjuster in (clockwise) counting the number of clicks, then reset it as required. Always make sure both adjusters are set equally.

Rear shock absorber

5 On all models the rear shock absorber is adjustable for spring pre-load and both rebound and compression damping.

6 Spring pre-load adjustment is made by turning the adjuster nut on the threads on the shock absorber body **(see illustration)**.

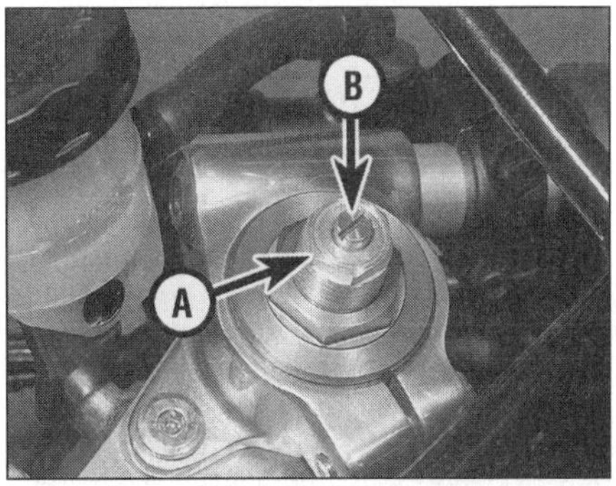

12.2 Spring pre-load adjuster (A), rebound damping adjuster (B)

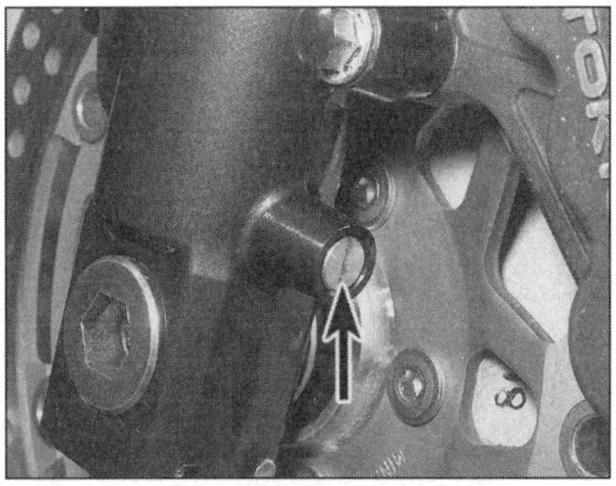

12.4 Compression damping adjuster (arrowed)

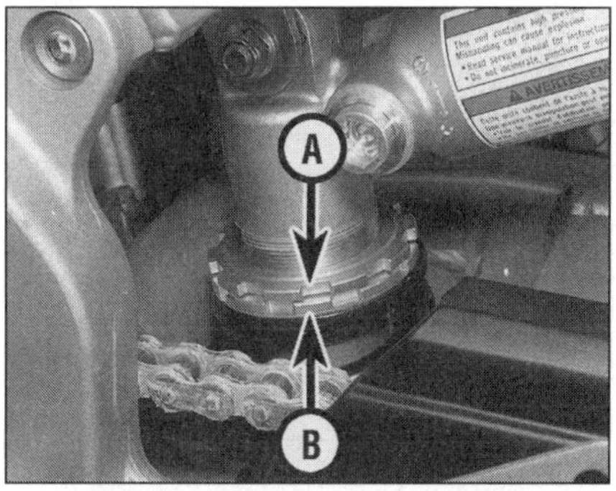

12.6 Pre-load adjuster locknut (A) and adjuster (B)

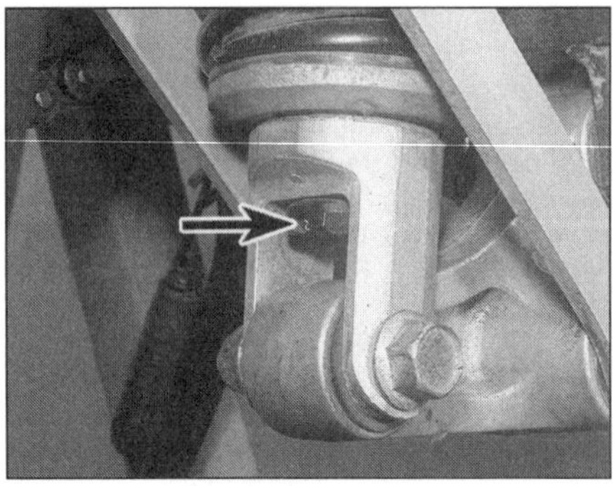

12.7 Rebound damping adjuster (arrowed) – F models

12.8 Rebound damping adjuster (arrowed) – G, H, J and A models

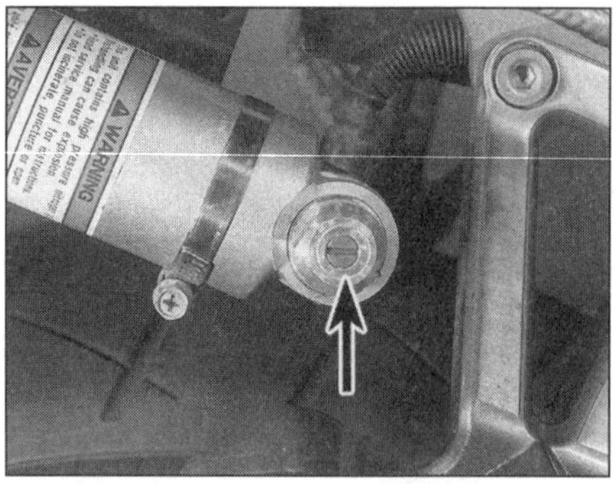

12.9a Compression damping adjuster (arrowed) – F models

12.9b Compression damping adjuster – G, H, J and A models

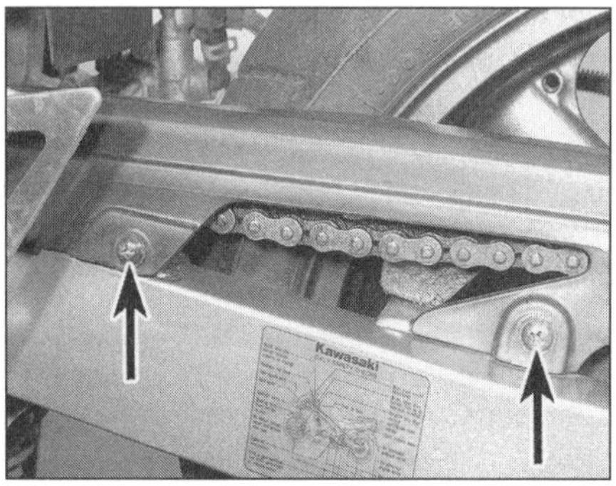

13.2 The chainguard is secured by two screws (arrowed)

Slacken the locknut, then turn the adjuster nut clockwise to increase pre-load and anti-clockwise to decrease it. On F models, the amount of pre-load is set by measuring the amount of spring compression from the relaxed position, i.e. when the adjuster is fully unscrewed from the spring. On G, H, J and A models, the amount of pre-load is set by measuring the length of the spring. The standard position and usable range of pre-load are listed in the Specifications at the beginning of the Chapter. Adjustment and measurement is made easier by removing the shock absorber (see Section 10). Tighten the locknut securely after adjustment.

7 On F models, rebound damping adjustment is made by turning the adjuster on the bottom of the shock absorber **(see illustration)**. The amount of damping is indicated by a number on the adjuster. There are four positions. The standard position is number 2. The weakest is number 1 and the strongest number 4. Turn the adjuster until the desired setting, indicated by the number, aligns with the index mark on the shock body and a click is felt.

8 On G, H, J and A models, rebound damping is adjusted using a screwdriver in the slot in the adjuster on the base of the shock absorber **(see illustration)**. The amount of damping is indicated by the number of clicks when turned anti-clockwise from the fully screwed-in position. There are twenty positions on G and H models and eighteen on J and A models. The standard position is eight clicks out on G and H models and ten clicks on J and A models. Turn the adjuster clockwise to increase damping and anti-clockwise to decrease it. To establish the current setting, turn the adjuster in (clockwise) counting the number of clicks, then reset it as required.

9 Compression damping is adjusted using a screwdriver in the slot in the adjuster on the reservoir body **(see illustrations)**. The amount of damping is indicated by the number of clicks when turned anti-clockwise from the fully screwed-in position. There are twenty-two positions on F models, and twenty on G, H, J and A models. The standard position is twelve clicks out on F models, nine clicks on G and H models and ten clicks on J and A models. Turn the adjuster clockwise to increase damping and anti-clockwise to decrease it. To establish the current setting, turn the adjuster in (clockwise) counting the number of clicks, then reset it as required.

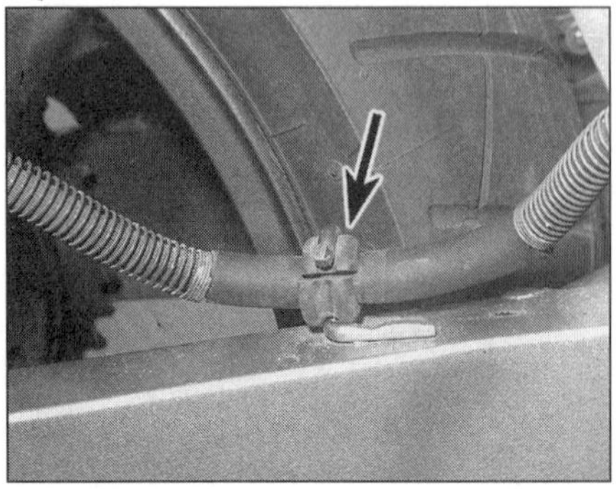

13.3a On F models release the brake hose grommet (arrowed) from the clamp

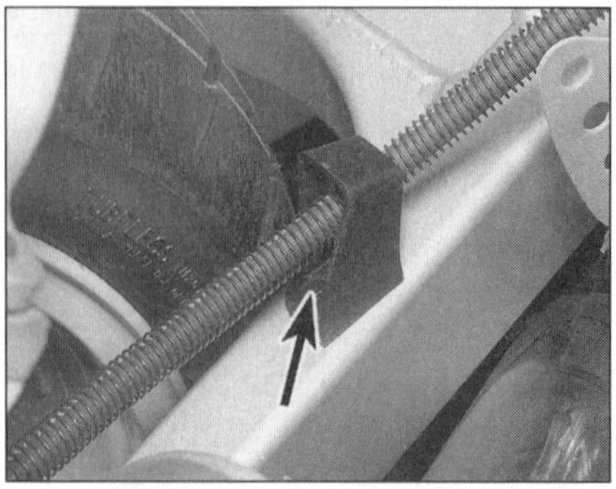

13.3b On G, H, J and A models, unscrew the bolt (arrowed) and detach the guide

13 Swingarm – removal and installation

Removal

1 Remove the rear wheel (see Chapter 7).

2 Remove the screws securing the chainguard to the swingarm and remove the guard, noting how it fits **(see illustration)**.

3 On F models, slip the brake hose with its grommet out of the clamp on the swingarm **(see illustration)**. On G, H, J and A models, unscrew the bolt securing the hose guide to the swingarm **(see illustration)**. **Note:** *On J and A models, there are two hose guides bolted to the swingarm.*

4 Undo the bolt securing the linkage rods to the swingarm and swing the linkage rods forwards. Remove the rear shock absorber (see Section 10).

5 Unscrew the nut on the left-hand end of the swingarm pivot bolt **(see illustration)**.
6 Support the swingarm, then withdraw the pivot bolt and remove the swingarm **(see illustration)**.
7 Remove the chain slider from the front of the swingarm if necessary, noting how it fits. If it is badly worn or damaged, a new slider should be fitted.
8 Inspect all components for wear or damage as described in Section 14.

Installation

9 If removed, install the chain slider and tighten its screw securely.
10 Remove the collar from the left-hand side and the cap from the right-hand side of the swingarm pivot, and lubricate the grease seals, bearings, and the pivot bolt with grease **(see illustration 14.4a)**. Re-install the collar and the cap.
11 Offer up the swingarm, and have an assistant hold it in place. Make sure the drive chain is looped over the front of the swingarm. Slide the pivot bolt through the swingarm from the right-hand side, then fit the nut onto its left-hand end. Counter-hold the bolt and tighten the nut to the torque setting specified at the beginning of the Chapter.
12 Install the rear shock absorber and linkage rods (see Section 10).
13 On F models, secure the brake hose in its clamp, using a new rubber grommet if the old one is damaged or deteriorated **(see illustration 13.3a)**. On all other models, mount the hose guide(s) onto the swingarm and tighten the bolt(s) securely (see Step 3).
14 Install the chainguard and tighten its screws securely **(see illustration 13.2)**.
15 Install the rear wheel (see Chapter 7).
16 Check and adjust the drive chain slack (see Chapter 1). Check the operation of the rear suspension before taking the machine on the road.

14 Swingarm – inspection and bearing renewal

Inspection

1 Thoroughly clean all components, removing all traces of dirt, corrosion and grease **(see illustrations)**.
2 Inspect all components closely, looking for obvious signs of wear such as heavy scoring, and cracks or distortion due to accident damage. Any damaged or worn component must be renewed.
3 Check the swingarm pivot bolt for straightness by rolling it on a flat surface such as a piece of plate glass (first wipe off all old grease and remove any corrosion using steel wool). If the equipment is available, place the pivot bolt in V-blocks and check the runout using a dial gauge. If the pivot bolt is bent, fit a new one.

13.5 Unscrew the swingarm pivot bolt nut (arrowed) . . .

13.6 . . . and withdraw the pivot bolt (arrowed)

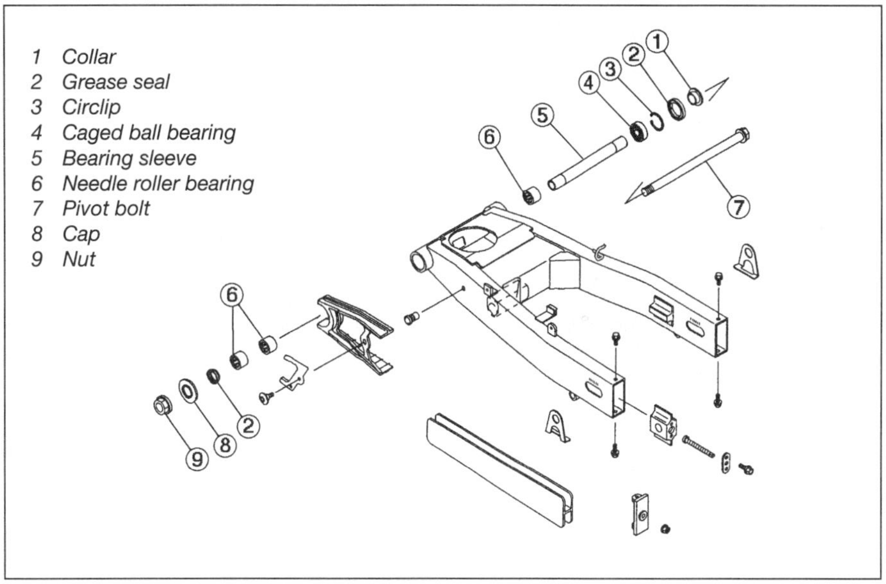

14.1a Swingarm components – F models

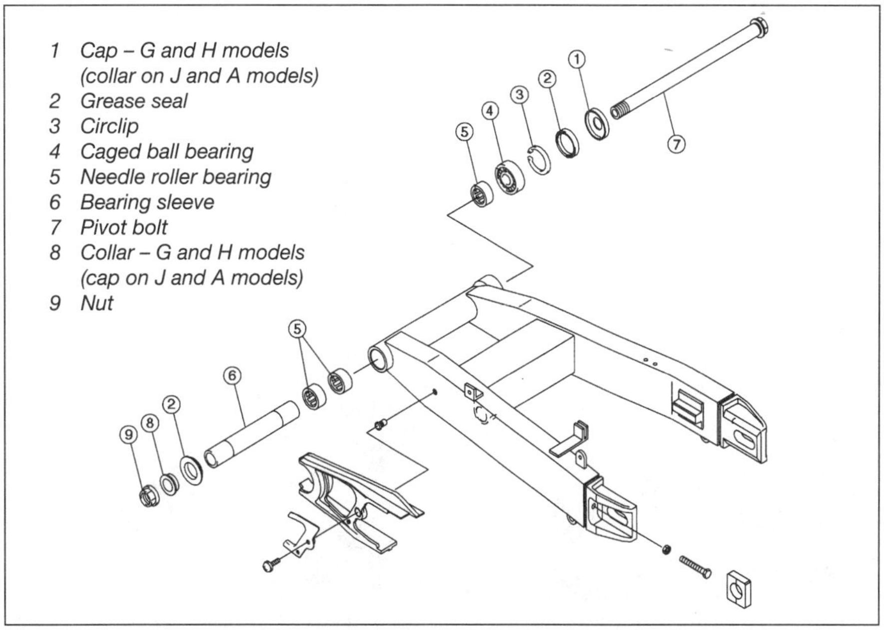

14.1b Swingarm components – G, H, J and A models

Bearing renewal

4 Remove the collar from the right-hand side of the swingarm pivot on F, J and A models and the left-hand side on G and H models. Remove the cap from the left-hand side on F, J and A models and the right-hand side on G and H models. Lever out the grease seal on each side of the swingarm **(see illustrations)**. Withdraw the bearing sleeve.

5 Referring to *Tools and Workshop Tips (Section 5)* in the Reference section at the end of this Manual, clean the bearings and inspect them for wear or damage. A caged ball bearing and a needle roller bearing are fitted in the right-hand side, and two needle roller bearings in the left-hand side. If the bearings do not run smoothly and freely or if there is excessive freeplay, they must be renewed. If necessary, remove the circlip from the right-hand side and carefully drift out the ball bearing. Only remove the needle bearings if you are going to fit new ones.

6 When installing new bearings, lubricate them liberally grease. Check the condition of the grease seals and renew them if they are damaged or deteriorated. It is advisable to renew them as a matter of course if they are removed.

7 On J and A models, clean the grease nipples on the linkage rod and swingarm pivots and pump some grease through them to ensure that they are not blocked. Fit new grease nipples if necessary.

15 Drive chain – removal, cleaning and installation

Removal – endless type chain

Note: *An endless chain has no riveted (soft) link – all links and pins are the same. The chain fitted as original equipment and supplied as a spare part from Kawasaki dealers is of the endless type.*

1 On F models, remove the left-hand lower fairing panel (see Chapter 8).

2 On G, H, J and A models, unscrew the bolt securing the speedometer sensor in the front sprocket cover and detach the sensor, noting how it fits **(see illustration)**.

14.4a Remove the collar and cap . . .

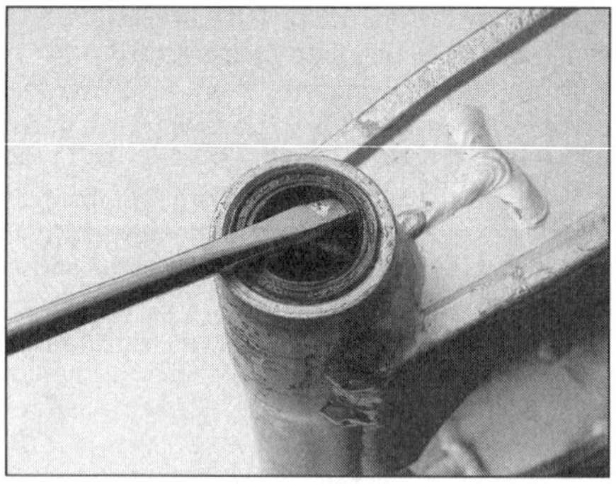

14.4b . . . then lever out the grease seals

3 Unscrew the bolts securing the front sprocket cover, noting the position of the wiring clamp, and remove the cover **(see illustration)**. On F models, also remove the Allen head stay bolt located just to the rear of the sprocket **(see illustration)**.

4 Remove the swingarm (see Section 13).

5 Slip the chain off the front sprocket and remove it from the bike.

Removal – riveted link chain

Note: *The riveted (soft) link can be identified by its identification markings on the side plate and usually slightly different colour. Also the staked ends of the link's two pins look as if they have been deeply centre-punched, instead of peened over as with all other pins.*

6 Locate the joining link in a suitable position to work on by rotating the back wheel; midway between the sprockets is ideal.

7 Slacken the drive chain as described in Chapter 1.

8 Split the chain at the joining link using an approved chain breaker tool intended for motorcycle use. There are a number of types available for motorcycle use and it is important to follow carefully the instructions supplied with the tool – see *Tools and Workshop Tips* in the Reference section for a typical example. Remove the chain from the bike, noting its routing through the swingarm.

Cleaning

9 Soak the chain in paraffin (kerosene) for approximately five or six minutes. If the chain is very dirty, use a soft-bristled brush to remove caked-on deposits, taking care to wear hand protection.

Caution: Don't use petrol (gasoline), solvent or other cleaning fluids. Don't use high-pressure water. Remove the chain, wipe it off, then blow dry it with compressed air immediately. The entire process shouldn't take longer than ten minutes – if it does, the O-rings in the chain rollers could be damaged.

Installation – endless chain

10 Installation is the reverse of removal. On G, H, J and A models, tighten the sprocket cover bolts to the torque setting specified at the beginning of the Chapter, and apply a suitable non-permanent thread locking compound to the speedometer sensor mounting bolt and tighten it to the specified torque **(see illustration 15.2)**.

11 Adjust the chain following the procedure described in Chapter 1.

Installation – riveted link chain

12 Thread the chain into position, making sure that it takes the correct route around the swingarm and sprockets and leave the two ends in a convenient place to work on. Obtain a new soft link – never attempt to reuse an old link.

13 Assemble the new soft link and rivet it securely in place using a chain riveting tool. Refer to *Tools and Workshop Tips* in the Reference section for details.

14 After riveting, check the soft link pin ends for any signs of cracking. If there is any evidence of cracking, the soft link, O-rings

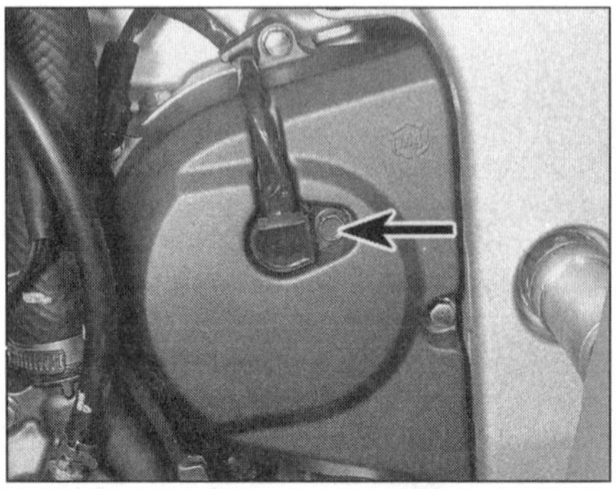

15.2 Unscrew the bolt (arrowed) and detach the sensor

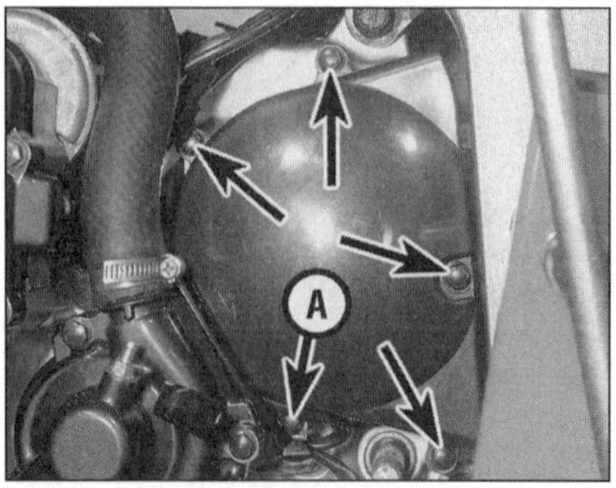

15.3a Unscrew the bolts (arrowed), noting the wiring clamp (A), and remove the cover

15.3b On F models unscrew the stay bolt

16.9a Bend down the locking tab . . .

16.9b . . . then unscrew the nut and remove the washer

16.11 Install the sprocket with the mark facing out

and side plate must be removed and the procedure repeated with a new soft link.

15 Install the sprocket cover and adjust the chain as described in Step 10. Adjust and lubricate the chain as described in Chapter 1.

Warning: NEVER install a drive chain which uses a clip-type master (split) link. If you do not have access to a chain riveting tool, have the chain fitted by a Kawasaki dealer.

16 Sprockets - check and renewal

Check

1 On F models, remove the fairing left-hand lower panel (see Chapter 8).

2 On all other models, unscrew the bolt securing the speedometer sensor in the front sprocket cover and detach the sensor, noting how it fits **(see illustration 15.2)**.

3 Unscrew the bolts securing the front sprocket cover, noting the position of the wiring clamp, and remove the cover **(see illustration 15.3a)**.

4 Check the wear pattern on both sprockets as described in Chapter 1, Section 8. If the sprocket teeth are worn excessively, renew the chain and both sprockets as a set. Whenever the sprockets are inspected, the drive chain should be inspected also (see Chapter 1).

5 Adjust and lubricate the chain following the procedures described in Chapter 1.

Renewal

Front sprocket

6 On F models, remove the fairing left-hand lower panel (see Chapter 8).

7 On all other models, unscrew the bolt securing the speedometer sensor in the front sprocket cover and detach the sensor, noting how it fits **(see illustration 15.2)**.

8 Unscrew the bolts securing the sprocket cover, noting the position of the wiring clamp, and remove the cover **(see illustration 15.3a)**. On F models, also remove the Allen head stay bolt located just to the rear of the sprocket **(see illustration 15.3b)**.

9 Bend down the rim of the lockwasher behind the sprocket nut using a suitable drift or screwdriver **(see illustration)**. Select first gear and have an assistant apply the rear brake, then unscrew the sprocket nut and remove the washer **(see illustration)**. Refer to Chapter 1 and adjust the drive chain until it is fully slack, then slip it off the rear sprocket.

10 Slip the chain off the front sprocket and slide the sprocket off the gearbox shaft.

11 Slide the new sprocket onto the shaft, with the 315 15T mark on F models, and the OUT mark on G, H, J and A models, facing out. Engage the chain on the sprocket **(see illustration)**. Refer to Chapter 1 and take up the slack in the chain by turning the adjusters, then temporarily tighten the axle nut.

12 Install a ***new*** lockwasher over the gearbox shaft splines. Lightly oil the shaft threads and the seating surface of the nut, then install the nut and tighten it to the torque setting specified at the beginning of the Chapter, using the rear brake to prevent the sprocket from turning **(see illustrations)**. Bend the rim of the washer up against one of the nut flats to lock the nut in place **(see illustration)**.

13 On F models, install the Allen head stay bolt. On all models, install the sprocket cover and the cover bolts and wiring clamp. On G, H, J and A models, tighten the sprocket cover bolts to the torque setting specified at the beginning of the Chapter, and apply a suitable non-permanent thread locking compound to the speedometer sensor mounting bolt and tighten it to the specified torque **(see illustration 15.2)**. Adjust and lubricate the chain following the procedures described in Chapter 1.

Rear sprocket

14 Remove the rear wheel (see Chapter 7).

15 Unscrew the nuts securing the sprocket to the coupling and remove the sprocket,

16.12a Fit the new washer onto the splines . . .

16.12b . . . then install the nut and tighten it to the specified torque

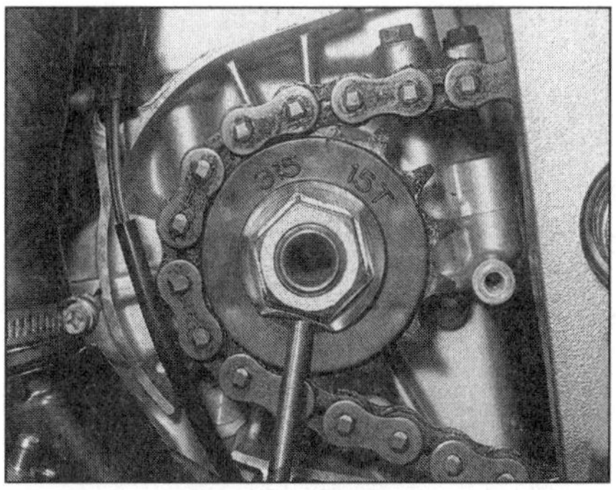

16.12c Lock the nut by bending the rim of the washer against it

16.15 Unscrew the nuts (arrowed) and remove the sprocket, noting the tooth number marking (A)

17.2 Lift the sprocket coupling out of the wheel . . .

17.3 . . . and remove the damper

noting which way round it fits **(see illustration)**.

16 Check that the sprocket studs are secure in the coupling. If any are loose, remove them all and clean their threads, then apply a suitable non-permanent thread locking compound and tighten them securely. To ease removal and tightening of the studs, thread two nuts onto the stud and use one as a locknut and the other to unscrew and tighten the studs (see *Tools and Workshop Tips* in the Reference section).

17 Install the sprocket onto the coupling with the stamped tooth number facing out, then fit the nuts **(see illustration 16.15)**. Tighten the nuts to the torque setting specified at the beginning of the Chapter.

18 Install the rear wheel (see Chapter 7), then adjust and lubricate the chain following the procedures described in Chapter 1.

17 Sprocket coupling/rubber damper - check and renewal

1 Remove the rear wheel (see Chapter 7).

2 Lift the sprocket coupling from the wheel **(see illustration)**. Check the coupling for cracks and damage, and renew it if necessary.

3 Remove the rubber damper from the sprocket coupling or wheel hub and check it for cracks, hardening and general deterioration **(see illustration)**. Fit a new damper if necessary.

4 Checking and renewal procedures for the coupling bearing are in Chapter 7.

5 Installation is the reverse of removal.

Chapter 7
Brakes, wheels and tyres

Contents

Degrees of difficulty

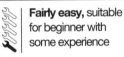

Easy, suitable for novice with little experience	**Fairly easy,** suitable for beginner with some experience	**Fairly difficult,** suitable for competent DIY mechanic	**Difficult,** suitable for experienced DIY mechanic	**Very difficult,** suitable for expert DIY or professional

Specifications

Brakes

Brake fluid type	DOT 4
Brake pad friction material thickness	
Front brake pads	
Standard	4.0 mm
Service limit (min)	1.0 mm
Rear brake pads	
Standard	5.0 mm
Service limit (min)	1.0 mm
Front disc thickness	
F models	
Standard	3.8 to 4.2 mm
Service limit (min)	3.5 mm
G, H, J and A models	
Standard	4.85 to 5.15 mm
Service limit (min)	4.5 mm
Rear disc minimum thickness	
F models	
Standard	5.8 to 6.2 mm
Service limit (min)	5.5 mm
G, H, J and A models	
Standard	4.8 to 5.15 mm
Service limit (min)	4.5 mm
Disc maximum runout (front and rear)	
F models	
Standard (max)	0.2 mm
Service limit (max)	0.3 mm
G, H, J and A models	
Standard (max)	0.15 mm
Service limit (max)	0.3 mm

Wheels

Maximum wheel runout (front and rear)	
Axial (side-to-side)	0.5 mm
Radial (out-of-round)	0.8 mm
Maximum axle runout (front and rear)	0.2 mm

Tyres

Tyre pressures and minimum tread depth	see *Daily (pre-ride)* checks
Tyre sizes*	
F models	
Front	120/60-ZR17
Rear	160/60-ZR17
G and H models	
Front	120/60-ZR17 (55W)
Rear	170/60-ZR17 (72W)
J and A models	
Front	120/65-ZR17 (56W)
Rear	180/55-ZR17 (73W)

**Refer to the owners handbook or the tyre information label on the swingarm for approved tyre brands.*

Torque settings

Brake caliper bleed valves	7.9 Nm
Brake hose banjo bolts	25 Nm
Front brake caliper half joining bolts	21 Nm
Front brake caliper mounting bolts	34 Nm
Front brake disc mounting bolts	
F, G and H models	23 Nm
J and A models	27 Nm
Front brake master cylinder clamp bolts	11 Nm
Front brake master cylinder reservoir bracket bolt (G, H, J and A models)	6.9 Nm
Front wheel axle	
F, G and H models	110 Nm
J models	125 Nm
A models	127 Nm
Front wheel axle clamp bolts	20 Nm
Rear brake caliper mounting bolts	25 Nm
Rear brake disc mounting bolts	
F, G and H models	23 Nm
J and A models	27 Nm
Rear brake master cylinder mounting bolts	
F, G and H models	23 Nm
J and A models	25 Nm
Rear wheel axle nut	
F, G and H models	110 Nm
J models	125 Nm
A models	127 Nm

1 General information

All models covered in this manual are fitted with cast alloy wheels designed for tubeless tyres only. Both front and rear brakes are hydraulically operated disc brakes.

The front brakes on F models are two four-piston calipers. Later models are fitted with two six-piston calipers; on J and A models the lower piston in each caliper has a smaller bore that the upper two. The rear brake on all models has is a single piston sliding caliper.

Caution: Disc brake components rarely require disassembly. Do not disassemble components unless absolutely necessary. If a hydraulic brake line is loosened, the entire system must be disassembled, drained, cleaned and then properly filled and bled upon reassembly. Do not use solvents on internal brake components. Solvents will cause the seals to swell and distort. Use only clean brake fluid or denatured alcohol for cleaning. Use care when working with brake fluid as it can injure your eyes and it will damage painted surfaces and plastic parts.

2 Front brake pads – renewal

Warning: The dust created by the brake system may contain asbestos, which is harmful to your health. Never blow it out with compressed air and don't inhale any of it. An approved filtering mask should be worn when working on the brakes.

Note: *The pads can be removed with the calipers in situ, however if difficulty is encountered removing the cover screws or the pad pin clip, the caliper should be* *displaced to improve access (see Section 3). There is no need to disconnect the hydraulic hose.*

1 Remove the screws or bolts securing the pad spring on the top of the caliper and lift off the spring, noting how it fits **(see illustration)**. Take care when removing the screws on F models as they are prone to becoming seized, and their heads could be easily rounded off. Remove the clip securing the pad retaining pin and withdraw the pin, then lift out the pads **(see illustrations)**.

2 Inspect the surface of each pad for contamination and check that the friction material has not worn level with or beyond the wear limit cutout in the top of each pad. Alternatively, measure the thickness of friction material remaining and compare it to the minimum specified at the beginning of the Chapter. If either pad is worn down to, or beyond, the wear limit, fouled with oil or grease, or heavily scored or damaged by dirt and debris, both pads must be renewed as a set. Note that it is not possible to degrease the friction material; if the pads are contaminated in any way they must be discarded.

3 If the pads are in good condition clean them carefully, using a fine wire brush which is completely free of oil and grease to remove all traces of road dirt and corrosion. Using a pointed instrument, clean out the grooves in the friction material and dig out any embedded particles of foreign matter.

4 Check the condition of the brake disc (see Section 4).

5 Remove all traces of corrosion from the pad pin. Inspect the pin and the pin clip for signs of damage and renew them if necessary.

6 Push the pistons as far back into the caliper as possible using hand pressure or a piece of wood as leverage. Due to the increased friction material thickness of new pads, it may be necessary to remove the master cylinder reservoir cover (F models) or cap (all other models), diaphragm plate and diaphragm and siphon out some fluid. If the pistons are seized in the caliper, the caliper must be overhauled (see Section 3).

7 Smear the backs of the pads and the shank of the pad pin with copper-based grease, making sure that none gets on the friction material of the pads. It is also advisable to apply some to the threads of the pad spring screws on F models as they are prone to becoming seized, and their heads could be easily rounded off.

8 Installation of the pads is the reverse of removal. Insert the pads into the caliper so that the friction material faces the disc, then slide the pad pin through the pads **(see illustrations 2.1d and c)**. Install the pad pin clip, then fit the spring and tighten the screws or bolts securely **(see illustration 2.1b and a)**.

9 Top up the master cylinder reservoir if necessary (see *Daily (pre-ride) checks*), and install the reservoir diaphragm, diaphragm plate and cover/cap.

2.1a Remove the pad spring screws (arrowed) or bolts and remove the spring . . .

2.1b . . . then pull out the retaining pin clip . . .

2.1c . . . remove the retaining pin . . .

2.1d . . . and lift out the pads

10 Operate the brake lever several times to bring the pads into contact with the disc. Check the operation of the brake before riding the motorcycle.

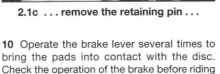

3 Front brake calipers – removal, overhaul and installation

Warning: If a caliper indicates the need for an overhaul (usually due to leaking fluid or sticky operation), all old brake fluid should be flushed from the system. Also, the dust created by the brake system may contain asbestos, which is harmful to your health. Never blow it out with compressed air and don't inhale any of it. An approved filtering mask should be worn when working on the brakes. Do not, under any circumstances, use petroleum-based solvents to clean brake parts. Use clean brake fluid, brake cleaner or denatured alcohol only.

Removal

1 If the calipers are being overhauled, remove the brake pads (see Section 2), then slacken and lightly retighten the four Allen bolts which join the caliper halves **(see illustration)**. If the calipers are just being removed, the pads can be left in place.

2 If the calipers are just being displaced and not completely removed or overhauled, do not disconnect the brake hoses. If the calipers are being overhauled, remove the brake hose banjo bolts **(see illustration 3.1)**. Note the alignment of each hose on the caliper and separate the hose from the caliper. Wrap a plastic bag tightly around the hose end to minimise fluid loss and prevent dirt entering the system, and secure the hose in an upright position. Discard the sealing washers as new ones must be used on installation. **Note:** *If you are planning to overhaul the caliper and don't have a source of compressed air to blow out the pistons, just loosen the banjo bolt at this stage and retighten it lightly. The bike's hydraulic system can then be used to force the pistons out of the body once the pads have been removed. Disconnect the hose once the pistons have been sufficiently displaced.*

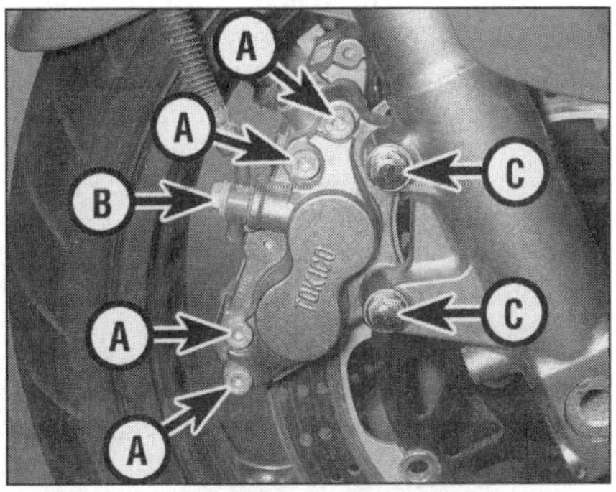

3.1 Caliper half joining bolts (A), brake hose banjo bolt (B), caliper mounting bolts (C)

7

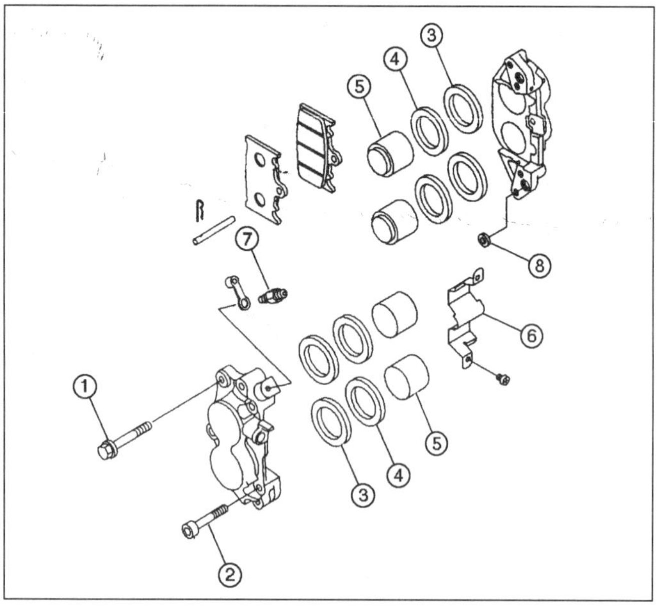

3.4a Front brake caliper components – F models

1 *Mounting bolt*
2 *Joining bolt*
3 *Piston seal*
4 *Dust seal*
5 *Piston*
6 *Pad spring*
7 *Bleed valve*
8 *Caliper seal*

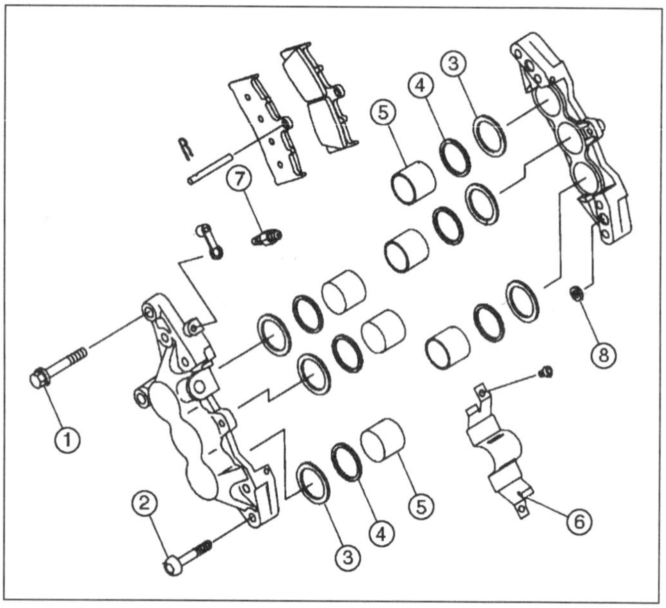

3.4b Front brake caliper components – G, H, J and A models

1 *Mounting bolt*
2 *Joining bolt*
3 *Piston seal*
4 *Dust seal*
5 *Piston*
6 *Pad spring*
7 *Bleed valve*
8 *Caliper seal*

3 Unscrew the caliper mounting bolts, and slide the caliper off the disc **(see illustration 3.1)**.

Overhaul

4 Clean the exterior of the caliper with denatured alcohol or brake system cleaner **(see illustrations)**.

5 Displace the pistons as far as possible from the caliper body, either by pumping them out by operating the front brake lever, or by forcing them out using compressed air. If the compressed air method is used, place a wad of rag between the pistons and the caliper to act as a cushion, then use compressed air directed into the fluid inlet to force the pistons out of the body **(see illustration)**. Use only low pressure to ease the pistons out and make sure both pistons are displaced at the same time. If the air pressure is too high and the pistons are forced out, the caliper and/or pistons may be damaged. Unscrew the Allen bolts and separate the caliper halves **(see illustration)**. Mark each piston head and caliper body with a felt marker to ensure that the pistons can be matched to their original bores on reassembly, then remove the pistons **(see illustration)**. **Note:** *On J and A models the lower piston in each caliper has a smaller bore that the upper two.* On F models, remove the inserts from the centre of the pistons. Remove the caliper seals from either half of the caliper body and discard them as new ones must be used.

Warning: Never place your fingers in front of the pistons in an attempt to catch or protect them when applying compressed air, as serious injury could result.

6 Using a wooden or plastic tool to avoid damaging the caliper bores, remove the dust seals from the bores **(see illustration)**. Discard them as new ones must be used on reassembly.

7 Remove and discard the piston seals in the same way.

8 Clean the pistons and bores with denatured alcohol, clean brake fluid or brake system

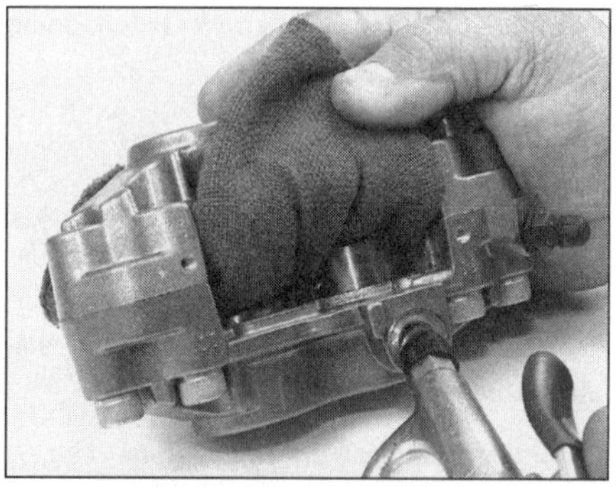

3.5a Place rags in the brake pad cavity and apply a blast of compressed air to break the pistons loose

3.5b Remove the four Allen bolts (arrowed) to separate the caliper halves

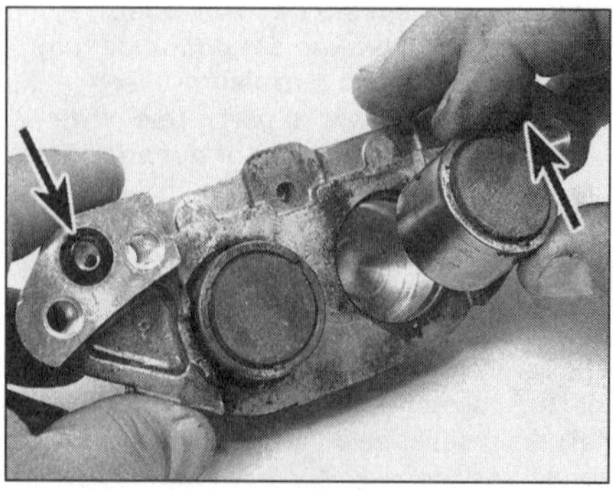

3.5c Remove the pistons from their bores and remove the caliper seals (arrowed)

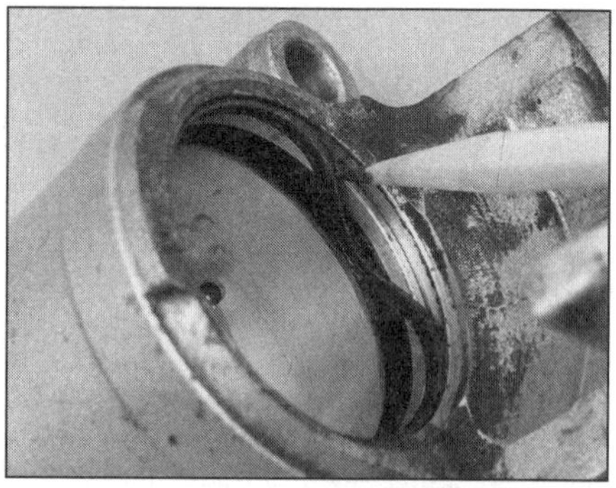

3.6 Use a plastic or wooden tool (a pencil works well) to remove the seals

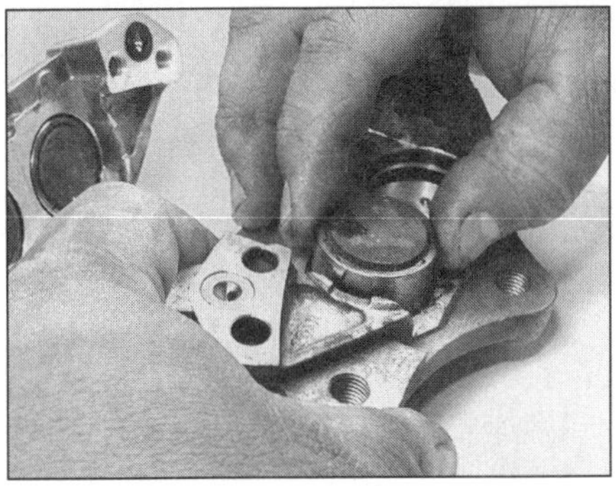

3.12 Dip each piston in fresh brake fluid, then push it straight into the bore with your thumbs

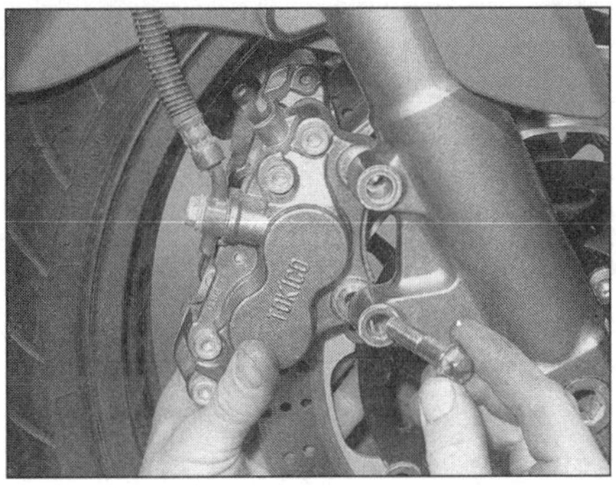

3.14 Fit the caliper onto the disc . . .

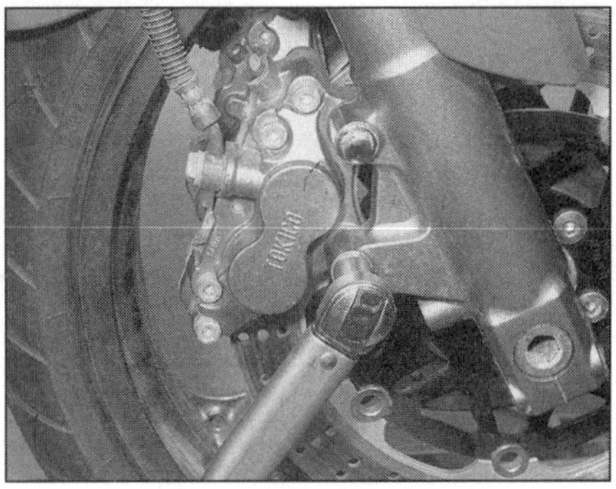

3.15 . . . and tighten the mounting bolts to the specified torque

cleaner. If compressed air is available, use it to dry the parts thoroughly (make sure it's filtered and unlubricated).

Caution: Do not, under any circumstances, use a petroleum-based solvent to clean brake parts.

9 Inspect the caliper bores and pistons for signs of corrosion, nicks and burrs and loss of plating. If surface defects are present, the caliper assembly must be renewed. If the caliper is in bad shape the master cylinder should also be checked.

10 Lubricate the new piston seals with clean brake fluid and install them in their grooves in the caliper bores. **Note:** *On J and A models the lower piston in each caliper has a smaller bore that the upper two. Ensure the correct size piston and dust seals are fitted in the appropriate bores.*

11 Lubricate the new dust seals with clean brake fluid and install them in their grooves in the caliper bores.

12 On F models, fit the inserts into the pistons. On all models, lubricate the pistons with clean brake fluid and install them closed-end first into the caliper bores **(see illustration)**. Using your thumbs, push the pistons all the way in, making sure they enter the bore squarely.

13 Fit new caliper seals into one half of the caliper body, then join the halves together and tighten the four Allen bolts lightly. They can be fully tightened after the calipers have been installed.

Installation

14 Install the caliper on the brake disc making sure the pads sit squarely either side of the disc (if they weren't removed) **(see illustration)**.

15 Install the caliper mounting bolts, and tighten them to the torque setting specified at the beginning of the Chapter **(see illustration)**.

16 If the calipers were overhauled, tighten the four Allen bolts to the specified torque setting.

17 If removed, connect the brake hose to the caliper, using new sealing washers on each side of the fitting **(see illustration)**. Align the hose as noted on removal. Tighten the banjo bolt to the torque setting specified at the beginning of the Chapter. Top up the master cylinder reservoir (see *Daily (pre-ride) checks*) and bleed the hydraulic system as described in Section 11.

18 If removed, install the brake pads (see Section 2).

19 Check for leaks and thoroughly test the operation of the brake before riding the motorcycle.

4 Front brake discs – inspection, removal and installation

Inspection

1 Visually inspect the surface of the disc for score marks and other damage. Light scratches are normal after use and won't affect brake operation, but deep grooves and heavy score marks will reduce braking efficiency and accelerate pad wear. If a disc is badly grooved it must be machined or renewed.

2 To check disc runout, position the bike on an auxiliary stand and support it so that the wheel is raised off the ground. Mount a dial gauge on the fork slider, with the plunger on the gauge touching the surface of the disc about 10 mm from the outer edge **(see illustration)**. Rotate the wheel and watch the gauge needle, comparing the reading with the limit listed in the Specifications at the beginning of the Chapter. If the runout is greater than the

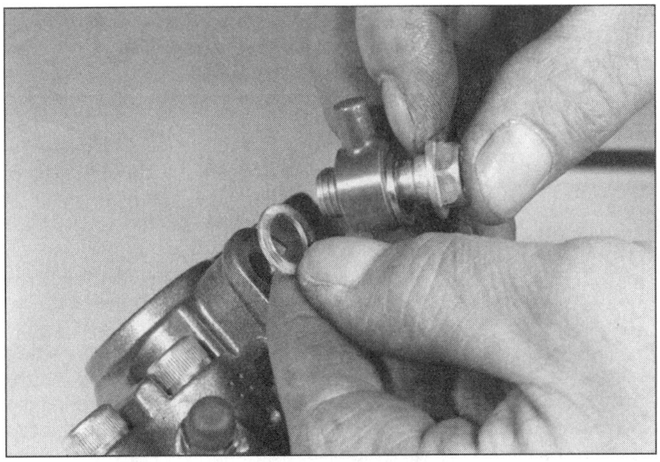

3.17 Always use new sealing washers on each side of the hose union

4.2 Set up a dial gauge, with the probe touching the disc, and turn the wheel to measure runout

4.3a The minimum thickness is stamped into the disc

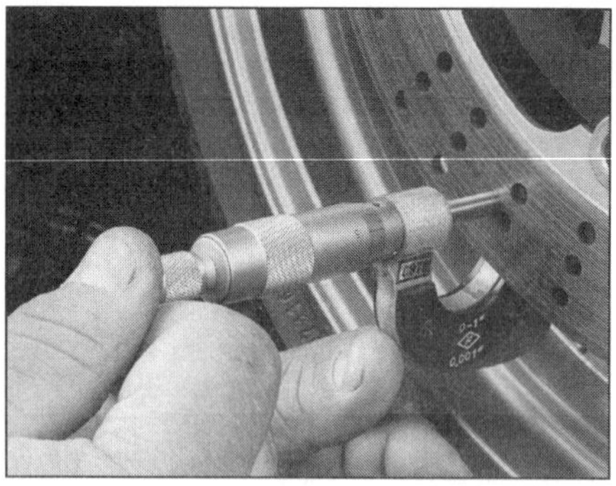

4.3b Use a micrometer to measure the thickness of the disc at several points

4.5 Unscrew the bolts (arrowed) and remove the disc

service limit, check the wheel bearings for play (see Chapter 1). If the bearings are worn, renew them (see Section 16) and repeat this check. If the disc runout is still excessive, it will have to be renewed, although machining by an engineer may be possible.

3 The disc must not be machined or allowed to wear down to a thickness less than the service limit as listed in this Chapter's Specifications and as marked on the disc itself **(see illustration)**. The thickness of the disc can be checked with a micrometer **(see illustration)**. If the thickness of the disc is less than the service limit, fit a new disc.

Removal

4 Remove the front wheel (see Section 14). ***Caution: Do not lay the wheel down and allow it to rest on the disc – the disc could become warped. Set the wheel on wood blocks so the disc doesn't support the weight of the wheel.***

5 Mark the relationship of the disc to the wheel, so it can be installed in the same position. Unscrew the disc retaining bolts, loosening them a little at a time in a criss-cross pattern to avoid distorting the disc, then remove the disc from the wheel **(see illustration)**.

Installation

6 Install the disc on the wheel, making sure the marked side is on the outside. Align the previously applied matchmarks (if you're reinstalling the original disc).

7 Tighten the bolts in a criss-cross pattern evenly and progressively to the torque setting specified at the beginning of the Chapter. Clean off all grease from the brake disc(s) using acetone or brake system cleaner. If a new brake disc has been installed, remove any protective coating from its working surfaces.

8 Install the wheel (see Section 14).

9 Operate the brake lever several times to bring the pads into contact with the disc. Check the operation of the brakes carefully before riding the bike.

5.3 Slacken the reservoir screws (arrowed)

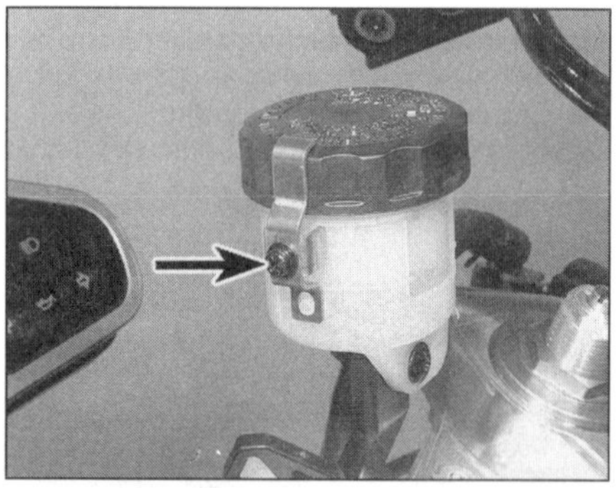

5.4a Remove the screw (arrowed) and take off the clamp . . .

5.4b . . . then remove the bracket bolt (arrowed)

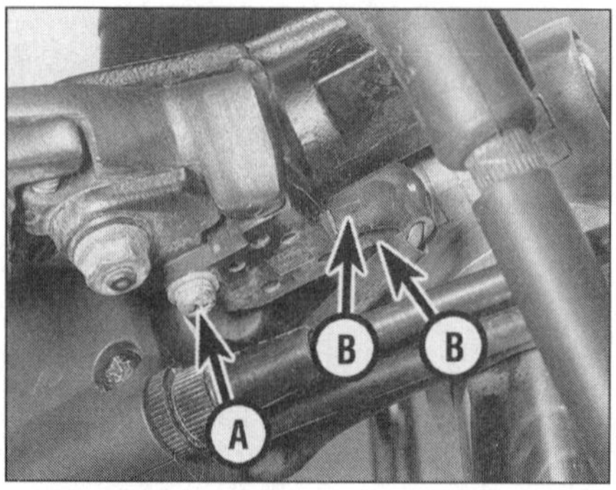

5.5 Disconnect the brake light switch connectors (B). The switch is secured by a screw (A)

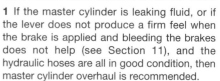

5 Front brake master cylinder – removal, overhaul and installation

1 If the master cylinder is leaking fluid, or if the lever does not produce a firm feel when the brake is applied and bleeding the brakes does not help (see Section 11), and the hydraulic hoses are all in good condition, then master cylinder overhaul is recommended.

2 Before disassembling the master cylinder, read through the entire procedure and make sure that you have the correct rebuild kit. Also, you will need some new DOT 4 brake fluid, some clean rags and internal circlip pliers. **Note:** *To prevent damage to the paint from spilled brake fluid, always cover the fuel tank when working on the master cylinder.* ***Caution: Disassembly, overhaul and reassembly of the brake master cylinder must be done in a spotlessly clean work area to avoid contamination and possible failure of the brake hydraulic system components.***

Removal

3 On F models, loosen, but do not remove, the screws holding the reservoir cover in place **(see illustration)**. Access to the front reservoir cap screws is restricted by the windshield. If a short or angled screwdriver is not available, remove the fairing to access the screws (see Chapter 8).

4 On G, H, J and A models, remove the screw securing the reservoir cap clamp and detach the clamp, then unscrew the bolt securing the master cylinder reservoir bracket to the top yoke **(see illustrations)**.

5 Disconnect the electrical connectors from the brake light switch **(see illustration)**.

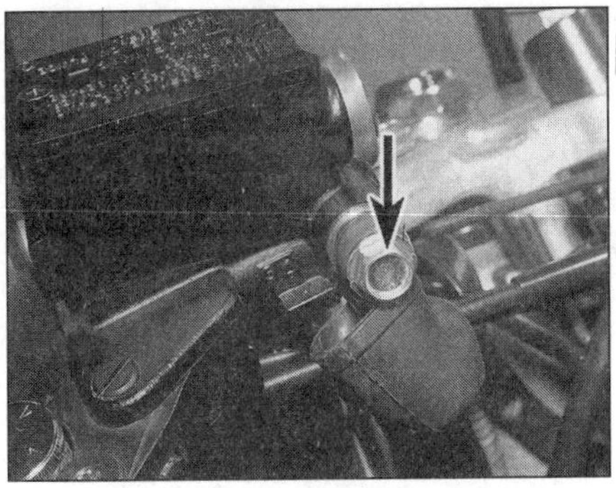
5.7a Brake hose banjo bolt (arrowed) – F models

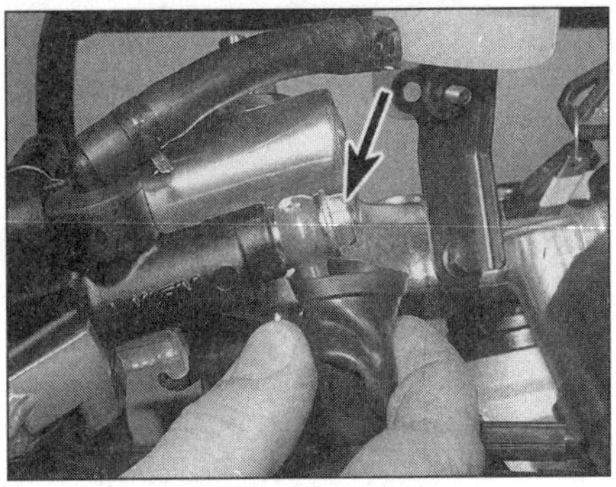
5.7b Brake hose banjo bolt (arrowed) – G, H, J and A models

5.8a Master cylinder clamp bolts (arrowed) – F models

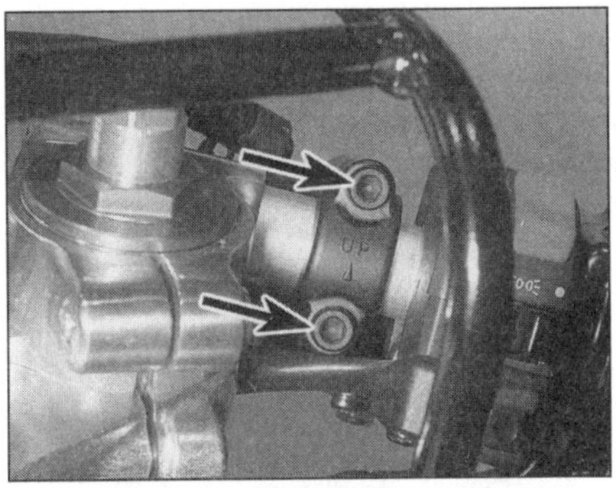
5.8b Master cylinder clamp bolts (arrowed) – G, H, J and A models

6 If the master cylinder is being overhauled, remove the front brake lever (see Chapter 6).

7 Where fitted, pull back the rubber boot, then unscrew the brake hose banjo bolt and separate the hose from the master cylinder, noting its alignment **(see illustrations)**. Wrap a plastic bag tightly around the end of the hose to minimise fluid loss and prevent dirt entering the system, and secure the hose in an upright position. Discard the sealing washers as new ones must be used on reassembly.

8 Unscrew the master cylinder clamp bolts, then lift the master cylinder assembly away from the handlebar **(see illustrations)**.

9 Remove the screw securing the brake light switch to the bottom of the master cylinder and remove the switch **(see illustration 5.5)**.

Caution: Do not tip the master cylinder upside down or brake fluid will run out.

Overhaul

10 Remove the reservoir cover or cap, the diaphragm plate and the rubber diaphragm **(see illustrations)**. Drain the brake fluid from the reservoir into a suitable container. On G, H, J and A models, release the clamp and detach the reservoir hose from its union on the master cylinder. Wipe any remaining fluid out of the reservoir with a clean rag.

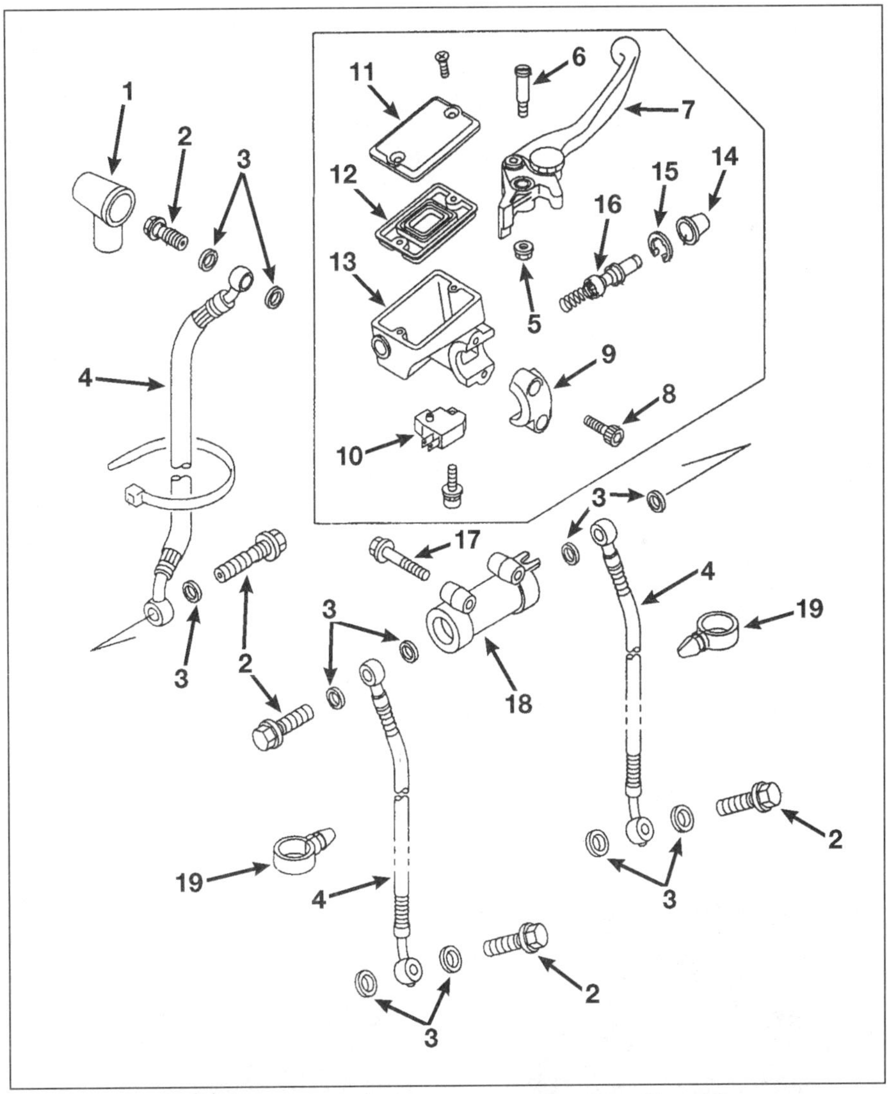

5.10a Front brake master cylinder components – F models

1 Rubber boot
2 Banjo bolt
3 Sealing washers
4 Brake hose
5 Nut
6 Brake lever pivot bolt
7 Brake lever
8 Clamp bolt
9 Clamp
10 Brake light switch
11 Reservoir cover and diaphragm plate
12 Diaphragm
13 Master cylinder/reservoir
14 Dust boot
15 Circlip
16 Piston assembly
17 Brake hose union bolt
18 Brake hose union
19 Brake hose guide

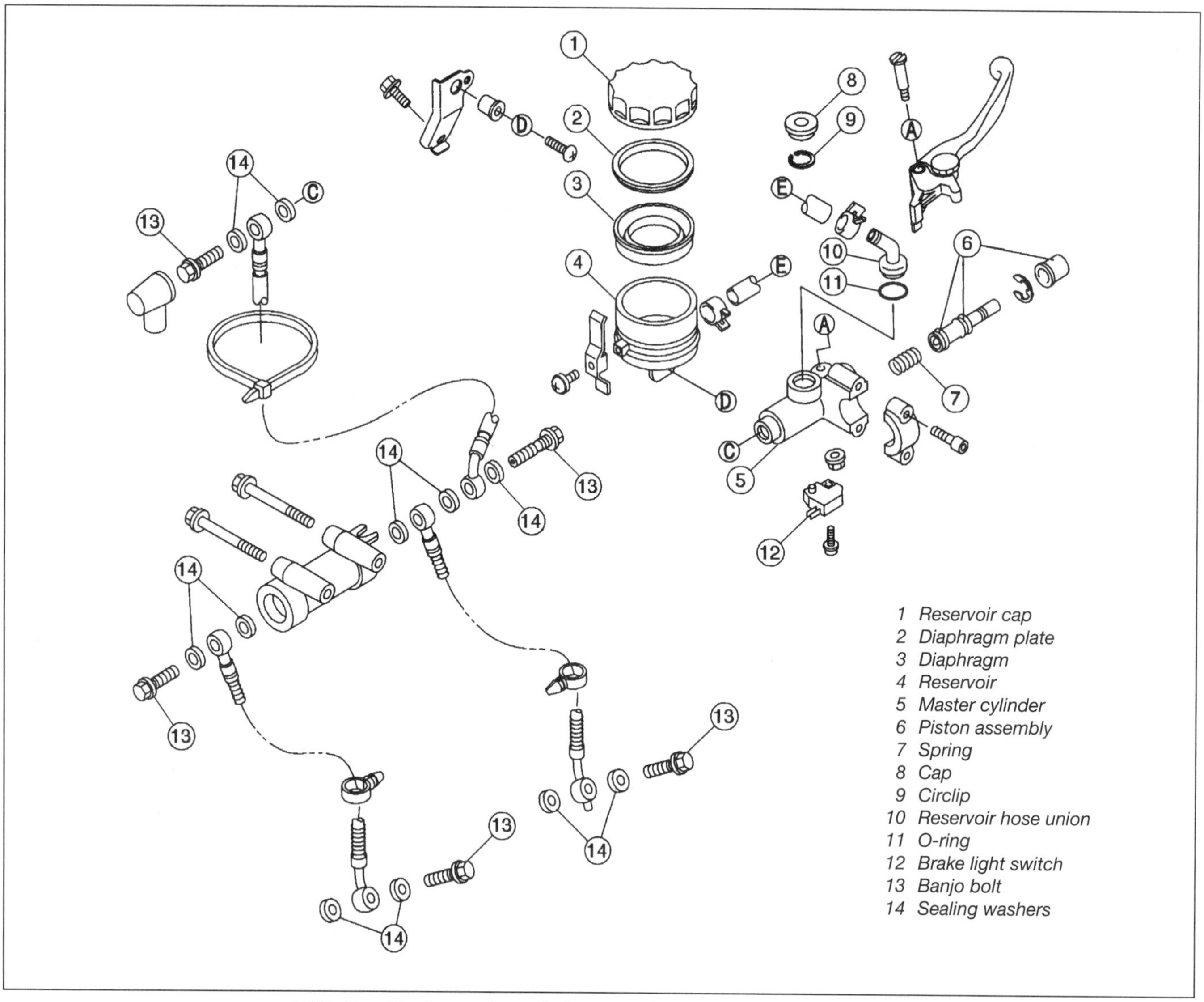

5.10b Front brake master cylinder components – G, H, J and A models

11 Carefully remove the dust boot from the end of the piston **(see illustration)**.

12 Using circlip pliers, remove the circlip and slide out the piston assembly and the spring, noting how they fit **(see illustration)**. Lay the parts out in the proper order to prevent confusion during reassembly **(see illustration)**.

13 On G, H, J and A models, if required, remove the rubber cap on the fluid reservoir hose union, then remove the circlip and detach the union from the master cylinder

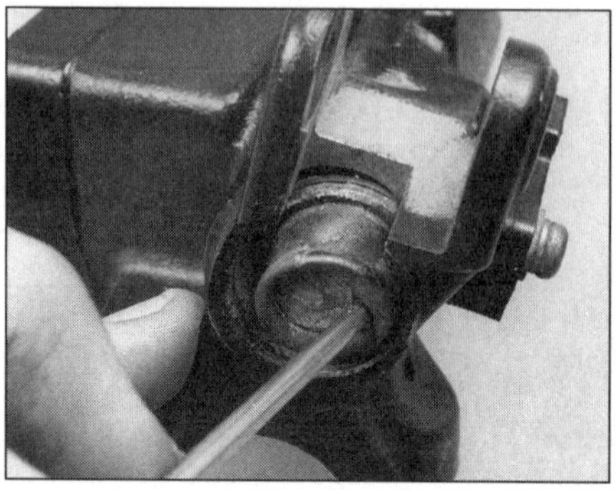

5.11 Remove the rubber boot from the end of the master cylinder piston . . .

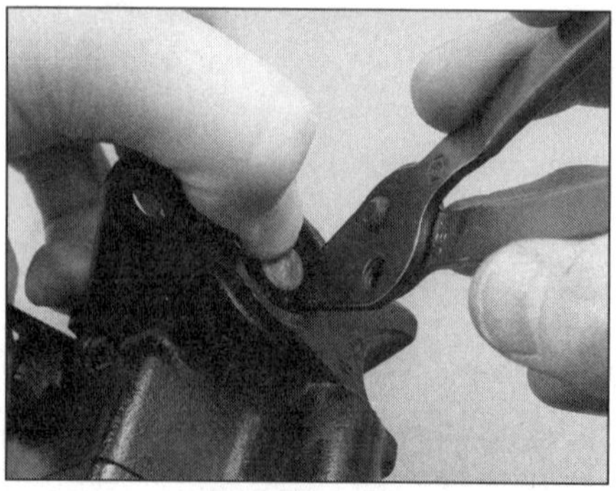

5.12a . . . then depress the piston and remove the circlip using a pair of internal circlip pliers

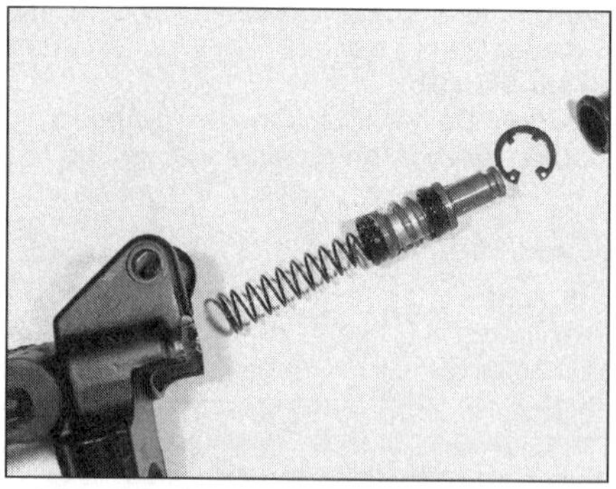

5.12b Lay out the internal parts as shown, even if new parts are being used, to avoid confusion on reassembly

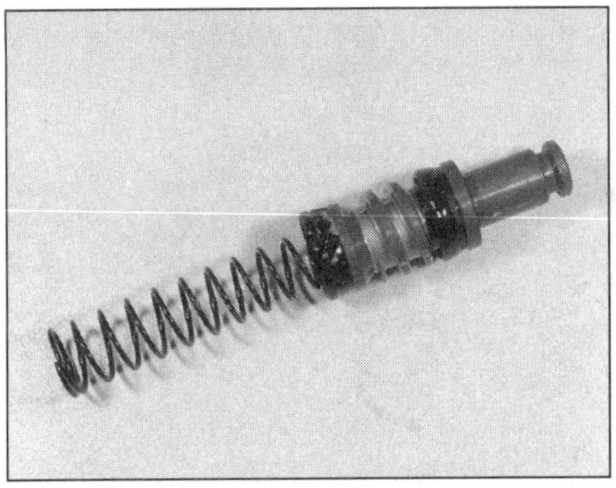

5.16 Make sure the lips of the cups face in the proper direction

(see illustration 5.10b). Discard the O-ring as a new one must be used. Inspect the reservoir hose for cracks or splits and renew if necessary.

14 Clean all parts with clean brake fluid or denatured alcohol. If compressed air is available, use it to dry the parts thoroughly (make sure it's filtered and unlubricated).

Caution: Do not, under any circumstances, use a petroleum-based solvent to clean brake parts.

15 Check the master cylinder bore for corrosion, scratches, nicks and score marks. If damage or wear is evident, a new master cylinder must be fitted. If the master cylinder is in poor condition, then the brake calipers should be checked as well. Check that the fluid inlet and outlet ports in the master cylinder are clear.

16 The dust boot, circlip, piston, seal, primary cup and spring are included in the rebuild kit. Use all of the new parts, regardless of the apparent condition of the old ones. If the seal and cup are not already on the piston, fit them according to the layout of the old piston assembly **(see illustration)**.

17 Install the spring in the master cylinder; if the spring is tapered, fit it wider end first so that the narrower end faces the piston.

18 Lubricate the cylinder bore, piston, seal and cup with clean brake fluid. Install the assembly

5.23 Install the clamp with the UP mark facing up

into the master cylinder, making sure it is the correct way round **(see illustration 5.12b)**. Make sure the lips on the cup do not turn inside out when they are slipped into the bore. Depress the piston and install the new circlip, making sure that it locates in the master cylinder groove **(see illustration 5.12a)**.

19 Install the rubber dust boot, making sure the lip is seated correctly in the piston groove **(see illustration 5.11)**.

20 On G, H, J and A models, if removed, fit a new O-ring onto the reservoir hose union, then press the union into the master cylinder and secure it with the circlip. Fit the rubber cap over the circlip.

21 Inspect the reservoir cover or cap rubber diaphragm and renew it if it is damaged or deteriorated.

Installation

22 Install the brake light switch **(see illustration 5.5)**.

23 Attach the master cylinder to the handlebar and fit the clamp with its UP mark facing up. Align the mating surfaces of the clamp with the mating surfaces of the handlebar switch halves on F models, and with the punch mark on the handlebar on all other models **(see illustration and 5.8a or b)**. Tighten the upper clamp bolt first, followed by the lower bolt, to the torque setting specified at the beginning of the Chapter.

24 Connect the brake hose to the master cylinder, using new sealing washers on each side of the union, and aligning the hose as noted on removal **(see illustrations 5.7a or b)**. Tighten the banjo bolt to the torque setting specified at the beginning of this Chapter. If fitted, install the rubber boot over the bolt.

25 If removed, install the brake lever (see Chapter 6).

26 On G, H, J and A models, mount the reservoir onto the top yoke and tighten its bracket bolt to the specified torque **(see illustration 5.4b)**. Connect the reservoir hose to the union and secure it with the clamp.

27 Connect the brake light switch wiring **(see illustration 5.5)**.

28 Fill the fluid reservoir with new DOT 4 brake fluid as described in *Daily (pre-ride) checks*. Refer to Section 11 of this Chapter and bleed the air from the system.

29 Fit the rubber diaphragm, making sure it is correctly seated, the diaphragm plate and the cover or cap onto the master cylinder reservoir. On G, H, J and A models, fit the reservoir cap clamp **(see illustration 5.4a)**.

30 Check the operation of the front brake before riding the motorcycle and check for any fluid leakage.

6 Rear brake pads – renewal

Warning: The dust created by the brake system may contain asbestos, which is harmful to your health. Never blow it out with compressed air and don't inhale any of it. An approved filtering mask should be worn when working on the brakes.

1 Unscrew the brake caliper mounting bolts and slide the caliper off the disc **(see illustration 7.1)**. Remove the clip from the end of the pad retaining pin, then withdraw the pad pin **(see illustrations)**. Lift the inner

6.1a Remove the clip . . .

6.1b . . . the pull out the retaining pin

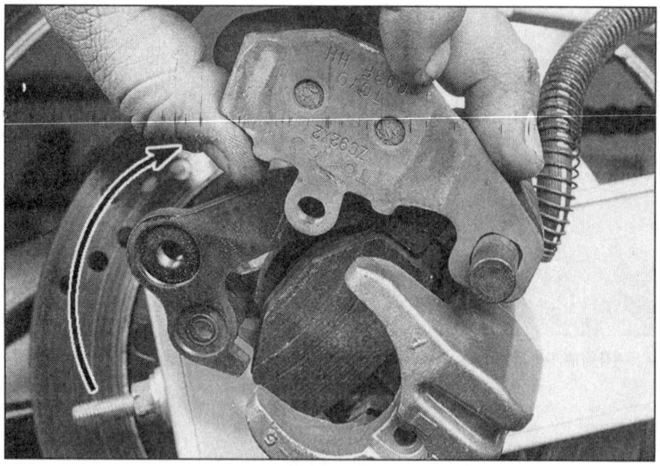

6.1c To remove the inner pad, pivot the free end up and slide the pad off the pin

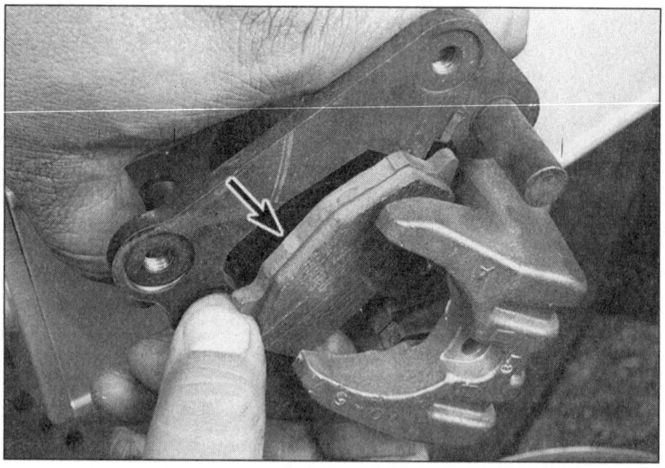

6.1d To remove the outer pad, push down on it (arrow) and pull the pad edge out from under the bracket

pad and slide it off its guide pin on the caliper mounting bracket, noting how it fits **(see illustration)**. Remove the outer pad from the caliper body, noting how the pad locates against the guide and the bracket **(see illustration)**.

2 Inspect the surface of each pad for contamination and check that the friction material has not worn level with or beyond the wear grooves in the pad face or the cutouts in the pad edge. If either pad is worn down to, or beyond, the service limit, fouled with oil or grease, or heavily scored or damaged by dirt and debris, both pads must be renewed as a set. Note that it is not possible to degrease the friction material; if the pads are contaminated in any way they must be discarded.

3 If the pads are in good condition clean them carefully, using a fine wire brush which is completely free of oil and grease to remove all traces of road dirt and corrosion. Using a pointed instrument, clean out the grooves in the friction material and dig out any embedded particles of foreign matter.

4 Check the condition of the brake disc (see Section 8).

5 Remove all traces of corrosion from the pad pin. Inspect the pin and the pin clip for signs of damage and renew them if necessary.

6 Push the pistons as far back into the caliper as possible using hand pressure or a piece of wood as leverage. Due to the increased friction material thickness of new pads, it may be necessary to remove the master cylinder reservoir cap, diaphragm plate and diaphragm and siphon out some fluid. If the piston is seized in the caliper, the caliper must be overhauled (see Section 7).

7 Smear the backs of the pads and the shank of the pad pin with copper-based grease, making sure that none gets on the friction material of the pads.

8 Installation of the pads is the reverse of removal. Make sure the pad spring and guide are correctly positioned. Insert the pads into the caliper so that the friction material faces the disc **(see illustrations 6.1d and c)**. Make sure the outer pad locates correctly against the guide and the bracket **(see illustration)**. Slide the pad pin through each pad and secure it with the clip **(see illustrations 6.1b and a)**.

9 Install the caliper on the brake disc making sure the pads sit squarely either side of the disc.

10 Install the caliper mounting bolts, and tighten them to the torque setting specified at the beginning of this Chapter **(see illustration 7.1)**.

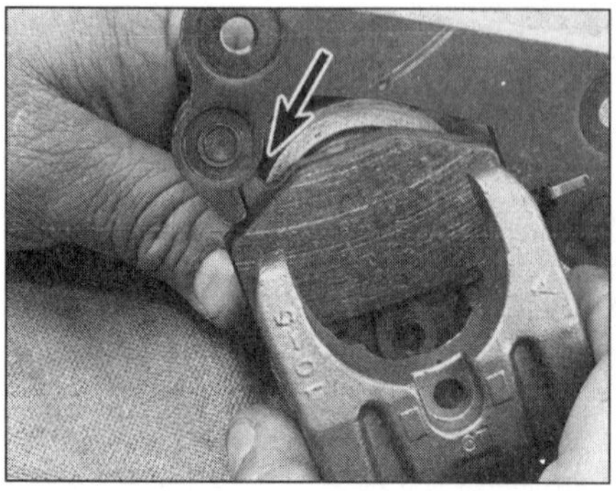

6.8 Make sure the outer pad locates correctly against the bracket (arrowed)

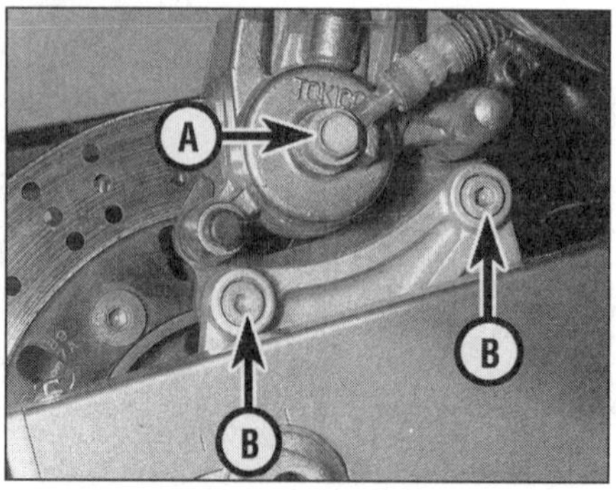

7.1 Brake hose banjo bolt (A), caliper mounting bolts (B)

11 Top up the master cylinder reservoir if necessary (see *Daily (pre-ride) checks*), and install the reservoir diaphragm, diaphragm plate and cap.

12 Operate the brake pedal several times to bring the pads into contact with the disc. Check the operation of the brake before riding the motorcycle.

7 Rear brake caliper – removal, overhaul and installation

Warning: If a caliper indicates the need for an overhaul (usually due to leaking fluid or sticky operation), all old brake fluid should be flushed from the system. Also, the dust created by the brake system may contain asbestos, which is harmful to your health. Never blow it out with compressed air and don't inhale any of it. An approved filtering mask should be worn when working on the brakes. Do not, under any circumstances, use petroleum-based solvents to clean brake parts. Use clean brake fluid, brake cleaner or denatured alcohol only.

Removal

1 If the caliper is just being displaced and not completely removed or overhauled, do not disconnect the brake hose. If the caliper is being overhauled, remove the brake hose banjo bolt **(see illustration)**. Note the alignment of the hose on the caliper and separate the hose from the caliper. Wrap a plastic bag tightly around the hose end to minimise fluid loss and prevent dirt entering the system, and secure the hose in an upright position. Discard the sealing washers as new ones must be used on installation. **Note:** *If you are planning to overhaul the caliper and don't have a source of compressed air to blow out the piston, just loosen the banjo bolt at this stage and retighten it lightly. The bike's* *hydraulic system can then be used to force the piston out of the body once the pads have been removed. Disconnect the hose once the piston has been sufficiently displaced.*

2 Unscrew the caliper mounting bolts, and slide the caliper assembly off the disc **(see illustration 7.1)**. If the caliper is being overhauled, remove the pads (see Section 6) and the pad anti-rattle spring, noting carefully how it fits **(see illustration)**.

Overhaul

3 Slide the caliper off the caliper bracket **(see illustrations)**.

4 Clean the exterior of the caliper with denatured alcohol or brake system cleaner.

5 Remove the piston from the caliper body, either by pumping it out by operating the rear brake pedal until the piston is displaced, or by forcing it out using compressed air. If the compressed air method is used, place a wad of rag over the piston to act as a cushion, then use compressed air directed into the fluid inlet to force the piston out of the body. Use only low pressure to ease the piston out. If the air pressure is too high and the piston is forced out, the caliper and/or piston may be damaged. On F models, remove the insert from the centre of the piston.

Warning: Never place your fingers in front of the piston in an attempt to catch or protect it when applying compressed air, as serious injury could result.

6 Using a wooden or plastic tool to avoid damaging the caliper bore, remove the dust seal from the bore **(see illustration 3.6)**. Discard it as a new one must be used on reassembly.

7 Remove and discard the piston seal in the same way.

8 Clean the piston and bore with denatured alcohol, clean brake fluid or brake system cleaner. If compressed air is available, use it to dry the parts thoroughly (make sure it's filtered and unlubricated).

Caution: Do not, under any circumstances, use a petroleum-based solvent to clean brake parts.

9 Inspect the caliper bore and piston for signs of corrosion, nicks and burrs and loss of plating. If surface defects are present, the caliper assembly must be renewed. If the caliper is in bad shape the master cylinder should also be checked.

10 Check that the caliper body is able to slide freely on the bracket slider pins. If not, clean off all traces of corrosion and hardened grease. Apply a smear of copper or silicone-based grease to the slider pins and reassemble the two components and check again **(see illustration)**. Fit new rubber boots if they are damaged or deteriorated **(see illustration)**.

11 Lubricate the new piston seal with clean brake fluid and install it in the groove in the caliper bore.

12 Lubricate the new dust seal with clean brake fluid and install it in the groove in the caliper bore.

13 On F models, fit the insert into the piston. On all models, lubricate the piston with clean brake fluid and install it closed-end first into the caliper bore **(see illustration)**. Using your thumbs, push the piston all the way in, making sure it enters the bore squarely.

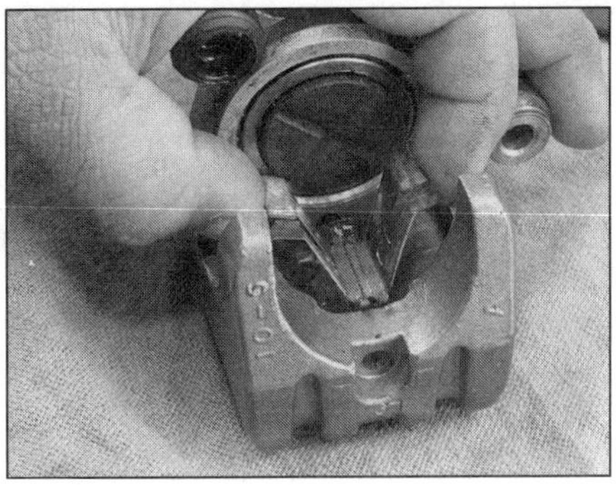

7.2 Remove the anti-rattle spring

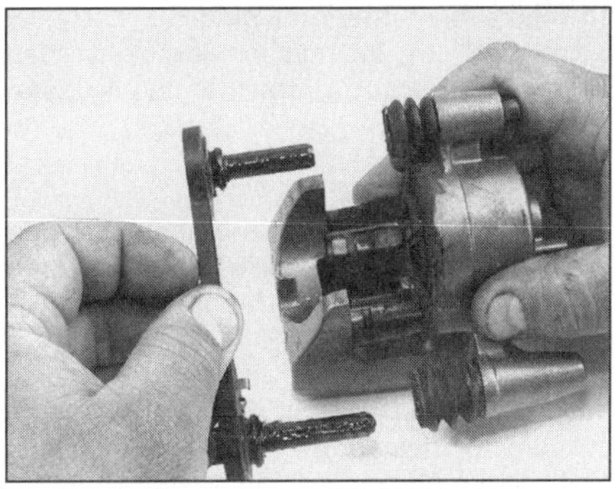

7.3a Pull the bracket out of the caliper

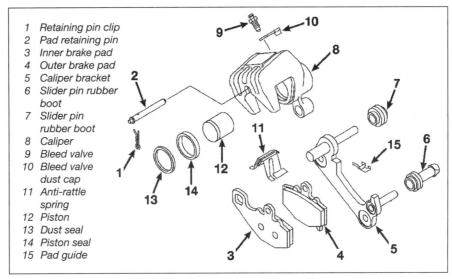

1 Retaining pin clip
2 Pad retaining pin
3 Inner brake pad
4 Outer brake pad
5 Caliper bracket
6 Slider pin rubber boot
7 Slider pin rubber boot
8 Caliper
9 Bleed valve
10 Bleed valve dust cap
11 Anti-rattle spring
12 Piston
13 Dust seal
14 Piston seal
15 Pad guide

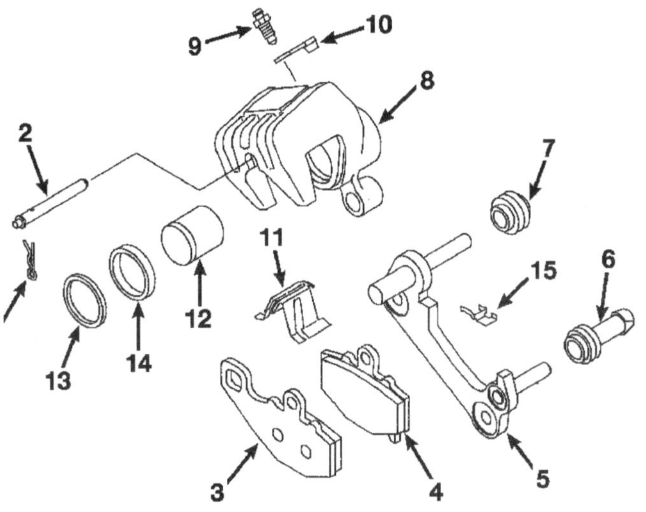

7.3b Rear brake caliper components

7.10a Apply the specified grease to the slider pins on the caliper bracket

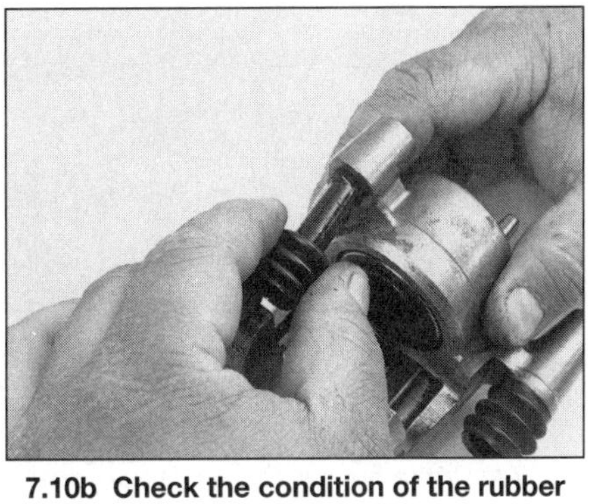

7.10b Check the condition of the rubber boots and replace them if necessary

7.13 Push the piston into the caliper bore making sure it is straight

14 Make sure the pad guide is correctly positioned on the caliper bracket, then slide the bracket onto the caliper **(see illustration 7.3a)**.

Installation

15 If removed, make sure that the pad anti-rattle spring is correctly fitted **(see illustration 7.2)**, then install the brake pads (see Section 6).

16 Install the caliper on the brake disc making sure the pads sit squarely either side of the disc, then tighten the caliper mounting bolts to the torque setting specified at the beginning of the Chapter **(see illustration 7.1)**.

17 Connect the brake hose to the caliper, using a new sealing washer on each side of the union. Align the hose as noted on removal and tighten the banjo bolt to the torque setting specified at the beginning of the Chapter **(see illustration 7.1)**.

18 Top up the master cylinder reservoir (see *Daily (pre-ride) checks*) and bleed the hydraulic system as described in Section 11.

19 Check for leaks and thoroughly test the operation of the brake before riding the motorcycle.

8 Rear brake disc – inspection, removal and installation

Inspection

1 Visually inspect the surface of the disc for score marks and other damage. Light scratches are normal after use and won't affect brake operation, but deep grooves and heavy score marks will reduce braking efficiency and accelerate pad wear. If a disc is badly grooved it must be machined or renewed.

2 To check disc runout, position the bike on an auxiliary stand and support it so that the rear wheel is raised off the ground. Mount a dial gauge on the swingarm, with the plunger on the gauge touching the surface of the disc about 10 mm from the outer edge **(see illustration 4.2)**. Rotate the wheel and watch the indicator needle, comparing the reading with the limit listed in the Specifications at the beginning of the Chapter. If the runout is greater than the service limit, check the bearings for play (see Chapter 1). If the bearings are worn, renew them (see Section 16) and repeat this check. If the disc runout is still excessive, it will have to be renewed, although machining by an engineer may be possible.

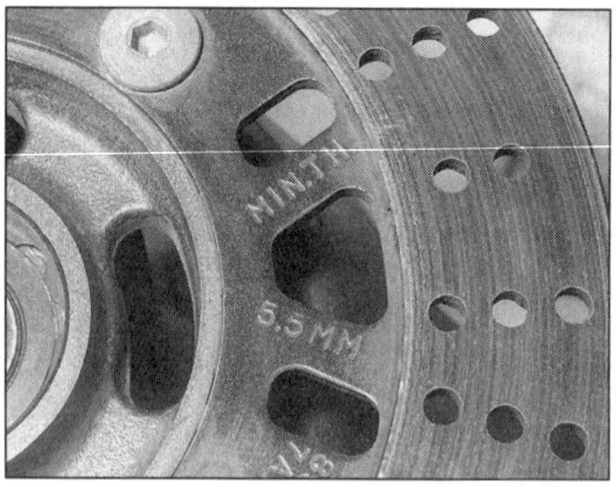
8.3 The minimum thickness is stamped into the disc

3 The disc must not be machined or allowed to wear down to a thickness less than the service limit listed in this Chapter's Specifications and as marked on the disc itself **(see illustration)**. The thickness of the disc can be checked with a micrometer **(see illustration 4.3b)**. If the thickness of the disc is less than the service limit, fit a new disc.

Removal

4 Remove the rear wheel (see Section 15).

5 Mark the relationship of the disc to the wheel, so it can be installed in the same position. Unscrew the disc retaining bolts, loosening them a little at a time in a criss-cross pattern to avoid distorting the disc, then remove the disc from the wheel **(see illustration)**.

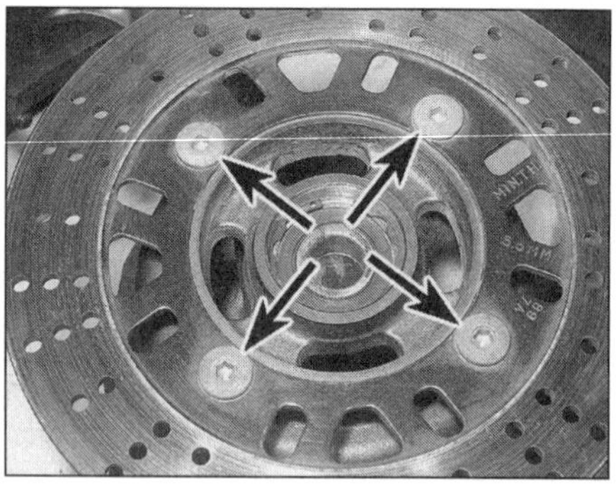
8.5 Unscrew the bolts (arrowed) and remove the disc

Installation

6 Install the disc on the wheel, making sure the marked side is on the outside. Align the previously applied matchmarks (if you're reinstalling the original disc).

7 Tighten the bolts in a criss-cross pattern evenly and progressively to the torque setting specified at the beginning of the Chapter. Clean off all grease from the brake disc using acetone or brake system cleaner. If a new brake disc has been installed, remove any protective coating from its working surfaces.

8 Install the wheel (see Section 15).

9 Operate the brake pedal several times to bring the pads into contact with the disc. Check the operation of the brake carefully before riding the bike.

9 Rear brake master cylinder – removal, overhaul and installation

1 If the master cylinder is leaking fluid, or if the pedal does not produce a firm feel when the brake is applied and bleeding the brakes does not help (see Section 11), and the hydraulic hose is in good condition, then master cylinder overhaul is recommended.

2 Before disassembling the master cylinder, read through the entire procedure and make sure that you have the correct rebuild kit. Also, you will need some new DOT 4 brake fluid, some clean rags and internal circlip pliers. **Note:** *To prevent damage to the paint from spilled brake fluid, always cover the surrounding components when working on the master cylinder.*

Caution: Disassembly, overhaul and reassembly of the brake master cylinder must be done in a spotlessly clean work area to avoid contamination and possible failure of the brake hydraulic system components.

Removal

3 Release the clamp securing the reservoir hose to the union on the master cylinder, then detach the hose and drain the fluid from the reservoir into a suitable container **(see illustration)**.

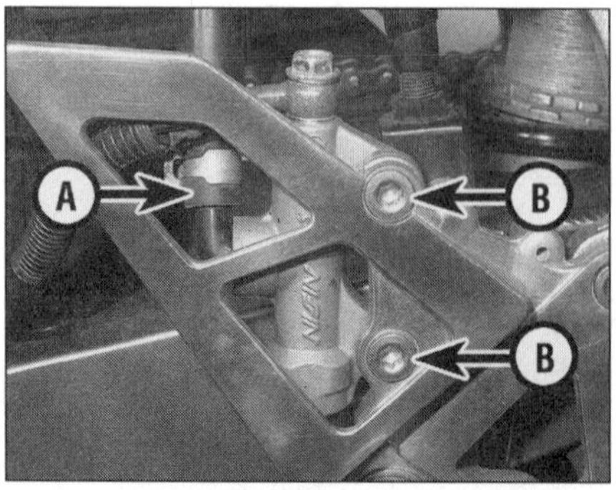

9.3 Slacken the clamp and detach the hose (A) from the union. Master cylinder mounting bolts (B)

4 Unscrew the brake hose banjo bolt and separate the brake hose from the master cylinder, noting its alignment **(see illustration)**. Wrap a plastic bag tightly around the end of the hose to minimise fluid loss and prevent dirt entering the system, and secure the hose in an upright position. Discard the sealing washers as new ones must be used on reassembly.

9.4 Brake hose banjo bolt (arrowed)

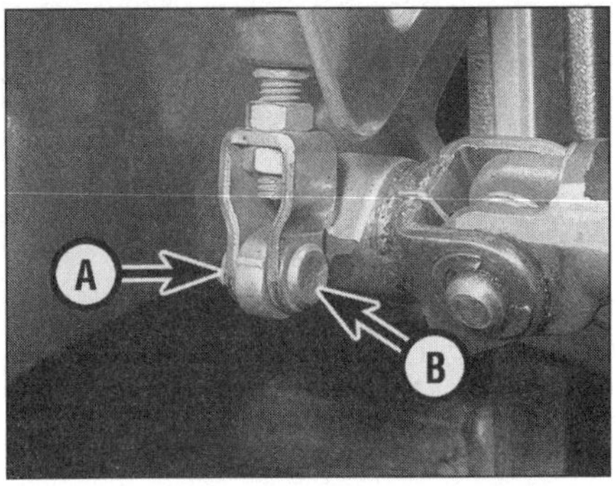

9.5 Remove the split pin (A) and withdraw the clevis pin (B)

5 Remove the split pin from the clevis pin securing the brake pedal to the master cylinder pushrod **(see illustration)**. Withdraw the clevis pin and separate the pedal from the pushrod. Discard the split pin as a new one must be used.

6 Unscrew the two bolts securing the master cylinder to the footrest bracket and remove the master cylinder **(see illustration 9.3)**. On G, H, J and A, the heel plate is also secured by the bolts.

Overhaul

7 If required, slacken the clevis locknut on the pushrod, then thread the clevis with its base nut off the pushrod, followed by the locknut **(see illustrations)**. If this is done, it is advisable to mark the position of the top of the locknut on the pushrod so that brake pedal height won't be affected when the clevis is later installed.

8 Dislodge the rubber dust boot from the base of the master cylinder to reveal the pushrod retaining circlip **(see illustration)**.

9 Depress the pushrod and, using circlip pliers, remove the circlip **(see illustration)**. Slide out the piston assembly and spring. If they are difficult to remove, apply low pressure compressed air to the fluid outlet. Lay the parts out in the proper order to prevent confusion during reassembly.

10 Clean all of the parts with clean brake fluid or denatured alcohol.

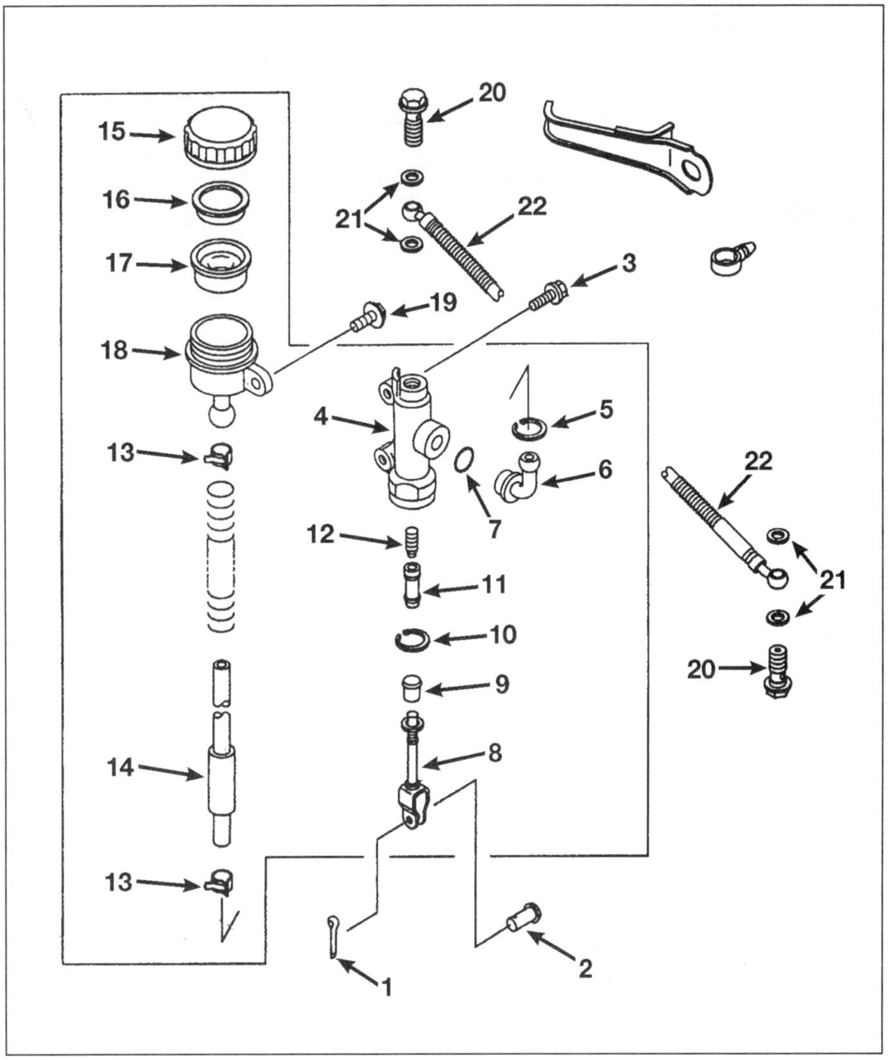

9.7a Rear brake master cylinder components

1 Split pin
2 Clevis pin
3 Master cylinder mounting bolt
4 Master cylinder
5 Circlip
6 Reservoir hose union
7 O-ring
8 Clevis/pushrod assembly
9 Dust boot
10 Circlip
11 Piston/cup assembly
12 Spring
13 Hose clamp
14 Brake hose
15 Reservoir cap
16 Diaphragm plate
17 Diaphragm
18 Reservoir
19 Reservoir mounting bolt
20 Banjo bolt
21 Sealing washers
22 Brake hose

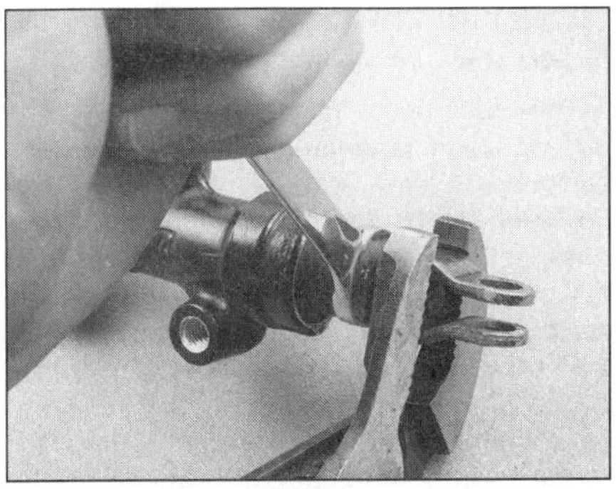

9.7b Hold the clevis and slacken the locknut

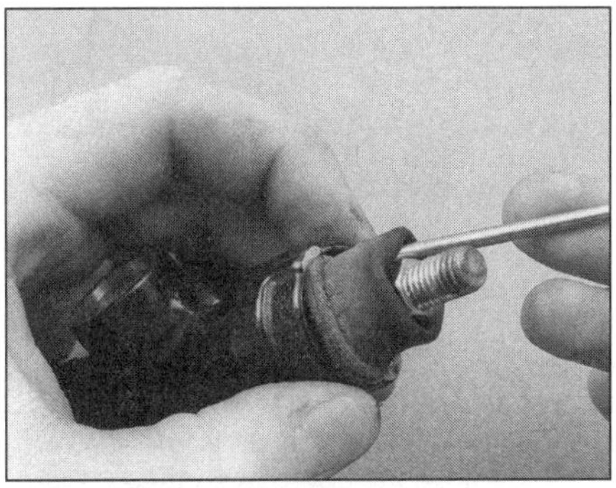

9.8 Remove the dust boot from the pushrod

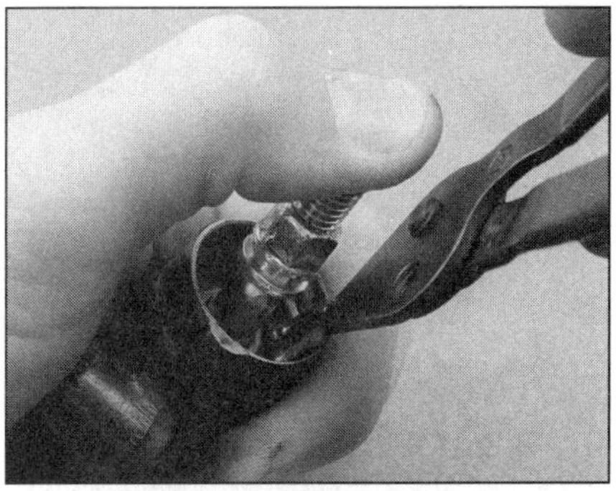

9.9 Depress the piston and remove the circlip from the cylinder

9.12 Remove the circlip that secures the reservoir hose union

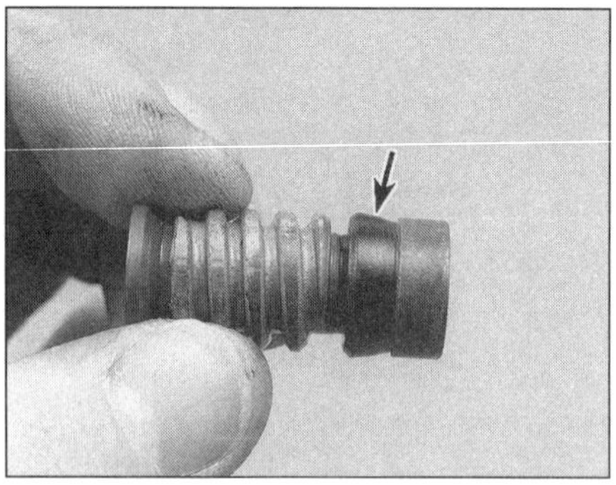

9.13 Make sure the lips of the cups (arrowed) face away from the pushrod end of the piston

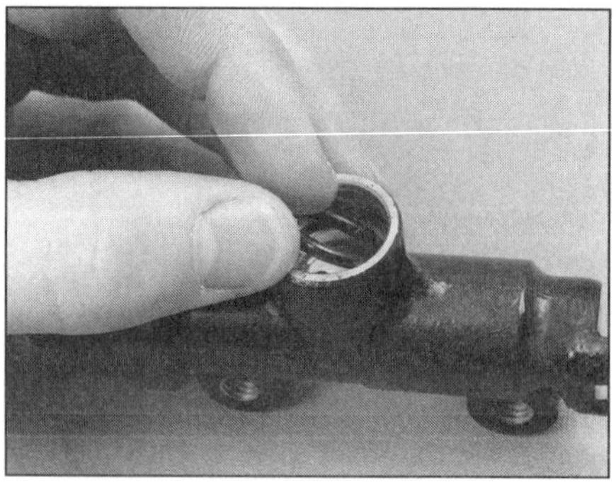

9.18 Use a new O-ring for the reservoir hose union

Caution: Do not, under any circumstances, use a petroleum-based solvent to clean brake parts. If compressed air is available, use it to dry the parts thoroughly (make sure it's filtered and unlubricated).

11 Check the master cylinder bore for corrosion, scratches, nicks and score marks. If damage or wear is evident, a new master cylinder must be fitted. If the master cylinder is in poor condition, then the caliper should be checked as well.

12 If required, remove the circlip securing the reservoir hose union and detach the union from the master cylinder **(see illustration)**. Discard the O-ring as a new one must be used. Inspect the reservoir hose for cracks or splits and renew if necessary.

13 The dust boot, circlip, piston, seal, primary cup and spring are included in the rebuild kit. Use all of the new parts, regardless of the apparent condition of the old ones. If the seal and cup are not already on the piston, fit them according to the layout of the old piston assembly **(see illustration)**.

14 Install the spring in the master cylinder wider end first so that the narrower end faces the piston.

15 Lubricate the piston, seal and cup with clean brake fluid. Install the assembly into the master cylinder, making sure it is the correct way round. Make sure the lips on the cup do not turn inside out when they are slipped into the bore.

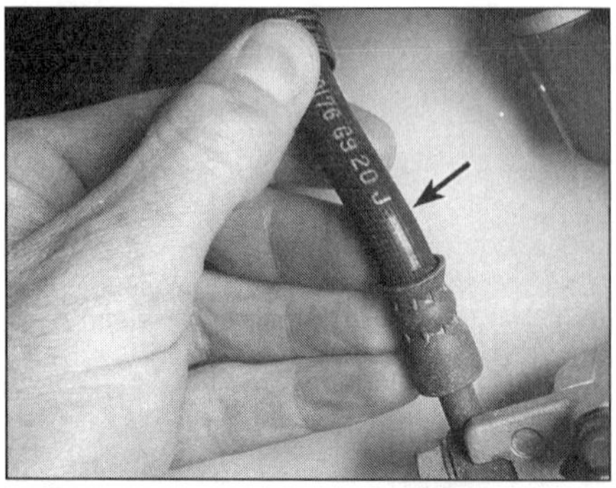

10.2 Flex the brake hoses and check for cracks, bulges and leaking fluid

16 Install and depress the pushrod, then fit a new circlip, making sure it is properly seated in the groove **(see illustration 9.9)**.

17 Install the rubber dust boot, making sure the lip is seated properly in the groove **(see illustration 9.8)**.

18 If removed, fit a new O-ring to the fluid reservoir hose union **(see illustration)**, then install the union onto the master cylinder and secure it with its circlip **(see illustration 9.12)**.

Installation

19 If removed, install the clevis locknut, the clevis and its base nut onto the master cylinder pushrod end. Position the clevis as noted on removal, then tighten the clevis locknut securely **(see illustration 9.7b)**. If required, the pedal height can be checked and altered to suit individual tastes (see Chapter 1, Section 10).

20 Install the master cylinder onto the footrest bracket. On G, H, J and A models, fit the heel plate. Install the mounting bolts and tighten them to the torque setting specified at the beginning of the Chapter **(see illustration 9.3)**.

21 Align the brake pedal with the master cylinder pushrod clevis, then slide in the clevis pin and secure it using a new split pin **(see illustration 9.5)**.

22 Connect the brake hose to the master cylinder, using a new sealing washer on each side of the banjo union. Ensure that the hose is positioned so that it butts against the lug and tighten the banjo bolt to the specified torque setting **(see illustration 9.4)**.

23 Connect the reservoir hose to the union on the master cylinder and secure it with the clamp **(see illustration 9.3)**. Check that the hose is secure and clamped at the reservoir end as well. If the clamps have weakened, use new ones.

24 Fill the fluid reservoir with new DOT 4 brake fluid (see *Daily (pre-ride) checks*) and bleed the system following the procedure in Section 11.

25 Check the operation of the brake carefully before riding the motorcycle.

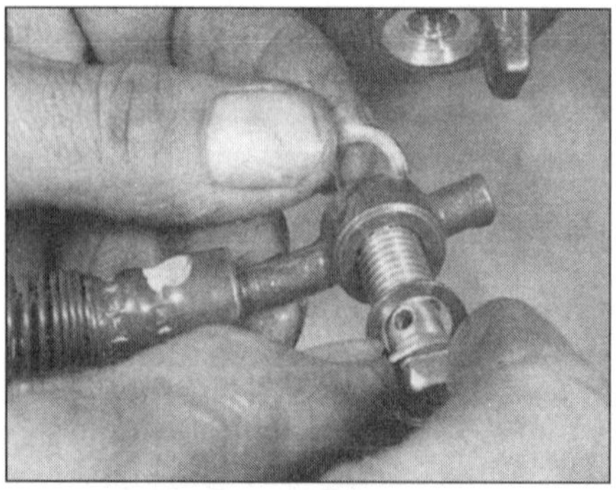

10.4 Remove the banjo bolt and separate the hose from the caliper; there is a sealing washer on each side of the fitting

10 Brake hoses and unions – inspection and renewal

Inspection

1 Brake hose condition should be checked regularly and new hoses fitted at the specified interval (see Chapter 1).

2 Twist and flex the rubber hoses while looking for cracks, bulges and seeping fluid **(see illustration)**. Check extra carefully around the areas where the hoses connect with the banjo fittings, as these are common areas for hose failure.

3 Inspect the banjo union fittings connected to the brake hoses. If the fittings are rusted, scratched or cracked, renew them.

Renewal

4 The brake hoses have banjo union fittings on each end **(see illustration)**. Cover the surrounding area with plenty of rags and unscrew the banjo bolt at each end of the hose, noting its alignment. Free the hose from any clips or guides and remove it. Discard the sealing washers on the hose banjo unions.

5 Position the new hose, making sure it isn't twisted or otherwise strained, and align the hose union with the lug on the component casting, where present. Otherwise align the hose as noted on removal. Install the hose banjo bolts using new sealing washers on

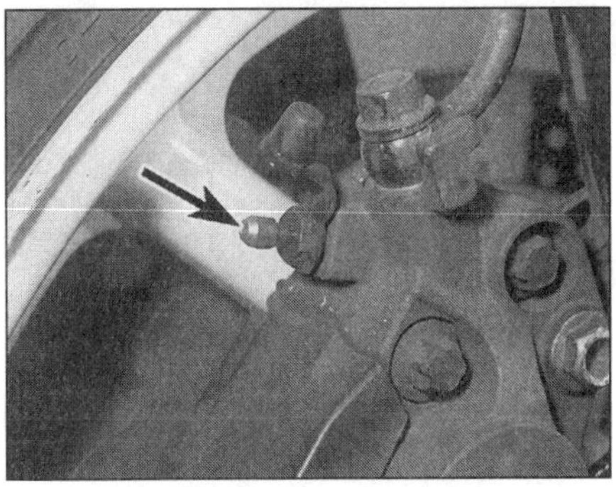

11.6a Brake caliper bleed valve (arrowed)

11.6b To bleed the brakes, you need a spanner, a short section of clear tubing, and a clear container half-filled with brake fluid

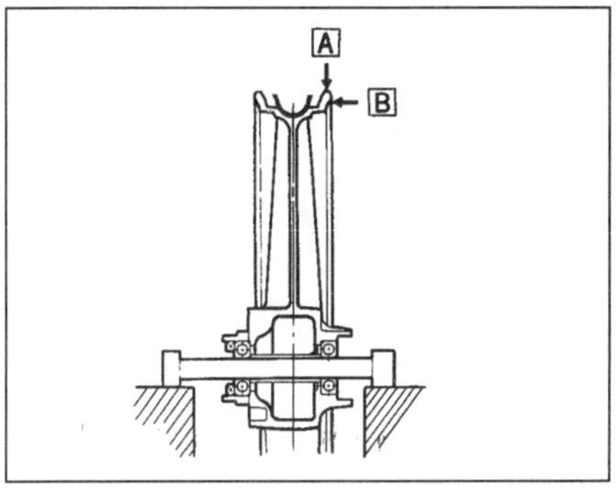

12.2 Check the wheel for radial (out-of-round) runout (A) and axial (side-to-side) runout (B)

both sides of the unions. Tighten the banjo bolts to the torque setting specified at the beginning of this Chapter. Make sure the hoses are correctly aligned and routed clear of all moving components.

6 Flush the old brake fluid from the system, refill with new DOT 4 brake fluid (see *Daily (pre-ride) checks*) and bleed the air from the system (see Section 11). Check the operation of the brakes carefully before riding the motorcycle.

11 Brake system – bleeding and fluid change

Bleeding

1 Bleeding the brakes is simply the process of removing all the air bubbles from the brake fluid reservoirs, the hoses and the brake calipers. Bleeding is necessary whenever a brake system hydraulic connection is loosened, when a new component or hose is fitted, or when the master cylinder or caliper is overhauled. Leaks in the system may also allow air to enter, but leaking brake fluid will reveal their presence and warn you of the need for repair.

2 To bleed the brakes, you will need some new DOT 4 brake fluid, a length of clear vinyl or plastic tubing, a small container partially filled with clean brake fluid, some rags and a spanner to fit the brake caliper bleed valves.

3 Cover the fuel tank and other painted components to prevent damage in the event that brake fluid is spilled.

4 On F models, remove the rider's seat for access to the rear brake fluid reservoir (see Chapter 8).

5 Remove the reservoir cover or cap, diaphragm plate and diaphragm and slowly pump the brake lever or pedal a few times, until no air bubbles can be seen floating up from the holes in the bottom of the reservoir. Doing this bleeds the air from the master cylinder end of the line. Loosely refit the reservoir cover.

6 Pull the dust cap off the bleed valve **(see illustration)**. Attach one end of the clear vinyl or plastic tubing to the bleed valve and submerge the other end in the brake fluid in the container **(see illustration)**.

7 Remove the reservoir cover and check the fluid level. Do not allow the fluid level to drop below the lower mark during the bleeding process.

8 Carefully pump the brake lever or pedal three or four times and hold it in (front) or down (rear) while opening the caliper bleed valve. When the valve is opened, brake fluid will flow out of the caliper into the clear tubing and the lever will move toward the handlebar or the pedal will move down.

9 Retighten the bleed valve, then release the brake lever or pedal gradually. Repeat the process until no air bubbles are visible in the brake fluid leaving the caliper and the lever or pedal is firm when applied. On completion, disconnect the bleeding equipment, then tighten the bleed valve to the torque setting specified at the beginning of the chapter and install the dust cap.

10 Install the diaphragm and cover assembly, wipe up any spilled brake fluid and check the entire system for leaks.

> **HAYNES HiNT** ***If it's not possible to produce a firm feel to the lever or pedal the fluid my be aerated. Let the brake fluid in the system stabilise for a few hours and then repeat the procedure when the tiny bubbles in the system have settled out. To speed this process up, tie the front brake lever to the handlebar or tie a weight to the rear brake pedal so that the system is pressurised.***

Fluid change

11 Changing the brake fluid is a similar process to bleeding the brakes and requires the same materials plus a suitable tool (poultry baster) for siphoning the fluid out of the reservoir – do not siphon by mouth. Ensure that the container is large enough to take all the old fluid when it is flushed out of the system.

12 Pull the dust cap off the bleed valve. Attach one end of the clear vinyl or plastic tubing to the bleed valve and submerge the other end in the brake fluid in the container. Remove the reservoir cover or cap, diaphragm plate and diaphragm and siphon the old fluid out of the reservoir. Fill the reservoir with new brake fluid, then follow Step 8.

13 Tighten the bleed valve, then release the brake lever or pedal gradually. Keep the reservoir topped-up with new fluid to above the LOWER level at all times or air may enter the system and greatly increase the length of the task. Repeat the process until new fluid can be seen emerging from the bleed valve.

> **HAYNES HiNT** ***Old brake fluid is invariably much darker in colour than new fluid, making it easy to see when all old fluid has been expelled from the system.***

14 Disconnect the hose, then tighten the bleed valve to the specified torque setting and install the dust cap. If changing the fluid in the front brake system, repeat the procedure on the other front caliper.

15 Top-up the reservoir, install the diaphragm, diaphragm plate and cap or cover, and wipe up any spilled brake fluid. Check the entire system for fluid leaks.

16 Check the operation of the brakes before riding the motorcycle.

12 Wheels – inspection and repair

1 In order to carry out a proper inspection of the wheels, it is necessary to support the bike upright so that the wheel being inspected is raised off the ground. Position the motorcycle on an auxiliary stand. Clean the wheels thoroughly to remove mud and dirt that may interfere with the inspection procedure or mask defects. Make a general check of the wheels (see Chapter 1) and tyres (see *Daily (pre-ride) checks*).

2 To check the runout, attach a dial gauge to the fork slider or the swingarm and position its stem against the side of the rim **(see illustration)**. Spin the wheel slowly and check

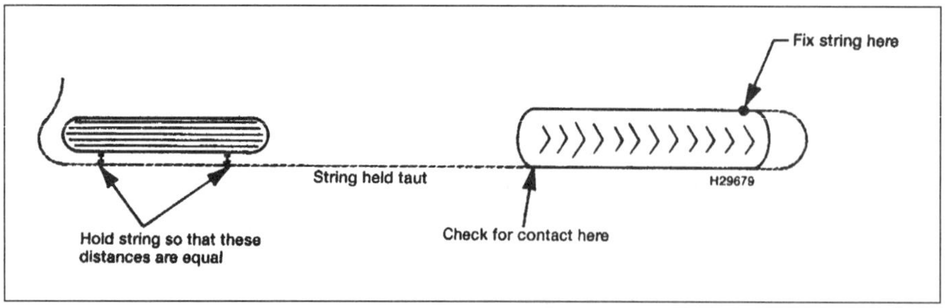

13.5 Wheel alignment check using string

the axial (side-to-side) runout of the rim. In order to accurately check radial (out of round) runout with the dial gauge, the wheel would have to be removed from the machine, and the tyre from the wheel. With the axle clamped in a vice and the dial gauge positioned on the top of the rim, the wheel can be rotated to check the runout.

3 An easier, though slightly less accurate, method is to attach a stiff wire pointer to the fork slider or the swingarm and position the end a fraction of an inch from the wheel (where the wheel and tyre join). If the wheel is true, the distance from the pointer to the rim will be constant as the wheel is rotated. **Note:** *If wheel runout is excessive, check the wheel bearings very carefully before renewing the wheel.*

4 The wheels should also be visually inspected for cracks, flat spots on the rim and other damage. Look very closely for dents in the area where the tyre bead contacts the rim. Dents in this area may prevent complete sealing of the tyre against the rim, which leads to deflation of the tyre over a period of time.

5 If damage is evident, or if runout in either direction exceeds the amount specified, a new wheel will have to be fitted. Never attempt to repair a damaged cast alloy wheel.

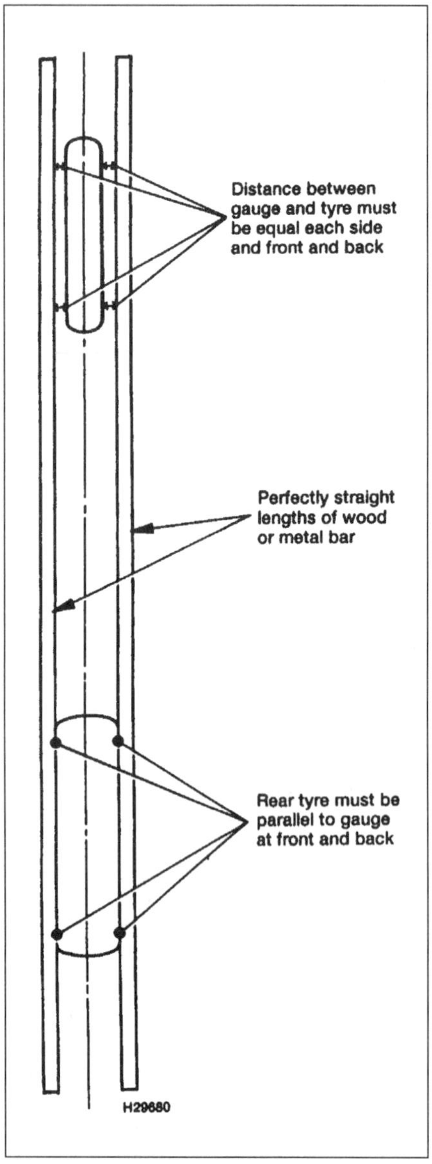

13.7 Wheel alignment check using a straight-edge

13 Wheels – alignment check

1 Misalignment of the wheels, which may be due to a cocked rear wheel or a bent frame or fork yokes, can cause strange and possibly serious handling problems. If the frame or yokes are at fault, repair by a frame specialist or replacement with new parts are the only alternatives.

2 To check the alignment you will need an assistant, a length of string or a perfectly straight piece of wood and a ruler. A plumb bob or other suitable weight will also be required.

3 In order to make a proper check of the wheels it is necessary to support the bike in an upright position, using an auxiliary stand. Measure the width of both tyres at their widest points. Subtract the smaller measurement from the larger measurement, then divide the difference by two. The result is the amount of offset that should exist between the front and rear tyres on both sides.

4 If a string is used, have your assistant hold one end of it about halfway between the floor and the rear axle, touching the rear sidewall of the tyre.

5 Run the other end of the string forward and pull it tight so that it is roughly parallel to the floor. Slowly bring the string into contact with the front sidewall of the rear tyre, then turn the front wheel until it is parallel with the string. Measure the distance from the front tyre sidewall to the string **(see illustration)**.

6 Repeat the procedure on the other side of the motorcycle. The distance from the front tyre sidewall to the string should be equal on both sides.

7 As was previously pointed out, a perfectly straight length of wood may be substituted for the string. The procedure is the same **(see illustration)**.

8 If the distance between the string and tyre is greater on one side, or if the rear wheel appears to be cocked, refer to Chapter 1, Section 2 and check that the chain adjuster markings coincide on each side of the swingarm.

9 If the front-to-back alignment is correct, the wheels still may be out of alignment vertically.

10 Using the plumb bob, or other suitable weight, and a length of string, check the rear wheel to make sure it is vertical. To do this, hold the string against the tyre upper sidewall and allow the weight to settle just off the floor. When the string touches both the upper and lower tyre sidewalls and is perfectly straight, the wheel is vertical. If it is not, place thin spacers under one leg of the stand.

11 Once the rear wheel is vertical, check the front wheel in the same manner. If both wheels are not perfectly vertical, the frame and/or major suspension components are bent.

14 Front wheel – removal and installation

Removal

1 Remove the fairing lower panels (see Chapter 8). Position the motorcycle on an auxiliary stand and support it under the crankcase so that the front wheel is off the ground. Always make sure the motorcycle is properly supported.

2 Remove the brake caliper mounting bolts and slide the calipers off the disc **(see illustration 3.14)**. Support the calipers with a piece of wire or a cable tie so that no strain is placed on their hydraulic hoses. There is no need to disconnect the hose from the caliper. **Note**: *Do not operate the front brake lever with the calipers removed.*

3 On F models, unscrew the knurled ring securing the speedometer cable to the

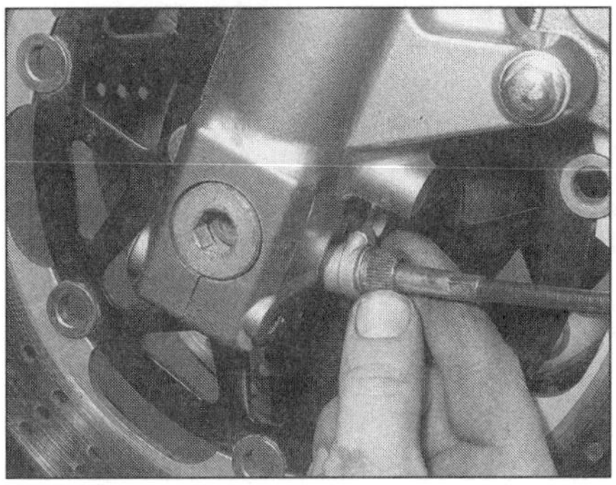

14.3 Unscrew the knurled ring and detach the speedometer cable

14.4 Slacken the axle clamp bolts (A), then unscrew the axle (B)

14.5 Withdraw the axle and remove the wheel

drive gear and detach the cable **(see illustration)**.

4 Slacken the axle clamp bolts on the bottom of the right-hand fork, then unscrew the axle **(see illustration)**.

5 Support the wheel, then withdraw the axle from the right-hand side and carefully lower the wheel **(see illustration)**.

Caution: Don't lay the wheel down and allow it to rest on a disc – the disc could become warped. Set the wheel on wood blocks so the disc doesn't support the weight of the wheel.

6 Check the axle for straightness by rolling it on a flat surface such as a piece of plate glass (first wipe off all old grease and remove any corrosion using steel wool). If the equipment is available, place the axle in V-blocks and measure the runout using a dial gauge. If the axle is bent or the runout exceeds the limit specified, renew it.

7 On F models, remove the collar from the right-hand side of the wheel and the speedometer drive gear from the left-hand side, noting how it fits **(see illustrations)**. On G, H, J and A models, remove the collar from each side of the wheel. Check the condition of the grease seals and wheel bearings (see Section 16).

Installation

8 Apply a smear of grease to the axle, the collars and on F models, the speedometer drive gear. On F models, fit the collar into the right-hand side of the wheel and the speedometer drive gear into the left-hand side, aligning the tabs on the drive gear with the slots in the drive collar in the wheel **(see illustrations 14.7a and b)**. On all other models, fit the collar into each side of the wheel. Each side of the wheel can be identified using the directional arrow cast into one of the spokes near the rim. The arrow denotes the normal direction of rotation of the wheel.

9 Manoeuvre the wheel into position, making sure the directional arrow is pointing in the normal direction of rotation. Apply a thin coat of grease to the axle.

10 If the wheel was removed because the forks were being removed, and the forks were subsequently overhauled, fit the axle nut into the bottom of the left-hand fork slider, but do not tighten the clamp bolts **(see illustration)**.

11 Lift the wheel into place between the fork sliders, making sure the collar(s)/speedometer drive gear remain in position. Slide the axle in from the right-hand side **(see illustration 14.5)**.

12 Counter-hold the axle nut and tighten the axle to the torque setting specified at the beginning of the Chapter **(see illustration)**.

13 On J and A models, place a wooden block in front of the wheel to stop the bike rolling forward, and pump the front forks four or five times to align the fork legs with the axle.

14 Tighten the axle clamp bolts on the bottom of the right-hand fork to the specified torque setting **(see illustration)**. If the axle nut was removed from the bottom of the left-hand fork for fork overhaul, now tighten the clamp bolts on the bottom of the left-hand fork to the specified torque.

14.7a Remove the collar . . .

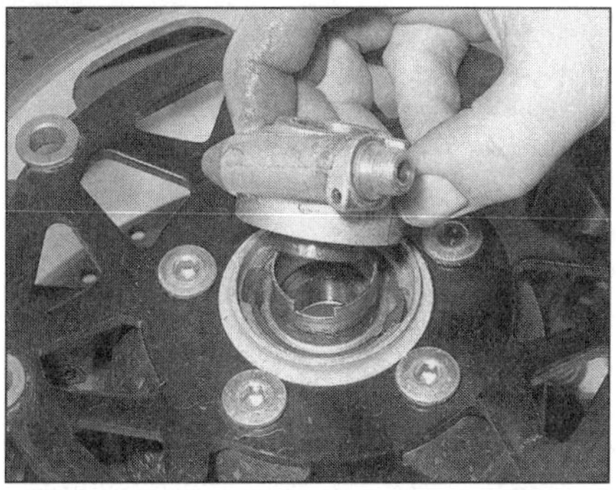

14.7b . . . and the speedometer drive gear

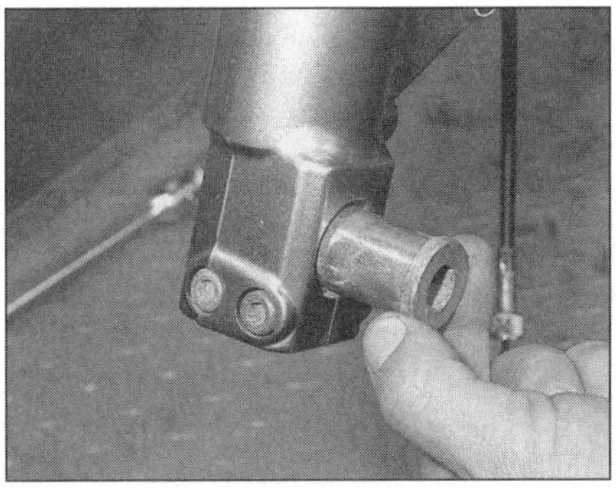

14.10 If removed, fit the axle nut into the left-hand fork

14.12 Tighten the axle nut to the specified torque . . .

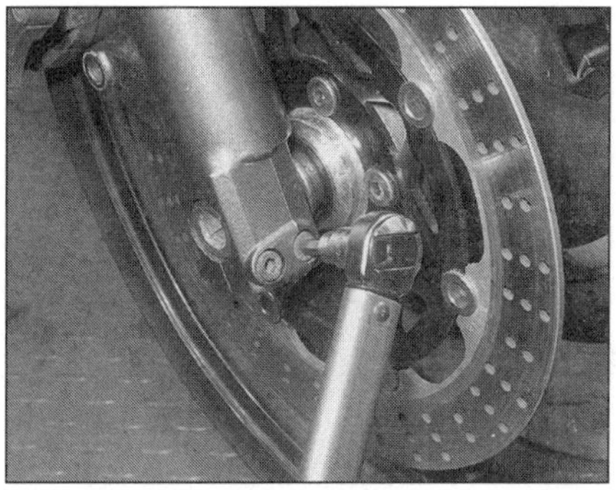

14.14 . . . followed by the clamp bolts

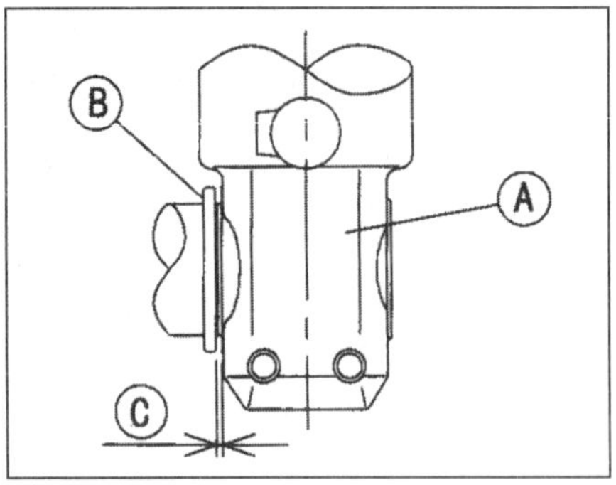

14.15 Check the clearance (C) between the fork leg (A) and the collar (B)

The standard clearance is 1.5 mm, although a clearance of 0.5 to 2.8 mm is acceptable.

15 On J and A models, check the clearance between the right-hand fork leg and the collar using a feeler gauge **(see illustration)**. If the clearance is outside the specifications, remove the wheel and check the axle and suspension components for damage.

16 Install the brake calipers, making sure the pads sit squarely on either side of the disc, then tighten the caliper mounting bolts to the specified torque setting **(see illustrations 3.14 and 3.15)**.

17 On F models, fit the speedometer cable into the drive housing, aligning the slot in the end of the cable with the drive tab, and tighten the knurled ring to secure it **(see illustration)**.

18 Apply the front brake a few times to bring the pads back into contact with the discs. Move the motorcycle off its stand, apply the front brake and pump the front forks a few times to settle all components in position.

19 Check for correct operation of the front brake before riding the motorcycle.

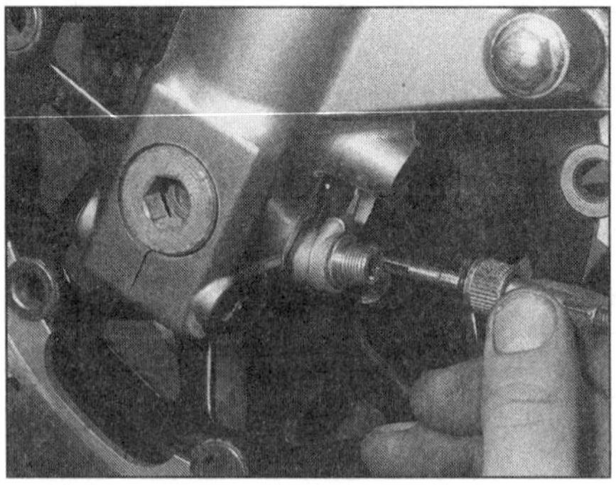

14.17 Locate the slot in the end of the cable onto the drive tab and tighten the ring

15 Rear wheel – removal and installation

Removal

1 Position the motorcycle on an auxiliary stand so that the wheel is off the ground. If required, remove the lower fairing panels so that the stand can be fitted (see Chapter 8).

2 Remove the split pin from the axle nut on the left-hand end of the axle **(see illustration)**. Unscrew the axle nut and remove the washer and the chain adjuster position marker **(see illustration)**.

3 Support the wheel then withdraw the axle from the right and lower the wheel to the ground **(see illustration)**. Retrieve the chain adjustment position marker. Note on G, H, J and A models, the left and right-hand position markers are different. Note how the caliper bracket locates against the swingarm, and support it so that it will not fall off its lug.

4 Disengage the chain from the sprocket and remove the wheel from the swingarm **(see illustration)**.

Caution: Do not lay the wheel down and allow it to rest on the disc or the sprocket – they could become warped. Set the wheel on wood blocks so the disc or the sprocket doesn't support the weight of the wheel. Do not operate the brake pedal with the wheel removed.

5 Check the axle for straightness by rolling it on a flat surface such as a piece of plate glass (if the axle is corroded, first remove the corrosion with steel wool). If the equipment is available, place the axle in V-blocks and check the runout using a dial gauge. If the axle is bent or the runout exceeds the limit specified at the beginning of the Chapter, renew it.

6 Remove the collar from each side of the wheel, noting which fit where **(see illustrations)**. Check the condition of the grease seals and wheel bearings (see Section 16).

15.2a Remove the split pin . . .

15.2b . . . then unscrew the nut and remove the washer and adjustment marker (F models shown)

15.3 Withdraw the axle with the adjustment marker (F models shown) . . .

15.4 . . . then disengage the chain

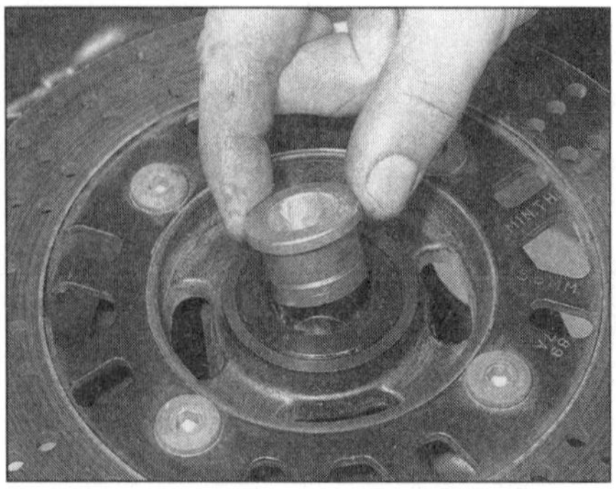

15.6a Remove the right-hand collar . . .

15.6b . . . and the left-hand collar

Installation

7 Apply a thin coat of grease to the lips of each grease seal, and also to the collars and the axle. Slide the right-hand chain adjustment position marker onto the axle, making sure it is the correct way round. On G, H, J and A models, ensure the flats on the head of the axle locate between the raised sides of the position marker **(see illustration)**.

8 Install the short collar into the left-hand side of the wheel and the long collar into the right-hand side **(see illustrations 15.6b and a)**. Manoeuvre the wheel so that it is between the ends of the swingarm and apply a thin coat of grease to the axle. Position the brake caliper bracket against the swingarm so that the lug on the swingarm fits into the slot in the bracket **(see illustration)**.

9 Engage the drive chain with the sprocket and lift the wheel into position **(see illustration 15.4)**. Make sure the collars and caliper bracket remain correctly in place, and that the brake disc fits squarely into the caliper with the pads positioned correctly either side of the disc.

10 Install the axle, with the adjustment marker, from the right, making sure it passes through the chain adjusters and the caliper bracket **(see illustration 15.3)**. Check that everything is correctly aligned, then fit the left-hand adjustment position marker, the washer and the axle nut **(see illustration 15.2b)**. Tighten the nut to the specified torque setting, counter-holding the axle head on the other side of the wheel **(see illustration)**. Secure the nut using a new split pin **(see illustration)**.

11 Adjust the chain slack as described in Chapter 1.

12 Operate the brake pedal several times to bring the pads into contact with the disc. Check the operation of the rear brake carefully before riding the bike.

16 Wheel bearings – removal, inspection and installation

Front wheel bearings

Note: *Always renew the wheel bearings in pairs, never individually. Avoid using a high pressure cleaner on the wheel bearing area.*

1 Remove the wheel (see Section 14).

2 Set the wheel on blocks so as not to allow the weight of the wheel to rest on the brake disc.

3 On F models, remove the circlip securing the speedometer drive collar in the left-hand side of the wheel, then remove the collar, noting how it fits **(see illustrations)**. Lever out the grease seal on the right-hand side of the wheel using a flat-bladed screwdriver, taking care not to damage the rim of the hub **(see illustration)**. Discard the seal as a new one should be used. Remove the circlip securing the right-hand bearing **(see illustration)**.

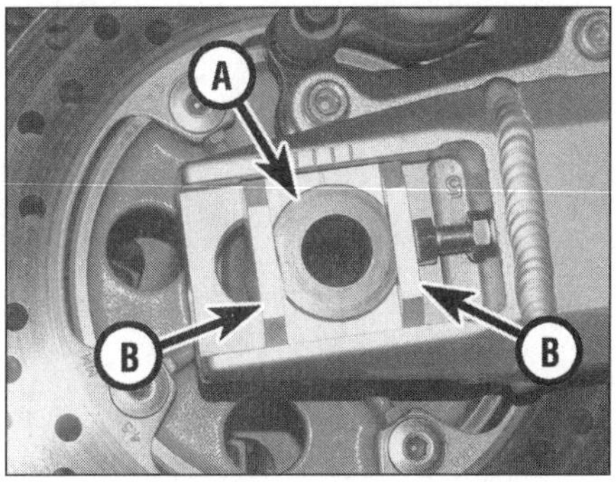

15.7 Locate the axle (A) between the sides (B) of the position marker – G, H, J and A models

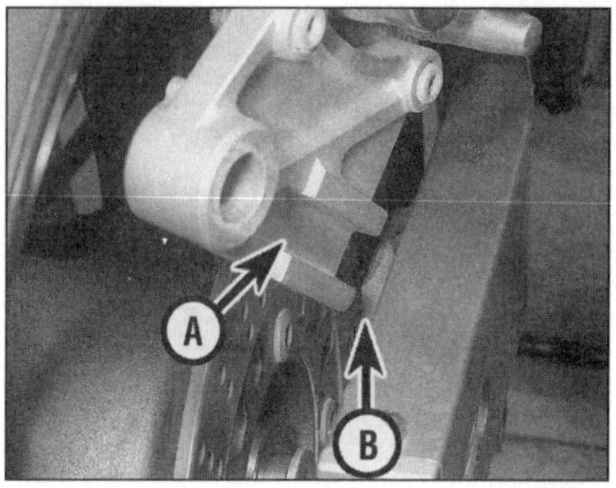

15.8 Make sure the caliper bracket slot (A) locates correctly onto the lug (B) on the swingarm

15.10a Tighten the nut to the specified torque . . .

15.10b . . . and secure it with a new split pin

16.3a Remove the circlip . . .

16.3b . . . and lift out the drive collar

16.3c Lever out the grease seal . . .

16.3d . . . and remove the circlip

7

16.5a Drive out the bearing using a drift and hammer as shown

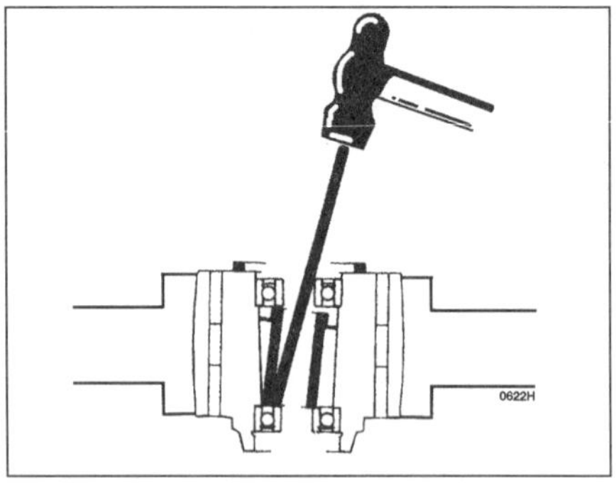

16.5b Locate the drift as shown when driving out the bearing

16.10 Drive the bearing in as described

4 On G, H, J and A models, lever out the grease seal on each side of the wheel using a flat-bladed screwdriver, taking care not to damage the rim **(see illustration 16.3c)**. Remove the circlip securing the right-hand bearing **(see illustration 16.3d)**.

> **HAYNES HiNT** ***Position a piece of wood against the wheel to prevent the screwdriver shaft damaging it when levering the grease seals out.***

5 Using a metal rod (preferably a brass drift punch) inserted through the centre of the one bearing, tap evenly around the inner race of the other bearing to drive it from the hub **(see illustrations)**. The bearing spacer will also come out.

6 Lay the wheel on its other side so that the remaining bearing faces down. Drive the bearing out of the wheel using the same technique as above.

7 If the bearings are of the unsealed type or are only sealed on one side, clean them with a high flash-point solvent (one which won't leave any residue) and blow them dry with compressed air (don't let the bearings spin as you dry them). Apply a few drops of oil to the bearing. **Note:** *If the bearing is sealed on both sides don't attempt to clean it.*

Refer to Tools and Workshop Tips (Section 5) for more information about bearings.

8 Hold the outer race of the bearing and rotate the inner race – if the bearing doesn't turn smoothly, has rough spots or is noisy, fit a new one.

9 If the bearing is good and can be re-used, wash it in solvent once again and dry it, then pack the bearing with grease.

10 Thoroughly clean the hub area of the wheel. Install the right-hand bearing into its recess in the hub, with the marked or sealed side facing outwards. Using the old bearing (if new ones are being fitted), a bearing driver or a socket large enough to contact the outer race of the bearing, drive it in until it's completely seated – the circlip groove should be completely exposed **(see illustration)**. Fit the circlip, making sure it seats properly in its groove **(see illustration 16.3d)**.

11 Turn the wheel over and install the bearing spacer. Drive the left-hand bearing into place as described above.

12 Apply a smear of grease to the lips of the seal(s), then press them into the wheel **(see illustration)**, using a seal or bearing driver, a suitable socket or a flat piece of wood to drive it into place if necessary **(see illustration 16.22)**. On F models, fit the speedometer drive collar into the left-hand side of the wheel, aligning the tabs on the collar with the cutouts in the hub **(see illustration 16.3b)**. Secure the collar with the circlip, making sure it seats properly in its groove **(see illustration 16.3a)**.

13 Clean off all grease from the brake discs using acetone or brake system cleaner then install the wheel (see Section 14).

16.12 Fit the grease seal as described

16.14 Lift the sprocket coupling out of the wheel

Rear wheel bearings

14 Remove the rear wheel (see Section 15). Lift the sprocket coupling out of the wheel, noting how it fits **(see illustration)**.

15 Set the wheel on blocks so as not to allow the weight of the wheel to rest on the brake disc.

16 Lever out the grease seal on the right-hand side of the wheel using a flat-bladed screwdriver, taking care not to damage the rim of the hub **(see illustration)**. Discard the seal as a new one should be used. Remove the circlip securing the right-hand bearing **(see illustration)**.

17 Using a metal rod (preferably a brass drift punch) inserted through the centre of one bearing, tap evenly around the inner race of the other bearing to drive it from the hub **(see**

16.16a Lever out the grease seal . . .

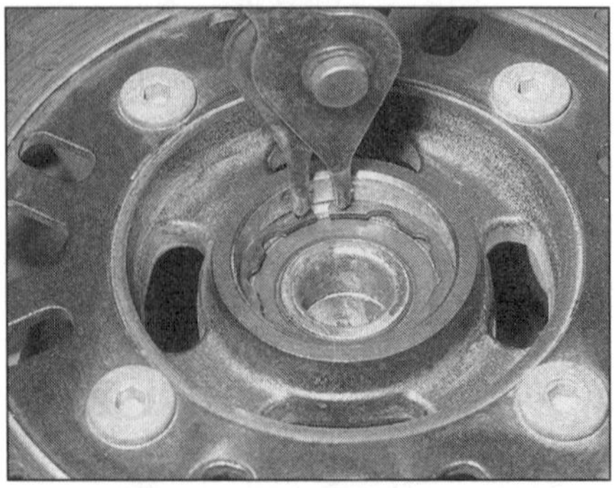

16.16b . . . and remove the circlip

16.22 A piece of wood can be used to fit the seal

16.25a Remove the spacer . . .

16.25b . . . then lever out the grease seal . . .

illustrations 16.5a and b). The bearing spacer will also come out.

18 Lay the wheel on its other side so that the remaining bearing faces down. Drive the bearing out of the wheel using the same technique as above.

19 Refer to Steps 7 to 9 above and check the bearings.

20 Thoroughly clean the hub area of the wheel. First install the right-hand bearing into its recess in the hub, with the marked or sealed side facing outwards. Using the old bearing (if new ones are being fitted), a bearing driver or a socket large enough to contact the outer race of the bearing, drive it in squarely until it's completely seated – the circlip groove should be completely exposed **(see illustration 16.10)**. Fit the circlip, making sure it seats properly in its groove.**(see illustration 16.16b)**.

21 Turn the wheel over and install the bearing spacer. Drive the left-hand side bearing into place as described above.

22 Apply a smear of grease to the lips of the new grease seal, and press it into the right-hand side of the wheel **(see illustration 16.12)**, using a seal or bearing driver, a suitable socket or a flat piece of wood to drive it into place if necessary **(see illustration)**.

23 Clean off all grease from the brake disc using acetone or brake system cleaner. Install the rear sprocket and sprocket coupling assembly onto the wheel, then install the wheel (see Section 15).

Sprocket coupling bearing

24 Remove the rear wheel (see Section 15). Lift the sprocket coupling out of the wheel, noting how it fits **(see illustration 16.14)**.

25 Remove the spacer from the inside of the coupling bearing, noting which way round it fits **(see illustration)**. Using a flat-bladed screwdriver, lever out the grease seal from the outside of the coupling **(see illustration)**. Remove the circlip securing the bearing **(see illustration)**.

26 Support the coupling on blocks of wood and drive the bearing out from the inside using a bearing driver or socket **(see illustration)**.

27 Refer to Steps 7 to 9 above and check the bearings.

28 Thoroughly clean the bearing recess then install the bearing into the recess in the coupling, with the marked or sealed side facing out. Using the old bearing (if new ones are being fitted), a bearing driver or a socket large enough to contact the outer race of the bearing, drive it in until it is completely seated – the circlip groove should be completely exposed. Fit the circlip, making sure it seats properly in its groove **(see illustration 16.25c)**.

29 Apply a smear of grease to the lips of the new seal, and press it into the coupling, using a seal or bearing driver, a suitable socket or a flat piece of wood to drive it into place if necessary **(see illustration)**. Install the spacer into the inside of the coupling, making sure it is the correct way round **(see illustration 16.25a)**.

30 Check the sprocket coupling/rubber damper (see Chapter 6).

31 Clean off all grease from the brake disc using acetone or brake system cleaner. Fit the sprocket coupling into the wheel **(see illustration 16.14)**, then install the wheel (see Section 15).

17 Tyres – general information and fitting

General information

1 The wheels fitted to all models are designed to take tubeless tyres only. Tyre sizes are given in the Specifications at the beginning of this chapter.

2 Refer to the *Daily (pre-ride) checks* listed at the beginning of this manual for tyre maintenance.

Fitting new tyres

3 When selecting new tyres, refer to the tyre information label on the swingarm and the tyre options listed in the owners handbook. Ensure that front and rear tyre types are compatible,

16.25c . . . and remove the circlip

16.26 Drive the bearing out from the inside

16.29 Fit the grease seal as described

the correct size and correct speed rating; if necessary seek advice from a Kawasaki dealer or tyre fitting specialist **(see illustration)**.

4 It is recommended that tyres are fitted by a motorcycle tyre specialist rather than attempted in the home workshop. This is particularly relevant in the case of tubeless tyres because the force required to break the seal between the wheel rim and tyre bead is substantial, and is usually beyond the capabilities of an individual working with normal tyre levers. Additionally, the specialist will be able to balance the wheels after tyre fitting.

5 Note that punctured tubeless tyres can in some cases be repaired. Kawasaki recommend that such repairs are carried out only by an authorised dealer. If repairs are made, they should be made internally (on the inside of the tyre) rather than externally. Kawasaki recommend that a repaired tyre should not be used at speeds above 60 mph (100 km/h) for the first 24 hours after the repair, and thereafter not above 110 mph (180 km/h).

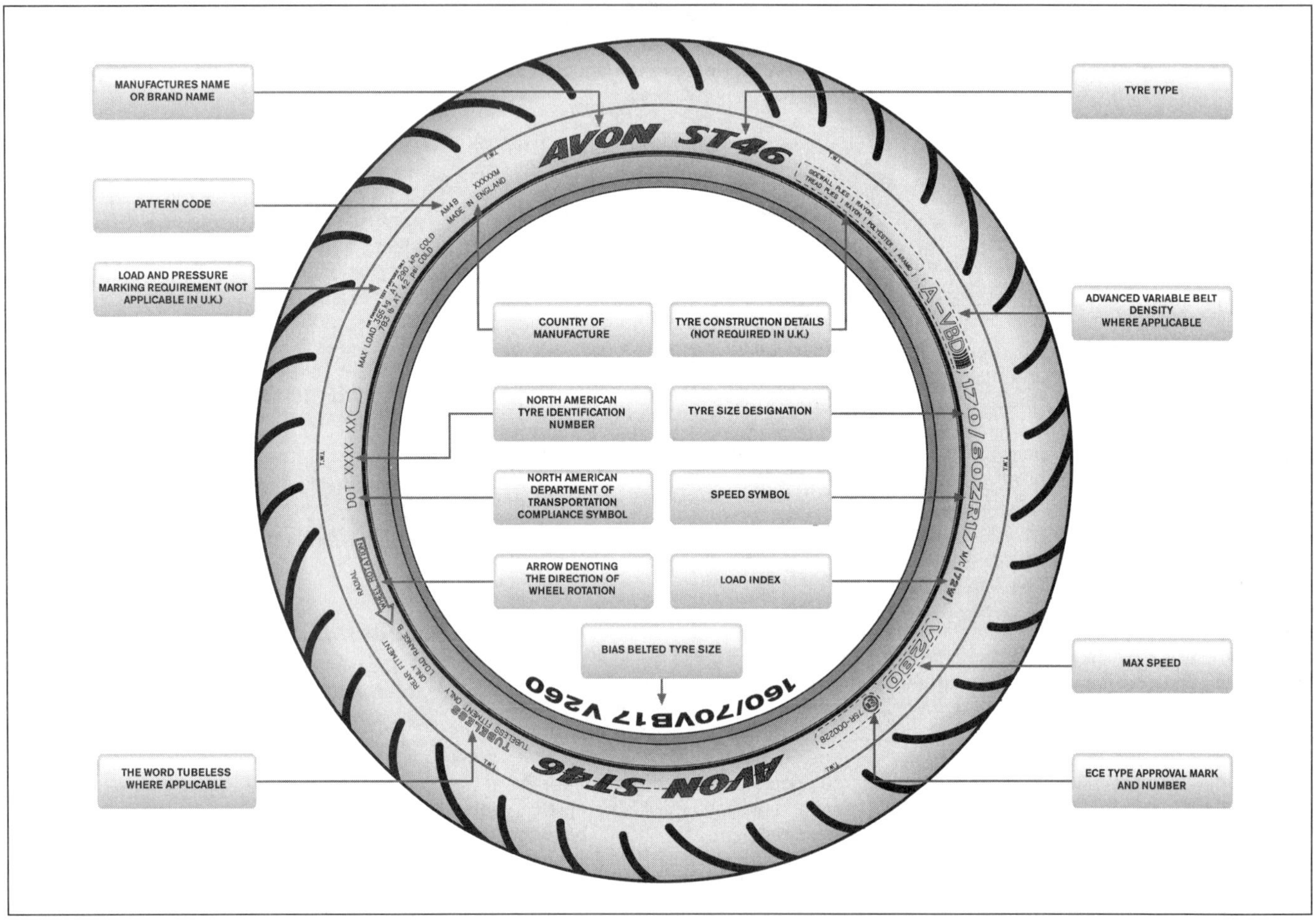

17.3 Common tyre sidewall markings

Chapter 8
Bodywork

Contents

Degrees of difficulty

Easy, suitable for novice with little experience	**Fairly easy,** suitable for beginner with some experience	**Fairly difficult,** suitable for competent DIY mechanic	**Difficult,** suitable for experienced DIY mechanic	**Very difficult,** suitable for expert DIY or professional

1 General information

This Chapter covers the procedures necessary to remove and install the body parts. Since many service and repair operations on these motorcycles require the removal of the body parts, the procedures are grouped here and referred to from other Chapters.

In the case of damage to the body parts, it is usually necessary to remove the broken component and replace it with a new (or used) one. The material that the body panels are composed of doesn't lend itself to conventional repair techniques. There are however some places that specialise in 'plastic welding', so it may be worthwhile seeking the advice of one of these specialists before consigning an expensive component to the bin.

When attempting to remove any body panel, first study it closely, noting any fasteners and associated fittings, to be sure of returning everything to its correct place on installation. In some cases the aid of an assistant will be required when removing panels, to help avoid the risk of damage to paintwork. Once the evident fasteners have been removed, try to withdraw the panel as described but DO NOT FORCE IT – if it will not release, check that all fasteners have been removed and try again. Where a panel engages another by means of tabs, be careful not to break the tab or its mating slot or to damage the paintwork. Remember that a few moments of patience at this stage will save you a lot of money in replacing broken fairing panels!

When installing a body panel, first study it closely, noting any fasteners and associated fittings removed with it, to be sure of returning everything to its correct place. Check that all fasteners are in good condition, including all trim nuts or clips and damping/rubber mounts; any of these must be replaced if faulty before the panel is reassembled. Check also that all mounting brackets are straight and repair or replace them if necessary before attempting to install the panel. Where assistance was required to remove a panel, make sure your assistant is on hand to install it.

Tighten the fasteners securely, but be careful not to overtighten any of them or the panel may break (not always immediately) due to the uneven stress. Where quick-release fasteners are fitted, turn them 90° anti-clockwise to release them, and 90° clockwise to secure them.

> HAYNES HiNT
> ***Note that a small amount of lubricant (liquid soap or similar) applied to the mounting rubber grommets of the seat cowling will assist the lugs to engage without the need for undue pressure.***

2 Seats – removal and installation

Removal

F models

1 To remove the pillion seat, insert the ignition key into the seat lock located in the left-hand side panel, and turn it clockwise to

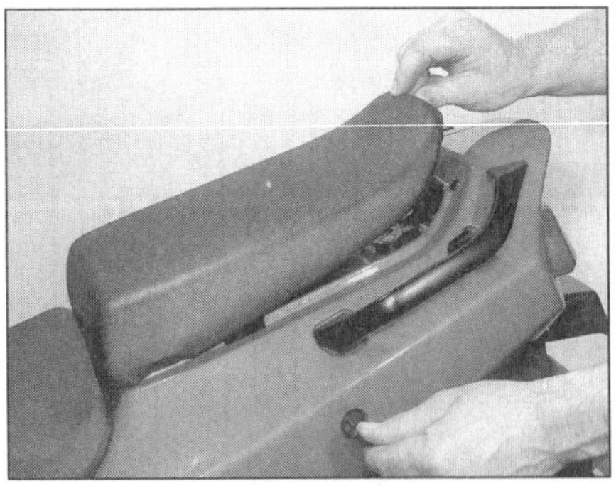

2.1 Unlock the seat and remove it as described

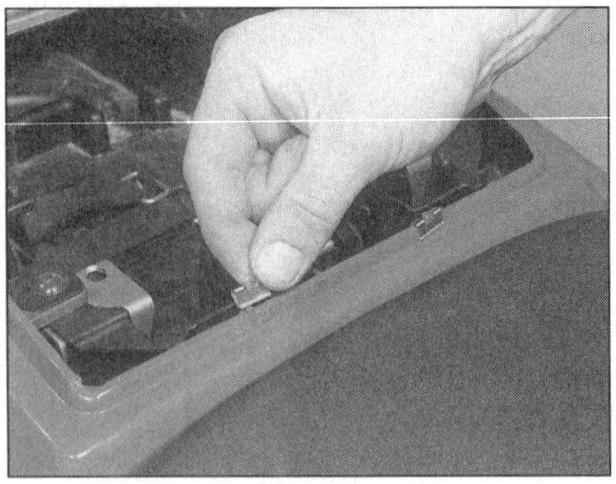

2.3a Remove the clips . . .

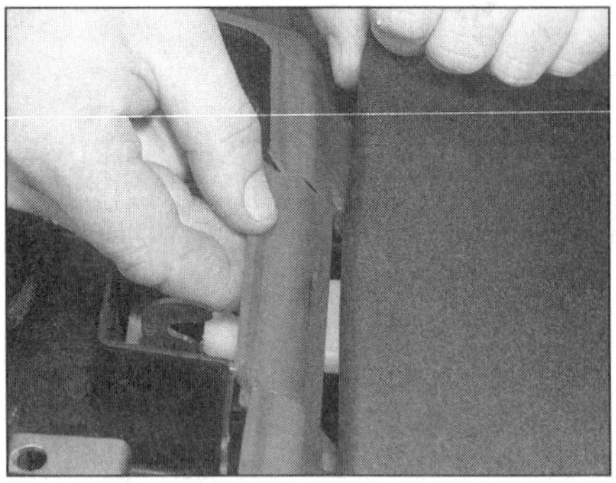

2.3b . . . and lift out the panel . . .

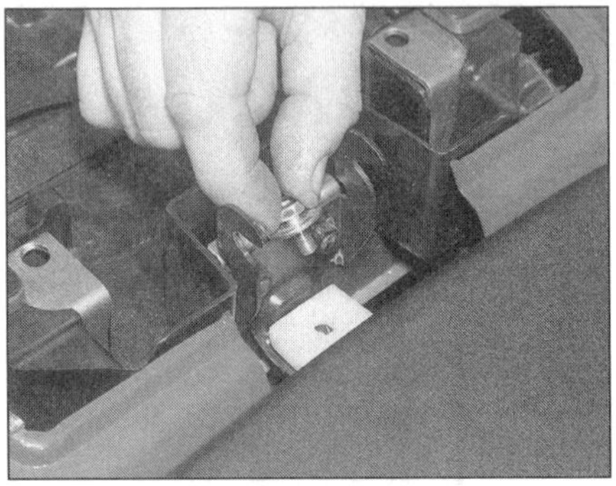

2.3c . . . then remove the bolt and remove the seat

2.6a Unscrew the bolt (arrowed) . . .

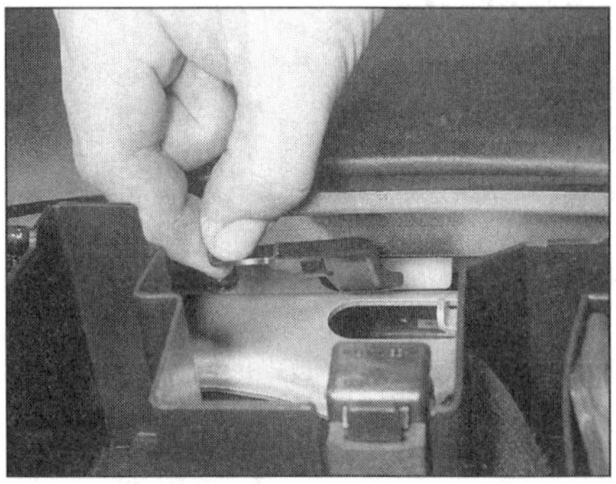

2.6b . . . and remove the bracket

unlock the seat **(see illustration)**. Lift the back of the seat up, then pull the seat forward, noting how it fits.

2 To remove the rider's seat, first remove the pillion seat.

3 Remove the two clips securing the trim panel at the rear of the seat, then remove the panel **(see illustrations)**. Remove the bolt securing the seat, then draw the seat back and up, noting how it fits **(see illustration)**.

G, H, J and A models

4 To remove the pillion seat, insert the ignition key into the seat lock located in the left-hand side panel, and turn it clockwise to unlock the seat **(see illustration 2.12)**. Lift the back of the seat up, then pull the seat back, noting how it fits.

5 To remove the rider's seat, first remove the pillion seat.

6 Unscrew the bolt securing the seat bracket and remove the bracket, noting how it fits **(see illustrations)**. Draw the seat back and up, noting how it fits.

Installation

F models

7 To install the rider's seat, locate the tab at the front of the seat under the fuel tank bracket, then secure the back of the seat with the bolt **(see illustration and 2.3c)**. Fit the trim panel and secure it with the clips **(see illustrations 2.3b and a)**.

8 To install the pillion seat, first install the rider's seat, if removed.

9 Locate the bar at the front of the seat under the hooks on the bracket, then position the peg over the latch and press down on the rear of the seat until the latch engages **(see illustration)**.

G, H, J and A models

10 To install the rider's seat, locate the tab at

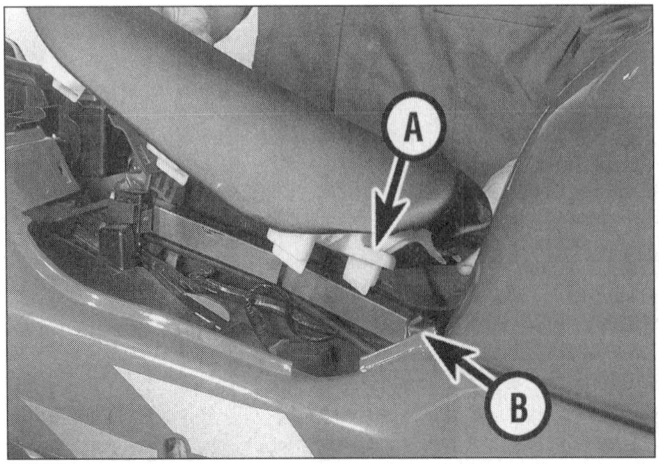

2.7 Locate the tab (A) under the bracket (B)

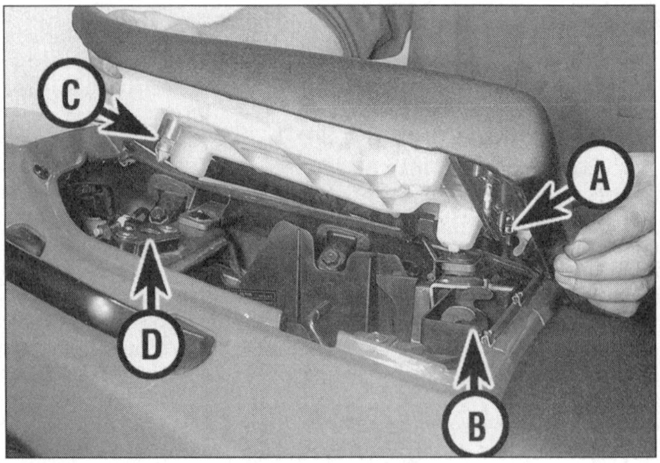

2.9 Locate the bar (A) under the hooks (B), then fit the peg (C) into the latch (D) and press down

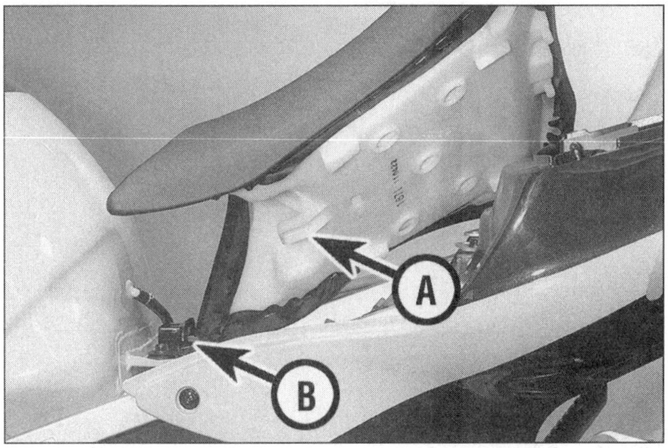

2.10 Locate the tab (A) under the bracket (B)

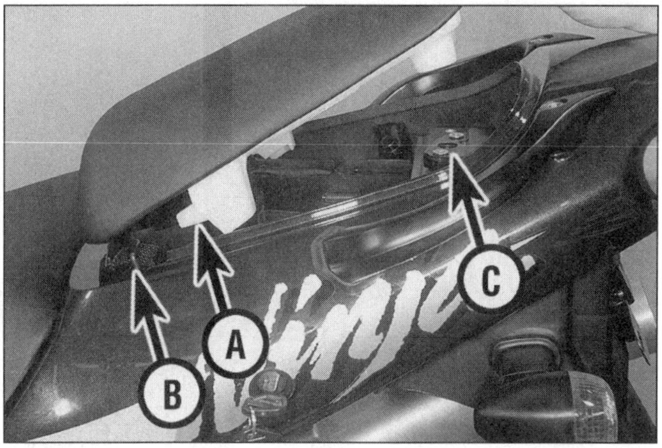

2.12 Locate the tab (A) on each side into the bracket (B), and the peg into the latch (C) and press down

the front of the seat under the fuel tank bracket, then fit the bracket into its slot in the back of the seat and secure it with the bolt **(see illustration and 2.6b and a)**.

11 To install the pillion seat, first install the rider's seat, if removed.

12 Locate the tabs at the front of the seat into their sockets on the bracket, then position the peg over the latch and press down on the rear of the seat until the latch engages **(see illustration)**.

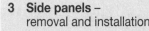

3 Side panels – removal and installation

Removal

F models

1 Remove the seats (see Section 2).

2 Unscrew the bolts securing each pillion grab-rail and remove the grab-rails, noting how they fit **(see illustration)**.

3 Disconnect the tail light assembly wiring connector **(see illustration)**.

4 Remove the six screws securing the side panels **(see illustration)**. Gently pull the front of each panel away from the fuel tank until the pegs disengage from the rubber grommets, then draw the side panels backwards and off the frame **(see illustrations)**.

5 If required, remove the tail light assembly

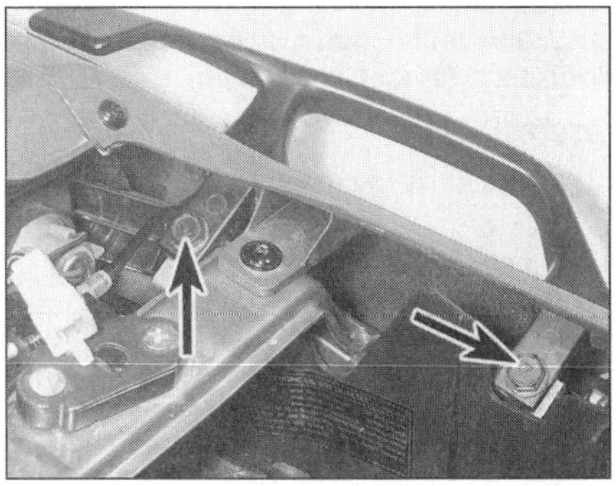

3.2 Unscrew the bolts (arrowed) and remove the grab-rail

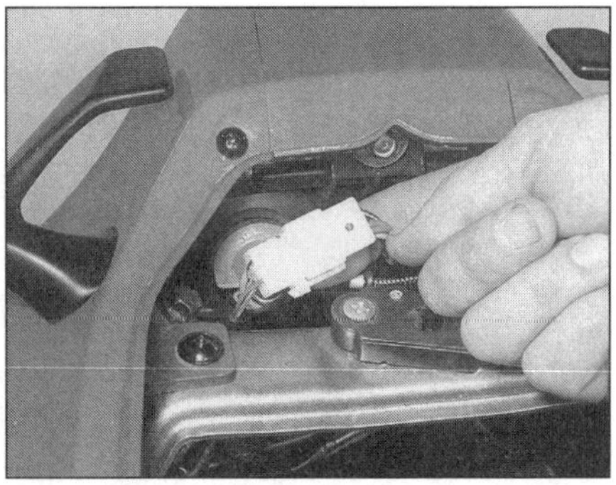

3.3 Disconnect the tail light wiring connector

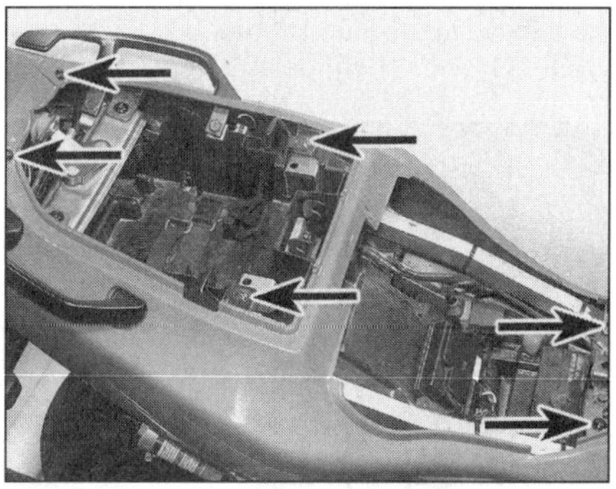

3.4a Remove the six screws (arrowed) . . .

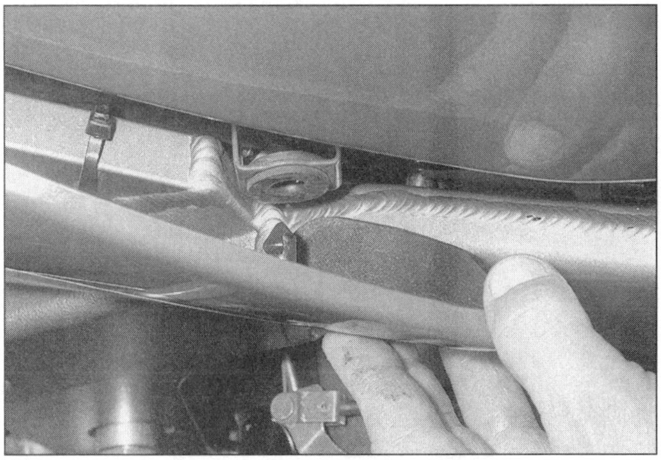

3.4b . . . then release the pegs at the front . . .

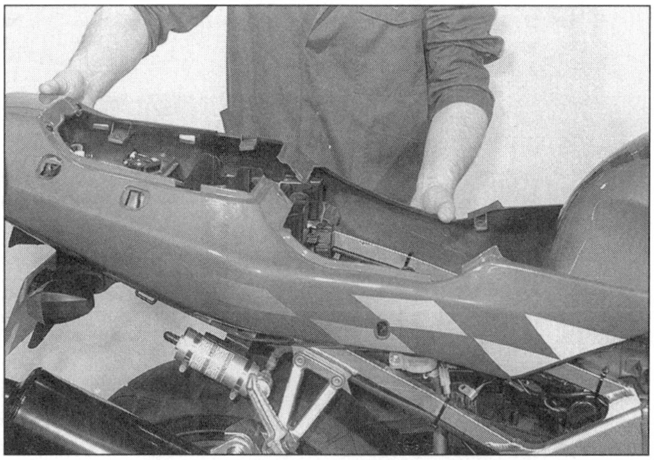

3.4c . . . and remove the side panels

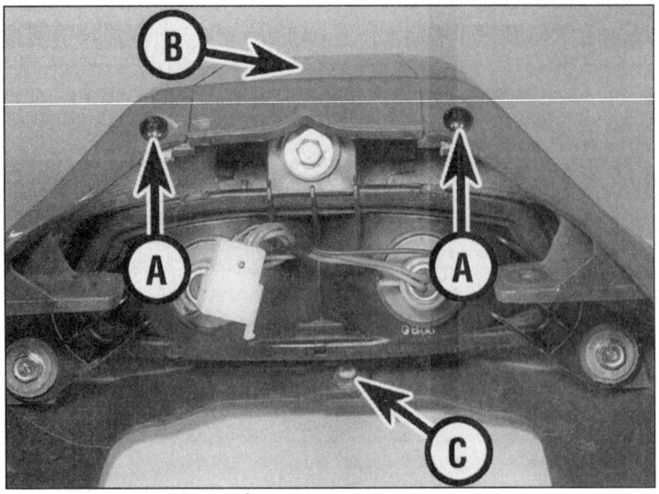

3.5 To separate the side panels, remove the tail light assembly, the screws (A), the centre piece (B) and the joining screw (C)

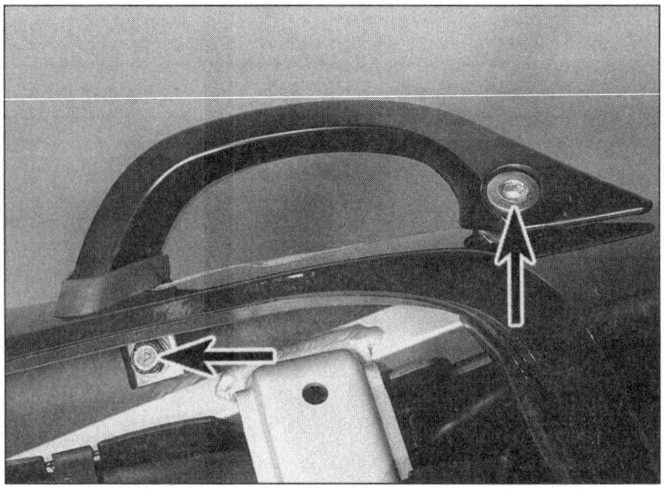

3.7 Unscrew the bolts (arrowed) and remove the grab-rail

(see Chapter 9). To separate the side panels, remove the two screws securing each side panel to the centre piece, and the screw joining the side panels, then remove the centre piece and separate the panels **(see illustration)**.

G, H, J and A models

6 Remove the seats (see Section 2).

7 Unscrew the bolts securing each pillion grab-rail and remove the grab-rails, noting how they fit **(see illustration)**.

8 On G and H models, remove the two screws securing the seat lock and detach the lock **(see illustration)**. On J and A models, disconnect the seat lock cable from the back of the lock mechanism.

9 Remove the four screws securing the side panels – one on each side at the front and one on each side on the underside **(see illustration)**. Draw the side panels backwards and off the frame.

Installation

10 Installation is the reverse of removal. **Note:** *On J and A models, ensure the seat lock cable is reconnected securely before installing the pillion seat.*

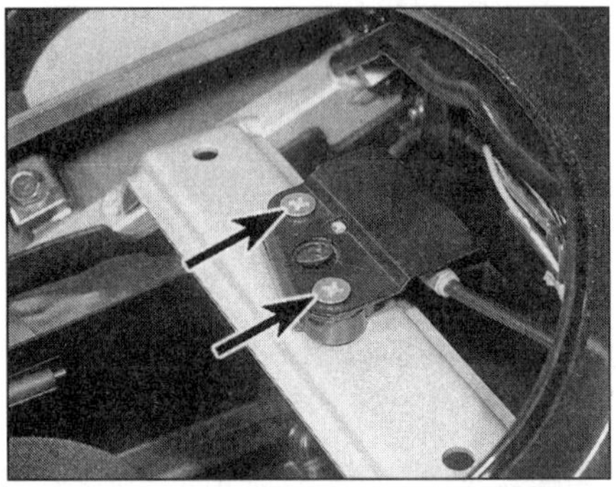

3.8 Remove the screws (arrowed) and detach the seat lock

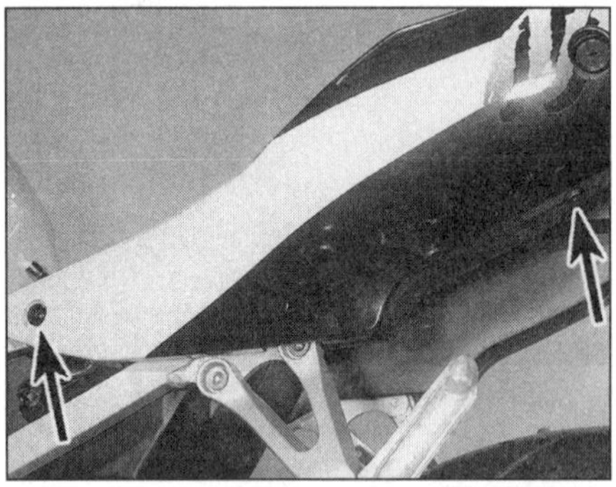

3.9 Remove the two screws (arrowed) on each side

4 Rear view mirrors – removal and installation

Removal

1 Unscrew the two nuts securing each mirror and remove the mirror along with its rubber insulator pads **(see illustration)**.

Installation

2 Installation is the reverse of removal.

5 Upper fairing – removal and installation

Removal

F models

1 Remove the screw securing each air duct trim panel, then ease the front of each panel up until the peg disengages from its rubber grommet **(see illustrations)**.

4.1 Each mirror is secured on the inside of the fairing by two nuts

5.1a Remove the screw . . .

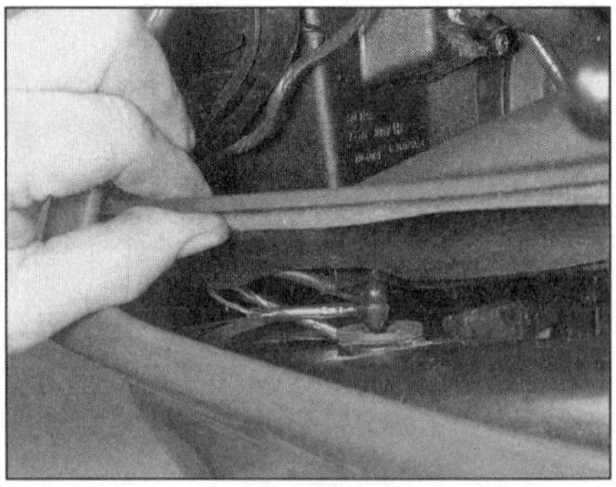

5.1b . . . and lift the panel to free the peg

5.3a Disconnect the headlight wiring connector . . .

5.3b . . . and the wiring connectors (arrowed) for each turn signal

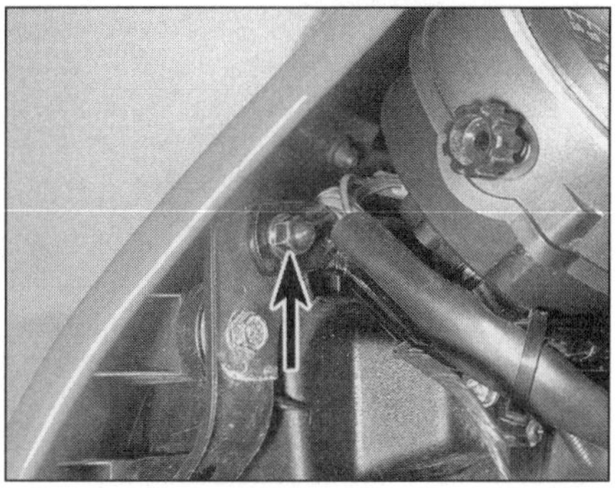

5.4 Remove the nut (arrowed) on each side

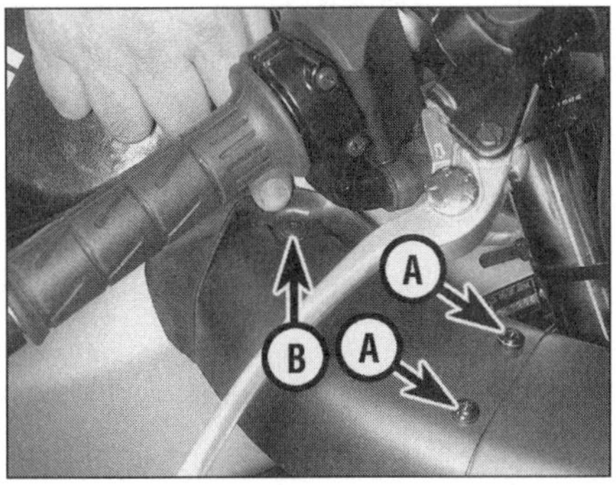

5.5a Remove the screws (A) and the trim clip (B) and remove the panel

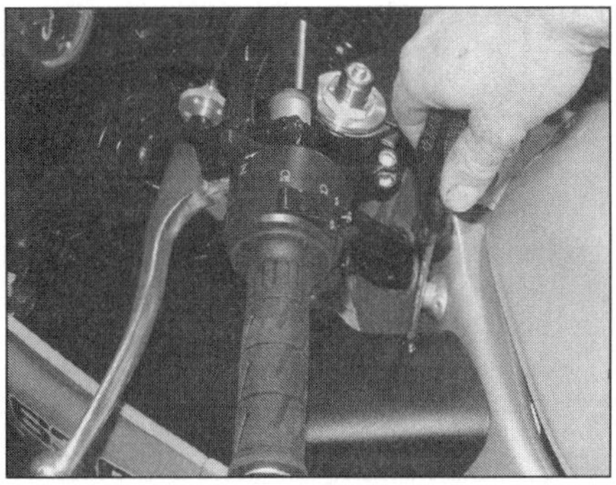

5.5b Remove the screw . . .

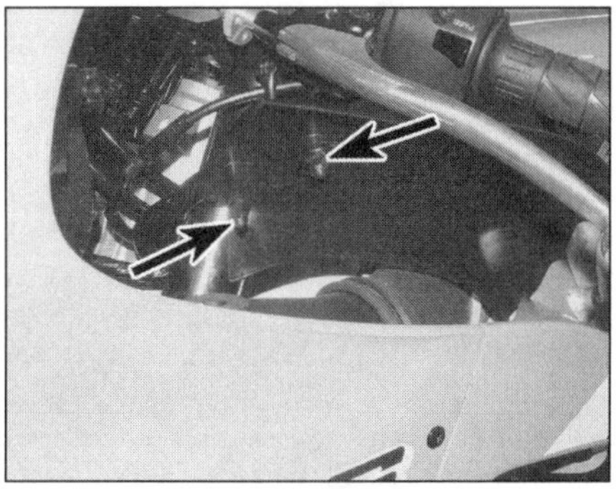

5.5c . . . then ease the panel up to release the pegs (arrowed)

2 Remove the rear view mirrors (see Section 4).

3 Disconnect the headlight wiring connector and the turn signal wiring connectors **(see illustrations)**. Cut any cable ties securing the turn signal wiring between the connectors and the turn signals themselves.

4 Remove the three screws on each side securing the upper fairing to the lower fairing panels **(see illustration 5.10a)**. Unscrew the nut on each side securing the fairing to the instrument cluster bracket **(see illustration)**. Carefully draw the fairing forward until the sidelight bulbholder becomes accessible (the sidelight is mounted on top of the headlight), then pull the bulbholder out of its socket. Draw the fairing off the bike.

G, H, J and A models

5 On G and H models, remove the screws and the trim clip, which is accessed by lifting the rubber cover at the rear, securing each air duct trim panel, then remove the panel **(see illustration)**. On J and A models, remove the screw securing each air duct trim panel, then ease the front of each panel up until the two pegs disengage from the rubber grommets **(see illustrations)**. Slip the spring band back off each air duct **(see illustration)**.

6 Detach the air duct hose from the rear section of the Y-piece inside the fairing **(see illustration)**. If it is difficult to access, disconnect it as it becomes accessible when drawing the fairing off the bike.

7 Remove the windshield (see Section 8).

8 Remove the rear view mirrors (see Section 4).

9 Disconnect the headlight/turn signal wiring connector **(see illustration)**.

10 Remove the three screws on each side

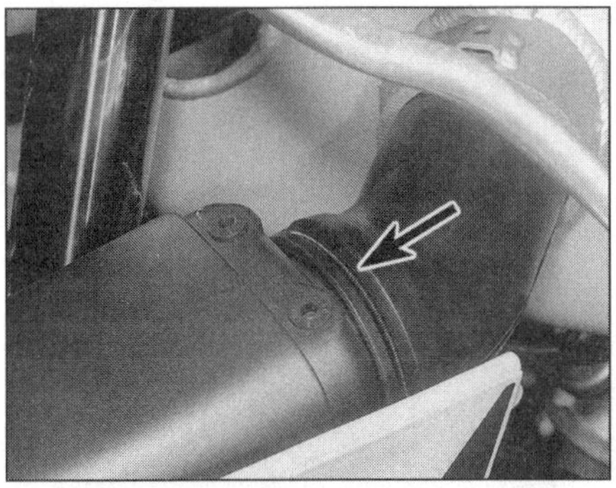

5.5d Slip the spring band (arrowed) back off the duct

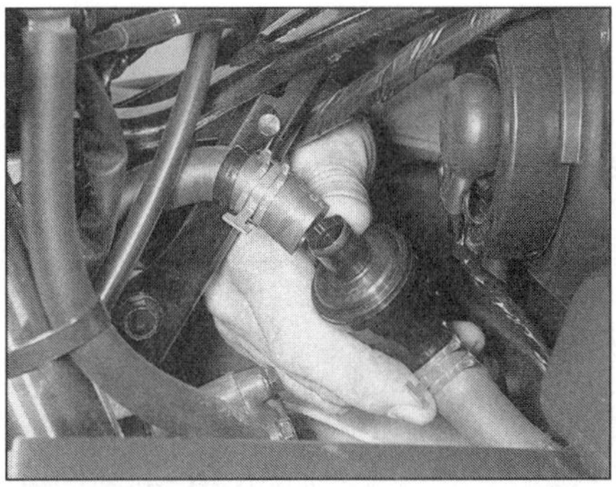

5.6 Disconnect the hose from the Y-piece

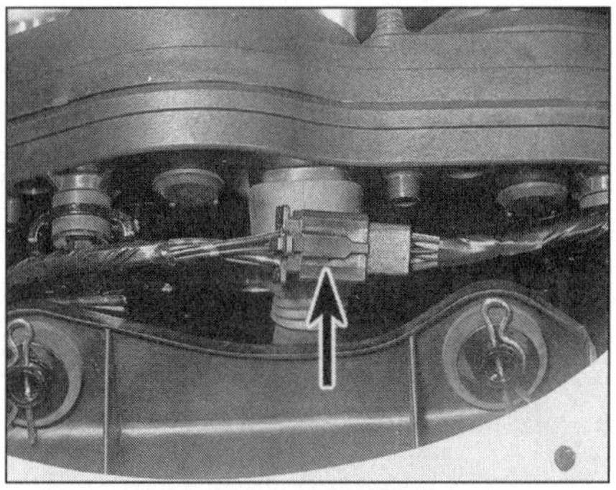

5.9 Disconnect the headlight/turn signal wiring connector

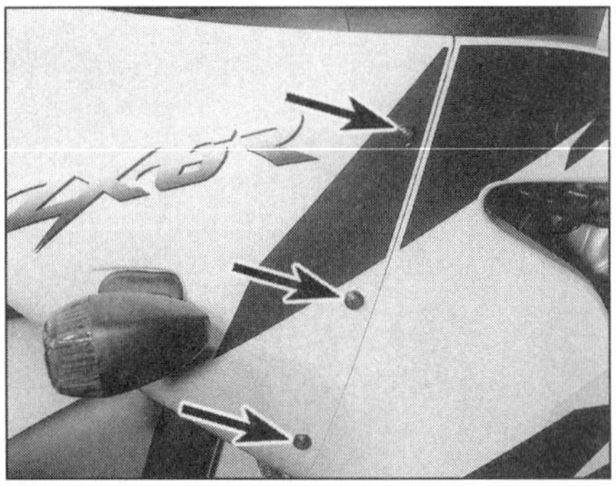

5.10a Remove the three screws (arrowed)

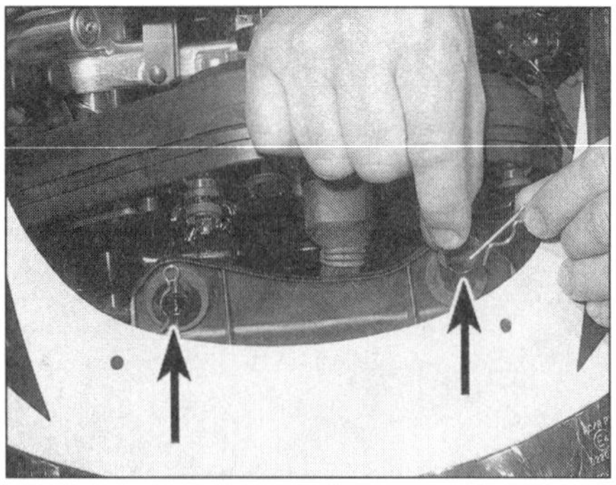

5.10b On G and H models, remove the two clips (arrowed)

5.10c On J and A models, remove the bolts

securing the upper fairing to the lower fairing panels **(see illustration)**. On G and H models, withdraw the clips and remove the washers securing the front of the fairing to the instrument cluster bracket **(see illustration)**. On J and A models, undo the bolts securing the front of the fairing to the instrument cluster bracket **(see illustration)**.

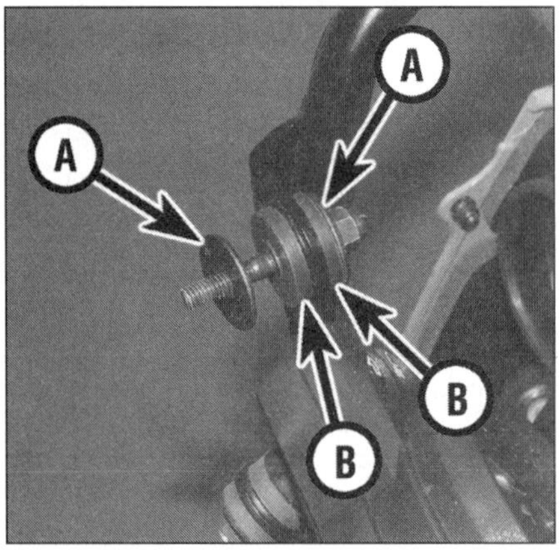

5.10d Note the position of the washers (A) and bushes (B)

Carefully draw the fairing forward and off the bike. On J and A models, note the position of the washers and rubber bushes on the instrument cluster bracket fitting **(see illustration)**.

Installation

11 Installation is the reverse of removal. Make sure the wiring connectors are correctly and securely connected.

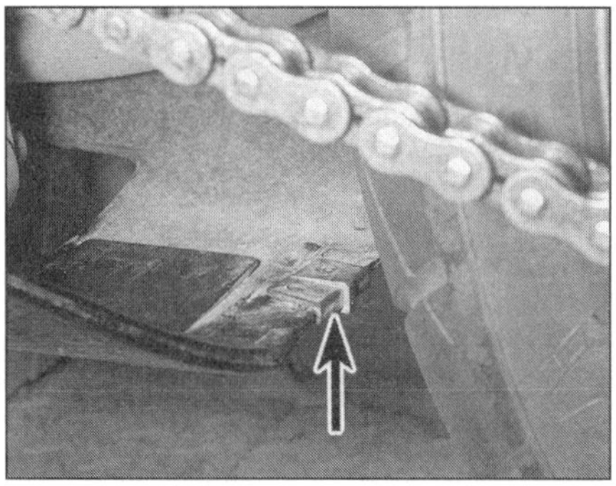

6.2 Remove the clip (arrowed), noting how it fits

6 Lower fairing panels – removal and installation

Removal

1 Each lower fairing panel is secured by four screws, three bolts, two locating pegs, and on F models, a clip.

2 On F models, first remove the clip which joins the two halves together at the back **(see illustration)**.

3 Remove the screws and the bolts, then carefully pull the lower front part of the panel away from the inner cover until the pegs disengage from the grommets, then remove the panel, noting how it fits **(see illustrations)**. If removing both panels, the inner cover can be removed after one lower panel has been removed, or it can be left attached to one of the panels.

Installation

4 Installation is the reverse of removal.

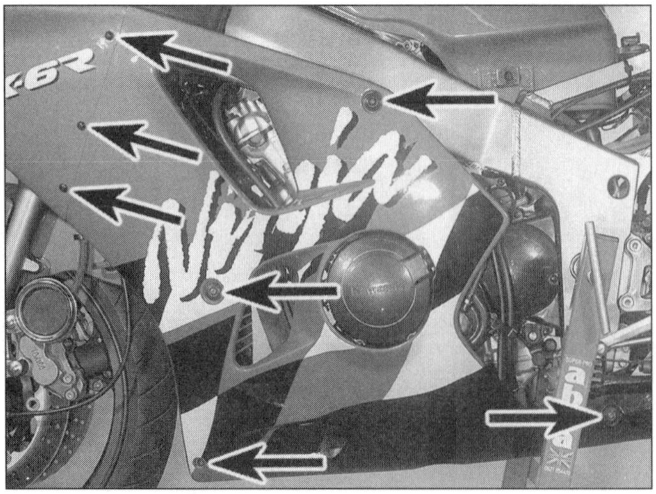

6.3a Remove the seven screws (arrowed) . . .

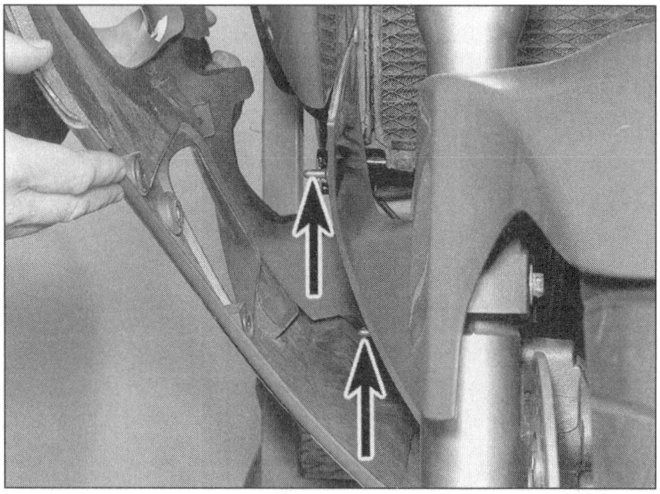

6.3b . . . then pull the panel away to release the pegs (arrowed)

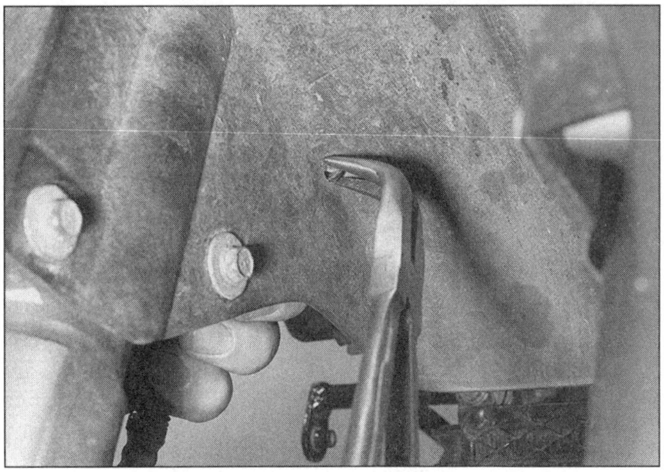
7.1a Squeeze the clips on the inside to release them

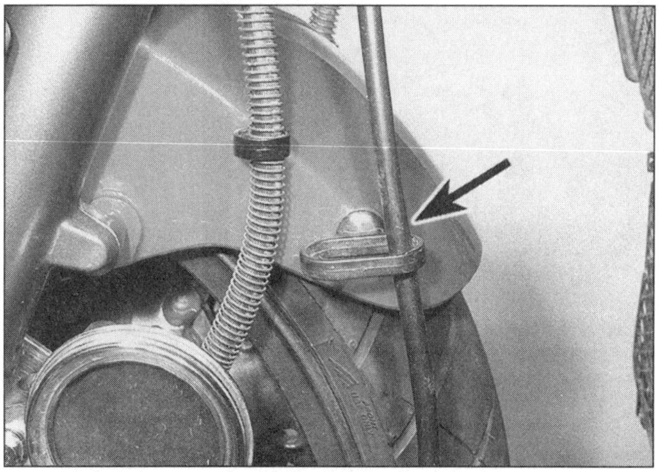
7.1b Release the cable from the guide or the guide from the mudguard (arrowed)

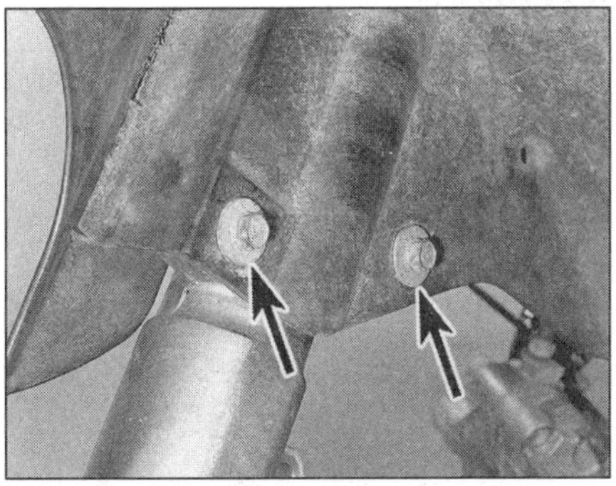
7.2a Unscrew the two bolts (arrowed) . . .

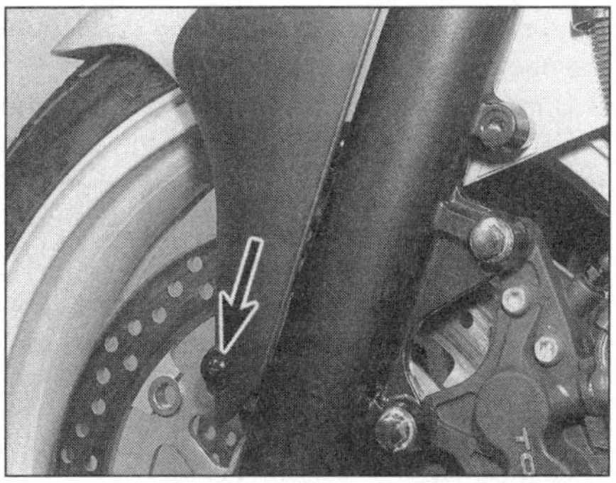
7.2b . . . and on G, H, J and A models the lower fixing screws (arrowed) . . .

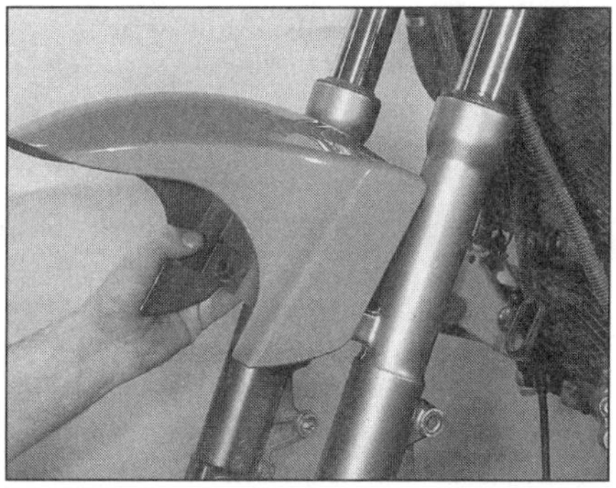
7.2c . . . and remove the mudguard

7 Front mudguard – removal and installation

Removal

Note: *The brake hose guides and mudguard mounting bolts are all accessed from inside the mudguard, and access with the front wheel in situ is restricted. If required, remove the front wheel to improve access (see Chapter 7).*

1 Release the front brake hose guides from the mudguard by pressing together the clips on the inside of the mudguard and pulling the guides out from the outside **(see illustration)**. On F models, either release the speedometer cable guide from the mudguard, or detach the cable from the drive housing on the front wheel and draw it out of the guide (if the wheel has not been removed) (see Chapter 9) **(see illustration)**.

2 Unscrew the two bolts securing each side of the mudguard to the fork slider **(see illustration)**. On G, H, J and A models, also remove the screw securing the lower part of each side **(see illustration)**. Remove the mudguard by drawing it forwards, noting how it fits **(see illustration)**.

Installation

3 Installation is the reverse of removal.

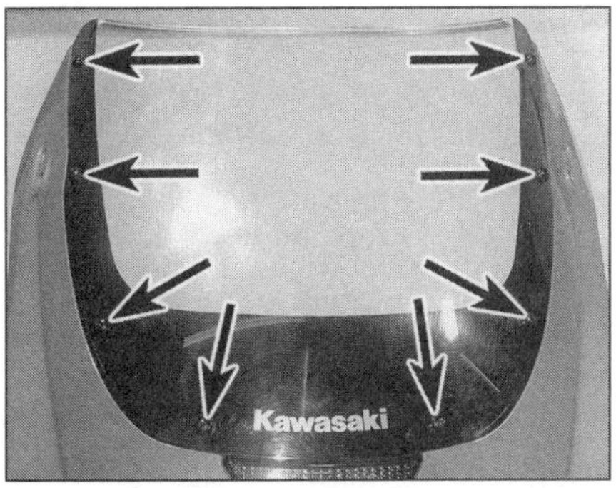

8.1a Windshield screws (arrowed) – F models

8.1b Windshield screws (arrowed) – G, H, J and A models

8 Windshield – removal and installation

Removal

1 Remove the screws securing the windshield to the fairing and remove the windshield, noting how it fits **(see illustrations)**.

Installation

2 Installation is the reverse of removal. Do not overtighten the screws.

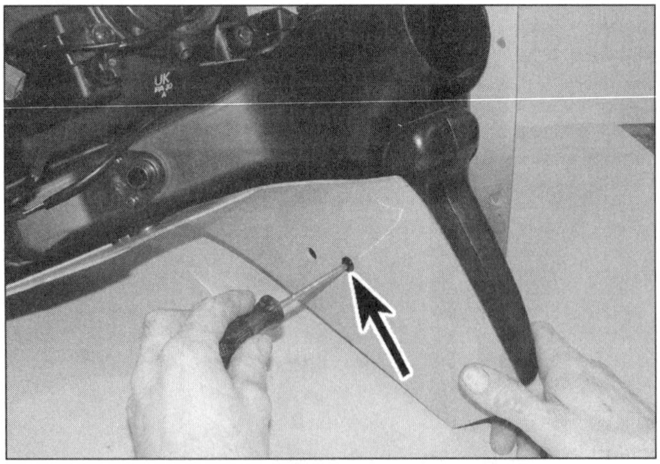

9.2a Undo the screw (arrowed) on each side of the upper fairing . . .

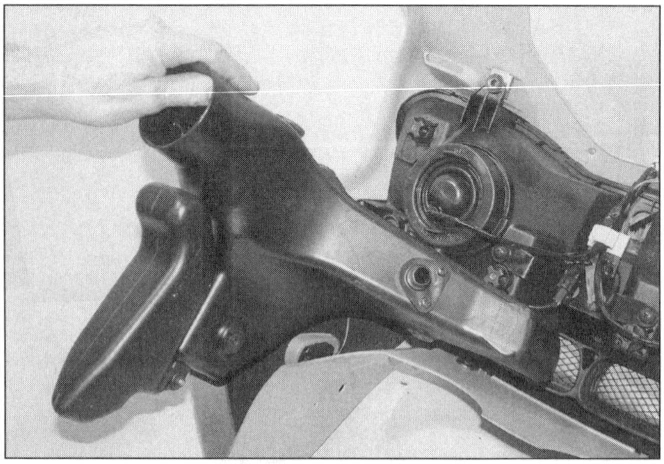

9.2b . . . and lift out the ducts

9 Air intake (J and A models) – removal and installation

Removal

1 Remove the upper fairing (see Section 5).

2 Undo the screws securing the left and right-hand air intake ducts to the fairing and lift out the ducts **(see illustrations)**.

3 Unscrew the two trim clips on the underside of the fairing and the trim clip on the underside of the headlight unit, then pull out the intake grille **(see illustrations)**.

Installation

4 Installation is the reverse of removal. Before fitting the trip clips, ensure the locating holes are correctly aligned. Press the clip tabs together then insert the clip into the hole. Press the trim clip in firmly, then push the clip centre in to lock the clip in place.

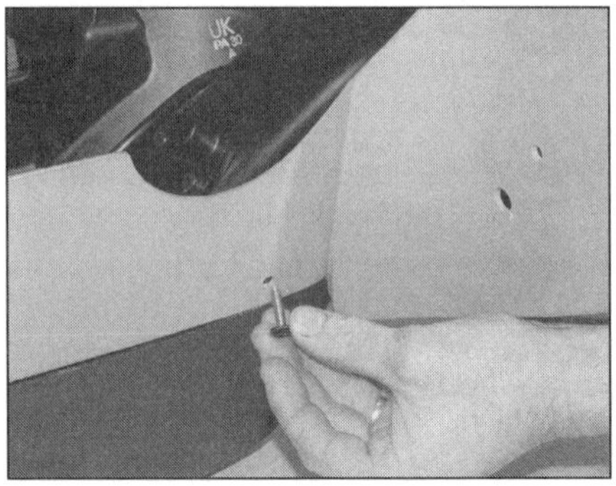

9.3a Unscrew the left and right-hand trim clips . . .

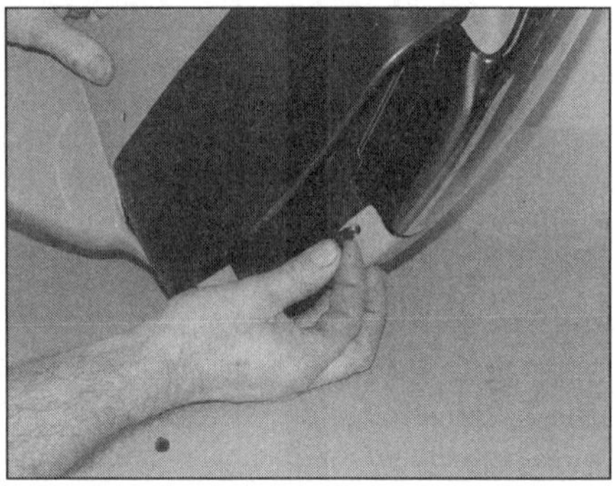

9.3b . . . and the trim clip under the headlight unit . . .

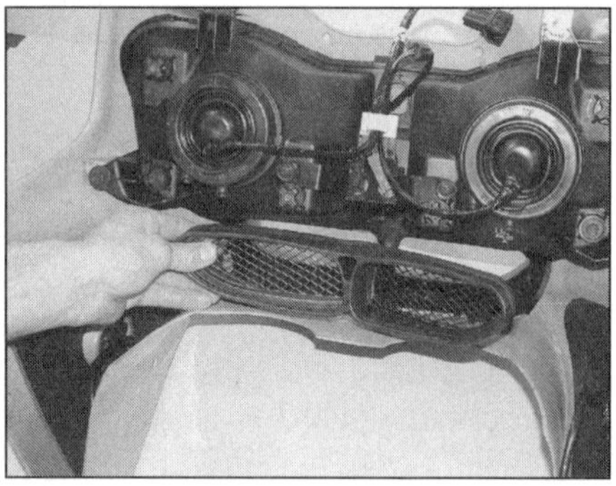

9.3c . . . then pull out the intake grille

Chapter 9
Electrical system

Contents

Degrees of difficulty

Easy, suitable for novice with little experience	**Fairly easy,** suitable for beginner with some experience	**Fairly difficult,** suitable for competent DIY mechanic	**Difficult,** suitable for experienced DIY mechanic	**Very difficult,** suitable for expert DIY or professional

Specifications

Battery

Capacity	
F models	12 V, 10 Ah
G, H, J and A models	12 V, 8 Ah
Voltage	
Fully charged	
F models	12.6 V or more
G, H, J and A models	12.8 V or more
Uncharged	
F models	less than 12.6 V
G and H models	less than 12.8 V
J and A models	less than 12.6 V
Charging rate	
F models	
Normal	1.2 A for 5 to 10 hrs
Quick	5.0 A for 1 hr
G, H, J and A models	
Normal	0.9 A for 5 to 10 hrs
Quick	4.0 A for 1 hr
Current leakage	1 mA (max)

Starter motor

Brush length	
F models	
Standard	12.0 mm
Service limit (min)	8.5 mm
G, H, J and A models	
Standard	7.0 mm
Service limit (min)	3.5 mm
Commutator diameter	
F models	
Standard	28.0 mm
Service limit (min)	27.0 mm
G, H, J and A models	
Standard	24.0 mm
Service limit (min)	23.0 mm

Alternator

Stator coil resistance	
F models	0.2 to 0.6 ohms
G, H, J and A models	0.3 to 0.4 ohms
Unregulated voltage output	
F models	45 V or more
G and H models	42.5 to 57.5 V @ 4000 rpm
J and A models	53.5 to 72.5 V @ 4000 rpm
Regulated voltage output	
F models	14 to 15 V
G, H, J and A models	14.2 to 15.2 V

Fuses

Main fuse	30 A
Accessory fuse	10 A
Fan fuse	10 A
Turn signal fuse	10 A
Horn fuse	10 A
Ignition fuse	10 A
Headlight fuse	10 A
Headlight relay fuse – J and A models	20 A
Tail light fuse	10 A

Bulbs

Headlight	60/55 W H4 halogen
Sidelight (UK models)	5.0 W
Brake/tail light	
UK models	21/5 W
US models	27/8 W
Turn signal lights	
UK models	21 W
US models	23 W
Instrument and warning lights – F models	
Instrument lights	1.7 W
Turn signal indicator light	3.4 W
Neutral indicator light	3.4 W
Oil pressure indicator light	3.4 W
High beam indicator light	3.4 W
Instrument and warning lights – G and H models	
Instrument lights	2 W
Turn signal indicator light	2 W
Neutral indicator light	2 W
Oil pressure indicator light	2 W
High beam indicator light	2 W
Instrument and warning lights – J and A models	
Instrument lights	0.7 W
Turn signal indicator light	1.1 W
Neutral indicator light	1.1 W
Oil pressure indicator light	1.1 W
High beam indicator light	1.1 W

Torque settings

Alternator cover bolts	12 Nm
Alternator rotor bolt	
F models	110 Nm
G and H models	120 Nm
J and A models	
Initial torque	70 Nm
Final torque	120 Nm
Alternator stator coil bolts	12 Nm
Alternator wiring clamp bolts	
F, G and H models	8.3 Nm
J and A models	7.0 Nm
Neutral switch	15 Nm
Oil pressure switch	15 Nm
Starter motor mounting bolts	
F models	9.8 Nm
G and H models	11 Nm
J and A models	12 Nm

1 General information

All models have a 12-volt electrical system charged by a three-phase alternator with a separate regulator/rectifier.

The regulator maintains the charging system output within the specified range to prevent overcharging, and the rectifier converts the ac (alternating current) output of the alternator to dc (direct current) to power the lights and other components and to charge the battery. The alternator rotor is mounted on the left-hand end of the crankshaft.

The starter motor is mounted on the top of the crankcase behind the cylinder block. The starting system includes the motor, the battery, the relay and the various wires and switches. If the engine kill switch is in the RUN position and the ignition (main) switch is ON, the starter relay allows the starter motor to operate only if the transmission is in neutral (neutral switch on) or, if the transmission is in gear and the clutch lever is pulled into the handlebar and the sidestand is up.

Note: *Keep in mind that electrical parts, once purchased, cannot be returned. To avoid unnecessary expense, make very sure the faulty component has been positively identified before buying a replacement part.*

2 Electrical system – fault finding

Warning: To prevent the risk of short circuits, the ignition (main) switch must always be OFF and the battery negative (-ve) terminal should be disconnected before any of the bike's other electrical components are disturbed. Don't forget to reconnect the terminal securely once work is finished or if battery power is needed for circuit testing.

1 A typical electrical circuit consists of an electrical component, the switches, relays, etc. related to that component and the wiring and connectors that hook the component to both the battery and the frame. To aid in locating a problem in any electrical circuit, refer to *Wiring diagrams* at the end of this Chapter.

2 Before tackling any troublesome electrical circuit, first study the wiring diagram (see end of Chapter) thoroughly to get a complete picture of what makes up that individual circuit. Trouble spots, for instance, can often be narrowed down by noting if other components related to that circuit are operating properly or not. If several components or circuits fail at one time, chances are the fault lies in the fuse or earth (ground) connection, as several circuits often are routed through the same fuse and earth (ground) connections.

3 Electrical problems often stem from simple causes, such as loose or corroded connections or a blown fuse. Prior to any electrical fault finding, always visually check the condition of the fuse, wires and connections in the problem circuit. Intermittent failures can be especially frustrating, since you can't always duplicate the failure when it's convenient to test. In such situations, a good practice is to clean all connections in the affected circuit, whether or not they appear to be good. All of the connections and wires should also be wiggled to check for looseness which can cause intermittent failure.

4 If testing instruments are going to be utilised, use the wiring diagram to plan where you will make the necessary connections in order to accurately pinpoint the trouble spot.

5 The basic tools needed for electrical fault finding include a battery and bulb test circuit, a continuity tester, a test light, and a jumper wire. A multimeter capable of reading volts, ohms and amps is also very useful as an alternative to the above, and is necessary for performing more extensive tests and checks.

HAYNES HINT *Refer to Fault Finding Equipment in the Reference section for details of how to use electrical test equipment.*

3 Battery – removal, installation, inspection and maintenance

Caution: Be extremely careful when handling or working around the battery. The electrolyte is very caustic and an explosive gas (hydrogen) is given off when the battery is charging.

Removal and installation

1 On F models, remove the two screws securing the front of the side panels to the fuel tank bracket, then remove the bolts securing the rear of the fuel tank, noting the earth (ground) wire secured by the left-hand bolt **(see illustration)**.

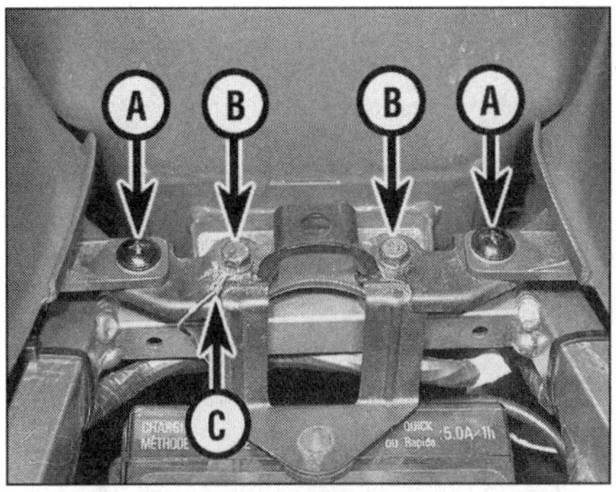

3.1a Unscrew the side panel bolts (A) and the fuel tank bolts (B), noting the earth wire (C) . . .

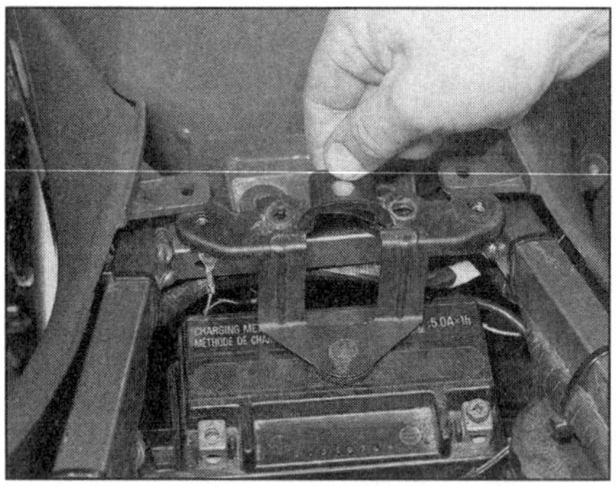

3.1b . . . and remove the bracket

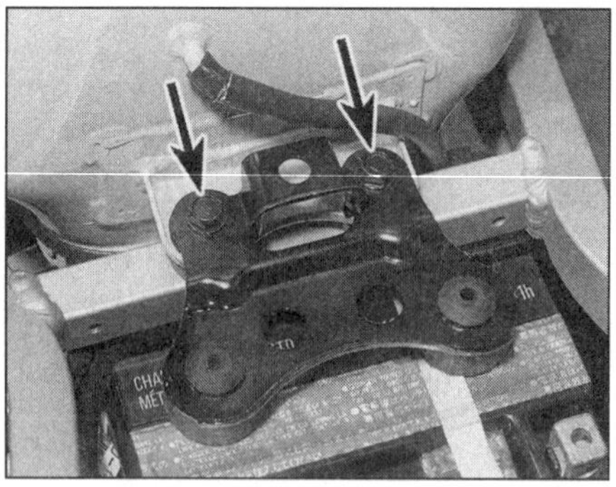

3.2 Unscrew the two bolts (arrowed) and remove the bracket

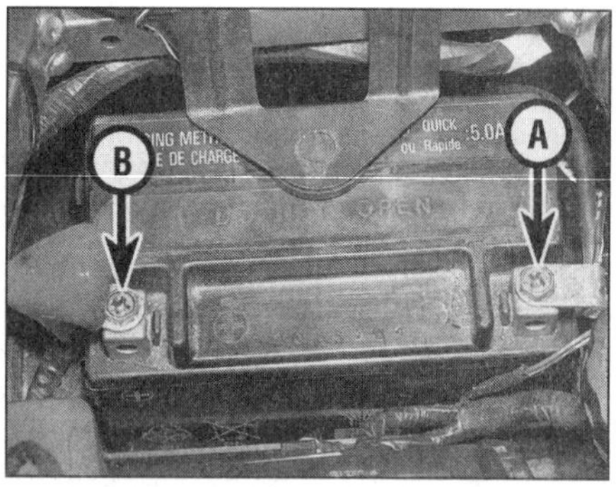

3.3a Unscrew the negative terminal bolt (A) first, then the positive terminal bolt (B) . . .

Remove the bracket, noting how it fits **(see illustration)**.

2 On G, H, J and A models, remove the two bolts securing the rear of the fuel tank and remove the bracket **(see illustration)**.

3 Unscrew the negative (-ve) terminal bolt first and disconnect the lead from the battery **(see illustration)**. Lift up the red insulating cover to access the positive (+ve) terminal, then unscrew the bolt and disconnect the lead. Lift the battery out of the bike **(see illustration)**.

4 On installation, clean the battery terminals and lead ends with a wire brush, knife, or steel wool. Reconnect the leads, connecting the positive (+ve) terminal first.

> **HAYNES HiNT** ***Battery corrosion can be kept to a minimum by applying a layer of petroleum jelly to the terminals after the cables have been connected.***

5 Install the bracket and tighten the fuel tank bolts. On F models, don't forget to secure the earth (ground) wire with the left-hand bolt **(see illustration)**. On F models install the side panel screws **(see illustration 3.1a)**.

Inspection and maintenance

6 The battery fitted to the models covered in this manual is of the maintenance free (sealed) type, therefore requiring no regular maintenance. However, the following checks should still be regularly performed.

7 Check the battery terminals and leads for tightness and corrosion. If corrosion is evident, unscrew the terminal bolts and disconnect the leads from the battery, disconnecting the negative (-ve) terminal first. Clean the terminals and lead ends with a wire brush, knife or steel wool. Reconnect the leads, connecting the negative (-ve) terminal last, and apply a thin coat of petroleum jelly to the connections to slow further corrosion.

8 The battery case should be kept clean to prevent current leakage, which can discharge the battery over a period of time (especially when it sits unused). Wash the outside of the case with a solution of baking soda and water. Rinse the battery thoroughly, then dry it.

9 Look for cracks in the case and replace the battery if any are found. If acid has been spilled on the frame or battery box, neutralise it with a baking soda and water solution, dry it thoroughly, then touch up any damaged paint.

10 If the motorcycle sits unused for long periods of time, disconnect the leads from the battery terminals, negative (-ve) terminal first. Refer to Section 4 and charge the battery once every month to six weeks.

11 The condition of the battery can be assessed by measuring the voltage present at the battery terminals. Connect the voltmeter (set to the 0 – 20 dc volts range) positive (+ve) probe to the battery positive (+ve) terminal, and the negative (-ve) probe to the battery negative (-ve) terminal. When fully charged there should be the voltage specified at the beginning of the Chapter. If the voltage falls below this the battery must be removed and recharged as described in Section 4.

4 Battery – charging

Caution: Be extremely careful when handling or working around the battery. The electrolyte is very caustic and an explosive gas (hydrogen) is given off when the battery is charging.

1 Remove the battery (see Section 3). Connect the charger to the battery, making sure that the positive (+ve) lead on the charger is connected to the positive (+ve) terminal on the battery, and the negative (-ve) lead is connected to the negative (-ve) terminal.

2 Charge the battery at the rate specified at the beginning of the Chapter. Exceeding this figure can cause the battery to overheat, buckling the plates and rendering it useless. Few owners will have access to an expensive current controlled charger, so if a normal domestic charger is used check that after a possible initial peak, the charge rate falls to a safe level **(see illustration)**. If the battery becomes hot during charging **stop**. Further charging will cause damage. **Note:** *In*

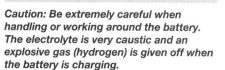

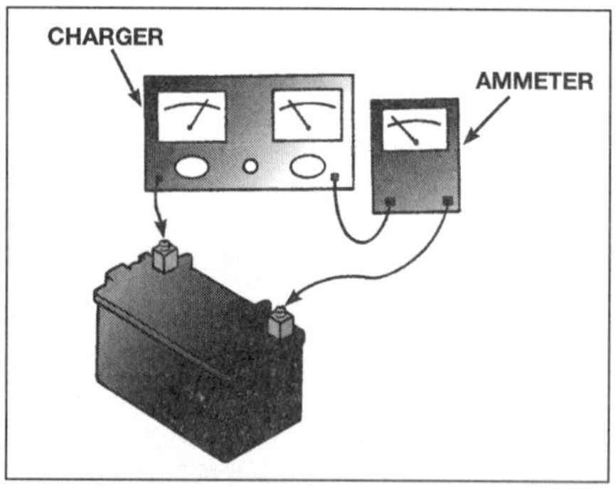

4.2 If the charger doesn't have an ammeter built in, connect one in series as shown. DO NOT connect the ammeter between the battery terminals or it will be ruined

3.3b . . . and remove the battery

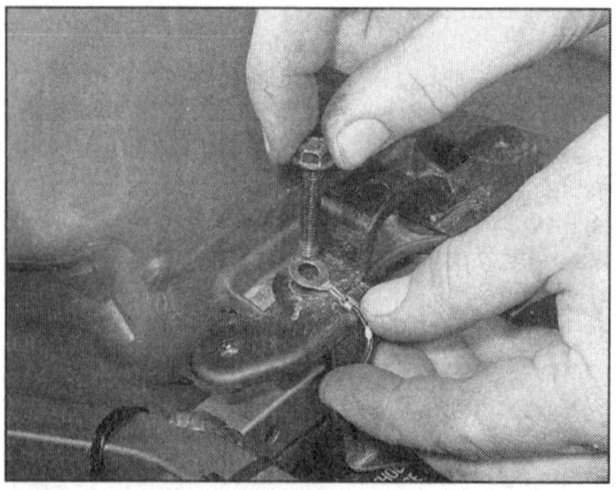

3.5 On F models secure the earth wire with the left-hand tank bolt

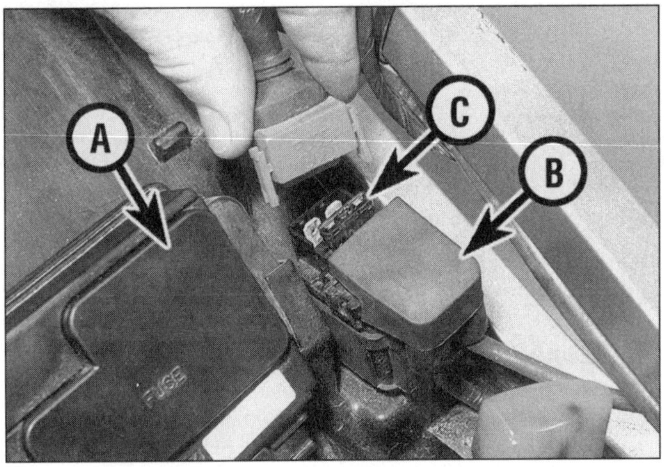

5.1a Fusebox (A), starter relay (B), main fuse (C)

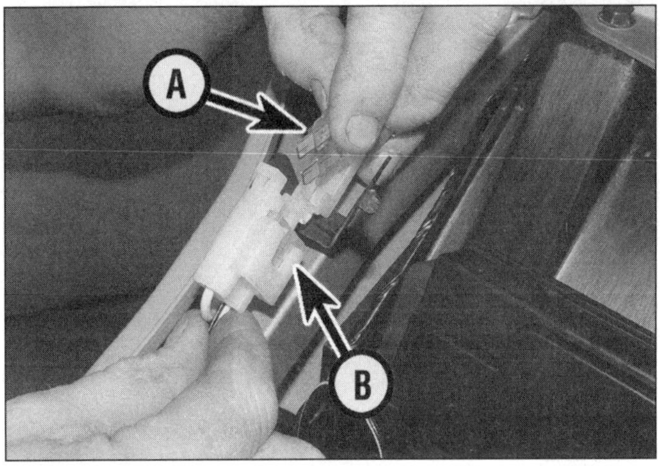

5.1b Headlight relay fuse (A) and spare fuse (B) – J and A models

emergencies the battery can be charged at the specified higher rate for a period of 1 hour. However, this is not recommended and the low amp charge is by far the safer method of charging the battery.

3 If the recharged battery discharges rapidly if left disconnected it is likely that an internal short caused by physical damage or sulphation has occurred. A new battery will be required. A sound item will tend to lose its charge at about 1% per day.

4 Install the battery (see Section 3).

5 If the motorcycle sits unused for long periods of time, charge the battery once every month to six weeks and leave it disconnected.

5 Fuses – check and replacement

1 The electrical system is protected by fuses of different ratings. All except the main fuse and, on J and A models the headlight relay fuse, are housed in the fusebox, which is located under the rider's seat **(see illustration)**. The main fuse is integral with the starter relay, which is to the left of the fusebox. On J and A models, the headlight relay fuse is behind the right-hand side panel **(see illustration)**.

2 To access the fuses, remove the seats (see Chapter 8) and unclip the fusebox lid **(see illustration)**. To access the main fuse, disconnect the starter relay wiring connector **(see illustration 5.1a)**.

3 The fuses can be removed and checked visually **(see illustration)**. If you can't pull the fuse out with your fingertips, use a pair of suitable pliers. A blown fuse is easily identified by a break in the element **(see illustration)**. Each fuse is clearly marked with its rating and must only be replaced by a fuse of the correct rating. A spare fuse of each rating is housed in the fusebox. If a spare fuse is used, always replace it so that a spare of each rating is carried on the bike at all times.

Warning: Never put in a fuse of a higher rating or bridge the terminals with any other substitute, however temporary it may be. Serious damage may be done to the circuit, or a fire may start.

4 If a fuse blows, be sure to check the wiring circuit very carefully for evidence of a short-circuit. Look for bare wires and chafed, melted or burned insulation. If the fuse is replaced before the cause is located, the new fuse will blow immediately.

5 Occasionally a fuse will blow or cause an open-circuit for no obvious reason. Corrosion of the fuse ends and fusebox terminals may occur and cause a poor contact. If this happens, remove the corrosion with a wire brush or steel wool, then spray the fuse end and terminals with electrical contact cleaner.

6 Refer to Section 25 for details of fuse circuit testing via the junction box connector.

6 Lighting system – check

1 The battery provides power for operation of the headlight, tail light, brake light and instrument cluster lights. If none of the lights operate, always check battery voltage before proceeding. Low battery voltage indicates either a faulty battery or a defective charging system. Refer to Section 3 for battery checks and Sections 30 and 31 for charging system tests. Also, check the condition of the fuses (see Section 5) and the headlight relay(s) (see Step 2).

Headlight

2 If the headlight fails to work, first check the fuse (see Section 5). If the fuse is good,

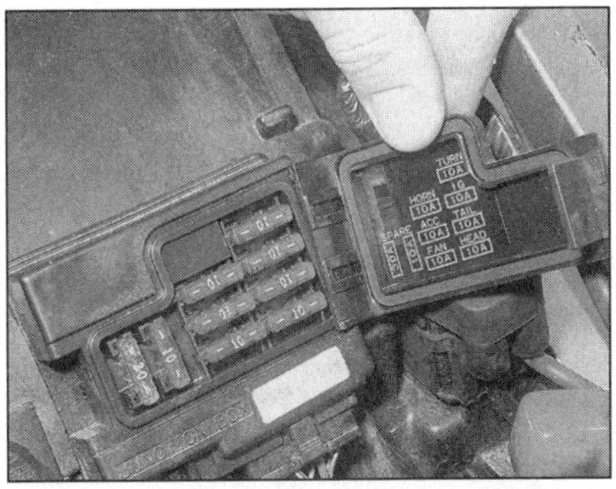

5.2 Unclip the lid to access the fuses in the fusebox

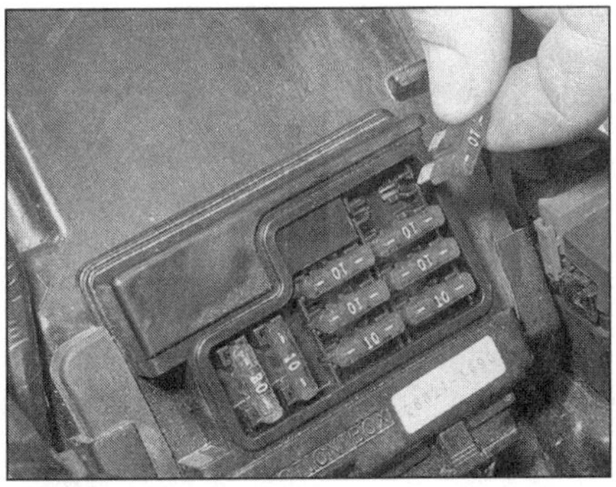

5.3a Remove the fuse and check it

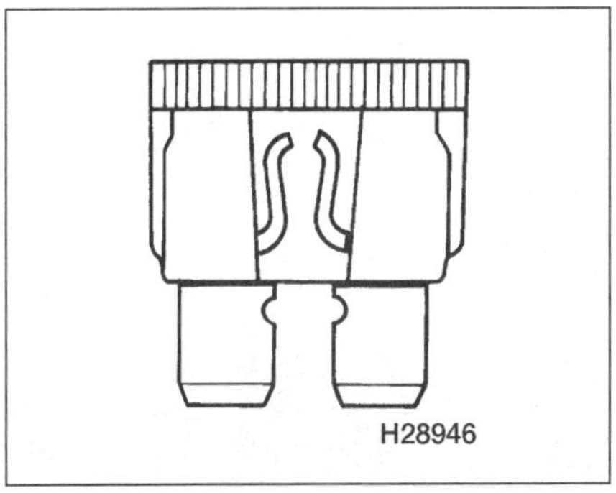

5.3b A blown fuse can be identified by a break in its element

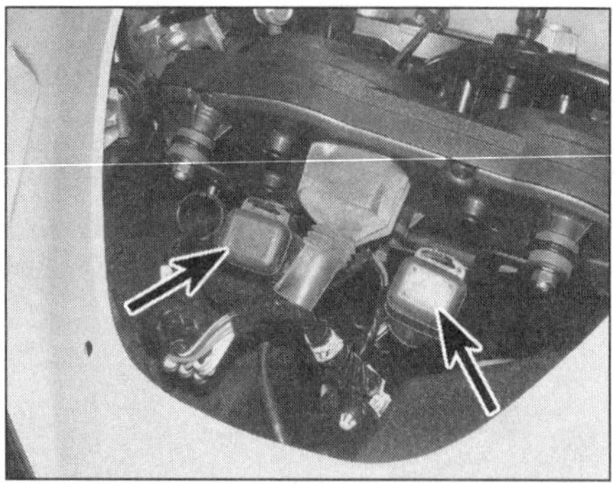

6.4a Headlight relay locations (arrowed) – J and A models

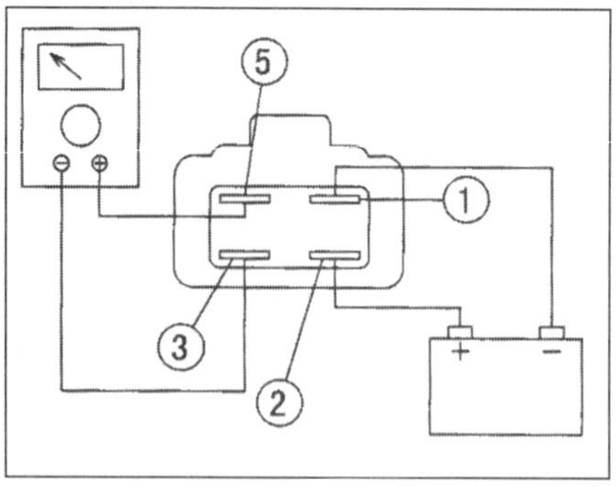

6.4b Headlight relay test – J and A models

Terminal numbering corresponds to text procedure

remove the bulb (see Section 7) and use jumper wires to connect the bulb directly to the battery terminals. If the light comes on, the problem lies in the wiring, one of the switches in the circuit or, where fitted, the relay (see wiring diagrams at the end of this Chapter). Refer to Section 20 for the switch testing procedures.

3 Refer to Section 25 to check the headlight circuit relay in the junction box (US models).

4 The twin headlights of J and A models are controlled through two relays, for high and low beam circuits, mounted on the instrument cluster bracket; remove the windshield (see Chapter 8) to access the relays. Disconnect each relay from its wiring connector and use a multimeter or continuity tester to check for continuity between the relay's No. 3 and No. 5 terminals **(see illustrations)**. There should be no continuity (infinite resistance). Now use jumper wires to connect the positive (+ve) terminal of a 12 volt battery to the relay's No. 2 terminal and the negative (-ve) battery terminal to the relay's No. 1 terminal; there should now be continuity (zero resistance). If there is no continuity, fit a new relay.

Tail light

5 If the tail light fails to work, check the bulbs and the bulb terminals first, then the fuse, then check for battery voltage at the red terminal on the supply side of the tail light wiring connector. If voltage is present, check the earth (ground) circuit for an open or poor connection.

6 If no voltage is indicated, check the wiring between the tail light and the ignition switch, then check the switch. Also check the lighting switch (UK models only).

Brake light

7 If the brake light fails to work, check the bulbs and the bulb terminals first, then the fuse, then check for battery voltage at the blue/red terminal on the supply side of the tail light wiring connector, with the brake lever pulled in or the pedal depressed. If voltage is present, check the earth (ground) circuit for an open or poor connection.

8 If no voltage is indicated, check the brake light switches, then the wiring between the tail light and the switches.

9 See Section 14 for brake switch checks and Section 9 for tail light bulb replacement.

Instrument and warning lights

10 See Section 17 for instrument and warning light bulb replacement.

Turn signal lights

11 See Section 11 for turn signal circuit check.

7 Headlight bulb and sidelight bulb – replacement

Note: *The headlight bulb is of the quartz-halogen type. Do not touch the bulb glass as skin acids will shorten the bulb's service life. If the bulb is accidentally touched, it should be wiped carefully when cold with a rag soaked in methylated spirit and dried before fitting.*

Warning: Allow the bulb time to cool before removing it if the headlight has just been on.

Headlight

1 Disconnect the wiring connector from the back of the headlight assembly and remove the rubber dust cover, noting how it fits **(see illustrations)**.

2 Release the bulb retaining clip, noting how it fits, then remove the bulb **(see illustrations)**.

3 Fit the new bulb, bearing in mind the information in the **Note** above. Make sure the tabs on the bulb fit correctly in the slots in the bulb housing, and secure it in position with the retaining clip.

4 Install the dust cover, making sure it is correctly seated and with the 'TOP' mark at the top, and connect the wiring connector.

5 Check the operation of the headlight.

7.1a Disconnect the wiring connector . . .

7.1b . . . and remove the rubber dust cover

7.2a Release the clip . . .

7.2b . . . and remove the bulb

HAYNES HiNT

Hint: Always use a paper towel or dry cloth when handling new bulbs to prevent injury if the bulb should break and to increase bulb life.

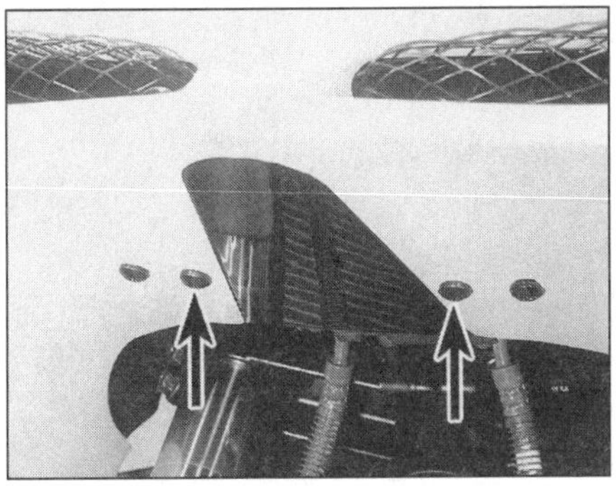

7.6 On G and H models, remove the two screws (arrowed) and remove the access panel

Sidelight (UK models)

6 On F, J and A models, remove the windshield (see Chapter 8). The sidelight is located above the headlight assembly. On G and H models, remove the access panel in the underside of the upper fairing **(see illustration)**. The sidelight is located in the base of the headlight.

7 Pull the bulbholder out of its socket, then carefully pull the bulb out of the holder **(see illustrations)**.

8 Install the new bulb in the bulbholder, then install the bulbholder by pressing it in. Make sure the rubber cover is correctly seated.

9 Check the operation of the sidelight. On F, J and A models, install the windshield (see Chapter 8). On G and H models, install the access panel **(see illustration 7.6)**.

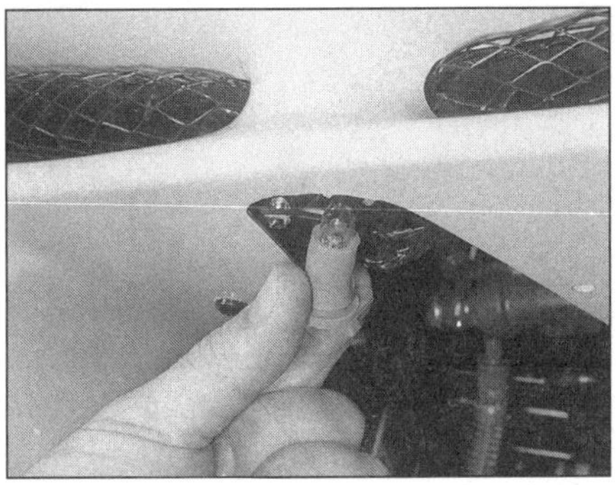

7.7a On G and H models withdraw the bulbholder . . .

8 Headlight assembly – removal and installation

Removal

F, G and H models

1 Remove the upper fairing (see Chapter 8).

2 Remove the four bolts securing the headlight unit to the fairing and remove the headlight, noting how it fits **(see illustrations)**.

J and A models

3 Remove the upper fairing and the air intake grille (see Chapter 8).

4 Undo the bolt on each side of the headlight unit, then lift the unit out of the fairing **(see illustration)**.

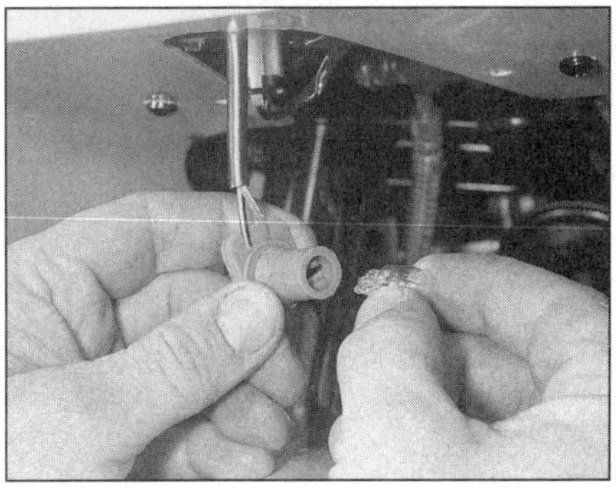

7.7b . . . and pull out the bulb

Installation

5 Installation is the reverse of removal. Make sure all the wiring is correctly connected and secured. Check the operation of the headlight and sidelight. Check the headlight aim (see Chapter 1).

9 Brake/tail light bulbs – replacement

1 Remove the pillion seat (see Chapter 8).

2 Turn the relevant bulbholder anti-clockwise and withdraw it from the tail light **(see illustration)**.

3 Push the bulb into the holder and twist it anti-clockwise to remove it **(see illustration)**.

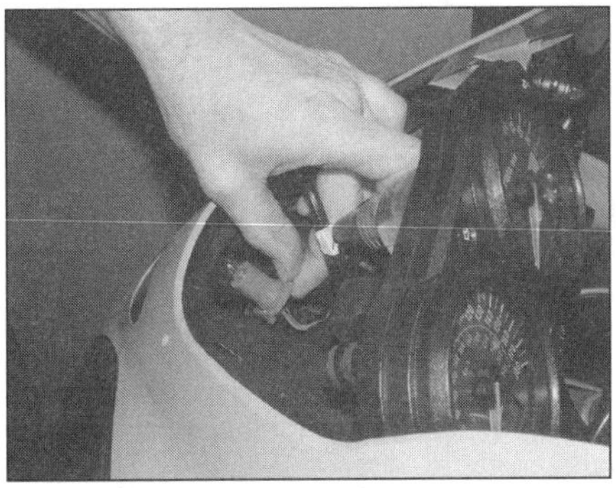

7.7c Sidelight location on J and A models

8.2a Headlight mounting bolts – F models

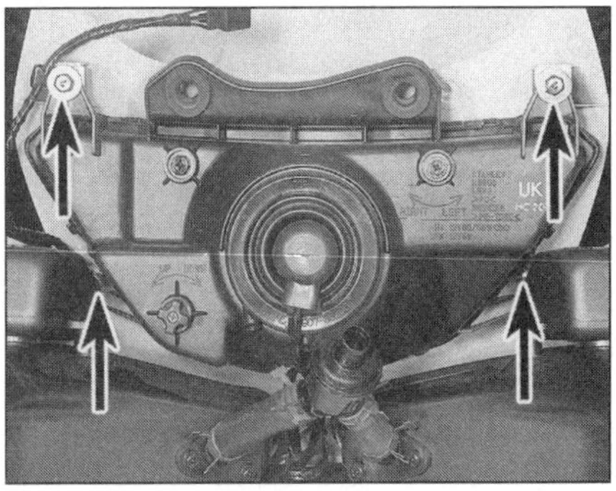

8.2b Headlight mounting bolts – G and H models

8.4 On J and A models the headlight unit is secured by one bolt (arrowed) on each side

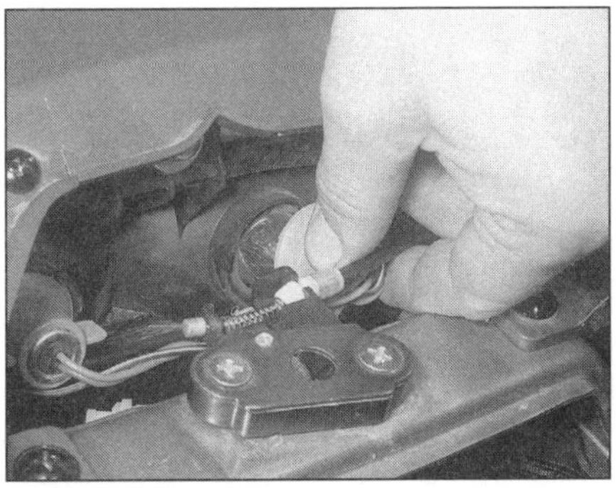

9.2 Remove the bulbholder from the tail light . . .

9.3 . . . and the bulb from the holder

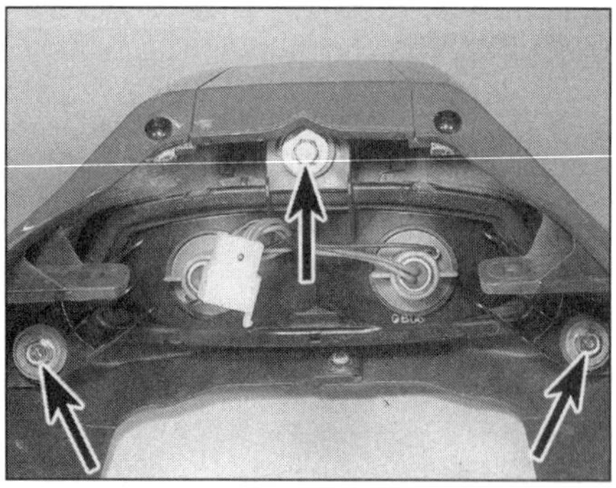

10.2 On F models, the tail light is secured to the side panels by three bolts (arrowed)

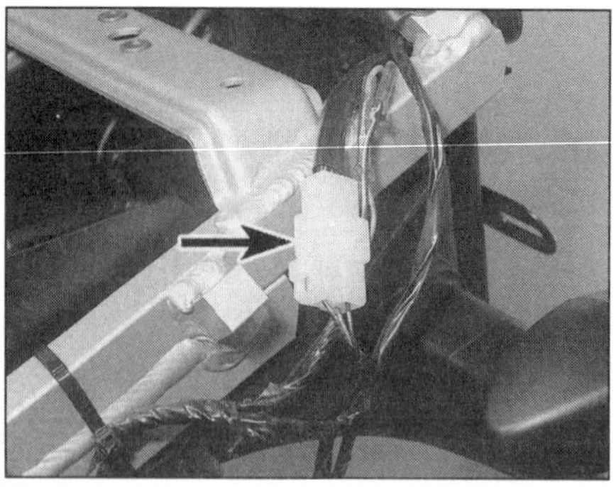

10.3a On G, H, J and A models, disconnect the wiring connector (arrowed) . . .

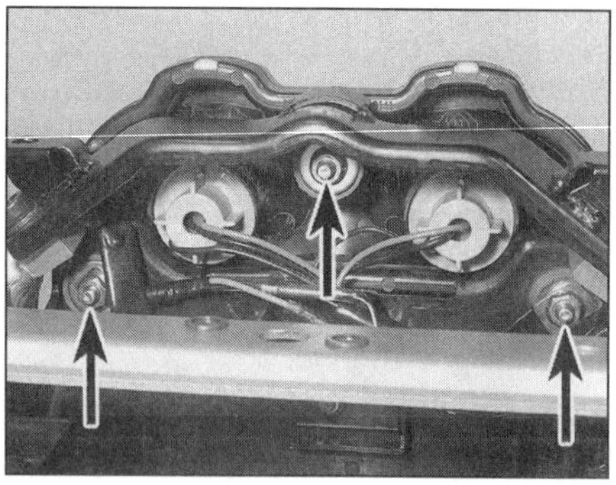

10.3b . . . then unscrew the nuts (arrowed) and remove the tail light from the back

Check the socket terminals for corrosion and clean them if necessary. Line up the pins of the new bulb with the slots in the socket, then push the bulb in and turn it clockwise until it locks into place. **Note:** *The pins on the bulb are offset so it can only be installed one way. It is a good idea to use a paper towel or dry cloth when handling the new bulb to prevent injury if the bulb should break and to increase bulb life.*

4 Install the bulbholder into the tail light and turn it clockwise to secure it.

5 Install the seat (see Chapter 8).

10 Tail light assembly – removal and installation

Removal

1 Remove the side panels (see Chapter 8).

2 On F models, remove the three bolts securing the tail light assembly and carefully withdraw it from the side panels **(see illustration)**. If required, turn the bulbholders anti-clockwise and withdraw them from the tail light.

3 On G, H, J and A models, disconnect the tail light assembly wiring connector, then unscrew the three nuts securing the assembly and remove it **(see illustrations)**. If required, turn the bulbholders anti-clockwise and withdraw them from the tail light.

Installation

4 Installation is the reverse of removal. Check the operation of the tail light bulbs and the brake lights.

11 Turn signal circuit – check

1 The battery provides power for operation of the turn signal lights, so if they do not operate, always check the battery voltage first. Low battery voltage indicates either a faulty battery or a defective charging system. Refer to Section 3 for battery checks and Sections 30 and 31 for charging system tests. Also, check the fuse (see Section 5) and the switch (see Section 20).

2 Most turn signal problems are the result of a burned-out bulb or corroded socket. This is especially true when the turn signals function properly in one direction, but fail to flash in the other direction. Check the bulbs and the sockets (see Section 12).

3 If the bulbs and sockets are good, remove the seats (see Chapter 8) to access the turn signal relay **(se illustrations)**. Disconnect the relay wiring connector, then turn the ignition ON and check for power at the brown/red (F models) or brown/yellow (G, H, J and A models) wire terminal in the connector. Turn the ignition OFF when the check is complete.

4 If no power is present at the relay, check the wiring from the relay to the ignition (main) switch for continuity.

5 If power was present at the relay, using the appropriate wiring diagram at the end of this Chapter, check the wiring between the relay, turn signal switch and turn signal lights for continuity. If the wiring and switch are sound, replace the relay with a new one.

6 If the turn signals work, but do so either too fast or too slow, and the bulbs, wiring and switches are all good, count the number of flashes in one minute – there should be between 75 and 95. If not, replace the relay with a new one.

12 Turn signal bulbs – replacement

1 Remove the screw securing the turn signal lens and remove the lens, noting how it fits **(see illustration)**. Remove the rubber gasket if it is free, and discard it if it is damaged or deteriorated.

2 Push the bulb into the holder and twist it

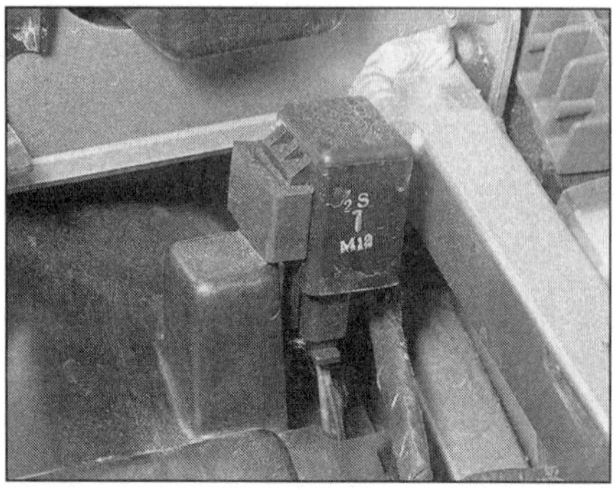

11.3a Turn signal relay – F models

11.3b Turn signal relay – G, H, J and A models

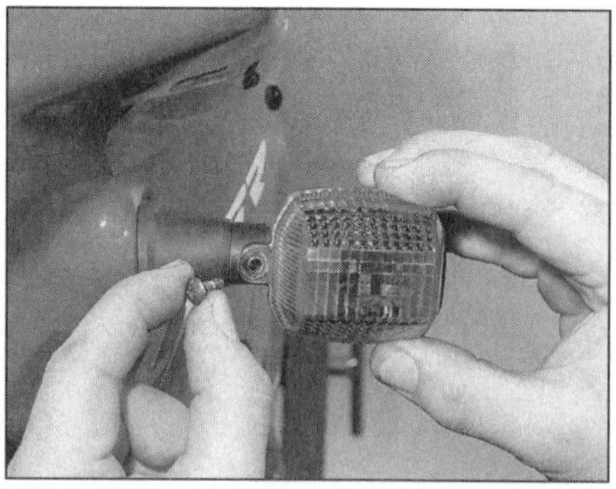

12.1 Remove the screw and detach the lens – F models . . .

anti-clockwise to remove it **(see illustration)**. Check the socket terminals for corrosion and clean them if necessary. Line up the pins of the new bulb with the slots in the socket, then push the bulb in and turn it clockwise until it locks into place.

3 Fit the lens onto the holder, using a new rubber gasket if required, and make sure it is properly seated and not pinched by the lens.

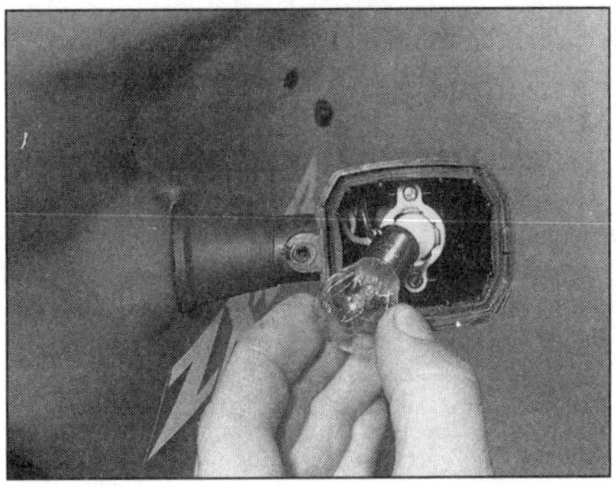

12.2 . . . then remove the bulb

13 Turn signal assemblies – removal and installation

Removal

1 To remove a front turn signal, first remove the upper fairing, then remove the screws securing the air intake duct to the inside of the fairing and remove the relevant duct (see Chapter 8). Now remove the screw securing the outer mounting plate and remove the plate, noting how it fits, then lever out the inner plate, again noting how it fits **(see illustrations)**. Remove the turn signal and feed the wiring through **(see illustration)**. If required, unscrew the nut securing the turn signal to the stalk and separate them **(see illustration)**.

2 To remove a rear turn signal, first remove the pillion seat (see Chapter 8) and disconnect the relevant wiring connectors **(see illustration)**. Unscrew the nut securing the turn signal to the inside of the mudguard **(see illustration)**. Remove the turn signal, noting the arrangement of the mounting base and damper, and feed the wiring through. If required, separate the turn signal from the stalk.

Installation

3 Installation is the reverse of removal. Check the operation of the turn signals.

14 Brake light switches – check and renewal

Circuit check

1 Before checking any electrical circuit, check the bulb (see Section 9) and tail light fuse (see Section 5).

2 Using a multimeter or test light connected to a good earth (ground), check for voltage at the brake light switch wiring connector **(see illustration 14.6 or 14.9b)**. On the front brake switch, the connectors fit directly onto the switch itself, however both wires are black so it may be necessary to test both wires before it is known which is the feed wire. Alternatively, disconnect the handlebar switch wiring connector (see Section 20) and trace the wire from the brake switch which joins the red/blue wire on the loom side of the main connector (see the *Wiring diagrams* at the end of this Chapter). When testing the rear brake switch, remove the seat (see Chapter 8), then trace the wiring from the switch to the connector and check for voltage at the brown terminal on the switch side of the connector (which must be still connected).

3 If there's no voltage present, check the wire between the switch and the ignition switch (see the *Wiring diagrams* at the end of this Chapter).

4 If voltage is available, touch the probe of the test light to the other terminal of the switch, then pull the brake lever in or depress the brake pedal. If no reading is obtained or the test light doesn't light up, renew the switch.

5 If a reading is obtained or the test light does light up, check the wiring between the switch and the brake light bulb (see the *Wiring diagrams* at the end of this Chapter).

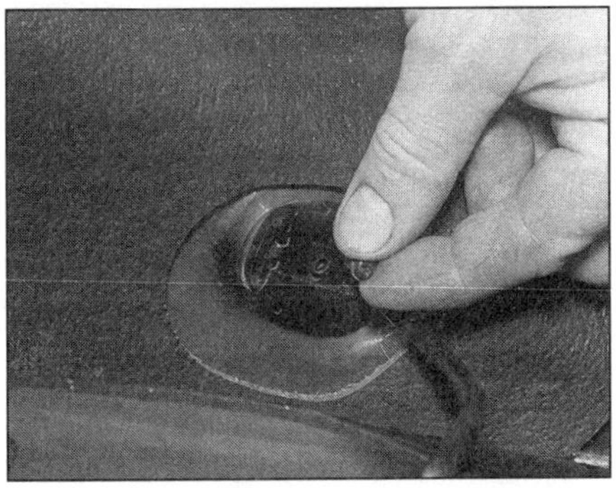

13.1a Remove the screw and the outer plate . . .

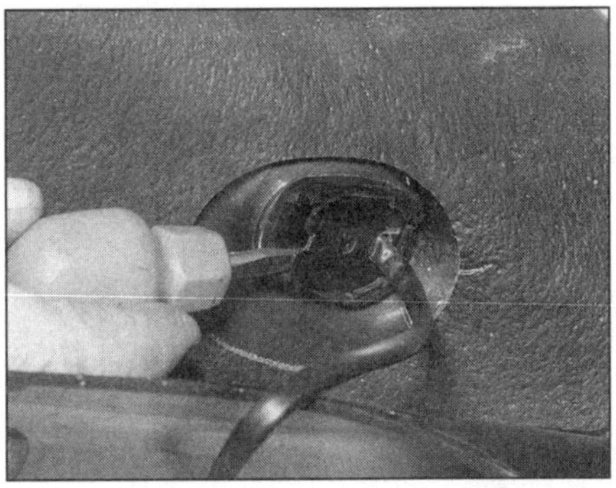

13.1b . . . then lever out the inner plate . . .

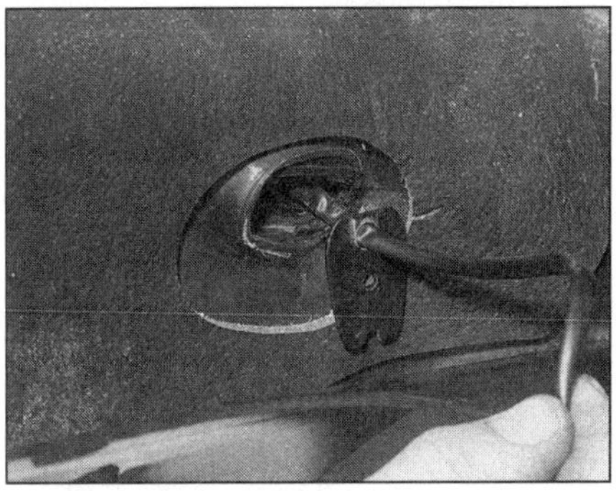

13.1c . . . and draw the wiring through

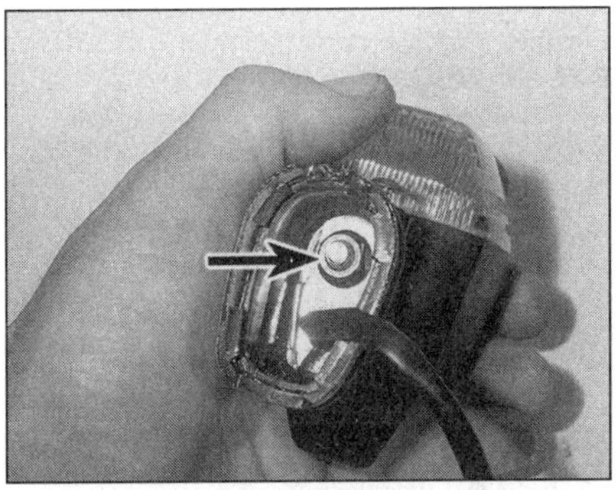

13.1d If required, unscrew the nut (arrowed) and separate the turn signal from its stalk

13.2a Disconnect the relevant wiring connectors . . .

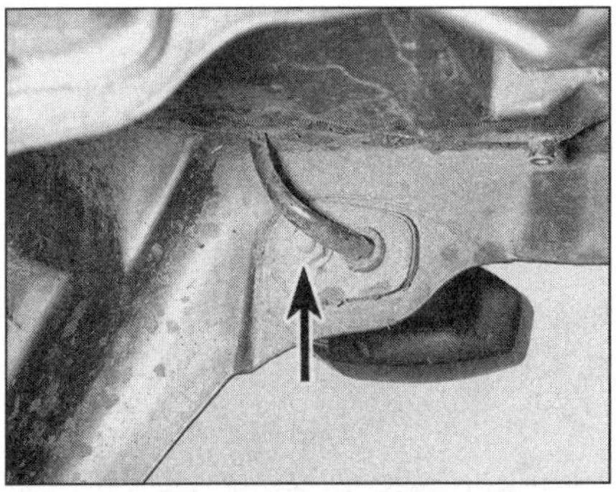

13.2b . . . then unscrew the nut (arrowed) and remove the turn signal

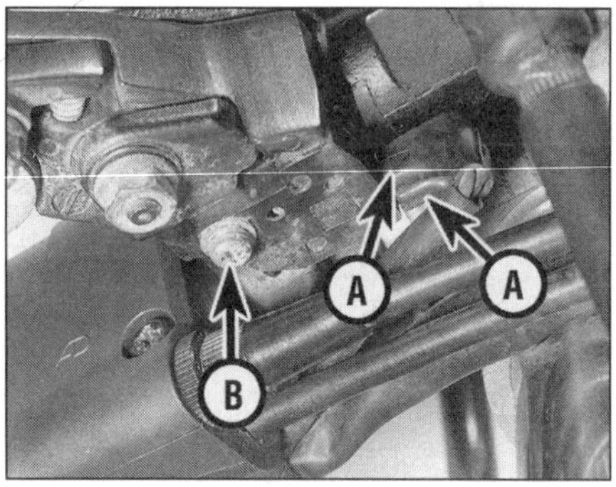

14.6 Front brake light switch wiring connectors (A) and mounting screw (B)

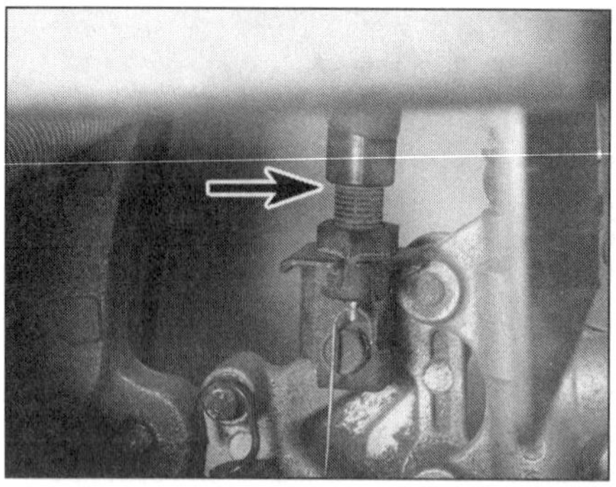
14.9a Rear brake light switch (arrowed)

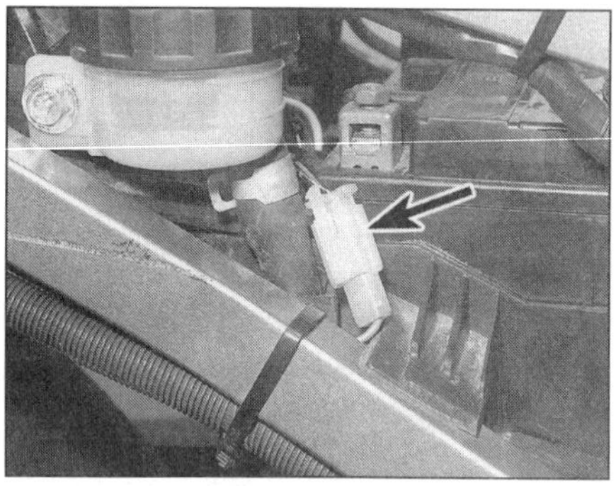
14.9b Disconnect the brake light switch wiring connector

Switch renewal

Front brake lever switch

6 The switch is mounted on the underside of the brake master cylinder. Disconnect the wiring connectors from the switch **(see illustration)**.

7 Remove the single screw securing the switch to the bottom of the master cylinder and remove the switch **(see illustration 14.6)**.

8 Installation is the reverse of removal. The switch isn't adjustable.

Rear brake pedal switch

9 The switch is mounted on the inside of the right-hand footrest bracket **(see illustration)**. Remove the seat for access to the connector (see Chapter 8). Trace the wiring from the switch and disconnect it at the connector **(see illustration)**.

10 Detach the lower end of the switch spring from the brake pedal, then unscrew and remove the switch. If access to the switch is too restricted, unscrew the two bolts securing the rider's right-hand footrest bracket to the frame, then swing the whole footrest/rear brake master cylinder assembly out, making sure no strain is placed on the brake and reservoir hoses.

11 Installation is the reverse of removal. If removed, tighten the footrest bracket bolts securely. Make sure the brake light is activated just before the rear brake pedal takes effect. If adjustment is necessary, hold the switch and turn the adjusting ring on the switch body until the brake light is activated when required.

15 Instrument cluster and speedometer cable – removal and installation

Instrument cluster

Removal

1 On F models, remove the upper fairing (see Chapter 8). On G, H, J and A models, it is only necessary to remove the windshield (see Chapter 8), though it is advisable to remove the entire upper fairing to avoid the possibility of damaging it should a spanner slip when unscrewing the nuts securing the cluster.

2 On F models, unscrew the knurled ring securing the speedometer cable to the back of the speedometer and detach the cable **(see illustration 15.8)**.

3 On F models, cut the cable tie securing the cluster wiring and disconnect the wiring connectors **(see illustration)**. On G, H, J and A models, draw back the rubber boot and disconnect wiring connector from the cluster **(see illustrations)**. On G and H models, if the connector is tight and difficult to pull off, disconnect it after displacing the cluster from its bracket.

4 Unscrew the three nuts securing the instrument cluster and carefully lift it away **(see illustrations)**.

Caution: Do not store the instrument cluster on its face or side – keep it the right way up or it could be damaged.

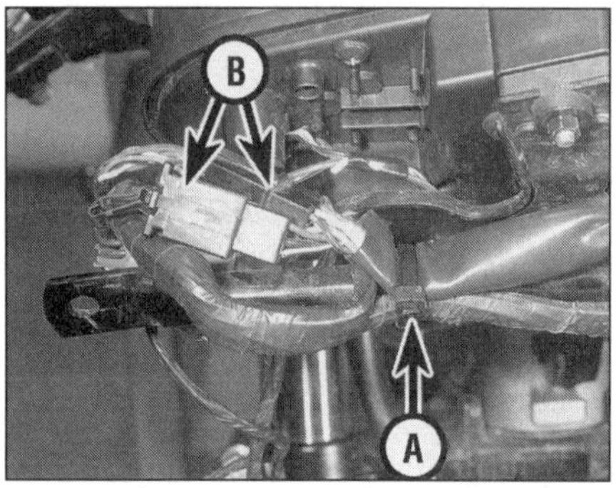

15.3a On F models, cut the cable tie (A) and disconnect the wiring connectors (B)

15.3b On G and H models, pull back the rubber boot and disconnect the wiring connector (arrowed)

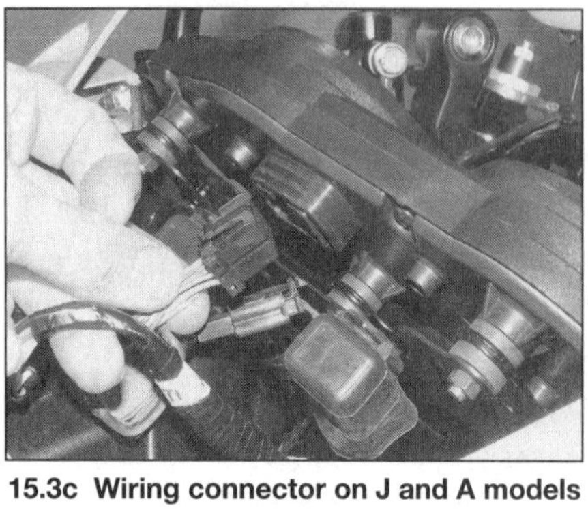
15.3c Wiring connector on J and A models

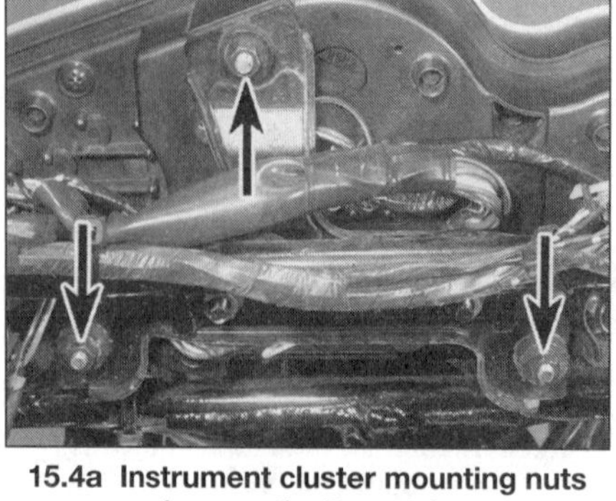
15.4a Instrument cluster mounting nuts (arrowed) – F models

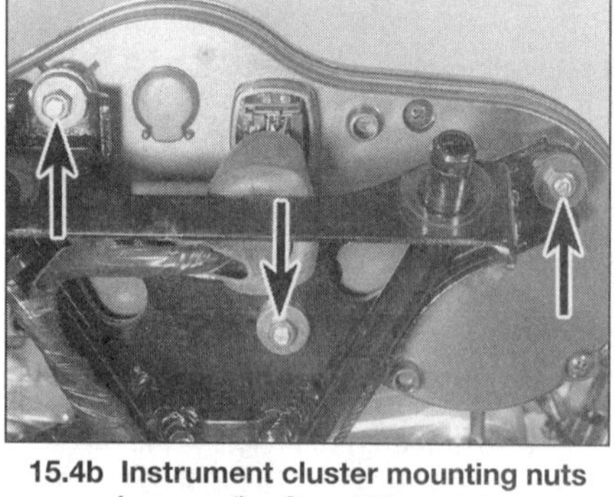
15.4b Instrument cluster mounting nuts (arrowed) – G and H models

15.4c Instrument cluster mounting nuts (arrowed) – J and A models

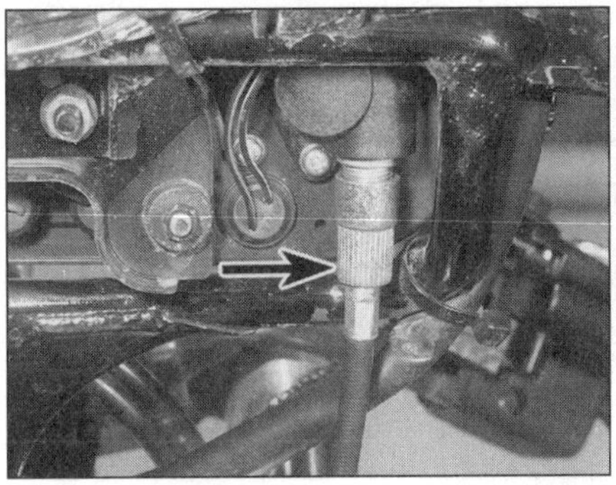

15.8 Unscrew the knurled ring (arrowed) and detach the cable from the instrument cluster . . .

15.9 . . . and the drive housing on the front wheel

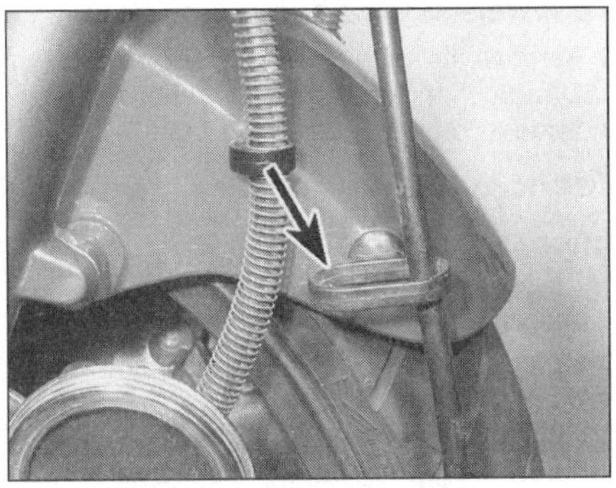

15.10 Withdraw the cable from its guide (arrowed)

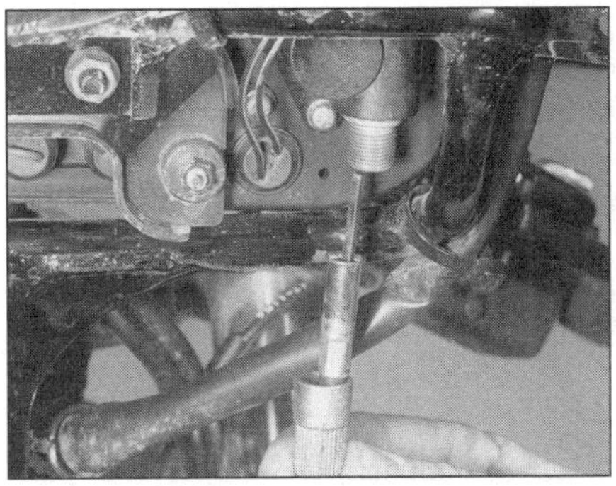

15.12 Fit the cable into the instrument cluster and tighten the ring

15.13 Align the slot in the end of the cable with the drive tab in the housing

5 Check the condition of the rubber mounting grommets in the bracket and replace them if they are damaged, hardened or deteriorated.

Installation

6 Installation is the reverse of removal. Make sure that the speedometer cable (where fitted) and wiring connectors are correctly routed and secured.

Speedometer cable (F models)

Removal

7 Remove the upper fairing (see Chapter 8).

8 Unscrew the knurled ring securing the speedometer cable to the back of the speedometer and detach the cable **(see illustration)**.

9 Unscrew the knurled ring securing the speedometer cable to the drive housing on the front wheel and detach the cable **(see illustration)**.

10 Withdraw the cable, releasing it from its guide on the front mudguard, and remove it from the bike, noting its correct routing **(see illustration)**.

Installation

11 Route the cable up through its guide to the back of the instrument cluster.

12 Connect the cable upper end to the speedometer and tighten the retaining ring securely **(see illustration)**.

13 Connect the cable lower end to the drive housing, aligning the slot in the cable end with the drive tab, and tighten the retaining ring securely **(see illustration)**.

14 Check that the cable doesn't restrict steering movement or interfere with any other components.

16 Instruments – check and renewal

Speedometer

Check – F models

1 Special instruments are required to properly check the operation of this meter. If it is believed to be faulty, take the motorcycle to a Kawasaki dealer for assessment.

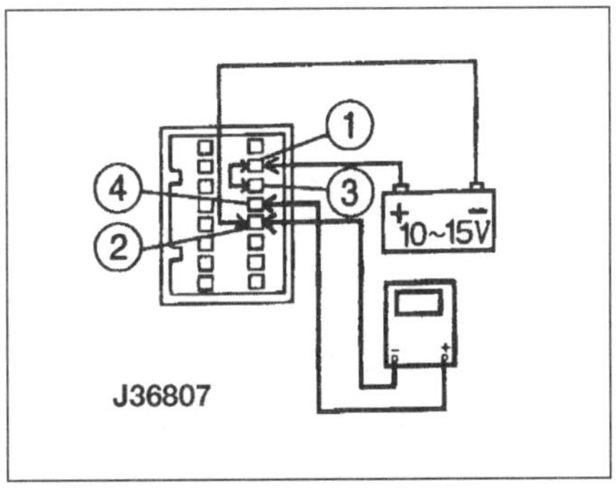

16.2a Speedometer test set-up – G and H models

Terminal numbering corresponds to text procedure

Check – G, H, J and A models

Note: *The connector terminals on the instrument cluster are very closely spaced – take great care when connecting test wires to them.*

2 Remove the instrument cluster (see Section 15). Using a 12V battery, connect the battery positive terminal to the No. 1 terminal on the cluster wiring connector, and the battery negative terminal to the No. 2 terminal **(see illustrations)**. Using a jumper wire, connect between the No. 1 and No. 3 terminals to form a bridge. Using a voltmeter set to the 25V range, connect the positive probe to the No. 4 terminal and the negative probe to the No. 2 terminal. If the voltage reading is less than 7V, the speedometer is faulty.

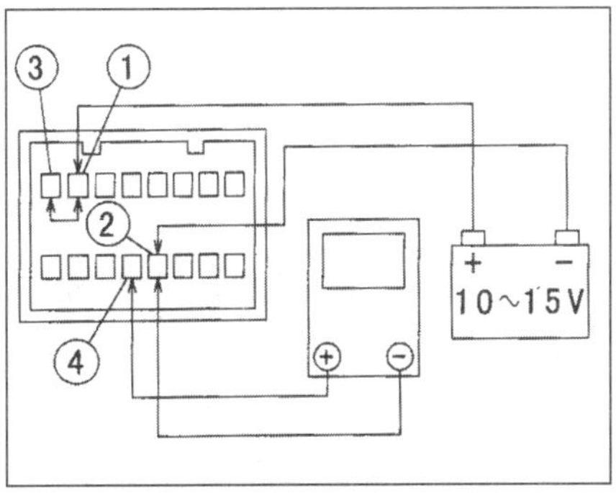

16.2b Speedometer test set-up – J and A models

Terminal numbering corresponds to text procedure

9

16.5a Remove the screw . . .

16.5b . . . and detach the trip knob

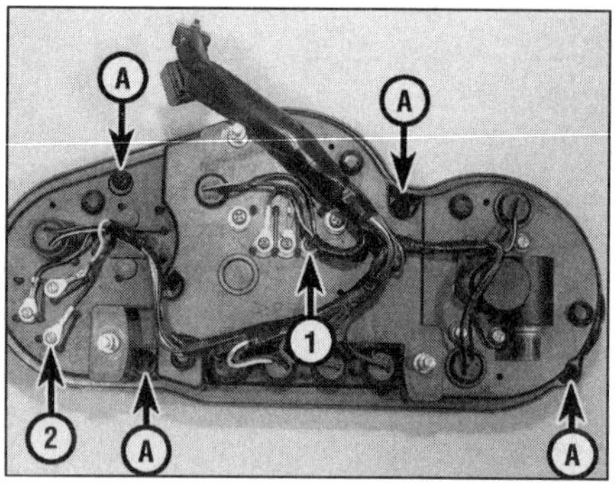

16.6a Remove the screws (A) . . .

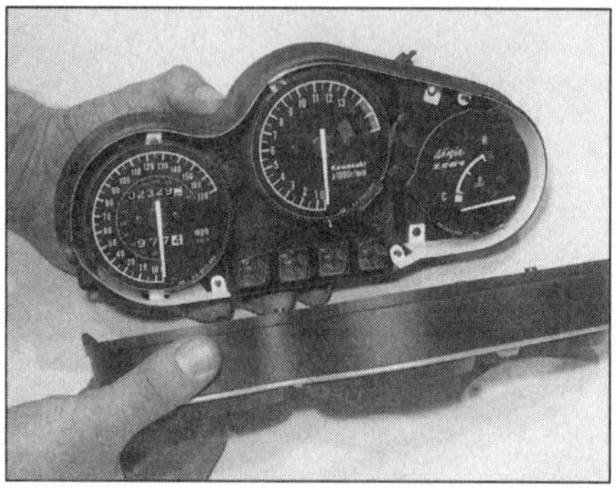

16.6b . . . and lift off the cover

3 If the voltage reading is as specified, the only other checks require special testing equipment – take the instrument cluster to a Kawasaki dealer. Also have them check the speed sensor. If the speedometer is faulty, the entire cluster must be replaced as no individual components are available.

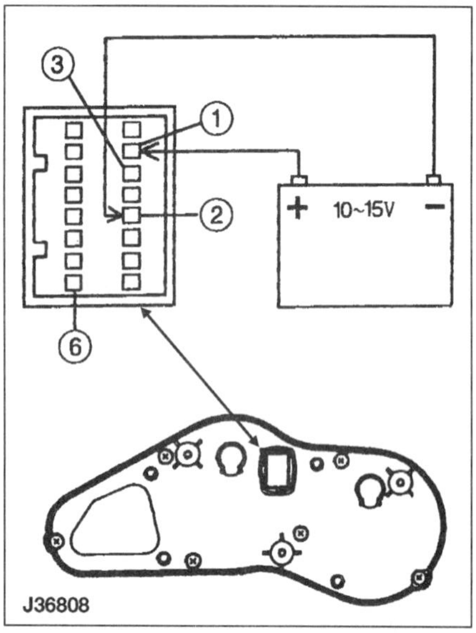

16.12a Tachometer test set-up – G and H models

Terminal numbering corresponds to text procedure

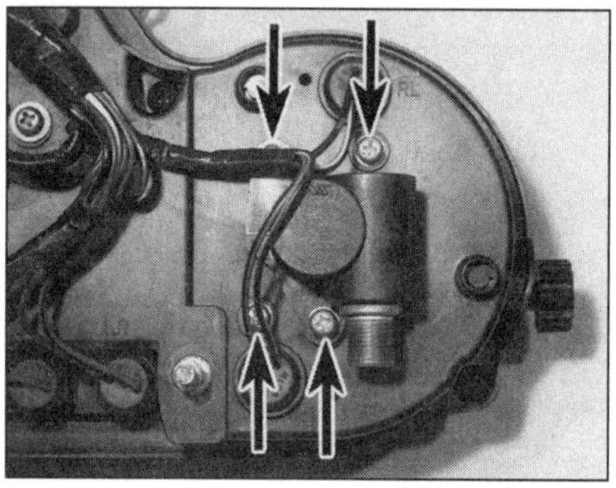

16.7 Remove the screws (arrowed) and lift out the speedometer

Renewal – F models

4 Remove the instrument cluster (see Section 15).

5 Using a very small Phillips screwdriver, remove the screw in the centre of the odometer trip knob and remove the knob **(see illustrations)**.

6 Remove the four screws on the back of the cluster and lift off the front cover **(see illustrations)**.

7 Remove the four screws securing the speedometer and lift the meter out of the casing **(see illustration)**.

8 Installation is the reverse of removal.

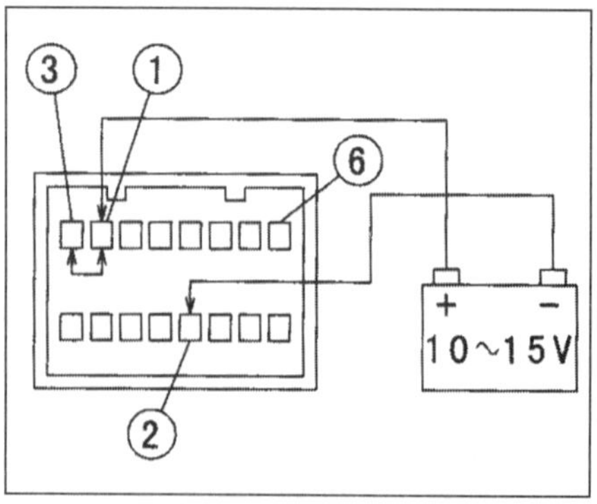

16.12b Tachometer test set-up – J and A models

Terminal numbering corresponds to text procedure

Renewal – G, H, J and A models

9 Remove the instrument cluster (see Section 15). The entire cluster must be renewed as no individual components are available.

Tachometer

Check – F models

10 Before checking the tachometer itself, refer to the *Wiring diagrams* at the end of the Chapter and check all components and wiring in the tachometer circuit.

11 If all the wiring and components are good, remove the upper fairing (see Chapter 8). Remove the screw securing the black wire for the tachometer **(wire No. 1 on illustration 16.6a)** and detach the wire, then retighten the screw. Using a jumper wire, and with the ignition switch ON, connect one end of it to the brown wire screw for the temperature gauge **(wire No. 2 on illustration 16.6a)**, then repeatedly connect and disconnect the other end to the screw for the tachometer black wire, while watching the tachometer. The needle should be seen to flicker. If the needle does not flicker the meter is faulty.

Check – G, H, J and A models

Note: *The connector terminals on the instrument cluster are very closely spaced – take great care when connecting test wires to them.*

12 Remove the instrument cluster (see Section 15). Using a 12V battery, connect the battery positive terminal to the No. 1 terminal on the cluster wiring connector, and the battery negative terminal to the No. 2 terminal **(see illustrations)**. Using a jumper wire, connect between the No. 1 and No. 3 terminals to form a bridge.

13 Using another jumper wire, connect one end to No. 1 terminal, then repeatedly connect and disconnect the other end of the No. 6 terminal, while watching the tachometer. The needle should be seen to flicker. If the needle does not flicker the tachometer is faulty.

14 If the needle does flicker, the only other checks require special testing equipment – take the instrument cluster to a Kawasaki dealer. If the tachometer is faulty, the entire cluster must be renewed as no individual components are available.

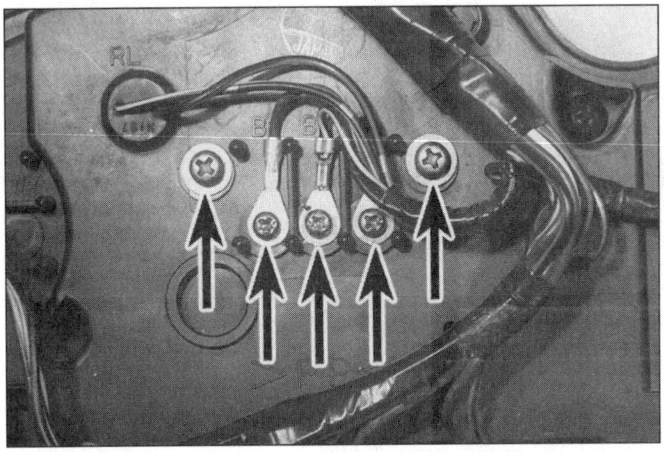

16.18 Remove the screws (arrowed) and lift out the tachometer

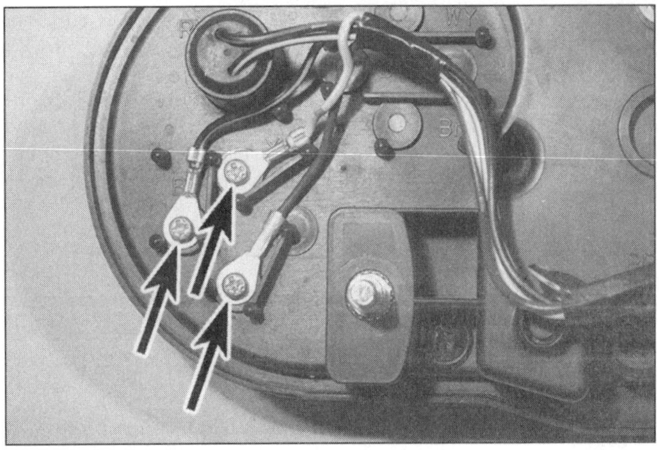

16.25 Remove the screws (arrowed) and lift out the temperature gauge

Renewal – F models

15 Remove the instrument cluster (see Section 15).

16 Using a small Phillips screwdriver, remove the screw in the centre of the odometer trip knob and remove the knob **(see illustrations 16.5a and b)**.

17 Remove the four screws on the back of the cluster and lift off the front cover **(see illustrations 16.6a and b)**.

18 Remove the five screws securing the tachometer, noting which wire fits where, and lift the meter out of the casing **(see illustration)**.

19 Installation is the reverse of removal. The correct location for each wire is indicated by lettering referring to the colour coding of the wires.

Renewal – G, H, J and A models

20 Remove the instrument cluster (see Section 15). The entire cluster must be renewed as no individual components are available.

Coolant temperature gauge

Check

21 See Chapter 3.

Renewal – F models

22 Remove the instrument cluster (see Section 15).

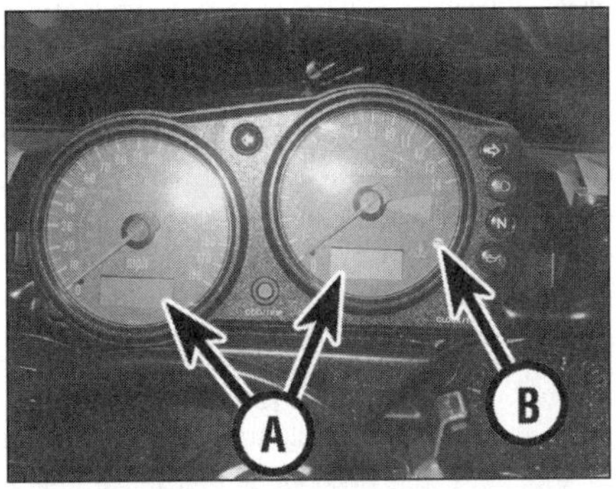

16.28 LCD segments (A) and warning light (B)

23 Using a small Phillips screwdriver, remove the screw in the centre of the odometer trip knob and remove the knob **(see illustrations 16.5a and b)**.

24 Remove the four screws on the back of the cluster and lift off the front cover **(see illustrations 16.6a and b)**.

25 Remove the three screws securing the temperature gauge, noting which wire fits where, and lift the gauge out of the casing **(see illustration)**.

26 Installation is the reverse of removal. The correct location for each wire is indicated by lettering referring to the colour coding of the wires.

Renewal – G, H, J and A models

27 Remove the instrument cluster (see Section 15). The entire cluster must be renewed as no individual components are available.

Liquid crystal display – G, H, J and A models

Check

Note: *The connector terminals on the instrument cluster are very closely spaced – take great care when connecting test wires to them.*

28 Remove the instrument cluster (see Section 15). Using a 12V battery, connect the battery positive terminal to the No. 1 terminal on the cluster wiring connector, and the battery negative terminal to the No. 2 terminal **(see illustrations 16.12a or b)**. Using a jumper wire, connect between the No. 1 and No. 3 terminals to form a bridge. All the LCD segments and the warning light should appear for three seconds **(see illustration)**. If the wiring to the connector is disconnected within that time, the LCD's should disappear immediately.

29 On G and H models, with the battery and jumper wire connected as described in Step 28, press the MODE button and keep it held down. The LCD segment in the speedometer should flick through its functions (ODO, TRIP, CLOCK). Set the display to CLOCK mode, and check that when the RESET button is pressed for more than two seconds the display changes to the clock set mode. Now set the display to TRIP mode, and check that when the RESET button is pressed for more than two seconds the figure resets to 0.0 (zero miles).

30 On J and A models, with the battery and jumper wire connected as described in Step 28, press the ODO/TRIP button and keep it held down. The LCD segment in the speedometer should flick through its functions (ODO, TRIP, ODO) at approximately 2-second intervals. Press the CLOCK/TEMP button and keep it held down. The LCD segment in the tachometer should flick through its functions (CLOCK, TEMPERATURE, CLOCK) at approximately 2-second intervals. Set the display to CLOCK mode, and check that when the RESET button is pressed again for more than two seconds the display starts flashing. It should now be possible to set the time on the clock.

31 If the LCD does not function as described, it is faulty. If the display functions as described, but the performance of any individual function is suspect (i.e. the odometer doesn't work, or displays inaccurate information), take the cluster to a Kawasaki dealer as special equipment is required to properly check these functions.

Renewal

32 Remove the instrument cluster (see Section 15). The entire cluster must be replaced as no individual components are available.

17 Instrument and warning light bulbs – replacement

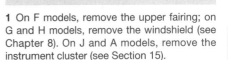

1 On F models, remove the upper fairing; on G and H models, remove the windshield (see Chapter 8). On J and A models, remove the instrument cluster (see Section 15).

17.2a Pull out the bulbholder . . .

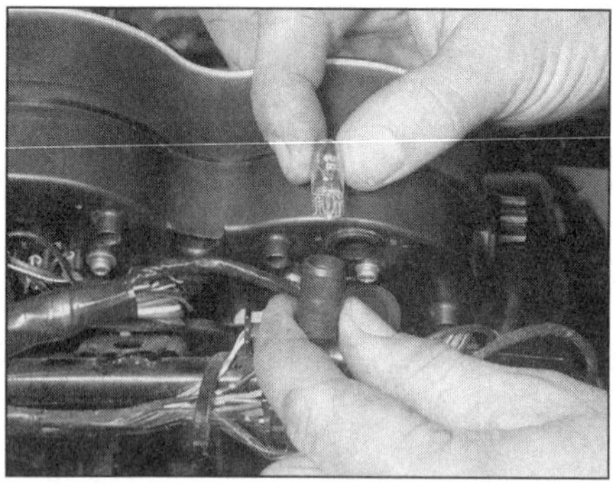

17.2b . . . and remove the bulb

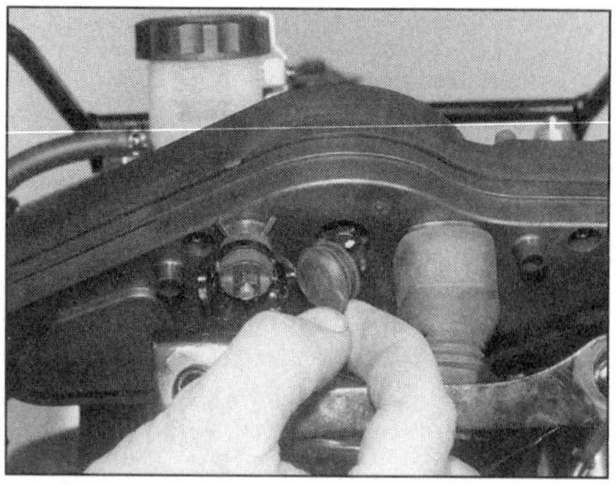

17.3a Remove the blanking plug . . .

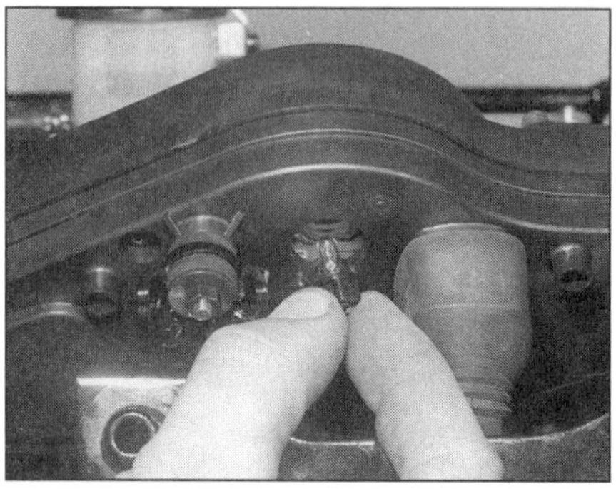

17.3b . . . then release the bulbholder . . .

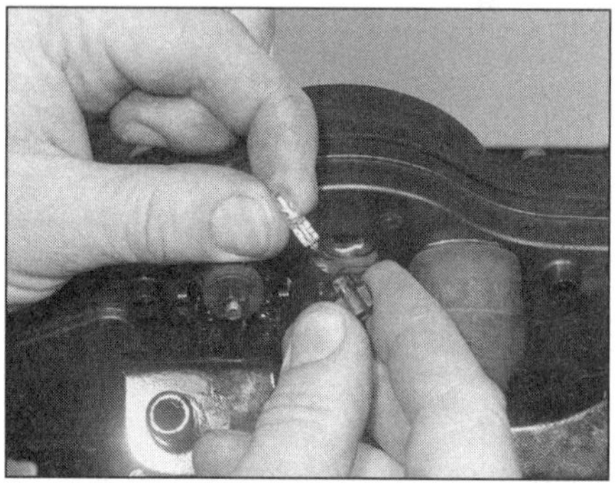

17.3c . . . and remove the bulb

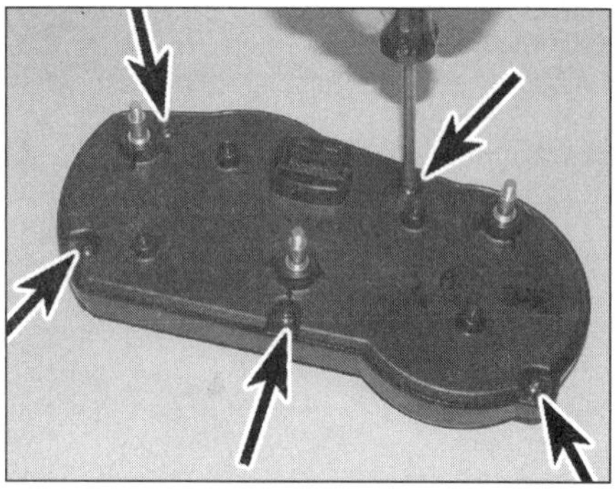

17.4a On J and A models, undo the cluster casing screws (arrowed) . . .

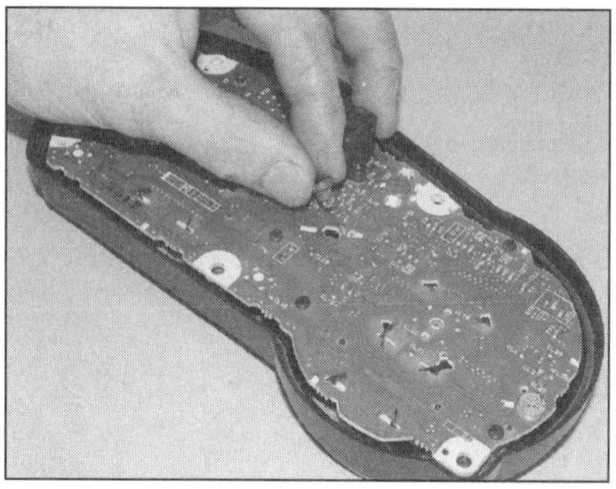

17.4b . . . and twist the bulbholder to remove it

2 On F models, carefully pull the bulbholder out of the instrument casing, then pull the bulb out of the bulbholder **(see illustrations)**.

3 On G and H models, remove the rubber blanking plug for the relevant bulb **(see illustration)**. Twist the bulbholder anticlockwise and withdraw it from the cluster, then pull the bulb out of the holder **(see illustrations)**.

4 On J and A models, undo the screws securing the two halves of the cluster casing and separate them **(see illustration)**. Use a screwdriver to twist the bulbholder to remove it from the circuitboard **(see illustration)**. The bulb is of the capless type and the bulb terminal wires pass through the bulbholder and are locked to hold the bulb in place. Note the position of the wires, then straighten them before pulling the bulb out of the holder.

5 If the socket contacts are dirty or corroded, scrape them clean and spray them with electrical contact cleaner before a new bulb is installed.

6 Carefully push the new bulb into the holder. On J and A models, lock the bulb terminal wires around the holder. Install the bulbholder. On G and H models, fit the rubber blanking plug. On J and A models, reassemble the instrument cluster.

7 Install the remaining components in the reverse order of removal.

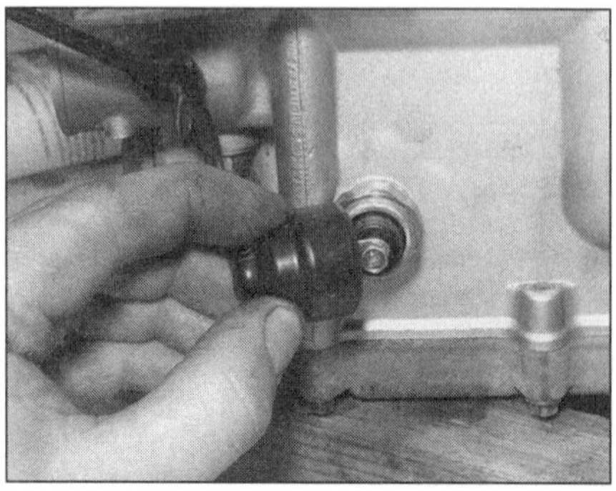

18.3a Pull back the rubber cover . . .

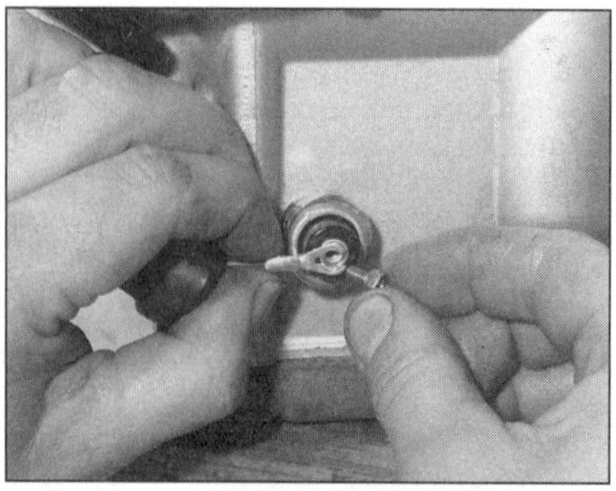

18.3b . . . then remove the screw and detach the wire

18 Oil pressure switch – check, removal and installation

Check

1 The oil pressure warning light should come on when the ignition (main) switch is turned ON and extinguish a few seconds after the engine is started. If the oil pressure warning light comes on whilst the engine is running, stop the engine immediately and carry out an oil level check, and if the level is correct, an oil pressure check (see Chapter 1).

2 If the oil pressure warning light does not come on when the ignition is turned on, check the bulb (see Section 17) and fuse (see Section 5).

3 The oil pressure switch is screwed into the front of the crankcase and is accessed by removing the right-hand lower fairing panel (see Chapter 8). Pull the rubber cover off the switch and remove the screw securing the wiring connector **(see illustrations)**. With the ignition switched ON, earth (ground) the wire on the crankcase and check that the warning light comes on. If the light comes on, the switch is defective and must be replaced.

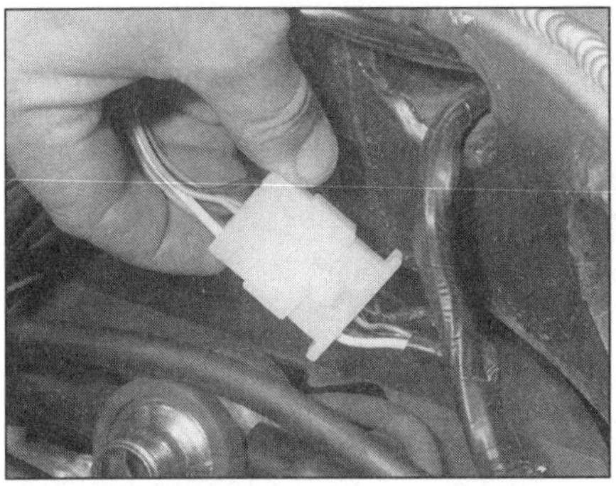

19.1 Disconnect the ignition switch wiring connector

4 If the light still does not come on, check for voltage at the wire terminal. If there is no voltage present, check the wire between the switch, the instrument cluster and fusebox for continuity (see the *Wiring diagrams* at the end of this Chapter).
5 If the warning light comes on whilst the engine is running, yet the oil pressure is satisfactory, remove the wire from the oil pressure switch. With the wire detached and the ignition switched ON the light should be out. If it is illuminated, the wire between the switch and instrument cluster must be earthed (grounded) at some point. If the wiring is good, the switch must be assumed faulty and replaced.

Removal

6 Remove the right-hand lower fairing panel (see Chapter 8). Drain the engine oil (see Chapter 1).
7 Pull the rubber cover off the switch and remove the screw securing the wiring connector **(see illustrations 18.3a and b)**.
8 Unscrew the oil pressure switch and withdraw it from the crankcase.

Installation

9 Apply a suitable silicone sealant (such as Kawasaki Bond 56019-120) to the upper portion of the switch threads near the switch body, leaving the bottom 3 to 4 mm of thread clean. Install the switch in the crankcase and tighten it to the torque setting specified at the beginning of the Chapter. Attach the wiring connector and secure it with the screw, then fit the rubber cover **(see illustrations 18.3b and a)**.

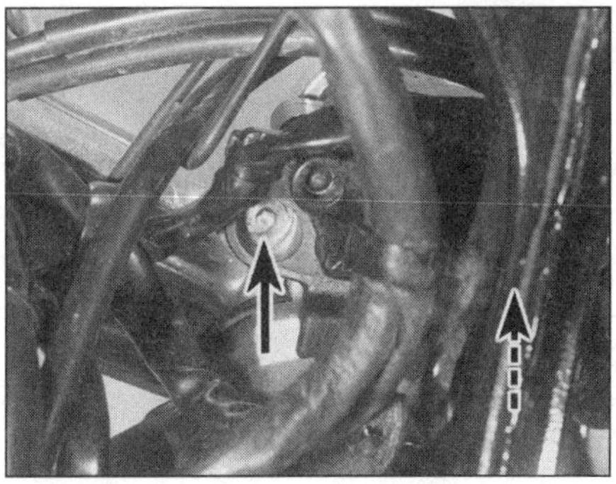

19.5 Ignition switch Torx bolts (arrowed)

10 Refill the engine using the specified grade and quantity of oil (see Chapter 1). Run the engine and check that the switch operates correctly.
11 Install the lower fairing panel (see Chapter 8).

19 Ignition (main) switch – check, removal and installation

Warning: To prevent the risk of short circuits, disconnect the battery negative (-ve) lead before making any ignition (main) switch checks.

Check

1 Remove the air filter housing (see Chapter 4). Trace the ignition (main) switch wiring back from the base of the switch and disconnect it at the white connector **(see illustration)**.
2 Using an ohmmeter or a continuity tester, check the continuity of the connector terminal pairs on the switch side of the connector (see the *Wiring diagrams* at the end of this Chapter). Continuity should exist between the terminals connected by a solid line on the diagram when the switch is in the indicated position.
3 If the switch fails any of the tests, renew it.

Removal

4 Remove the upper fairing (see Chapter 8) and the air filter housing (see Chapter 4). Trace the ignition (main) switch wiring back from the base of the switch and disconnect it at the white connector **(see illustration 19.1)**. Draw the wiring through to the switch, noting its routing.
5 Special shear-head security Torx bolts are used to mount the ignition switch **(see illustration)**. Remove the two security bolts using a centre punch and hammer to initially slacken them. Alternatively, drill the bolt heads off. New bolts must be used on installation. Access to the bolts is best obtained by displacing the instrument cluster bracket from the steering head – it is secured by two bolts. If required, first remove the instrument cluster (see Section 15), though with care the bracket can be displaced with the cluster still mounted.

Installation

6 Installation is the reverse of removal. Using new shear-head Torx bolts, tighten them until either the tool slips round on the bolt head, or until the bolt head sheers off. Make sure wiring is securely connected and correctly routed.

20 Handlebar switches – check

1 Generally speaking, the switches are reliable and trouble-free. Most troubles, when they do occur, are caused by dirty or corroded contacts, but wear and breakage of internal parts is a possibility that should not be overlooked. If breakage does occur, the entire switch and related wiring harness will have to be replaced with a new one, as individual parts are not available.
2 The switches can be checked for continuity using an ohmmeter or a continuity test light. Always disconnect the battery negative (-ve) cable, which will prevent the possibility of a short circuit, before making the checks.
3 Trace the wiring harness of the switch in question back to its connector and disconnect it. On F models, the connectors are on the front of the instrument cluster – remove the upper fairing for access **(see illustrations)**. On all other models, the connectors are behind the steering stem **(see illustration)** – remove the fuel tank and air filter housing for access (see Chapter 4).

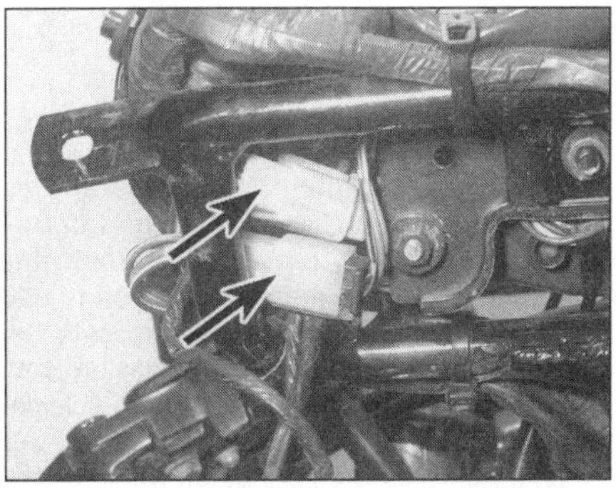

20.3a Right handlebar switch wiring connectors (arrowed) – F models

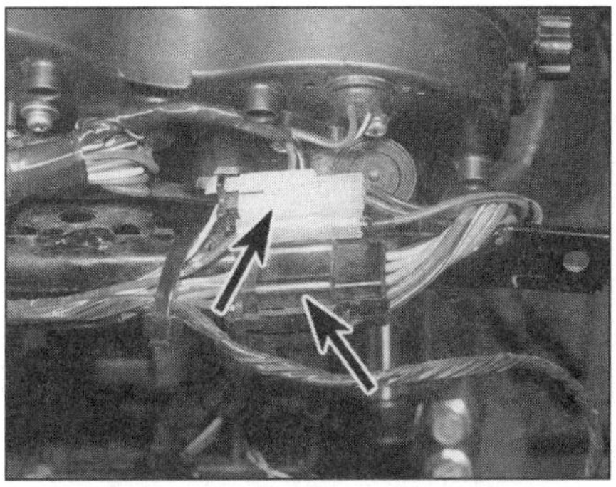

20.3b Left handlebar switch wiring connectors (arrowed) – F models

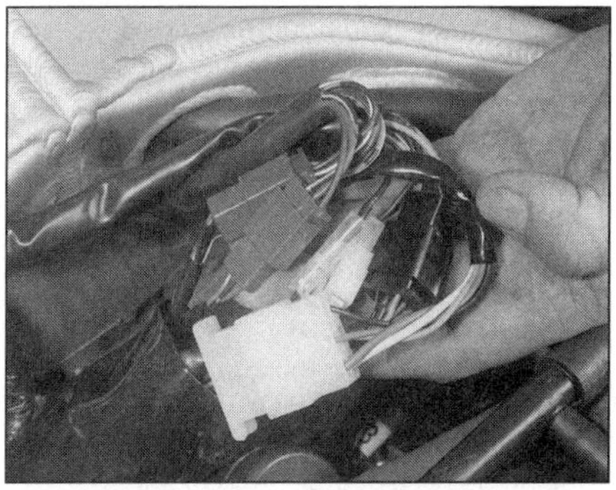

20.3c Handlebar switch and ignition switch wiring connectors – G, H, J and A models

22.2a Neutral switch (arrowed)

22.2b Pull off the wiring connector

4 Check for continuity between the terminals of the switch harness with the switch in the various positions (i.e. switch off – no continuity, switch on – continuity) – see the *Wiring diagrams* at the end of this Chapter.

5 If the continuity check indicates a problem exists, refer to Section 21, remove the switch and spray the switch contacts with electrical contact cleaner. If they are accessible, the contacts can be cleaned with a knife or crocus cloth. If switch components are damaged or broken, it will be obvious when the switch is disassembled.

21 Handlebar switches – removal and installation

Removal

1 If the switch is to be removed from the bike, rather than just displaced from the handlebar, trace the wiring harness of the switch in question back to its connector and disconnect it. On F models, the connectors are on the front of the instrument cluster – remove the upper fairing for access **(see illustrations 20.3a and b)**. On all other models, the connectors are behind the steering stem **(see illustration 20.3c)** – remove the air filter housing for access (see Chapter 4). Work back along the harness, freeing it from all the relevant clips and ties, whilst noting its correct routing.

2 Disconnect the two wires from the brake light switch (if removing the right-hand switch) or the connector from the clutch switch (if removing the left-hand switch) **(see illustration 14.6 or 24.4)**.

3 Unscrew the two handlebar switch screws and separate the halves. On F models, detach the throttle cables from the right-hand switch housing (see Chapter 4). On all models, detach the choke cable from the left-hand switch housing (see Chapter 3).

Installation

4 Installation is the reverse of removal. Refer to Chapter 4 for the installation of the throttle and choke cables. Make sure the locating pin in the switch housing locates in the hole in the handlebar.

22 Neutral switch – check, removal and installation

Check

1 Before checking the electrical circuit, check the bulb (see Section 17) and fuse (see Section 5).

2 The switch is located in the left-hand side of the transmission casing, below the front sprocket cover **(see illustration)**. Detach the wiring connector from the switch **(see illustration)**. Make sure the transmission is in neutral.

3 With the connector disconnected and the ignition switched ON, the neutral light should be out. If not, the wire between the connector and instrument cluster must be earthed (grounded) at some point.

4 Check for continuity between the switch terminal and the crankcase. With the transmission in neutral, there should be continuity. With the transmission in gear, there should be no continuity. If the tests prove otherwise, then the switch is faulty.

5 If the continuity tests prove the switch is good, check for voltage at the wire terminal using a test light. If there's no voltage present, check the wire between the switch, the instrument cluster and fusebox (see the *Wiring diagrams* at the end of this Chapter).

Removal

6 If required for improved access, remove the left-hand lower fairing panel (see Chapter 8).

7 Detach the wiring connector from the switch **(see illustration 22.2b)**.

8 Unscrew the switch and withdraw it from the transmission casing.

Installation

9 Check the condition of the sealing washer and use a new one if the old one is damaged or distorted.

10 Install the switch with the washer and tighten it to the torque setting specified at the beginning of the Chapter.

11 Check the operation of the neutral light.

12 If removed, install the lower fairing panel (see Chapter 8).

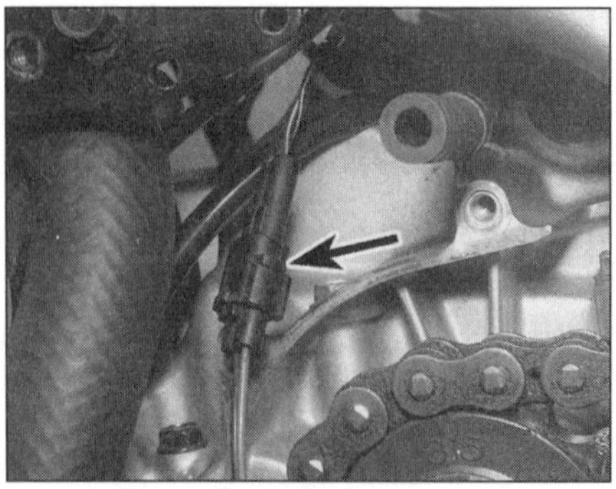

23.2 Sidestand switch wiring connector (arrowed)

23 Sidestand switch – check and renewal

Check

1 The sidestand switch is mounted on the sidestand bracket. The switch is part of the safety circuit which prevents or stops the engine running if the transmission is in gear whilst the sidestand is down, and prevents the engine from starting if the transmission is in gear unless the sidestand is up and the clutch lever is pulled in.

2 Trace the wiring back from the switch to its connector just above the sprocket cover and disconnect it **(see illustration)**.

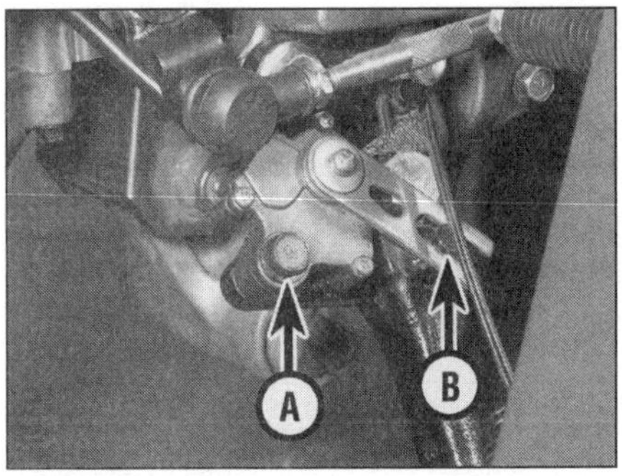

23.7 Sidestand switch mounting bolt (A). Note how the arm locates around the lug (B)

3 Check the operation of the switch using an ohmmeter or continuity test light. Connect the meter probes to the terminals on the switch side of the connector. With the sidestand up there should be continuity (zero resistance) between the terminals, and with the stand down there should be no continuity (infinite resistance).

4 If the switch does not perform as expected, it is defective and must be renewed.

5 If the switch is good, check the wiring between the various components in the starter safety circuit (see the *Wiring diagrams* at the end of this book).

Renewal

6 The sidestand switch is mounted on the sidestand bracket. If required for improved access, remove the left-hand lower fairing panel (see Chapter 8). Trace the wiring back from the switch to its connector and disconnect it **(see illustration 23.2)**. Free the wiring from its clip, noting its correct routing.

7 Unscrew the switch bolt and remove the switch from the stand, noting how it fits **(see illustration)**.

8 Fit the new switch onto the sidestand, making sure the slot in the switch lever arm locates over the lug on the sidestand **(see illustration 23.7)**. Apply a suitable non-permanent thread locking compound to the switch bolt and tighten it securely.

9 Make sure the wiring is correctly routed up to the connector and retained by the clip.

10 Reconnect the wiring connector and check the operation of the sidestand switch.

11 If removed, install the lower fairing panel (see Chapter 8).

24 Clutch switch – check and renewal

Check

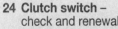

1 The clutch switch is housed in the clutch lever bracket. The switch is part of the safety circuit which prevents or stops the engine running if the transmission is in gear whilst the sidestand is down, and prevents the engine from starting if the transmission is in gear unless the sidestand is up and the clutch lever is pulled in. The switch isn't adjustable.

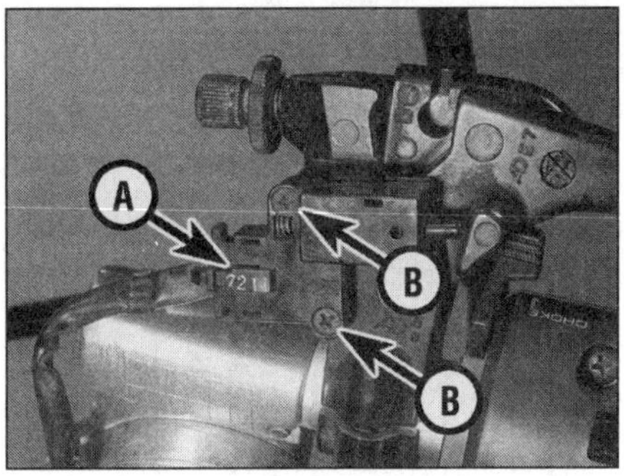

24.4 Clutch switch wiring connector (A), mounting screws (B)

2 To check the switch, disconnect the wiring connector **(see illustration 24.4)**. Connect the positive probe of an ohmmeter or a continuity test light to the black wire terminal on the switch, and the negative probe to black/red wire terminal. Note the meter readings first with the clutch lever out and then with the lever pulled in. Now connect the negative probe to the black/yellow wire terminal and again note the readings with the lever out and in. With the probes connected one way there should be continuity with the clutch lever released, and no continuity with the lever pulled in. With the probes connected the other way there should be no continuity with the lever released and continuity with the lever pulled in.

3 If the switch is good, check the other components in the starter circuit as described in the relevant sections of this Chapter. If all components are good, check the wiring between the various components (see the *Wiring diagrams* at the end of this book).

Renewal

4 Disconnect the wiring connector from the clutch switch **(see illustration)**. Remove the two screws securing the switch to the underside of the clutch lever bracket and remove the switch, noting how it fits. To access the screws, depending on the tools available it may be necessary to slacken the clutch lever bracket clamp bolts and swivel the bracket on the handlebar – if doing this it is advisable to first detach the cable from the lever (see Chapter 2).

5 Installation is the reverse of removal.

25 Junction box – check and renewal

Check

1 Remove the seats (see Chapter 8).

2 The junction box contains the starter circuit relay, the headlight circuit relay (US F, G, H and J models), and diodes, as well as the fusebox. The starter circuit relay and interlock diodes are part of the safety circuit which prevents or stops the engine running if the transmission is in gear whilst the sidestand is down, and prevents the engine from starting if the transmission is in gear unless the sidestand is up and the clutch is pulled in. Slide the junction box out of its holder and disconnect the wiring connectors **(see illustration 25.6)**.

3 Using an ohmmeter or continuity tester and a 12V battery with jumper wires, connect the meter probes and the battery (when specified) to the terminals on the junction box

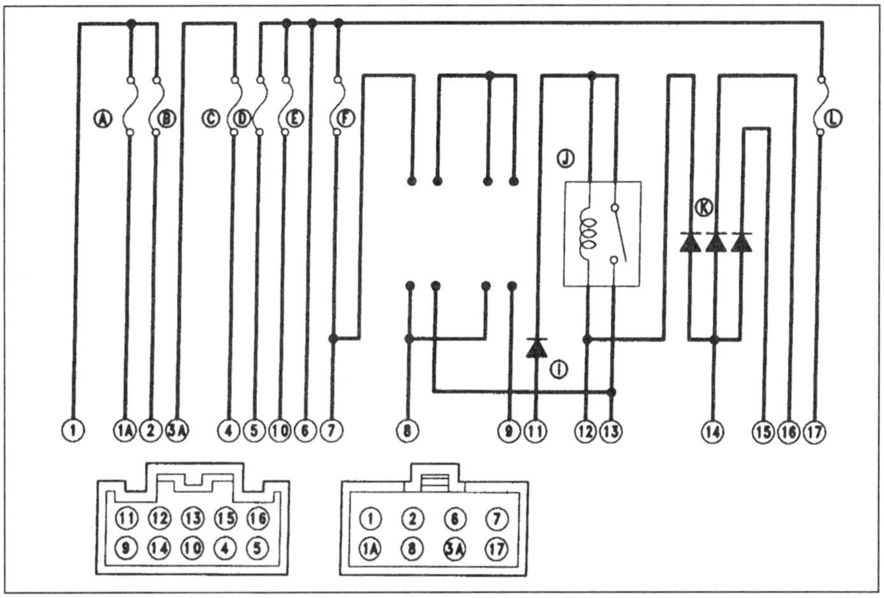

25.3a Junction box internal circuitry and terminal identification – UK models

A Accessory fuse
B Fan fuse
C Turn signal relay fuse
D Horn fuse
E Ignition fuse
F Headlight fuse
I Starter diode
J Starter circuit relay
K Starter circuit diodes
L Tail light fuse

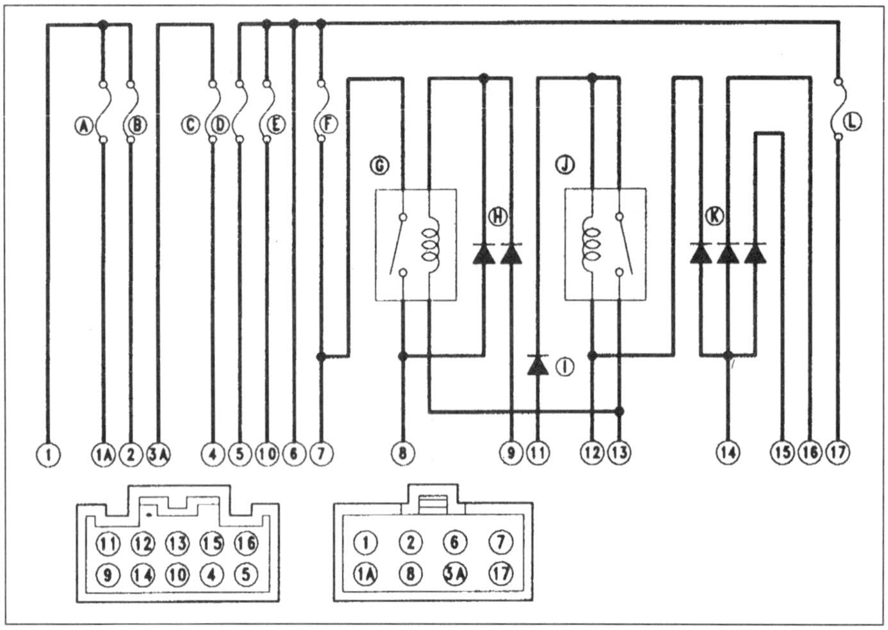

25.3b Junction box internal circuitry and terminal identification – US models

A Accessory fuse
B Fan fuse
C Turn signal relay fuse
D Horn fuse
E Ignition fuse
F Headlight fuse
G Headlight circuit relay
H Headlight diodes
I Starter diode
J Starter circuit relay
K Starter circuit diodes
L Tail light fuse

Tester Connection	Tester Reading (Ω)
1 - 1A	0
1 - 2	0
3A - 4	0
6 - 5	0
6 - 10	0
6 - 7	0
6 - 17	0

Tester Connection	Tester Reading (Ω)
1A - 8	∞
2 - 8	∞
3A - 8	∞
6 - 2	∞
6 - 3A	∞
17 - 3A	∞

25.3c Junction box fuse test connections

see illustration 25.3a or 25.3b for terminal identification

connectors as indicated in the various tables **(see illustrations)**. If the results achieved after all terminal pairs have been tested do not agree with the results specified in the tables, the junction box is faulty and must be renewed.

4 When testing the diode circuits, test each of the following terminal pairs in one direction, then reverse the probes and test the pair in the other direction.

13 – 8 (US F, G, H and J models only)
13 – 9 (US F, G, H and J models only)
12 – 11
12 – 14
15 – 14
16 – 14

There should be continuity in one direction, and no continuity in the other. If not, the junction box is faulty and must be renewed.

5 If the junction box is good, check the other components in that circuit as described in the relevant sections of this Chapter. If all components are good, check the wiring between the various components (see the *Wiring diagrams* at the end of this book).

Renewal

6 Remove the seats (see Chapter 8). Slide the junction box out of its holder and disconnect the wiring connectors **(see illustration)**.

7 Ensure the wiring connector terminals are clean, then push the connectors on firmly. Install the new box in its holder and fit the seats.

25.6 Slide the junction box out of its holder and disconnect the wiring connectors

	Tester Connection	Tester Reading (Ω)
Headlight Relay	*7 - 8	∞
	*7 - 13	∞
	(+) (-) *13 - 9	Not ∞ **

	Tester Connection	Tester Reading (Ω)
Starter Circuit Relay	9 - 11	∞
	12 - 13	∞
	(+) (-) 13 - 11	∞
	(+) (-) 12 - 11	Not ∞ **

	Battery Connection (+) (-)	Tester Connection	Tester Reading (Ω)
Headlight Relay	*9 - 13	*7 - 8	0
Starter Circuit Relay	11 - 12	(+) (-) 13 - 11	Not ∞ **

25.3d Junction box starter circuit and headlight circuit relay test connections

see illustration 25.3a or 25.3b for terminal identification
** The headlight circuit relay is fitted to US models only*
*** The actual reading varies depending on the meter used*

26 Horn – check and renewal

Check

1 On F, G and H models, the horn is mounted on the bottom fork yoke **(see illustration 26.5)**. On J and A models, the horn is mounted to the frame in front of the radiator **(see illustration)**. Remove the upper fairing for access if required (see Chapter 8).
2 Unplug the wiring connectors from the horn. Using two jumper wires, apply battery voltage directly to the terminals on the horn. If the horn sounds, check the switch (see Section 21) and the wiring between the switch and the horn (see the *wiring diagrams* at the end of this Chapter).
3 If the horn doesn't sound, renew it.

Renewal

4 If required, remove the upper fairing for access (see Chapter 8).
5 Disconnect the wiring connectors from the horn, then unscrew the bolts securing the horn bracket and remove it from the bike **(see illustration)**.
6 Install the horn and securely tighten the bolts. Connect the wiring connectors to the horn. Install the upper fairing (see Chapter 8).

27 Starter relay – check and renewal

Check

1 If the starter circuit is faulty, first check the fuse (see Section 5).
2 The starter relay is located under the rider's seat. Remove the seats for access (see Chapter 8). Lift the rubber terminal cover and unscrew the bolt securing the starter motor lead **(see illustration)**; position the lead away

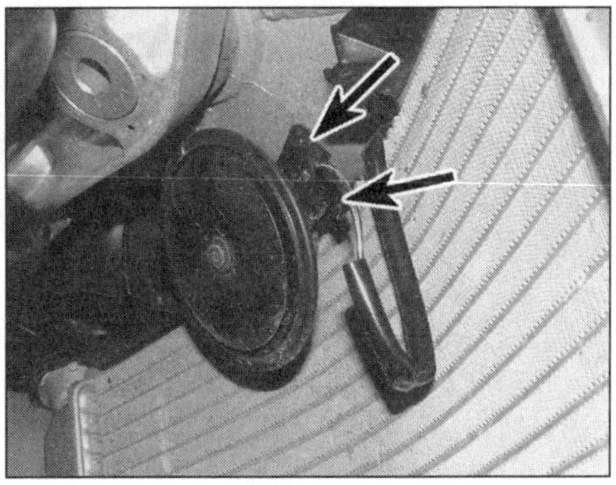

26.1 Location of the horn and wiring connectors (arrowed) – J and A models

from the relay terminal. With the ignition switch ON, the engine kill switch in the RUN position and the transmission in neutral, press the starter switch. The relay should be heard to click.
3 If the relay doesn't click, switch off the ignition and remove the relay (see Step 8) and test it as follows.
4 Set a multimeter to the ohms x 1 scale and connect it across the relay's starter motor and battery lead terminals **(see illustration)**. There should be no continuity (infinite resistance). Using a fully-charged 12 volt battery and two insulated jumper wires, connect the positive (+ve) battery terminal to the yellow/red wire terminal of the relay, and the negative (-ve) battery terminal to the black/yellow wire terminal. At this point the relay should be heard to click and the multimeter read 0 ohms (continuity). If this is the case the relay is proved good. If the relay does not click when battery voltage is applied and still indicates no continuity (infinite resistance) across its terminals, it is faulty and must be renewed.
5 If the relay is good, check for battery voltage between the yellow/red wire and the black/yellow wire when the starter button is pressed. Check the other components in the starter circuit as described in the relevant sections of this Chapter. If all components are good, check the wiring between the various

26.5 Disconnect the wiring connectors (A), then unscrew the bolts (B) and remove the horn – F, G, and H models

components (see the *Wiring diagrams* at the end of this book).

Renewal

6 Remove the seats (see Chapter 8).
7 Disconnect the battery terminals, remembering to disconnect the negative (-ve) terminal first.
8 Disconnect the relay wiring connector, then lift the rubber terminal cover and unscrew the bolts securing the starter motor and battery leads to the relay and detach the leads **(see illustration)**. Remove the relay with its rubber sleeve from its mounting lug on the frame.
9 Installation is the reverse of removal. Make sure the terminal bolts are securely tightened. Connect the negative (-ve) lead last when reconnecting the battery.

28 Starter motor – removal and installation

Removal

1 Make sure the ignition switch is OFF. Remove the fuel tank (see Chapter 4). The starter motor is mounted on top of the crankcase behind the cylinder block.
2 Peel back the rubber terminal cover,

27.2 Lift the rubber cover to access the starter motor and battery terminals (arrowed)

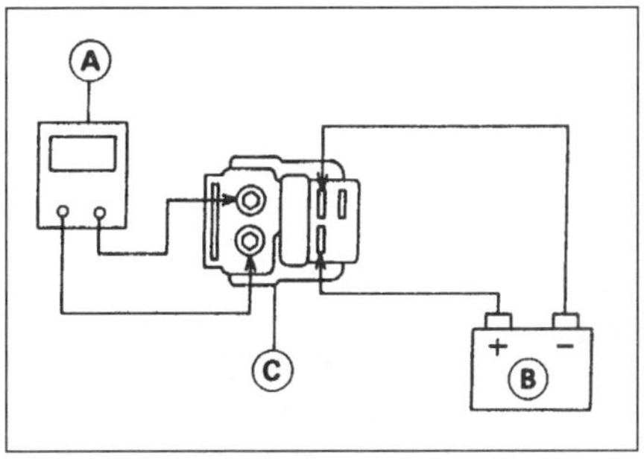

27.4 Starter relay test

A *Multimeter*
B *12V battery*
C *Starter relay*

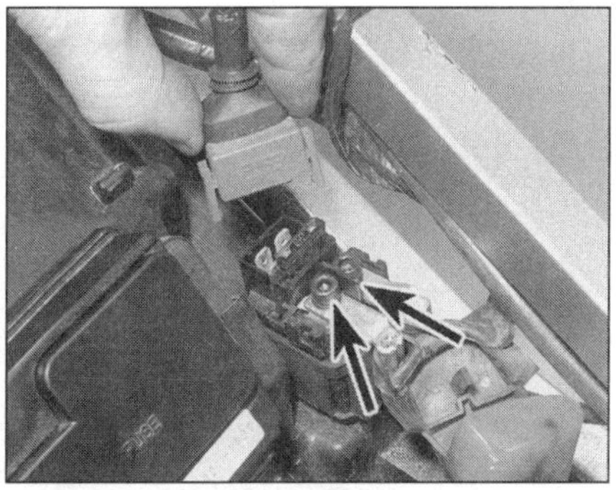

27.8 Disconnect the wiring connector, then remove the bolts (arrowed) and detach the leads

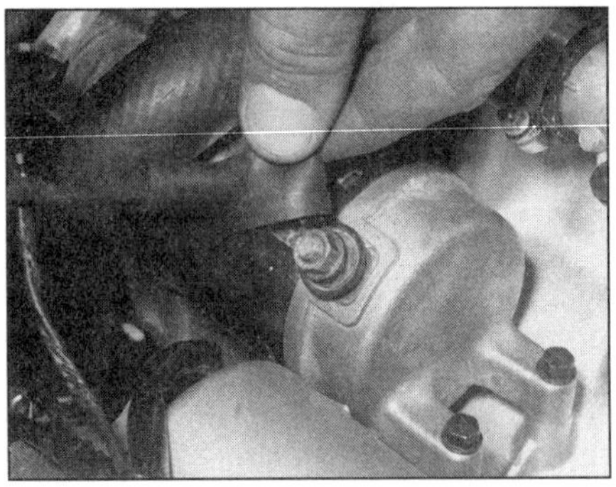

28.2a Pull back the rubber cover . . .

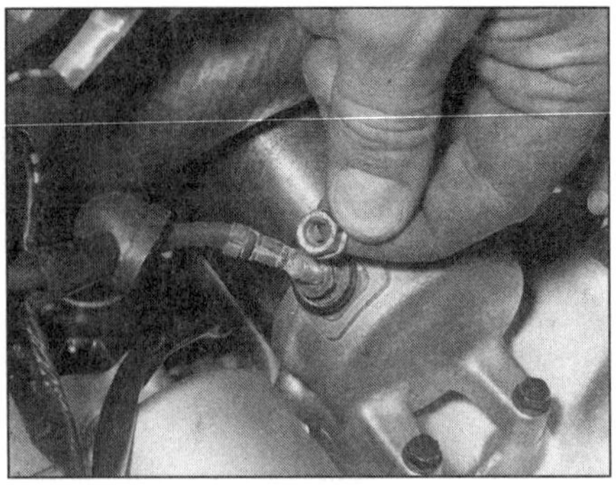

28.2b . . . then unscrew the nut and detach the lead

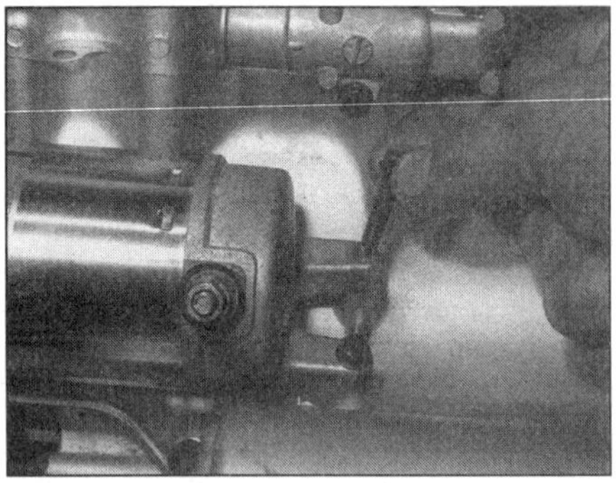

28.3 Unscrew the bolts and remove the starter motor

then remove the nut securing the starter lead to the motor and detach the lead **(see illustrations)**.

3 Unscrew the two bolts securing the starter motor to the crankcase **(see illustration)**. Slide the starter motor out from the crankcase and remove it from the machine.

4 Remove the O-ring on the end of the starter motor and discard it as a new one must be used **(see illustration)**.

Installation

5 Install a new O-ring on the end of the starter motor and ensure it is seated in its groove **(see illustration 28.4)**. Apply a smear of engine oil or grease to the O-ring to aid installation. Make sure the mating surfaces between the starter motor mounting lugs and the crankcase are clean to ensure a good earth (ground) contact.

6 Manoeuvre the motor into position and slide it into the crankcase **(see illustration)**. Ensure that the starter motor teeth mesh correctly with those of the starter idle/reduction gear. Install the mounting bolts and tighten them to the torque setting specified at the beginning of the Chapter **(see illustration 28.3)**.

7 Connect the starter lead to the motor and secure it with the nut **(see illustrations 28.2b and a)**. Make sure the rubber cover is correctly seated over the terminal.

8 Install the seats (see Chapter 8).

28.4 Remove the old O-ring and fit a new one

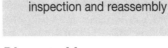

29 Starter motor – disassembly, inspection and reassembly

Disassembly

F models

1 Remove the starter motor (see Section 28).

2 Note the alignment marks between the main housing and the front and rear covers, or make your own if they aren't clear **(see illustration)**.

3 Unscrew the two long bolts and withdraw them from the starter motor. Discard their O-rings as new ones must be used.

4 Remove the front cover from the motor. Remove the cover O-ring from the main housing and discard it as a new one must be used.

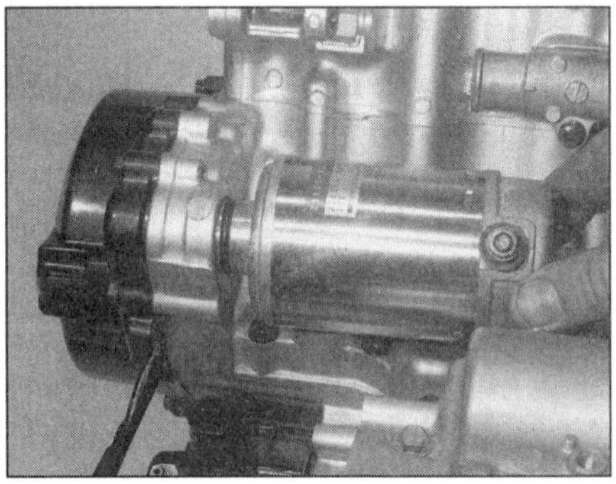

28.6 Slide the motor into the crankcase

5 Remove the rear cover and brushplate assembly from the motor, making sure that the brushes do not get caught up and damaged on the commutator **(see illustration)**. Remove the cover O-ring from the main housing and discard it as a new one must be used. Remove the washer from the rear end of the armature shaft or from inside the rear cover after the brushplate assembly has been removed.

6 Withdraw the armature from the main housing.

7 Noting the correct fitted location of each component, unscrew the terminal nut from the rear cover and remove it along with the insulating rubber and O-ring. Remove the brushplate assembly and withdraw the terminal bolt from the main housing **(see illustration)**.

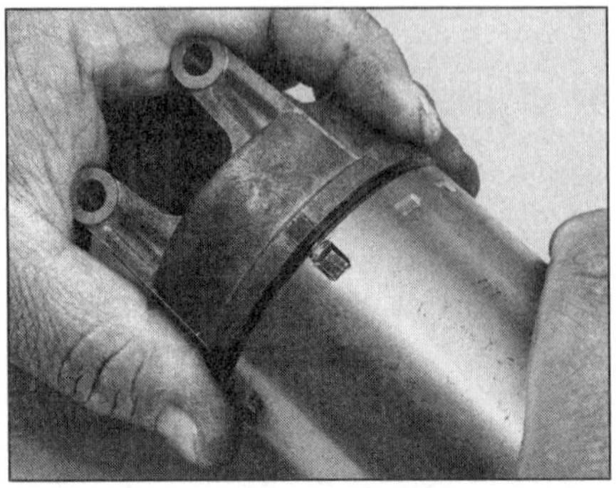

29.2 Mark the relationship of the end covers to the main housing

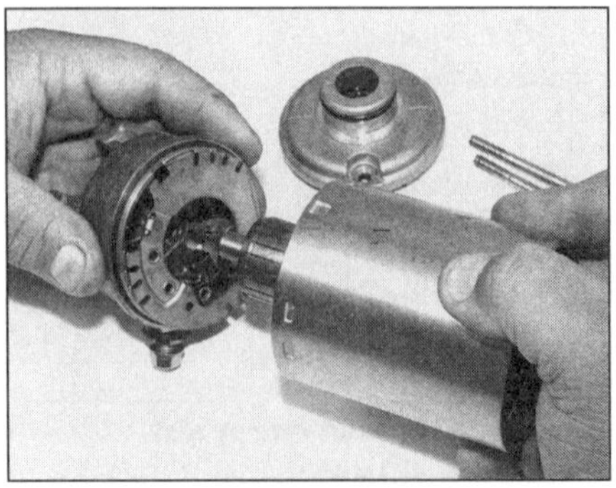

29.5 Carefully separate the rear cover from the main housing

29.7 Remove the brushplate and terminal bolt from the rear cover

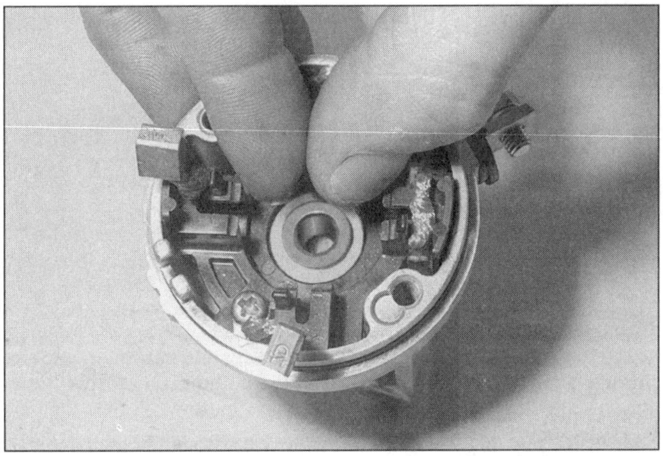

29.13 Slide out the brushes and remove the springs

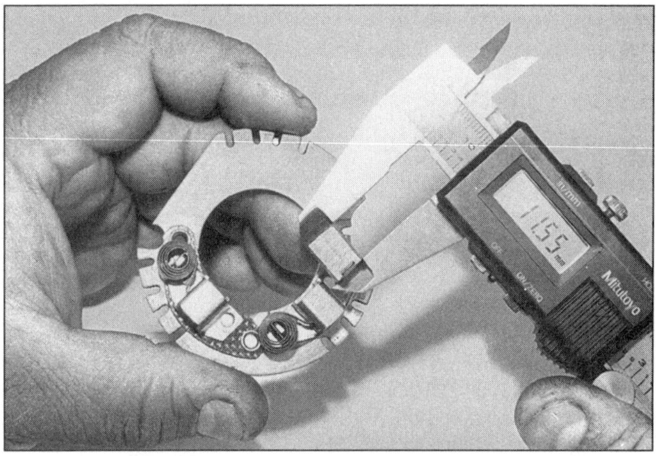

29.16 Measure the length of the brushes

8 Lift the brush springs and slide the brushes out from their holders.

G, H, J and A models

9 Remove the starter motor (see Section 28).

10 Note the alignment marks between the main housing and the front and rear covers, or make your own if they aren't clear.

11 Unscrew the two long bolts and withdraw them from the starter motor. Discard their O-rings as new ones must be used.

12 Remove the front cover from the motor. Remove the cover O-ring from the main housing and discard it as a new one must be used. Remove the washer and tabbed washer from either the front cover or from the armature shaft.

13 Carefully remove the rear cover and brushplate assembly from the motor. Make sure that the brushes do not get caught up and damaged on the commutator and take care not to lose the brush springs. Slide the brushes out from their holders and remove the springs for safekeeping **(see illustration)**.

14 Remove the cover O-ring from the main housing and discard it as a new one must be used.

15 Withdraw the armature from the main housing.

Inspection

16 The parts of the starter motor that are most likely to require attention are the brushes. Measure the length of the brushes and compare the results to the brush length listed in this Chapter's Specifications **(see illustration)**. If the brushes are not worn excessively, cracked, chipped, or otherwise damaged, they may be re-used. On F models, if either of the brushes are worn beyond the service limit, fit a new brush plate and terminal bolt. On G, H, J and A models, only the brush springs are available individually; the brushes, brushplates and rear cover are supplied as an assembly.

17 Inspect the commutator bars on the armature for scoring, scratches and discoloration. The commutator can be cleaned and polished with crocus cloth or very fine emery paper, but do not use sandpaper. After cleaning, wipe away any residue, particularly from the grooves between the segments, with a cloth soaked in electrical system cleaner or denatured alcohol.

18 Using an ohmmeter or a continuity test light, check for continuity between the commutator bars **(see illustration)**. Continuity should exist between each bar and all of the others. Also, check for continuity between the commutator bars and the armature shaft **(see illustration)**. There should be no continuity (infinite resistance) between the commutator and the shaft. If the checks indicate otherwise, the armature is defective.

19 On F models, check for continuity between the positive brush and the terminal bolt, and between the negative brush and the brushplate **(see illustration)**. There should be continuity (zero or very close to zero resistance). With the components assembled in the rear cover (see below), check for continuity between the terminal bolt and the rear cover and between the bolt and the brushplate. There should be no continuity (infinite resistance).

20 On G, H, J and A models, check for continuity between the positive brushes and the terminal bolt, and between the negative brushes and the rear cover (the negative brushes are attached to the negative brushplate, which is the upper plate in the rear cover, secured by two screws). There should be continuity (zero or very close to zero resistance). Check for continuity between the terminal bolt and the rear cover. There should be no continuity (infinite resistance).

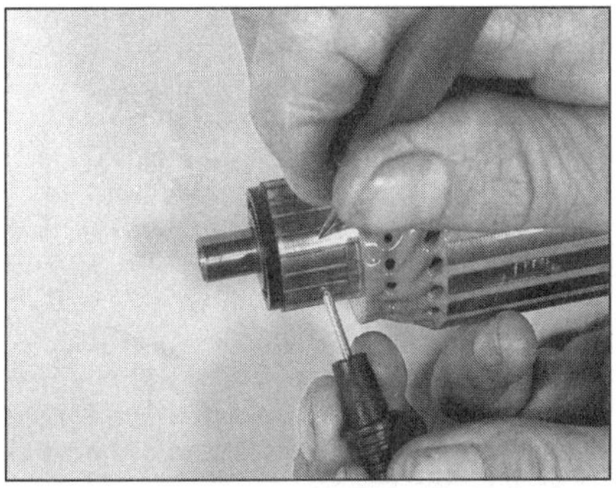

29.18a There should be continuity between the commutator bars

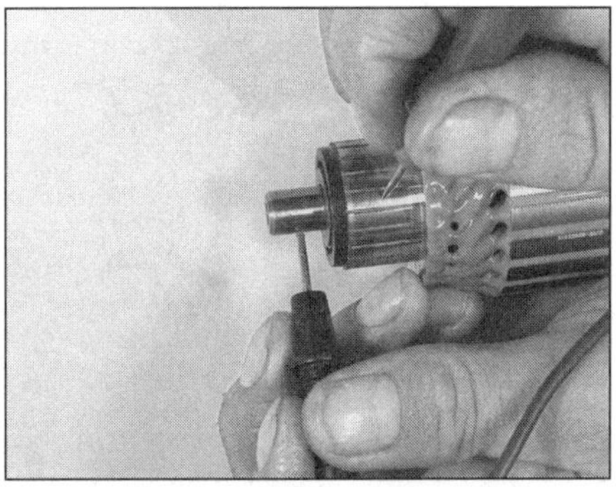

29.18b There should be no continuity between the commutator and the armature shaft

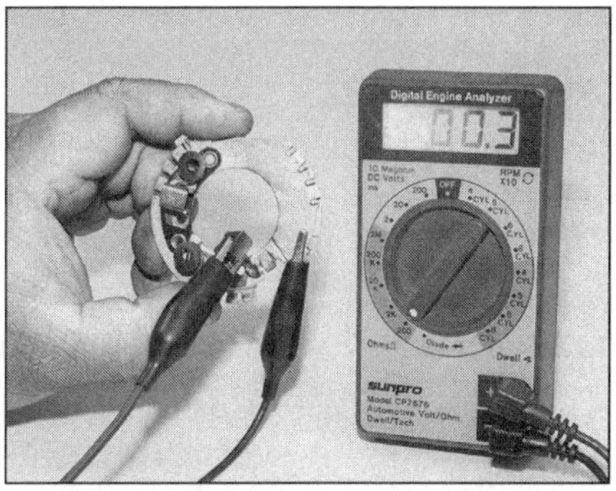

29.19 There should be virtually no resistance between the negative brush and the brushplate

29.23a Fit the terminal bolt into the rear cover . . .

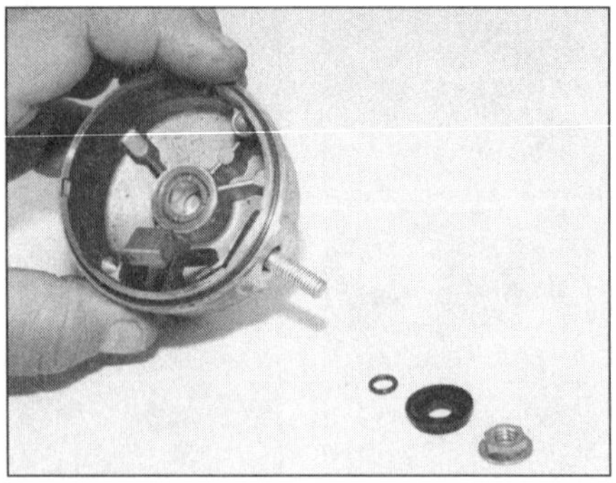

29.23b . . . then fit the O-ring and the insulator and tighten the nut

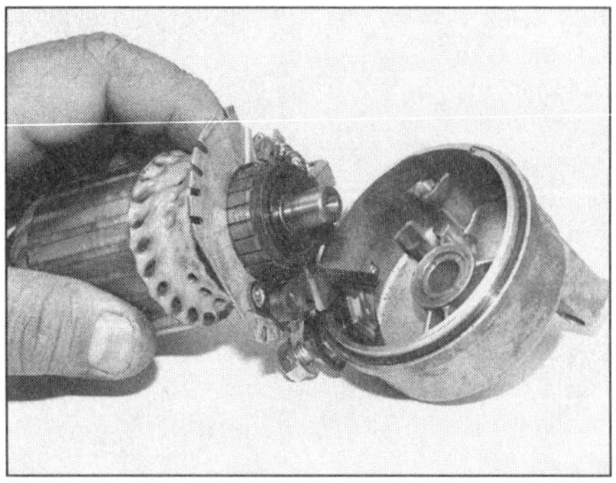

29.24 Push the brushes into their holders while sliding the commutator through the plate

21 Check the front end of the armature shaft for worn, cracked, chipped and broken teeth. If the shaft is damaged or worn, a new starter motor will have to be fitted.

22 Inspect the end covers for signs of cracks or wear. Inspect the magnets in the main housing and the housing itself for cracks.

Reassembly

F models

23 Insert the terminal bolt through the rear cover, then fit the O-ring and the insulating rubber over the terminal, then fit the nut and tighten it **(see illustrations)**.

24 Slide the brushes back into position in their holders and place the brush spring ends onto the brushes. Fit the brushplate onto the armature, pulling back the brushes as you do to allow the commutator through the plate **(see illustration)**. Take care not to damage the brushes when installing the brushplate onto the armature, and make sure they are correctly seated against the commutator after installation.

25 Slide the washer onto the rear end of the armature shaft, then fit the armature and brushplate assembly in the rear cover, making sure its tab is correctly located in the slot in the cover **(see illustrations)**. Check that each brush is securely pressed against the commutator by its spring and is free to move easily in its holder.

26 Fit a new O-ring onto the main housing, then fit the housing over the armature and onto the rear cover, aligning the marks made on removal.

29.25a Do not forget to fit the washer on the shaft

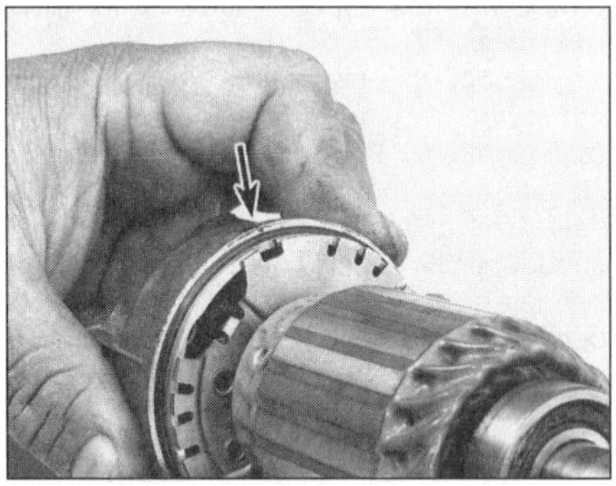

29.25b Make sure the notch in the brushplate is aligned with the notch in the armature housing

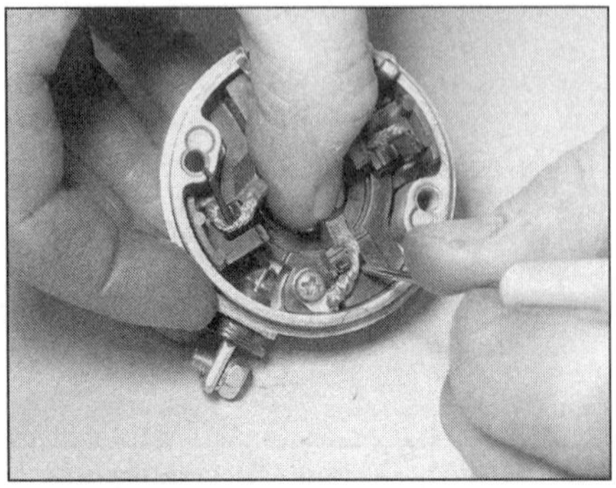

29.30 Slide the brushes into their holders and secure them with clips

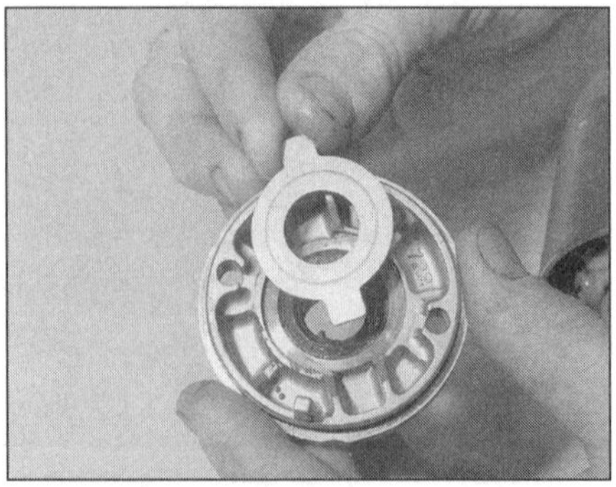

29.32 Fit the tabbed washer into the front cover

27 Fit a new O-ring onto the front of the main housing. Apply a smear of grease to the lips of the seal in the front cover. Install the front cover, aligning the marks made on removal.

28 Slide a new O-ring onto each of the long bolts. Check the marks made on removal are correctly aligned, then install the long bolts and tighten them securely.

29 Install the starter motor (see Section 29).

G, H, J and A models

30 Slide the brushes back into position in their holders and secure them against the spring pressure using crocodile clips to allow the armature to be fitted into the rear cover **(see illustration)**. Fit the armature into the rear cover, taking care not to damage the brushes when doing so, then remove the clips. Make sure the brushes spring out and are correctly seated against the commutator. Check that each brush is securely pressed against the commutator by its spring and is free to move easily in its holder.

31 Fit a new O-ring onto the main housing, then fit the housing over the armature and onto the rear cover, aligning the marks made on removal.

32 Fit a new O-ring onto the front of the main housing. Apply a smear of grease to the lips of the seal in the front cover. Fit the washer onto the armature shaft and the tabbed washer into the front cover **(see illustration)**. Install the front cover, aligning the marks made on removal (there is also a tab on the inside of the cover which aligns with the terminal bolt in the rear cover).

33 Slide a new O-ring onto each of the long bolts. Check the marks made on removal are correctly aligned, then install the long bolts and tighten them securely.

34 Install the starter motor (see Section 29).

30 Charging system testing – general information and precautions

1 If the performance of the charging system is suspect, the system as a whole should be checked first, followed by testing of the individual components. **Note:** *Before beginning the checks, make sure the battery is* *fully charged and that all system connections are clean and tight.*

2 Checking the output of the charging system and the performance of the various components within the charging system requires the use of a multimeter (with voltage, current and resistance checking facilities).

3 When making the checks, follow the procedures carefully to prevent incorrect connections or short circuits, as irreparable damage to electrical system components may result if short circuits occur.

4 If a multimeter is not available, the job of checking the charging system should be left to a Kawasaki dealer.

31 Charging system – leakage, output and resistance tests

1 If the charging system of the machine is thought to be faulty, remove the seats (see Chapter 8) and perform the following checks.

Leakage test

Caution: Always connect an ammeter in series, never in parallel with the battery, otherwise it will be damaged. Do not turn the ignition ON or operate the starter motor when the ammeter is connected – a sudden surge in current will blow the meter's fuse.

2 Turn the ignition switch OFF and disconnect the lead from the battery negative (-ve) terminal.

3 Set the multimeter to the Amps function and connect its negative (-ve) probe to the battery negative (-ve) terminal, and positive (+ve) probe to the disconnected negative (-ve) lead **(see illustration)**. Always set the meter to a high amps range initially and then bring it down to the mA (milli Amps) range; if there is a high current flow in the circuit it may blow the meter's fuse.

4 If the current leakage indicated exceeds the amount specified at the beginning of the Chapter, there is probably a short circuit in the wiring. Disconnect the meter and connect the negative (-ve) lead to the battery, tightening it securely,

5 If leakage is indicated, use the wiring diagrams at the end of this book to systematically disconnect individual electrical components and repeat the test until the source is identified.

Regulated voltage output test

6 Start the engine and warm it up to normal operating temperature. Stop the engine. Remove the seats (see Chapter 8).

7 To check the voltage output connect a multimeter set to the 0-20 volts DC scale (voltmeter) across the terminals of the battery (positive (+ve) lead to battery positive (+ve) terminal, negative (-ve) lead to battery negative (-ve) terminal). Start the engine and slowly increase engine speed to 5000 rpm and note the reading obtained. The regulated voltage should be as specified at the beginning of the Chapter. If the voltage is outside these limits, check the alternator and the regulator (see Sections 32 and 33). **Note:** *If the voltage is below the limit, then it is more likely that the alternator is faulty. If the voltage is above the limit, it is more likely that the regulator is faulty.*

> **HAYNES HiNT** ***Clues to a faulty regulator are constantly blowing bulbs, with brightness varying considerably with engine speed, and battery overheating, necessitating frequent topping up of the electrolyte level.***

Unregulated output test

8 Start the engine and warm it up to normal operating temperature. Stop the engine.

9 Remove the fuel tank (see Chapter 4). Trace the alternator wiring from the alternator cover and disconnect it at the connector **(see illustration)**. Either position the alternator end of the wiring connector so that it is accessible with the tank reinstalled, or rig up a remote fuel tank.

10 Using a multimeter set to 0-250 V AC range, connect the meter probes to one pair of terminals on the alternator side of the connector. Start the engine and increase its speed to 4000 rpm. Check the voltage output and compare it to the minimum specified at the beginning of the Chapter. Connect the meter to each pair of terminals in turn, taking three readings in all. If any of the readings are below the minimum specified, check the stator coil resistance (see below). If the readings are good, check the regulator (see Section 33).

Alternator stator coil test

11 Remove the fuel tank (see Chapter 4). Trace the alternator wiring from the alternator cover and disconnect it at the connector **(see illustration 31.9)**.

12 Using a multimeter set to the ohms x 1 scale, check the resistance between each of the wires on the alternator side of the connector, taking a total of three readings **(see illustration)**. Also check for continuity between each terminal and earth (ground). If the stator coil windings are in good condition there should be the resistance specified at the beginning of the Chapter between each of the terminals, and no continuity (infinite resistance) between any of the terminals and earth (ground). If not, the alternator stator coil assembly is at fault and should be replaced. If the resistance readings are as specified but the alternator output is low when tested as above, replace the rotor. **Note:** *Before condemning the stator coils, check the fault is not due to damaged wiring between the connector and coils.*

32 Alternator rotor and stator – removal and installation

Removal

1 Remove the left-hand lower fairing panel (see Chapter 8), the coolant reservoir (see Chapter 3) and the fuel tank (see Chapter 4).

2 Trace the alternator wiring from the alternator cover and disconnect it at the connector **(see illustration 31.9)**. Free the wiring from any clips or guides and feed it through to the alternator cover.

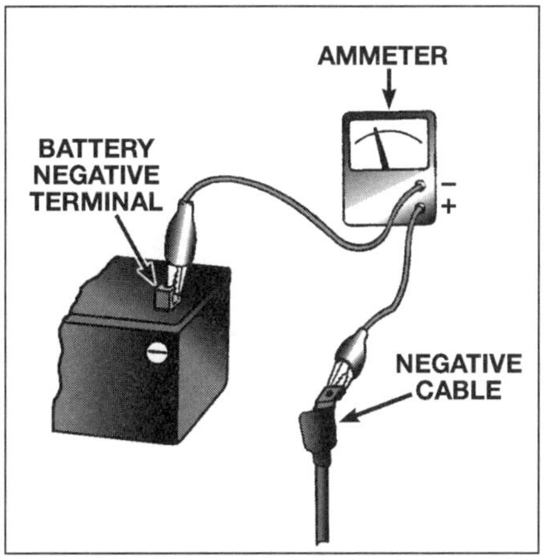

31.3 Checking the charging system leakage rate – connect the ammeter as shown

31.9 Disconnect the alternator wiring connector

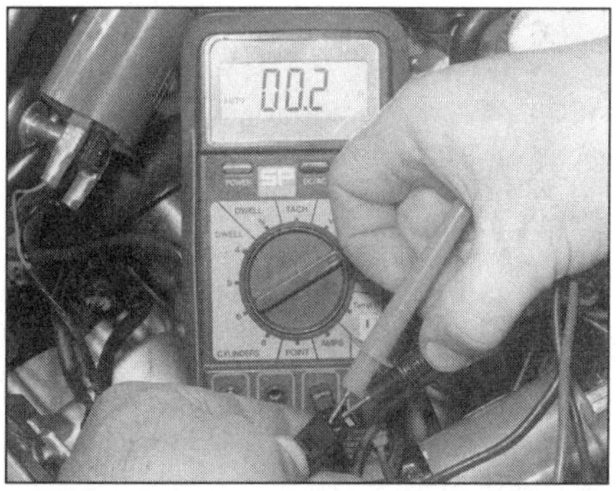

31.12 Checking stator coil resistance

32.3 Unscrew the bolts (arrowed) and remove the cover

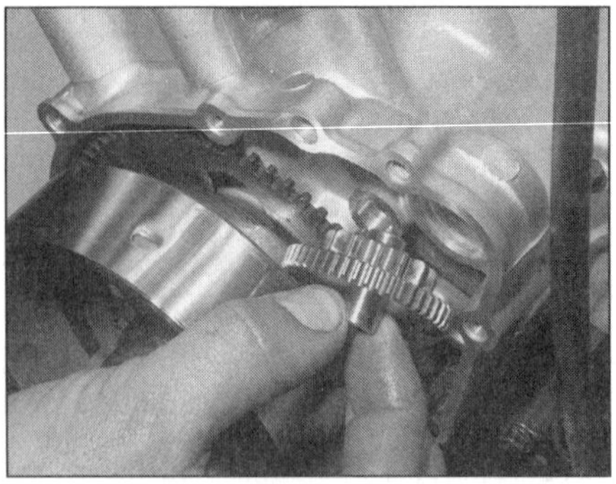

32.4 Remove the idle/reduction gear assembly

32.5 Using a holding tool to slacken the rotor bolt

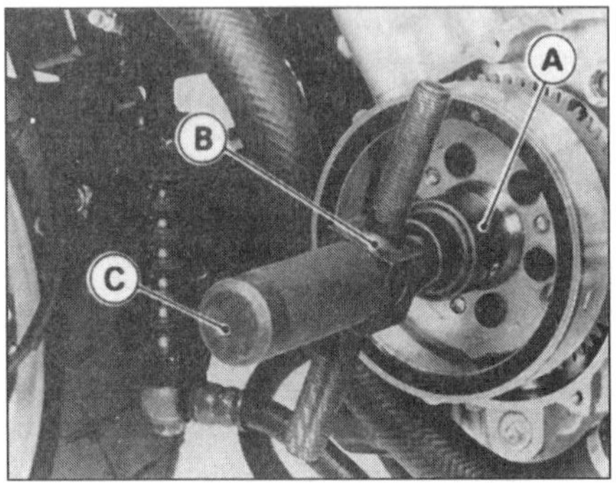

32.6a Rotor puller tool – F models

A Adapter B Puller C Puller head

32.6b Rotor puller tool (A) – G, H, J and A models

3 Working in a criss-cross pattern, slacken the alternator cover retaining bolts evenly **(see illustration)**. Lift the cover away from the engine, being prepared to catch any residual oil which may be released as the cover is removed. Remove the gasket and discard it. Remove the dowels from either the cover or the crankcase if they are loose.

4 Withdraw the shaft from the starter idle/reduction gear and remove the gear, noting how it fits **(see illustration)**.

5 To remove the rotor bolt it is necessary to stop the rotor from turning. If a rotor holding strap or tool is not available, place the transmission in gear and have an assistant apply the rear brake, then unscrew the bolt and remove the washer, noting which way round it fits **(see illustration)**. If using a holding tool, first wipe off any residue oil from the outside of the rotor.

6 To remove the rotor from the shaft it is necessary to use a rotor puller (Kawasaki service tools pt. no. 57001-1223 and 57001-1216 on F models, or pt. no. 57001-1405 on all other models, or a commercially available equivalent). Thread the rotor puller into the centre of the rotor and turn it until the rotor is displaced from the shaft **(see illustrations)**. On F models, remove the Woodruff key from the crankshaft for safekeeping if it is loose. If required, separate the starter clutch from the rotor (see Chapter 2).

7 To remove the stator from the cover, unscrew the three bolts securing the stator, and the bolts securing the wiring clamp, then remove the assembly, noting how the rubber wiring grommet fits **(see illustration)**.

Installation

8 Install the stator into the cover, aligning the rubber wiring grommet with the groove in the case **(see illustration 32.7)**. Apply a suitable non-permanent thread locking compound to the stator bolts, then install the bolts and tighten them to the torque setting specified at the beginning of the Chapter. Apply a suitable silicone sealant to the wiring grommet, then install it into the cut-out in the cover. Secure the wiring with its clamp and tighten the bolts to the specified torque.

9 If removed, install the starter clutch onto the rotor, and fit the starter driven gear into the starter clutch (see Chapter 2). Clean the tapered end of the crankshaft and the corresponding mating surface on the inside of the rotor with a suitable solvent and dry the surfaces – this is essential to ensure a good fit between the two components **(see illustration)**. Apply a smear of molybdenum disulphide grease to the mating surface of the starter driven gear and the crankshaft. On F models, fit the Woodruff key into its slot in the crankshaft.

10 Make sure that no metal objects have attached themselves to the magnet on the inside of the rotor, then install the rotor onto the shaft, on F models aligning the slot in the rotor with the Woodruff key, making sure it locates properly.

11 Install the rotor bolt washer with its chamfered side facing out.

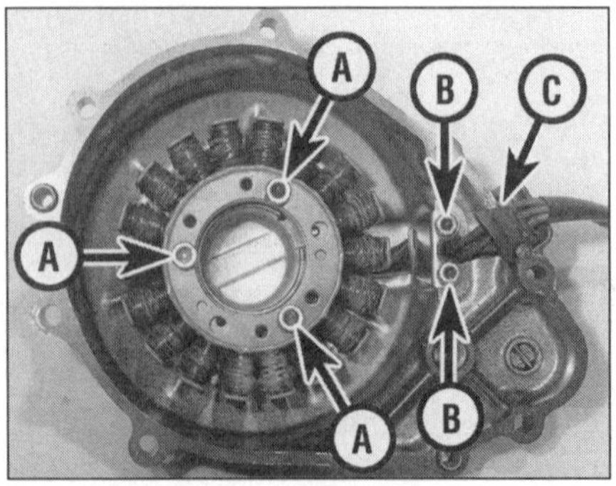

32.7 The stator is secured by three bolts (A) and the wiring clamp by two bolts (B). Note the wiring grommet (C)

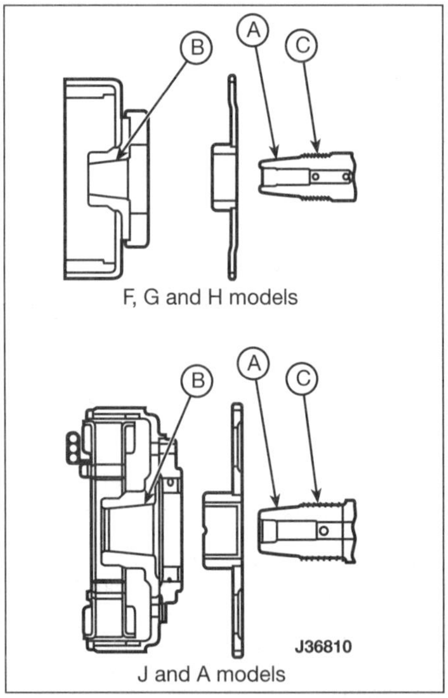

32.9 Clean any oil and dirt off the crankshaft taper (A) and the rotor taper (B), then dry both surfaces. Apply a smear of molybdenum disulphide grease to the parallel section of the crankshaft (C)

12 On F, G and H models, use the method employed on removal to prevent the rotor from turning, then install the bolt and tighten it to the torque setting specified at the beginning of the Chapter **(see illustrations)**.

13 On J and A models, use the method employed on removal to prevent the rotor from turning, then install the bolt and tighten it to the initial torque setting. Now undo the bolt and remove the washer. Check that the rotor is properly seated on the crankshaft by installing the rotor puller **(see illustration 32.6b)** and applying a torque of 20 Nm. If the rotor stays in place it is properly seated, and the washer and bolt can be refitted and tightened to the final torque setting. If the rotor was displaced during the test, there is a problem between its mating surface and the crankshaft taper: inspect the shaft and rotor internal taper for dirt or damage.

14 On all models, lubricate the idle/reduction gear shaft with clean engine oil, then install the idle/reduction gear followed by its shaft, making sure the smaller pinion on the idle/reduction gear faces in and meshes correctly with the teeth of the starter driven gear, and the teeth of the larger pinion mesh correctly with the teeth of the starter motor shaft **(see illustration 32.4)**.

15 Apply a suitable silicone sealant to the wiring grommet in the cover and to the crankcase half joints **(see illustration)**. If removed, fit the dowels into the crankcase. Install the alternator cover using a new gasket, making sure it locates correctly onto the dowels **(see illustration)**. Tighten the cover bolts evenly in a criss-cross sequence to the specified torque.

16 Reconnect the wiring at the connector and secure it with any clips or ties **(see illustration 31.9)**.

17 Install the fuel tank (see Chapter 4), the coolant reservoir (see Chapter 3) and the lower fairing panel (see Chapter 8).

32.12a Fit the washer and bolt . . .

32.12b . . . and tighten the bolt to the specified torque

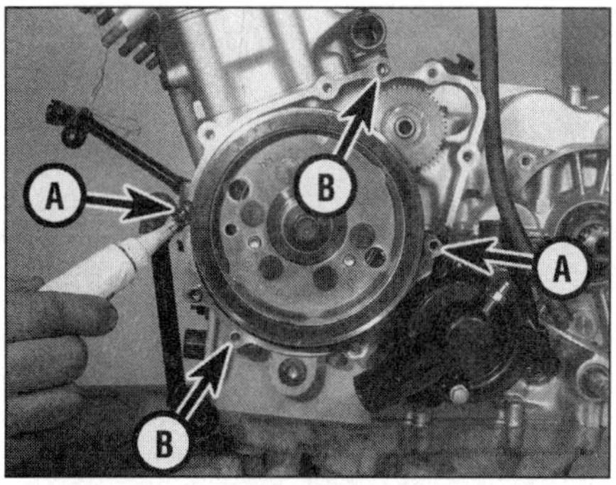

32.15a Apply the sealant to the crankcase joints (A), and check the dowels (B) are installed . . .

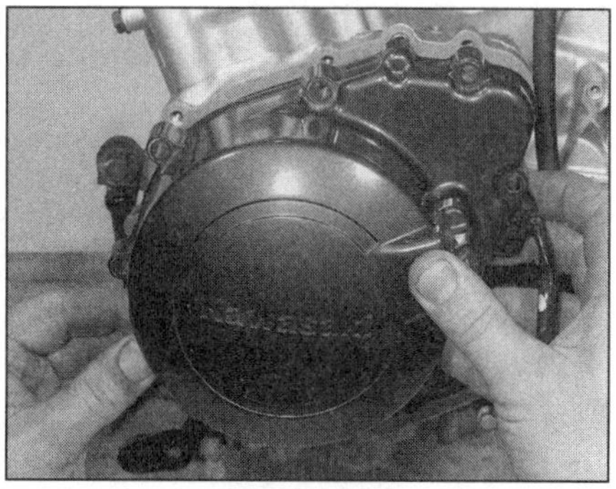

32.15b . . . then fit the cover using a new gasket

33 Regulator/rectifier – check and renewal

Check

1 The regulator/rectifier is mounted behind the left-hand side panel on F models, and on the right-hand side above the front of the swingarm on G, H, J and A models. Remove the side panels on F models, and the seats on all other models (see Chapter 8). On F models, disconnect the wiring connector from the unit **(see illustration)**. On all other models, trace the wiring from the regulator/rectifier unit and disconnect it at the connector(s) **(see illustrations)**. **Note:** *On J and A models there are two wiring connectors.*

2 To test the rectifier circuit, use a multimeter set to the appropriate resistance scale and check the resistance between the various terminals of the regulator/rectifier connector(s)

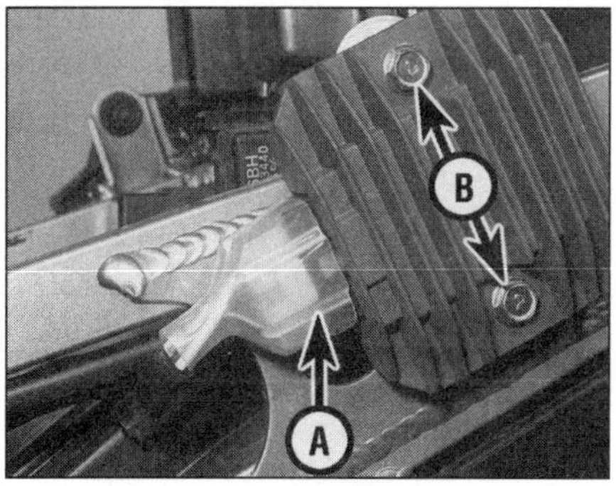

33.1a Regulator/rectifier wiring connector (A), mounting bolts (B) – F models

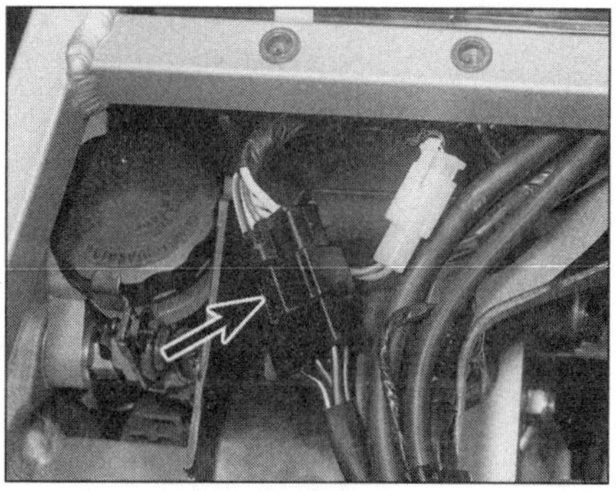

33.1b Regulator/rectifier wiring connector (arrowed) – G and H models

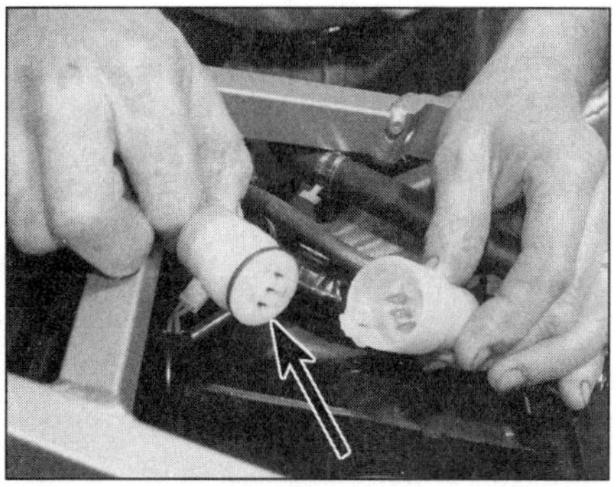

33.1c Regulator/rectifier wiring connector to main loom (arrowed) – J and A models

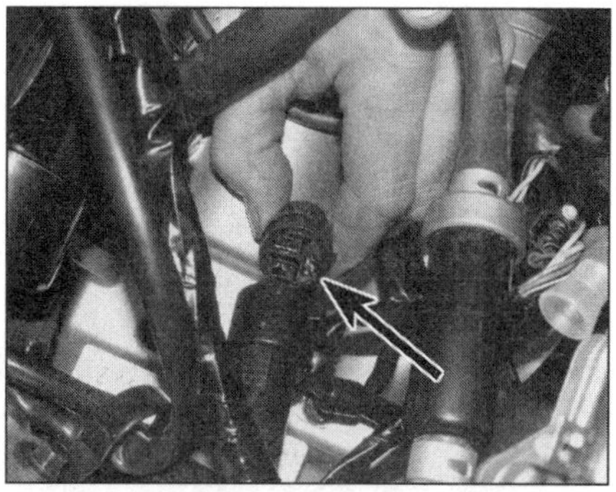

33.1d Regulator/rectifier wiring connector to alternator (arrowed) – J and A models

Number	Connections: Meter (+) to	Connections: Meter (-) to	Reading	Meter Range
1	Y1	W	∞	x 10Ω or x100Ω
2	Y2			
3	Y3			
4	Y1	BK/Y	1/2 scale	
5	Y2			
6	Y3			
7	W	Y1		
8		Y2		
9		Y3		
10	BK/Y	Y1	∞	
11		Y2		
12		Y3		

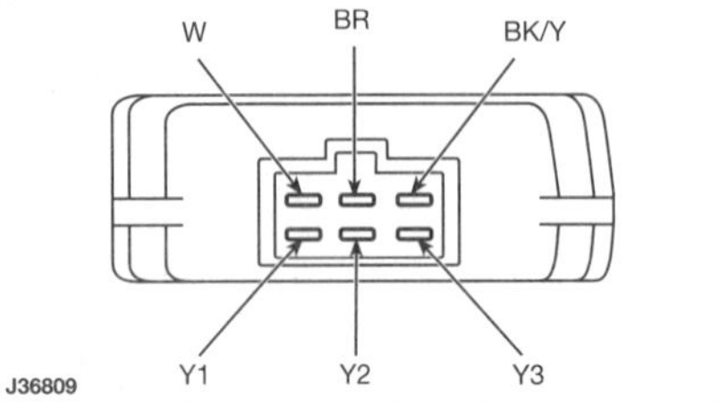

33.2a Rectifier test details and terminal identification – F, G and H models

W White wire | *Y1 Yellow 1 wire*
BR Brown wire | *Y2 Yellow 2 wire*
BK/Y Black/yellow wire | *Y3 Yellow 3 wire*

Number	Connections: Tester (+)	Connections: Tester (-)	Reading	Tester Range
1	BK1	BK/BL	∞	x 10Ω or x100Ω
2	BK2			
3	BK3			
4	BK1	BK/W	1/2 scale or less	
5	BK2			
6	BK3			
7	BK/BL	BK1		
8		BK2		
9		BK3		
10	BK/W	BK1	∞	
11		BK2		
12		BK3		

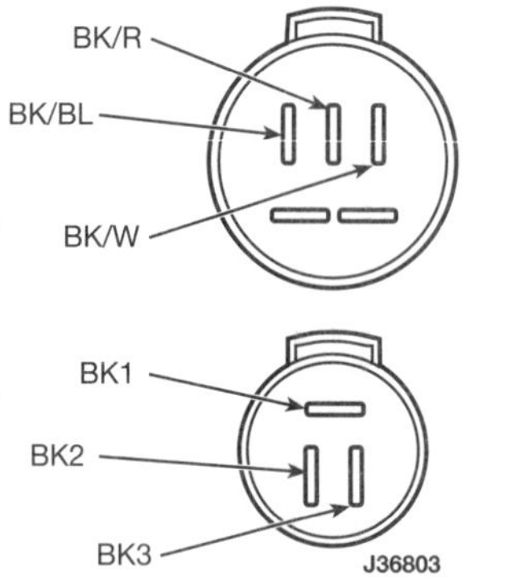

33.2b Rectifier test details and terminal identification – J and A models

BK/BL Black/blue wire | *BK/W Black/white wire* | *BK2 Black 2 wire*
BK/R Black/red wire | *BK1 Black 1 wire* | *BK3 Black 3 wire*

as shown in the table **(see illustrations)**. If the readings do not compare closely with those shown in the table the regulator/rectifier unit can be considered faulty. **Note:** *The use of certain multimeters could lead to false readings being obtained. Therefore, if the above check shows the regulator/rectifier unit to be faulty take the unit to a Kawasaki dealer for confirmation of its condition before replacing it.*

3 To test the regulator circuit, three fully-charged 12V batteries, each with a set of auxiliary leads, and a test light are required. If these are not available, carry out a charging system test (see Section 31). If the conditions arise from that test that indicate a faulty regulator, take it to a Kawasaki dealer for further testing. Clues to a faulty regulator are constantly blowing bulbs, with brightness varying considerably with engine speed, and battery overheating, necessitating frequent topping up of the electrolyte level.

4 Referring to the three circuit diagrams shown, set each circuit up in turn **(see illustrations)**. Where dotted lines are shown to the terminals on the connector, check the circuit for each of the terminals in turn using the same lead, thereby taking three readings for each circuit. In the first test circuit (A), the bulb should not light up. In the second test circuit (B), the bulb should not light up. In the third test circuit (C) the bulb should light up. If any of the tests prove otherwise, the regulator/rectifier is faulty and must be replaced.

5 The tests outlined above are not foolproof. If the test results indicate that the unit is good, and all other components in the charging circuit have been checked and proven good, but there is still a problem, the regulator/rectifier may well be faulty. If this is the case, either take the unit to a Kawasaki dealer for testing, or substitute the suspect unit with one that is known to be good and recheck the system.

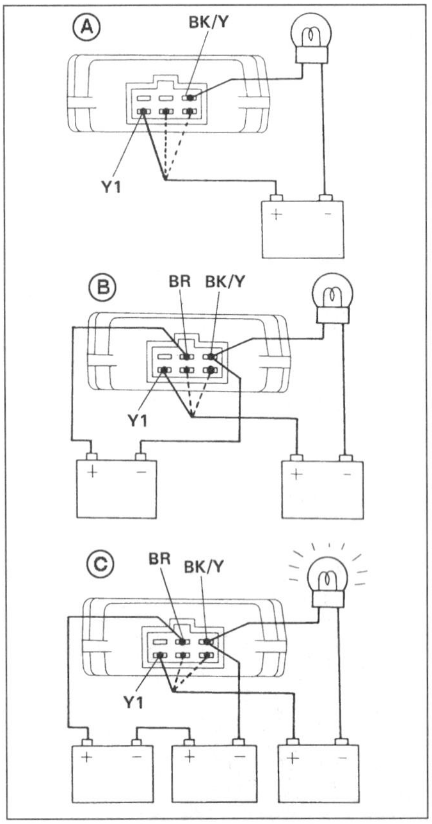

33.4a Regulator test circuit set-up – F, G and H models

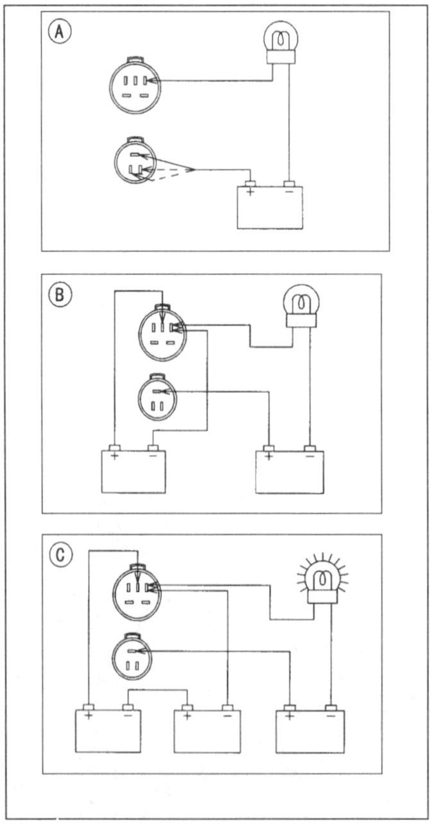

33.4b Regulator test circuit set-up – J and A models

Renewal

6 The regulator/rectifier is mounted behind the left-hand side panel on F models, and on the right-hand side above the front of the swingarm on G, H, J and A models. Remove the side panels on F models, and the seats on all other models (see Chapter 8). On F models, disconnect the wiring connector from the unit **(see illustration 33.1a)**. On all other models, trace the wiring from the regulator/rectifier unit and disconnect it at the connector(s) **(see illustrations 33.1b, 33.1c and 33.1d)**.

7 Unscrew the two bolts securing the regulator/rectifier and remove it.

8 Install the new unit and tighten its bolts securely. Connect the wiring connector(s).

9 Install the side panels and/or seats (see Chapter 8).

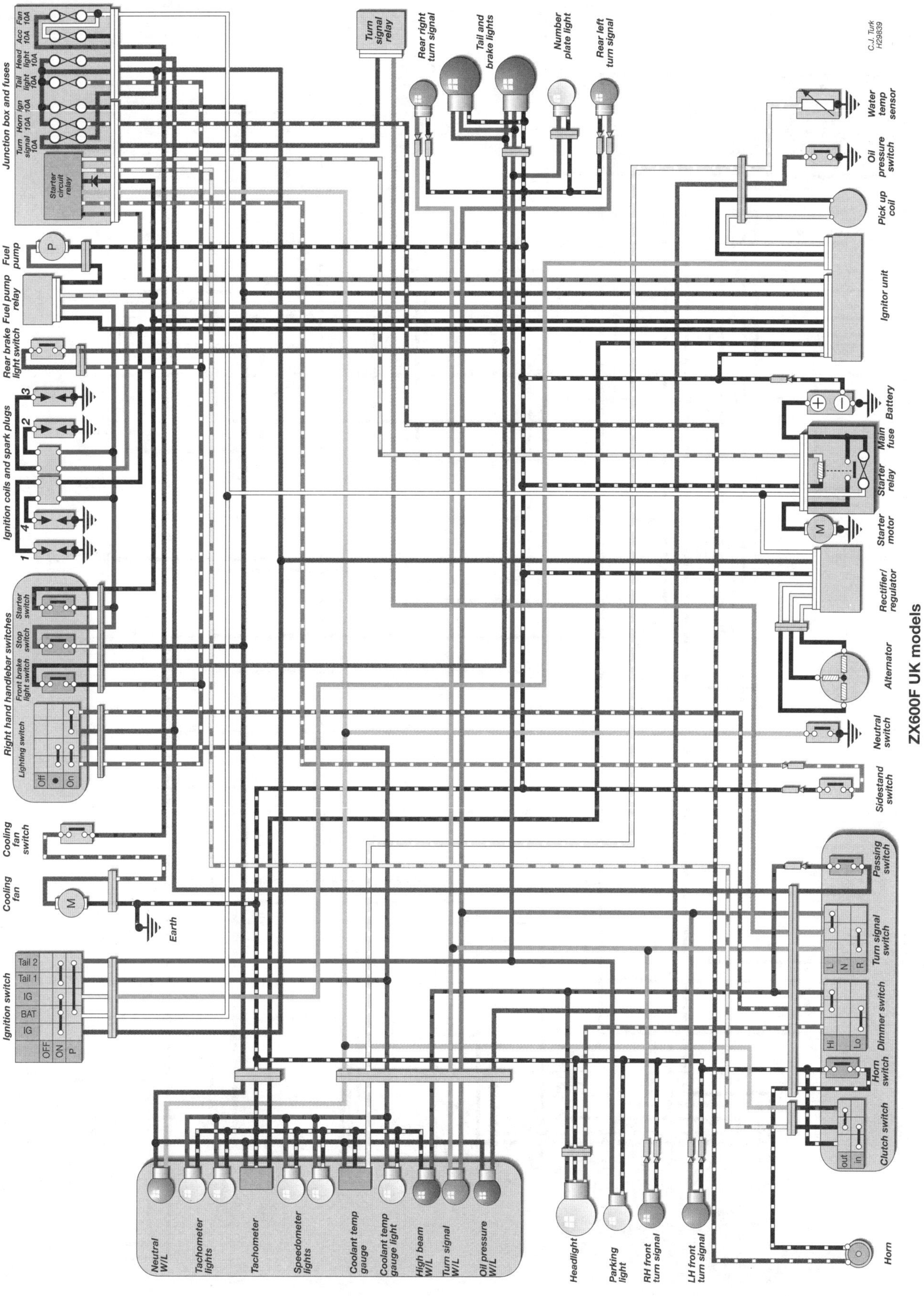
ZX600F UK models
Junction box and fuses
Turn signal 10A
Horn 10A
Ign 10A
Tail light 10A
Head light 10A
Acc 10A
Fan 10A
Starter circuit relay
Fuel pump
Fuel pump relay
Rear brake light switch
Ignition coils and spark plugs
1
2
3
4
Right hand handlebar switches
Starter switch
Stop switch
Front brake light switch
Lighting switch
Off
On
Cooling fan switch
Cooling fan
Earth
Ignition switch
Tail 2
Tail 1
IG
BAT
IG
OFF
ON
P
Neutral W/L
Tachometer lights
Tachometer
Speedometer lights
Coolant temp gauge
Coolant temp gauge light
High beam W/L
Turn signal W/L
Oil pressure W/L
Headlight
Parking light
RH front turn signal
LH front turn signal
Horn
Turn signal relay
Rear right turn signal
Tail and brake lights
Number plate light
Rear left turn signal
C.J. Turk
H29839
Water temp sensor
Oil pressure switch
Pick up coil
Ignitor unit
Battery
Main fuse
Starter relay
Starter motor
Rectifier/ regulator
Alternator
Neutral switch
Sidestand switch
Passing switch
Turn signal switch
L
N
R
Dimmer switch
Hi
Lo
Horn switch
Clutch switch
out
in

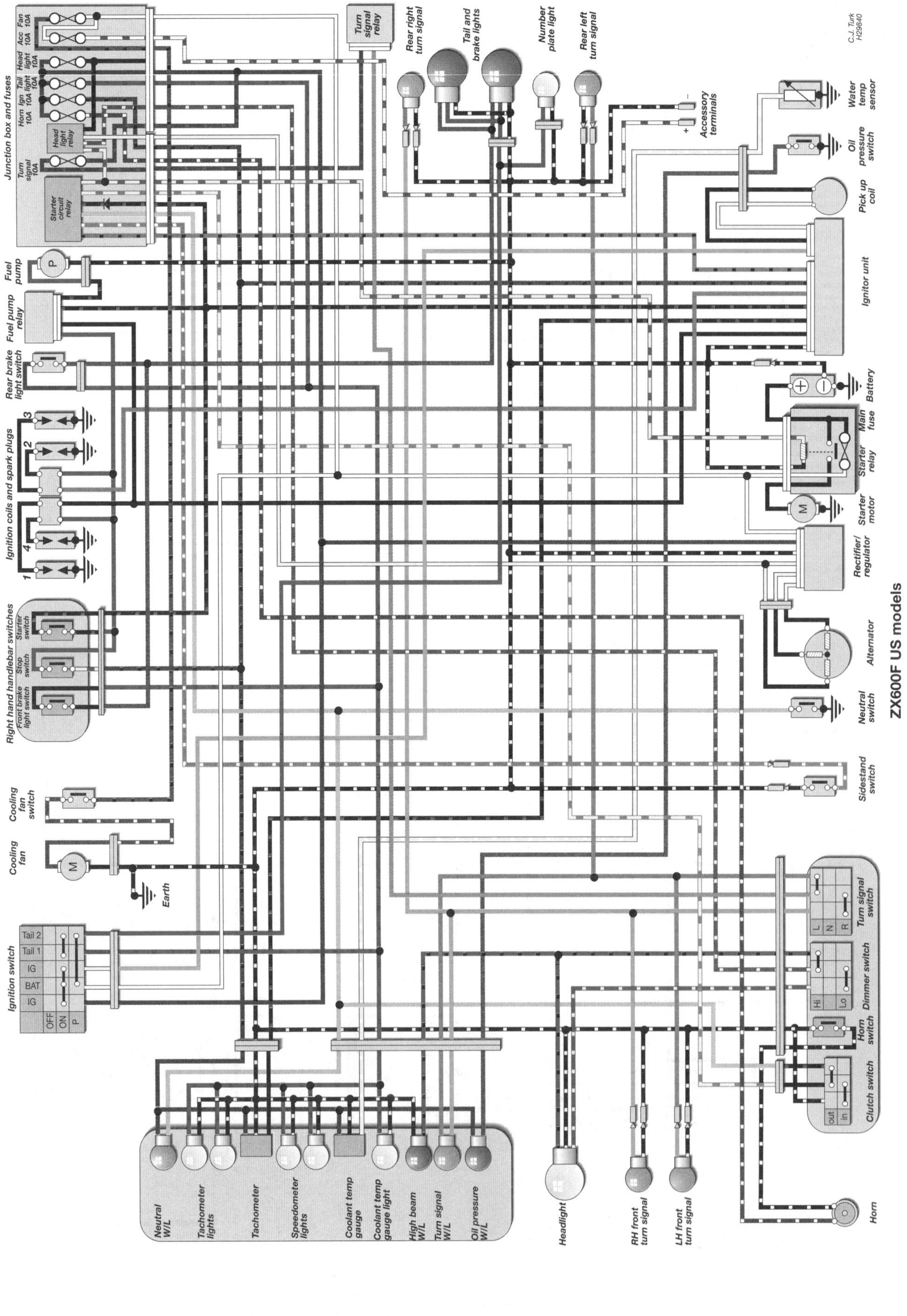

ZX600F US models

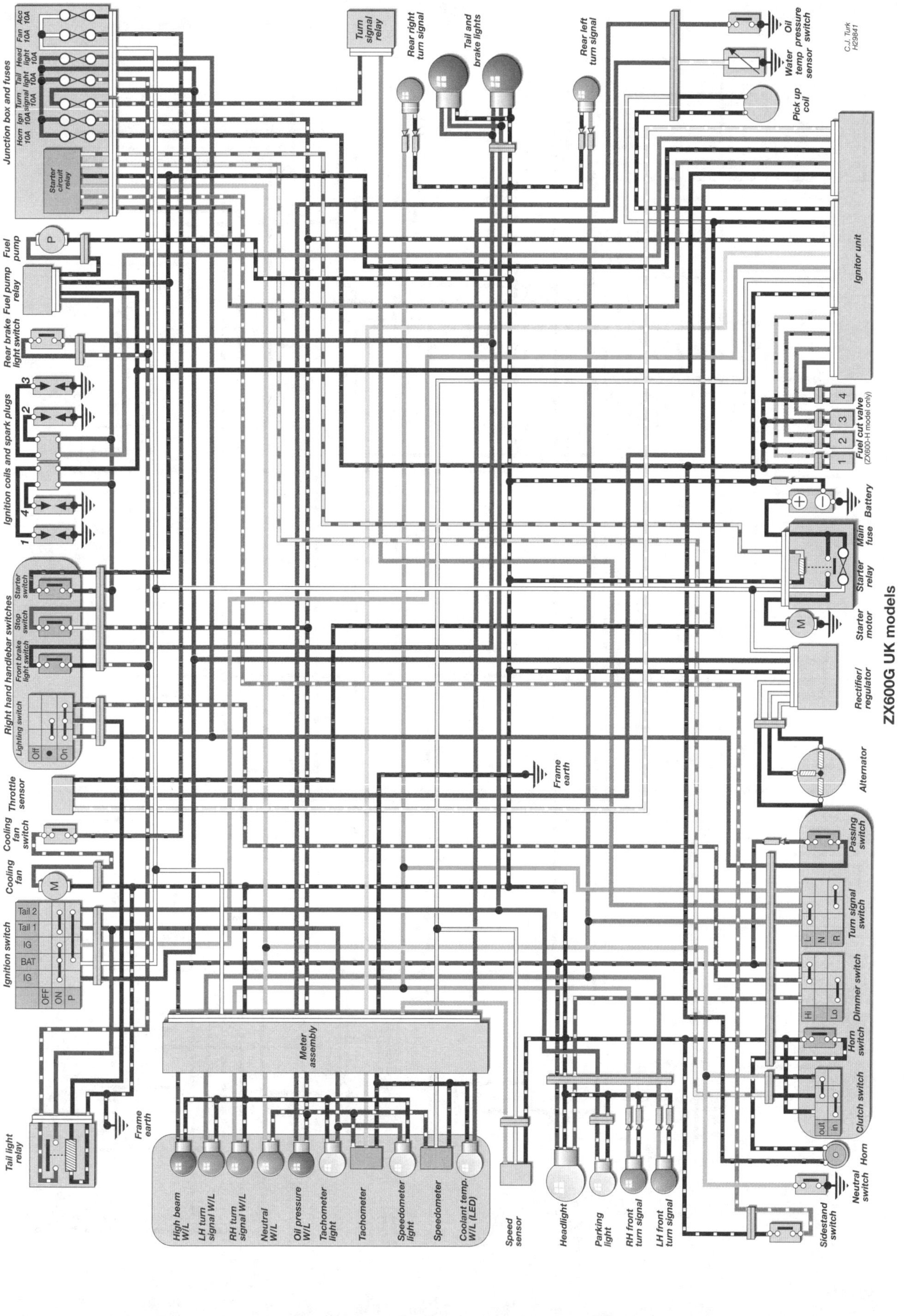
Junction box and fuses
Horn 10A
Ign 10A
Turn signal 10A
Tail light 10A
Head light 10A
Fan 10A
Acc 10A
Starter circuit relay
Turn signal relay
Rear right turn signal
Tail and brake lights
Rear left turn signal
Oil pressure switch
Water temp sensor
Pick up coil
C.J. Turk
H29841
Fuel pump
P
Fuel pump relay
Rear brake light switch
Ignition coils and spark plugs
1
2
3
4
Ignitor unit
Fuel cut valve
(ZX600-H model only)
Battery
Main fuse
Starter relay
Starter motor
M
Rectifier/ regulator
ZX600G UK models
Alternator
Right hand handlebar switches
Starter switch
Stop switch
Front brake light switch
Lighting switch
Off
On
Throttle sensor
Frame earth
Cooling fan switch
Cooling fan
Ignition switch
Tail 2
Tail 1
IG
BAT
IG
OFF
ON
P
Passing switch
Turn signal switch
L
N
R
Dimmer switch
Hi
Lo
Horn switch
Clutch switch
out
in
Meter assembly
Tail light relay
Frame earth
High beam W/L
LH turn signal W/L
RH turn signal W/L
Neutral W/L
Oil pressure W/L
Tachometer light
Tachometer
Speedometer light
Speedometer
Coolant temp. W/L (LED)
Speed sensor
Headlight
Parking light
RH front turn signal
LH front turn signal
Horn
Neutral switch
Sidestand switch

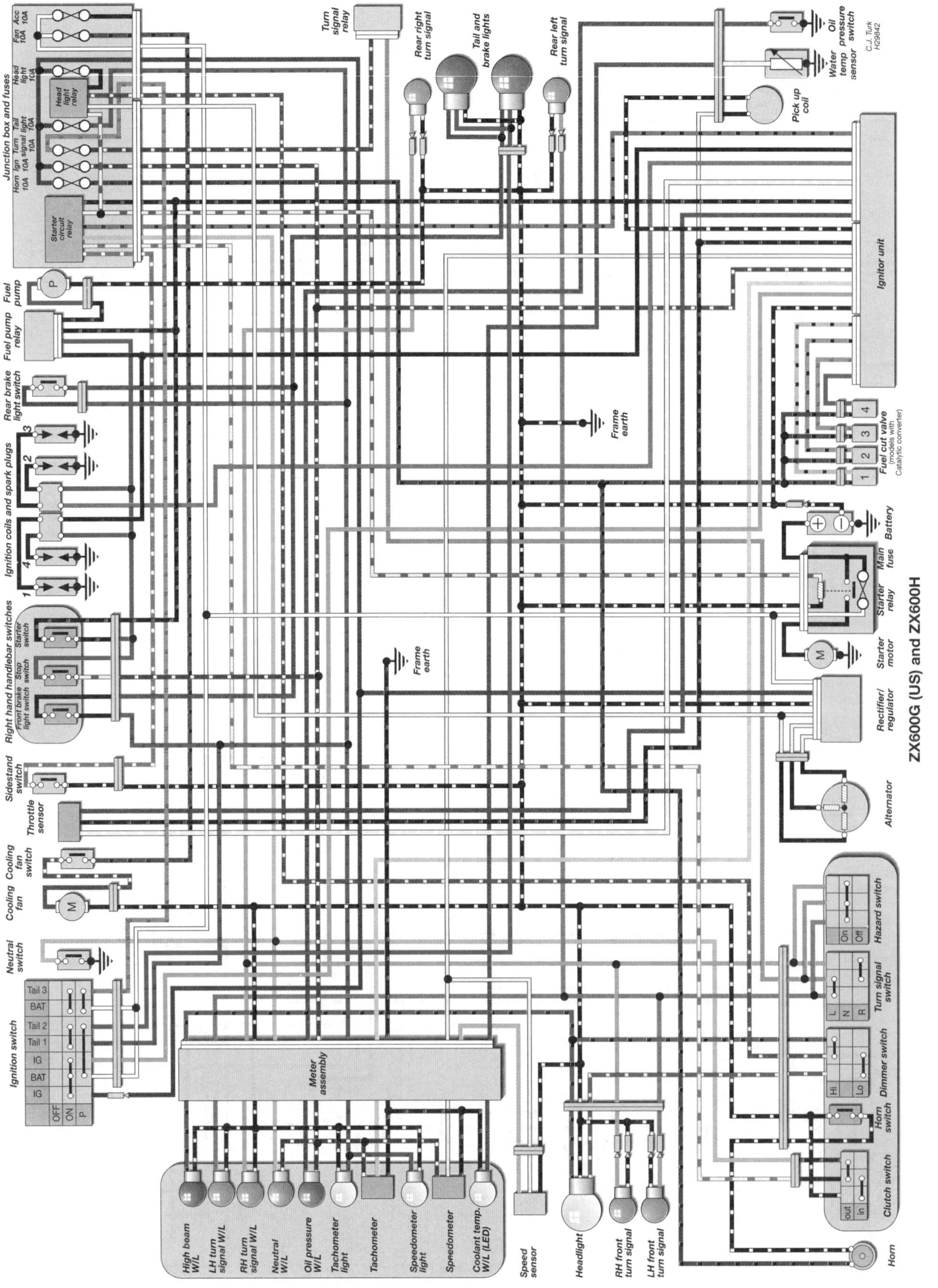
Junction box and fuses
Fan 10A
Acc 10A
Head light 10A
Head light relay
Tail light 10A
Turn signal 10A
Ign 10A
Horn 10A
Starter circuit relay
Fuel pump
Fuel pump relay
Rear brake light switch
Ignition coils and spark plugs
Right hand handlebar switches
Starter switch
Stop switch
Front brake light switch
Sidestand switch
Throttle sensor
Cooling fan switch
Cooling fan
Neutral switch
Ignition switch
Tail 3
BAT
Tail 2
Tail 1
IG
BAT
IG
OFF
ON
P
Meter assembly
High beam W/L
LH turn signal W/L
RH turn signal W/L
Neutral W/L
Oil pressure W/L
Tachometer light
Tachometer
Speedometer light
Speedometer
Coolant temp. W/L (LED)
Speed sensor
Headlight
RH front turn signal
LH front turn signal
Horn
Clutch switch
Horn switch
Dimmer switch
Turn signal switch
Hazard switch
Alternator
Rectifier/ regulator
Starter motor
Starter relay
Main fuse
Battery
Fuel cut valve (models with Catalytic converter)
Ignitor unit
Frame earth
Pick up coil
Water temp sensor
Oil pressure switch
C.J. Turk H29842
Rear left turn signal
Tail and brake lights
Rear right turn signal
Turn signal relay
ZX600G (US) and ZX600H

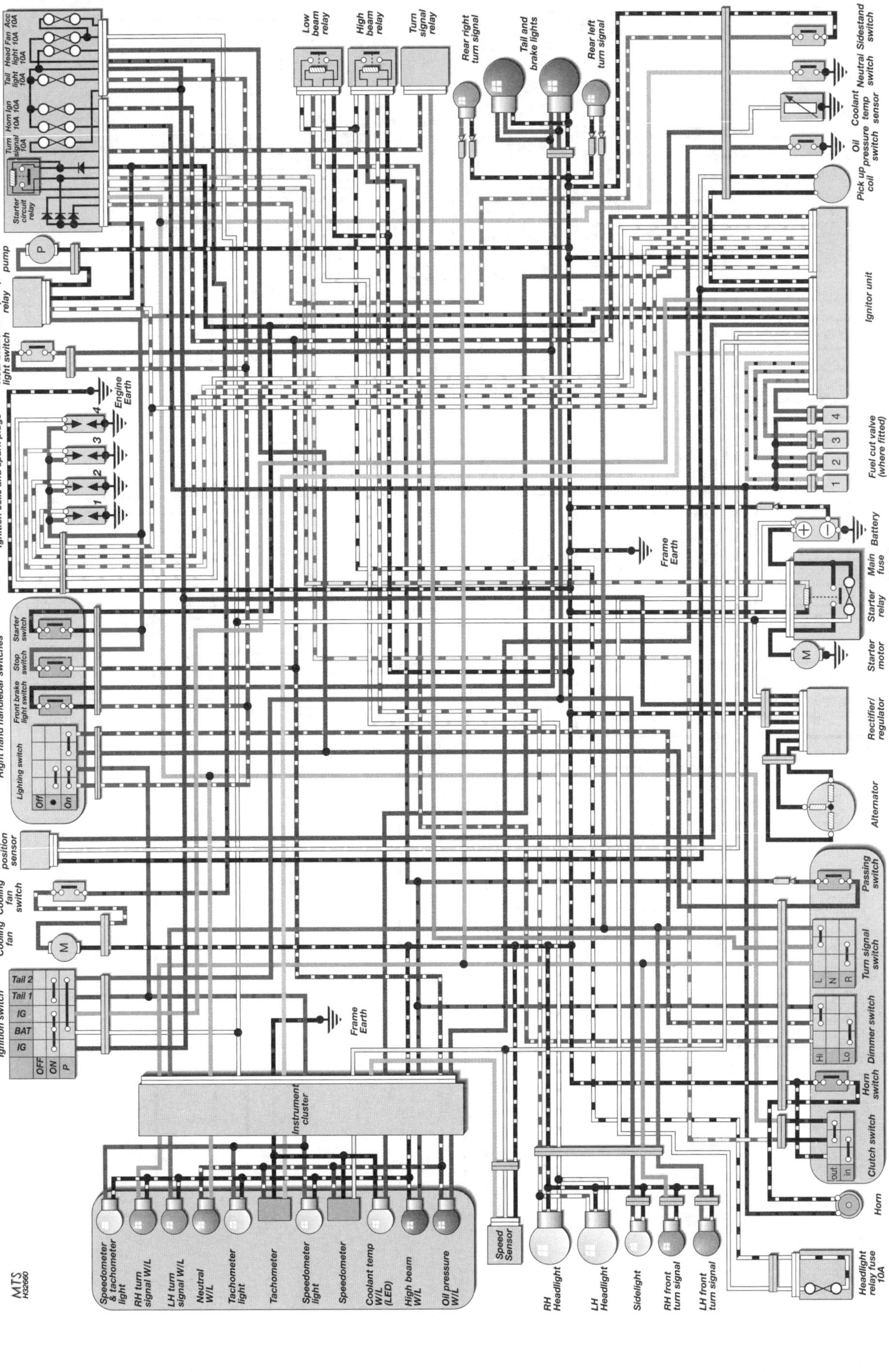

ZX600J and ZX636A Europe models

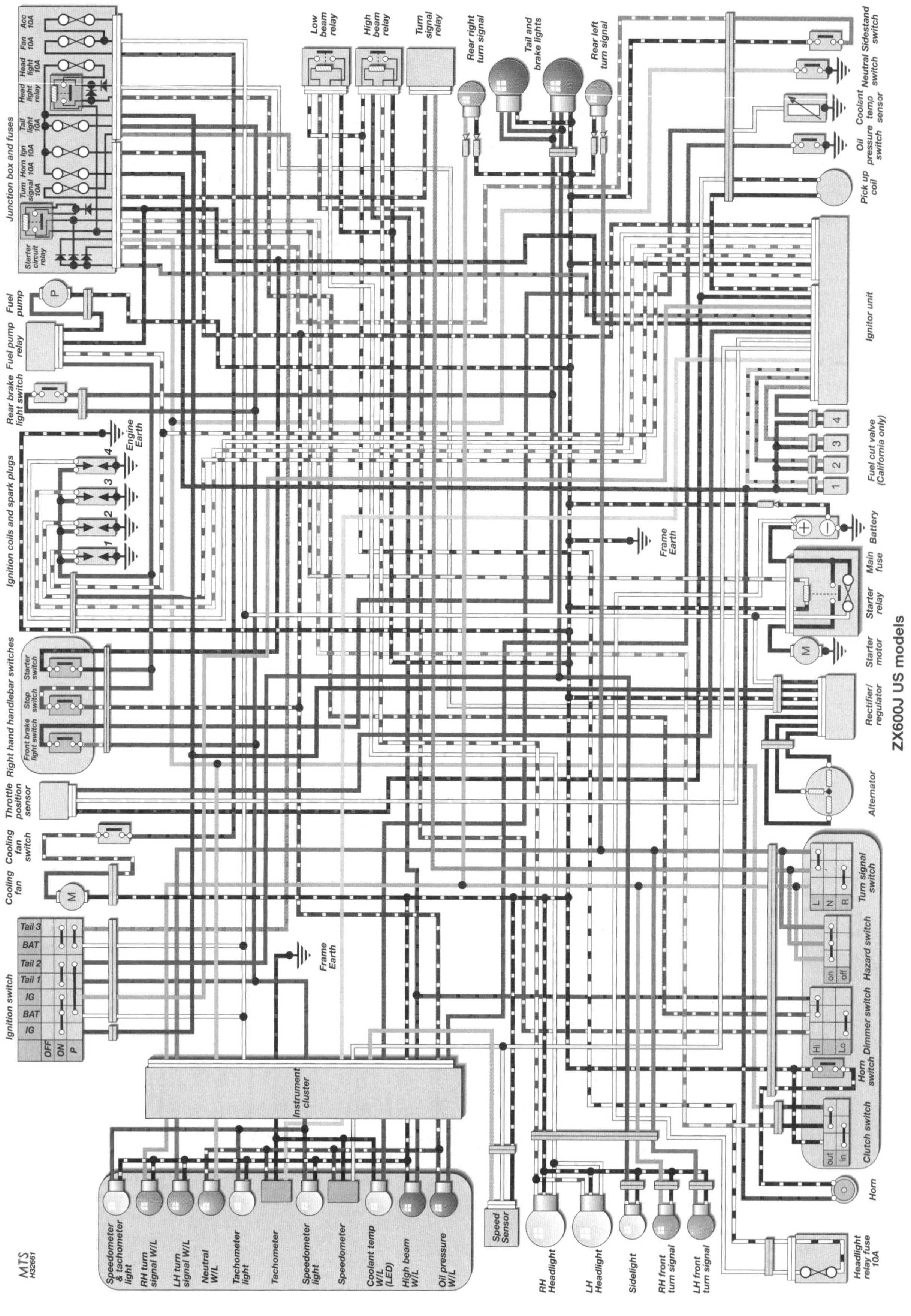
Junction box and fuses
Starter circuit relay
Turn signal 10A
Horn 10A
Ign 10A
Tail light 10A
Head light relay
Head light 10A
Fan 10A
Acc 10A
Fuel pump
Fuel pump relay
Rear brake light switch
Engine Earth
Ignition coils and spark plugs
Right hand handlebar switches
Starter switch
Stop switch
Front brake light switch
Throttle position sensor
Cooling fan switch
Cooling fan
Ignition switch
Tail 3
BAT
Tail 2
Tail 1
IG
BAT
IG
OFF
ON
P
Frame Earth
Instrument cluster
Speedometer & tachometer light
RH turn signal W/L
LH turn signal W/L
Neutral W/L
Tachometer light
Tachometer
Speedometer light
Speedometer
Coolant temp W/L (LED)
High beam W/L
Oil pressure W/L
MTS H32661
Speed Sensor
RH Headlight
LH Headlight
Sidelight
RH front turn signal
LH front turn signal
Low beam relay
High beam relay
Turn signal relay
Rear right turn signal
Tail and brake lights
Rear left turn signal
Frame Earth
Sidestand switch
Neutral switch
Coolant temp sensor
Oil pressure switch
Pick up coil
Ignitor unit
Fuel cut valve (California only)
Battery
Main fuse
Starter relay
Starter motor
Rectifier/ regulator
Alternator
ZX600J US models
Turn signal switch
L
N
R
Hazard switch
on
off
Dimmer switch
Hi
Lo
Horn switch
Clutch switch
out
in
Horn
Headlight relay fuse 10A

Reference

- Building up a tool kit and equipping your workshop ● Using tools
- Understanding bearing, seal, fastener and chain sizes and markings
- Repair techniques

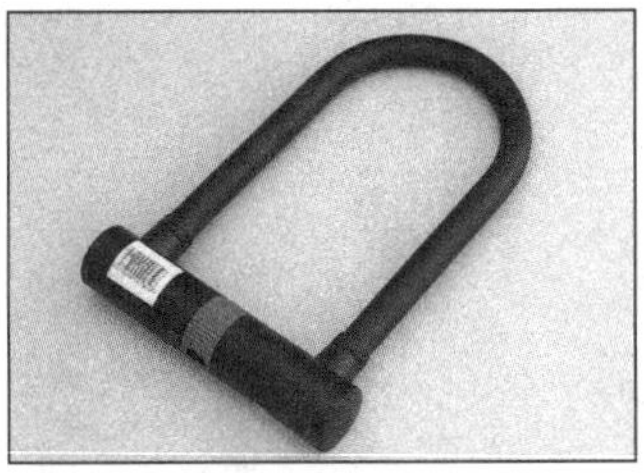

- Locks and chains
- U-locks ● Disc locks
- Alarms and immobilisers
- Security marking systems ● Tips on how to prevent bike theft

- Engine oils
- Transmission (gear) oils
- Coolant/anti-freeze
- Fork oils and suspension fluids ● Brake/clutch fluids
- Spray lubes, degreasers and solvents

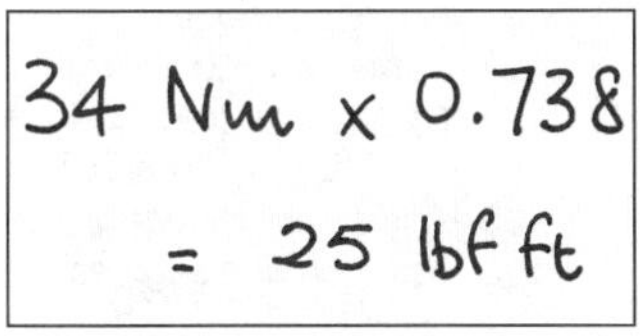

- Formulae for conversion of the metric (SI) units used throughout the manual into Imperial measures

- A guide to the UK MOT test ● Which items are tested ● How to prepare your motorcycle for the test and perform a pre-test check

- How to prepare your motorcycle for going into storage and protect essential systems ● How to get the motorcycle back on the road

- Common faults and their likely causes ● How to check engine cylinder compression ● How to make electrical tests and use test meters

- Component names, technical terms and common abbreviations explained

Buying tools

A toolkit is a fundamental requirement for servicing and repairing a motorcycle. Although there will be an initial expense in building up enough tools for servicing, this will soon be offset by the savings made by doing the job yourself. As experience and confidence grow, additional tools can be added to enable the repair and overhaul of the motorcycle. Many of the specialist tools are expensive and not often used so it may be preferable to hire them, or for a group of friends or motorcycle club to join in the purchase.

As a rule, it is better to buy more expensive, good quality tools. Cheaper tools are likely to wear out faster and need to be renewed more often, nullifying the original saving.

> ***Warning: To avoid the risk of a poor quality tool breaking in use, causing injury or damage to the component being worked on, always aim to purchase tools which meet the relevant national safety standards.***

The following lists of tools do not represent the manufacturer's service tools, but serve as a guide to help the owner decide which tools are needed for this level of work. In addition, items such as an electric drill, hacksaw, files, soldering iron and a workbench equipped with a vice, may be needed. Although not classed as tools, a selection of bolts, screws, nuts, washers and pieces of tubing always come in useful.

For more information about tools, refer to the Haynes *Motorcycle Workshop Practice TechBook* (Bk. No. 3470).

Manufacturer's service tools

Inevitably certain tasks require the use of a service tool. Where possible an alternative tool or method of approach is recommended, but sometimes there is no option if personal injury or damage to the component is to be avoided. Where required, service tools are referred to in the relevant procedure.

Service tools can usually only be purchased from a motorcycle dealer and are identified by a part number. Some of the commonly-used tools, such as rotor pullers, are available in aftermarket form from mail-order motorcycle tool and accessory suppliers.

Maintenance and minor repair tools

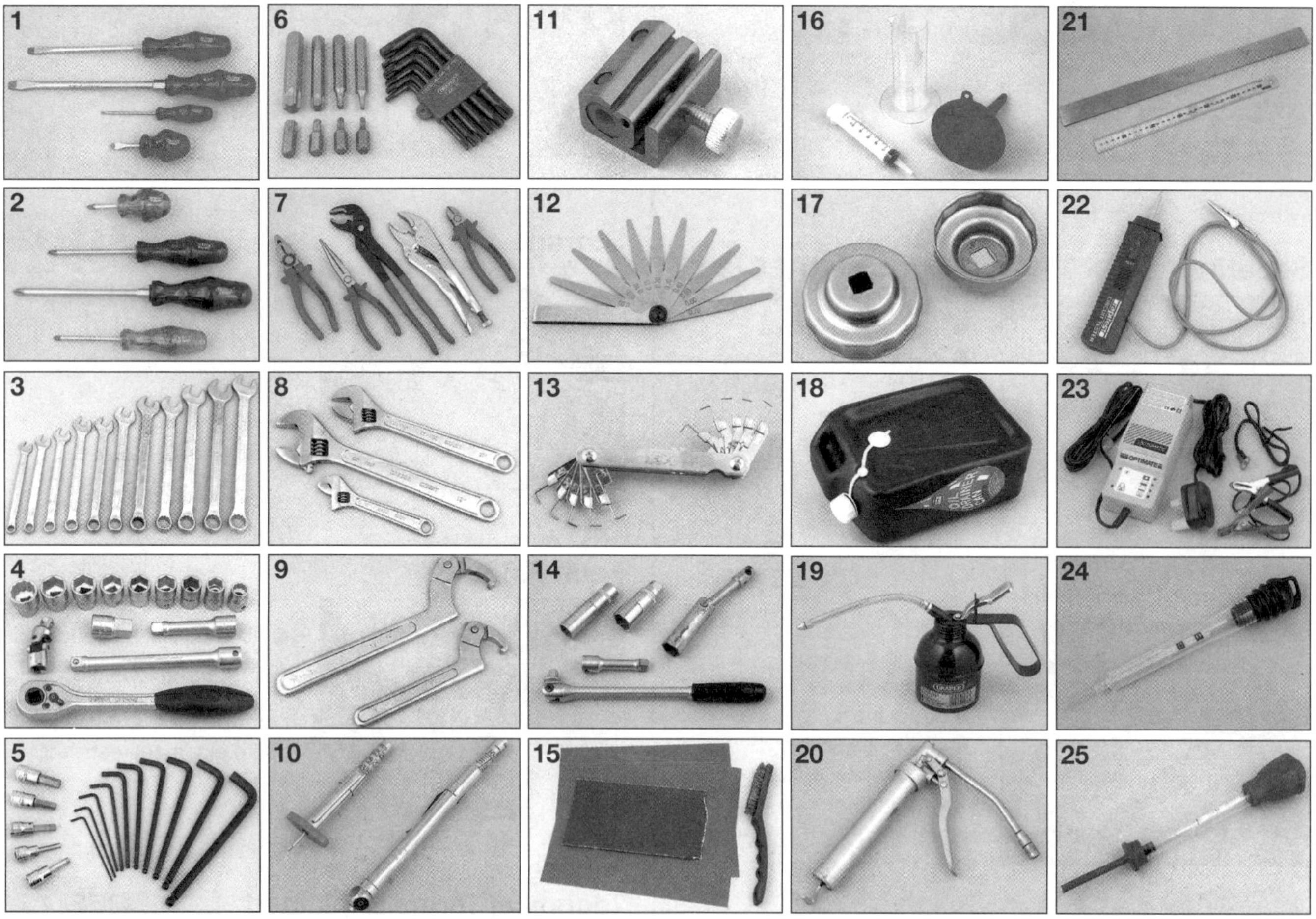

1 *Set of flat-bladed screwdrivers*
2 *Set of Phillips head screwdrivers*
3 *Combination open-end and ring spanners*
4 *Socket set (3/8 inch or 1/2 inch drive)*
5 *Set of Allen keys or bits*
6 *Set of Torx keys or bits*
7 *Pliers, cutters and self-locking grips (Mole grips)*
8 *Adjustable spanners*
9 *C-spanners*
10 *Tread depth gauge and tyre pressure gauge*
11 *Cable oiler clamp*
12 *Feeler gauges*
13 *Spark plug gap measuring tool*
14 *Spark plug spanner or deep plug sockets*
15 *Wire brush and emery paper*
16 *Calibrated syringe, measuring vessel and funnel*
17 *Oil filter adapters*
18 *Oil drainer can or tray*
19 *Pump type oil can*
20 *Grease gun*
21 *Straight-edge and steel rule*
22 *Continuity tester*
23 *Battery charger*
24 *Hydrometer (for battery specific gravity check)*
25 *Anti-freeze tester (for liquid-cooled engines)*

Repair and overhaul tools

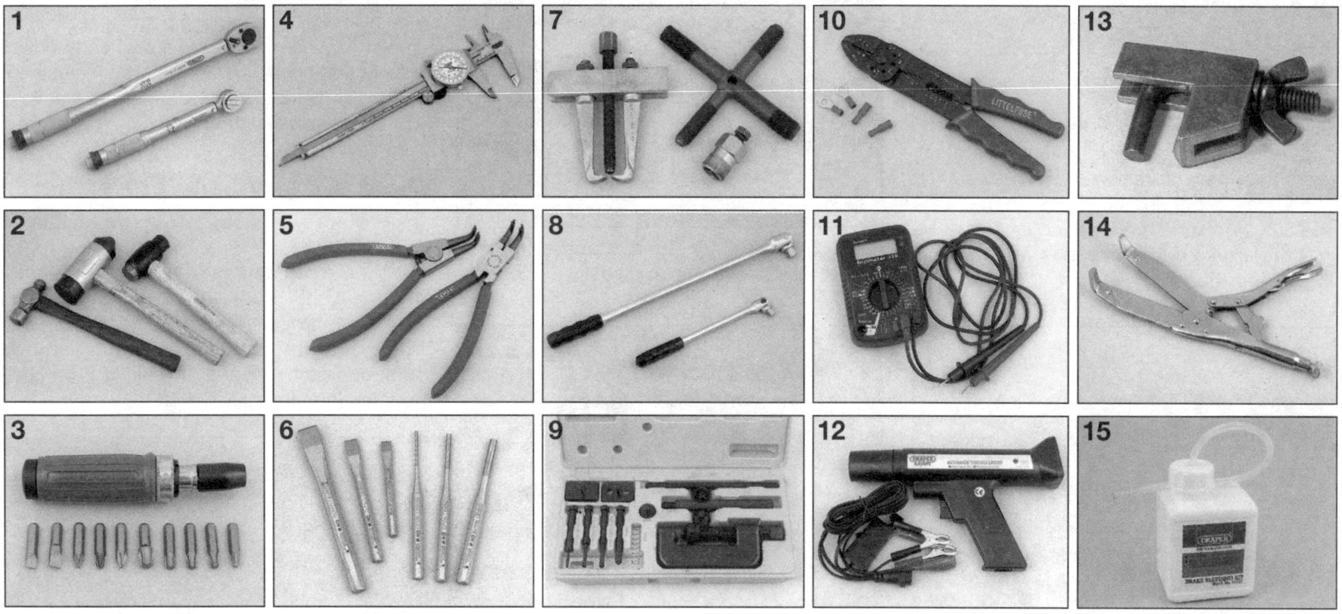

1 *Torque wrench (small and mid-ranges)*
2 *Conventional, plastic or soft-faced hammers*
3 *Impact driver set*
4 *Vernier gauge*
5 *Circlip pliers (internal and external, or combination)*
6 *Set of cold chisels and punches*
7 *Selection of pullers*
8 *Breaker bars*
9 *Chain breaking/ riveting tool set*
10 *Wire stripper and crimper tool*
11 *Multimeter (measures amps, volts and ohms)*
12 *Stroboscope (for dynamic timing checks)*
13 *Hose clamp (wingnut type shown)*
14 *Clutch holding tool*
15 *One-man brake/clutch bleeder kit*

Specialist tools

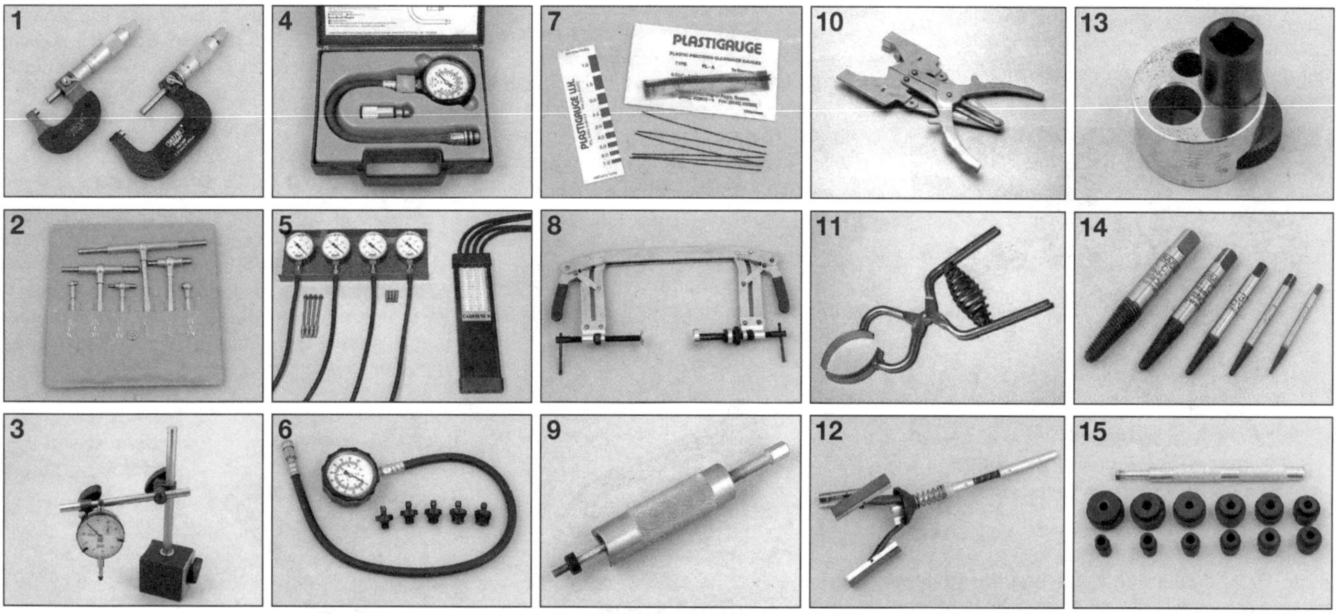

1 *Micrometers (external type)*
2 *Telescoping gauges*
3 *Dial gauge*
4 *Cylinder compression gauge*
5 *Vacuum gauges (left) or manometer (right)*
6 *Oil pressure gauge*
7 *Plastigauge kit*
8 *Valve spring compressor (4-stroke engines)*
9 *Piston pin drawbolt tool*
10 *Piston ring removal and installation tool*
11 *Piston ring clamp*
12 *Cylinder bore hone (stone type shown)*
13 *Stud extractor*
14 *Screw extractor set*
15 *Bearing driver set*

1 Workshop equipment and facilities

The workbench

● Work is made much easier by raising the bike up on a ramp - components are much more accessible if raised to waist level. The hydraulic or pneumatic types seen in the dealer's workshop are a sound investment if you undertake a lot of repairs or overhauls **(see illustration 1.1)**.

1.1 Hydraulic motorcycle ramp

● If raised off ground level, the bike must be supported on the ramp to avoid it falling. Most ramps incorporate a front wheel locating clamp which can be adjusted to suit different diameter wheels. When tightening the clamp, take care not to mark the wheel rim or damage the tyre - use wood blocks on each side to prevent this.

● Secure the bike to the ramp using tie-downs **(see illustration 1.2)**. If the bike has only a sidestand, and hence leans at a dangerous angle when raised, support the bike on an auxiliary stand.

1.2 Tie-downs are used around the passenger footrests to secure the bike

● Auxiliary (paddock) stands are widely available from mail order companies or motorcycle dealers and attach either to the wheel axle or swingarm pivot **(see illustration 1.3)**. If the motorcycle has a centrestand, you can support it under the crankcase to prevent it toppling whilst either wheel is removed **(see illustration 1.4)**.

1.3 This auxiliary stand attaches to the swingarm pivot

1.4 Always use a block of wood between the engine and jack head when supporting the engine in this way

Fumes and fire

● Refer to the Safety first! page at the beginning of the manual for full details. Make sure your workshop is equipped with a fire extinguisher suitable for fuel-related fires (Class B fire - flammable liquids) - it is not sufficient to have a water-filled extinguisher.

● Always ensure adequate ventilation is available. Unless an exhaust gas extraction system is available for use, ensure that the engine is run outside of the workshop.

● If working on the fuel system, make sure the workshop is ventilated to avoid a build-up of fumes. This applies equally to fume build-up when charging a battery. Do not smoke or allow anyone else to smoke in the workshop.

Fluids

● If you need to drain fuel from the tank, store it in an approved container marked as suitable for the storage of petrol (gasoline) **(see illustration 1.5)**. Do not store fuel in glass jars or bottles.

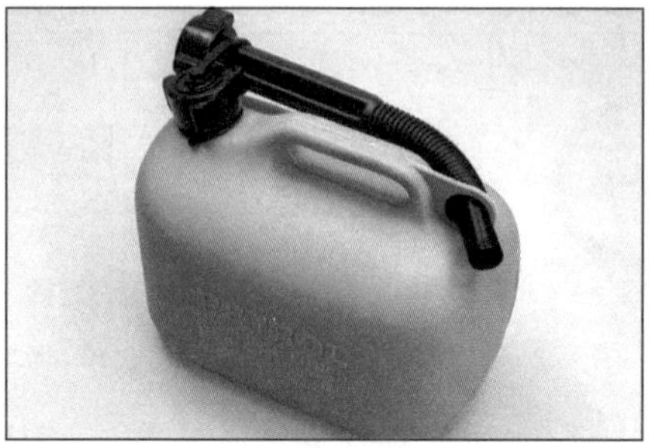

1.5 Use an approved can only for storing petrol (gasoline)

● Use proprietary engine degreasers or solvents which have a high flash-point, such as paraffin (kerosene), for cleaning off oil, grease and dirt - never use petrol (gasoline) for cleaning. Wear rubber gloves when handling solvent and engine degreaser. The fumes from certain solvents can be dangerous - always work in a well-ventilated area.

Dust, eye and hand protection

● Protect your lungs from inhalation of dust particles by wearing a filtering mask over the nose and mouth. Many frictional materials still contain asbestos which is dangerous to your health. Protect your eyes from spouts of liquid and sprung components by wearing a pair of protective goggles **(see illustration 1.6)**.

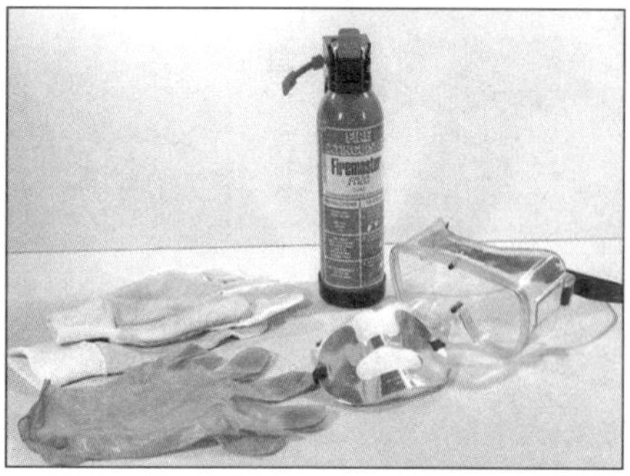

1.6 A fire extinguisher, goggles, mask and protective gloves should be at hand in the workshop

● Protect your hands from contact with solvents, fuel and oils by wearing rubber gloves. Alternatively apply a barrier cream to your hands before starting work. If handling hot components or fluids, wear suitable gloves to protect your hands from scalding and burns.

What to do with old fluids

● Old cleaning solvent, fuel, coolant and oils should not be poured down domestic drains or onto the ground. Package the fluid up in old oil containers, label it accordingly, and take it to a garage or disposal facility. Contact your local authority for location of such sites or ring the oil care hotline.

OIL CARE
FOLLOW THE CODE
OIL BANK LINE
0800 66 33 66
www.oilbankline.org.uk

Note: It is antisocial and illegal to dump oil down the drain. To find the location of your local oil recycling bank, call this number free.

In the USA, note that any oil supplier must accept used oil for recycling.

2 Fasteners - screws, bolts and nuts

Fastener types and applications

Bolts and screws

- Fastener head types are either of hexagonal, Torx or splined design, with internal and external versions of each type **(see illustrations 2.1 and 2.2)**; splined head fasteners are not in common use on motorcycles. The conventional slotted or Phillips head design is used for certain screws. Bolt or screw length is always measured from the underside of the head to the end of the item **(see illustration 2.11)**.

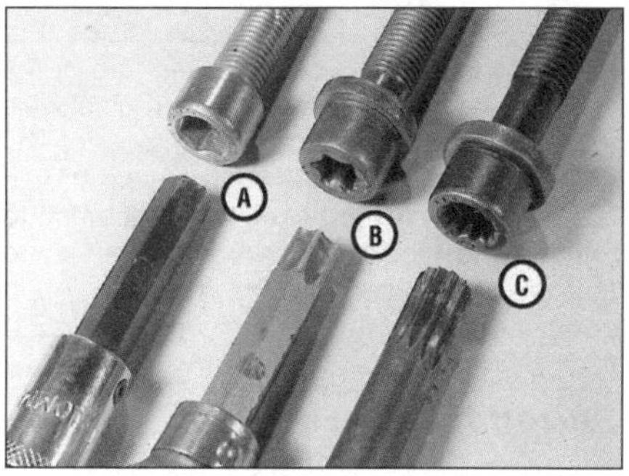

2.1 Internal hexagon/Allen (A), Torx (B) and splined (C) fasteners, with corresponding bits

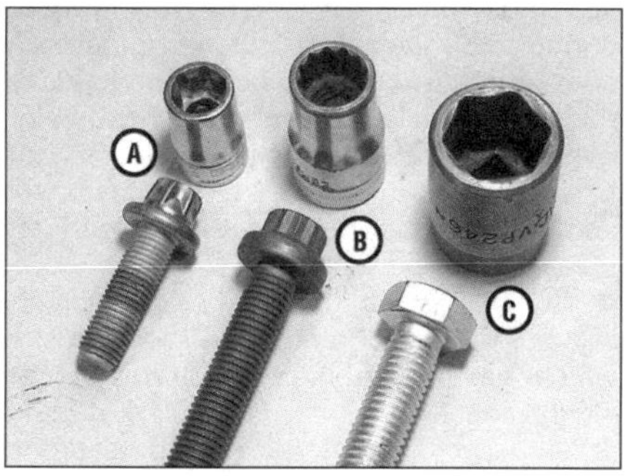

2.2 External Torx (A), splined (B) and hexagon (C) fasteners, with corresponding sockets

- Certain fasteners on the motorcycle have a tensile marking on their heads, the higher the marking the stronger the fastener. High tensile fasteners generally carry a 10 or higher marking. Never replace a high tensile fastener with one of a lower tensile strength.

Washers (see illustration 2.3)

- Plain washers are used between a fastener head and a component to prevent damage to the component or to spread the load when torque is applied. Plain washers can also be used as spacers or shims in certain assemblies. Copper or aluminium plain washers are often used as sealing washers on drain plugs.

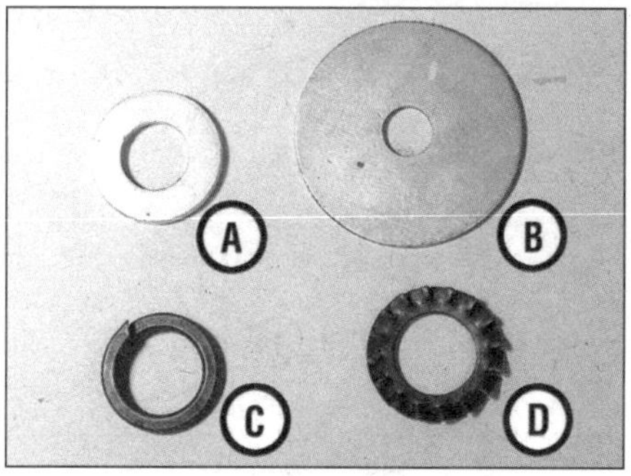

2.3 Plain washer (A), penny washer (B), spring washer (C) and serrated washer (D)

- The split-ring spring washer works by applying axial tension between the fastener head and component. If flattened, it is fatigued and must be renewed. If a plain (flat) washer is used on the fastener, position the spring washer between the fastener and the plain washer.
- Serrated star type washers dig into the fastener and component faces, preventing loosening. They are often used on electrical earth (ground) connections to the frame.
- Cone type washers (sometimes called Belleville) are conical and when tightened apply axial tension between the fastener head and component. They must be installed with the dished side against the component and often carry an OUTSIDE marking on their outer face. If flattened, they are fatigued and must be renewed.
- Tab washers are used to lock plain nuts or bolts on a shaft. A portion of the tab washer is bent up hard against one flat of the nut or bolt to prevent it loosening. Due to the tab washer being deformed in use, a new tab washer should be used every time it is disturbed.
- Wave washers are used to take up endfloat on a shaft. They provide light springing and prevent excessive side-to-side play of a component. Can be found on rocker arm shafts.

Nuts and split pins

- Conventional plain nuts are usually six-sided **(see illustration 2.4)**. They are sized by thread diameter and pitch. High tensile nuts carry a number on one end to denote their tensile strength.

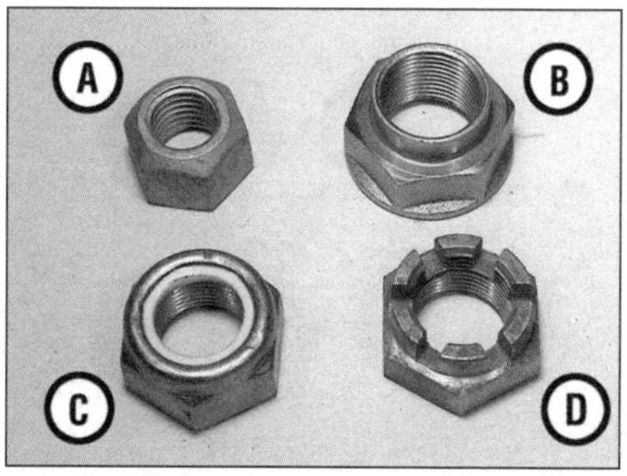

2.4 Plain nut (A), shouldered locknut (B), nylon insert nut (C) and castellated nut (D)

- Self-locking nuts either have a nylon insert, or two spring metal tabs, or a shoulder which is staked into a groove in the shaft - their advantage over conventional plain nuts is a resistance to loosening due to vibration. The nylon insert type can be used a number of times, but must be renewed when the friction of the nylon insert is reduced, ie when the nut spins freely on the shaft. The spring tab type can be reused unless the tabs are damaged. The shouldered type must be renewed every time it is disturbed.
- Split pins (cotter pins) are used to lock a castellated nut to a shaft or to prevent slackening of a plain nut. Common applications are wheel axles and brake torque arms. Because the split pin arms are deformed to lock around the nut a new split pin must always be used on installation - always fit the correct size split pin which will fit snugly in the shaft hole. Make sure the split pin arms are correctly located around the nut **(see illustrations 2.5 and 2.6)**.

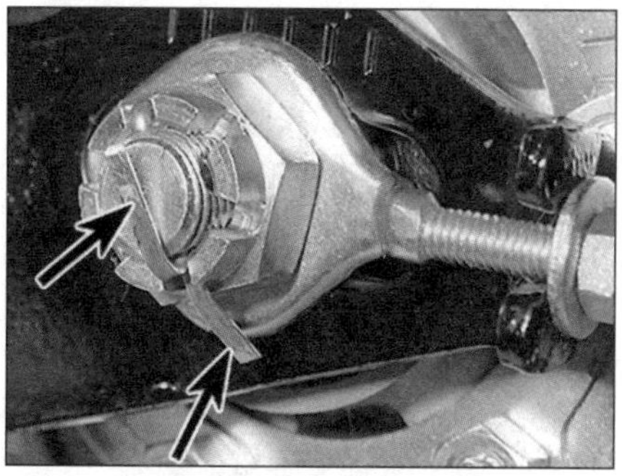
2.5 Bend split pin (cotter pin) arms as shown (arrows) to secure a castellated nut

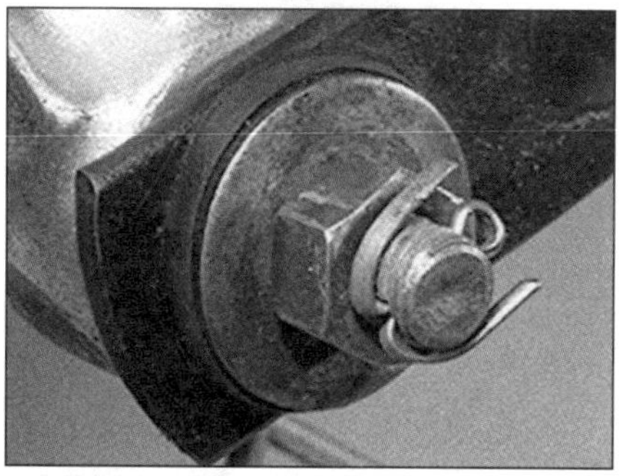
2.6 Bend split pin (cotter pin) arms as shown to secure a plain nut

> ***Caution: If the castellated nut slots do not align with the shaft hole after tightening to the torque setting, tighten the nut until the next slot aligns with the hole - never slacken the nut to align its slot.***

- R-pins (shaped like the letter R), or slip pins as they are sometimes called, are sprung and can be reused if they are otherwise in good condition. Always install R-pins with their closed end facing forwards **(see illustration 2.7)**.

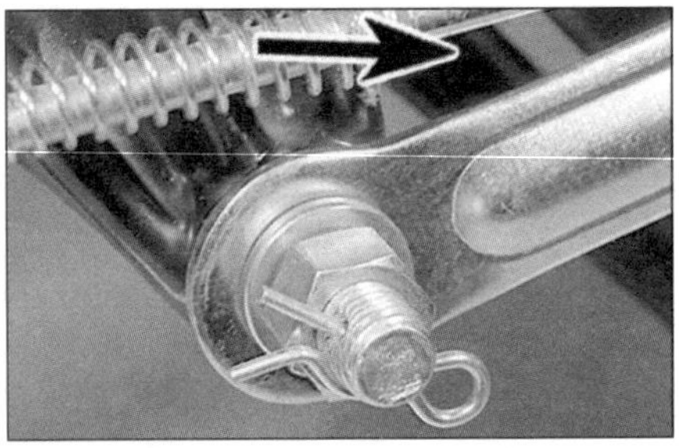

2.7 Correct fitting of R-pin. Arrow indicates forward direction

Circlips (see illustration 2.8)

● Circlips (sometimes called snap-rings) are used to retain components on a shaft or in a housing and have corresponding external or internal ears to permit removal. Parallel-sided (machined) circlips can be installed either way round in their groove, whereas stamped circlips (which have a chamfered edge on one face) must be installed with the chamfer facing away from the direction of thrust load **(see illustration 2.9)**.

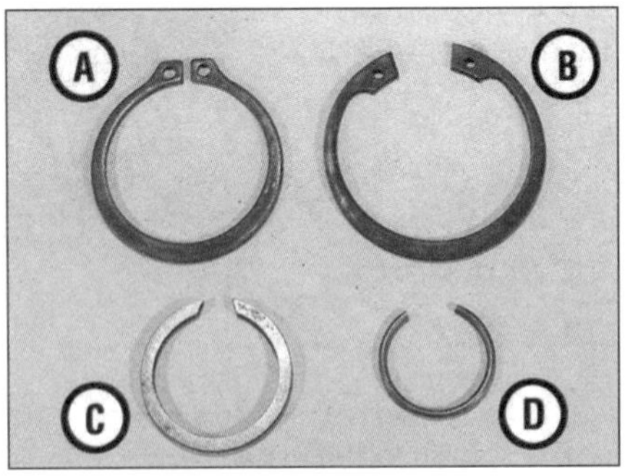

2.8 External stamped circlip (A), internal stamped circlip (B), machined circlip (C) and wire circlip (D)

● Always use circlip pliers to remove and install circlips; expand or compress them just enough to remove them. After installation, rotate the circlip in its groove to ensure it is securely seated. If installing a circlip on a splined shaft, always align its opening with a shaft channel to ensure the circlip ends are well supported and unlikely to catch **(see illustration 2.10)**.

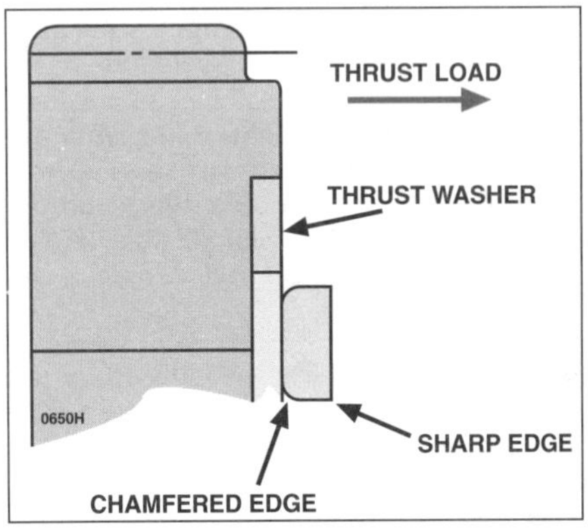

2.9 Correct fitting of a stamped circlip

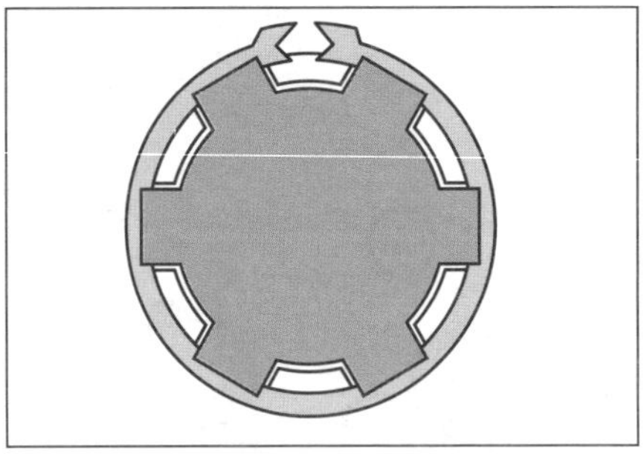

2.10 Align circlip opening with shaft channel

● Circlips can wear due to the thrust of components and become loose in their grooves, with the subsequent danger of becoming dislodged in operation. For this reason, renewal is advised every time a circlip is disturbed.

● Wire circlips are commonly used as piston pin retaining clips. If a removal tang is provided, long-nosed pliers can be used to dislodge them, otherwise careful use of a small flat-bladed screwdriver is necessary. Wire circlips should be renewed every time they are disturbed.

Thread diameter and pitch

● Diameter of a male thread (screw, bolt or stud) is the outside diameter of the threaded portion **(see illustration 2.11)**. Most motorcycle manufacturers use the ISO (International Standards Organisation) metric system expressed in millimetres, eg M6 refers to a 6 mm diameter thread. Sizing is the same for nuts, except that the thread diameter is measured across the valleys of the nut.

● Pitch is the distance between the peaks of the thread **(see illustration 2.11)**. It is expressed in millimetres, thus a common bolt size may be expressed as 6.0 x 1.0 mm (6 mm thread diameter and 1 mm pitch). Generally pitch increases in proportion to thread diameter, although there are always exceptions.

● Thread diameter and pitch are related for conventional fastener applications and the accompanying table can be used as a guide. Additionally, the AF (Across Flats), spanner or socket size dimension of the bolt or nut **(see illustration 2.11)** is linked to thread and pitch specification. Thread pitch can be measured with a thread gauge **(see illustration 2.12)**.

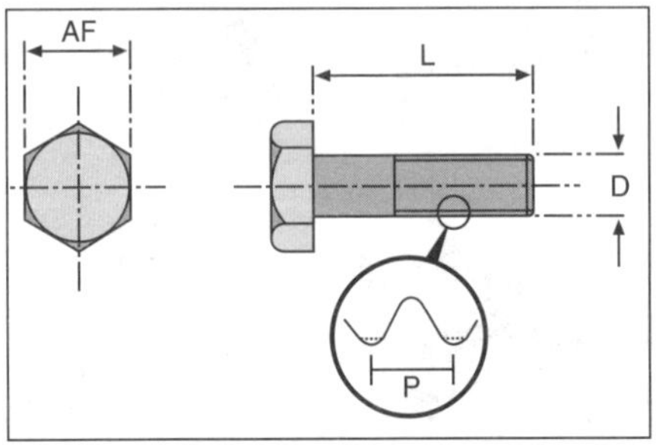

2.11 Fastener length (L), thread diameter (D), thread pitch (P) and head size (AF)

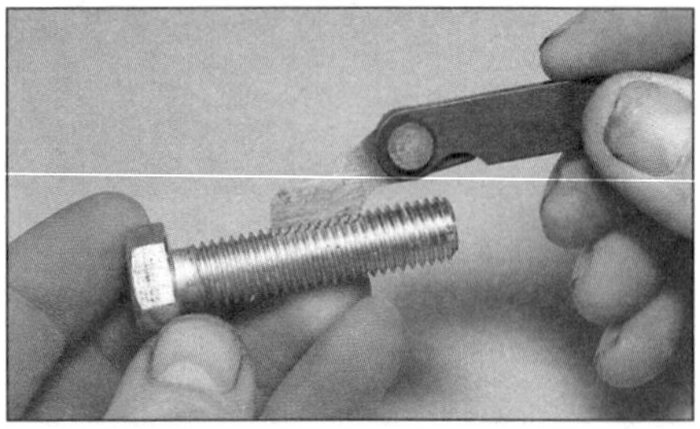

2.12 Using a thread gauge to measure pitch

AF size	Thread diameter x pitch (mm)
8 mm	M5 x 0.8
8 mm	M6 x 1.0
10 mm	M6 x 1.0
12 mm	M8 x 1.25
14 mm	M10 x 1.25
17 mm	M12 x 1.25

● The threads of most fasteners are of the right-hand type, ie they are turned clockwise to tighten and anti-clockwise to loosen. The reverse situation applies to left-hand thread fasteners, which are turned anti-clockwise to tighten and clockwise to loosen. Left-hand threads are used where rotation of a component might loosen a conventional right-hand thread fastener.

Seized fasteners

● Corrosion of external fasteners due to water or reaction between two dissimilar metals can occur over a period of time. It will build up sooner in wet conditions or in countries where salt is used on the roads during the winter. If a fastener is severely corroded it is likely that normal methods of removal will fail and result in its head being ruined. When you attempt removal, the fastener thread should be heard to crack free and unscrew easily - if it doesn't, stop there before damaging something.

● A smart tap on the head of the fastener will often succeed in breaking free corrosion which has occurred in the threads **(see illustration 2.13)**.

● An aerosol penetrating fluid (such as WD-40) applied the night beforehand may work its way down into the thread and ease removal. Depending on the location, you may be able to make up a Plasticine well around the fastener head and fill it with penetrating fluid.

2.13 A sharp tap on the head of a fastener will often break free a corroded thread

● If you are working on an engine internal component, corrosion will most likely not be a problem due to the well lubricated environment. However, components can be very tight and an impact driver is a useful tool in freeing them **(see illustration 2.14)**.

2.14 Using an impact driver to free a fastener

● Where corrosion has occurred between dissimilar metals (eg steel and aluminium alloy), the application of heat to the fastener head will create a disproportionate expansion rate between the two metals and break the seizure caused by the corrosion. Whether heat can be applied depends on the location of the fastener - any surrounding components likely to be damaged must first be removed **(see illustration 2.15)**. Heat can be applied using a paint stripper heat gun or clothes iron, or by immersing the component in boiling water - wear protective gloves to prevent scalding or burns to the hands.

2.15 Using heat to free a seized fastener

● As a last resort, it is possible to use a hammer and cold chisel to work the fastener head unscrewed **(see illustration 2.16)**. This will damage the fastener, but more importantly extreme care must be taken not to damage the surrounding component.

Caution: Remember that the component being secured is generally of more value than the bolt, nut or screw - when the fastener is freed, do not unscrew it with force, instead work the fastener back and forth when resistance is felt to prevent thread damage.

2.16 Using a hammer and chisel to free a seized fastener

Broken fasteners and damaged heads

● If the shank of a broken bolt or screw is accessible you can grip it with self-locking grips. The knurled wheel type stud extractor tool or self-gripping stud puller tool is particularly useful for removing the long studs which screw into the cylinder mouth surface of the crankcase or bolts and screws from which the head has broken off **(see illustration 2.17)**. Studs can also be removed by locking two nuts together on the threaded end of the stud and using a spanner on the lower nut **(see illustration 2.18)**.

2.17 Using a stud extractor tool to remove a broken crankcase stud

2.18 Two nuts can be locked together to unscrew a stud from a component

● A bolt or screw which has broken off below or level with the casing must be extracted using a screw extractor set. Centre punch the fastener to centralise the drill bit, then drill a hole in the fastener **(see illustration 2.19)**. Select a drill bit which is approximately half to three-quarters the

2.19 When using a screw extractor, first drill a hole in the fastener . . .

diameter of the fastener and drill to a depth which will accommodate the extractor. Use the largest size extractor possible, but avoid leaving too small a wall thickness otherwise the extractor will merely force the fastener walls outwards wedging it in the casing thread.

● If a spiral type extractor is used, thread it anti-clockwise into the fastener. As it is screwed in, it will grip the fastener and unscrew it from the casing **(see illustration 2.20)**.

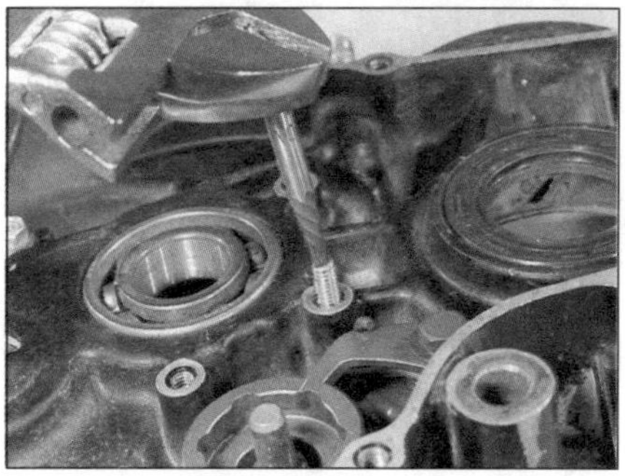

2.20 . . . then thread the extractor anti-clockwise into the fastener

● If a taper type extractor is used, tap it into the fastener so that it is firmly wedged in place. Unscrew the extractor (anti-clockwise) to draw the fastener out.

Warning: Stud extractors are very hard and may break off in the fastener if care is not taken - ask an engineer about spark erosion if this happens.

● Alternatively, the broken bolt/screw can be drilled out and the hole retapped for an oversize bolt/screw or a diamond-section thread insert. It is essential that the drilling is carried out squarely and to the correct depth, otherwise the casing may be ruined - if in doubt, entrust the work to an engineer.

● Bolts and nuts with rounded corners cause the correct size spanner or socket to slip when force is applied. Of the types of spanner/socket available always use a six-point type rather than an eight or twelve-point type - better grip

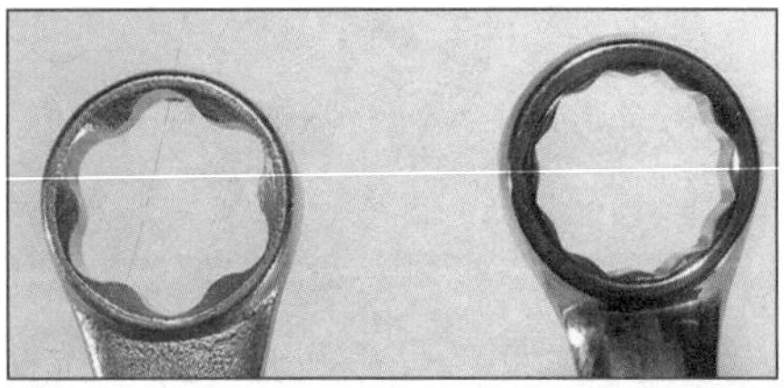

2.21 Comparison of surface drive ring spanner (left) with 12-point type (right)

is obtained. Surface drive spanners grip the middle of the hex flats, rather than the corners, and are thus good in cases of damaged heads **(see illustration 2.21)**.

- Slotted-head or Phillips-head screws are often damaged by the use of the wrong size screwdriver. Allen-head and Torx-head screws are much less likely to sustain damage. If enough of the screw head is exposed you can use a hacksaw to cut a slot in its head and then use a conventional flat-bladed screwdriver to remove it. Alternatively use a hammer and cold chisel to tap the head of the fastener around to slacken it. Always replace damaged fasteners with new ones, preferably Torx or Allen-head type.

HAYNES HiNT

A dab of valve grinding compound between the screw head and screw-driver tip will often give a good grip.

Thread repair

- Threads (particularly those in aluminium alloy components) can be damaged by overtightening, being assembled with dirt in the threads, or from a component working loose and vibrating. Eventually the thread will fail completely, and it will be impossible to tighten the fastener.
- If a thread is damaged or clogged with old locking compound it can be renovated with a thread repair tool (thread chaser) **(see illustrations 2.22 and 2.23)**; special thread

2.22 A thread repair tool being used to correct an internal thread

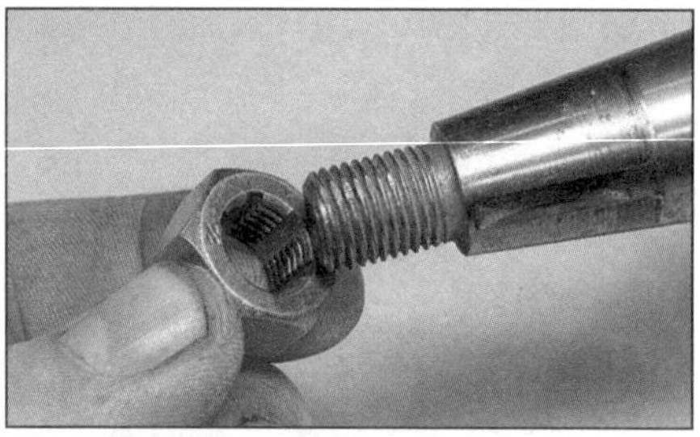

2.23 A thread repair tool being used to correct an external thread

chasers are available for spark plug hole threads. The tool will not cut a new thread, but clean and true the original thread. Make sure that you use the correct diameter and pitch tool. Similarly, external threads can be cleaned up with a die or a thread restorer file **(see illustration 2.24)**.

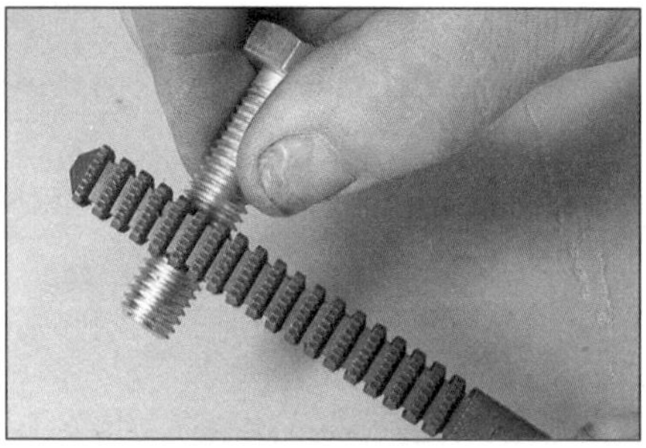

2.24 Using a thread restorer file

- It is possible to drill out the old thread and retap the component to the next thread size. This will work where there is enough surrounding material and a new bolt or screw can be obtained. Sometimes, however, this is not possible - such as where the bolt/screw passes through another component which must also be suitably modified, also in cases where a spark plug or oil drain plug cannot be obtained in a larger diameter thread size.
- The diamond-section thread insert (often known by its popular trade name of Heli-Coil) is a simple and effective method of renewing the thread and retaining the original size. A kit can be purchased which contains the tap, insert and installing tool **(see illustration 2.25)**. Drill out the damaged thread with the size drill specified **(see illustration 2.26)**. Carefully retap the thread **(see illustration 2.27)**. Install the

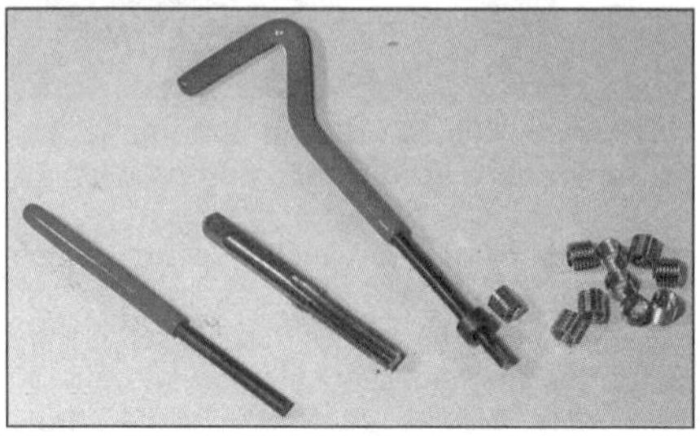

2.25 Obtain a thread insert kit to suit the thread diameter and pitch required

2.26 To install a thread insert, first drill out the original thread . . .

2.27 . . . tap a new thread . . .

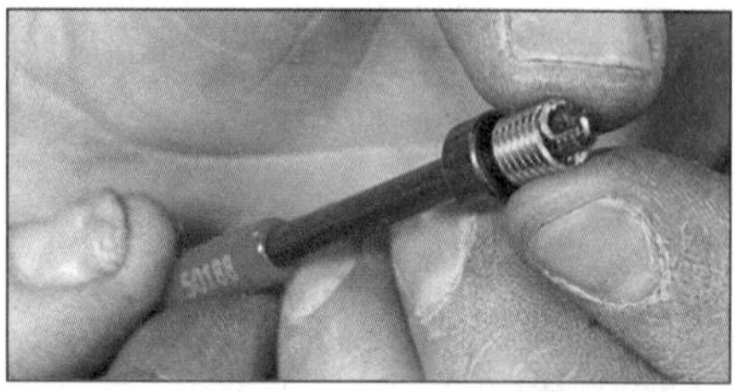

2.28 . . . fit insert on the installing tool . . .

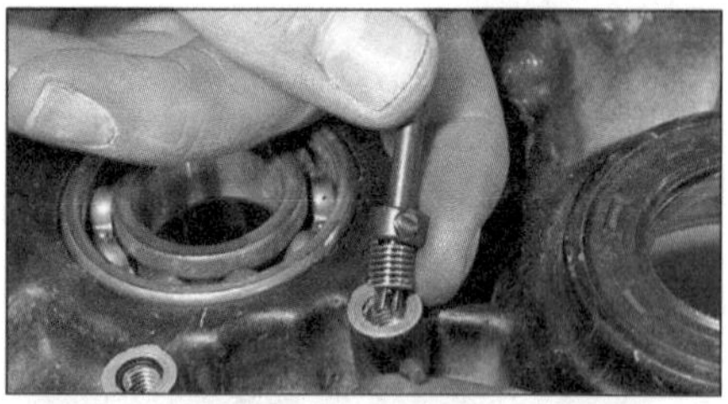

2.29 . . . and thread into the component . . .

2.30 . . . break off the tang when complete

insert on the installing tool and thread it slowly into place using a light downward pressure **(see illustrations 2.28 and 2.29)**. When positioned between a 1/4 and 1/2 turn below the surface withdraw the installing tool and use the break-off tool to press down on the tang, breaking it off **(see illustration 2.30)**.

- There are epoxy thread repair kits on the market which can rebuild stripped internal threads, although this repair should not be used on high load-bearing components.

Thread locking and sealing compounds

- Locking compounds are used in locations where the fastener is prone to loosening due to vibration or on important safety-related items which might cause loss of control of the motorcycle if they fail. It is also used where important fasteners cannot be secured by other means such as lockwashers or split pins.
- Before applying locking compound, make sure that the threads (internal and external) are clean and dry with all old compound removed. Select a compound to suit the component being secured - a non-permanent general locking and sealing type is suitable for most applications, but a high strength type is needed for permanent fixing of studs in castings. Apply a drop or two of the compound to the first few threads of the fastener, then thread it into place and tighten to the specified torque. Do not apply excessive thread locking compound otherwise the thread may be damaged on subsequent removal.
- Certain fasteners are impregnated with a dry film type coating of locking compound on their threads. Always renew this type of fastener if disturbed.
- Anti-seize compounds, such as copper-based greases, can be applied to protect threads from seizure due to extreme heat and corrosion. A common instance is spark plug threads and exhaust system fasteners.

3 Measuring tools and gauges

Feeler gauges

- Feeler gauges (or blades) are used for measuring small gaps and clearances **(see illustration 3.1)**. They can also be used to measure endfloat (sideplay) of a component on a shaft where access is not possible with a dial gauge.
- Feeler gauge sets should be treated with care and not bent or damaged. They are etched with their size on one face. Keep them clean and very lightly oiled to prevent corrosion build-up.

3.1 Feeler gauges are used for measuring small gaps and clearances - thickness is marked on one face of gauge

- When measuring a clearance, select a gauge which is a light sliding fit between the two components. You may need to use two gauges together to measure the clearance accurately.

Micrometers

- A micrometer is a precision tool capable of measuring to 0.01 or 0.001 of a millimetre. It should always be stored in its case and not in the general toolbox. It must be kept clean and never dropped, otherwise its frame or measuring anvils could be distorted resulting in inaccurate readings.
- External micrometers are used for measuring outside diameters of components and have many more applications than internal micrometers. Micrometers are available in different size ranges, eg 0 to 25 mm, 25 to 50 mm, and upwards in 25 mm steps; some large micrometers have interchangeable anvils to allow a range of measurements to be taken. Generally the largest precision measurement you are likely to take on a motorcycle is the piston diameter.
- Internal micrometers (or bore micrometers) are used for measuring inside diameters, such as valve guides and cylinder bores. Telescoping gauges and small hole gauges are used in conjunction with an external micrometer, whereas the more expensive internal micrometers have their own measuring device.

External micrometer

Note: *The conventional analogue type instrument is described. Although much easier to read, digital micrometers are considerably more expensive.*

- Always check the calibration of the micrometer before use. With the anvils closed (0 to 25 mm type) or set over a test gauge (for the larger types) the scale should read zero **(see illustration 3.2)**; make sure that the anvils (and test piece) are clean first. Any discrepancy can be adjusted by referring to the instructions supplied with the tool. Remember that the micrometer is a precision measuring tool - don't force the anvils closed, use the ratchet (4) on the end of the micrometer to close it. In this way, a measured force is always applied.

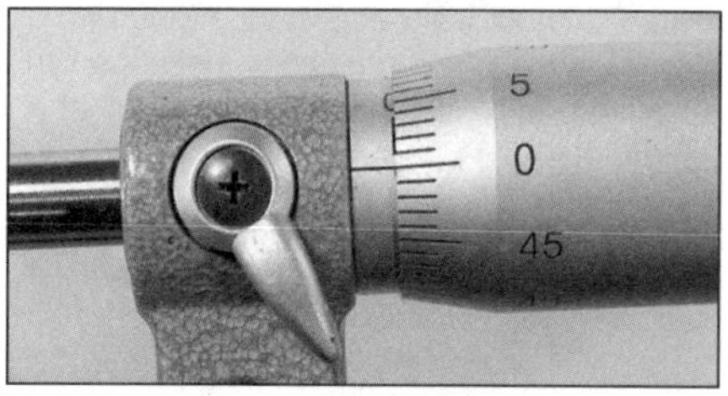

3.2 Check micrometer calibration before use

- To use, first make sure that the item being measured is clean. Place the anvil of the micrometer (1) against the item and use the thimble (2) to bring the spindle (3) lightly into contact with the other side of the item **(see illustration 3.3)**. Don't tighten the thimble down because this will damage the micrometer - instead use the ratchet (4) on the end of the micrometer. The ratchet mechanism applies a measured force preventing damage to the instrument.
- The micrometer is read by referring to the linear scale on the sleeve and the annular scale on the thimble. Read off the sleeve first to obtain the base measurement, then add the fine measurement from the thimble to obtain the overall reading. The linear scale on the sleeve represents the measuring range of the micrometer (eg 0 to 25 mm). The annular scale

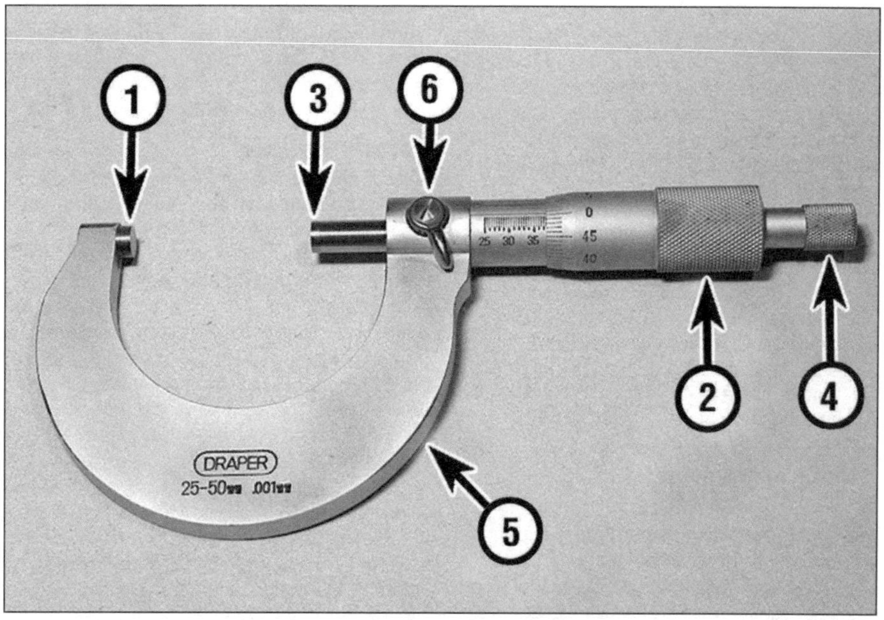

3.3 Micrometer component parts

1 Anvil
2 Thimble
3 Spindle
4 Ratchet
5 Frame
6 Locking lever

on the thimble will be in graduations of 0.01 mm (or as marked on the frame) - one full revolution of the thimble will move 0.5 mm on the linear scale. Take the reading where the datum line on the sleeve intersects the thimble's scale. Always position the eye directly above the scale otherwise an inaccurate reading will result.

In the example shown the item measures 2.95 mm **(see illustration 3.4)**:

Linear scale	2.00 mm
Linear scale	0.50 mm
Annular scale	0.45 mm
Total figure	**2.95 mm**

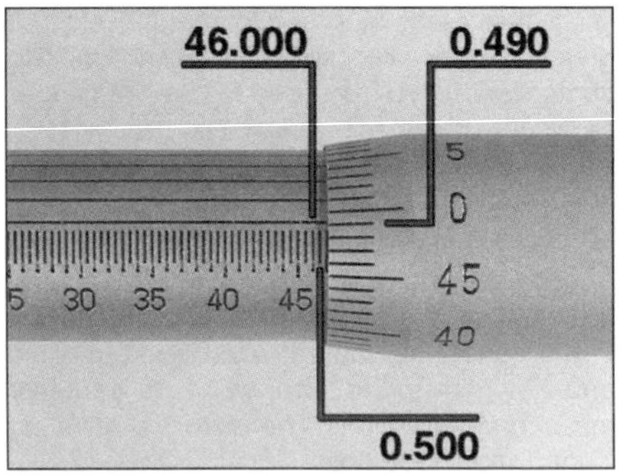

3.5 Micrometer reading of 46.99 mm on linear and annular scales . . .

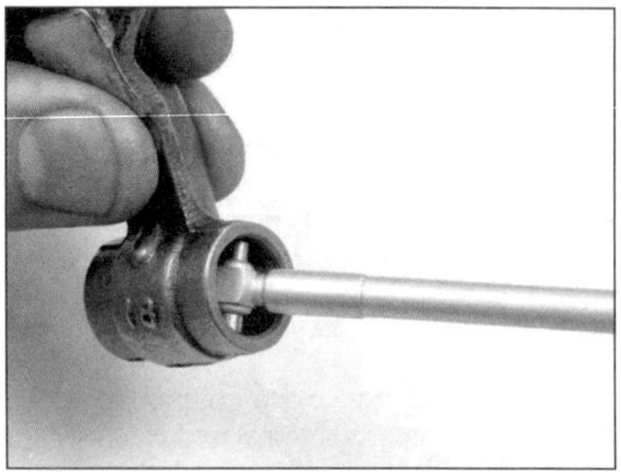
3.7 Expand the telescoping gauge in the bore, lock its position . . .

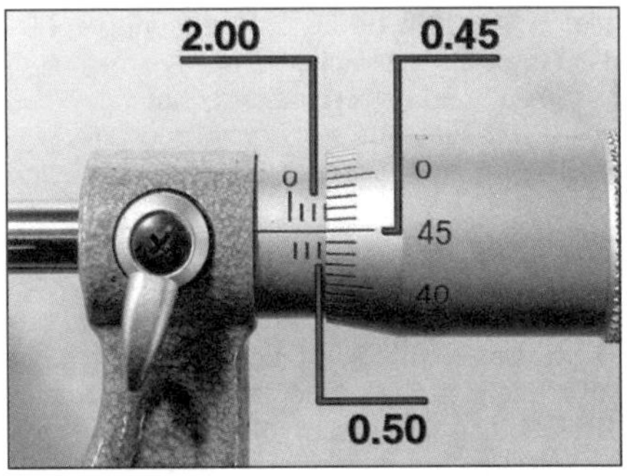

3.4 Micrometer reading of 2.95 mm

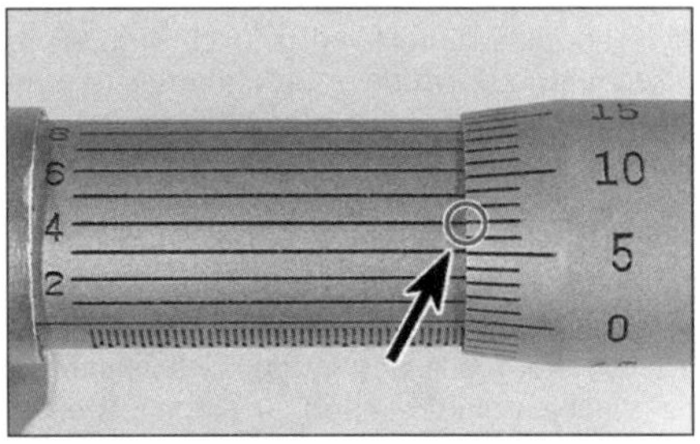
3.6 . . . and 0.004 mm on vernier scale

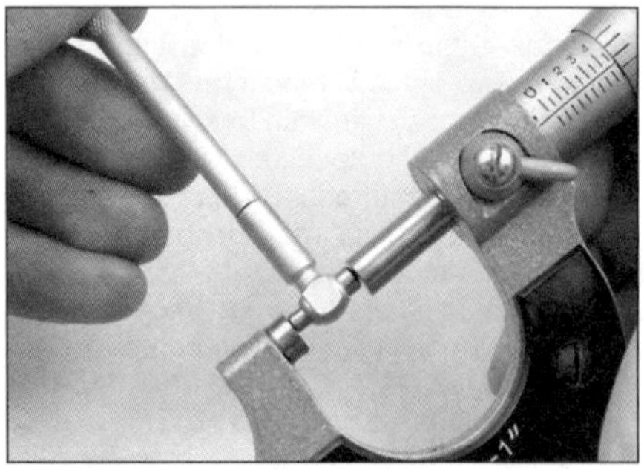
3.8 . . . then measure the gauge with a micrometer

Most micrometers have a locking lever (6) on the frame to hold the setting in place, allowing the item to be removed from the micrometer.

● Some micrometers have a vernier scale on their sleeve, providing an even finer measurement to be taken, in 0.001 increments of a millimetre. Take the sleeve and thimble measurement as described above, then check which graduation on the vernier scale aligns with that of the annular scale on the thimble **Note:** *The eye must be perpendicular to the scale when taking the vernier reading - if necessary rotate the body of the micrometer to ensure this.* Multiply the vernier scale figure by 0.001 and add it to the base and fine measurement figures.

In the example shown the item measures 46.994 mm **(see illustrations 3.5 and 3.6)**:

Linear scale (base)	46.000 mm
Linear scale (base)	00.500 mm
Annular scale (fine)	00.490 mm
Vernier scale	00.004 mm
Total figure	**46.994 mm**

Internal micrometer

● Internal micrometers are available for measuring bore diameters, but are expensive and unlikely to be available for home use. It is suggested that a set of telescoping gauges and small hole gauges, both of which must be used with an external micrometer, will suffice for taking internal measurements on a motorcycle.

● Telescoping gauges can be used to measure internal diameters of components. Select a gauge with the correct size range, make sure its ends are clean and insert it into the bore. Expand the gauge, then lock its position and withdraw it from the bore **(see illustration 3.7)**. Measure across the gauge ends with a micrometer **(see illustration 3.8)**.

● Very small diameter bores (such as valve guides) are measured with a small hole gauge. Once adjusted to a slip-fit inside the component, its position is locked and the gauge withdrawn for measurement with a micrometer **(see illustrations 3.9 and 3.10)**.

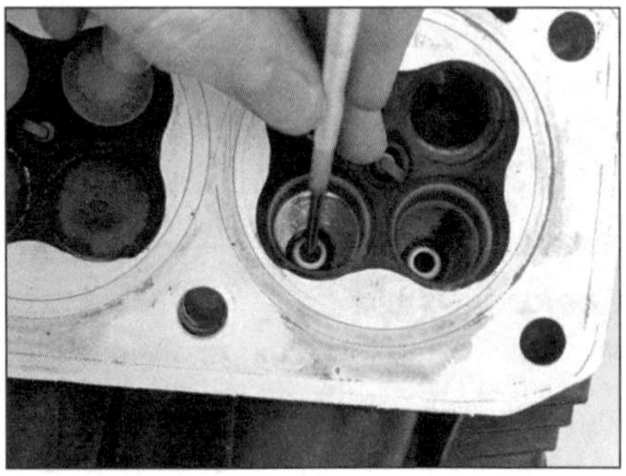
3.9 Expand the small hole gauge in the bore, lock its position . . .

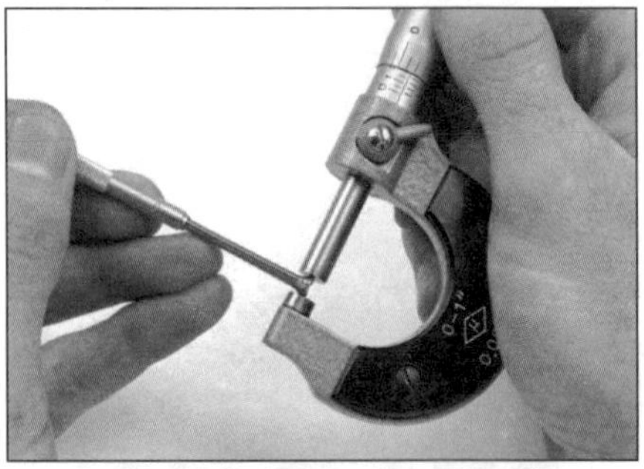
3.10 . . . then measure the gauge with a micrometer

Vernier caliper

Note: *The conventional linear and dial gauge type instruments are described. Digital types are easier to read, but are far more expensive.*

● The vernier caliper does not provide the precision of a micrometer, but is versatile in being able to measure internal and external diameters. Some types also incorporate a depth gauge. It is ideal for measuring clutch plate friction material and spring free lengths.

● To use the conventional linear scale vernier, slacken off the vernier clamp screws (1) and set its jaws over (2), or inside (3), the item to be measured **(see illustration 3.11)**. Slide the jaw into contact, using the thumbwheel (4) for fine movement of the sliding scale (5) then tighten the clamp screws (1). Read off the main scale (6) where the zero on the sliding scale (5) intersects it, taking the whole number to the left of the zero; this provides the base measurement. View along the sliding scale and select the division which lines up exactly with any of the divisions on the main scale, noting that the divisions usually represents 0.02 of a millimetre. Add this fine measurement to the base measurement to obtain the total reading.

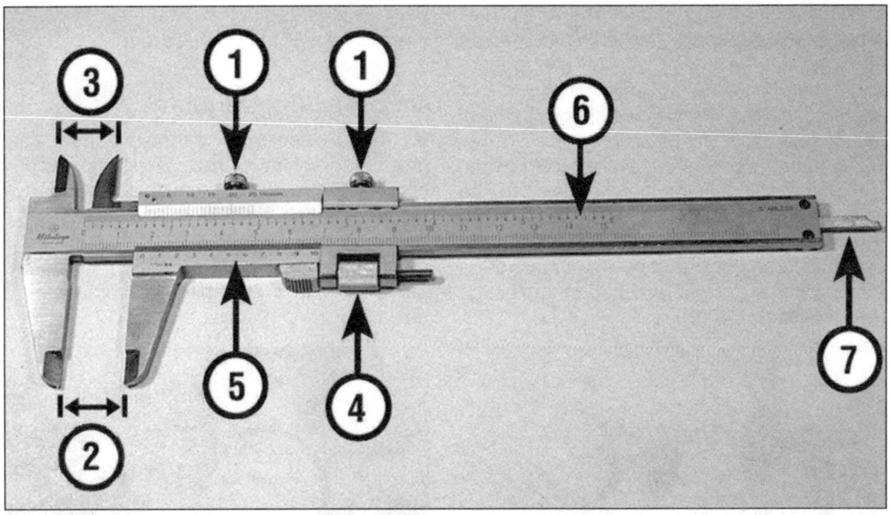

3.11 Vernier component parts (linear gauge)

1 *Clamp screws*
2 *External jaws*
3 *Internal jaws*
4 *Thumbwheel*
5 *Sliding scale*
6 *Main scale*
7 *Depth gauge*

In the example shown the item measures 55.92 mm **(see illustration 3.12)**:

Base measurement	55.00 mm
Fine measurement	00.92 mm
Total figure	**55.92 mm**

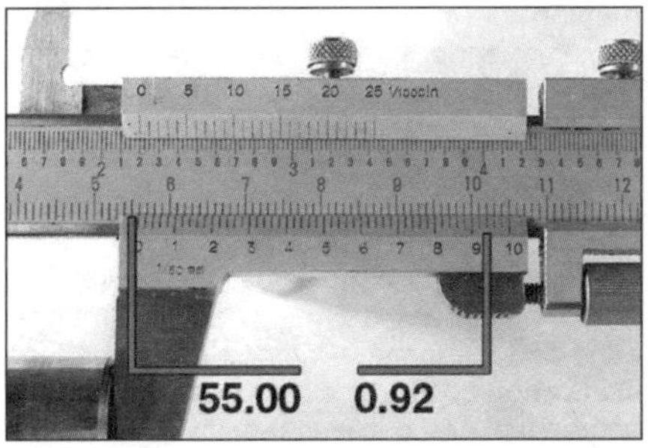

3.12 Vernier gauge reading of 55.92 mm

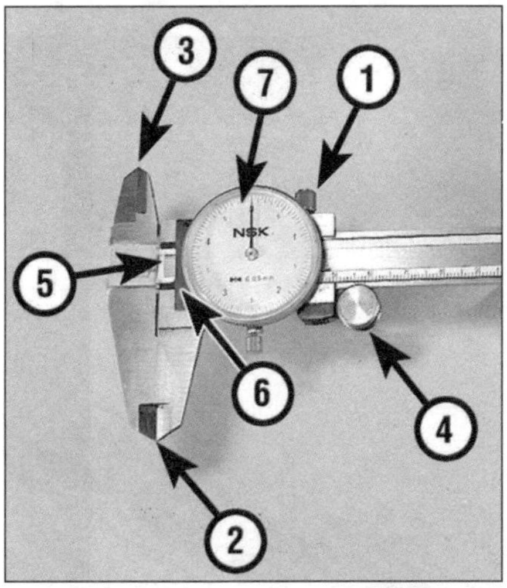

3.13 Vernier component parts (dial gauge)

1 *Clamp screw*
2 *External jaws*
3 *Internal jaws*
4 *Thumbwheel*
5 *Main scale*
6 *Sliding scale*
7 *Dial gauge*

● Some vernier calipers are equipped with a dial gauge for fine measurement. Before use, check that the jaws are clean, then close them fully and check that the dial gauge reads zero. If necessary adjust the gauge ring accordingly. Slacken the vernier clamp screw (1) and set its jaws over (2), or inside (3), the item to be measured **(see illustration 3.13)**. Slide the jaws into contact, using the thumbwheel (4) for fine movement. Read off the main scale (5) where the edge of the sliding scale (6) intersects it, taking the whole number to the left of the zero; this provides the base measurement. Read off the needle position on the dial gauge (7) scale to provide the fine measurement; each division represents 0.05 of a millimetre. Add this fine measurement to the base measurement to obtain the total reading.

In the example shown the item measures 55.95 mm **(see illustration 3.14)**:

Base measurement	55.00 mm
Fine measurement	00.95 mm
Total figure	**55.95 mm**

3.14 Vernier gauge reading of 55.95 mm

Plastigauge

● Plastigauge is a plastic material which can be compressed between two surfaces to measure the oil clearance between them. The width of the compressed Plastigauge is measured against a calibrated scale to determine the clearance.

● Common uses of Plastigauge are for measuring the clearance between crankshaft journal and main bearing inserts, between crankshaft journal and big-end bearing inserts, and between camshaft and bearing surfaces. The following example describes big-end oil clearance measurement.

● Handle the Plastigauge material carefully to prevent distortion. Using a sharp knife, cut a length which corresponds with the width of the bearing being measured and place it carefully across the journal so that it is parallel with the shaft **(see illustration 3.15)**. Carefully install both bearing shells and the connecting rod. Without rotating the rod on the journal tighten its bolts or nuts (as applicable) to the specified torque. The connecting rod and bearings are then disassembled and the crushed Plastigauge examined.

3.15 Plastigauge placed across shaft journal

● Using the scale provided in the Plastigauge kit, measure the width of the material to determine the oil clearance **(see illustration 3.16)**. Always remove all traces of Plastigauge after use using your fingernails.

Caution: Arriving at the correct clearance demands that the assembly is torqued correctly, according to the settings and sequence (where applicable) provided by the motorcycle manufacturer.

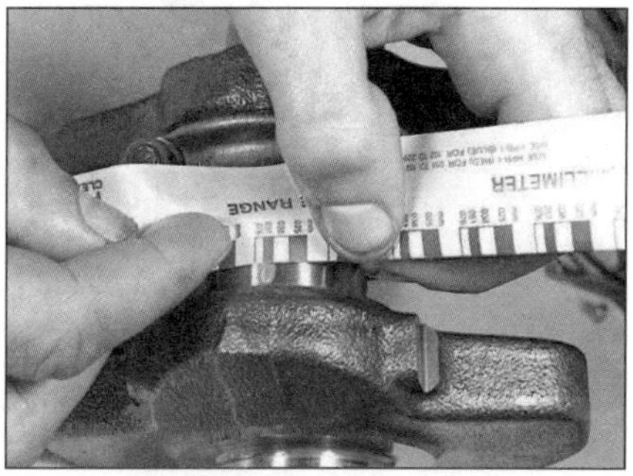

3.16 Measuring the width of the crushed Plastigauge

Dial gauge or DTI (Dial Test Indicator)

● A dial gauge can be used to accurately measure small amounts of movement. Typical uses are measuring shaft runout or shaft endfloat (sideplay) and setting piston position for ignition timing on two-strokes. A dial gauge set usually comes with a range of different probes and adapters and mounting equipment.

● The gauge needle must point to zero when at rest. Rotate the ring around its periphery to zero the gauge.

● Check that the gauge is capable of reading the extent of movement in the work. Most gauges have a small dial set in the face which records whole millimetres of movement as well as the fine scale around the face periphery which is calibrated in 0.01 mm divisions. Read off the small dial first to obtain the base measurement, then add the measurement from the fine scale to obtain the total reading.

In the example shown the gauge reads 1.48 mm **(see illustration 3.17)**:

Base measurement	1.00 mm
Fine measurement	0.48 mm
Total figure	**1.48 mm**

3.17 Dial gauge reading of 1.48 mm

● If measuring shaft runout, the shaft must be supported in vee-blocks and the gauge mounted on a stand perpendicular to the shaft. Rest the tip of the gauge against the centre of the shaft and rotate the shaft slowly whilst watching the gauge reading **(see illustration 3.18)**. Take several measurements along the length of the shaft and record the maximum gauge reading as the amount of runout in the shaft. **Note:** *The reading obtained will be total runout at that point - some manufacturers specify that the runout figure is halved to compare with their specified runout limit.*

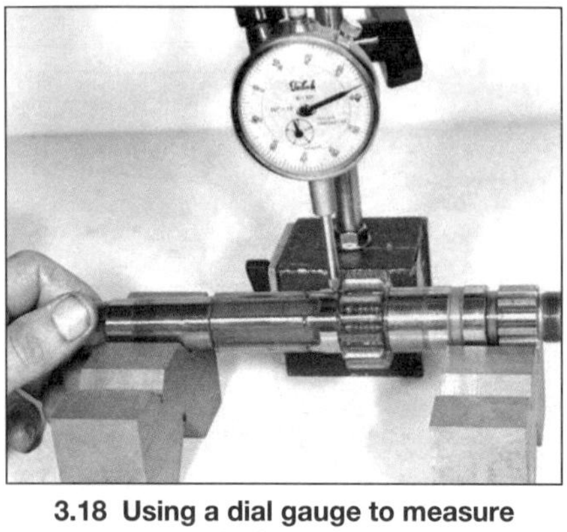

3.18 Using a dial gauge to measure shaft runout

● Endfloat (sideplay) measurement requires that the gauge is mounted securely to the surrounding component with its probe touching the end of the shaft. Using hand pressure, push and pull on the shaft noting the maximum endfloat recorded on the gauge **(see illustration 3.19)**.

3.19 Using a dial gauge to measure shaft endfloat

● A dial gauge with suitable adapters can be used to determine piston position BTDC on two-stroke engines for the purposes of ignition timing. The gauge, adapter and suitable length probe are installed in the place of the spark plug and the gauge zeroed at TDC. If the piston position is specified as 1.14 mm BTDC, rotate the engine back to 2.00 mm BTDC, then slowly forwards to 1.14 mm BTDC.

Cylinder compression gauges

● A compression gauge is used for measuring cylinder compression. Either the rubber-cone type or the threaded adapter type can be used. The latter is preferred to ensure a perfect seal against the cylinder head. A 0 to 300 psi (0 to 20 Bar) type gauge (for petrol/gasoline engines) will be suitable for motorcycles.

● The spark plug is removed and the gauge either held hard against the cylinder head (cone type) or the gauge adapter screwed into the cylinder head (threaded type) **(see illustration 3.20)**. Cylinder compression is measured with the engine turning over, but not running - carry out the compression test as described in *Fault Finding Equipment*. The gauge will hold the reading until manually released.

3.20 Using a rubber-cone type cylinder compression gauge

Oil pressure gauge

● An oil pressure gauge is used for measuring engine oil pressure. Most gauges come with a set of adapters to fit the thread of the take-off point **(see illustration 3.21)**. If the take-off point specified by the motorcycle manufacturer is an external oil pipe union, make sure that the specified replacement union is used to prevent oil starvation.

3.21 Oil pressure gauge and take-off point adapter (arrow)

● Oil pressure is measured with the engine running (at a specific rpm) and often the manufacturer will specify pressure limits for a cold and hot engine.

Straight-edge and surface plate

● If checking the gasket face of a component for warpage, place a steel rule or precision straight-edge across the gasket face and measure any gap between the straight-edge and component with feeler gauges **(see illustration 3.22)**. Check diagonally across the component and between mounting holes **(see illustration 3.23)**.

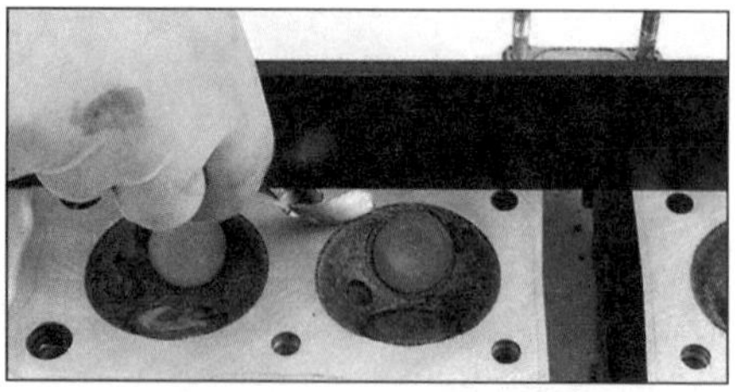

3.22 Use a straight-edge and feeler gauges to check for warpage

3.23 Check for warpage in these directions

- Checking individual components for warpage, such as clutch plain (metal) plates, requires a perfectly flat plate or piece or plate glass and feeler gauges.

4 Torque and leverage

What is torque?

- Torque describes the twisting force about a shaft. The amount of torque applied is determined by the distance from the centre of the shaft to the end of the lever and the amount of force being applied to the end of the lever; distance multiplied by force equals torque.
- The manufacturer applies a measured torque to a bolt or nut to ensure that it will not slacken in use and to hold two components securely together without movement in the joint. The actual torque setting depends on the thread size, bolt or nut material and the composition of the components being held.
- Too little torque may cause the fastener to loosen due to vibration, whereas too much torque will distort the joint faces of the component or cause the fastener to shear off. Always stick to the specified torque setting.

Using a torque wrench

- Check the calibration of the torque wrench and make sure it has a suitable range for the job. Torque wrenches are available in Nm (Newton-metres), kgf m (kilograms-force metre), lbf ft (pounds-feet), lbf in (inch-pounds). Do not confuse lbf ft with lbf in.
- Adjust the tool to the desired torque on the scale **(see illustration 4.1)**. If your torque wrench is not calibrated in the units specified, carefully convert the figure (see *Conversion Factors*). A manufacturer sometimes gives a torque setting as a range (8 to 10 Nm) rather than a single figure - in this case set the tool midway between the two settings. The same torque may be expressed as 9 Nm ± 1 Nm. Some torque wrenches have a method of locking the setting so that it isn't inadvertently altered during use.

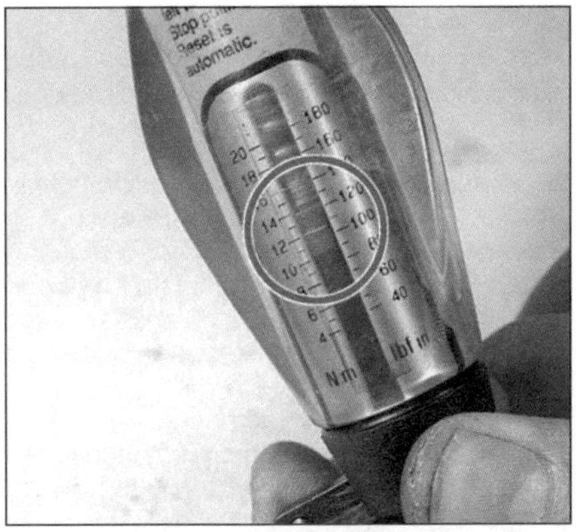

4.1 Set the torque wrench index mark to the setting required, in this case 12 Nm

- Install the bolts/nuts in their correct location and secure them lightly. Their threads must be clean and free of any old locking compound. Unless specified the threads and flange should be dry - oiled threads are necessary in certain circumstances and the manufacturer will take this into account in the specified torque figure. Similarly, the manufacturer may also specify the application of thread-locking compound.
- Tighten the fasteners in the specified sequence until the torque wrench clicks, indicating that the torque setting has been reached. Apply the torque again to double-check the setting. Where different thread diameter fasteners secure the component, as a rule tighten the larger diameter ones first.
- When the torque wrench has been finished with, release the lock (where applicable) and fully back off its setting to zero - do not leave the torque wrench tensioned. Also, do not use a torque wrench for slackening a fastener.

Angle-tightening

- Manufacturers often specify a figure in degrees for final tightening of a fastener. This usually follows tightening to a specific torque setting.
- A degree disc can be set and attached to the socket **(see illustration 4.2)** or a protractor can be used to mark the angle of movement on the bolt/nut head and the surrounding casting **(see illustration 4.3)**.

4.2 Angle tightening can be accomplished with a torque-angle gauge . . .

4.3 . . . or by marking the angle on the surrounding component

Loosening sequences

- Where more than one bolt/nut secures a component, loosen each fastener evenly a little at a time. In this way, not all the stress of the joint is held by one fastener and the components are not likely to distort.
- If a tightening sequence is provided, work in the REVERSE of this, but if not, work from the outside in, in a criss-cross sequence **(see illustration 4.4)**.

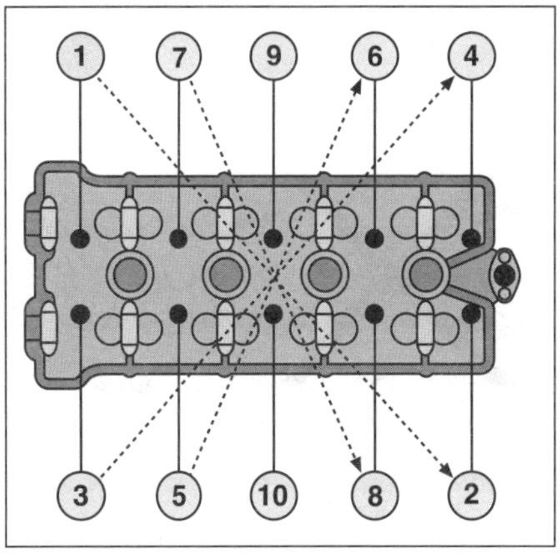

4.4 When slackening, work from the outside inwards

Tightening sequences

- If a component is held by more than one fastener it is important that the retaining bolts/nuts are tightened evenly to prevent uneven stress build-up and distortion of sealing faces. This is especially important on high-compression joints such as the cylinder head.
- A sequence is usually provided by the manufacturer, either in a diagram or actually marked in the casting. If not, always start in the centre and work outwards in a criss-cross pattern **(see illustration 4.5)**. Start off by securing all bolts/nuts finger-tight, then set the torque wrench and tighten each fastener by a small amount in sequence until the final torque is reached. By following this practice,

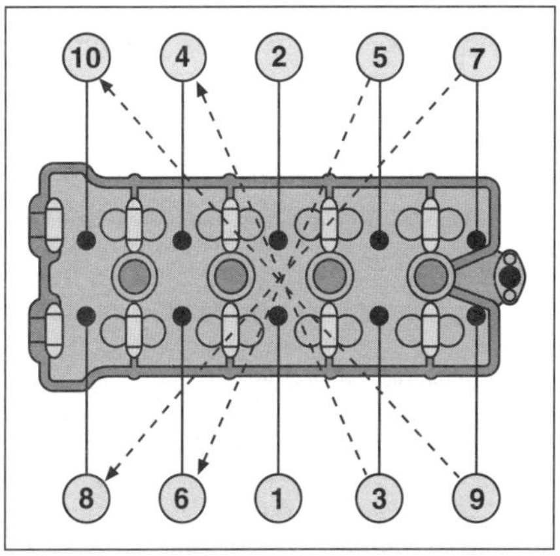

4.5 When tightening, work from the inside outwards

the joint will be held evenly and will not be distorted. Important joints, such as the cylinder head and big-end fasteners often have two- or three-stage torque settings.

Applying leverage

● Use tools at the correct angle. Position a socket wrench or spanner on the bolt/nut so that you pull it towards you when loosening. If this can't be done, push the spanner without curling your fingers around it **(see illustration 4.6)** - the spanner may slip or the fastener loosen suddenly, resulting in your fingers being crushed against a component.

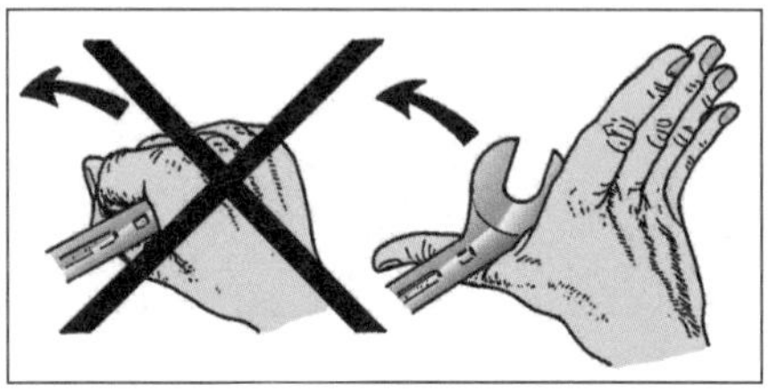

4.6 If you can't pull on the spanner to loosen a fastener, push with your hand open

● Additional leverage is gained by extending the length of the lever. The best way to do this is to use a breaker bar instead of the regular length tool, or to slip a length of tubing over the end of the spanner or socket wrench.

● If additional leverage will not work, the fastener head is either damaged or firmly corroded in place (see *Fasteners*).

5 Bearings

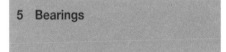

Bearing removal and installation

Drivers and sockets

● Before removing a bearing, always inspect the casing to see which way it must be driven out - some casings will have retaining plates or a cast step. Also check for any identifying markings on the bearing and if installed to a certain depth, measure this at this stage. Some roller bearings are sealed on one side - take note of the original fitted position.

● Bearings can be driven out of a casing using a bearing driver tool (with the correct size head) or a socket of the correct diameter. Select the driver head or socket so that it contacts the outer race of the bearing, not the balls/rollers or inner race. Always support the casing around the bearing housing with wood blocks, otherwise there is a risk of fracture. The bearing is driven out with a few blows on the driver or socket from a heavy mallet. Unless access is severely restricted (as with wheel bearings), a pin-punch is not recommended unless it is moved around the bearing to keep it square in its housing.

● The same equipment can be used to install bearings. Make sure the bearing housing is supported on wood blocks and line up the bearing in its housing. Fit the bearing as noted on removal - generally they are installed with their marked side facing outwards. Tap the bearing squarely into its housing using a driver or socket which bears only on the bearing's outer race - contact with the bearing balls/rollers or inner race will destroy it **(see illustrations 5.1 and 5.2)**.

● Check that the bearing inner race and balls/rollers rotate freely.

5.1 Using a bearing driver against the bearing's outer race

5.2 Using a large socket against the bearing's outer race

Pullers and slide-hammers

● Where a bearing is pressed on a shaft a puller will be required to extract it **(see illustration 5.3)**. Make sure that the puller clamp or legs fit securely behind the bearing and are unlikely to slip out. If pulling a bearing off a gear shaft for example, you may have to locate the puller behind a gear pinion if there is no access to the race and draw the gear pinion off the shaft as well **(see illustration 5.4)**.

5.3 This bearing puller clamps behind the bearing and pressure is applied to the shaft end to draw the bearing off

Caution: Ensure that the puller's centre bolt locates securely against the end of the shaft and will not slip when pressure is applied. Also ensure that puller does not damage the shaft end.

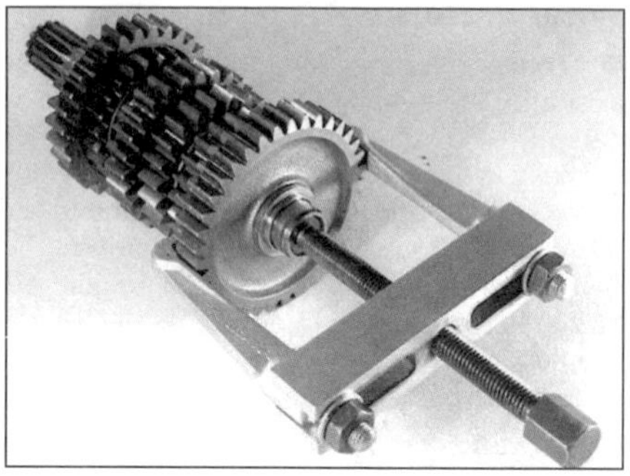

5.4 Where no access is available to the rear of the bearing, it is sometimes possible to draw off the adjacent component

● Operate the puller so that its centre bolt exerts pressure on the shaft end and draws the bearing off the shaft.

● When installing the bearing on the shaft, tap only on the bearing's inner race - contact with the balls/rollers or outer race with destroy the bearing. Use a socket or length of tubing as a drift which fits over the shaft end **(see illustration 5.5)**.

5.5 When installing a bearing on a shaft use a piece of tubing which bears only on the bearing's inner race

● Where a bearing locates in a blind hole in a casing, it cannot be driven or pulled out as described above. A slide-hammer with knife-edged bearing puller attachment will be required. The puller attachment passes through the bearing and when tightened expands to fit firmly behind the bearing **(see illustration 5.6)**. By operating the slide-hammer part of the tool the bearing is jarred out of its housing **(see illustration 5.7)**.

● It is possible, if the bearing is of reasonable weight, for it to drop out of its housing if the casing is heated as described opposite. If this

5.6 Expand the bearing puller so that it locks behind the bearing . . .

5.7 . . . attach the slide hammer to the bearing puller

method is attempted, first prepare a work surface which will enable the casing to be tapped face down to help dislodge the bearing - a wood surface is ideal since it will not damage the casing's gasket surface. Wearing protective gloves, tap the heated casing several times against the work surface to dislodge the bearing under its own weight **(see illustration 5.8)**.

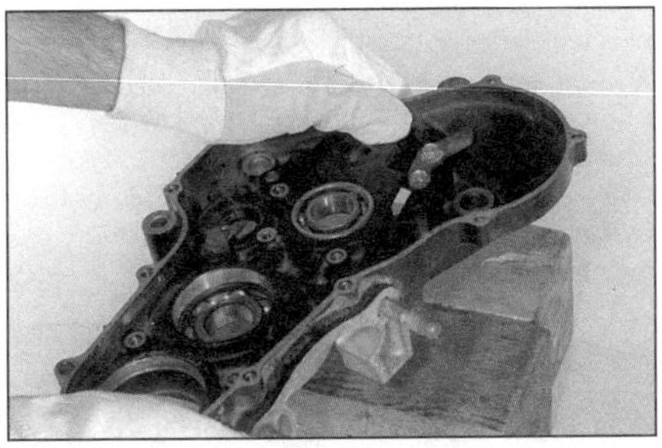

5.8 Tapping a casing face down on wood blocks can often dislodge a bearing

- Bearings can be installed in blind holes using the driver or socket method described above.

Drawbolts

- Where a bearing or bush is set in the eye of a component, such as a suspension linkage arm or connecting rod small-end, removal by drift may damage the component. Furthermore, a rubber bushing in a shock absorber eye cannot successfully be driven out of position. If access is available to a engineering press, the task is straightforward. If not, a drawbolt can be fabricated to extract the bearing or bush.

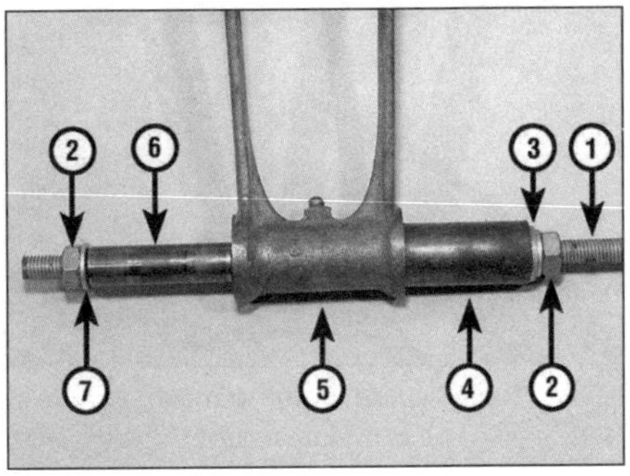

5.9 Drawbolt component parts assembled on a suspension arm

1 *Bolt or length of threaded bar*
2 *Nuts*
3 *Washer (external diameter greater than tubing internal diameter)*
4 *Tubing (internal diameter sufficient to accommodate bearing)*
5 *Suspension arm with bearing*
6 *Tubing (external diameter slightly smaller than bearing)*
7 *Washer (external diameter slightly smaller than bearing)*

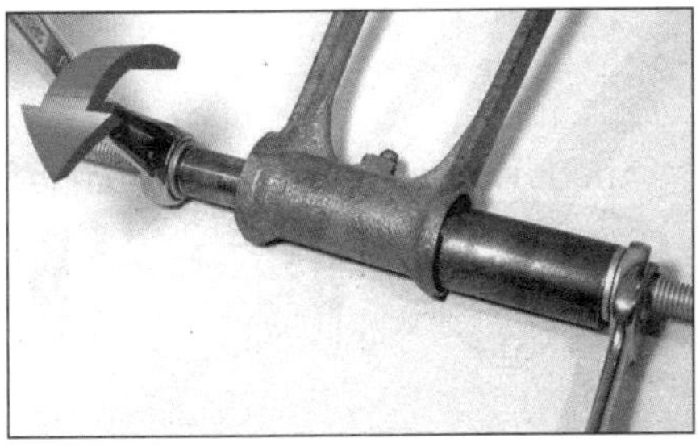

5.10 Drawing the bearing out of the suspension arm

- To extract the bearing/bush you will need a long bolt with nut (or piece of threaded bar with two nuts), a piece of tubing which has an internal diameter larger than the bearing/bush, another piece of tubing which has an external diameter slightly smaller than the bearing/bush, and a selection of washers **(see illustrations 5.9 and 5.10)**. Note that the pieces of tubing must be of the same length, or longer, than the bearing/bush.
- The same kit (without the pieces of tubing) can be used to draw the new bearing/bush back into place **(see illustration 5.11)**.

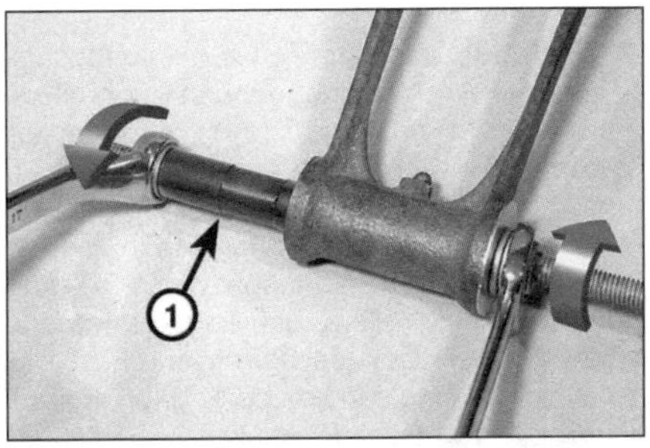

5.11 Installing a new bearing (1) in the suspension arm

Temperature change

- If the bearing's outer race is a tight fit in the casing, the aluminium casing can be heated to release its grip on the bearing. Aluminium will expand at a greater rate than the steel bearing outer race. There are several ways to do this, but avoid any localised extreme heat (such as a blow torch) - aluminium alloy has a low melting point.
- Approved methods of heating a casing are using a domestic oven (heated to 100°C) or immersing the casing in boiling water **(see illustration 5.12)**. Low temperature range localised heat sources such as a paint stripper heat gun or clothes iron can also be used **(see illustration 5.13)**. Alternatively, soak a rag in boiling water, wring it out and wrap it around the bearing housing.

> ***Warning: All of these methods require care in use to prevent scalding and burns to the hands. Wear protective gloves when handling hot components.***

5.12 A casing can be immersed in a sink of boiling water to aid bearing removal

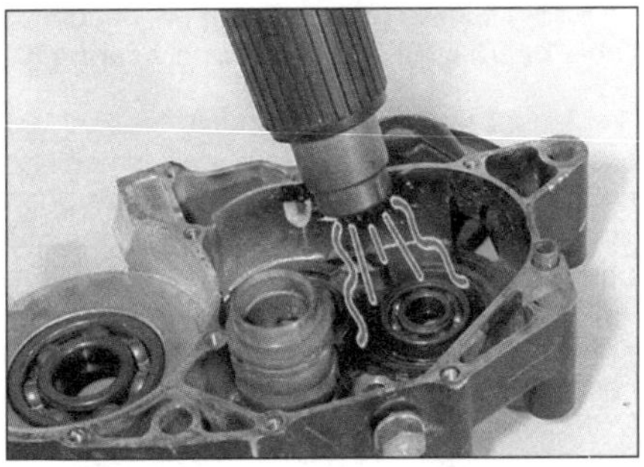

5.13 Using a localised heat source to aid bearing removal

- If heating the whole casing note that plastic components, such as the neutral switch, may suffer - remove them beforehand.
- After heating, remove the bearing as described above. You may find that the expansion is sufficient for the bearing to fall out of the casing under its own weight or with a light tap on the driver or socket.
- If necessary, the casing can be heated to aid bearing installation, and this is sometimes the recommended procedure if the motorcycle manufacturer has designed the housing and bearing fit with this intention.

● Installation of bearings can be eased by placing them in a freezer the night before installation. The steel bearing will contract slightly, allowing easy insertion in its housing. This is often useful when installing steering head outer races in the frame.

Bearing types and markings

● Plain shell bearings, ball bearings, needle roller bearings and tapered roller bearings will all be found on motorcycles **(see illustrations 5.14 and 5.15)**. The ball and roller types are usually caged between an inner and outer race, but uncaged variations may be found.

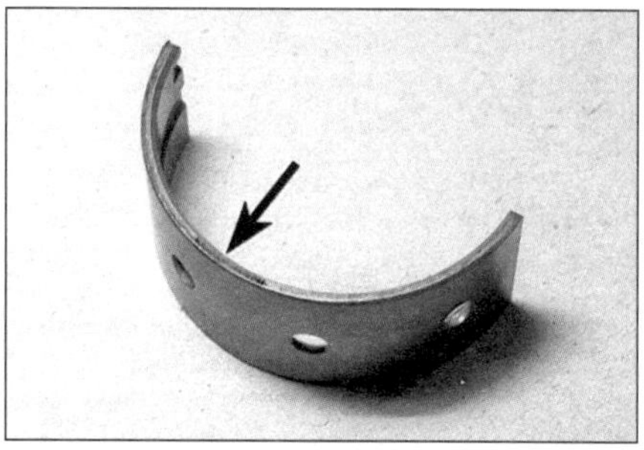

5.14 Shell bearings are either plain or grooved. They are usually identified by colour code (arrow)

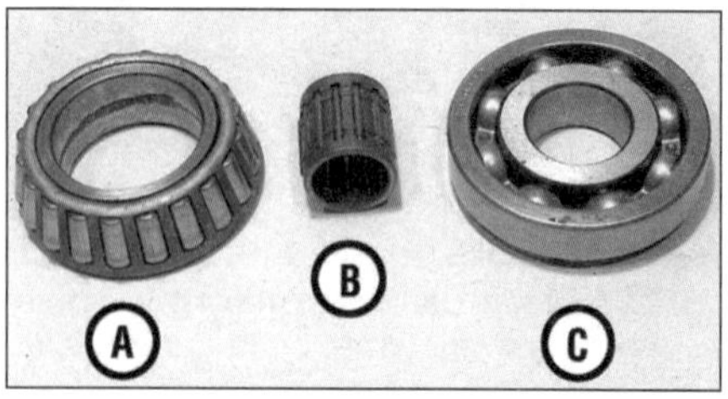

5.15 Tapered roller bearing (A), needle roller bearing (B) and ball journal bearing (C)

● Shell bearings (often called inserts) are usually found at the crankshaft main and connecting rod big-end where they are good at coping with high loads. They are made of a phosphor-bronze material and are impregnated with self-lubricating properties.

● Ball bearings and needle roller bearings consist of a steel inner and outer race with the balls or rollers between the races. They require constant lubrication by oil or grease and are good at coping with axial loads. Taper roller bearings consist of rollers set in a tapered cage set on the inner race; the outer race is separate. They are good at coping with axial loads and prevent movement along the shaft - a typical application is in the steering head.

● Bearing manufacturers produce bearings to ISO size standards and stamp one face of the bearing to indicate its internal and external diameter, load capacity and type **(see illustration 5.16)**.

● Metal bushes are usually of phosphor-bronze material. Rubber bushes are used in suspension mounting eyes. Fibre bushes have also been used in suspension pivots.

5.16 Typical bearing marking

Bearing fault finding

● If a bearing outer race has spun in its housing, the housing material will be damaged. You can use a bearing locking compound to bond the outer race in place if damage is not too severe.

● Shell bearings will fail due to damage of their working surface, as a result of lack of lubrication, corrosion or abrasive particles in the oil **(see illustration 5.17)**. Small particles of dirt in the oil may embed in the bearing material whereas larger particles will score the bearing and shaft journal. If a number of short journeys are made, insufficient heat will be generated to drive off condensation which has built up on the bearings.

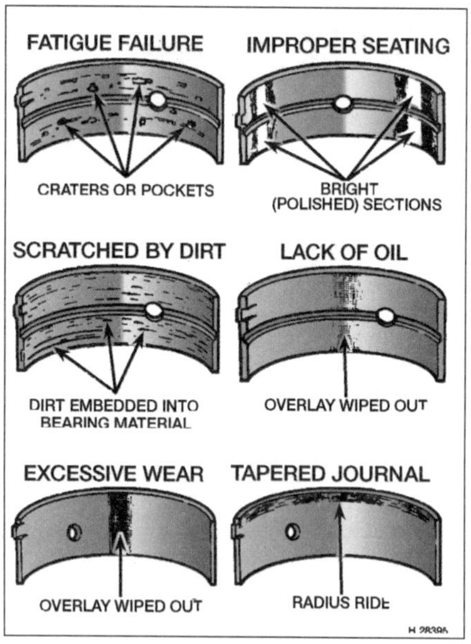

5.17 Typical bearing failures

● Ball and roller bearings will fail due to lack of lubrication or damage to the balls or rollers. Tapered-roller bearings can be damaged by overloading them. Unless the bearing is sealed on both sides, wash it in paraffin (kerosene) to remove all old grease then allow it to dry. Make a visual inspection looking to dented balls or rollers, damaged cages and worn or pitted races **(see illustration 5.18)**.

● A ball bearing can be checked for wear by listening to it when spun. Apply a film of light oil to the bearing and hold it close to the ear - hold the outer race with one hand and spin the inner race with the other hand **(see illustration 5.19)**. The bearing should be almost silent when spun; if it grates or rattles it is worn.

5.18 Example of ball journal bearing with damaged balls and cages

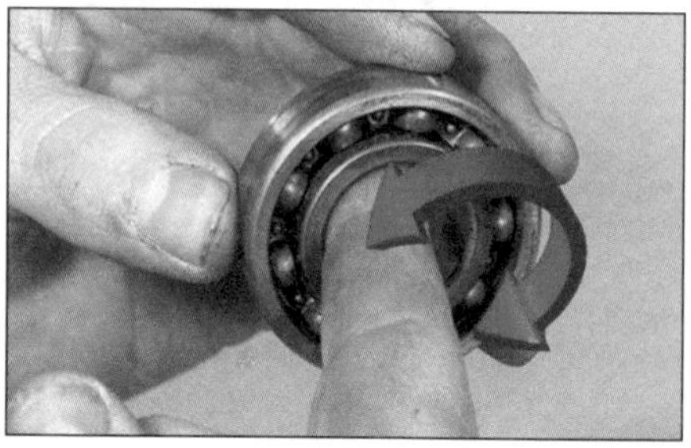

5.19 Hold outer race and listen to inner race when spun

6 Oil seals

Oil seal removal and installation

● Oil seals should be renewed every time a component is dismantled. This is because the seal lips will become set to the sealing surface and will not necessarily reseal.

● Oil seals can be prised out of position using a large flat-bladed screwdriver **(see illustration 6.1)**. In the case of crankcase seals, check first that the seal is not lipped on the inside, preventing its removal with the crankcases joined.

6.1 Prise out oil seals with a large flat-bladed screwdriver

● New seals are usually installed with their marked face (containing the seal reference code) outwards and the spring side towards the fluid being retained. In certain cases, such as a two-stroke engine crankshaft seal, a double lipped seal may be used due to there being fluid or gas on each side of the joint.

- Use a bearing driver or socket which bears only on the outer hard edge of the seal to install it in the casing - tapping on the inner edge will damage the sealing lip.

Oil seal types and markings

- Oil seals are usually of the single-lipped type. Double-lipped seals are found where a liquid or gas is on both sides of the joint.
- Oil seals can harden and lose their sealing ability if the motorcycle has been in storage for a long period - renewal is the only solution.
- Oil seal manufacturers also conform to the ISO markings for seal size - these are moulded into the outer face of the seal **(see illustration 6.2)**.

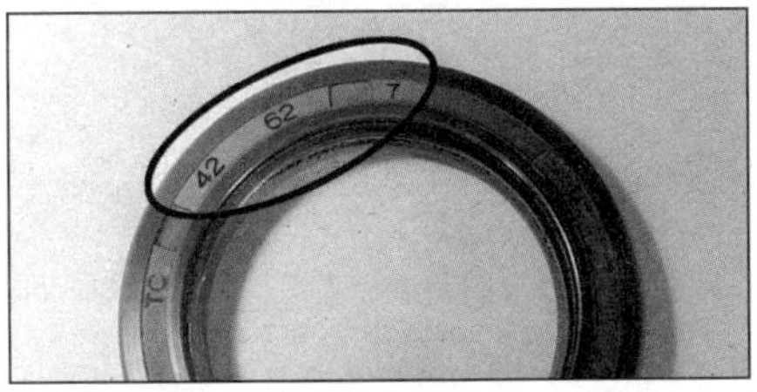

6.2 These oil seal markings indicate inside diameter, outside diameter and seal thickness

7 Gaskets and sealants

Types of gasket and sealant

- Gaskets are used to seal the mating surfaces between components and keep lubricants, fluids, vacuum or pressure contained within the assembly. Aluminium gaskets are sometimes found at the cylinder joints, but most gaskets are paper-based. If the mating surfaces of the components being joined are undamaged the gasket can be installed dry, although a dab of sealant or grease will be useful to hold it in place during assembly.
- RTV (Room Temperature Vulcanising) silicone rubber sealants cure when exposed to moisture in the atmosphere. These sealants are good at filling pits or irregular gasket faces, but will tend to be forced out of the joint under very high torque. They can be used to replace a paper gasket, but first make sure that the width of the paper gasket is not essential to the shimming of internal components. RTV sealants should not be used on components containing petrol (gasoline).
- Non-hardening, semi-hardening and hard setting liquid gasket compounds can be used with a gasket or between a metal-to-metal joint. Select the sealant to suit the application: universal non-hardening sealant can be used on virtually all joints; semi-hardening on joint faces which are rough or damaged; hard setting sealant on joints which require a permanent bond and are subjected to high temperature and pressure. **Note:** *Check first if the paper gasket has a bead of sealant impregnated in its surface before applying additional sealant.*
- When choosing a sealant, make sure it is suitable for the application, particularly if being applied in a high-temperature area or in the vicinity of fuel. Certain manufacturers produce sealants in either clear, silver or black colours to match the finish of the engine. This has a particular application on motorcycles where much of the engine is exposed.
- Do not over-apply sealant. That which is squeezed out on the outside of the joint can be wiped off, whereas an excess of sealant on the inside can break off and clog oilways.

Breaking a sealed joint

- Age, heat, pressure and the use of hard setting sealant can cause two components to stick together so tightly that they are difficult to separate using finger pressure alone. Do not resort to using levers unless there is a pry point provided for this purpose **(see illustration 7.1)** or else the gasket surfaces will be damaged.
- Use a soft-faced hammer **(see illustration 7.2)** or a wood block and conventional hammer to strike the component near the mating surface. Avoid hammering against cast extremities since they may break off. If this method fails, try using a wood wedge between the two components.

Caution: If the joint will not separate, double-check that you have removed all the fasteners.

7.1 If a pry point is provided, apply gently pressure with a flat-bladed screwdriver

7.2 Tap around the joint with a soft-faced mallet if necessary - don't strike cooling fins

Removal of old gasket and sealant

- Paper gaskets will most likely come away complete, leaving only a few traces stuck on the sealing faces of the components. It is imperative that all traces are removed to ensure correct sealing of the new gasket.
- Very carefully scrape all traces of gasket away making sure that the sealing surfaces are not gouged or scored by the scraper **(see illustrations 7.3, 7.4 and 7.5)**. Stubborn deposits can be removed by spraying with an aerosol gasket remover. Final preparation of

Most components have one or two hollow locating dowels between the two gasket faces. If a dowel cannot be removed, do not resort to gripping it with pliers - it will almost certainly be distorted. Install a close-fitting socket or Phillips screwdriver into the dowel and then grip the outer edge of the dowel to free it.

7.3 Paper gaskets can be scraped off with a gasket scraper tool . . .

7.4 . . . a knife blade . . .

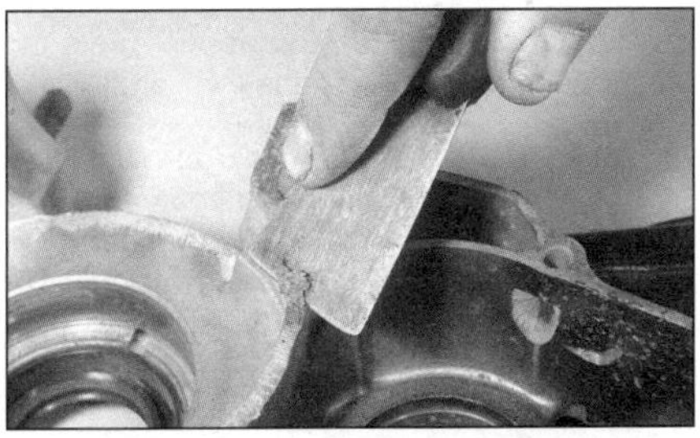

7.5 . . . or a household scraper

7.6 Fine abrasive paper is wrapped around a flat file to clean up the gasket face

7.7 A kitchen scourer can be used on stubborn deposits

the gasket surface can be made with very fine abrasive paper or a plastic kitchen scourer **(see illustrations 7.6 and 7.7)**.

- Old sealant can be scraped or peeled off components, depending on the type originally used. Note that gasket removal compounds are available to avoid scraping the components clean; make sure the gasket remover suits the type of sealant used.

8 Chains

Breaking and joining final drive chains

- Drive chains for all but small bikes are continuous and do not have a clip-type connecting link. The chain must be broken using a chain breaker tool and the new chain securely riveted together using a new soft rivet-type link. Never use a clip-type connecting link instead of a rivet-type link, except in an emergency. Various chain breaking and riveting tools are available, either as separate tools or combined as illustrated in the accompanying photographs - read the instructions supplied with the tool carefully.

Warning: The need to rivet the new link pins correctly cannot be overstressed - loss of control of the motorcycle is very likely to result if the chain breaks in use.

- Rotate the chain and look for the soft link. The soft link pins look like they have been

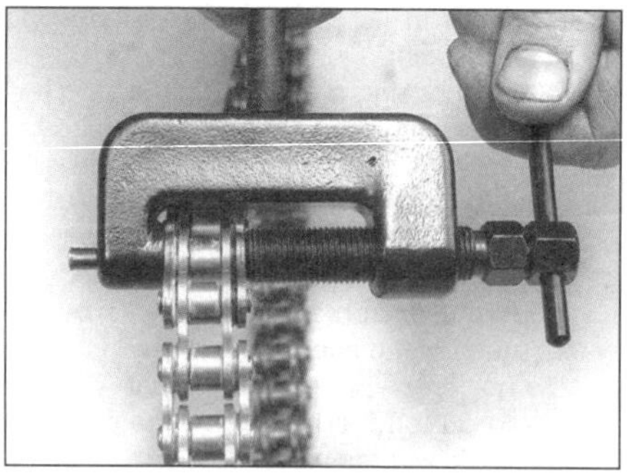

8.1 Tighten the chain breaker to push the pin out of the link . . .

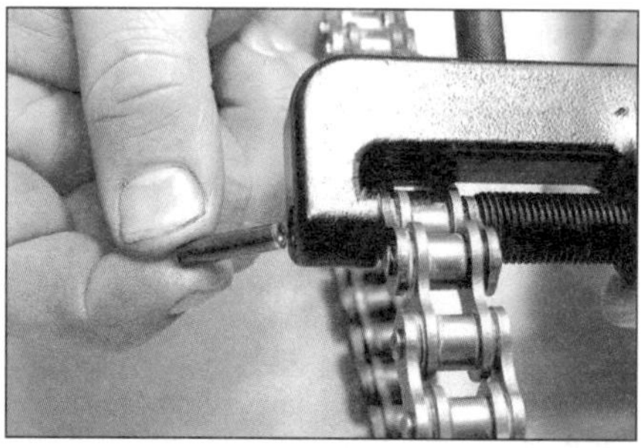

8.2 . . . withdraw the pin, remove the tool . . .

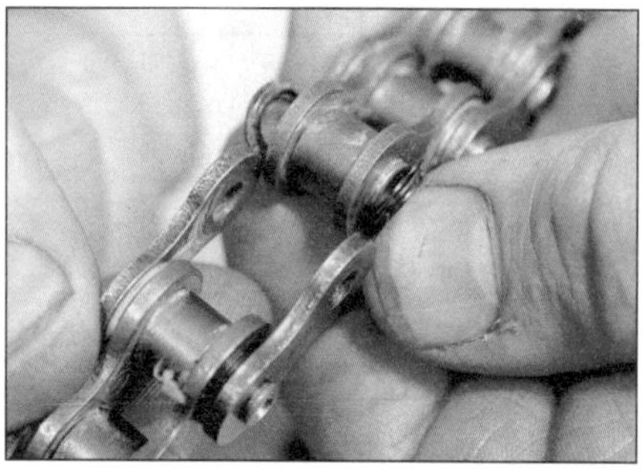

8.3 . . . and separate the chain link

deeply centre-punched instead of peened over like all the other pins **(see illustration 8.9)** and its sideplate may be a different colour. Position the soft link midway between the sprockets and assemble the chain breaker tool over one of the soft link pins **(see illustration 8.1)**. Operate the tool to push the pin out through the chain **(see illustration 8.2)**. On an O-ring chain, remove the O-rings **(see illustration 8.3)**. Carry out the same procedure on the other soft link pin.

Caution: Certain soft link pins (particularly on the larger chains) may require their ends to be filed or ground off before they can be pressed out using the tool.

- Check that you have the correct size and strength (standard or heavy duty) new soft link - do not reuse the old link. Look for the size marking on the chain sideplates **(see illustration 8.10)**.
- Position the chain ends so that they are engaged over the rear sprocket. On an O-ring

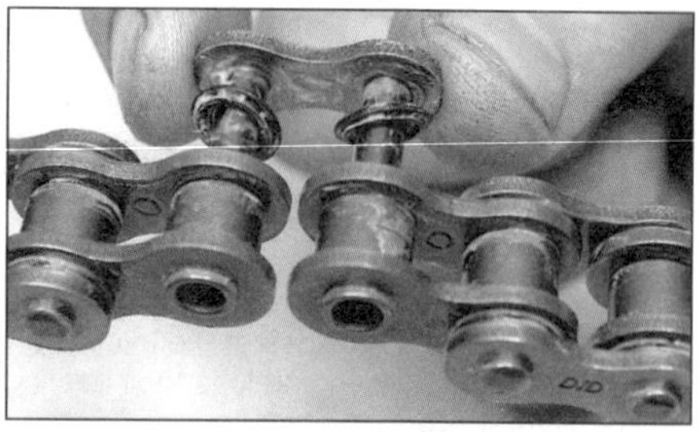

8.4 Insert the new soft link, with O-rings, through the chain ends . . .

8.5 . . . install the O-rings over the pin ends . . .

8.6 . . . followed by the sideplate

chain, install a new O-ring over each pin of the link and insert the link through the two chain ends **(see illustration 8.4)**. Install a new O-ring over the end of each pin, followed by the sideplate (with the chain manufacturer's marking facing outwards) **(see illustrations 8.5 and 8.6)**. On an unsealed chain, insert the link through the two chain ends, then install the sideplate with the chain manufacturer's marking facing outwards.

- Note that it may not be possible to install the sideplate using finger pressure alone. If using a joining tool, assemble it so that the plates of the tool clamp the link and press the sideplate over the pins **(see illustration 8.7)**. Otherwise, use two small sockets placed over

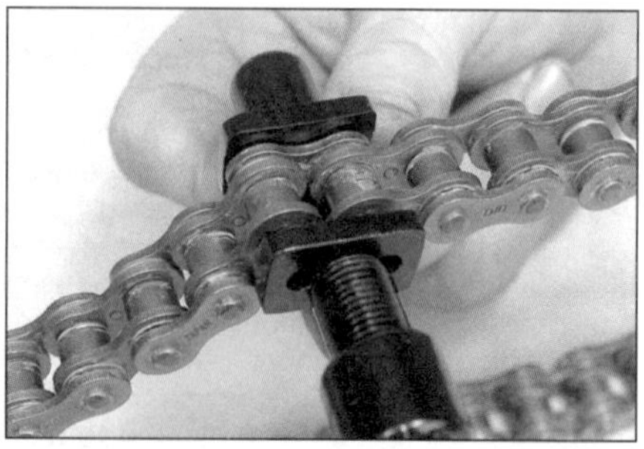

8.7 Push the sideplate into position using a clamp

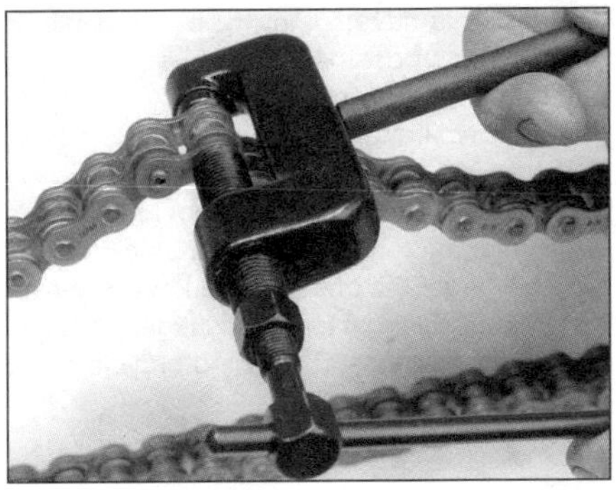

8.8 Assemble the chain riveting tool over one pin at a time and tighten it fully

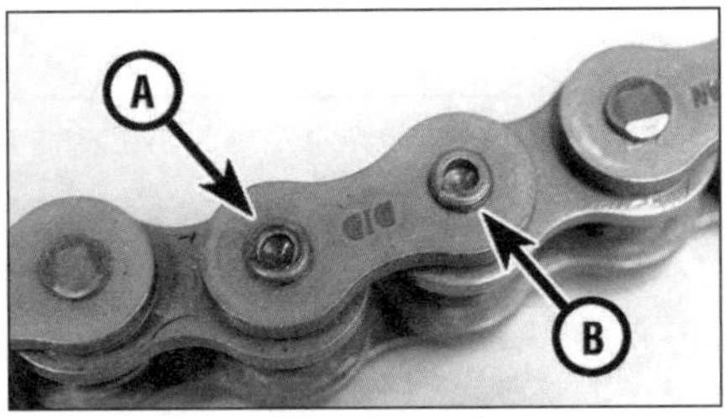

8.9 Pin end correctly riveted (A), pin end unriveted (B)

the rivet ends and two pieces of the wood between a G-clamp. Operate the clamp to press the sideplate over the pins.

● Assemble the joining tool over one pin (following the maker's instructions) and tighten the tool down to spread the pin end securely **(see illustrations 8.8 and 8.9)**. Do the same on the other pin.

> ***Warning: Check that the pin ends are secure and that there is no danger of the sideplate coming loose. If the pin ends are cracked the soft link must be renewed.***

Final drive chain sizing

● Chains are sized using a three digit number, followed by a suffix to denote the chain type **(see illustration 8.10)**. Chain type is either standard or heavy duty (thicker sideplates), and also unsealed or O-ring/X-ring type.

● The first digit of the number relates to the pitch of the chain, ie the distance from the centre of one pin to the centre of the next pin **(see illustration 8.11)**. Pitch is expressed in eighths of an inch, as follows:

8.10 Typical chain size and type marking

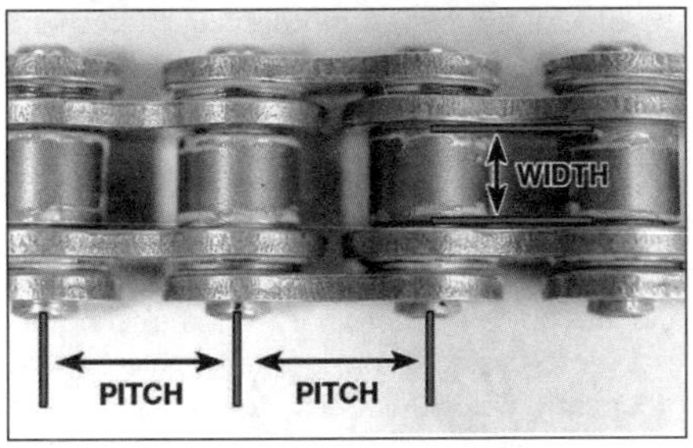

8.11 Chain dimensions

Sizes commencing with a 4 (eg 428) have a pitch of 1/2 inch (12.7 mm)

Sizes commencing with a 5 (eg 520) have a pitch of 5/8 inch (15.9 mm)

Sizes commencing with a 6 (eg 630) have a pitch of 3/4 inch (19.1 mm)

● The second and third digits of the chain size relate to the width of the rollers, again in imperial units, eg the 525 shown has 5/16 inch (7.94 mm) rollers **(see illustration 8.11)**.

9 Hoses

Clamping to prevent flow

● Small-bore flexible hoses can be clamped to prevent fluid flow whilst a component is worked on. Whichever method is used, ensure that the hose material is not permanently distorted or damaged by the clamp.

*a) A brake hose clamp available from auto accessory shops **(see illustration 9.1)**.*

*b) A wingnut type hose clamp **(see illustration 9.2)**.*

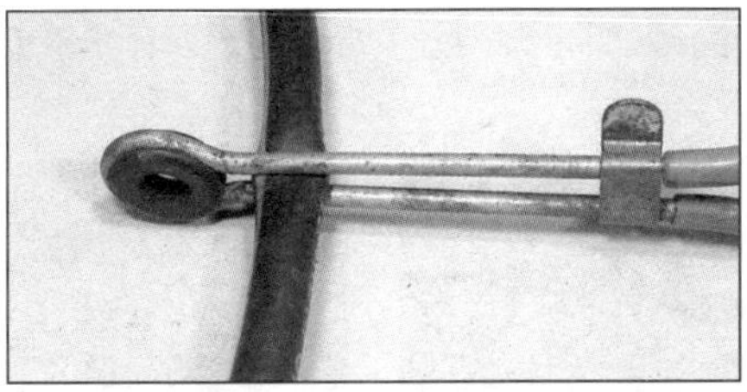

9.1 Hoses can be clamped with an automotive brake hose clamp . . .

9.2 . . . a wingnut type hose clamp . . .

*c) Two sockets placed each side of the hose and held with straight-jawed self-locking grips **(see illustration 9.3)**.*

*d) Thick card each side of the hose held between straight-jawed self-locking grips **(see illustration 9.4)**.*

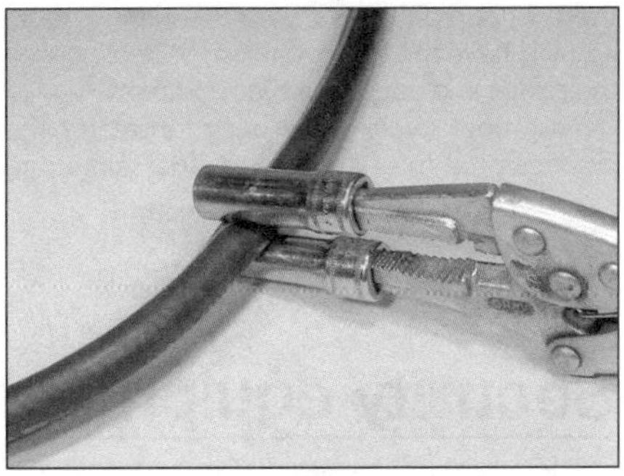

9.3 . . . two sockets and a pair of self-locking grips . . .

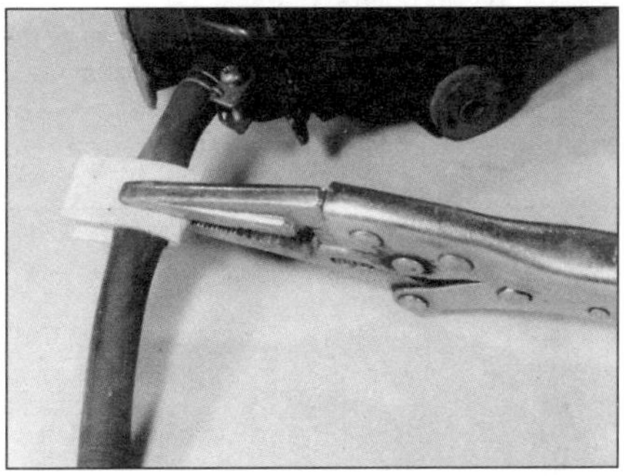

9.4 . . . or thick card and self-locking grips

Freeing and fitting hoses

● Always make sure the hose clamp is moved well clear of the hose end. Grip the hose with your hand and rotate it whilst pulling it off the union. If the hose has hardened due to age and will not move, slit it with a sharp knife and peel its ends off the union **(see illustration 9.5)**.

● Resist the temptation to use grease or soap on the unions to aid installation; although it helps the hose slip over the union it will equally aid the escape of fluid from the joint. It is preferable to soften the hose ends in hot water and wet the inside surface of the hose with water or a fluid which will evaporate.

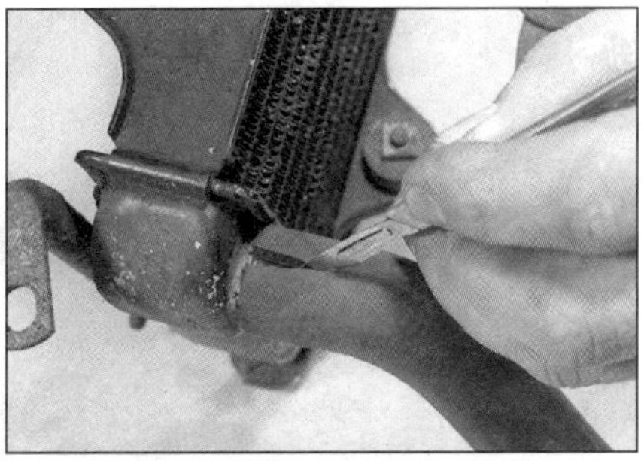

9.5 Cutting a coolant hose free with a sharp knife

Introduction

In less time than it takes to read this introduction, a thief could steal your motorcycle. Returning only to find your bike has gone is one of the worst feelings in the world. Even if the motorcycle is insured against theft, once you've got over the initial shock, you will have the inconvenience of dealing with the police and your insurance company.

The motorcycle is an easy target for the professional thief and the joyrider alike and the official figures on motorcycle theft make for depressing reading; on average a motorcycle is stolen every 16 minutes in the UK!

Motorcycle thefts fall into two categories, those stolen 'to order' and those taken by opportunists. The thief stealing to order will be on the look out for a specific make and model and will go to extraordinary lengths to obtain that motorcycle. The opportunist thief on the other hand will look for easy targets which can be stolen with the minimum of effort and risk.

Whilst it is never going to be possible to make your machine 100% secure, it is estimated that around half of all stolen motorcycles are taken by opportunist thieves. Remember that the opportunist thief is always on the look out for the easy option: if there are two similar motorcycles parked side-by-side, they will target the one with the lowest level of security. By taking a few precautions, you can reduce the chances of your motorcycle being stolen.

Security equipment

There are many specialised motorcycle security devices available and the following text summarises their applications and their good and bad points.

Once you have decided on the type of security equipment which best suits your needs, we recommended that you read one of the many equipment tests regularly carried out by the motorcycle press. These tests compare the products from all the major manufacturers and give impartial ratings on their effectiveness, value-for-money and ease of use.

No one item of security equipment can provide complete protection. It is highly recommended that two or more of the items described below are combined to increase the security of your motorcycle (a lock and chain plus an alarm system is just about ideal). The more security measures fitted to the bike, the less likely it is to be stolen.

1

Ensure the lock and chain you buy is of good quality and long enough to shackle your bike to a solid object

Lock and chain

Pros: *Very flexible to use; can be used to secure the motorcycle to almost any immovable object. On some locks and chains, the lock can be used on its own as a disc lock (see below).*

Cons: *Can be very heavy and awkward to carry on the motorcycle, although some types will be supplied with a carry bag which can be strapped to the pillion seat.*

- Heavy-duty chains and locks are an excellent security measure **(see illustration 1)**. Whenever the motorcycle is parked, use the lock and chain to secure the machine to a solid, immovable object such as a post or railings. This will prevent the machine from being ridden away or being lifted into the back of a van.

- When fitting the chain, always ensure the chain is routed around the motorcycle frame or swingarm **(see illustrations 2 and 3)**. Never merely pass the chain around one of the wheel rims; a thief may unbolt the wheel and lift the rest of the machine into a van, leaving you with just the wheel! Try to avoid having excess chain free, thus making it difficult to use cutting tools, and keep the chain and lock off the ground to prevent thieves attacking it with a cold chisel. Position the lock so that its lock barrel is facing downwards; this will make it harder for the thief to attack the lock mechanism.

2

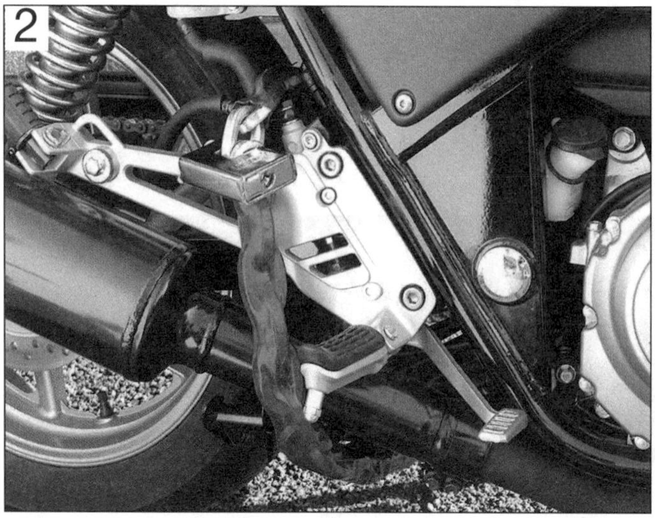

Pass the chain through the bike's frame, rather than just through a wheel . . .

3

. . . and loop it around a solid object

U-locks

Pros: *Highly effective deterrent which can be used to secure the bike to a post or railings. Most U-locks come with a carrier which allows the lock to be easily carried on the bike.*

Cons: *Not as flexible to use as a lock and chain.*

- These are solid locks which are similar in use to a lock and chain. U-locks are lighter than a lock and chain but not so flexible to use. The length and shape of the lock shackle limit the objects to which the bike can be secured **(see illustration 4)**.

U-locks can be used to secure the bike to a solid object – ensure you purchase one which is long enough

Disc locks

Pros: *Small, light and very easy to carry; most can be stored underneath the seat.*

Cons: *Does not prevent the motorcycle being lifted into a van. Can be very embarrassing if you forget to remove the lock before attempting to ride off!*

A typical disc lock attached through one of the holes in the disc

- Disc locks are designed to be attached to the front brake disc. The lock passes through one of the holes in the disc and prevents the wheel rotating by jamming against the fork/brake caliper **(see illustration 5)**. Some are equipped with an alarm siren which sounds if the disc lock is moved; this not only acts as a theft deterrent but also as a handy reminder if you try to move the bike with the lock still fitted.

- Combining the disc lock with a length of cable which can be looped around a post or railings provides an additional measure of security **(see illustration 6)**.

Alarms and immobilisers

Pros: *Once installed it is completely hassle-free to use. If the system is 'Thatcham' or 'Sold Secure-approved', insurance companies may give you a discount.*

Cons: *Can be expensive to buy and complex to install. No system will prevent the motorcycle from being lifted into a van and taken away.*

- Electronic alarms and immobilisers are available to suit a variety of budgets. There are three different types of system available: pure alarms, pure immobilisers, and the more expensive systems which are combined alarm/immobilisers **(see illustration 7)**.
- An alarm system is designed to emit an audible warning if the motorcycle is being tampered with.
- An immobiliser prevents the motorcycle being started and ridden away by disabling its electrical systems.
- When purchasing an alarm/immobiliser system, check the cost of installing the system unless you are able to do it yourself. If the motorcycle is not used regularly, another consideration is the current drain of the system. All alarm/immobiliser systems are powered by the motorcycle's battery; purchasing a system with a very low current drain could prevent the battery losing its charge whilst the motorcycle is not being used.

A disc lock combined with a security cable provides additional protection

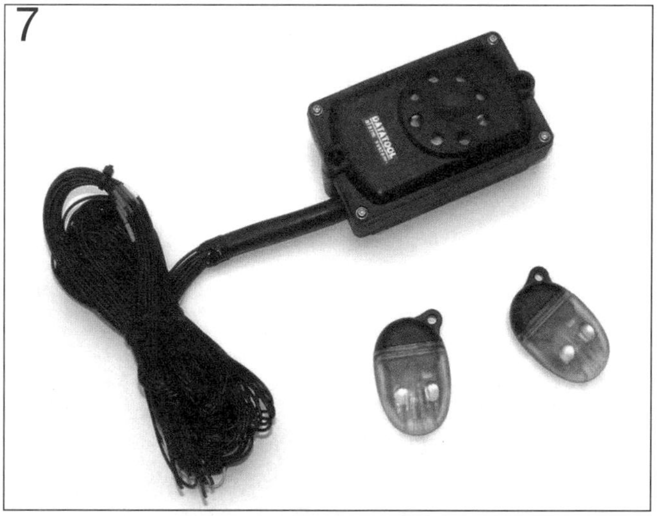

A typical alarm/immobiliser system

8

Indelible markings can be applied to most areas of the bike – always apply the manufacturer's sticker to warn off thieves

9

Chemically-etched code numbers can be applied to main body panels . . .

10

. . . again, always ensure that the kit manufacturer's sticker is applied in a prominent position

Security marking kits

Pros: *Very cheap and effective deterrent. Many insurance companies will give you a discount on your insurance premium if a recognised security marking kit is used on your motorcycle.*

Cons: *Does not prevent the motorcycle being stolen by joyriders.*

● There are many different types of security marking kits available. The idea is to mark as many parts of the motorcycle as possible with a unique security number **(see illustrations 8, 9 and 10)**. A form will be included with the kit to register your personal details and those of the motorcycle with the kit manufacturer. This register is made available to the police to help them trace the rightful owner of any motorcycle or components which they recover should all other forms of identification have been removed. Always apply the warning stickers provided with the kit to deter thieves.

Ground anchors, wheel clamps and security posts

Pros: *An excellent form of security which will deter all but the most determined of thieves.*

Cons: *Awkward to install and can be expensive.*

● Whilst the motorcycle is at home, it is a good idea to attach it securely to the floor or a solid wall, even if it is kept in a securely locked garage. Various types of ground anchors, security posts and wheel clamps are available for this purpose **(see illustration 11)**. These security devices are either bolted to a solid concrete or brick structure or can be cemented into the ground.

11

Permanent ground anchors provide an excellent level of security when the bike is at home

Security at home

A high percentage of motorcycle thefts are from the owner's home. Here are some things to consider whenever your motorcycle is at home:

✔ Where possible, always keep the motorcycle in a securely locked garage. Never rely solely on the standard lock on the garage door, these are usual hopelessly inadequate. Fit an additional locking mechanism to the door and consider having the garage alarmed. A security light, activated by a movement sensor, is also a good investment.

✔ Always secure the motorcycle to the ground or a wall, even if it is inside a securely locked garage.

✔ Do not regularly leave the motorcycle outside your home, try to keep it out of sight wherever possible. If a garage is not available, fit a motorcycle cover over the bike to disguise its true identity.

✔ It is not uncommon for thieves to follow a motorcyclist home to find out where the bike is kept. They will then return at a later date. Be aware of this whenever you are returning home on your motorcycle. If you suspect you are being followed, do not return home, instead ride to a garage or shop and stop as a precaution.

✔ When selling a motorcycle, do not provide your home address or the location where the bike is normally kept. Arrange to meet the buyer at a location away from your home. Thieves have been known to pose as potential buyers to find out where motorcycles are kept and then return later to steal them.

Security away from the home

As well as fitting security equipment to your motorcycle here are a few general rules to follow whenever you park your motorcycle.

✔ Park in a busy, public place.

✔ Use car parks which incorporate security features, such as CCTV.

✔ At night, park in a well-lit area, preferably directly underneath a street light.

✔ Engage the steering lock.

✔ Secure the motorcycle to a solid, immovable object such as a post or railings with an additional lock. If this is not possible, secure the bike to a friend's motorcycle. Some public parking places provide security loops for motorcycles.

✔ Never leave your helmet or luggage attached to the motorcycle. Take them with you at all times.

Lubricants and fluids

A wide range of lubricants, fluids and cleaning agents is available for motor-cycles. This is a guide as to what is available, its applications and properties.

Four-stroke engine oil

● Engine oil is without doubt the most important component of any four-stroke engine. Modern motorcycle engines place a lot of demands on their oil and choosing the right type is essential. Using an unsuitable oil will lead to an increased rate of engine wear and could result in serious engine damage. Before purchasing oil, always check the recommended oil specification given by the manufacturer. The manufacturer will state a recommended 'type or classification' and also a specific 'viscosity' range for engine oil.

● The oil 'type or classification' is identified by its API (American Petroleum Institute) rating. The API rating will be in the form of two letters, e.g. SG. The S identifies the oil as being suitable for use in a petrol (gasoline) engine (S stands for spark ignition) and the second letter, ranging from A to J, identifies the oil's performance rating. The later this letter, the higher the specification of the oil; for example API SG oil exceeds the requirements of API SF oil. **Note:** *On some oils there may also be a second rating consisting of another two letters, the first letter being C, e.g. API SF/CD. This rating indicates the oil is also suitable for use in a diesel engines (the C stands for compression ignition) and is thus of no relevance for motorcycle use.*

● The 'viscosity' of the oil is identified by its SAE (Society of Automotive Engineers) rating. All modern engines require multigrade oils and the SAE rating will consist of two numbers, the first followed by a W, e.g. 10W/40. The first number indicates the viscosity rating of the oil at low temperatures (W stands for winter – tested at –20°C) and the second number represents the viscosity of the oil at high temperatures (tested at 100°C). The lower the number, the thinner the oil. For example an oil with an SAE 10W/40 rating will give better cold starting and running than an SAE 15W/40 oil.

● As well as ensuring the 'type' and 'viscosity' of the oil match the recommendations, another consideration to make when buying engine oil is whether to purchase a standard mineral-based oil, a semi-synthetic oil (also known as a synthetic blend or synthetic-based oil) or a fully-synthetic oil. Although all oils will have a similar rating and viscosity, their cost will vary considerably; mineral-based oils are the cheapest, the fully-synthetic oils the most expensive with the semi-synthetic oils falling somewhere in-between. This decision is very much up to the owner, but it should be noted that modern synthetic oils have far better lubricating and cleaning qualities than traditional mineral-based oils and tend to retain these properties for far longer. Bearing in mind the operating conditions inside a modern, high-revving motorcycle engine it is highly recommended that a fully synthetic oil is used. The extra expense at each service could save you money in the long term by preventing premature engine wear.

● As a final note always ensure that the oil is specifically designed for use in motorcycle engines. Engine oils designed primarily for use in car engines sometimes contain additives or friction modifiers which could cause clutch slip on a motorcycle fitted with a wet-clutch.

Two-stroke engine oil

● Modern two-stroke engines, with their high power outputs, place high demands on their oil. If engine seizure is to be avoided it is essential that a high-quality oil is used. Two-stroke oils differ hugely from four-stroke oils. The oil lubricates only the crankshaft and piston(s) (the transmission has its own lubricating oil) and is used on a total-loss basis where it is burnt completely during the combustion process.

● The Japanese have recently introduced a classification system for two-stroke oils, the JASO rating. This rating is in the form of two letters, either FA, FB or FC – FA is the lowest classification and FC the highest. Ensure the oil being used meets or exceeds the recommended rating specified by the manufacturer.

● As well as ensuring the oil rating matches the recommendation, another consideration to make when buying engine oil is whether to purchase a standard mineral-based oil, a semi-synthetic oil (also known as a synthetic blend or synthetic-based oil) or a fully-synthetic oil. The cost of each type of oil varies considerably; mineral-based oils are the cheapest, the fully-synthetic oils the most expensive with the semi-synthetic oils falling somewhere in-between. This decision is very much up to the owner, but it should be noted that modern synthetic oils have far better lubricating properties and burn cleaner than traditional mineral-based oils. It is therefore recommended that a fully synthetic oil is used. The extra expense could save you money in the long term by preventing premature engine wear, engine performance will be improved, carbon deposits and exhaust smoke will be reduced.

● Always ensure that the oil is specifically designed for use in an injector system. Many high quality two-stroke oils are designed for competition use and need to be pre-mixed with fuel. These oils are of a much higher viscosity and are not designed to flow through the injector pumps used on road-going two-stroke motorcycles.

Transmission (gear) oil

● On a two-stroke engine, the transmission and clutch are lubricated by their own separate oil bath which must be changed in accordance with the Maintenance Schedule.

● Although the engine and transmission units of most four-strokes use a common lubrication supply, there are some exceptions where the engine and gearbox have separate oil reservoirs and a dry clutch is used.

● Motorcycle manufacturers will either recommend a monograde transmission oil or a four-stroke multigrade engine oil to lubricate the transmission.

● Transmission oils, or gear oils as they are often called, are designed specifically for use in transmission systems. The viscosity of these oils is represented by an SAE number, but the scale of measurement applied is different to that used to grade engine oils. As a rough guide a SAE90 gear oil will be of the same viscosity as an SAE50 engine oil.

Shaft drive oil

● On models equipped with shaft final drive, the shaft drive gears are will have their own oil supply. The manufacturer will state a recommended 'type or classification' and also a specific 'viscosity' range in the same manner as for four-stroke engine oil.

● Gear oil classification is given by the number which follows the API GL (GL standing for gear lubricant) rating, the higher the number, the higher the specification of the oil, e.g. API GL5 oil is a higher specification than API GL4 oil. Ensure the oil meets or exceeds the classification specified and is of the correct viscosity. The viscosity of gear oils is also represented by an SAE number but the scale of measurement used is different to that used to grade engine oils. As a rough guide an SAE90 gear oil will be of the same viscosity as an SAE50 engine oil.

● If the use of an EP (Extreme Pressure) gear oil is specified, ensure the oil purchased is suitable.

Fork oil and suspension fluid

● Conventional telescopic front forks are hydraulic and require fork oil to work. To ensure the forks function correctly, the fork oil must be changed in accordance with the Maintenance Schedule.

● Fork oil is available in a variety of viscosities, identified by their SAE rating; fork oil ratings vary from light (SAE 5) to heavy (SAE 30). When purchasing fork oil, ensure the viscosity rating matches that specified by the manufacturer.

● Some lubricant manufacturers also produce a range of high-quality suspension fluids which are very similar to fork oil but are designed mainly for competition use. These fluids may have a different viscosity rating system which is not to be confused with the SAE rating of normal fork oil. Refer to the manufacturer's instructions if in any doubt.

Brake and clutch fluid

● All disc brake systems and some clutch systems are hydraulically operated. To ensure correct operation, the hydraulic fluid must be changed in accordance with the Maintenance Schedule.

● Brake and clutch fluid is classified by its DOT rating with most motorcycle manufacturers specifying DOT 3 or 4 fluid. Both fluid types are glycol-based and can be mixed together without adverse effect; DOT 4 fluid exceeds the requirements of DOT 3 fluid. Although it is safe to use DOT 4 fluid in a system designed for use with DOT 3 fluid, never use DOT 3 fluid in a system which specifies the use of DOT 4 as this will adversely affect the system's performance. The type required for the system will be marked on the fluid reservoir cap.

● Some manufacturers also produce a DOT 5 hydraulic fluid. DOT 5 hydraulic fluid is silicone-based and is not compatible with the glycol-based DOT 3 and 4 fluids. Never mix DOT 5 fluid with DOT 3 or 4 fluid as this will seriously affect the performance of the hydraulic system.

Coolant/antifreeze

● When purchasing coolant/antifreeze, always ensure it is suitable for use in an aluminium engine and contains corrosion inhibitors to prevent possible blockages of the internal coolant passages of the system. As a general rule, most coolants are designed to be used neat and should not be diluted whereas antifreeze can be mixed with distilled water to provide a coolant solution of the required strength. Refer to the manufacturer's instructions on the bottle.

● Ensure the coolant is changed in accordance with the Maintenance Schedule.

Chain lube

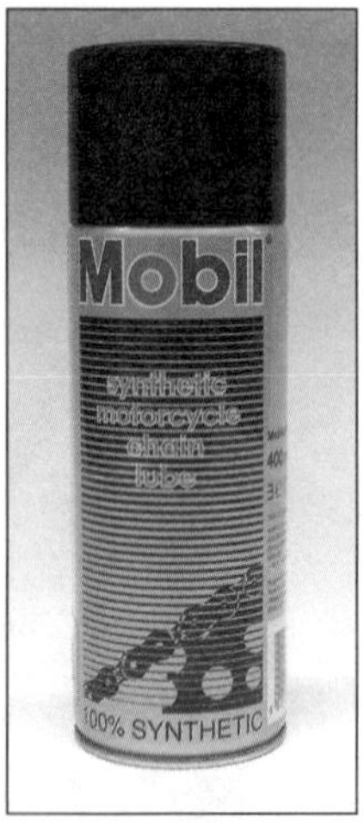

● Chain lube is an aerosol-type spray lubricant specifically designed for use on motorcycle final drive chains. Chain lube has two functions, to minimise friction between the final drive chain and sprockets and to prevent corrosion of the chain. Regular use of a good-quality chain lube will extend the life of the drive chain and sprockets and thus maximise the power being transmitted from the transmission to the rear wheel.

● When using chain lube, always allow some time for the solvents in the lube to evaporate before riding the motorcycle. This will minimise the amount of lube which will 'fling' off from the chain when the motorcycle is used. If the motorcycle is equipped with an 'O-ring' chain, ensure the chain lube is labelled as being suitable for use on 'O-ring' chains.

Degreasers and solvents

● There are many different types of solvents and degreasers available to remove the grime and grease which accumulate around the motorcycle during normal use. Degreasers and solvents are usually available as an aerosol-type spray or as a liquid which you apply with a brush. Always closely follow the manufacturer's instructions and wear eye protection during use. Be aware that many solvents are flammable and may give off noxious fumes; take adequate precautions when using them (*see Safety First!*).

● For general cleaning, use one of the many solvents or degreasers available from most motorcycle accessory shops. These solvents are usually applied then left for a certain time before being washed off with water.

Brake cleaner is a solvent specifically designed to remove all traces of oil, grease and dust from braking system components. Brake cleaner is designed to evaporate quickly and leaves behind no residue.

Carburettor cleaner is an aerosol-type solvent specifically designed to clear carburettor blockages and break down the hard deposits and gum often found inside carburettors during overhaul.

Contact cleaner is an aerosol-type solvent designed for cleaning electrical components. The cleaner will remove all traces of oil and dirt from components such as switch contacts or fouled spark plugs and then dry, leaving behind no residue.

Gasket remover is an aerosol-type solvent designed for removing stubborn gaskets from engine components during overhaul. Gasket remover will minimise the amount of scraping required to remove the gasket and therefore reduce the risk of damage to the mating surface.

Spray lubricants

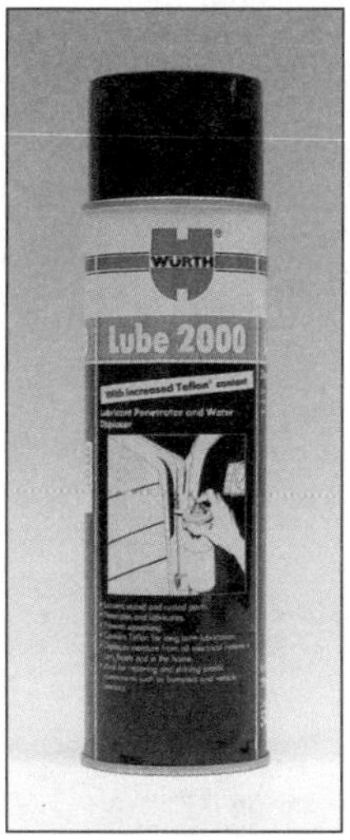

● Aerosol-based spray lubricants are widely available and are excellent for lubricating lever pivots and exposed cables and switches. Try to use a lubricant which is of the dry-film type as the fluid evaporates, leaving behind a dry-film of lubricant. Lubricants which leave behind an oily residue will attract dust and dirt which will increase the rate of wear of the cable/lever.

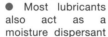

● Most lubricants also act as a moisture dispersant and a penetrating fluid. This means they can also be used to 'dry out' electrical components such as wiring connectors or switches as well as helping to free seized fasteners.

Greases

● Grease is used to lubricate many of the pivot-points. A good-quality multi-purpose grease is suitable for most applications but some manufacturers will specify the use of specialist greases for use on components such as swingarm and suspension linkage bushes. These specialist greases can be purchased from most motorcycle (or car) accessory shops; commonly specified types include molybdenum disulphide grease, lithium-based grease, graphite-based grease, silicone-based grease and high-temperature copper-based grease.

Gasket sealing compounds

● Gasket sealing compounds can be used in conjunction with gaskets, to improve their sealing capabilities, or on their own to seal metal-to-metal joints. Depending on their type, sealing compounds either set hard or stay relatively soft and pliable.

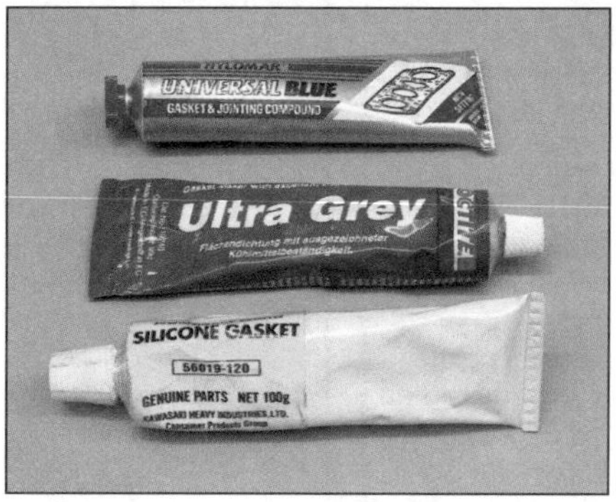

● When purchasing a gasket sealing compound, ensure that it is designed specifically for use on an internal combustion engine. General multi-purpose sealants available from DIY stores may appear visibly similar but they are not designed to withstand the extreme heat or contact with fuel and oil encountered when used on an engine (*see 'Tools and Workshop Tips' for further information*).

Thread locking compound

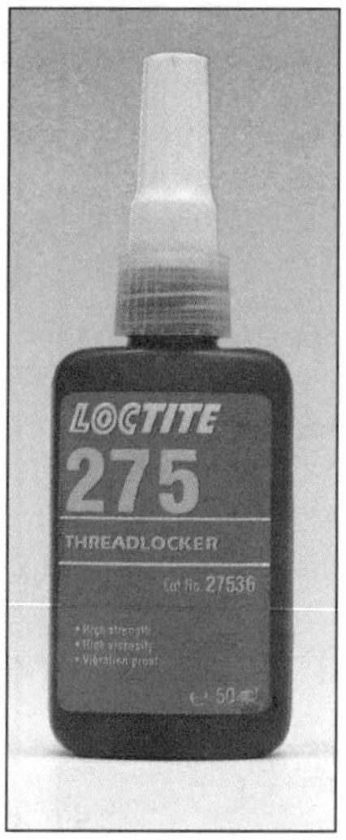

● Thread locking compounds are used to secure certain threaded fasteners in position to prevent them from loosening due to vibration. Thread locking compounds can be purchased from most motorcycle (and car) accessory shops. Ensure the threads of the both components are completely clean and dry before sparingly applying the locking compound (*see 'Tools and Workshop Tips' for further information*).

Fuel additives

● Fuel additives which protect and clean the fuel system components are widely available. These additives are designed to remove all traces of deposits that build up on the carburettors/injectors and prevent wear, helping the fuel system to operate more efficiently. If a fuel additive is being used, check that it is suitable for use with your motorcycle, especially if your motorcycle is equipped with a catalytic converter.

● Octane boosters are also available. These additives are designed to improve the performance of highly-tuned engines being run on normal pump-fuel and are of no real use on standard motorcycles.

Conversion Factors

Length (distance)

Inches (in)	x 25.4	= Millimetres (mm)	x 0.0394	= Inches (in)
Feet (ft)	x 0.305	= Metres (m)	x 3.281	= Feet (ft)
Miles	x 1.609	= Kilometres (km)	x 0.621	= Miles

Volume (capacity)

Cubic inches (cu in; in^3)	x 16.387	= Cubic centimetres (cc; cm^3)	x 0.061	= Cubic inches (cu in; in^3)
Imperial pints (Imp pt)	x 0.568	= Litres (l)	x 1.76	= Imperial pints (Imp pt)
Imperial quarts (Imp qt)	x 1.137	= Litres (l)	x 0.88	= Imperial quarts (Imp qt)
Imperial quarts (Imp qt)	x 1.201	= US quarts (US qt)	x 0.833	= Imperial quarts (Imp qt)
US quarts (US qt)	x 0.946	= Litres (l)	x 1.057	= US quarts (US qt)
Imperial gallons (Imp gal)	x 4.546	= Litres (l)	x 0.22	= Imperial gallons (Imp gal)
Imperial gallons (Imp gal)	x 1.201	= US gallons (US gal)	x 0.833	= Imperial gallons (Imp gal)
US gallons (US gal)	x 3.785	= Litres (l)	x 0.264	= US gallons (US gal)

Mass (weight)

Ounces (oz)	x 28.35	= Grams (g)	x 0.035	= Ounces (oz)
Pounds (lb)	x 0.454	= Kilograms (kg)	x 2.205	= Pounds (lb)

Force

Ounces-force (ozf; oz)	x 0.278	= Newtons (N)	x 3.6	= Ounces-force (ozf; oz)
Pounds-force (lbf; lb)	x 4.448	= Newtons (N)	x 0.225	= Pounds-force (lbf; lb)
Newtons (N)	x 0.1	= Kilograms-force (kgf; kg)	x 9.81	= Newtons (N)

Pressure

Pounds-force per square inch (psi; lbf/in^2; lb/in^2)	x 0.070	= Kilograms-force per square centimetre (kgf/cm^2; kg/cm^2)	x 14.223	= Pounds-force per square inch (psi; lbf/in^2; lb/in^2)
Pounds-force per square inch (psi; lbf/in^2; lb/in^2)	x 0.068	= Atmospheres (atm)	x 14.696	= Pounds-force per square inch (psi; lbf/in^2; lb/in^2)
Pounds-force per square inch (psi; lbf/in^2; lb/in^2)	x 0.069	= Bars	x 14.5	= Pounds-force per square inch (psi; lbf/in^2; lb/in^2)
Pounds-force per square inch (psi; lbf/in^2; lb/in^2)	x 6.895	= Kilopascals (kPa)	x 0.145	= Pounds-force per square inch (psi; lbf/in^2; lb/in^2)
Kilopascals (kPa)	x 0.01	= Kilograms-force per square centimetre (kgf/cm^2; kg/cm^2)	x 98.1	= Kilopascals (kPa)
Millibar (mbar)	x 100	= Pascals (Pa)	x 0.01	= Millibar (mbar)
Millibar (mbar)	x 0.0145	= Pounds-force per square inch (psi; lbf/in^2; lb/in^2)	x 68.947	= Millibar (mbar)
Millibar (mbar)	x 0.75	= Millimetres of mercury (mmHg)	x 1.333	= Millibar (mbar)
Millibar (mbar)	x 0.401	= Inches of water (inH_2O)	x 2.491	= Millibar (mbar)
Millimetres of mercury (mmHg)	x 0.535	= Inches of water (inH_2O)	x 1.868	= Millimetres of mercury (mmHg)
Inches of water (inH_2O)	x 0.036	= Pounds-force per square inch (psi; lbf/in^2; lb/in^2)	x 27.68	= Inches of water (inH_2O)

Torque (moment of force)

Pounds-force inches (lbf in; lb in)	x 1.152	= Kilograms-force centimetre (kgf cm; kg cm)	x 0.868	= Pounds-force inches (lbf in; lb in)
Pounds-force inches (lbf in; lb in)	x 0.113	= Newton metres (Nm)	x 8.85	= Pounds-force inches (lbf in; lb in)
Pounds-force inches (lbf in; lb in)	x 0.083	= Pounds-force feet (lbf ft; lb ft)	x 12	= Pounds-force inches (lbf in; lb in)
Pounds-force feet (lbf ft; lb ft)	x 0.138	= Kilograms-force metres (kgf m; kg m)	x 7.233	= Pounds-force feet (lbf ft; lb ft)
Pounds-force feet (lbf ft; lb ft)	x 1.356	= Newton metres (Nm)	x 0.738	= Pounds-force feet (lbf ft; lb ft)
Newton metres (Nm)	x 0.102	= Kilograms-force metres (kgf m; kg m)	x 9.804	= Newton metres (Nm)

Power

Horsepower (hp)	x 745.7	= Watts (W)	x 0.0013	= Horsepower (hp)

Velocity (speed)

Miles per hour (miles/hr; mph)	x 1.609	= Kilometres per hour (km/hr; kph)	x 0.621	= Miles per hour (miles/hr; mph)

Fuel consumption*

Miles per gallon (mpg)	x 0.354	= Kilometres per litre (km/l)	x 2.825	= Miles per gallon (mpg)

Temperature

Degrees Fahrenheit = (°C x 1.8) + 32

Degrees Celsius (Degrees Centigrade; °C) = (°F - 32) x 0.56

** It is common practice to convert from miles per gallon (mpg) to litres/100 kilometres (l/100km), where mpg x l/100 km = 282*

About the MOT Test

In the UK, all vehicles more than three years old are subject to an annual test to ensure that they meet minimum safety requirements. A current test certificate must be issued before a machine can be used on public roads, and is required before a road fund licence can be issued. Riding without a current test certificate will also invalidate your insurance.

For most owners, the MOT test is an annual cause for anxiety, and this is largely due to owners not being sure what needs to be checked prior to submitting the motorcycle for testing. The simple answer is that a fully roadworthy motorcycle will have no difficulty in passing the test.

This is a guide to getting your motorcycle through the MOT test. Obviously it will not be possible to examine the motorcycle to the same standard as the professional MOT tester, particularly in view of the equipment required for some of the checks. However, working through the following procedures will enable you to identify any problem areas before submitting the motorcycle for the test.

It has only been possible to summarise the test requirements here, based on the regulations in force at the time of printing. Test standards are becoming increasingly stringent, although there are some exemptions for older vehicles. More information about the MOT test can be obtained from the TSO publications, *How Safe is your Motorcycle* and *The MOT Inspection Manual for Motorcycle Testing.*

Many of the checks require that one of the wheels is raised off the ground. If the motorcycle doesn't have a centre stand, note that an auxiliary stand will be required. Additionally, the help of an assistant may prove useful.

Certain exceptions apply to machines under 50 cc, machines without a lighting system, and Classic bikes - if in doubt about any of the requirements listed below seek confirmation from an MOT tester prior to submitting the motorcycle for the test.

Check that the frame number is clearly visible.

> **HAYNES HiNT** ***If a component is in borderline condition, the tester has discretion in deciding whether to pass or fail it. If the motorcycle presented is clean and evidently well cared for, the tester may be more inclined to pass a borderline component than if the motorcycle is scruffy and apparently neglected.***

Electrical System

Lights, turn signals, horn and reflector

✔ With the ignition on, check the operation of the following electrical components. **Note:** *The electrical components on certain small-capacity machines are powered by the generator, requiring that the engine is run for this check.*

a) Headlight and tail light. Check that both illuminate in the low and high beam switch positions.

b) Position lights. Check that the front position (or sidelight) and tail light illuminate in this switch position.

c) Turn signals. Check that all flash at the correct rate, and that the warning light(s) function correctly. Check that the turn signal switch works correctly.

d) Hazard warning system (where fitted). Check that all four turn signals flash in this switch position.

e) Brake stop light. Check that the light comes on when the front and rear brakes are independently applied. Models first used on or after 1st April 1986 must have a brake light switch on each brake.

f) Horn. Check that the sound is continuous and of reasonable volume.

✔ Check that there is a red reflector on the rear of the machine, either mounted separately or as part of the tail light lens.

✔ Check the condition of the headlight, tail light and turn signal lenses.

Headlight beam height

✔ The MOT tester will perform a headlight beam height check using specialised beam setting equipment **(see illustration 1)**. This equipment will not be available to the home mechanic, but if you suspect that the headlight is incorrectly set or may have been maladjusted in the past, you can perform a rough test as follows.

✔ Position the bike in a straight line facing a brick wall. The bike must be off its stand, upright and with a rider seated. Measure the height from the ground to the centre of the headlight and mark a horizontal line on the wall at this height. Position the motorcycle 3.8 metres from the wall and draw a vertical line up the wall central to the centreline of the motorcycle. Switch to dipped beam and check that the beam pattern falls slightly lower than the horizontal line and to the left of the vertical line **(see illustration 2)**.

1

Headlight beam height checking equipment

2

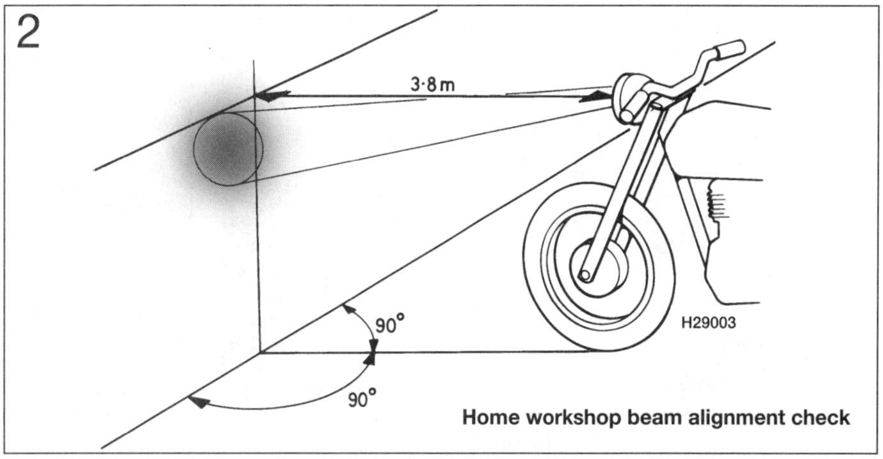

Home workshop beam alignment check

Exhaust System and Final Drive

Exhaust

✔ Check that the exhaust mountings are secure and that the system does not foul any of the rear suspension components.

✔ Start the motorcycle. When the revs are increased, check that the exhaust is neither holed nor leaking from any of its joints. On a linked system, check that the collector box is not leaking due to corrosion.

✔ Note that the exhaust decibel level ("loudness" of the exhaust) is assessed at the discretion of the tester. If the motorcycle was first used on or after 1st January 1985 the silencer must carry the BSAU 193 stamp, or a marking relating to its make and model, or be of OE (original equipment) manufacture. If the silencer is marked NOT FOR ROAD USE, RACING USE ONLY or similar, it will fail the MOT.

Final drive

✔ On chain or belt drive machines, check that the chain/belt is in good condition and does not have excessive slack. Also check that the sprocket is securely mounted on the rear wheel hub. Check that the chain/belt guard is in place.

✔ On shaft drive bikes, check for oil leaking from the drive unit and fouling the rear tyre.

Steering and Suspension

Steering

✔ With the front wheel raised off the ground, rotate the steering from lock to lock. The handlebar or switches must not contact the fuel tank or be close enough to trap the rider's hand. Problems can be caused by damaged lock stops on the lower yoke and frame, or by the fitting of non-standard handlebars.

✔ When performing the lock to lock check, also ensure that the steering moves freely without drag or notchiness. Steering movement can be impaired by poorly routed cables, or by overtight head bearings or worn bearings. The tester will perform a check of the steering head bearing lower race by mounting the front wheel on a surface plate, then performing a lock to lock check with the weight of the machine on the lower bearing **(see illustration 3)**.

✔ Grasp the fork sliders (lower legs) and attempt to push and pull on the forks **(see illustration 4)**. Any play in the steering head bearings will be felt. Note that in extreme cases, wear of the front fork bushes can be misinterpreted for head bearing play.

3

Front wheel mounted on a surface plate for steering head bearing lower race check

✔ Check that the handlebars are securely mounted.

✔ Check that the handlebar grip rubbers are secure. They should by bonded to the bar left end and to the throttle cable pulley on the right end.

Front suspension

✔ With the motorcycle off the stand, hold the front brake on and pump the front forks up and down **(see illustration 5)**. Check that they are adequately damped.

4

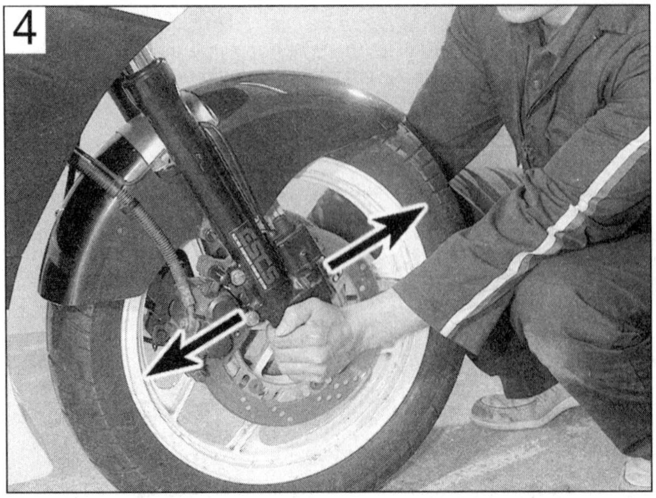

Checking the steering head bearings for freeplay

5

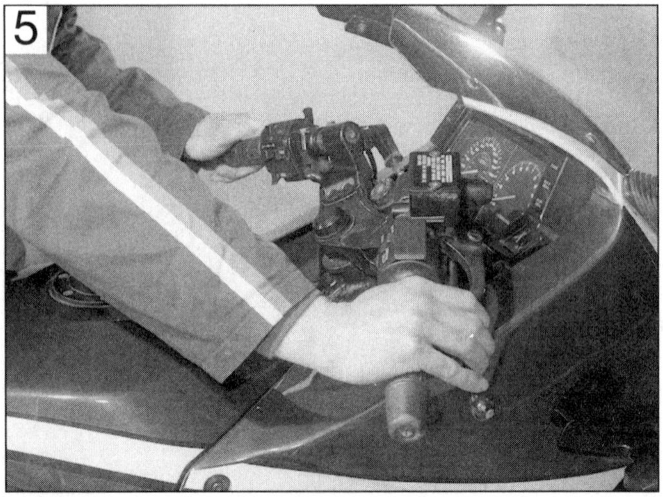

Hold the front brake on and pump the front forks up and down to check operation

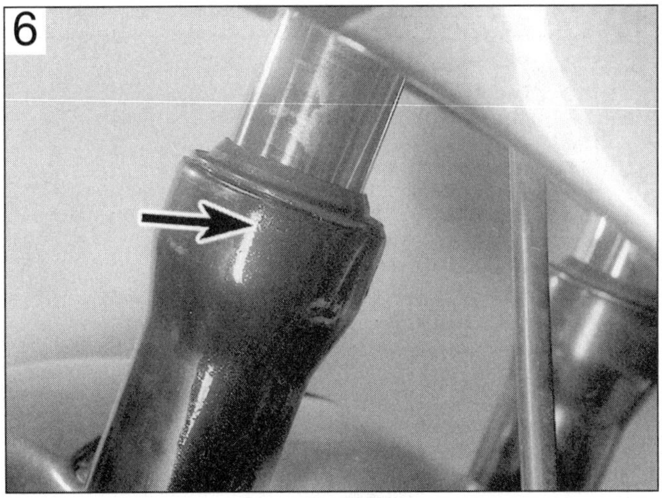

Inspect the area around the fork dust seal for oil leakage (arrow)

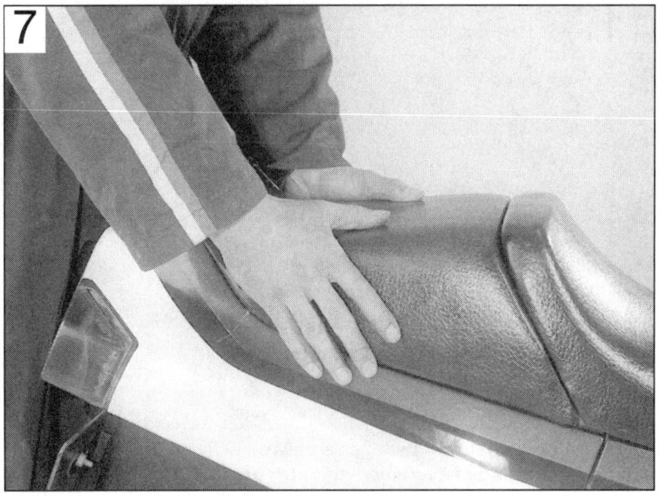

Bounce the rear of the motorcycle to check rear suspension operation

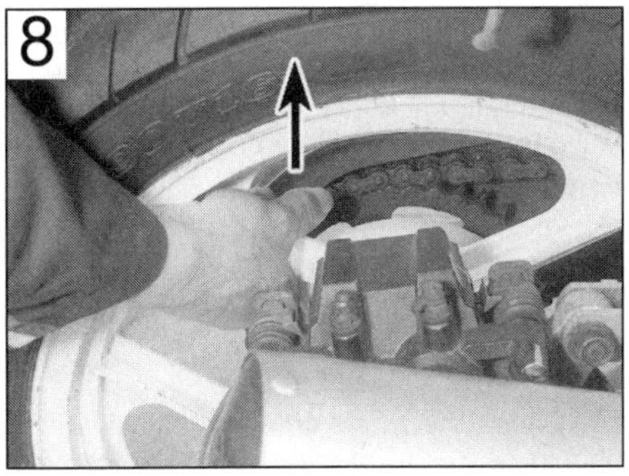

Checking for rear suspension linkage play

✔ Inspect the area above and around the front fork oil seals **(see illustration 6)**. There should be no sign of oil on the fork tube (stanchion) nor leaking down the slider (lower leg). On models so equipped, check that there is no oil leaking from the anti-dive units.

✔ On models with swingarm front suspension, check that there is no freeplay in the linkage when moved from side to side.

Rear suspension

✔ With the motorcycle off the stand and an assistant supporting the motorcycle by its handlebars, bounce the rear suspension **(see illustration 7)**. Check that the suspension components do not foul on any of the cycle parts and check that the shock absorber(s) provide adequate damping.

✔ Visually inspect the shock absorber(s) and check that there is no sign of oil leakage from its damper. This is somewhat restricted on certain single shock models due to the location of the shock absorber.

✔ With the rear wheel raised off the ground, grasp the wheel at the highest point and attempt to pull it up **(see illustration 8)**. Any play in the swingarm pivot or suspension linkage bearings will be felt as movement. **Note:** *Do not confuse play with actual suspension movement.* Failure to lubricate suspension linkage bearings can lead to bearing failure **(see illustration 9)**.

✔ With the rear wheel raised off the ground, grasp the swingarm ends and attempt to move the swingarm from side to side and forwards and backwards - any play indicates wear of the swingarm pivot bearings **(see illustration 10)**.

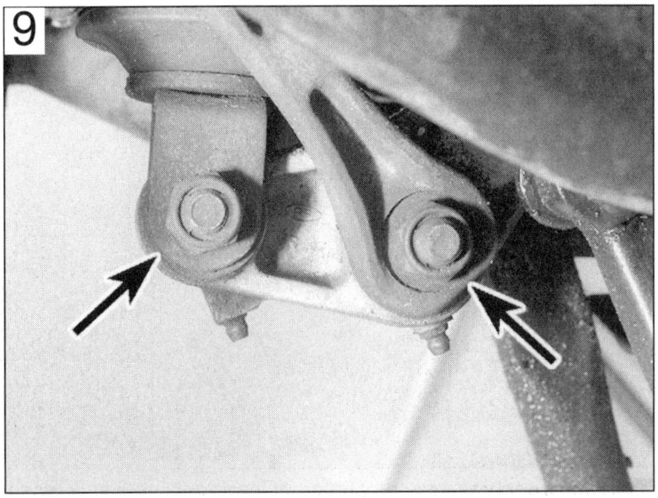

Worn suspension linkage pivots (arrows) are usually the cause of play in the rear suspension

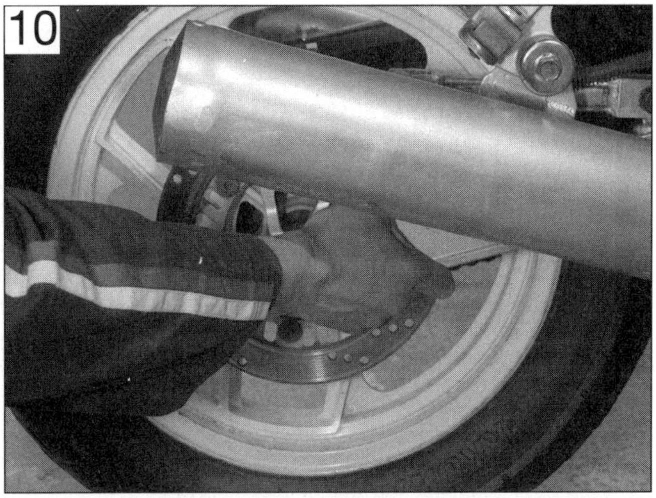

Grasp the swingarm at the ends to check for play in its pivot bearings

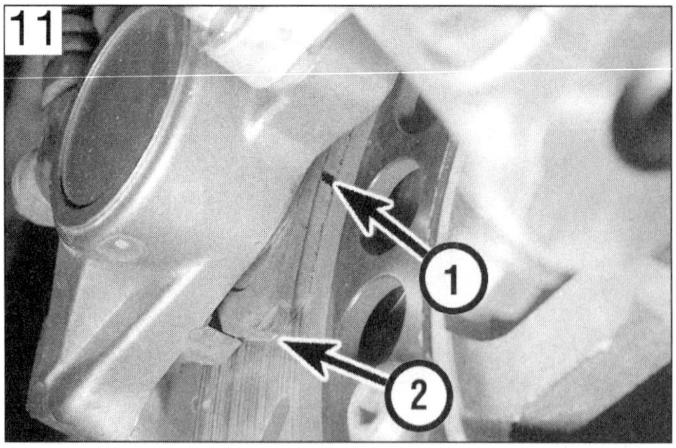

Brake pad wear can usually be viewed without removing the caliper. Most pads have wear indicator grooves (1) and some also have indicator tangs (2)

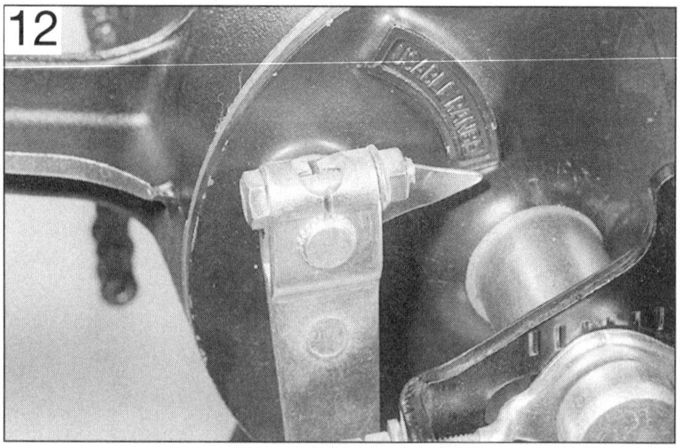

On drum brakes, check the angle of the operating lever with the brake fully applied. Most drum brakes have a wear indicator pointer and scale.

Brakes, Wheels and Tyres

Brakes

✔ With the wheel raised off the ground, apply the brake then free it off, and check that the wheel is about to revolve freely without brake drag.

✔ On disc brakes, examine the disc itself. Check that it is securely mounted and not cracked.

✔ On disc brakes, view the pad material through the caliper mouth and check that the pads are not worn down beyond the limit **(see illustration 11)**.

✔ On drum brakes, check that when the brake is applied the angle between the operating lever and cable or rod is not too great **(see illustration 12)**. Check also that the operating lever doesn't foul any other components.

✔ On disc brakes, examine the flexible hoses from top to bottom. Have an assistant hold the brake on so that the fluid in the hose is under pressure, and check that there is no sign of fluid leakage, bulges or cracking. If there are any metal brake pipes or unions, check that these are free from corrosion and damage. Where a brake-linked anti-dive system is fitted, check the hoses to the anti-dive in a similar manner.

✔ Check that the rear brake torque arm is secure and that its fasteners are secured by self-locking nuts or castellated nuts with split-pins or R-pins **(see illustration 13)**.

✔ On models with ABS, check that the self-check warning light in the instrument panel works.

✔ The MOT tester will perform a test of the motorcycle's braking efficiency based on a calculation of rider and motorcycle weight. Although this cannot be carried out at home, you can at least ensure that the braking systems are properly maintained. For hydraulic disc brakes, check the fluid level, lever/pedal feel (bleed of air if its spongy) and pad material. For drum brakes, check adjustment, cable or rod operation and shoe lining thickness.

Wheels and tyres

✔ Check the wheel condition. Cast wheels should be free from cracks and if of the built-up design, all fasteners should be secure. Spoked wheels should be checked for broken, corroded, loose or bent spokes.

✔ With the wheel raised off the ground, spin the wheel and visually check that the tyre and wheel run true. Check that the tyre does not foul the suspension or mudguards.

✔ With the wheel raised off the ground, grasp the wheel and attempt to move it about the axle (spindle) **(see illustration 14)**. Any play felt here indicates wheel bearing failure.

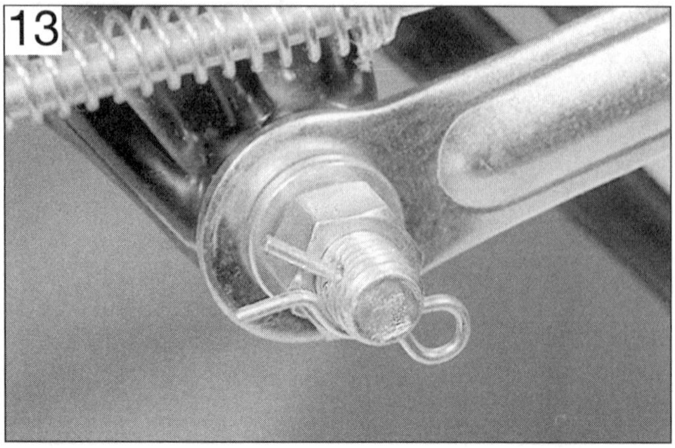

Brake torque arm must be properly secured at both ends

Check for wheel bearing play by trying to move the wheel about the axle (spindle)

Checking the tyre tread depth

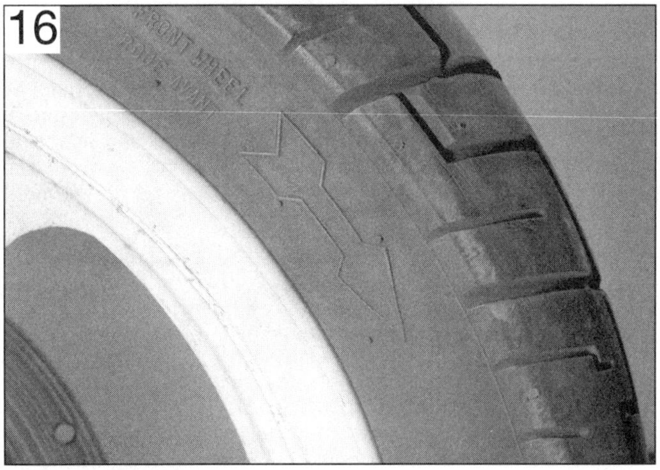

Tyre direction of rotation arrow can be found on tyre sidewall

Castellated type wheel axle (spindle) nut must be secured by a split pin or R-pin

Two straightedges are used to check wheel alignment

✔ Check the tyre tread depth, tread condition and sidewall condition **(see illustration 15)**.

✔ Check the tyre type. Front and rear tyre types must be compatible and be suitable for road use. Tyres marked NOT FOR ROAD USE, COMPETITION USE ONLY or similar, will fail the MOT.

✔ If the tyre sidewall carries a direction of rotation arrow, this must be pointing in the direction of normal wheel rotation **(see illustration 16)**.

✔ Check that the wheel axle (spindle) nuts (where applicable) are properly secured. A self-locking nut or castellated nut with a split-pin or R-pin can be used **(see illustration 17)**.

✔ Wheel alignment is checked with the motorcycle off the stand and a rider seated. With the front wheel pointing straight ahead, two perfectly straight lengths of metal or wood and placed against the sidewalls of both tyres **(see illustration 18)**. The gap each side of the front tyre must be equidistant on both sides. Incorrect wheel alignment may be due to a cocked rear wheel (often as the result of poor chain adjustment) or in extreme cases, a bent frame.

General checks and condition

✔ Check the security of all major fasteners, bodypanels, seat, fairings (where fitted) and mudguards.

✔ Check that the rider and pillion footrests, handlebar levers and brake pedal are securely mounted.

✔ Check for corrosion on the frame or any load-bearing components. If severe, this may affect the structure, particularly under stress.

Sidecars

A motorcycle fitted with a sidecar requires additional checks relating to the stability of the machine and security of attachment and swivel joints, plus specific wheel alignment (toe-in) requirements. Additionally, tyre and lighting requirements differ from conventional motorcycle use. Owners are advised to check MOT test requirements with an official test centre.

Preparing for storage

Before you start

If repairs or an overhaul is needed, see that this is carried out now rather than left until you want to ride the bike again.

Give the bike a good wash and scrub all dirt from its underside. Make sure the bike dries completely before preparing for storage.

Engine

- Remove the spark plug(s) and lubricate the cylinder bores with approximately a teaspoon of motor oil using a spout-type oil can **(see illustration 1)**. Reinstall the spark plug(s). Crank the engine over a couple of times to coat the piston rings and bores with oil. If the bike has a kickstart, use this to turn the engine over. If not, flick the kill switch to the OFF position and crank the engine over on the starter **(see illustration 2)**. If the nature on the ignition system prevents the starter operating with the kill switch in the OFF position, remove the spark plugs and fit them back in their caps; ensure that the plugs are earthed (grounded) against the cylinder head when the starter is operated **(see illustration 3)**.

Warning: It is important that the plugs are earthed (grounded) away from the spark plug holes otherwise there is a risk of atomised fuel from the cylinders igniting.

HAYNES HiNT ***On a single cylinder four-stroke engine, you can seal the combustion chamber completely by positioning the piston at TDC on the compression stroke.***

- Drain the carburettor(s) otherwise there is a risk of jets becoming blocked by gum deposits from the fuel **(see illustration 4)**.
- If the bike is going into long-term storage, consider adding a fuel stabiliser to the fuel in the tank. If the tank is drained completely, corrosion of its internal surfaces may occur if left unprotected for a long period. The tank can be treated with a rust preventative especially for this purpose. Alternatively, remove the tank and pour half a litre of motor oil into it, install the filler cap and shake the tank to coat its internals with oil before draining off the excess. The same effect can also be achieved by spraying WD40 or a similar water-dispersant around the inside of the tank via its flexible nozzle.
- Make sure the cooling system contains the correct mix of antifreeze. Antifreeze also contains important corrosion inhibitors.
- The air intakes and exhaust can be sealed off by covering or plugging the openings. Ensure that you do not seal in any condensation; run the engine until it is hot,

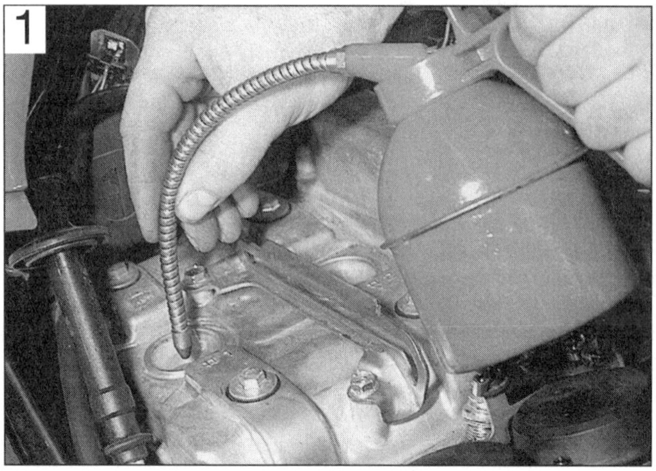

Squirt a drop of motor oil into each cylinder

Flick the kill switch to OFF . . .

. . . and ensure that the metal bodies of the plugs (arrows) are earthed against the cylinder head

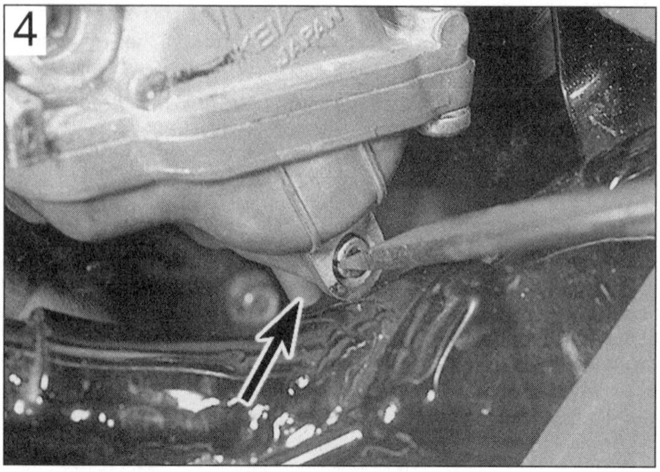

Connect a hose to the carburettor float chamber drain stub (arrow) and unscrew the drain screw

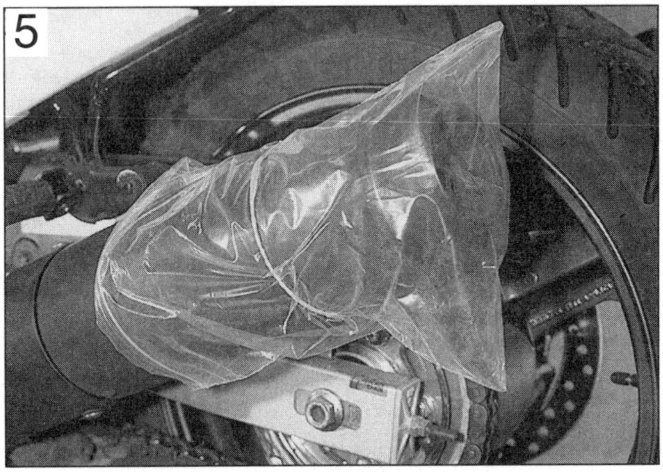

Exhausts can be sealed off with a plastic bag

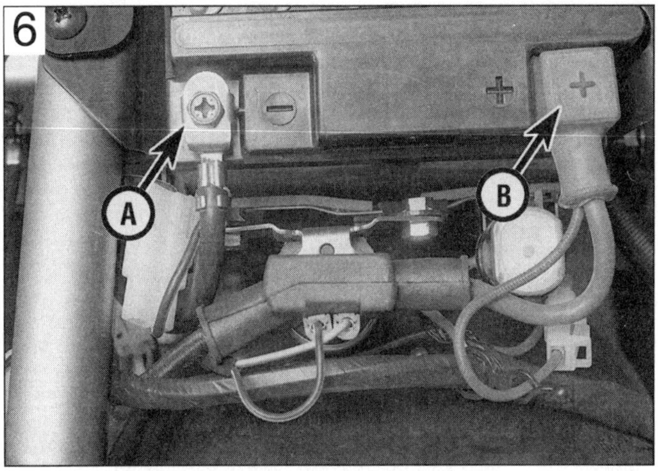

Disconnect the negative lead (A) first, followed by the positive lead (B)

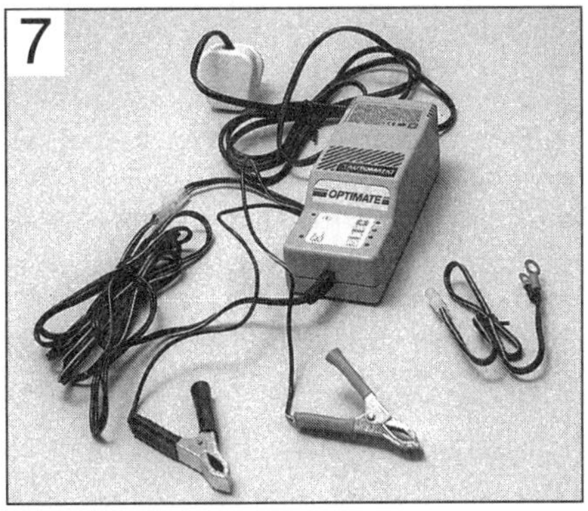

Use a suitable battery charger - this kit also assess battery condition

then switch off and allow to cool. Tape a piece of thick plastic over the silencer end(s) **(see illustration 5)**. Note that some advocate pouring a tablespoon of motor oil into the silencer(s) before sealing them off.

Battery

● Remove it from the bike - in extreme cases of cold the battery may freeze and crack its case **(see illustration 6)**.

● Check the electrolyte level and top up if necessary (conventional refillable batteries). Clean the terminals.

● Store the battery off the motorcycle and away from any sources of fire. Position a wooden block under the battery if it is to sit on the ground.

● Give the battery a trickle charge for a few hours every month **(see illustration 7)**.

Tyres

● Place the bike on its centrestand or an auxiliary stand which will support the motorcycle in an upright position. Position wood blocks under the tyres to keep them off the ground and to provide insulation from damp. If the bike is being put into long-term storage, ideally both tyres should be off the ground; not only will this protect the tyres, but will also ensure that no load is placed on the steering head or wheel bearings.

● Deflate each tyre by 5 to 10 psi, no more or the beads may unseat from the rim, making subsequent inflation difficult on tubeless tyres.

Pivots and controls

● Lubricate all lever, pedal, stand and footrest pivot points. If grease nipples are fitted to the rear suspension components, apply lubricant to the pivots.

● Lubricate all control cables.

Cycle components

● Apply a wax protectant to all painted and plastic components. Wipe off any excess, but don't polish to a shine. Where fitted, clean the screen with soap and water.

● Coat metal parts with Vaseline (petroleum jelly). When applying this to the fork tubes, do not compress the forks otherwise the seals will rot from contact with the Vaseline.

● Apply a vinyl cleaner to the seat.

Storage conditions

● Aim to store the bike in a shed or garage which does not leak and is free from damp.

● Drape an old blanket or bedspread over the bike to protect it from dust and direct contact with sunlight (which will fade paint). This also hides the bike from prying eyes. Beware of tight-fitting plastic covers which may allow condensation to form and settle on the bike.

Getting back on the road

Engine and transmission

● Change the oil and replace the oil filter. If this was done prior to storage, check that the oil hasn't emulsified - a thick whitish substance which occurs through condensation.

● Remove the spark plugs. Using a spout-type oil can, squirt a few drops of oil into the cylinder(s). This will provide initial lubrication as the piston rings and bores comes back into contact. Service the spark plugs, or fit new ones, and install them in the engine.

● Check that the clutch isn't stuck on. The plates can stick together if left standing for some time, preventing clutch operation. Engage a gear and try rocking the bike back and forth with the clutch lever held against the handlebar. If this doesn't work on cable-operated clutches, hold the clutch lever back against the handlebar with a strong elastic band or cable tie for a couple of hours **(see illustration 8)**.

● If the air intakes or silencer end(s) were blocked off, remove the bung or cover used.

● If the fuel tank was coated with a rust

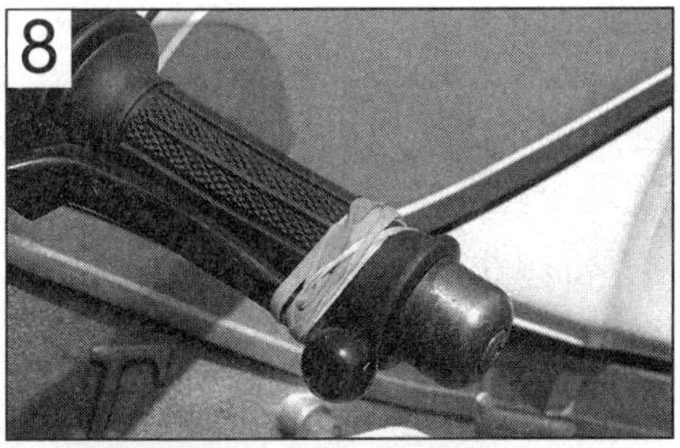

Hold clutch lever back against the handlebar with elastic bands or a cable tie

preventative, oil or a stabiliser added to the fuel, drain and flush the tank and dispose of the fuel sensibly. If no action was taken with the fuel tank prior to storage, it is advised that the old fuel is disposed of since it will go off over a period of time. Refill the fuel tank with fresh fuel.

Frame and running gear

- Oil all pivot points and cables.
- Check the tyre pressures. They will definitely need inflating if pressures were reduced for storage.
- Lubricate the final drive chain (where applicable).
- Remove any protective coating applied to the fork tubes (stanchions) since this may well destroy the fork seals. If the fork tubes weren't protected and have picked up rust spots, remove them with very fine abrasive paper and refinish with metal polish.
- Check that both brakes operate correctly. Apply each brake hard and check that it's not possible to move the motorcycle forwards, then check that the brake frees off again once released. Brake caliper pistons can stick due to corrosion around the piston head, or on the sliding caliper types, due to corrosion of the slider pins. If the brake doesn't free after repeated operation, take the caliper off for examination. Similarly drum brakes can stick due to a seized operating cam, cable or rod linkage.
- If the motorcycle has been in long-term storage, renew the brake fluid and clutch fluid (where applicable).
- Depending on where the bike has been stored, the wiring, cables and hoses may have been nibbled by rodents. Make a visual check and investigate disturbed wiring loom tape.

Battery

- If the battery has been previously removal and given top up charges it can simply be reconnected. Remember to connect the positive cable first and the negative cable last.
- On conventional refillable batteries, if the battery has not received any attention, remove it from the motorcycle and check its electrolyte level. Top up if necessary then charge the battery. If the battery fails to hold a charge and a visual checks show heavy white sulphation of the plates, the battery is probably defective and must be renewed. This is particularly likely if the battery is old. Confirm battery condition with a specific gravity check.
- On sealed (MF) batteries, if the battery has not received any attention, remove it from the motorcycle and charge it according to the information on the battery case - if the battery fails to hold a charge it must be renewed.

Starting procedure

- If a kickstart is fitted, turn the engine over a couple of times with the ignition OFF to distribute oil around the engine. If no kickstart is fitted, flick the engine kill switch OFF and the ignition ON and crank the engine over a couple of times to work oil around the upper cylinder components. If the nature of the ignition system is such that the starter won't work with the kill switch OFF, remove the spark plugs, fit them back into their caps and earth (ground) their bodies on the cylinder head. Reinstall the spark plugs afterwards.
- Switch the kill switch to RUN, operate the choke and start the engine. If the engine won't start don't continue cranking the engine - not only will this flatten the battery, but the starter motor will overheat. Switch the ignition off and try again later. If the engine refuses to start, go through the fault finding procedures in this manual. **Note:** *If the bike has been in storage for a long time, old fuel or a carburettor blockage may be the problem. Gum deposits in carburettors can block jets - if a carburettor cleaner doesn't prove successful the carburettors must be dismantled for cleaning.*
- Once the engine has started, check that the lights, turn signals and horn work properly.
- Treat the bike gently for the first ride and check all fluid levels on completion. Settle the bike back into the maintenance schedule.

This Section provides an easy reference-guide to the more common faults that are likely to afflict your machine. Obviously, the opportunities are almost limitless for faults to occur as a result of obscure failures, and to try and cover all eventualities would require a book. Indeed, a number have been written on the subject.

Successful troubleshooting is not a mysterious 'black art' but the application of a bit of knowledge combined with a systematic and logical approach to the problem. Approach any troubleshooting by first accurately identifying the symptom and then checking through the list of possible causes, starting with the simplest or most obvious and progressing in stages to the most complex.

Take nothing for granted, but above all apply liberal quantities of common sense.

The main symptom of a fault is given in the text as a major heading below which are listed the various systems or areas which may contain the fault. Details of each possible cause for a fault and the remedial action to be taken are given, in brief, in the paragraphs below each heading. Further information should be sought in the relevant Chapter.

1 Engine doesn't start or is difficult to start

Starter motor doesn't rotate

- ☐ Engine kill switch OFF.
- ☐ Fuse blown. Check main fuse (Chapter 9).
- ☐ Battery voltage low. Check and recharge battery (Chapter 9).
- ☐ Starter motor defective. Make sure the wiring to the starter is secure. Make sure the starter relay clicks when the start button is pushed. If the relay clicks, then the fault is in the wiring or motor.
- ☐ Starter relay faulty. Check it according to the procedure in Chapter 9.
- ☐ Starter switch not contacting. The contacts could be wet, corroded or dirty. Disassemble and clean the switch (Chapter 9).
- ☐ Wiring open or shorted. Check all wiring connections and harnesses to make sure that they are dry, tight and not corroded. Also check for broken or frayed wires that can cause a short to ground (earth) (see wiring diagram, Chapter 9).
- ☐ Ignition (main) switch defective. Check the switch according to the procedure in Chapter 9. Replace the switch with a new one if it is defective.
- ☐ Engine kill switch defective. Check for wet, dirty or corroded contacts. Clean or replace the switch as necessary (Chapter 9).
- ☐ Faulty neutral, side stand or clutch switch. Check the wiring to each switch and the switch itself according to the procedures in Chapter 9.
- ☐ Faulty starter circuit relay. Refer to junction box checks in Chapter 9.

Starter motor rotates but engine does not turn over

- ☐ Starter motor clutch defective. Inspect and repair or replace (Chapter 2).
- ☐ Damaged idler or starter gears. Inspect and replace the damaged parts (Chapter 2).

Starter works but engine won't turn over (seized)

- ☐ Seized engine caused by one or more internally damaged components. Failure due to wear, abuse or lack of lubrication. Damage can include seized valves, followers, camshafts, pistons, crankshaft, connecting rod bearings, or transmission gears or bearings. Refer to Chapter 2 for engine disassembly.

No fuel flow

- ☐ No fuel in tank.
- ☐ Fuel pump failure or in-line filter blockage (see Chapters 9 and 1 respectively).
- ☐ Fuel tank breather obstructed (not California models).
- ☐ Fuel tap filter clogged. Remove the tap and clean it and the filter (Chapter 1).
- ☐ Fuel line clogged. Pull the fuel line loose and carefully blow through it.
- ☐ Float needle valve clogged. For all of the valves to be clogged, either a very bad batch of fuel with an unusual additive has been used, or some other foreign material has entered the tank. Many times after a machine has been stored for many months without running, the fuel turns to a varnish-like liquid and forms deposits on the inlet needle valves and jets. The carburettors should be removed and overhauled if draining the float chambers doesn't solve the problem.

Engine flooded

- ☐ Float height too high. Check as described in Chapter 4.
- ☐ Float needle valve worn or stuck open. A piece of dirt, rust or other debris can cause the valve to seat improperly, causing excess fuel to be admitted to the float chamber. In this case, the float chamber should be cleaned and the needle valve and seat inspected. If the needle and seat are worn, then the leaking will persist and the parts should be replaced with new ones (Chapter 4).
- ☐ Starting technique incorrect. Under normal circumstances (i.e., if all the carburettor functions are sound) the machine should start with little or no throttle. When the engine is cold, the choke should be operated and the engine started without opening the throttle. When the engine is at operating temperature, only a very slight amount of throttle should be necessary. If the engine is flooded, turn the fuel tap OFF and hold the throttle open while cranking the engine. This will allow additional air to reach the cylinders. Remember to turn the fuel tap back ON after the engine starts.

No spark or weak spark

- ☐ Ignition switch OFF.
- ☐ Engine kill switch turned to the OFF position.
- ☐ Battery voltage low. Check and recharge the battery as necessary (Chapter 9).
- ☐ Spark plugs dirty, defective or worn out. Locate reason for fouled plugs using spark plug condition chart and follow the plug maintenance procedures (Chapter 1).
- ☐ Spark plug caps or secondary (HT) wiring faulty. Check condition. Replace either or both components if cracks or deterioration are evident (Chapter 5).
- ☐ Spark plug caps not making good contact. Make sure that the plug caps fit snugly over the plug ends.
- ☐ IC igniter defective. Check the igniter, referring to Chapter 5 for details.
- ☐ Pick-up coil defective. Check the unit, referring to Chapter 5 for details.
- ☐ Ignition HT coils defective. Check the coils, referring to Chapter 5.
- ☐ Ignition or kill switch shorted. This is usually caused by water, corrosion, damage or excessive wear. The switches can be disassembled and cleaned with electrical contact cleaner. If cleaning does not help, replace the switches (Chapter 9).
- ☐ Wiring shorted or broken between:
- ☐ Ignition (main) switch and engine kill switch (or blown fuse)
- ☐ IC igniter and engine kill switch
- ☐ IC igniter and ignition HT coils
- ☐ Ignition HT coils and spark plugs
- ☐ IC igniter and pick-up coil
- ☐ Make sure that all wiring connections are clean, dry and tight. Look for chafed and broken wires (Chapters 5 and 9).

Compression low

- ☐ Spark plugs loose. Remove the plugs and inspect their threads. Reinstall and tighten to the specified torque (Chapter 1).
- ☐ Cylinder head not sufficiently tightened down. If the cylinder head is suspected of being loose, then there's a chance that the gasket or head is damaged if the problem has persisted for any length of time. The head bolts should be tightened to the proper torque in the correct sequence (Chapter 2).
- ☐ Improper valve clearance. This means that the valve is not closing completely and compression pressure is leaking past the valve. Check and adjust the valve clearances (Chapter 1).
- ☐ Cylinder and/or piston worn. Excessive wear will cause compression pressure to leak past the rings. This is usually accompanied by worn rings as well. A top-end overhaul is necessary (Chapter 2).
- ☐ Piston rings worn, weak, broken, or sticking. Broken or sticking piston rings usually indicate a lubrication or carburation problem that causes excess carbon deposits or seizures to form on the pistons and rings. Top-end overhaul is necessary (Chapter 2).
- ☐ Piston ring-to-groove clearance excessive. This is caused by excessive wear of the piston ring lands. Piston replacement is necessary (Chapter 2).
- ☐ Cylinder head gasket damaged. If the head is allowed to become loose, or if excessive carbon build-up on the piston crown and combustion chamber causes extremely high compression, the head gasket may leak. Retorquing the head is not always sufficient to restore the seal, so gasket replacement is necessary (Chapter 2).
- ☐ Cylinder head warped. This is caused by overheating or improperly tightened head bolts. Machine shop resurfacing or head replacement is necessary (Chapter 2).
- ☐ Valve spring broken or weak. Caused by component failure or wear; the springs must be replaced (Chapter 2).

1 Engine doesn't start or is difficult to start (continued)

- ☐ Valve not seating properly. This is caused by a bent valve (from over-revving or improper valve adjustment), burned valve or seat (improper carburation) or an accumulation of carbon deposits on the seat (from carburation or lubrication problems). The valves must be cleaned and/or replaced and the seats serviced if possible (Chapter 2).
- ☐ Stalls after starting
- ☐ Improper choke action. Make sure the choke linkage shaft is getting a full stroke and staying in the out position (Chapter 4).
- ☐ Ignition malfunction. See Chapter 5.
- ☐ Carburettor malfunction. See Chapter 4.
- ☐ Fuel contaminated. The fuel can be contaminated with either dirt or water, or can change chemically if the machine is allowed to sit for several months or more. Drain the tank and float chambers (Chapter 4).
- ☐ Intake air leak. Check for loose carburettor-to-intake manifold connections, loose or missing vacuum gauge adapter screws or hoses, or loose carburettor tops (Chapter 4).
- ☐ Engine idle speed incorrect. Turn idle adjusting screw until the engine idles at the specified rpm (Chapter 1).

Rough idle

- ☐ Ignition malfunction. See Chapter 5.
- ☐ Idle speed incorrect. See Chapter 1.
- ☐ Carburettors not synchronised. Adjust carburettors with vacuum gauge or manometer set as described in Chapter 1.
- ☐ Carburettor malfunction. See Chapter 4.
- ☐ Fuel contaminated. The fuel can be contaminated with either dirt or water, or can change chemically if the machine is allowed to sit for several months or more. Drain the tank and float chambers (Chapter 4).
- ☐ Intake air leak. Check for loose carburettor-to-intake manifold connections, loose or missing vacuum gauge adapter screws or hoses, or loose carburettor tops (Chapter 4).
- ☐ Air filter clogged. Replace the air filter element (Chapter 1).

2 Poor running at low speeds

Spark weak

- ☐ Battery voltage low. Check and recharge battery (Chapter 9).
- ☐ Spark plugs fouled, defective or worn out. Refer to Chapter 1 for spark plug maintenance.
- ☐ Spark plug cap or HT wiring defective. Refer to Chapters 1 and 5 for details on the ignition system.
- ☐ Spark plug caps not making contact.
- ☐ Incorrect spark plugs. Wrong type, heat range or cap configuration. Check and install correct plugs listed in Chapter 1.
- ☐ IC igniter defective. See Chapter 5.
- ☐ Pick-up coil defective. See Chapter 5.
- ☐ Ignition HT coils defective. See Chapter 5.

Fuel/air mixture incorrect

- ☐ Pilot screws out of adjustment (Chapter 4).
- ☐ Pilot jet or air passage clogged. Remove and overhaul the carburettors (Chapter 4).
- ☐ Air bleed holes clogged. Remove carburettor and blow out all passages (Chapter 4).
- ☐ Air filter clogged, poorly sealed or missing (Chapter 1).
- ☐ Air filter housing poorly sealed. Look for cracks, holes or loose clamps and replace or repair defective parts.
- ☐ Fuel level too high or too low. Check the float height (Chapter 4).
- ☐ Fuel pump faulty. Check output rate (Chapter 9).
- ☐ Fuel tank breather obstructed (not California models).
- ☐ Carburettor intake manifolds loose. Check for cracks, breaks, tears or loose clamps. Replace the rubber intake manifold joints if split or perished.

Compression low

- ☐ Spark plugs loose. Remove the plugs and inspect their threads. Reinstall and tighten to the specified torque (Chapter 1).
- ☐ Cylinder head not sufficiently tightened down. If the cylinder head is suspected of being loose, then there's a chance that the gasket and head are damaged if the problem has persisted for any length of time. The head bolts should be tightened to the proper torque in the correct sequence (Chapter 2).
- ☐ Improper valve clearance. This means that the valve is not closing completely and compression pressure is leaking past the valve. Check and adjust the valve clearances (Chapter 1).
- ☐ Cylinder and/or piston worn. Excessive wear will cause compression pressure to leak past the rings. This is usually accompanied by worn rings as well. A top end overhaul is necessary (Chapter 2).
- ☐ Piston rings worn, weak, broken, or sticking. Broken or sticking piston rings usually indicate a lubrication or carburation problem that causes excess carbon deposits or seizures to form on the pistons and rings. Top-end overhaul is necessary (Chapter 2).
- ☐ Piston ring-to-groove clearance excessive. This is caused by excessive wear of the piston ring lands. Piston replacement is necessary (Chapter 2).
- ☐ Cylinder head gasket damaged. If the head is allowed to become loose, or if excessive carbon build-up on the piston crown and combustion chamber causes extremely high compression, the head gasket may leak. Retorquing the head is not always sufficient to restore the seal, so gasket replacement is necessary (Chapter 2).
- ☐ Cylinder head warped. This is caused by overheating or improperly tightened head bolts. Machine shop resurfacing or head replacement is necessary (Chapter 2).
- ☐ Valve spring broken or weak. Caused by component failure or wear; the springs must be replaced (Chapter 2).
- ☐ Valve not seating properly. This is caused by a bent valve (from over-revving or improper valve adjustment), burned valve or seat (improper carburation) or an accumulation of carbon deposits on the seat (from carburation, lubrication problems). The valves must be cleaned and/or replaced and the seats serviced if possible (Chapter 2).

Poor acceleration

- ☐ Carburettors leaking or dirty. Overhaul the carburettors (Chapter 4).
- ☐ Timing not advancing. The pick-up coil or the IC igniter may be defective. If so, they must be replaced with new ones, as they can't be repaired.
- ☐ Carburettors not synchronised. Adjust them with a vacuum gauge set or manometer (Chapter 1).
- ☐ Engine oil viscosity too high. Using a heavier oil than that recommended in Chapter 1 can damage the oil pump or lubrication system and cause drag on the engine.
- ☐ Brakes dragging. Usually caused by debris which has entered the brake piston seals, or from a warped disc or bent axle. Repair as necessary (Chapter 7).

3 Poor running or no power at high speed

Firing incorrect

- ☐ Air filter restricted. Clean or replace filter (Chapter 1).
- ☐ Spark plugs fouled, defective or worn out. See Chapter 1 for spark plug maintenance.
- ☐ Spark plug caps or HT wiring defective. See Chapters 1 and 5 for details of the ignition system.
- ☐ Spark plug caps not in good contact. See Chapter 5.
- ☐ Incorrect spark plugs. Wrong type, heat range or cap configuration. Check and install correct plugs listed in Chapter 1.
- ☐ IC igniter defective. See Chapter 5.
- ☐ Ignition coils defective. See Chapter 5.

Fuel/air mixture incorrect

- ☐ Main jet clogged. Dirt, water or other contaminants can clog the main jets. Clean the fuel tap filter, the in-line filter, the float chamber area, and the jets and carburettor orifices (Chapter 4).
- ☐ Main jet wrong size. The standard jetting is for sea level atmospheric pressure and oxygen content.
- ☐ Throttle shaft-to-carburettor body clearance excessive. Refer to Chapter 4 for inspection and part replacement procedures.
- ☐ Air bleed holes clogged. Remove and overhaul carburettors (Chapter 4).
- ☐ Air filter clogged, poorly sealed, or missing (Chapter 1).
- ☐ Air filter housing poorly sealed. Look for cracks, holes or loose clamps, and replace or repair defective parts.
- ☐ Fuel level too high or too low. Check the float height (Chapter 4).
- ☐ Fuel pump faulty. Check output rate (Chapter 9).
- ☐ Fuel tank breather obstructed (not California models).
- ☐ Carburettor intake manifolds loose. Check for cracks, breaks, tears or loose clamps. Replace the rubber intake manifolds if they are split or perished (Chapter 4).

Compression low

- ☐ Spark plugs loose. Remove the plugs and inspect their threads. Reinstall and tighten to the specified torque (Chapter 1).
- ☐ Cylinder head not sufficiently tightened down. If the cylinder head is suspected of being loose, then there's a chance that the gasket and head are damaged if the problem has persisted for any length of time. The head bolts should be tightened to the proper torque in the correct sequence (Chapter 2).
- ☐ Improper valve clearance. This means that the valve is not closing completely and compression pressure is leaking past the valve. Check and adjust the valve clearances (Chapter 1).
- ☐ Cylinder and/or piston worn. Excessive wear will cause compression pressure to leak past the rings. This is usually accompanied by worn rings as well. A top-end overhaul is necessary (Chapter 2).
- ☐ Piston rings worn, weak, broken, or sticking. Broken or sticking piston rings usually indicate a lubrication or carburation problem that causes excess carbon deposits or seizures to form on the pistons and rings. Top-end overhaul is necessary (Chapter 2).
- ☐ Piston ring-to-groove clearance excessive. This is caused by excessive wear of the piston ring lands. Piston replacement is necessary (Chapter 2).
- ☐ Cylinder head gasket damaged. If the head is allowed to become loose, or if excessive carbon build-up on the piston crown and combustion chamber causes extremely high compression, the head gasket may leak. Retorquing the head is not always sufficient to restore the seal, so gasket replacement is necessary (Chapter 2).
- ☐ Cylinder head warped. This is caused by overheating or improperly tightened head bolts. Machine shop resurfacing or head replacement is necessary (Chapter 2).
- ☐ Valve spring broken or weak. Caused by component failure or wear; the springs must be replaced (Chapter 2).
- ☐ Valve not seating properly. This is caused by a bent valve (from over-revving or improper valve adjustment), burned valve or seat (improper carburation) or an accumulation of carbon deposits on the seat (from carburation or lubrication problems). The valves must be cleaned and/or replaced and the seats serviced if possible (Chapter 2).

Knocking or pinking

- ☐ Carbon build-up in combustion chamber. Use of a fuel additive that will dissolve the adhesive bonding the carbon particles to the crown and chamber is the easiest way to remove the build-up. Otherwise, the cylinder head will have to be removed and decarbonised (Chapter 2).
- ☐ Incorrect or poor quality fuel. Old or improper grades of fuel can cause detonation. This causes the piston to rattle, thus the knocking or pinking sound. Drain old fuel and always use the recommended fuel grade.
- ☐ Spark plug heat range incorrect. Uncontrolled detonation indicates the plug heat range is too hot. The plug in effect becomes a glow plug, raising cylinder temperatures. Install the proper heat range plug (Chapter 1).
- ☐ Improper air/fuel mixture. This will cause the cylinder to run hot, which leads to detonation. Clogged jets or an air leak can cause this imbalance. See Chapter 4.

Miscellaneous causes

- ☐ Throttle valve doesn't open fully. Adjust the throttle grip freeplay (Chapter 1).
- ☐ Clutch slipping. May be caused by loose or worn clutch components. Refer to Chapter 2 for clutch overhaul procedures.
- ☐ Timing not advancing.
- ☐ Engine oil viscosity too high. Using a heavier oil than the one recommended in Chapter 1 can damage the oil pump or lubrication system and cause drag on the engine.
- ☐ Brakes dragging. Usually caused by debris which has entered the brake piston seals, or from a warped disc or bent axle. Repair as necessary.

4 Overheating

Engine overheats

- ☐ Coolant level low. Check and add coolant (see *'Daily (pre-ride) checks'*).
- ☐ Leak in cooling system. Check cooling system hoses and radiator for leaks and other damage. Repair or replace parts as necessary (Chapter 3).
- ☐ Thermostat sticking open or closed. Check and replace as described in Chapter 3.
- ☐ Faulty radiator cap. Remove the cap and have it pressure tested.
- ☐ Coolant passages clogged. Have the entire system drained and flushed, then refill with fresh coolant.
- ☐ Water pump defective. Remove the pump and check the components (Chapter 3).
- ☐ Clogged radiator fins. Clean them by blowing compressed air through the fins from the backside.
- ☐ Cooling fan or fan switch fault (Chapter 3).

Firing incorrect

- ☐ Spark plugs fouled, defective or worn out. See Chapter 1 for spark plug maintenance.
- ☐ Incorrect spark plugs.
- ☐ Faulty ignition HT coils (Chapter 5).

Fuel/air mixture incorrect

- ☐ Main jet clogged. Dirt, water and other contaminants can clog the main jets. Clean the fuel tap filter, the fuel pump in-line filter, the float chamber area and the jets and carburettor orifices (Chapter 4).
- ☐ Main jet wrong size. The standard jetting is for sea level atmospheric pressure and oxygen content.
- ☐ Air filter clogged, poorly sealed or missing (Chapter 1).
- ☐ Air filter housing poorly sealed. Look for cracks, holes or loose clamps and replace or repair.
- ☐ Fuel level too low. Check float height (Chapter 4).
- ☐ Fuel pump faulty. Check output rate (Chapter 9).
- ☐ Fuel tank breather obstructed (not California models).
- ☐ Carburettor intake manifolds loose. Check for cracks, breaks, tears or loose clamps. Replace the rubber intake manifold joints if split or perished.

Compression too high

- ☐ Carbon build-up in combustion chamber. Use of a fuel additive that will dissolve the adhesive bonding the carbon particles to the piston crown and chamber is the easiest way to remove the build-up. Otherwise, the cylinder head will have to be removed and decarbonised (Chapter 2).
- ☐ Improperly machined head surface or installation of incorrect gasket during engine assembly.

Engine load excessive

- ☐ Clutch slipping. Can be caused by damaged, loose or worn clutch components. Refer to Chapter 2 for overhaul procedures.
- ☐ Engine oil level too high. The addition of too much oil will cause pressurisation of the crankcase and inefficient engine operation. Check Specifications and drain to proper level (Chapter 1).
- ☐ Engine oil viscosity too high. Using a heavier oil than the one recommended in Chapter 1 can damage the oil pump or lubrication system as well as cause drag on the engine.
- ☐ Brakes dragging. Usually caused by debris which has entered the brake piston seals, or from a warped disc or bent axle. Repair as necessary.

Lubrication inadequate

- ☐ Engine oil level too low. Friction caused by intermittent lack of lubrication or from oil that is overworked can cause overheating. The oil provides a definite cooling function in the engine. Check the oil level (see *'Daily (pre-ride) checks'*).
- ☐ Poor quality engine oil or incorrect viscosity or type. Oil is rated not only according to viscosity but also according to type. Some oils are not rated high enough for use in this engine. Check the Specifications section and change to the correct oil (Chapter 1).

Miscellaneous causes

- ☐ Modification to exhaust system. Most aftermarket exhaust systems cause the engine to run leaner, which make them run hotter. When installing an accessory exhaust system, always rejet the carburettors.

5 Clutch problems

Clutch slipping

- ☐ Cable freeplay insufficient. Check and adjust cable (Chapter 1).
- ☐ Friction plates worn or warped. Overhaul the clutch assembly (Chapter 2).
- ☐ Plain plates warped (Chapter 2).
- ☐ Clutch springs broken or weak. Old or heat-damaged (from slipping clutch) springs should be replaced with new ones (Chapter 2).
- ☐ Clutch release mechanism defective. Replace any defective parts (Chapter 2).
- ☐ Clutch centre or housing unevenly worn. This causes improper engagement of the plates. Replace the damaged or worn parts (Chapter 2).

Clutch not disengaging completely

- ☐ Cable freeplay excessive. Check and adjust cable (Chapter 1).
- ☐ Clutch plates warped or damaged. This will cause clutch drag, which in turn will cause the machine to creep. Overhaul the clutch assembly (Chapter 2).
- ☐ Clutch spring tension uneven. Usually caused by a sagged or broken spring. Check and replace the springs as a set (Chapter 2).
- ☐ Engine oil deteriorated. Old, thin, worn out oil will not provide proper lubrication for the plates, causing the clutch to drag. Replace the oil and filter (Chapter 1).
- ☐ Engine oil viscosity too high. Using a heavier oil than recommended in Chapter 1 can cause the plates to stick together, putting a drag on the engine. Change to the correct weight oil (Chapter 1).
- ☐ Clutch release mechanism defective. Overhaul the clutch cover components (Chapter 2).
- ☐ Loose clutch centre nut. Causes housing and centre misalignment putting a drag on the engine. Engagement adjustment continually varies. Overhaul the clutch assembly (Chapter 2).

6 Gearchange problems

Doesn't go into gear or lever doesn't return

- ☐ Clutch not disengaging. See Section 27.
- ☐ Selector fork(s) bent or seized. Overhaul the transmission (Chapter 2).
- ☐ Gear(s) stuck on shaft. Most often caused by a lack of lubrication or excessive wear in transmission bearings and bushings. Overhaul the transmission (Chapter 2).
- ☐ Selector drum binding. Caused by lubrication failure or excessive wear. Replace the drum and bearing (Chapter 2).
- ☐ Gearchange lever centralising spring weak or broken (Chapter 2).
- ☐ Gearchange lever broken. Splines stripped out of lever or shaft, caused by allowing the lever to get loose or from dropping the machine. Replace necessary parts (Chapter 2).
- ☐ Gearchange shaft bent. Could be caused by dropping the motorcycle. Check and replace if necessary (see Chapter 2).
- ☐ Gearchange mechanism selector and/or stopper arm broken or worn. Full engagement and rotary movement of shift drum results. Replace the arm (Chapter 2).
- ☐ Stopper arm spring broken. Allows arm to float, causing sporadic shift operation. Replace spring (Chapter 2).

Jumps out of gear

- ☐ Shift fork(s) worn. Overhaul the transmission (Chapter 2).
- ☐ Gear groove(s) worn. Overhaul the transmission (Chapter 2).
- ☐ Gear dogs or dog slots worn or damaged. The gears should be inspected and replaced. No attempt should be made to service the worn parts.

Overselects

- ☐ Stopper arm spring weak or broken (Chapter 2).
- ☐ Gearchange shaft centralising spring post broken or distorted (Chapter 2).

7 Abnormal engine noise

Knocking or pinking

- ☐ Carbon build-up in combustion chamber. Use of a fuel additive that will dissolve the adhesive bonding the carbon particles to the piston crown and chamber is the easiest way to remove the build-up. Otherwise, the cylinder head will have to be removed and decarbonised (Chapter 2).
- ☐ Incorrect or poor quality fuel. Old or improper fuel can cause detonation. This causes the pistons to rattle, thus the knocking or pinking sound. Drain the old fuel and always use the recommended grade fuel (Chapter 4).
- ☐ Spark plug heat range incorrect. Uncontrolled detonation indicates that the plug heat range is too hot. The plug in effect becomes a glow plug, raising cylinder temperatures. Install the proper heat range plug (Chapter 1).
- ☐ Improper air/fuel mixture. This will cause the cylinders to run hot and lead to detonation. Clogged jets or an air leak can cause this imbalance. See Chapter 4.

Piston slap or rattling

- ☐ Cylinder-to-piston clearance excessive. Caused by improper assembly. Inspect and overhaul top-end parts (Chapter 2).
- ☐ Connecting rod bent. Caused by over-revving, trying to start a badly flooded engine or from ingesting a foreign object into the combustion chamber. Replace the damaged parts (Chapter 2).
- ☐ Piston pin or piston pin bore worn or seized from wear or lack of lubrication. Replace damaged parts (Chapter 2).
- ☐ Piston ring(s) worn, broken or sticking. Overhaul the top-end (Chapter 2).
- ☐ Piston seizure damage. Usually from lack of lubrication or overheating. Replace the pistons and bore the cylinders, as necessary (Chapter 2).
- ☐ Connecting rod upper or lower end clearance excessive. Caused by excessive wear or lack of lubrication. Replace worn parts.

Valve noise

- ☐ Incorrect valve clearances. Adjust the clearances by referring to Chapter 1.
- ☐ Valve spring broken or weak. Check and replace weak valve springs (Chapter 2).
- ☐ Camshaft or cylinder head worn or damaged. Lack of lubrication at high rpm is usually the cause of damage. Insufficient oil or failure to change the oil at the recommended intervals are the chief causes. Since there are no replaceable bearings in the head, the head itself will have to be replaced if there is excessive wear or damage (Chapter 2).

Other noise

- ☐ Cylinder head gasket leaking.
- ☐ Exhaust pipe leaking at cylinder head connection. Caused by improper fit of pipe(s) or loose exhaust flange. All exhaust fasteners should be tightened evenly and carefully. Failure to do this will lead to a leak.
- ☐ Crankshaft runout excessive. Caused by a bent crankshaft (from over-revving) or damage from an upper cylinder component failure. Can also be attributed to dropping the machine on either of the crankshaft ends.
- ☐ Engine mounting bolts loose. Tighten all engine mount bolts (Chapter 2).
- ☐ Crankshaft bearings worn (Chapter 2).
- ☐ Cam chain tensioner defective. Replace according to the procedure in Chapter 2.
- ☐ Cam chain, sprockets or guides worn (Chapter 2).

8 Abnormal driveline noise

Clutch noise

- ☐ Clutch housing/friction plate clearance excessive (Chapter 2).
- ☐ Loose or damaged clutch pressure plate and/or bolts (Chapter 2).

Transmission noise

- ☐ Bearings worn. Also includes the possibility that the shafts are worn. Overhaul the transmission (Chapter 2).
- ☐ Gears worn or chipped (Chapter 2).
- ☐ Metal chips jammed in gear teeth. Probably pieces from a broken clutch, gear or selector mechanism that were picked up by the gears. This will cause early bearing failure (Chapter 2).
- ☐ Engine oil level too low. Causes a howl from transmission. Also affects engine power and clutch operation. Check the oil level (see *'Daily (pre-ride) checks'*).

Final drive noise

- ☐ Chain not adjusted properly (Chapter 1).
- ☐ Engine sprocket or rear sprocket loose. Tighten fasteners (Chapter 6).
- ☐ Sprocket(s) worn. Replace sprocket(s) (Chapter 6).
- ☐ Rear sprocket warped. Replace (Chapter 6).
- ☐ Wheel coupling damper worn. Replace damper (Chapter 6).

9 Abnormal frame and suspension noise

Front end noise

- ☐ Low fluid level or improper viscosity oil in forks. This can sound like spurting and is usually accompanied by irregular fork action (Chapter 6).
- ☐ Spring weak or broken. Makes a clicking or scraping sound. Fork oil, when drained, will have a lot of metal particles in it (Chapter 6).
- ☐ Steering head bearings loose or damaged. Clicks when braking. Check and adjust or replace as necessary (Chapters 1 and 6).
- ☐ Fork clamp bolts in yokes loose. Make sure all clamp pinch bolts are tight (Chapter 6).
- ☐ Fork tube bent. Good possibility if machine has been dropped. Replace tube with a new one (Chapter 6).
- ☐ Front axle or axle clamp bolt loose. Tighten them to the specified torque (Chapter 6).

Shock absorber noise

- ☐ Fluid level incorrect. Indicates a leak caused by defective seal. Shock will be covered with oil. Replace shock or seek advice on repair from a Kawasaki dealer (Chapter 6).
- ☐ Defective shock absorber with internal damage. This is in the body of the shock and can't be remedied. The shock must be replaced with a new one (Chapter 6).
- ☐ Bent or damaged shock body. Replace the shock with a new one (Chapter 6).

Brake noise

- ☐ Squeal caused by dust on brake pads. Usually found in combination with glazed pads. Clean using brake cleaning solvent (Chapter 7).
- ☐ Contamination of brake pads. Oil, brake fluid or dirt causing brake to chatter or squeal. Clean or replace pads (Chapter 7).
- ☐ Pads glazed. Caused by excessive heat from prolonged use or from contamination. Do not use sandpaper, emery cloth, carborundum cloth or any other abrasive to roughen the pad surfaces as abrasives will stay in the pad material and damage the disc. A very fine flat file can be used, but pad replacement is suggested as a cure (Chapter 7).
- ☐ Disc warped. Can cause a chattering, clicking or intermittent squeal. Usually accompanied by a pulsating lever and uneven braking. Replace the disc (Chapter 7).
- ☐ Loose or worn wheel bearings. Check and replace as needed (Chapter 7).

10 Oil pressure warning light comes on

Engine lubrication system

- ☐ Engine oil pump defective, blocked oil strainer gauze or failed relief valve. Carry out oil pressure check (Chapter 2).
- ☐ Engine oil level low. Inspect for leak or other problem causing low oil level and add recommended oil (see *'Daily (pre-ride) checks'*).
- ☐ Engine oil viscosity too low. Very old, thin oil or an improper weight of oil used in the engine. Change to correct oil (see *'Daily (pre-ride) checks'*).
- ☐ Camshaft or journals worn. Excessive wear causing drop in oil pressure. Replace cam and/or/cylinder head. Abnormal wear could be caused by oil starvation at high rpm from low oil level or improper weight or type of oil (see *'Daily (pre-ride) checks'*).
- ☐ Crankshaft and/or bearings worn. Same problems as paragraph 4. Check and replace crankshaft and/or bearings (Chapter 2).

Electrical system

- ☐ Oil pressure switch defective. Check the switch according to the procedure in Chapter 9. Replace it if it is defective.
- ☐ Oil pressure warning light circuit defective. Check for pinched, shorted, disconnected or damaged wiring (Chapter 9).

11 Excessive exhaust smoke

White smoke

- ☐ Piston oil ring worn. The ring may be broken or damaged, causing oil from the crankcase to be pulled past the piston into the combustion chamber. Replace the rings with new ones (Chapter 2).
- ☐ Cylinders worn, cracked, or scored. Caused by overheating or oil starvation. The cylinders will have to be rebored and new pistons installed.
- ☐ Valve oil seal damaged or worn. Replace oil seals with new ones (Chapter 2).
- ☐ Valve guide worn. Perform a complete valve job (Chapter 2).
- ☐ Engine oil level too high, which causes the oil to be forced past the rings. Drain oil to the proper level (see *'Daily (pre-ride) checks'*).
- ☐ Head gasket broken between oil return and cylinder. Causes oil to be pulled into the combustion chamber. Replace the head gasket and check the head for warpage (Chapter 2).
- ☐ Abnormal crankcase pressurisation, which forces oil past the rings. Clogged breather hose is usually the cause.

Black smoke

- ☐ Air filter clogged. Clean or replace the element (Chapter 1).
- ☐ Main jet too large or loose. Compare the jet size to the Specifications (Chapter 4).
- ☐ Choke cable or linkage shaft stuck, causing fuel to be pulled through choke circuit (Chapter 4).
- ☐ Fuel level too high. Check and adjust the float height(s) as necessary (Chapter 4).
- ☐ Float needle valve held off needle seat. Clean the float chambers and fuel line and replace the needles and seats if necessary (Chapter 4).

Brown smoke

- ☐ Main jet too small or clogged. Lean condition caused by wrong size main jet or by a restricted orifice. Clean float chambers and jets and compare jet size to Specifications (Chapter 4).
- ☐ Fuel flow insufficient. Float needle valve stuck closed due to chemical reaction with old fuel. Float height incorrect. Restricted fuel line. Clean line and float chamber and adjust floats if necessary.
- ☐ Carburettor intake manifold clamps loose (Chapter 4).
- ☐ Air filter poorly sealed or not installed (Chapter 1).

12 Poor handling or stability

Handlebar hard to turn

- ☐ Steering head bearing adjuster nut too tight. Check adjustment as described in Chapter 1.
- ☐ Bearings damaged. Roughness can be felt as the bars are turned from side-to-side. Replace bearings and races (Chapter 6).
- ☐ Races dented or worn. Denting results from wear in only one position (eg, straight ahead), from a collision or hitting a pothole or from dropping the machine. Replace races and bearings (Chapter 6
- ☐ Steering stem lubrication inadequate. Causes are grease getting hard from age or being washed out by high pressure car washes. Disassemble steering head and repack bearings (Chapter 6).
- ☐ Steering stem bent. Caused by a collision, hitting a pothole or by dropping the machine. Replace damaged part. Don't try to straighten the steering stem (Chapter 6).
- ☐ Front tyre air pressure too low (see *'Daily (pre-ride) checks'*).

Handlebar shakes or vibrates excessively

- ☐ Tyres worn or out of balance (Chapter 7).
- ☐ Swingarm bearings worn. Replace worn bearings by referring to Chapter 6.
- ☐ Wheel rim(s) warped or damaged. Inspect wheels for runout (Chapter 7).
- ☐ Wheel bearings worn. Worn front or rear wheel bearings can cause poor tracking. Worn front bearings will cause wobble (Chapter 7).
- ☐ Handlebar clamp bolts loose (Chapter 6).
- ☐ Fork clamp bolts in yokes loose. Tighten them to the specified torque (Chapter 6).
- ☐ Engine mounting bolts loose. Will cause excessive vibration with increased engine rpm (Chapter 2).

Handlebar pulls to one side

- ☐ Frame bent. Definitely suspect this if the machine has been dropped. May or may not be accompanied by cracking near the bend. Replace the frame (Chapter 6).
- ☐ Wheels out of alignment. Caused by improper location of axle spacers or from bent steering stem or frame (Chapter 6).
- ☐ Swingarm bent or twisted. Caused by age (metal fatigue) or impact damage. Replace the arm (Chapter 6).
- ☐ Steering stem bent. Caused by impact damage or by dropping the motorcycle. Replace the steering stem (Chapter 6).
- ☐ Fork tube bent. Disassemble the forks and replace the damaged parts (Chapter 6).
- ☐ Fork oil level uneven. Check and add or drain as necessary (Chapter 6).

Poor shock absorbing qualities

- ☐ Too hard:
  Fork oil level excessive (Chapter 6).
  Fork oil viscosity too high. Use a lighter oil (see the Specifications in Chapter 6).
  Fork tube bent. Causes a harsh, sticking feeling (Chapter 6).
  Shock shaft or body bent or damaged (Chapter 6).
  Fork internal damage (Chapter 6).
  Shock internal damage.
  Tyre pressure too high (Chapter 1).
- ☐ Too soft:
  Fork or shock oil insufficient and/or leaking (Chapter 6).
  Fork oil level too low (Chapter 6).
  Fork oil viscosity too light (Chapter 6).
  Fork springs weak or broken (Chapter 6).
  Shock internal damage or leakage (Chapter 6).

13 Braking problems

Brakes are spongy, don't hold

- ☐ Air in brake line. Caused by inattention to master cylinder fluid level or by leakage. Locate problem and bleed brakes (Chapter 7).
- ☐ Pad or disc worn (Chapters 1 and 7).
- ☐ Brake fluid leak. See paragraph 1.
- ☐ Contaminated pads. Caused by contamination with oil, grease, brake fluid, etc. Clean or replace pads. Clean disc thoroughly with brake cleaner (Chapter 7).
- ☐ Brake fluid deteriorated. Fluid is old or contaminated. Drain system, replenish with new fluid and bleed the system (Chapter 7).
- ☐ Master cylinder internal parts worn or damaged causing fluid to bypass (Chapter 7).
- ☐ Master cylinder bore scratched by foreign material or broken spring. Repair or replace master cylinder (Chapter 7).
- ☐ Disc warped. Replace disc (Chapter 7).

Brake lever or pedal pulsates

- ☐ Disc warped. Replace disc (Chapter 7).
- ☐ Axle bent. Replace axle (Chapter 7).
- ☐ Brake caliper bolts loose (Chapter 7).
- ☐ Brake caliper sliders damaged or sticking (rear caliper), causing caliper to bind. Lubricate the sliders or replace them if they are corroded or bent (Chapter 7).
- ☐ Wheel warped or otherwise damaged (Chapter 7).
- ☐ Wheel bearings damaged or worn (Chapter 7).

Brakes drag

- ☐ Master cylinder piston seized. Caused by wear or damage to piston or cylinder bore (Chapter 7).
- ☐ Lever balky or stuck. Check pivot and lubricate (Chapter 7).
- ☐ Brake caliper binds. Caused by inadequate lubrication or damage to caliper sliders (Chapter 7).
- ☐ Brake caliper piston seized in bore. Caused by wear or ingestion of dirt past deteriorated seal (Chapter 7).
- ☐ Brake pad damaged. Pad material separated from backing plate. Usually caused by faulty manufacturing process or from contact with chemicals. Replace pads (Chapter 7).
- ☐ Pads improperly installed (Chapter 7).

14 Electrical problems

Battery dead or weak

- ☐ Battery faulty. Caused by sulphated plates which are shorted through sedimentation. Also, broken battery terminal making only occasional contact (Chapter 9).
- ☐ Battery cables making poor contact (Chapter 9).
- ☐ Load excessive. Caused by addition of high wattage lights or other electrical accessories.
- ☐ Ignition (main) switch defective. Switch either earths (grounds) internally or fails to shut off system. Replace the switch (Chapter 9).
- ☐ Regulator/rectifier defective (Chapter 9).
- ☐ Alternator stator coil open or shorted (Chapter 9).
- ☐ Wiring faulty. Wiring earthed (grounded) or connections loose in ignition, charging or lighting circuits (Chapter 9).

Battery overcharged

- ☐ Regulator/rectifier defective. Overcharging is noticed when battery gets excessively warm (Chapter 9).
- ☐ Battery defective. Replace battery with a new one (Chapter 9).
- ☐ Battery amperage too low, wrong type or size. Install manufacturer's specified amp-hour battery to handle charging load (Chapter 9).

Checking engine compression

● Low compression will result in exhaust smoke, heavy oil consumption, poor starting and poor performance. A compression test will provide useful information about an engine's condition and if performed regularly, can give warning of trouble before any other symptoms become apparent.

● A compression gauge will be required, along with an adapter to suit the spark plug hole thread size. Note that the screw-in type gauge/adapter set up is preferable to the rubber cone type.

● Before carrying out the test, first check the valve clearances as described in Chapter 1.

1 Run the engine until it reaches normal operating temperature, then stop it and remove the spark plug(s), taking care not to scald your hands on the hot components.

2 Install the gauge adapter and compression gauge in No. 1 cylinder spark plug hole **(see illustration 1)**.

Screw the compression gauge adapter into the spark plug hole, then screw the gauge into the adapter

3 On kickstart-equipped motorcycles, make sure the ignition switch is OFF, then open the throttle fully and kick the engine over a couple of times until the gauge reading stabilises.

4 On motorcycles with electric start only, the procedure will differ depending on the nature of the ignition system. Flick the engine kill switch (engine stop switch) to OFF and turn the ignition switch ON; open the throttle fully and crank the engine over on the starter motor for a couple of revolutions until the gauge reading stabilises. If the starter will not operate with the kill switch OFF, turn the ignition switch OFF and refer to the next paragraph.

5 Install the plugs back in their caps and arrange the plug electrodes so that their metal bodies are earthed (grounded) against the cylinder head; this is essential to prevent damage to the ignition system **(see illustration 2)**. Disconnect the fuel pump wring connector (see Chapter 4). Position the plugs well away from the plug holes otherwise there is a risk of atomised fuel escaping from the plug holes and igniting. As a safety precaution, cover the cylinder head with rag. Turn the ignition switch and kill switch ON, open the throttle fully and crank the engine over on the starter motor for a couple of revolutions until the gauge reading stabilises.

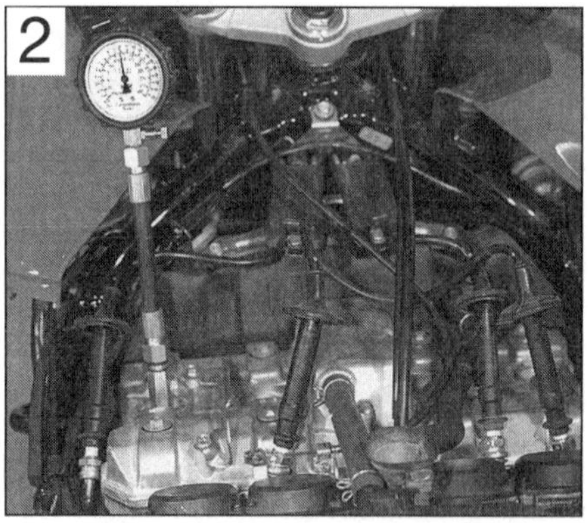

All spark plugs must be earthed (grounded) against the cylinder head

Caution: Do not lay the plugs against the magnesium engine covers (such as the valve cover on J and A models) as they could be damaged. If necessary, hold the spark plug with an insulated tool (see illustration).

6 After one or two revolutions the pressure should build up to a maximum figure and then stabilise. Take a note of this reading and on multi-cylinder engines repeat the test on the remaining cylinders.

7 The correct pressures are given in Chapter 1 Specifications. If the results fall within the specified range and on multi-cylinder engines all are relatively equal, the engine is in good condition. If there is a marked difference between the readings, or if the readings are lower than specified, inspection of the top-end components will be required.

8 Low compression pressure may be due to worn cylinder bores, pistons or rings, failure of the cylinder head gasket, worn valve seals, or poor valve seating.

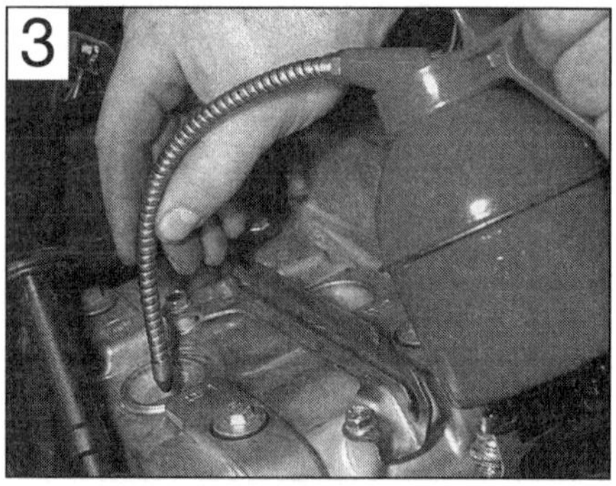

Bores can be temporarily sealed with a squirt of motor oil

9 To distinguish between cylinder/piston wear and valve leakage, pour a small quantity of oil into the bore to temporarily seal the piston rings, then repeat the compression tests **(see illustration 3)**. If the readings show a noticeable increase in pressure this confirms that the cylinder bore, piston, or rings are worn. If, however, no change is indicated, the cylinder head gasket or valves should be examined.

10 High compression pressure indicates excessive carbon build-up in the combustion chamber and on the piston crown. If this is the case the cylinder head should be removed and the deposits removed. Note that excessive carbon build-up is less likely with the used on modern fuels.

Checking battery open-circuit voltage

Warning: The gases produced by the battery are explosive - never smoke or create any sparks in the vicinity of the battery. Never allow the electrolyte to contact your skin or clothing - if it does, wash it off and seek immediate medical attention.

4
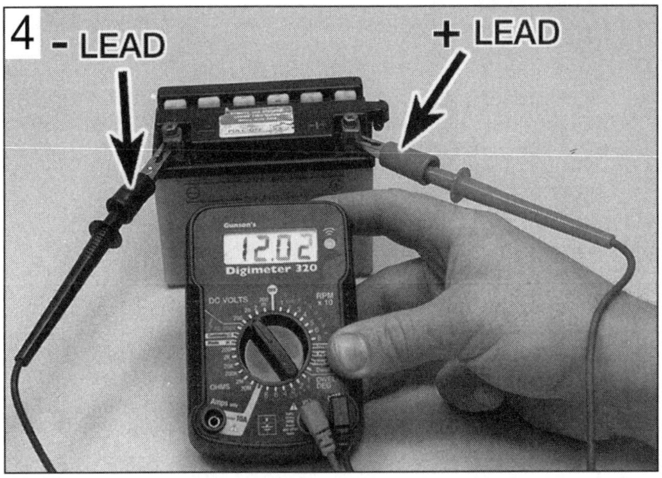

Measuring open-circuit battery voltage

5
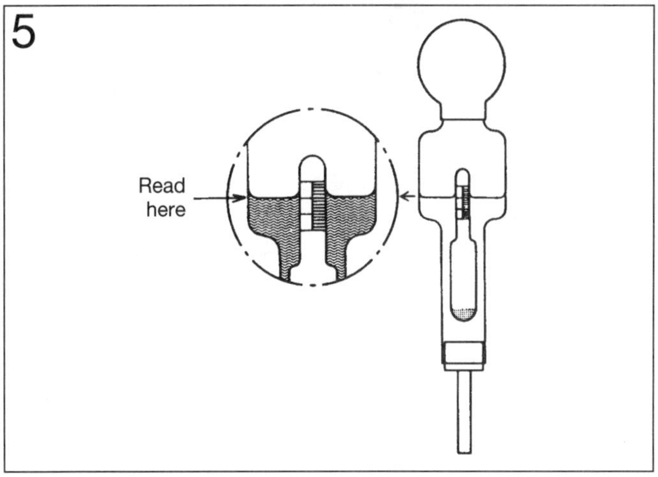

Float-type hydrometer for measuring battery specific gravity

● Before any electrical fault is investigated the battery should be checked.

● You'll need a dc voltmeter or multimeter to check battery voltage. Check that the leads are inserted in the correct terminals on the meter, red lead to positive (+ve), black lead to negative (-ve). Incorrect connections can damage the meter.

● A sound fully-charged 12 volt battery should produce between 12.3 and 12.6 volts across its terminals (12.8 volts for a maintenance-free battery). On machines with a 6 volt battery, voltage should be between 6.1 and 6.3 volts.

1 Set a multimeter to the 0 to 20 volts dc range and connect its probes across the battery terminals. Connect the meter's positive (+ve) probe, usually red, to the battery positive (+ve) terminal, followed by the meter's negative (-ve) probe, usually black, to the battery negative terminal (-ve) **(see illustration 4)**.

2 If battery voltage is low (below 10 volts on a 12 volt battery or below 4 volts on a six volt battery), charge the battery and test the voltage again. If the battery repeatedly goes flat, investigate the motorcycle's charging system.

Checking battery specific gravity (SG)

Warning: The gases produced by the battery are explosive - never smoke or create any sparks in the vicinity of the battery. Never allow the electrolyte to contact your skin or clothing - if it does, wash it off and seek immediate medical attention.

● The specific gravity check gives an indication of a battery's state of charge.

● A hydrometer is used for measuring specific gravity. Make sure you purchase one which has a small enough hose to insert in the aperture of a motorcycle battery.

● Specific gravity is simply a measure of the electrolyte's density compared with that of water. Water has an SG of 1.000 and fully-charged battery electrolyte is about 26% heavier, at 1.260.

● Specific gravity checks are not possible on maintenance-free batteries. Testing the open-circuit voltage is the only means of determining their state of charge.

1 To measure SG, remove the battery from the motorcycle and remove the first cell cap. Draw some electrolyte into the hydrometer and note the reading **(see illustration 5)**. Return the electrolyte to the cell and install the cap.

2 The reading should be in the region of 1.260 to 1.280. If SG is below 1.200 the battery needs charging. Note that SG will vary with temperature; it should be measured at 20°C (68°F). Add 0.007 to the reading for every 10°C above 20°C, and subtract 0.007 from the reading for every 10°C below 20°C. Add 0.004 to the reading for every 10°F above 68°F, and subtract 0.004 from the reading for every 10°F below 68°F.

3 When the check is complete, rinse the hydrometer thoroughly with clean water.

6
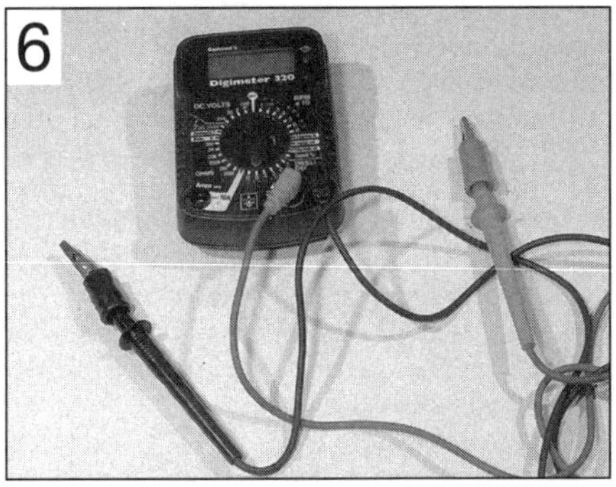

Digital multimeter can be used for all electrical tests

Checking for continuity

● The term continuity describes the uninterrupted flow of electricity through an electrical circuit. A continuity check will determine whether an **open-circuit** situation exists.

● Continuity can be checked with an ohmmeter, multimeter, continuity tester or battery and bulb test circuit **(see illustrations 6, 7 and 8)**.

7
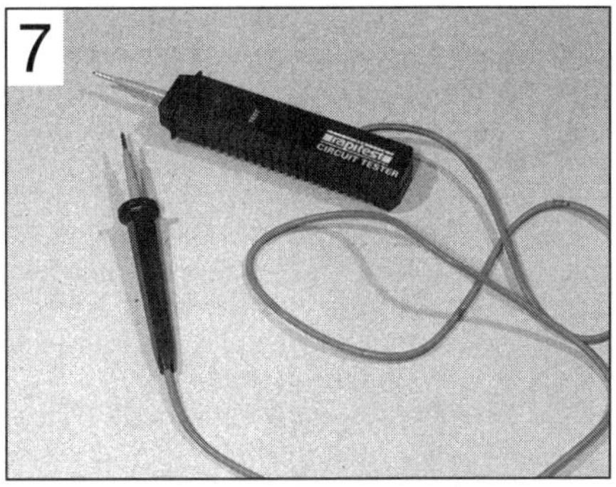

Battery-powered continuity tester

8
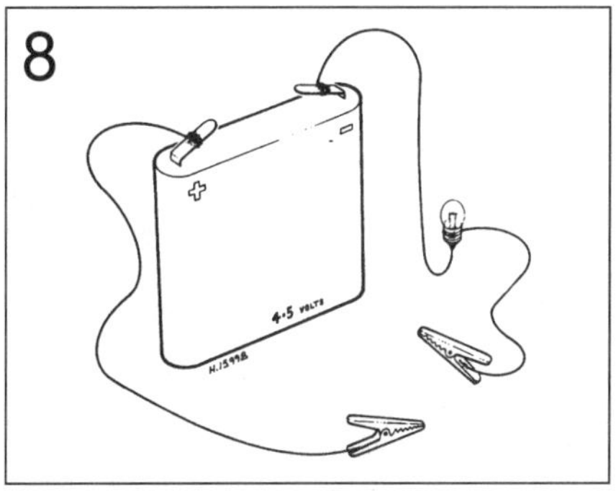

Battery and bulb test circuit

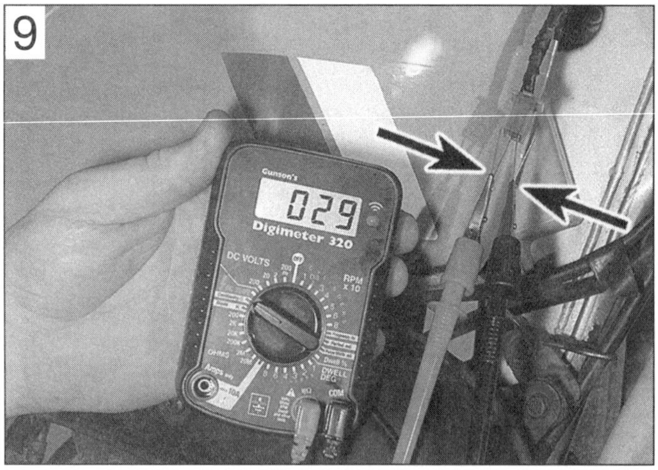

Continuity check of front brake light switch using a meter - note split pins used to access connector terminals

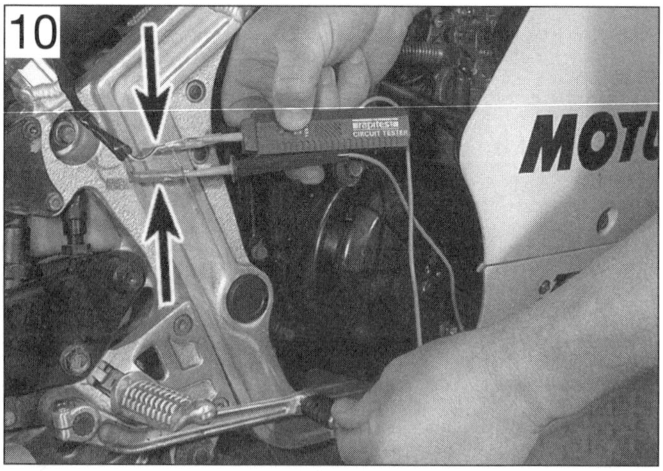

Continuity check of rear brake light switch using a continuity tester

- All of these instruments are self-powered by a battery, therefore the checks are made with the ignition OFF.
- As a safety precaution, always disconnect the battery negative (-ve) lead before making checks, particularly if ignition switch checks are being made.
- If using a meter, select the appropriate ohms scale and check that the meter reads infinity (∞). Touch the meter probes together and check that meter reads zero; where necessary adjust the meter so that it reads zero.
- After using a meter, always switch it OFF to conserve its battery.

Switch checks

1 If a switch is at fault, trace its wiring up to the wiring connectors. Separate the wire connectors and inspect them for security and condition. A build-up of dirt or corrosion here will most likely be the cause of the problem - clean up and apply a water dispersant such as WD40.

2 If using a test meter, set the meter to the ohms x 10 scale and connect its probes across the wires from the switch **(see illustration 9)**. Simple ON/OFF type switches, such as brake light switches, only have two wires whereas combination switches, like the ignition switch, have many internal links. Study the wiring diagram to ensure that you are connecting across the correct pair of wires. Continuity (low or no measurable resistance - 0 ohms) should be indicated with the switch ON and no continuity (high resistance) with it OFF.

3 Note that the polarity of the test probes doesn't matter for continuity checks, although care should be taken to follow specific test procedures if a diode or solid-state component is being checked.

4 A continuity tester or battery and bulb circuit can be used in the same way. Connect its probes as described above **(see illustration 10)**. The light should come on to indicate continuity in the ON switch position, but should extinguish in the OFF position.

Wiring checks

- Many electrical faults are caused by damaged wiring, often due to incorrect routing or chaffing on frame components.
- Loose, wet or corroded wire connectors can also be the cause of electrical problems, especially in exposed locations.

1 A continuity check can be made on a single length of wire by disconnecting it at each end and connecting a meter or continuity tester across both ends of the wire **(see illustration 11)**.

2 Continuity (low or no resistance - 0 ohms) should be indicated if the wire is good. If no continuity (high resistance) is shown, suspect a broken wire.

Checking for voltage

- A voltage check can determine whether current is reaching a component.
- Voltage can be checked with a dc voltmeter, multimeter set on the dc volts scale, test light or buzzer **(see illustrations 12 and 13)**. A meter has the advantage of being able to measure actual voltage.
- When using a meter, check that its leads are inserted in the correct terminals on the meter, red to positive (+ve), black to negative (-ve). Incorrect connections can damage the meter.
- A voltmeter (or multimeter set to the dc volts scale) should always be connected in parallel (across the load). Connecting it in series will not harm the meter, but the reading will not be meaningful.
- Voltage checks are made with the ignition ON.

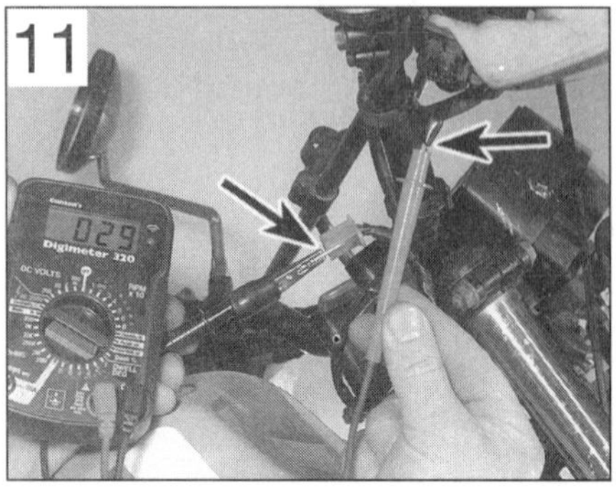

Continuity check of front brake light switch sub-harness

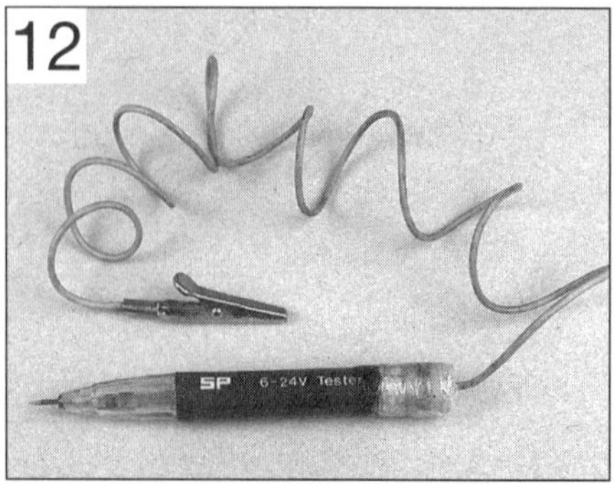

A simple test light can be used for voltage checks

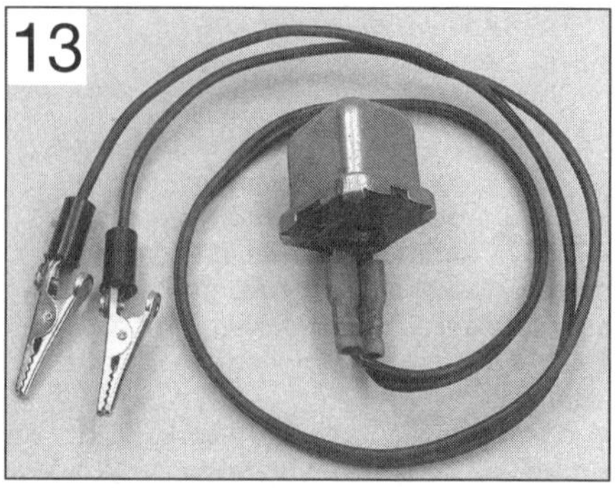

A buzzer is useful for voltage checks

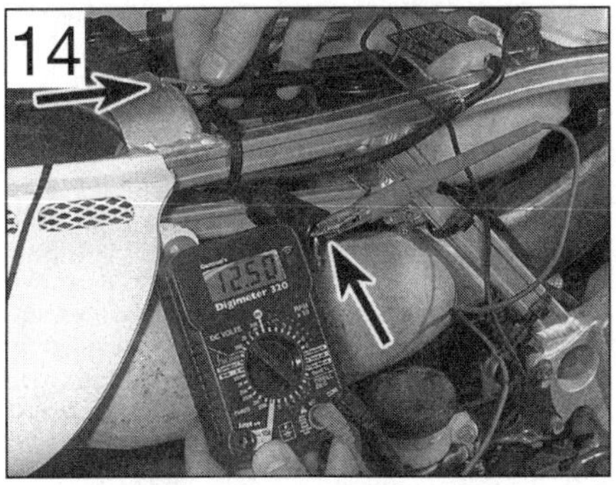

Checking for voltage at the rear brake light power supply wire using a meter . . .

1 First identify the relevant wiring circuit by referring to the wiring diagram at the end of this manual. If other electrical components share the same power supply (ie are fed from the same fuse), take note whether they are working correctly - this is useful information in deciding where to start checking the circuit.

2 If using a meter, check first that the meter leads are plugged into the correct terminals on the meter (see above). Set the meter to the dc volts function, at a range suitable for the battery voltage. Connect the meter red probe (+ve) to the power supply wire and the black probe to a good metal earth (ground) on the motorcycle's frame or directly to the battery negative (-ve) terminal **(see illustration 14)**. Battery voltage should be shown on the meter

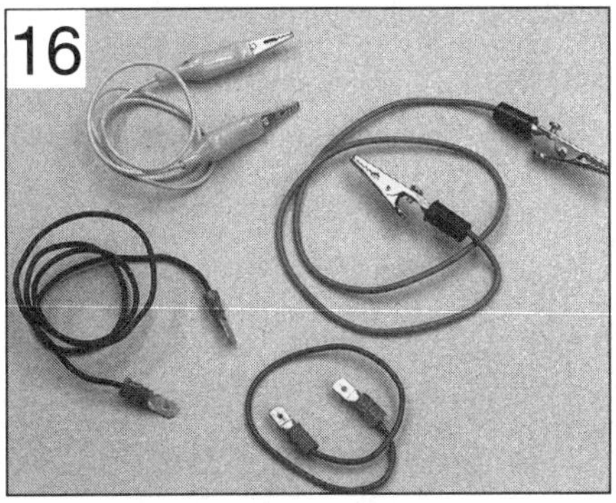

A selection of jumper wires for making earth (ground) checks

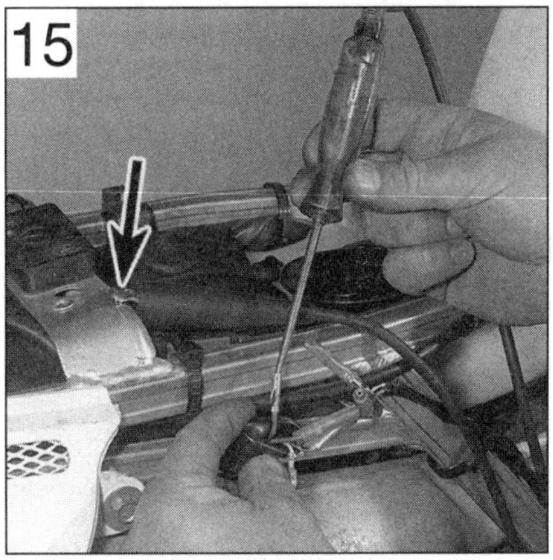

. . . or a test light - note the earth connection to the frame (arrow)

with the ignition switched ON.

3 If using a test light or buzzer, connect its positive (+ve) probe to the power supply terminal and its negative (-ve) probe to a good earth (ground) on the motorcycle's frame or directly to the battery negative (-ve) terminal **(see illustration 15)**. With the ignition ON, the test light should illuminate or the buzzer sound.

4 If no voltage is indicated, work back towards the fuse continuing to check for voltage. When you reach a point where there is voltage, you know the problem lies between that point and your last check point.

Checking the earth (ground)

- Earth connections are made either directly to the engine or frame (such as sensors, neutral switch etc. which only have a positive feed) or by a separate wire into the earth circuit of the wiring harness. Alternatively a short earth wire is sometimes run directly from the component to the motorcycle's frame.
- Corrosion is often the cause of a poor earth connection.
- If total failure is experienced, check the security of the main earth lead from the negative (-ve) terminal of the battery and also the main earth (ground) point on the wiring harness. If corroded, dismantle the connection and clean all surfaces back to bare metal.

1 To check the earth on a component, use an insulated jumper wire to temporarily bypass its earth connection **(see illustration 16)**. Connect one end of the jumper wire between the earth terminal or metal body of the component and the other end to the motorcycle's frame.

2 If the circuit works with the jumper wire installed, the original earth circuit is faulty. Check the wiring for open-circuits or poor connections. Clean up direct earth connections, removing all traces of corrosion and remake the joint. Apply petroleum jelly to the joint to prevent future corrosion.

Tracing a short-circuit

- A short-circuit occurs where current shorts to earth (ground) bypassing the circuit components. This usually results in a blown fuse.

- A short-circuit is most likely to occur where the insulation has worn through due to wiring chafing on a component, allowing a direct path to earth (ground) on the frame.

1 Remove any bodypanels necessary to access the circuit wiring.

2 Check that all electrical switches in the circuit are OFF, then remove the circuit fuse and connect a test light, buzzer or voltmeter (set to the dc scale) across the fuse terminals. No voltage should be shown.

3 Move the wiring from side to side whilst observing the test light or meter. When the test light comes on, buzzer sounds or meter shows voltage, you have found the cause of the short. It will usually shown up as damaged or burned insulation.

4 Note that the same test can be performed on each component in the circuit, even the switch.

A

ABS (Anti-lock braking system) A system, usually electronically controlled, that senses incipient wheel lockup during braking and relieves hydraulic pressure at wheel which is about to skid.
Aftermarket Components suitable for the motorcycle, but not produced by the motorcycle manufacturer.
Allen key A hexagonal wrench which fits into a recessed hexagonal hole.
Alternating current (ac) Current produced by an alternator. Requires converting to direct current by a rectifier for charging purposes.
Alternator Converts mechanical energy from the engine into electrical energy to charge the battery and power the electrical system.
Ampere (amp) A unit of measurement for the flow of electrical current. Current = Volts ÷ Ohms.
Ampere-hour (Ah) Measure of battery capacity.
Angle-tightening A torque expressed in degrees. Often follows a conventional tightening torque for cylinder head or main bearing fasteners **(see illustration)**.

Angle-tightening cylinder head bolts

Antifreeze A substance (usually ethylene glycol) mixed with water, and added to the cooling system, to prevent freezing of the coolant in winter. Antifreeze also contains chemicals to inhibit corrosion and the formation of rust and other deposits that would tend to clog the radiator and coolant passages and reduce cooling efficiency.
Anti-dive System attached to the fork lower leg (slider) to prevent fork dive when braking hard.
Anti-seize compound A coating that reduces the risk of seizing on fasteners that are subjected to high temperatures, such as exhaust clamp bolts and nuts.
API American Petroleum Institute. A quality standard for 4-stroke motor oils.
Asbestos A natural fibrous mineral with great heat resistance, commonly used in the composition of brake friction materials. Asbestos is a health hazard and the dust created by brake systems should never be inhaled or ingested.
ATF Automatic Transmission Fluid. Often used in front forks.
ATU Automatic Timing Unit. Mechanical device for advancing the ignition timing on early engines.
ATV All Terrain Vehicle. Often called a Quad.
Axial play Side-to-side movement.
Axle A shaft on which a wheel revolves. Also known as a spindle.

B

Backlash The amount of movement between meshed components when one component is held still. Usually applies to gear teeth.
Ball bearing A bearing consisting of a hardened inner and outer race with hardened steel balls between the two races.
Bearings Used between two working surfaces to prevent wear of the components and a build-up of heat. Four types of bearing are commonly used on motorcycles: plain shell bearings, ball bearings, tapered roller bearings and needle roller bearings.
Bevel gears Used to turn the drive through 90°. Typical applications are shaft final drive and camshaft drive **(see illustration)**.

Bevel gears are used to turn the drive through 90°

BHP Brake Horsepower. The British measurement for engine power output. Power output is now usually expressed in kilowatts (kW).
Bias-belted tyre Similar construction to radial tyre, but with outer belt running at an angle to the wheel rim.
Big-end bearing The bearing in the end of the connecting rod that's attached to the crankshaft.
Bleeding The process of removing air from an hydraulic system via a bleed nipple or bleed screw.
Bottom-end A description of an engine's crankcase components and all components contained there-in.
BTDC Before Top Dead Centre in terms of piston position. Ignition timing is often expressed in terms of degrees or millimetres BTDC.
Bush A cylindrical metal or rubber component used between two moving parts.
Burr Rough edge left on a component after machining or as a result of excessive wear.

C

Cam chain The chain which takes drive from the crankshaft to the camshaft(s).
Canister The main component in an evaporative emission control system (California market only); contains activated charcoal granules to trap vapours from the fuel system rather than allowing them to vent to the atmosphere.
Castellated Resembling the parapets along the top of a castle wall. For example, a castellated wheel axle or spindle nut.
Catalytic converter A device in the exhaust system of some machines which converts certain pollutants in the exhaust gases into less harmful substances.
Charging system Description of the components which charge the battery, ie the alternator, rectifer and regulator.
Circlip A ring-shaped clip used to prevent endwise movement of cylindrical parts and shafts. An internal circlip is installed in a groove in a housing; an external circlip fits into a groove on the outside of a cylindrical piece such as a shaft. Also known as a snap-ring.
Clearance The amount of space between two parts. For example, between a piston and a cylinder, between a bearing and a journal, etc.
Coil spring A spiral of elastic steel found in various sizes throughout a vehicle, for example as a springing medium in the suspension and in the valve train.
Compression Reduction in volume, and increase in pressure and temperature, of a gas, caused by squeezing it into a smaller space.
Compression damping Controls the speed the suspension compresses when hitting a bump.
Compression ratio The relationship between cylinder volume when the piston is at top dead centre and cylinder volume when the piston is at bottom dead centre.
Continuity The uninterrupted path in the flow of electricity. Little or no measurable resistance.
Continuity tester Self-powered bleeper or test light which indicates continuity.
Cp Candlepower. Bulb rating commonly found on US motorcycles.
Crossply tyre Tyre plies arranged in a criss-cross pattern. Usually four or six plies used, hence 4PR or 6PR in tyre size codes.
Cush drive Rubber damper segments fitted between the rear wheel and final drive sprocket to absorb transmission shocks **(see illustration)**.

Cush drive rubbers dampen out transmission shocks

D

Degree disc Calibrated disc for measuring piston position. Expressed in degrees.
Dial gauge Clock-type gauge with adapters for measuring runout and piston position. Expressed in mm or inches.
Diaphragm The rubber membrane in a master cylinder or carburettor which seals the upper chamber.
Diaphragm spring A single sprung plate often used in clutches.
Direct current (dc) Current produced by a dc generator.

Decarbonisation The process of removing carbon deposits - typically from the combustion chamber, valves and exhaust port/system.
Detonation Destructive and damaging explosion of fuel/air mixture in combustion chamber instead of controlled burning.
Diode An electrical valve which only allows current to flow in one direction. Commonly used in rectifiers and starter interlock systems.
Disc valve (or rotary valve) A induction system used on some two-stroke engines.
Double-overhead camshaft (DOHC) An engine that uses two overhead camshafts, one for the intake valves and one for the exhaust valves.
Drivebelt A toothed belt used to transmit drive to the rear wheel on some motorcycles. A drivebelt has also been used to drive the camshafts. Drivebelts are usually made of Kevlar.
Driveshaft Any shaft used to transmit motion. Commonly used when referring to the final driveshaft on shaft drive motorcycles.

E

Earth return The return path of an electrical circuit, utilising the motorcycle's frame.
ECU (Electronic Control Unit) A computer which controls (for instance) an ignition system, or an anti-lock braking system.
EGO Exhaust Gas Oxygen sensor. Sometimes called a Lambda sensor.
Electrolyte The fluid in a lead-acid battery.
EMS (Engine Management System) A computer controlled system which manages the fuel injection and the ignition systems in an integrated fashion.
Endfloat The amount of lengthways movement between two parts. As applied to a crankshaft, the distance that the crankshaft can move side-to-side in the crankcase.
Endless chain A chain having no joining link. Common use for cam chains and final drive chains.
EP (Extreme Pressure) Oil type used in locations where high loads are applied, such as between gear teeth.
Evaporative emission control system Describes a charcoal filled canister which stores fuel vapours from the tank rather than allowing them to vent to the atmosphere. Usually only fitted to California models and referred to as an EVAP system.
Expansion chamber Section of two-stroke engine exhaust system so designed to improve engine efficiency and boost power.

F

Feeler blade or gauge A thin strip or blade of hardened steel, ground to an exact thickness, used to check or measure clearances between parts.
Final drive Description of the drive from the transmission to the rear wheel. Usually by chain or shaft, but sometimes by belt.
Firing order The order in which the engine cylinders fire, or deliver their power strokes, beginning with the number one cylinder.
Flooding Term used to describe a high fuel level in the carburettor float chambers, leading to fuel overflow. Also refers to excess fuel in the combustion chamber due to incorrect starting technique.
Free length The no-load state of a component when measured. Clutch, valve and fork spring lengths are measured at rest, without any preload.
Freeplay The amount of travel before any action takes place. The looseness in a linkage, or an assembly of parts, between the initial application of force and actual movement. For example, the distance the rear brake pedal moves before the rear brake is actuated.
Fuel injection The fuel/air mixture is metered electronically and directed into the engine intake ports (indirect injection) or into the cylinders (direct injection). Sensors supply information on engine speed and conditions.
Fuel/air mixture The charge of fuel and air going into the engine. See **Stoichiometric ratio.**
Fuse An electrical device which protects a circuit against accidental overload. The typical fuse contains a soft piece of metal which is calibrated to melt at a predetermined current flow (expressed as amps) and break the circuit.

G

Gap The distance the spark must travel in jumping from the centre electrode to the side electrode in a spark plug. Also refers to the distance between the ignition rotor and the pickup coil in an electronic ignition system.
Gasket Any thin, soft material - usually cork, cardboard, asbestos or soft metal - installed between two metal surfaces to ensure a good seal. For instance, the cylinder head gasket seals the joint between the block and the cylinder head.
Gauge An instrument panel display used to monitor engine conditions. A gauge with a movable pointer on a dial or a fixed scale is an analogue gauge. A gauge with a numerical readout is called a digital gauge.
Gear ratios The drive ratio of a pair of gears in a gearbox, calculated on their number of teeth.
Glaze-busting see **Honing**
Grinding Process for renovating the valve face and valve seat contact area in the cylinder head.
Gudgeon pin The shaft which connects the connecting rod small-end with the piston. Often called a piston pin or wrist pin.

H

Helical gears Gear teeth are slightly curved and produce less gear noise that straight-cut gears. Often used for primary drives.

Installing a Helicoil thread insert in a cylinder head

Helicoil A thread insert repair system. Commonly used as a repair for stripped spark plug threads **(see illustration).**
Honing A process used to break down the glaze on a cylinder bore (also called glaze-busting). Can also be carried out to roughen a rebored cylinder to aid ring bedding-in.
HT (High Tension) Description of the electrical circuit from the secondary winding of the ignition coil to the spark plug.
Hydraulic A liquid filled system used to transmit pressure from one component to another. Common uses on motorcycles are brakes and clutches.
Hydrometer An instrument for measuring the specific gravity of a lead-acid battery.
Hygroscopic Water absorbing. In motorcycle applications, braking efficiency will be reduced if DOT 3 or 4 hydraulic fluid absorbs water from the air - care must be taken to keep new brake fluid in tightly sealed containers.

I

lbf ft Pounds-force feet. An imperial unit of torque. Sometimes written as ft-lbs.
lbf in Pound-force inch. An imperial unit of torque, applied to components where a very low torque is required. Sometimes written as in-lbs.
IC Abbreviation for Integrated Circuit.
Ignition advance Means of increasing the timing of the spark at higher engine speeds. Done by mechanical means (ATU) on early engines or electronically by the ignition control unit on later engines.
Ignition timing The moment at which the spark plug fires, expressed in the number of crankshaft degrees before the piston reaches the top of its stroke, or in the number of millimetres before the piston reaches the top of its stroke.
Infinity (∞) Description of an open-circuit electrical state, where no continuity exists.
Inverted forks (upside down forks) The sliders or lower legs are held in the yokes and the fork tubes or stanchions are connected to the wheel axle (spindle). Less unsprung weight and stiffer construction than conventional forks.

J

JASO Quality standard for 2-stroke oils.
Joule The unit of electrical energy.
Journal The bearing surface of a shaft.

K

Kickstart Mechanical means of turning the engine over for starting purposes. Only usually fitted to mopeds, small capacity motorcycles and off-road motorcycles.
Kill switch Handebar-mounted switch for emergency ignition cut-out. Cuts the ignition circuit on all models, and additionally prevent starter motor operation on others.
km Symbol for kilometre.
kmh Abbreviation for kilometres per hour.

L

Lambda (λ) sensor A sensor fitted in the exhaust system to measure the exhaust gas oxygen content (excess air factor).

Lapping see **Grinding**.
LCD Abbreviation for Liquid Crystal Display.
LED Abbreviation for Light Emitting Diode.
Liner A steel cylinder liner inserted in a aluminium alloy cylinder block.
Locknut A nut used to lock an adjustment nut, or other threaded component, in place.
Lockstops The lugs on the lower triple clamp (yoke) which abut those on the frame, preventing handlebar-to-fuel tank contact.
Lockwasher A form of washer designed to prevent an attaching nut from working loose.
LT Low Tension Description of the electrical circuit from the power supply to the primary winding of the ignition coil.

M

Main bearings The bearings between the crankshaft and crankcase.
Maintenance-free (MF) battery A sealed battery which cannot be topped up.
Manometer Mercury-filled calibrated tubes used to measure intake tract vacuum. Used to synchronise carburettors on multi-cylinder engines.
Micrometer A precision measuring instrument that measures component outside diameters **(see illustration)**.

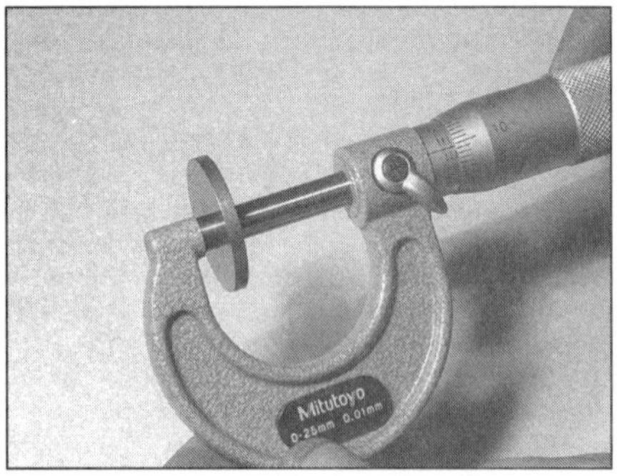

Tappet shims are measured with a micrometer

MON (Motor Octane Number) A measure of a fuel's resistance to knock.
Monograde oil An oil with a single viscosity, eg SAE80W.
Monoshock A single suspension unit linking the swingarm or suspension linkage to the frame.
mph Abbreviation for miles per hour.
Multigrade oil Having a wide viscosity range (eg 10W40). The W stands for Winter, thus the viscosity ranges from SAE10 when cold to SAE40 when hot.
Multimeter An electrical test instrument with the capability to measure voltage, current and resistance. Some meters also incorporate a continuity tester and buzzer.

N

Needle roller bearing Inner race of caged needle rollers and hardened outer race. Examples of uncaged needle rollers can be found on some engines. Commonly used in rear suspension applications and in two-stroke engines.
Nm Newton metres.
NOx Oxides of Nitrogen. A common toxic pollutant emitted by petrol engines at higher temperatures.

O

Octane The measure of a fuel's resistance to knock.
OE (Original Equipment) Relates to components fitted to a motorcycle as standard or replacement parts supplied by the motorcycle manufacturer.
Ohm The unit of electrical resistance. Ohms = Volts ÷ Current.
Ohmmeter An instrument for measuring electrical resistance.
Oil cooler System for diverting engine oil outside of the engine to a radiator for cooling purposes.
Oil injection A system of two-stroke engine lubrication where oil is pump-fed to the engine in accordance with throttle position.
Open-circuit An electrical condition where there is a break in the flow of electricity - no continuity (high resistance).
O-ring A type of sealing ring made of a special rubber-like material; in use, the O-ring is compressed into a groove to provide the sealing action.
Oversize (OS) Term used for piston and ring size options fitted to a rebored cylinder.
Overhead cam (sohc) engine An engine with single camshaft located on top of the cylinder head.
Overhead valve (ohv) engine An engine with the valves located in the cylinder head, but with the camshaft located in the engine block or crankcase.
Oxygen sensor A device installed in the exhaust system which senses the oxygen content in the exhaust and converts this information into an electric current. Also called a Lambda sensor.

P

Plastigauge A thin strip of plastic thread, available in different sizes, used for measuring clearances. For example, a strip of Plastigauge is laid across a bearing journal. The parts are assembled and dismantled; the width of the crushed strip indicates the clearance between journal and bearing.
Polarity Either negative or positive earth (ground), determined by which battery lead is connected to the frame (earth return). Modern motorcycles are usually negative earth.
Pre-ignition A situation where the fuel/air mixture ignites before the spark plug fires. Often due to a hot spot in the combustion chamber caused by carbon build-up. Engine has a tendency to 'run-on'.
Pre-load (suspension) The amount a spring is compressed when in the unloaded state. Preload can be applied by gas, spacer or mechanical adjuster.
Premix The method of engine lubrication on older two-stroke engines. Engine oil is mixed with the petrol in the fuel tank in a specific ratio. The fuel/oil mix is sometimes referred to as "petroil".
Primary drive Description of the drive from the crankshaft to the clutch. Usually by gear or chain.
PS Pfedestärke - a German interpretation of BHP.
PSI Pounds-force per square inch. Imperial measurement of tyre pressure and cylinder pressure measurement.
PTFE Polytetrafluroethylene. A low friction substance.
Pulse secondary air injection system A process of promoting the burning of excess fuel present in the exhaust gases by routing fresh air into the exhaust ports.

Q

Quartz halogen bulb Tungsten filament surrounded by a halogen gas. Typically used for the headlight **(see illustration)**.

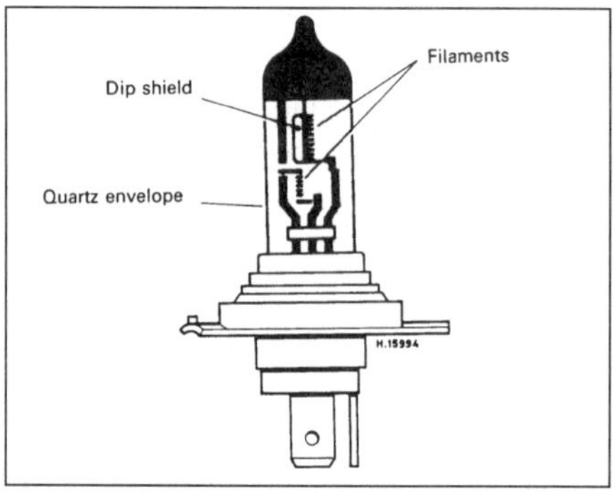

Quartz halogen headlight bulb construction

R

Rack-and-pinion A pinion gear on the end of a shaft that mates with a rack (think of a geared wheel opened up and laid flat). Sometimes used in clutch operating systems.
Radial play Up and down movement about a shaft.
Radial ply tyres Tyre plies run across the tyre (from bead to bead) and around the circumference of the tyre. Less resistant to tread distortion than other tyre types.
Radiator A liquid-to-air heat transfer device designed to reduce the temperature of the coolant in a liquid cooled engine.
Rake A feature of steering geometry - the angle of the steering head in relation to the vertical **(see illustration)**.

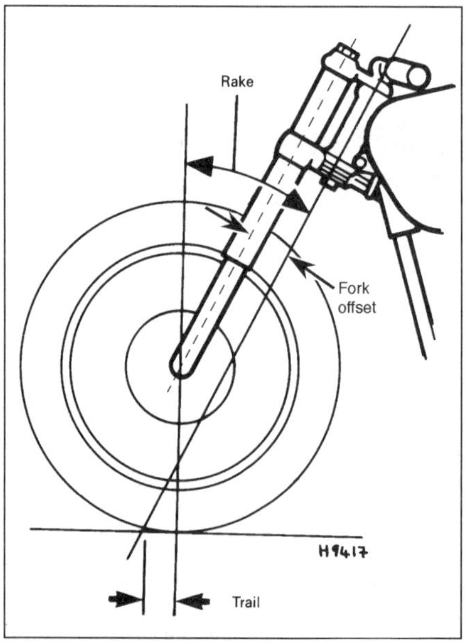

Steering geometry

Rebore Providing a new working surface to the cylinder bore by boring out the old surface. Necessitates the use of oversize piston and rings.
Rebound damping A means of controlling the oscillation of a suspension unit spring after it has been compressed. Resists the spring's natural tendency to bounce back after being compressed.
Rectifier Device for converting the ac output of an alternator into dc for battery charging.
Reed valve An induction system commonly used on two-stroke engines.
Regulator Device for maintaining the charging voltage from the generator or alternator within a specified range.
Relay A electrical device used to switch heavy current on and off by using a low current auxiliary circuit.
Resistance Measured in ohms. An electrical component's ability to pass electrical current.
RON (Research Octane Number) A measure of a fuel's resistance to knock.
rpm revolutions per minute.
Runout The amount of wobble (in-and-out movement) of a wheel or shaft as it's rotated. The amount a shaft rotates 'out-of-true'. The out-of-round condition of a rotating part.

S

SAE (Society of Automotive Engineers) A standard for the viscosity of a fluid.
Sealant A liquid or paste used to prevent leakage at a joint. Sometimes used in conjunction with a gasket.
Service limit Term for the point where a component is no longer useable and must be renewed.
Shaft drive A method of transmitting drive from the transmission to the rear wheel.
Shell bearings Plain bearings consisting of two shell halves. Most often used as big-end and main bearings in a four-stroke engine. Often called bearing inserts.
Shim Thin spacer, commonly used to adjust the clearance or relative positions between two parts. For example, shims inserted into or under tappets or followers to control valve clearances. Clearance is adjusted by changing the thickness of the shim.
Short-circuit An electrical condition where current shorts to earth (ground) bypassing the circuit components.
Skimming Process to correct warpage or repair a damaged surface, eg on brake discs or drums.
Slide-hammer A special puller that screws into or hooks onto a component such as a shaft or bearing; a heavy sliding handle on the shaft bottoms against the end of the shaft to knock the component free.
Small-end bearing The bearing in the upper end of the connecting rod at its joint with the gudgeon pin.
Spalling Damage to camshaft lobes or bearing journals shown as pitting of the working surface.
Specific gravity (SG) The state of charge of the electrolyte in a lead-acid battery. A measure of the electrolyte's density compared with water.
Straight-cut gears Common type gear used on gearbox shafts and for oil pump and water pump drives.
Stanchion The inner sliding part of the front forks, held by the yokes. Often called a fork tube.
Stoichiometric ratio The optimum chemical air/fuel ratio for a petrol engine, said to be 14.7 parts of air to 1 part of fuel.
Sulphuric acid The liquid (electrolyte) used in a lead-acid battery. Poisonous and extremely corrosive.
Surface grinding (lapping) Process to correct a warped gasket face, commonly used on cylinder heads.

T

Tapered-roller bearing Tapered inner race of caged needle rollers and separate tapered outer race. Examples of taper roller bearings can be found on steering heads.
Tappet A cylindrical component which transmits motion from the cam to the valve stem, either directly or via a pushrod and rocker arm. Also called a cam follower.
TCS Traction Control System. An electronically-controlled system which senses wheel spin and reduces engine speed accordingly.
TDC Top Dead Centre denotes that the piston is at its highest point in the cylinder.
Thread-locking compound Solution applied to fastener threads to prevent slackening. Select type to suit application.
Thrust washer A washer positioned between two moving components on a shaft. For example, between gear pinions on gearshaft.
Timing chain See **Cam Chain.**
Timing light Stroboscopic lamp for carrying out ignition timing checks with the engine running.
Top-end A description of an engine's cylinder block, head and valve gear components.
Torque Turning or twisting force about a shaft.
Torque setting A prescribed tightness specified by the motorcycle manufacturer to ensure that the bolt or nut is secured correctly. Undertightening can result in the bolt or nut coming loose or a surface not being sealed. Overtightening can result in stripped threads, distortion or damage to the component being retained.
Torx key A six-point wrench.
Tracer A stripe of a second colour applied to a wire insulator to distinguish that wire from another one with the same colour insulator. For example, Br/W is often used to denote a brown insulator with a white tracer.
Trail A feature of steering geometry. Distance from the steering head axis to the tyre's central contact point.
Triple clamps The cast components which extend from the steering head and support the fork stanchions or tubes. Often called fork yokes.
Turbocharger A centrifugal device, driven by exhaust gases, that pressurises the intake air. Normally used to increase the power output from a given engine displacement.
TWI Abbreviation for Tyre Wear Indicator. Indicates the location of the tread depth indicator bars on tyres.

U

Universal joint or U-joint (UJ) A double-pivoted connection for transmitting power from a driving to a driven shaft through an angle. Typically found in shaft drive assemblies.
Unsprung weight Anything not supported by the bike's suspension (ie the wheel, tyres, brakes, final drive and bottom (moving) part of the suspension).

V

Vacuum gauges Clock-type gauges for measuring intake tract vacuum. Used for carburettor synchronisation on multi-cylinder engines.
Valve A device through which the flow of liquid, gas or vacuum may be stopped, started or regulated by a moveable part that opens, shuts or partially obstructs one or more ports or passageways. The intake and exhaust valves in the cylinder head are of the poppet type.
Valve clearance The clearance between the valve tip (the end of the valve stem) and the rocker arm or tappet/follower. The valve clearance is measured when the valve is closed. The correct clearance is important - if too small the valve won't close fully and will burn out, whereas if too large noisy operation will result.
Valve lift The amount a valve is lifted off its seat by the camshaft lobe.
Valve timing The exact setting for the opening and closing of the valves in relation to piston position.
Vernier caliper A precision measuring instrument that measures inside and outside dimensions. Not quite as accurate as a micrometer, but more convenient.
VIN Vehicle Identification Number. Term for the bike's engine and frame numbers.
Viscosity The thickness of a liquid or its resistance to flow.
Volt A unit for expressing electrical "pressure" in a circuit. Volts = current x ohms.

W

Water pump A mechanically-driven device for moving coolant around the engine.
Watt A unit for expressing electrical power. Watts = volts x current.
Wear limit see **Service limit**
Wet liner A liquid-cooled engine design where the pistons run in liners which are directly surrounded by coolant **(see illustration)**.

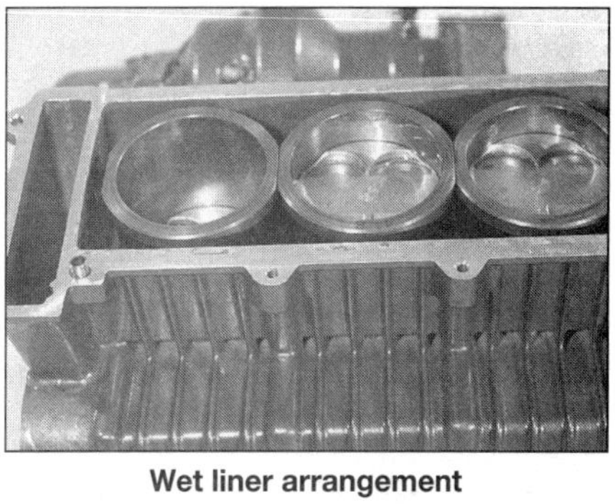

Wet liner arrangement

Wheelbase Distance from the centre of the front wheel to the centre of the rear wheel.
Wiring harness or loom Describes the electrical wires running the length of the motorcycle and enclosed in tape or plastic sheathing. Wiring coming off the main harness is usually referred to as a sub harness.
Woodruff key A key of semi-circular or square section used to locate a gear to a shaft. Often used to locate the alternator rotor on the crankshaft.
Wrist pin Another name for gudgeon or piston pin.

Note: *References throughout this index are in the form - "Chapter number" • "Page number"*

D

E

L

M

N

O

P

R

S

T

V

W

Haynes Motorcycle Manuals - The Complete List

Title	Book No
BMW 2-valve Twins (70 - 96)	♦ **0249**
BMW K100 & 75 2-valve Models (83 - 96)	♦ **1373**
BMW R850, 1100 & 1150 4-valve Twins (93 - 04)	♦ **3466**
BSA Bantam (48 - 71)	**0117**
BSA Unit Singles (58 - 72)	**0127**
BSA Pre-unit Singles (54 - 61)	**0326**
BSA A7 & A10 Twins (47 - 62)	**0121**
BSA A50 & A65 Twins (62 - 73)	0155
DUCATI 600, 750 & 900 2-valve V-Twins (91 - 96)	♦ 3290
Ducati MK III & Desmo Singles (69 - 76)	◇ 0445
Ducati 748, 916 & 996 4-valve V-Twins (94 - 01)	♦ 3756
GILERA Runner, DNA, Stalker & Ice (97 - 04)	4163
HARLEY-DAVIDSON Sportsters (70 - 03)	♦ 2534
Harley-Davidson Big Twins (73 - on)	2536
Harley-Davidson Twin Cam 88 (99 - 03)	♦ 2478
HONDA NB, ND, NP & NS50 Melody (81 - 85)	◇ 0622
Honda NE/NB50 Vision & SA50 Vision Met-in (85 - 95)	◇ 1278
Honda MB, MBX, MT & MTX50 (80 - 93)	0731
Honda C50, C70 & C90 (67 - 99)	0324
Honda XR80R & XR100R (85 - 04)	2218
Honda XL/XR 80, 100, 125, 185 & 200 2-valve Models (78 - 87)	0566
Honda H100 & H100S Singles (80 - 92)	◇ 0734
Honda CB/CD125T & CM125C Twins (77 - 88)	◇ 0571
Honda CG125 (76 - 00)	◇ 0433
Honda NS125 (86 - 93)	◇ 3056
Honda MBX/MTX125 & MTX200 (83 - 93)	◇ 1132
Honda CD/CM185 200T & CM250C 2-valve Twins (77 - 85)	0572
Honda XL/XR 250 & 500 (78 - 84)	0567
Honda XR250L, XR250R & XR400R (86 - 03)	2219
Honda CB250 & CB400N Super Dreams (78 - 84)	◇ 0540
Honda CR Motocross Bikes (86 - 01)	2222
Honda CBR400RR Fours (88 - 99)	◇ ♦ 3552
Honda VFR400 (NC30) & RVF400 (NC35) V-Fours (89 - 98)	◇ ♦ 3496
Honda CB500 (93 - 01)	◇ ♦ 3753
Honda CB400 & CB550 Fours (73 - 77)	0262
Honda CX/GL500 & 650 V-Twins (78 - 86)	0442
Honda CBX550 Four (82 - 86)	◇ 0940
Honda XL600R & XR600R (83 - 00)	2183
Honda XL600/650V Transalp & XRV750 Africa Twin (87 - 02)	◇ ♦ 3919
Honda CBR600F1 & 1000F Fours (87 - 96)	♦ 1730
Honda CBR600F2 & F3 Fours (91 - 98)	♦ 2070
Honda CBR600F4 (99 - 02)	♦ 3911
Honda CB600F Hornet (98 - 02)	◇ ♦ 3915
Honda CB650 sohc Fours (78 - 84)	0665
Honda NTV600 Revere, NTV650 & NT650V Deauville (88 - 01)	◇ ♦ 3243
Honda Shadow VT600 & 750 (USA) (88 - 03)	2312
Honda CB750 sohc Four (69 - 79)	0131
Honda V45/65 Sabre & Magna (82 - 88)	0820
Honda VFR750 & 700 V-Fours (86 - 97)	♦ 2101
Honda VFR800 V-Fours (97 - 01)	♦ 3703
Honda CB750 & CB900 dohc Fours (78 - 84)	0535
Honda VTR1000 (FireStorm, Super Hawk) & XL1000V (Varadero) (97 - 00)	♦ 3744
Honda CBR900RR FireBlade (92 - 99)	♦ 2161
Honda CBR900RR FireBlade (00 - 03)	♦ 4060
Honda CBR1100XX Super Blackbird (97 - 02)	♦ 3901
Honda ST1100 Pan European V-Fours (90 - 01)	♦ 3384
Honda Shadow VT1100 (USA) (85 - 98)	2313
Honda GL1000 Gold Wing (75 - 79)	0309
Honda GL1100 Gold Wing (79 - 81)	0669
Honda Gold Wing 1200 (USA) (84 - 87)	2199

Title	Book No
Honda Gold Wing 1500 (USA) (88 - 00)	2225
KAWASAKI AE/AR 50 & 80 (81 - 95)	1007
Kawasaki KC, KE & KH100 (75 - 99)	1371
Kawasaki KMX125 & 200 (86 - 02)	◇ 3046
Kawasaki 250, 350 & 400 Triples (72 - 79)	0134
Kawasaki 400 & 440 Twins (74 - 81)	0281
Kawasaki 400, 500 & 550 Fours (79 - 91)	0910
Kawasaki EN450 & 500 Twins (Ltd/Vulcan) (85 - 04)	2053
Kawasaki EX & ER500 (GPZ500S & ER-5) Twins (87 - 99)	♦ 2052
Kawasaki ZX600 (Ninja ZX-6, ZZ-R600) Fours (90 - 00)	♦ 2146
Kawasaki ZX-6R Ninja Fours (95 - 02)	♦ 3541
Kawasaki ZX600 (GPZ600R, GPX600R, Ninja 600R & RX) & ZX750 (GPX750R, Ninja 750R) Fours (85 - 97)	♦ 1780
Kawasaki 650 Four (76 - 78)	0373
Kawasaki Vulcan 700/750 & 800 (85 - 01)	♦ 2457
Kawasaki 750 Air-cooled Fours (80 - 91)	0574
Kawasaki ZR550 & 750 Zephyr Fours (90 - 97)	♦ 3382
Kawasaki ZX750 (Ninja ZX-7 & ZXR750) Fours (89 - 96)	♦ 2054
Kawasaki Ninja ZX-7R & ZX-9R (ZX750P, ZX900B/C/D/E) (94 - 00)	♦ 3721
Kawasaki 900 & 1000 Fours (73 - 77)	0222
Kawasaki ZX900, 1000 & 1100 Liquid-cooled Fours (83 - 97)	♦ 1681
MOTO GUZZI 750, 850 & 1000 V-Twins (74 - 78)	0339
MZ ETZ Models (81 - 95)	◇ 1680
NORTON 500, 600, 650 & 750 Twins (57 - 70)	0187
Norton Commando (68 - 77)	0125
PEUGEOT Speedfight, Trekker & Vivacity (96 - 02)	◇ 3920
PIAGGIO (Vespa) Scooters (91 - 03)	◇ 3492
SUZUKI GT, ZR & TS50 (77 - 90)	◇ 0799
Suzuki TS50X (84 - 00)	◇ 1599
Suzuki 100, 125, 185 & 250 Air-cooled Trail bikes (79 - 89)	0797
Suzuki GP100 & 125 Singles (78 - 93)	◇ 0576
Suzuki GS, GN, GZ & DR125 Singles (82 - 99)	◇ 0888
Suzuki 250 & 350 Twins (68 - 78)	0120
Suzuki GT250X7, GT200X5 & SB200 Twins (78 - 83)	◇ 0469
Suzuki GS/GSX250, 400 & 450 Twins (79 - 85)	0736
Suzuki GS500 Twin (89 - 02)	♦ 3238
Suzuki GS550 (77 - 82) & GS750 Fours (76 - 79)	0363
Suzuki GS/GSX550 4-valve Fours (83 - 88)	1133
Suzuki SV650 (99 - 02)	♦ 3912
Suzuki GSX-R600 & 750 (96 - 00)	♦ 3553e
Suzuki GSX-R600 (01 - 02), GSX-R750 (00 - 02) & GSX-R1000 (01 - 02)	♦ 3986e
Suzuki GSF600 & 1200 Bandit Fours (95 - 04)	♦ 3367
Suzuki GS850 Fours (78 - 88)	0536
Suzuki GS1000 Four (77 - 79)	0484
Suzuki GSX-R750, GSX-R1100 (85 - 92), GSX600F, GSX750F, GSX1100F (Katana) Fours (88 - 96)	♦ 2055
Suzuki GSX600/750F & GSX750 (98 - 02)	♦ 3987
Suzuki GS/GSX1000, 1100 & 1150 4-valve Fours (79 - 88)	0737
Suzuki TL1000S/R & DL1000 V-Strom (97 - 04)	♦ 4083
Suzuki GSX1300R Hayabusa (99 - 04)	♦ 4184
TRIUMPH Tiger Cub & Terrier (52 - 68)	0414
Triumph 350 & 500 Unit Twins (58 - 73)	0137
Triumph Pre-Unit Twins (47 - 62)	0251
Triumph 650 & 750 2-valve Unit Twins (63 - 83)	0122
Triumph Trident & BSA Rocket 3 (69 - 75)	0136
Triumph Fuel Injected Triples (97 - 00)	♦ 3755
Triumph Triples & Fours (carburettor engines) (91 - 99)	♦ 2162
VESPA P/PX125, 150 & 200 Scooters (78 - 03)	0707
Vespa Scooters (59 - 78)	0126
YAMAHA DT50 & 80 Trail Bikes (78 - 95)	◇ 0800
Yamaha T50 & 80 Townmate (83 - 95)	◇ 1247
Yamaha YB100 Singles (73 - 91)	◇ 0474

Title	Book No
Yamaha RS/RXS100 & 125 Singles (74 - 95)	0331
Yamaha RD & DT125LC (82 - 87)	◇ 0887
Yamaha TZR125 (87 - 93) & DT125R (88 - 02)	◇ 1655
Yamaha TY50, 80, 125 & 175 (74 - 84)	◇ 0464
Yamaha XT & SR125 (82 - 02)	◇ 1021
Yamaha Trail Bikes (81 - 00)	2350
Yamaha 250 & 350 Twins (70 - 79)	0040
Yamaha XS250, 360 & 400 sohc Twins (75 - 84)	0378
Yamaha RD250 & 350LC Twins (80 - 82)	0803
Yamaha RD350 YPVS Twins (83 - 95)	1158
Yamaha RD400 Twin (75 - 79)	0333
Yamaha XT, TT & SR500 Singles (75 - 83)	0342
Yamaha XZ550 Vision V-Twins (82 - 85)	0821
Yamaha FJ, FZ, XJ & YX600 Radian (84 - 92)	2100
Yamaha XJ600S (Diversion, Seca II) & XJ600N Fours (92 - 03)	♦ 2145
Yamaha YZF600R Thundercat & FZS600 Fazer (96 - 03)	♦ 3702
Yamaha YZF-R6 (98 - 02)	♦ 3900
Yamaha 650 Twins (70 - 83)	0341
Yamaha XJ650 & 750 Fours (80 - 84)	0738
Yamaha XS750 & 850 Triples (76 - 85)	0340
Yamaha TDM850, TRX850 & XTZ750 (89 - 99)	◇ ♦ 3540
Yamaha YZF750R & YZF1000R Thunderace (93 - 00)	♦ 3720
Yamaha FZR600, 750 & 1000 Fours (87 - 96)	♦ 2056
Yamaha XV (Virago) V-Twins (81 - 03)	♦ 0802
Yamaha XVS650 & 1100 Dragstar/V-Star (97 - 04)	♦ 4195
Yamaha XJ900F Fours (83 - 94)	♦ 3239
Yamaha XJ900S Diversion (94 - 01)	♦ 3739
Yamaha YZF-R1 (98 - 01)	♦ 3754
Yamaha FJ1100 & 1200 Fours (84 - 96)	♦ 2057
Yamaha XJR1200 & 1300 (95 - 03)	♦ 3981
Yamaha V-Max (85 - 03)	♦ 4072
ATVs	
Honda ATC70, 90, 110, 185 & 200 (71 - 85)	0565
Honda TRX300 Shaft Drive ATVs (88 - 00)	2125
Honda TRX300EX & TRX400EX ATVs (93 - 04)	2318
Honda Foreman 400 and 450 ATVs (95 - 02)	2465
Kawasaki Bayou 220/250/300 & Prairie 300 ATVs (86 - 03)	2351
Polaris ATVs (85 - 97)	2302
Polaris ATVs (98 - 03)	2508
Yamaha YFS200 Blaster ATV (88 - 98)	2317
Yamaha YFB250 Timberwolf ATVs (92 - 00)	2217
Yamaha YFM350 & YFM400 (ER and Big Bear) ATVs (87 - 03)	2126
Yamaha Banshee and Warrior ATVs (87 - 03)	2314
ATV Basics	10450
TECHBOOK SERIES	
Motorcycle Basics TechBook (2nd Edition)	3515
Motorcycle Electrical TechBook (3rd Edition)	3471
Motorcycle Fuel Systems TechBook	3514
Motorcycle Maintenance TechBook	4071
Motorcycle Workshop Practice TechBook (2nd Edition)	3470
GENERAL MANUALS	
Twist and Go (automatic transmission) Scooters Service and Repair Manual	4082

◇ = not available in the USA *♦ = Superbike*

The manuals on this page are available through good motorcyle dealers and accessory shops.
In case of difficulty, contact: **Haynes Publishing**
(UK) **+44 1963 442030** (USA) **+1 805 498 6703**
(FR) **+33 1 47 17 66 29** (SV) **+46 18 124016**
(Australia/New Zealand) **+61 3 9763 8100**

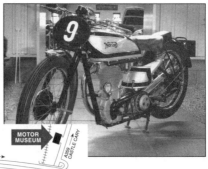